Advances in Computer Vision and Pattern Recognition

More information about this series at http://www.springer.com/series/4205

Kevin W. Bowyer · Mark J. Burge
Editors

Handbook of Iris Recognition

Second Edition

 Springer

Editors
Kevin W. Bowyer
Department of Computer Science
  and Engineering
University of Notre Dame
Notre Dame, IN
USA

Mark J. Burge
Noblis, Inc.
Washington, DC
USA

ISSN 2191-6586   ISSN 2191-6594   (electronic)
Advances in Computer Vision and Pattern Recognition
ISBN 978-1-4471-6782-2   ISBN 978-1-4471-6784-6   (eBook)
DOI 10.1007/978-1-4471-6784-6

Library of Congress Control Number: 2016940358

This Springer imprint is published by Springer Nature
The registered company is Springer-Verlag London Ltd.

Divine Iris, what god sent you to me with a message?

—Homer, Iliad

Let every eye negotiate for itself and trust no agent.

—William Shakespeare,
Much Ado About Nothing

Foreword

Four years after the publication of the first edition of the Handbook of Iris Recognition, we are pleased to present this updated and reorganized edition featuring four new and four revised chapters. We hope that you will enjoy the new edition.

Kevin W. Bowyer and Mark J. Burge, January 2016

The arrival of this Handbook in 2012 suitably marks a number of milestones and anniversaries for iris recognition. The most breathtaking of these is the fact that now on a daily basis more than 100 trillion, or 10-to-the-14th-power, iris comparisons are performed. This juggernaut (a Hindi word, appropriately) was unleashed by the Indian Government to check for duplicate identities as the Universal Identification Authority of India, or UIDAI, enrolls the iris patterns of all its 1.2 billion citizens within 3 years. This vastly ambitious program requires enrolling about 1 million persons everyday, across 36,000 stations operated by 83 agencies. Its purpose is to issue each citizen a biometrically provable unique entitlement number (Aadhaar) by which benefits may be claimed, and social inclusion enhanced; thus the slogan of UIDAI is: "To give the poor an identity." With about 200 million persons enrolled so far, against whom the daily intake of another million must be compared for de-duplication, the daily number of iris cross-comparisons is about 10-to-the-14th-power, and growing. Similar national projects are also underway in Indonesia and in several smaller countries.

Also breathtaking (but perhaps mainly just for me personally) is the fact that this year is only the 20-year anniversary of the first academic paper proposing an actual method for iris recognition. In August 1992, having recently arrived at Cambridge University as a Research Fellow, I submitted a paper about the method to *IEEE Transactions on Pattern Analysis and Machine Intelligence* (PAMI) entitled: "High confidence visual recognition of persons by a test of statistical independence." The core theoretical idea was that the *failure* of a test of independence could be a very strong basis for pattern recognition, if there is sufficiently high entropy (enough degrees-of-freedom of random variation) among samples from different classes, as I was able to demonstrate with a set of 592 iris images. The PAMI paper was published in 1993, shortly before my corresponding US

Patent 5,291,560 was also issued. That original algorithm was widely licensed through a series of companies (IriScan, Iridian, Sarnoff, Sensar, LG-Iris, Panasonic, Oki, BI2, IrisGuard, Unisys, Sagem, Enschede, Securimetrics, and L1 now owned by Safran/Morpho). With various improvements over the years, this algorithm remains today the basis of all significant public deployments of iris recognition. But academic research on many aspects of this technology has exploded in recent years. To quote from the excellent survey chapter by Bowyer, Hollingsworth, and Flynn in this book: during just the 3-year period, 2008–2010, there were more papers published about iris recognition than during the entire 15-year period, 1992–2007.

The conjecture that perhaps the iris could serve as a fingerprint has a much longer history, and this year marks the 60-year anniversary of the following statement in Adler's classic clinical textbook *Physiology of the Eye* (Chap. 6, page 143): "In fact, the markings of the iris are so distinctive that it has been proposed to use photographs as a means of identification, instead of fingerprints." Apparently, Adler referred to a proposal by the British ophthalmologist Doggart. In the 1980s, two American ophthalmologists, Flom and Safir managed to patent Adler's and Doggart's conjecture, but they had no actual algorithm or implementation to perform it and so the patent was conjecture. The roots of the conjecture stretch back even further: In 1892, Alphonse Bertillon documented nuances in "Tableau de l'iris humain"; and divination of all sorts of things based on iris patterns goes back to ancient Egypt, Babylonia, and Greece. Iris divination persists today, as "iridology."

Optical systems for iris image acquisition have enjoyed impressive engineering advances, enabling generally a more flexible user interface and a more comfortable distance between camera and subject than the "in-your-face" experience and the "stop-and-stare" interface of the first cameras. Pioneering work by Jim Matey and his team at Sarnoff Labs led to the current generation of systems capturing "iris-at-a-distance" and "iris-on-the-move," in which capture volume is nearly a cubic meter and on-the-move means walking at 1 m/s, enabling throughput rates of a person per second. There has been a "long-distance race" to demonstrate the longest standoff distance, with some claims extending to the tens of meters. The camera is then essentially a telescope, but the need to project enough radiant light safely onto the target to overcome its inverse square law dilution is a limitation. These developments bring two wry thoughts to my mind: First, I recall that when I originally began giving live demonstrations of iris recognition, the capture volume was perhaps a cubic inch; the hardware was a wooden box containing a video camera, a video display, a near-infrared light source, and a voice interface that replayed the name of a person when visually identified. Second, I read that the Hubble Space Telescope is to be decommissioned, and I wonder whether we might convert it into the Hubble Iris Camera for the ultimate "iris-at-a-distance" demonstration….

In the first dozen years after the 1993 PAMI paper, it was always very difficult to persuade leaders of the established biometrics community to take an interest in the claim that the iris algorithm had extraordinary resistance against False Matches, as well as enormous matching speed. The encoding of an iris pattern into a sign bit sequence enables not only extremely fast XOR matching (e.g., on a 32-bit machine,

32 parallel bits from each of two IrisCodes can be simultaneously compared in a single machine instruction, in almost a single clock cycle at say 3 GHz). But even more importantly, the Bernoulli nature of random bit pair comparisons generates binomial distributions for the (dis)similarity scores between different eyes. The binomial distribution (for "imposter" comparisons) is dominated by combinatorial terms with geometric tails that attenuate extremely rapidly. For example, if you accept as a match any IrisCode pair for which no more than 32 % of the bits disagree, then the False Match likelihood is about 1 in a million; but if your criterion is just slightly stricter, say that no more than 28 % of the bits may disagree, then the False Match likelihood is about 1 in a billion (i.e., reduced by a further thousand-fold as result of a mere 4-percentile point [0.04] reduction in threshold). These claims became contentious in the year 2000 when the Director of the US "National Biometric Test Center" (NBTC) in San Jose wrote that in their testing of an iris recognition prototype at NBTC, many False Matches have been observed. I received copies of all the images, ran all-against-all cross-comparisons, and sure enough, there were many apparent False Matches. But when I inspected these putative False Match images visually, it became clear that they were all in fact True Matches but with changed identities. The Director of the NBTC later confirmed this and generously acknowledged: "Clearly we were getting scammed by some of our student volunteers (at $25 a head, they were changing names and coming through multiple times)."

Another obstacle to confirmation of the extreme resistance of this biometric to False Matches was the decision in the first large-scale test (ICE 2006: *Iris Challenge Evaluation*) to evaluate at a False Match Rate of 1 in a thousand (FMR = 0.001). In this very nondemanding region of an ROC plot, most biometrics will appear equally powerful. Indeed, since ROC curves converge into the corners at either extreme, if one tested at say FMR = 0.01, then probably the length of one's big toe would seem as discriminating as the iris. The long tradition of face recognition tests had typically used the FMR = 0.001 benchmark for obvious reasons: face recognition cannot perform at more demanding FMR levels. Thus the ICE 2006 Report drew the extraordinary conclusion that face and iris were equally powerful biometrics. Imagine how well face recognition would hold up in the 100 trillion daily cross-comparisons done by UIDAI. And if iris were operating at the FMR = 0.001 level, then everyday in UIDAI there would be 100 billion False Matches—a number equal to the number of stars in our galaxy, or of neurons in the human brain.

A critical feature of iris recognition is that it produces very flat ROC or DET curves. By threshold adjustment, the FMR can be shifted over four or five orders of magnitude while the FnMR hardly changes. Thus at FMR = 0.001 iris may appear unremarkable, as in ICE 2006, and so Newton and Phillips (2007) disputed "the conventional wisdom" that iris was a very powerful biometric. But hardly any price is paid in iris FnMR when its FMR is shifted by several log units, to 0.0000001 or smaller, as required for national-scale deployments. Fortunately, tests by NIST subsequent to ICE have understood this point about the likelihood ratio (the slope of the ROC curve) and have pushed iris testing into the billions of cross-comparisons (IREX-I) and indeed now 1,200 billion cross-comparisons (IREX-III). IREX-I confirmed (7.3.2) that "there is little variation in FnMR across the five decades of FMR," and also confirmed exactly the exponential decline in FMR with minuscule (percentile point) reductions in threshold as I had tabulated in earlier papers. IREX-III results (presented by Patrick Grother in London, October 2011) included a comparison of iris and face performance using the best face algorithms from 2010 on a database of 1.6 million mugshot face images (compliant with a police mugshot standard), and also 1.6 million DoD detainee iris images. These NIST tests showed that for any plausible FnMR target, iris recognition makes 100,000 times fewer False Matches than face.

I am delighted to see the range of topics included in this Handbook, which reflects in part the richness of our subject and all the connections it draws among biology, photonics, optical engineering, security engineering, mathematics, algorithms, and standardization. Especially, hot current topics include iris image quality metrics, with the recent NIST report (IREX-II or IQCE) on quality-performance covariates and their predictive powers across matchers, and current development of an ISO/IEC Standard (29794-6) for quality. One area that remains rather unexplored is the role of information theory, which lies at the heart of our subject since it measures both the complexity of random variation (the key to biometric collision avoidance), and discriminating power.

Twenty years is a remarkably short time to get from 0 to 100 trillion iris comparisons per day. But also, 20 years is perhaps a generation. It feels as though the real potential of this technology is just beginning to be understood (as can probably also be said about its limitations). This Handbook—the first book to be devoted entirely to iris recognition—is full of excellent contributions from a new generation of researchers. If I have been a torchbearer, I am all too happy to "pass the torch" to them while remaining, I hope, still on the field amidst increasing numbers of colleagues captivated by the entropy of the eye.

Cambridge   John Daugman
February 2012

Preface to the Second Edition

Creating the Second Edition of the Handbook of Iris Recognition is somehow more challenging and ambitious than creating the first edition. This is because iris recognition continues to develop simultaneously in both practical applications and fundamental research. On the practical application side, iris recognition is increasingly used with success in demanding, large-scale applications. Perhaps, the most prominent example of this is the Aadhaar program administered by the Unique ID Authority of India. Over one billion persons have already been enrolled in the Aadhaar program. This is over three times the population size of the United States! The Aadhaar program registers people with both fingerprint and iris. A report from the Center for Global Development compared fingerprint and iris recognition results from the program and stated—"UID's data suggest that iris scans are far more inclusive than fingerprints … They are also more precise for authentication, in terms of having a lower tradeoff curve between errors of acceptance and rejection." This sort of comparison statement would once have been highly controversial, but now seems broadly accepted. Another long-running application of iris recognition is the United Arab Emirates' border-crossing application that has been in place for well over a decade. And a more recent application is the use of iris recognition to create a duplicate-free voter registration list for new elections in Somaliland.

On the research side, many fundamental and fascinating questions are being addressed in the research community. Advances on these topics hold the promise of improving future applications of iris recognition. A number of current topics in the iris recognition research community have the aim of improving the use of iris recognition at high accuracy for whole populations. Examples of this can be seen in new chapters added to the Second Edition, authored by Czajka, by Nigam, Vatsa and Singh, and by Bolme and coworkers.

The new chapter by Czajka explores the issue of "liveness testing" for iris recognition, based on the dynamic nature of the pupil. The new chapter by Nigam, Vatsa, and Singh explores and catalogs various eye conditions that will be encountered in serving whole populations, and discusses the effects of these conditions on iris recognition. The new chapter by Bolme and coworkers looks in depth at the issue of correcting for images where the iris is seen in an off-angle view. The new chapter by Rathgeb and coworkers gives a system-level view of the flow of processing in an iris recognition system, along with an introduction to the open-source implementation provided by their lab. The revised chapter by Proença updates the corresponding chapter that appeared in the first edition. Proença is research community's best-known advocate in the for performing iris recognition using visible-light images rather than near-infrared images, and exploiting the use of visible-light imaging to allow less-constrained image acquisition.

The new iris segmentation chapter by Jillela and Ross also updates a corresponding chapter in the first edition. In many ways, the potential for improvement in iris recognition accuracy seems to be greater through improvements in segmentation than through improvements in coding or matching. This chapter gives an appreciation of the difficulty of the problem as well as of the current state of the art. The new chapter by Galbally and coworkers replaces the corresponding chapter in the first edition. This chapter is an excellent example of the collaborative spirit in the iris recognition research community. The two major research groups in the area of iris image reconstruction from iris codes have teamed up to provide an introduction to the state of the art on this topic.

Organization and Features

As already mentioned above, there are four new chapters added to the Second Edition of the Handbook of Iris Recognition. This results in over 100 pages of new material. In addition, four other chapters have undergone major revision and updating, resulting in another 100 pages of revised material. The result is a combination of broader coverage of topics than in the first edition, as well as deeper coverage of selected topics.

This Second Edition of the Handbook of Iris Recognition includes a Foreword by the Father of Iris Recognition, Professor John Daugman, along with 23 contributed chapters. The 59 contributing authors come from a wide range of different companies, government agencies, and universities. They also come from many different countries, including Austria, Canada, Denmark, Germany, Hong Kong, India, Lithuania, Poland, Portugal, Singapore, the United Kingdom, and the USA.

Target Audiences

There are multiple target audiences for the Handbook of Iris Recognition, brought together by the theme of needing a better understanding of the current state of the art in this field. Anyone new to the field of iris recognition and needing to quickly get a big-picture view of the field should find the Handbook quite useful.

Any potential consumer of iris recognition technology wanting a sober appraisal of the current state of the art should find it here. Any researcher looking for ideas of where and how to usefully advance the state of the art in iris recognition should find a wealth of ideas here.

Acknowledgments

Special thanks are due to authors of chapters in the first edition who took on the task of revising and updating their chapter: Hugo Proença for the chapter on visible-light iris recognition, Raghavender Jillela and Arun Ross for the chapter on methods for iris segmentation, and Javier Galbally, Marios Savvides, Shreyas Venugopalan, and Arun Ross for the chapter on iris image reconstruction from binary templates. Special thanks are due as well to the authors of new chapters: Adam Czajka for the chapter on iris liveness detection, Ishan Nigam, Mayank Vatsa, and Richa Singh for the chapter on the menagerie of ophthalmic disorders that affect iris recognition, Christian Rathgeb, Andreas Uhl, Peter Wild, and Heinz Hofbauer for the chapter on design decisions for an iris recognition SDK, and David S. Bolme, Hector Santos-Villalobos, Joseph Thompson, Mahmut Karakaya, and Chris Bensing Boehnen for the chapter on methods of correcting off-angle iris images. All of these authors have done an excellent job of improving the coverage and quality of the Handbook.

We again thank our editors at Springer for their patience and encouragement. We again would like to thank our families for their support over the evening and weekend time needed to make the Handbook a reality.

Notre Dame, IN, USA   Kevin W. Bowyer
Washington, DC, USA   Mark J. Burge
January 2016

Preface to the First Edition

Iris Recognition became a practical area of technology and study with John Daugman's pioneering work about two decades ago. The development of the field was at first slow, but has expanded dramatically in recent years. There are now various national identity schemes in progress that make use of Iris Recognition technology. There is also a large and vibrant research community focused on Iris Recognition, studying ways to make it even more accurate in even larger scale applications. The primary goal of this book is to give an authoritative introduction to the current state of the art in Iris Recognition technology. The field has already, in large part, moved past the study of alternative segmentation algorithms and texture filters applied to pristine iris images. One major current emphasis is how to deal with varying quality iris images acquired with less-explicit user cooperation. Another major current emphasis is on methods for improving accuracy in the context of varying quality images. Still another major current emphasis is on a better understanding of the basic science underlying iris recognition. Each of these emphases is represented by multiple chapters in this book.

Organization and Features

This book includes a Foreword by Professor John Daugman, along with a collection of 17 chapters contributed by researchers from around the world. It includes theoretical studies, such as the chapter by Clark, Culp, Herron and Ross on Iris Dynamics and the chapter by Kong, Zhang and Kamel on the Iris Code. It also includes very empirical studies, such as the chapter by Baker, Bowyer, Flynn, and Phillips on Iris Template Aging and the chapter by Phillips and Flynn analyzing results from the Iris Challenge Evaluation 2006. The 44 authors contributing to the book come from companies, government agencies, and universities. They also come from many different countries, including Lithuania, Canada, Singapore, Denmark, Portugal, Hong Kong, the United Kingdom, and the USA.

Target Audiences

The target audience for this book is anyone who wants a better understanding of the current state of the art in Iris Recognition. Practitioners in industry should find new insights and possibilities in the breadth of topics covered. Managers and executives in government should find a more sober appraisal of the field than that exists in the marketing literature of the industry. Researchers in government, industry, and academia should find new ideas for productive research efforts.

Acknowledgements

We would like to thank the editors at Springer for their patience and advice during the development of this project. We also would like to thank all of the contributors to this book for their prompt replies on various points. We would like to thank all of our collaborators at our respective institutions for the vibrant research atmosphere that they have provided. Finally, we would like to thank our families, for without their continual support and encouragement this book would not have been possible.

Notre Dame, IN, USA   Kevin W. Bowyer
Washington, DC, USA   Mark J. Burge
January 2013

Contents

Contributors

David Ackerman SRI, Princeton, NJ, USA

Sarah E. Baker University of Notre Dame, Notre Dame, IN, USA

Algirdas Bastys Vilnius University, Vilnius, Lithuania

Vishnu Naresh Boddeti Carnegie Mellon University, Pittsburgh, PA, USA

Chris Bensing Boehnen Oak Ridge National Laboratory, Oak Ridge, TN, USA

David S. Bolme Oak Ridge National Laboratory, Oak Ridge, TN, USA

Kevin W. Bowyer University of Notre Dame, Notre Dame, IN, USA

Mark J. Burge Noblis, Falls Church, VA, USA; The MITRE Corporation, McLean, VA, USA

Rama Chellappa University of Maryland, College Park, Maryland, MD, USA

Antwan Clark West Virginia University, Morgantown, WV, USA

Ryan Connaughton University of Notre Dame, Notre Dame, IN, USA

Adam Czajka Warsaw University of Technology, Warsaw, Poland; Research and Academic Computer Network (NASK), Warsaw, Poland

Patrick J. Flynn University of Notre Dame, Notre Dame, IN, USA

Javier Galbally European Commission-Joint Research Centre, Ispra, VA, Italy

Patrick Grother National Institute of Standards and Technology, Gaithersburg, MD, USA

Isom Herron Rensselaer Polytechnic Institute, Troy, NY, USA

Heinz Hofbauer Multimedia Signal Processing and Security Lab, Department of Computer Sciences, University of Salzburg, Salzburg, Austria

Karen P. Hollingsworth University of Notre Dame, Notre Dame, IN, USA

Xiaofei Hu Wake Forest University, Winston-Salem, NC, USA

Raghavender Jillela Digital Signal Corporation, Chantilly, VA, USA

Mohamed Kamel Pattern Analysis and Machine Intelligence Research Group, University of Waterloo, Ontario, Canada

Mahmut Karakaya Oak Ridge National Laboratory, Oak Ridge, TN, USA

Josh Klontz The MITRE Corporation, McLean, VA, USA

Adams Wai Kin Kong Biometrics and Forensics Laboratory, School of Computer Science and Engineering, Nanyang Technological University, Singapore, Singapore

Justas Kranauskas Vilnius University, Vilnius, Lithuania

Volker Krüger Aalborg University, Aalborg, Denmark

Scott Kulp Climate Central, Princeton, NJ, USA

Matthew Monaco Noblis, Falls Church, VA, USA

F. Nicolo ZOLL Medical Corporation, Pittsburgh, PA, USA

Ishan Nigam IIIT, Delhi, India

Vishal Patel Department of Electrical and Computer Engineering Rutgers, The State University of New Jersey, Piscataway, NJ, USA

Paúl Pauca Wake Forest University, Winston-Salem, NC, USA

P. Jonathon Phillips National Institute of Standards and Technology, Gaithersburg, MD, USA

Jaishanker K. Pillai University of Maryland, College Park, Maryland, MD, USA

Robert Plemmons Wake Forest University, Winston-Salem, NC, USA

Hugo Proença IT: Instituto de Telecomunicações, University of Beira Interior, Covilhã, Portugal

George Quinn National Institute of Standards and Technology, Gaithersburg, MD, USA

Nalini Ratha IBM Watson Research Center, Hawthorne, NY, USA

Christian Rathgeb Biometrics and Internet Security Research Group, Hochschule Darmstadt, Darmstadt, Germany

Arun A. Ross Integrated Pattern Recognition and Biometrics Lab (i-PRoBe), Michigan State University, East Lansing, MI, USA

Hector Santos-Villalobos Oak Ridge National Laboratory, Oak Ridge, TN, USA

Marios Savvides Cylab Biometrics Center, Carnegie Mellon University, Pittsburgh, PA, USA

N. Schmid West Virginia University, Morgantown, WV, USA

Richa Singh IIIT, Delhi, India

Jonathon M. Smereka Carnegie Mellon University, Pittsburgh, PA, USA

Elham Tabassi National Institute of Standards and Technology, Gaithersburg, MD, USA

Joseph Thompson Oak Ridge National Laboratory, Oak Ridge, TN, USA

Jason Thornton MIT Lincoln Laboratory, Lexington, MA, USA

Andreas Uhl Multimedia Signal Processing and Security Lab, Department of Computer Sciences, University of Salzburg, Salzburg, Austria

Mayank Vatsa IIIT, Delhi, India

Shreyas Venugopalan Cylab Biometrics Center, Carnegie Mellon University, Pittsburgh, PA, USA

B.V.K. Vijaya Kumar Carnegie Mellon University, Pittsburgh, PA, USA

H. Wechsler George Mason University, Fairfax, VA, USA

Peter Wild Safety and Security Department, AIT Austrian Institute of Technology GmbH, Seibersdorf, Austria

David Zhang Biometrics Research Centre Department of Computing, The Hong Kong Polytechnic University, Kowloon, Hong Kong

J. Zuo Symantec Corp, San Francisco, CA, USA

Chapter 1
Introduction to the Handbook of Iris Recognition

Kevin W. Bowyer and Mark J. Burge

Abstract Iris recognition is both a technology already in successful use in ambitious nation-scale applications and also a vibrant, active research area with many difficult and exciting problems yet to be solved. This chapter gives a brief introduction to iris recognition and an overview of the chapters in the Second Edition of the Handbook of Iris Recognition.

1.1 The Current State of Iris Recognition

The use of iris texture analysis for biometric identification is now well established. The United Arab Emirates has been using iris recognition for border control since 2001 [23], and famously claims "some 2.7 billion iris cross-comparisons being done every day" [8]. India is using iris recognition as part of its Unique ID program, along with fingerprint recognition. By 2016, the number of people enrolled in India's Unique ID program exceeded three times the population size of the United States [15]. The National Institute of Standards and Technology (NIST) in the United States has produced a series of seven IREX reports on iris recognition technology, with more planned for the future [27]. A market analysis report predicts that the worldwide market for iris recognition technology will experience a cumulative annual growth rate of 23.5 % over the period 2015–2019 [29]. The various high-profile uses of iris recognition, the sequence of IREX technical reports by NIST, and the rosy market forecast for iris recognition technology, might lead casual observers to think that iris recognition is a solved problem, and no longer an active research area. This would be far from the truth. The transition of iris recognition from laboratory technology

K.W. Bowyer (✉)
University of Notre Dame,
384 Fitzpatrick Hall, Notre Dame, IN 46556, USA
e-mail: kwb@cse.nd.edu

M.J. Burge
Noblis, Falls Church, VA, USA
e-mail: mark.burge@noblis.org

© Springer-Verlag London 2016
K.W. Bowyer and M.J. Burge (eds.), *Handbook of Iris Recognition*,
Advances in Computer Vision and Pattern Recognition,
DOI 10.1007/978-1-4471-6784-6_1

1

to nation-scale applications has actually spurred the need for research to solve many difficult and interesting problems. The research frontiers in iris recognition are moving to more difficult and demanding sorts of problems, where results need to prove out on larger and more real-world datasets.

As just one example of this, as iris recognition begins to be used in large-scale commercial applications, the problem of *liveness testing*—being sure that the iris image comes from a live iris rather than some fake iris—becomes a practical and important question. The problem of liveness detection is the focus of the new chapter, contributed by Adam Czajka, added to the Second Edition. Liveness detection is also touched on in the new chapter by Galbally, Savvides, Venugopalan and Ross. The Second Edition also includes: a new chapter by Rathgeb, Uhl, Wild and Hofbauer that details the design decisions involved in implementing a software system for iris recognition; a new chapter by Bolme, Santos-Villalobos, Thompson, Karakaya, and Boehnen that introduces state-of-the-art approaches to correcting off-angle iris images; a new chapter by Nigam, Vatsa and Singh discussing the range of different medical conditions of the eye that can affect iris recognition; a revised and updated chapter by Jillela and Ross on methods for iris segmentation; and a revised and updated chapter by Proença on iris recognition in visible-wavelength illumination.

Even with the new and revised chapters in the Second Edition, there are some interesting current research problems that are not represented by their own chapter. One such research problem is the effects of contact lenses on iris recognition accuracy. Cosmetic contact lenses present challenges that are more complex than is widely appreciated and even plain, clear, prescription contact lenses have been documented to cause a small degradation in iris recognition accuracy [2]. There is a known approach, due to Daugman [6], for detecting whether or not a person is wearing a cosmetic contact lens for which the synthetic texture is created by a "dot-matrix" process. However, there are other means of manufacturing cosmetic contact lenses that are not detected by this approach. An example image representing a non-dot-matrix type of cosmetic lens is shown in Fig. 1.1.

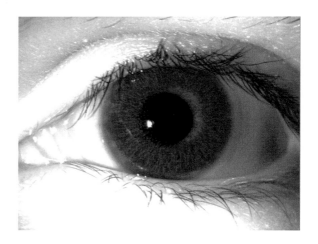

Fig. 1.1 Example iris image exhibiting texture from cosmetic contact lens. Note the slivers of natural iris texture visible by the sclera boundary near the nose and by pupil boundary away from the nose. Note also that the texture pattern is not created in a dot-matrix style, and so would not be detected by Daugman's method

Fig. 1.2 Example iris image exhibiting "AV" lettering printed on contact lens. Note the "AV" lettering near the iris-sclera boundary on the side near the nose

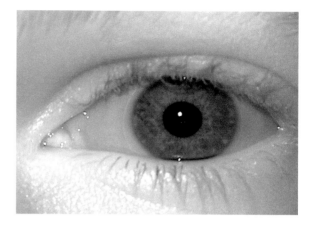

The problem of automatically detecting cosmetic contact lenses is important because cosmetic contacts obscure the natural iris texture. With current iris matching technologies, attempting to match two images of the same iris when there is either (a) a cosmetic contact lens worn in one image and not in the other, or (b) the same type of cosmetic contact lens worn in both images, is almost certain to generate a false non-match result [9].

The issue of contact lenses effecting iris recognition accuracy applies across all types of contacts, not just cosmetic lenses. Figure 1.2 shows an example image in which the "AV" logo printed on the lens is visible. In general, the logo will appear in a different place in different images of the iris, leading to a slightly degraded match between two images of the same eye wearing the same contact.

The typical "soft contacts" are the most popular type of contacts, but not the only type. There are also rigid gas permeable lenses, or "hard lenses". These can cause some large artifacts in the iris image, an example of which is shown in Fig. 1.3.

Fig. 1.3 Example iris image exhibiting a rigid gas permeable ("hard") contact lens

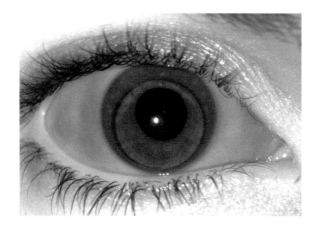

Fig. 1.4 Example iris image
exhibiting bright and dark
arcs due to poor contact lens
fit

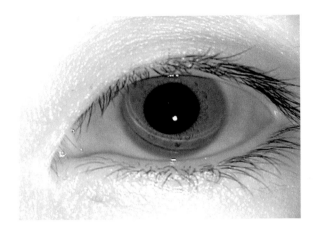

It is not only lenses that have printing on them or hard lenses that can cause
problems. Clear, prescription contacts that do not properly fit the eye can cause
dramatic artifacts in the iris image. An example of this appears in Fig. 1.4. In this
case, the bright and dark arcs that appear in the image are artifacts caused by a poorly
fitting contact lens.

It is important to note that even in the absence of all the special circumstances
mentioned above, Baker et al. [2] have shown that plain, clear prescription contacts
still have an effect of slightly degrading the match quality. For example, the lens
shown in Fig. 1.5 shows some circular banding artifact that can affect the match
quality.

The problem of automatically detecting whether a cosmetic contact lens appears
in an iris recognition image can be approached in various ways. The most popular
approach is to develop texture features and a classifier that will classify iris images as

Fig. 1.5 Example plain
contact lens image exhibiting
artifacts in the image. Note
the circular banding, most
prominent near the iris-sclera
boundary on the *bottom* of
the eye

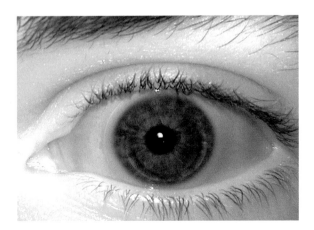

(a) showing artificial texture corresponding to a cosmetic contact lens, or (b) showing only natural iris texture. Early work on this problem was done with the same brand(s) of cosmetic lenses in both the training dataset and the test dataset. This makes the problem easier than it is in real applications. The harder version of the problem looks at the accuracy obtained when the contact lens manufacturer represented in the test set does not appear in the training set. This corresponds to the real-world problem of cosmetic lenses from a new manufacturer being encountered in an application before the application can be retuned for them. Doyle [9] presents results of cosmetic contact lens detection in this style, showing that (1) some manufacturers' cosmetic lens patterns present a harder generalization problem than others, and (2) in general, having more different manufacturers' lenses present in the training dataset results in better generalization to new manufacturers' lenses. Doyle also looks at generalization across different sensors; that is, training on images from one sensor and testing on images from another sensor.

In addition to the various types of image artifacts that may be caused by contact lenses, there are also a variety of medical and biological conditions that can degrade the accuracy of iris recognition. The example iris image in Fig. 1.6 shows an iris that was damaged in an accident. The pupillary boundary (between the pupil and the iris) of this iris has a distinctly noncircular shape. This shape will naturally present problems to iris segmentation algorithms that make the assumption of a circular boundary.

Figure 1.7 shows an image that represents a condition called *persistent pupillary membrane*. This condition does not present problems with a person's sight. But the strands that connect from the pupil out over the iris are the remains of a fetal membrane and not a part of the actual iris texture. The persistent pupillary membrane strands can potentially complicate iris segmentation and can (rarely) retract and so change the imaged iris texture.

Fig. 1.6 Example iris image showing accidental damage. Note the irregular shape of the boundary of the pupil

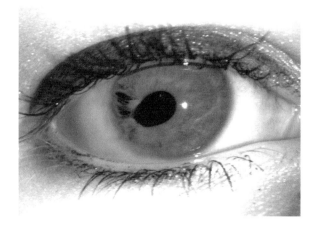

Fig. 1.7 Example iris image
showing effects of persistent
pupillary membrane

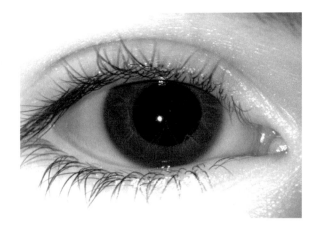

Fig. 1.8 Example iris image
showing an artificial eye.
Note the scattered specular
highlights. Also the pupil
size is the same in difference
images of this eye

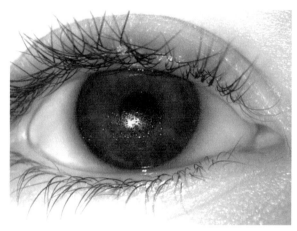

Figure 1.8 shows an example iris image in which the person has an artificial eye.
The specular highlights can be very different across different images of this eye,
potentially complicating the segmentation.

Two additional examples of naturally occuring eye conditions that cause
catastrophic failure for current iris segmentation algorithms were documented in
a trial voter registration effort for the country of Somaliland [4]. The trial of iris-
based voter registration was motivated by Somaliland's experience using face and
fingerprint to develop the voting register for their 2010 election [19]. The conclusion from the 2010 election was that face and fingerprint were not powerful enough
to reduce duplicate registrations to an acceptable level. Bowyer, Ortiz and Sgroi
describe a combination of automated and manual iris matching that resulted in zero
errors in detecting the duplicate registrations seeded into a trial dataset [4]. One
example image that resulted in catastrophic segmentation errors is shown in Fig. 1.9.

Fig. 1.9 Example iris image showing a dense cataract in the pupil region. N This condition causes catastrophic segmentation failure, so that two different images of this iris have a false non-match result

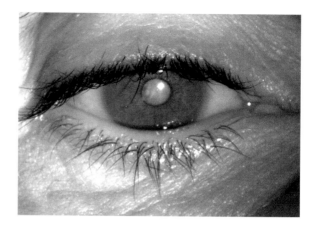

Fig. 1.10 Example iris image showing corneal disease that impacts the pupil region. This condition causes catastrophic segmentation failure, so that two different images of this iris have a false non-match result

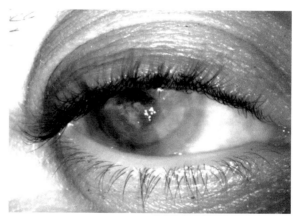

The eye condition is tentatively identified as a dense cataract. This condition has the effect of making the pupil region a bright spot in the image. The pupil appearing as a bright region forces segmentation algorithms that assume that the pupil will be a predominantly dark region to bypass the actual pupil region in favor of some next-best region. Three different images of this eye, segmented by each of two commercial algorithms, resulted in six different catastrophic segmentation failures, so that images of this iris always generated a false non-match [4].

The second example is shown in Fig. 1.10. The eye condition in this image is tentatively identified as corneal disease impacting the pupil region. This condition, like the one above, causes catastrophic segmentation failures with current segmentation algorithms, so that two different images of this iris result in a false non-match.

The preceding examples are just a few of the many different special conditions that iris recognition systems will need to deal with as the technology is used in nation-scale applications. The chapter by Nigam, Vatsa and Singh gives a more systematic and thorough discussion of this area.

Fig. 1.11 Note the small, elongated specular highlight in the iris region on the side near the nose. This is caused by reflection of the illumination off of the nose. It may appear in different places in different images of the iris, depending on the geometric relation between illuminator, nose and iris, and on the specularity of the nose surface

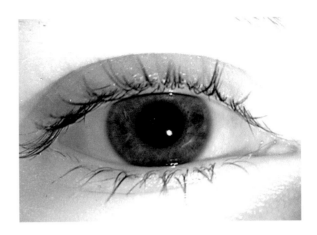

There are also many smaller, more subtle "everyday" issues that make the analysis of iris images challenging. Figure 1.11 shows an image in which there is a specular highlight in the iris region due to reflection of the illuminator off the side of the nose. Such inter-reflections are often visible on the side of the iris near the nose.

1.2 Overview of the Second Edition

The remaining chapters of the Second Edition fall into three broad sections. We briefly outline the sections here, and then introduce the individual chapters in later subsections. The first section comprises five chapters that deal with different preliminary topics. A survey of the iris recognition research literature by Bowyer, Hollingsworth and Flynn gives a sense of the different subfields and trends in the research community. The chapter by Ackermann presents a detailed summary of the theory and considerations that go into designing an iris imaging system. This chapter is a must read for anyone who wants to design an iris imaging system, or even to better understand how one works. A chapter by Quinn, Grother, and Tabassi presents the standard storage formats for iris images. There is a robust standards activity in the area of biometrics in general and iris recognition in particular. Two chapters deal with different sorts of analyses of iris quality metrics. Schmid, Zuo, Nicolo and Wechsler look at iris image quality metrics in the context of adaptive authentication. Flynn and Phillips explore the interaction of quality metrics and demographics.

The next section comprises ten chapters dealing with various core topics in iris segmentation and matching. We include here the topics of iris recognition with illumination outside the near-infrared spectrum, and of periocular matching. The newly revised and extended chapter by Jillela and Ross contains detailed coverage of all the major issues that arise in segmentation of typical iris images. The chapter by Bastys, Kranauskas and Krüger details their approach to iris image matching. This is a non-Daugman style approach, based on Taylor expansion features. The chapter by Kumar, Thornton, Savvides, Boddeti and Smereka details a different non-Daugman style approach to iris matching, based on correlation filters. The chapter by Kong, Zhang and Kamel gives a theoretical analysis of Daugman-style iris codes. The chapter by Pillai, Patel, Chellappa and Ratha discusses iris matching in the context of cancellable iris templates. The chapter by Burge and Monaco discusses iris matching in situations involving iris images acquired with different illumination spectra. They consider both fusion of results from multiple different spectra, and matching across different spectra. The next three chapters deal with different aspects of periocular matching. The chapter by Jillela, Ross, Boddeti, Kumar and coworkers deals with periocular segmentation issues. The chapter by Klontz and Burge deals with periocluar matching. The chapter by Proença deals with iris amd pericular matching in visible-wavelength illuminated images, as the core element iris recognition with least constraints on user cooperation. The chapter by Rathgeb, Uhl, Wild and Hofbauer describes an open source software for iris segmentation and matching, the Salzburg Iris Toolkit, and the design considerations that go into creating such a system.

The final section comprises seven chapters that deal with a variety of advanced topics. The chapter by Connaughton, Bowyer and Flynn describes an approach to fusing face and iris recognition using data from an early version of the Iris On the Move (IOM) system. The chapter by Clark, Kulp, Herron, and Ross presents an approach to more detailed modeling of the dynamics of the pupil. The chapter by Czajka introduces an approach to exploiting the dynamics of the pupil to create an effective liveness detection algorithm. The chapter by Galbally, Savvides, Venugopalan and Ross details two different approaches to reverse engineering a plausible iris image from an iris code, and also discusses means of detecting such synthetic images. The chapter by Bolme, Santos-Villalobos, Thompson, Karakaya and Boehnen analyzes different approaches to the problem of correcting an off-angle iris image so that it appears as a frontal-view image. The chapter by Nigam, Vatsa and Singh catalogs a number of medical conditions of the eye and explains how they can affect the accuracy of iris recognition. Finally, the chapter by Baker, Bowyer, Flynn and Phillips presents results of experiments that suggest that iris template aging does occur.

1.2.1 A Survey of Iris Biometrics Research: 2008–2010

The field of iris biometrics research is growing and fast changing. In this chapter, Bowyer, Hollingsworth and Flynn update their 2008 survey paper [3] to cover selected subareas of iris biometrics research through approximately 2010. The growth in iris biometrics research has been so explosive that, even covering this relatively short time period, the number of references in this chapter exceeds that in the 2008 survey. This survey should be useful to any researcher who wishes to acquire a "big picture" view of the current state of iris biometrics research, or who wishes to delve into greater detail about a specific line of iris biometrics research.

1.2.2 Optics of Iris Imaging Systems

Ackermann presents a detailed overview of the concerns that enter into the design
of a system for imaging the iris. He begins with a statement of basic assumptions
about the iris itself—"An iris ... is about 11 ± 1.5 mm in diameter and sits behind
the partially reflective cornea. We note that the diffuse reflectivity of an iris, referred
to as its albedo, is dependent on illumination wavelength and is typically low, around
10%, in the near-infrared (NIR) band." Ackermann reviews basic concepts of optic
design in the context or imaging the iris, and discusses how considerations of lens
quality, focal length, depth of field, spatial resolution, signal and noise, and currently
available imaging technology enter into the design of a system to image the iris. This
leads to a comparison of the tradeoffs in designing a system to image the iris at 0.3 m
versus imaging the iris at 3 m. The issues involved in the optics of imaging the iris
are nontrivial, given the need to image small detail within an already small object
with sufficient contrast to support reliable texture analysis. While this chapter does
not discuss segmentation of the iris region in an image, or the matching of iris texture
patterns, the imaging details summarized are fundamental information for all of the
higher-level processing that follows image acquisition.

1.2.3 Standard Iris Storage Formats

Iris biometric technology is becoming widely used, as evidenced for example in
India's Unique ID program. As the iris biometric industry grows, standards become
increasingly important. Quinn and coworkers from the National Institute of Standards
and Technology present an overview of work in the development of standards for data
storage formats in iris biometrics. They discuss issues of storage size constraints,
standard storage formats, compression and its effects on matching accuracy. It is
important to see the distinction between standard data formats that allow interchange
of iris data and potentially non-standard biometric templates. As the authors state,
"Standardized iris images (i.e. iris records), are not iris templates. Rather, they are
specialized interoperable images designed for the efficient storage and transmission
of iris data." One interesting conclusion of work in this area is that biometrically
useful iris image data can be stored in as little as 2 kilobytes.

1.2.4 Iris Quality Metrics for Adaptive Authentication

The topic of quality metrics for iris images is one that has attracted substantial
attention in the research community. It seems even more important for systems that
are meant to allow image acquisition under less-constrained conditions. Schmid
and coworkers discuss both common quality metrics and some of their own more

novel metrics. These include metrics for quality of iris segmentation, interlacing, illumination, lighting, occlusion, area in pixels, dilation ratio, off-angle and blur. They show results using the ICE 2005 dataset that demonstrate that matches between images with better values of a metric result in a better ROC curve. They also present a method to combine quality metrics for an image into an overall score for that image, a method to use the scores for two images to give a confidence level for their match, and a method to use the quality metrics to improve the performance the matching algorithm.

1.2.5   Quality and Demographic Investigation of ICE

Phillips and Flynn present the results of "mining" the quality scores submitted for iris images as part of the Iris Challenge Evaluation 2006. ICE 2006 [22] was a relatively large-scale evaluation of iris biometric performance, done using images acquired with the LG 2200 system. Three participants in the ICE 2006 evaluation submitted the optional quality metric for images. The quality score was required to be an integer in the range of 0 to 100, with 100 representing highest quality. The authors present results looking at correlation of quality scores between left and right irises, correlation between quality scores and subject demographics, and between quality scores and biometric performance. They note that the correlation coefficients for the pairs of quality scores are rather low, all less than 0.35. They also note that the distributions of three different quality scores over the allowed 0 to 100 range are qualitatively different. These two facts argue for the quality metrics in the three different systems being focused on different phenomena.

1.2.6   Methods for Iris Segmentation

In a substantially expanded new version of their chapter in the first edition, Jillela and Ross give a detailed overview of the main issues and algorithms involved in iris image segmentation. They begin by observing that the iris segmentation problem is somewhat different for iris images acquired in visible-wavelength illumination and in near-infrared illumination. (This issue is a major theme in the later chapter by Proença.) They show example images that illustrate the various challenges involved in accurate iris image segmentation, from occlusion by eyelids and eyelashes, to specular highlights from illumination, to off-angle views of the iris, to motion blur. They present the historical two main approaches to the core segmentation of pupil and iris boundaries: Daugman's integro-differential operator and the Hough transform approach proposed by Wildes. Then more modern approaches are also summarized, including geodesic active contours, variational level sets, and Fourier-based approximation. Differences that occur for iris segmentation in visible-wavelength images are described. Issues that arise when images are acquired with different levels of constraints on the user are discussed. Various steps for refining the basic iris segmentation are presented, such as finding areas of eyelash occlusion. Also, an approach to predicting when there is an error in the iris segmentation is introduced. This chapter is an excellent starting point for anyone wanting to understand the main elements of iris image segmentation.

1.2.7   Iris Recognition with Taylor Expansion-Based Features

Bastys and coworkers describe two alternative descriptions of iris texture and their use in iris matching. The texture descriptions are based on using the first- and second-order Taylor series expansion. One representation is a phase-based description based on binarization of the Taylor expansion at two scales. The other representation is based on local extrema in the first two Taylor series expansion coefficients. A sector-based elastic similarity metric is used for comparing two irises, to allow for minor segmentation inaccuracies. The two proposed texture representations show different relative performance on three datasets used for evaluation: CASIA II, ICE 2005, and Multiple Biometric Grand Challenge (MBGC) [26] Portal Challenge. However, the fusion of the two approaches is consistently better than either one on all three datasets. The authors point out that "despite the intuitive similarity to the Gabor features, the Taylor coefficients have greater localization in the space domain", and although this is "at the expense of poor feature resolution in the frequency domain", this problem may be less important because "periodic texture patterns that are well localised in frequency domain are rare" in the iris.

1.2.8   Application of Correlation Filters for Iris Recognition

In this chapter, Kumar and coworkers present an approach to iris recognition developed around a different technical core than that used in Daugman's approach. Daugman's approach revolves around creating an iris code based on applying a Gabor filter at a grid of locations on the iris image. Kumar and coworkers develop an approach that uses correlation filters as the basis for iris segmentation and matching. The use of correlation filters is motivated by the desire to handle iris images of degraded quality, of the type that might occur when the iris is imaged from a greater and less-controlled distance than is typical in current commercial iris biometric systems. They present an overview of major concepts in the design of correlation filters, show how to use a cross-correlation method for iris segmentation, show how to perform correlation-based matching of unwrapped iris images, and how to use Bayesian graphical models to improve iris matching in the presence of nonlinear deformations. In dealing with nonlinear deformations, they consider the unwrapped iris image as a grid of sub-images that can deform differently from each other.

1.2.9 Introduction to the IrisCode Theory

Kong and coworkers present an updated version of their theoretical analysis of the IrisCode approach [16]. In this context, IrisCode refers specifically to the Daugman-style approach to iris biometrics, in which a binary code is used that summarizes the features of the biometric. But the theoretical analysis is aimed at illuminating issues that are deeper than just the use of a binary code. Are the 0 and 1 bits in the iris code equally probable? Is the impostor distribution truly binomial? The authors summarize their theoretical analysis as follows—"we will prove that the IrisCode is a clustering algorithm with four prototypes; the locus of a Gabor function is a two-dimensional ellipse with respect to a phase parameter and can be approximated by a circle in many cases; the Gabor function can be considered as a phase-steerable filter, and the bitwise Hamming distance can be regarded as a bitwise phase distance." As an illustration, they present a method that encodes $n > 2$ bits from a single texture filter result. This chapter is an important contribution in a relatively under-studied area of iris biometrics.

1.2.10 Robust and Secure Iris Recognition

The area of "cancelable biometrics" deals with the study of systems that enroll a template based on a transformation of the original biometric. This is an area that was pioneered by researchers at IBM Research. In this approach, if the enrolled template is compromised and used by an impersonator, the enrollment can be cancelled and a different transformation used to create a new enrollment. Pillai and coworkers develop techniques in sparse representation and random projections to create "a unified framework for image quality estimation, recognition and privacy in iris biometrics". They also exploit the approach of considering an iris image in sectors, matching sectors individually and then fusing results. In the context of recognition using iris videos, the sectors may come from different frames of the video, depending on how quality varies in different frames. They present results in this area based on the Multiple Biometric Grand Challenge (MBGC) [26] iris video dataset.

1.2.11 Multispectral Iris Fusion and Cross-Spectrum Matching

Burge and Monaco attack the difficult problem of cross-spectrum iris matching. They report on methods of matching iris images acquired in near-infrared illumination to an iris acquired under normal visible illumination. They approach this problem by creating an estimated near-infrared (NIR) iris image from the color iris image using features derived from the color and structure of the visible-light iris image. They report on experiments performed with images acquired using a custom camera system that is capable of simultaneously acquiring registered images at four wavelengths (i.e., 460, 550, 670 and 800 nm). Their results show that, for lighter-colored portions of the iris, texture content increases with the frequency of the illumination, and that similarly, for darker colored portions of the iris, texture content decreases.

1.2.12 Methods for Periocular Segmentation

Jillela, Ross, Boddeti, Kumar and coauthors present an analysis of five different approaches to segmenting the periocular region. Definitions of the periocular region vary, but it generally refers to a rectangular region centered around the eye. The Face and Ocular Challenge Series (FOCS) Dataset is used in comparing the results of the five approaches. The images in the FOCS dataset are characterized by large variations in illumination, eyelid and eyelash occlusion, defocus blur, motion blur and resolution. The five approaches compared are Daugman's integro-differential operator, a Hough transform based approach, geodesic active contours, active contours without edges, and a directional ray detection method. The active contour approaches are found to yield better results than the other approaches.

1.2.13 Periocular Recognition from Low Quality Iris Images

Klontz and Burge show that especially in cases where the iris has not been acquired with sufficient quality to compute an IrisCode, the periocular region can provide additional discriminative information for biometric identification. They investigate periocular recognition on the FOCS dataset using three distinct classes of features: photometric, keypoint, and frequency-based. They examine the performance of these features alone, in combination, and when fused with classic IrisCodes.

1.2.14 Iris Recognition in the Visible Wavelength

All commercial iris recognition systems that we are aware of, and the vast majority of academic research on iris recognition, is based on using iris images acquired with near-infrared illumination. Under appropriate near-infrared illuminated, there effectively are no "light" and "dark" irises, and all irises have readily visible texture. Hugo Proença is perhaps the most vocal proponent of performing iris recognition using images acquired with visible-wavelength illumination rather than near-infrared illumination. In this updated and extended new chapter, he presents the argument for using visible-wavelength images. The main element of the argument is that using ambient visible-wavelength illumination is key to performing recognition in less-constrained environments that do not assume the subject's active cooperation in the image acquisition. Proença discusses the pros and cons of near-infrared and visible-wavelength images, and describes a state-of-the-art system for automatic acquisition of periocular and iris images in an unconstrained outdoor environment. Information content in images, image segmentation and feature encoding are contrasted for visible-wavelength and near-infrared images. Ocular recognition algorithms are discussed in some detail, and an ensemble of two experts is proposed. Overall, this chapter tackles a very ambitious form of biometric recognition, "non-cooperative ocular recognition" in unconstrained environments that do not assume user cooperation. Proença concludes that there are "... two key properties of an ocular recognition ensemble: 1) the weak (periocular) recognizer should provide as much independent scores (responses) as possible with respect to the strong (iris) recognizer; and 2) experts should not share particular sensitivity to the same data covariates, in order to actually improve recognition robustness".

1.2.15 Design Decisions for an Iris Recognition SDK

Rathgeb and coworkers have created one of the main two current open source software development kits (SDKs) for iris recognition. Their system is called the University of Salzburg Iris Toolkit [24]. The Open Source for Iris (OSIris) SDK is the other [28]. The Salzburg Iris Toolkit is written in C++. It includes different alternative algorithms for the important steps in the iris recognition pipeline. It has been successfully installed and used by a number of different research groups. One value of the University of Salzburg Toolkit is that it can provide benchmark performance results from an open source system as a comparison for new research results. A related value of the system is that it allows researchers to implement their own solution for only one step in the iris recognition pipeline, and yet still be able to demonstrate end-to-end recognition results by substituting their implementation for the corresponding Salzburg Toolkit module. The Toolkit also includes software for manually marking iris boundaries in order to create "ground truth" for an iris dataset. This can be of value to any researcher using a new iris image dataset that does not yet have any ground truth iris segmentation available.

1.2.16 Fusion of Face and Iris Biometrics

Connaughton and coworkers report the results of a multi-biometric face and iris study performed using video clips acquired with an Iris On the Move (IOM) system [18]. The dataset includes 1,886 videos covering 363 different subjects. One interesting aspect of this work is that it explicitly includes several different senses of the term multi-biometrics. One, it combines results of iris and face, since both are available in the near-infrared video obtained with the IOM system. Second, it uses multisample approaches, combining information from individual frames of a video. Third, it uses a multi-algorithm approach, combing results from multiple face matchers and from multiple iris matchers. Thus they have a large number of results of varying types to consider at the fusion stage. They find that fusion of iris across a video segment performance better than fusion of face across a video segment, but that fusion of both performs better still.

1.2.17 A Theoretical Model for Describing Iris Dynamics

It was once believed that the degree of pupil dilation did not impact the performance of iris biometrics. However, Hollingsworth et al. [14] showed experimental evidence that the difference in pupil dilation between the images being matched does in fact have a significant effect. The larger the difference in dilation ratio between two images of the same iris, the greater the likelihood of a false non-match result. This same basic conclusion was also found later in a NIST IREX study [13]. This has led to a desire for a better understanding of the basic process of pupil dilation. Clark and coworkers give an overview of work related to the effects of pupil dilation on iris biometrics, and present a theoretical study of the nonlinear dynamics involved in iris deformation during changes in dilation. They give a detailed mathematical development of the dynamics of iris deformation and present finite element model simulation results for the case of the iris being isotropic material and for the case of the iris being orthotropic material. The authors acknowledge that there is much more work still to be done in this area, as "there is a need to explore testing our model extensively on actual data to draw a more accurate comparison" and "there is a need to build a mathematical model that also takes into consideration the dynamics in the thickness of the iris".

1.2.18 Iris Liveness Detection by Modeling Dynamic Pupil Features

Czajka presents an extension of his previous work in the area of liveness detection for iris recognition. The problem of "liveness detection" is, as the name suggests, to determine whether the image acquisition is being performed on a live iris, as opposed to an image, a video, a fake eyeball, or other possible source of spoofing. In Czajkas approach, this is done by monitoring the pupil dilation change in response to a change in the level of visible light. Czajkas presentation in this chapter is commendable for its consistent effort to use the most recent ISO/IEC definitions of terminology. Czajka's chapter also provides a detailed review of related work in the more general area of liveness detection for iris biometrics.

Czajka formulates the problem in terms of determining whether a sample video is (a) the response of a live eye in the presence of static visible-light illumination level or (b) the response of a live eye in the presence of planned changes in illumination level. An additional dimension of this work is to reach a decision with the shortest length of video that allows a reliable decision. A new experimental dataset was acquired specifically for this work. Iris videos were acquired at 25 frames per second, for 30 seconds, for each iris of 26 different subjects. For 25 of the subjects, 4 videos were acquired for each eye, and for the remaining subject 2 videos were acquired for each eye. Planned changes in visible-light illumination were carried out in each video. In the analysis of the videos, circular pupil and iris segmentation is used to estimate pupil dilation. Experiments are performed on a leave-one-subject-out basis, which gives added confidence in the results. The conclusion is that "three-second observation is enough to get the perfect recognition of authentic and odd reactions of the pupil ...". This chapter should be essential reading for anyone interested in anti-spoofing techniques in iris recognition.

1.2.19 Iris Image Reconstruction from Binary Templates

Reconstructing a biometric sample, in this case an iris image, from a biometric template, in this case an iris code, is sometimes termed "inverse biometrics". The iris recognition research community has long assumed that it is not possible to reconstruct the original iris texture from an iris code. This assumption seems plausible because the Daugman-style iris code is composed of just the sign of the real and imaginary parts of the Gabor filter responses at a set of sample points on the iris, and this seems to not be enough information from which to reconstruct the original iris texture. However, two research groups have recently published approaches to generating a synthetic iris image from an iris code. The first group to make a significant contribution in the area of inverse biometrics for the iris code was Shreyas Venugopalan and Marios Savvides [30]. The First Edition of the Handbook contained a chapter by Venugopalan and Savvides describing their work on this topic. Not long after their work, Javier Galbally and Arun Ross, along with additional collaborators at the Universidad Autonoma de Madrid, published another approach to generating synthetic iris images from an iris code [12]. For the Second Edition of the Handbook, we are incredibly fortunate that Venugopalan and Savvides and Galbally and Ross have joined forces to collaborate in providing an up-to-date summary of their work in this area, replacing the previous chapter in the First Edition.

Perhaps the key point to understand about this work is that, as stated in the chapter, "the final objective is not to reconstruct a biometric sample which visually resembles the original one (in order to deceive a human observer), but rather, that it is incorrectly recognized as the original sample by an automatic authentication algorithm". Thus, the synthetic iris image generated by either approach described in the chapter is **not** intended to look visually the same as the original iris image that generated the iris code. Rather, it is "only" intended to be a synthetic image that will generate an iris code similar to the iris code generated by the original image. In this case, "similar" means close enough to generate a false match to the original image. This is all that is needed to spoof an iris recognition system.

In addition to describing how to generate a synthetic iris image from an iris code, the authors describe an approach to automatically discriminate between synthetic iris images of this type and real iris images. The approach is able to achieve roughly 90 % accurate discrimination between synthetic and real iris images. Thus this chapter presents both a potential path to iris spoofing and a means to detect such a spoofing attempt.

1.2.20   Off-Angle Iris Correction Methods

Bolme and coworkers extend a line of work coming out of Oak Ridge National Lab that tackles the difficult problem of correcting off-angle iris images so that they appear as frontal images. This problem is important because current iris matchers work well with approximately frontal images, but accuracy tends to degrade substantially with images that are more than 20–30° off-angle. The approach of correcting an off-angle image to an approximately frontal view allows the correction to be used as a preprocessing step with various iris matchers.

Iris recognition has historically been based on the idealized view of the iris as a flat, planar surface. Bolme and coworkers move beyond this idealization and attempt to deal with the fundamentally more complex reality of the iris. The iris has 3D structure that can lead to self-occlusions and shadows that can vary based on the illumination and viewing angle. Also, the iris is viewed through the cornea, a 3-D structure that adds its own distortions based on the geometry of the cornea and the view.

Bolme and coworkers experiment with four approaches to correcting off-angle images. One is a simple affine correction to make the iris appear circular. This is a baseline that does not take into account the 3D structure of the iris and cornea. The second approach is to measure the texture displacement between off-angle and frontal using optical flow. The third is to learn corrections using a genetic algorithm. And the fourth is to employ a sophisticated ray-tracing model of the corneal refraction to compensate for optical distortions in off-angle views. They find that the genetic algorithm approach produces better results than the other approaches at 30, 40 and 50° off-angle, although it also introduces some noticeable artifacts in the corrected images. While there is still much work to be done in this area, the results presented in this chapter show improvement in handling off-angle images through correcting them to a frontal view.

1.2.21 Ophthalmic Disorder Menagerie and Iris Recognition

Nigam, Vatsa and Singh catalog what they term an "Ophthalmic Disorder Menagerie" and discuss how the various disorders affect the performance of iris recognition. This chapter effectively emphasizes the breadth of different special cases that an iris recognition system must confront in a nation-scale application. They consider three broad categories within their menagerie: (a) disorders of the eye that affect the iris, (b) pupil dilation/constriction as an effect of drugs, and (c) ophthalmic surgeries. They show visible-light iris images illustrating a number of examples in the different categories.

Nigam, Vatsa and Singh have collected a number of their own special purpose datasets that are described in the chapter. One dataset contains iris images of subjects before and after consuming alcohol; changes in dilation appear to the main effect in this case. Other datasets contain images of subjects with and without cataracts, before and after being given eyedrops to cause dilation. Another dataset contains images of subjects before and after surgery to remove cataracts, with the post-surgery images acquired one week after surgery. They state that each of these dataset will be made available to other researches upon request.

They also discuss the effect of the various eye conditions both upon the iris segmentation stage and the iris matching stage. Not surprisingly, the segmentation stage is a challenge for many of the disorders that affect the iris. Even when segmentation of the iris region is not a problem, large dilation difference degrades matching and pre/post surgery differences degrade matching.

1.2.22 Template Aging in Iris Biometrics

Mansfield and Wayman, in the 2002 report on best practices in biometric testing [17], define template aging as follows - "Template ageing refers to the increase in error rates caused by time related changes in the biometric pattern, its presentation, and the sensor". It has been widely accepted since the inception of iris recognition that iris texture is stable over a person's lifetime in a way that results in iris recognition not being subject to template aging. Baker et al. published a paper [1] in the 2009 *International Conference on Biometrics* with experimental results showing that the false non-match rate increases for matching images taken roughly 4 years apart compared to images taken only a few months apart. In 2011, Fenker and Bowyer published a study on a different dataset that reaches essentially the same conclusion [10]. In this chapter, Baker and coworkers present an extended analysis on a larger dataset than used in their original study. The conclusions of this study have become controversial, since they challenge an element of conventional wisdom about iris recognition.

Several additional research groups have reported observing a template aging effect, using different sensors, different datasets and different analysis techniques than Baker [1] or Fenker [10]. As one example, Sazonova et al [25] analyzed data from 46 subjects with at least a year between the earliest and latest images for each subject. Match scores were generated with the Masek matcher and the Neurotechnology VeriEye matcher [20]. Match scores were analyzed with a regression model that includes the effect of time lapse, and another regression model that includes the effect of time lapse and also the effect of various quality metrics. The VeriEye matcher had a verification rate of 97.5 % at a false match rate of 0 % for one to 180 days of time lapse, and a verification rate of 93.3 % at the same threshold for image pairs with 721–1,021 days of time lapse. In other words, roughly 2 years of added time lapse resulted in the false non-match rate more than doubling, increasing from 2.5 % to 6.7 %.

As another example, Czajka [5] analyzed a dataset of 571 iris images corresponding to 58 different eyes, in which the short-term time lapse is considered to be 2 years, and the long-term time lapse is considered to be 5–9 years. Match scores were generated with the VeriEye matcher, the Mirlin matcher [11], and a custom Zak-Gabor matcher. VeriEye is found to be the most accurate of the three matchers. Czajka reports that "The genuine scores are approximately 14 % lower when the time lapse between samples starts from 5 years and reaches more than 8 years, and this observation is supported by the outcome of one-way unbalanced analysis of variance".

The NIST IREX VI report [21] released in 2013 reported rather different conclusions about iris template aging. The first result listed in the Executive Summary of the report is—"Our best estimate of iris recognition ageing is derived from a 7876 person subset of an operational registered traveler deployment who have used the system on forty or more occasions over at least 4 years and up to 9 years. The estimate is a population-average from a linear mixed-effects regression model. It states Hamming distances (HD) increase at a rate of $(8 \pm 2) \times 10^{-7}$ per day." Similarly, the Conclusions section of the Executive Summary states—"... we find no evidence of a widespread iris ageing effect. Specifically, the population statistics (mean and variance) are constant over periods of up to 9 years. This is consistent with the ability to enroll most individuals and see no degradation in overall recognition accuracy. Furthermore, we compute an ageing rate for how quickly recognition degrades with changes in the iris anatomy; this estimate suggests that iris recognition of average individuals will remain viable over decades."

As the IREX VI report was analyzed, and the dataset to obtain its "best estimate" was looked at in more detail, a number of errors and omissions have come to light. IREX VI is clear that the OPS-XING dataset that it analyzes contains only match scores accepted by the application as authentic matches. There is no impostor distribution to be examined. IREX VI is also clear that its (assumed) authentic scores are truncated at a Hamming Distance of 0.27. However, IREX VI incorrectly assumes that this truncation does not cause problems for regression analysis, when in fact a "truncated regression" technique should be employed in order to handle the fact that the higher Hamming distance values have been truncated. Also, the IREX VI report does not reveal that the dataset is, in the technical terminology of regression analysis, "censored" as well as truncated. The censoring arises because the Hamming distance scores have been normalized to account for the varying number of bits contributing to different HD scores, according to a technique described by Daugman [7]. The normalization sometimes results in a negative HD score. The dataset analyzed in IREX VI records all of the negative scores as zero; this is the censoring. A separate specialized regression technique would be needed to account for the censored data. IREX VI does not take into account either the truncation or the censoring.

IREX VI also states that the dataset results from 1-to-N matching—"The scores are Hamming distances (HDs) from a 1:N search of a live image against the enrolled database" [21]. In fact, the scores result from "1-to-First" matching rather than 1-to-N. The importance of this distinction is that 1-to-First search will have a greater probability of recording a false match as an assumed authentic score.

An even more fundamental problem not revealed in IREX VI is that the dataset is actually a composite of datasets collected in a number of different cities and that the HD trend over time varies significantly between cities. The variation in the HD behavior between cities is, as far as we know at this point, unexplained. Regardless of a possible eventual explanation, it is hard to imagine a justification for performing regression on a composite of datasets known to have different trends over time. In the end, the errors and unknowns with regard to the IREX VI report make it hard to determine what, if any, meaning can be assigned to its "best estimate" of iris aging.

References

1. S.E. Baker, K.W. Bowyer, P.J.J. Flynn, Empirical evidence for correct iris match score degradation with increased time-lapse between gallery and probe matches, in *Advances in Biometrics*. Lecture Notes in Computer Science, vol. 5558 (2009), pp. 1170–1179
2. S.E. Baker et al., Degradation of iris recognition performance due to non-cosmetic prescription contact lenses. Comput. Vis. Image Underst. **114**(9), 1030–1044 (2010)
3. K. Bowyer, K. Hollingsworth, P.J. Flynn, Image understanding for iris biometrics: a survey. Comput. Vis. Image Underst. **110**(2), 281–307 (2008)
4. K. Bowyer, E. Ortiz, A. Sgroi, Trial Somaliland voting register de-duplication using iris recognition, in *IEEE Automatic Face and Gesture Recognition Conference Workshops* (2015)
5. A. Czajka, Influence of iris template ageing on recognition reliability. Commun. Comput. Inf. Sci. **452**, 284–299 (2014)
6. J. Daugman, Demodulation by complex-valued wavelets for stochastic pattern recognition. Int. J. Wavelets Multiresol. Inf. Process. **1**(1), 1–17 (2003)
7. J. Daugman, New methods in iris recognition. IEEE Trans. Syst. Man Cybern. Part B: Cybern. **37**(5), 1167–1175 (2007)
8. J. Daugman, I. Malhas, Iris recognition border-crossing system in the UAE. Biometrics, 49053 (2004)
9. J. Doyle, K. Bowyer, Robust detection of textured contact lenses in iris recognition using BSIF. IEEE Access **3**, 1672–1683 (2015)
10. S.P. Fenker, Experimental evidence of a template aging effect in iris biometrics (2011)
11. FotoNation, Iris Recognition
12. J. Galbally et al., Iris image reconstruction from binary templates: An efficient probabilistic approach based on genetic algorithms. Comput. Vis. Image Underst. **117**, 1512–1525 (2013)
13. P. Grother et al., IREX I: performance of iris recognition algorithms on standard images (NIST Interagency Report 7629, in *PoLAR* (2009)
14. K. Hollingsworth, K. Bowyer, P.J. Flynn, Pupil dilation degrades iris biometric performance. Comput. Vis. Image Underst. **113**(1), 150–157 (2009)

15. G. of India, Unique Identification Authority of India
16. A.W.K. Kong, D. Zhang, M.S. Kamel, An analysis of IrisCode. IEEE Trans. Image Process. **19**(2), 522–532 (2010)
17. A.J. Mansfield, J.L. Wayman, Best practices in testing and reporting performance of biometric devices ver 2.01. Natl. Phys. Lab. **14**(02), 1–36 (2002)
18. J.R. Matey et al., Iris on the move: acquisition of images for iris recognition in less constrained environments. Proc. IEEE **94**(11), 1936–1947 (2006)
19. D. Mathieson, R. Wager, Somaliland national election commission: report on the preparation of the voting register (2010)
20. NeuroTechnology, VeriEye SDK
21. G.P. et al., IREX VI: Temporal stability of iris recognition accuracy (NIST Interagency Report 7948), in *PoLAR* (2013)
22. P.J. Phillips et al., FRVT 2006 and ICE 2006 large-scale experimental results. IEEE Trans. Pattern Anal. Mach. Intell. **32**(5), 831–846 (2010)
23. A.N. Al-Raisi, A.M. Al-Khouri, Iris recognition and the challenge of homeland and border control security in UAE. Telemat. Inform. **25**(2), 117–132 (2008)
24. C. Rathgeb, A. Uhl, P. Wild, USIT—University of Salzburg Iris-Toolkit
25. N. Sazonova et al., A study on quality-adjusted impact of time lapse on iris recognition, in *SPIE 8371B: Biometric Technology for Human Identification* (2012)
26. J.A. Scallan, S. Weimer, Overview of the multiple biometrics grand challenge, in *Advances in Biometrics*, ed. by M. Tistarelli, M. Nixon, vol. 5558 (Springer, Berlin/Heidelberg, 2009), pp. 705–714
27. N. I. of Standards and T. (NIST), IREX: IRis EXchange
28. G. Sutra et al., A biometric reference system for iris: OSIRIS version 4.1
29. Technavio, Global Iris Recognition Market: 2015–2019 (2015)
30. S. Venugopalan, M. Savvides, How to generate spoofed irises from an iris code template. IEEE Trans. Inf. Forensics Secur. **6**, 385–394 (2011)

Chapter 2
A Survey of Iris Biometrics Research: 2008–2010

Kevin W. Bowyer, Karen P. Hollingsworth and Patrick J. Flynn

Abstract A recent survey of iris biometric research from its inception through 2007, roughly 15 years of research, lists approximately 180 publications. This new survey is intended to update the previous one, and covers iris biometrics research over the period of roughly 2008–2010. Research in iris biometrics has expanded so much that although covering only 3 years and intentionally being selective about coverage, this new survey lists a larger number of references than the inception through 2007 survey.

2.1 Introduction

Iris biometrics research is an exciting, broad, and rapidly expanding field. At the same time, there are successful practical applications that illustrate the power of iris biometrics; there are also many fundamental research issues to be solved on the way to larger scale and more complex applications.

A survey that appeared in 2008 covered the field from its inception in the early 1990s through roughly the end of 2007 [20]. This new survey is intended to update the previous one, covering roughly the period 2008 through 2010. However, as illustrated in Fig. 2.1, there has been tremendous growth in the literature in this area, Due to this growth, this new survey does not attempt as exhaustive a coverage of the field as the previous survey. We focus primarily on papers that appeared in SpringerLink or in IEEE Xplore, as these appear to currently be the two major sources of publications

K.W. Bowyer (✉) · K.P. Hollingsworth · P.J. Flynn
University of Notre Dame,
384 Fitz Hall, Notre Dame, IN 46556, USA
e-mail: kwb@cse.nd.edu

K.P. Hollingsworth
e-mail: kholling@cse.nd.edu

P.J. Flynn
e-mail: flynn@cse.nd.edu

© Springer-Verlag London 2016
K.W. Bowyer and M.J. Burge (eds.), *Handbook of Iris Recognition*,
Advances in Computer Vision and Pattern Recognition,
DOI 10.1007/978-1-4471-6784-6_2

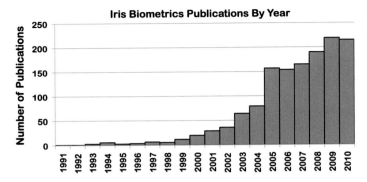

Fig. 2.1 Iris Biometrics Papers in Google Scholar from 1990 through 2010. This data was taken using Google Scholar's "advanced search" facility, searching for "iris biometrics pupil" appearing in articles, excluding patents, in the Engineering, Computer Science and Mathematics literature

in this field. We also omit coverage of some subareas of work judged to be of less importance. These omissions are explained at the appropriate points in the survey.

The main body of this survey is organized into the following sections:

Section 2.2—Iris Image Acquisition

Section 2.3—Iris Region Segmentation

Section 2.4—Texture Coding and Matching

Section 2.5—Multi-biometrics Involving the Iris

Section 2.6—Privacy and Security

Section 2.7—Datasets and Evaluations

Section 2.8—Performance Under Varying Conditions

Section 2.9—Applications

Section 2.10—Theoretical Analyses

Papers are grouped into a section according to their perceived main area of contribution. In some instances, a paper is mentioned in more than one section. The survey ends with a short discussion and a list of recommended readings.

There are several overview or introductory type articles that can be mentioned in this section. Gorodnichy [58] gives a good overview/introduction to biometrics, emphasizing evaluation of biometric system performance based on a dynamic, or life cycle view of operational systems. Bhattacharyya et al. [13] give a short, high-level overview of biometrics, primarily emphasizing iris biometrics. Phillips and Newton [143] present a short "point of view" type article on biometric evaluation, emphasizing issues such as the number of persons represented in the dataset and the longitudinal time over which biometric samples are collected. Each of these articles contains important elements for anyone new to the field of biometrics.

2.2   Iris Image Acquisition

There are still major research issues in the area of iris image acquisition. One issue involves imaging the iris with a sensor system that allows the person to be more "at a distance" and "on the move." Matey and Kennell [118] present a comprehensive tutorial on the issues involved in acquiring iris images at a distance of greater than one meter. The tutorial includes a partial list of commercial iris recognition devices released between 1995 and 2008 and a description of several successful applications of iris biometrics. The authors describe acquisition issues including the wavelength of light used, the type of light source, the amount of light reflected by the iris back to the sensor, required characteristics of the lens, signal-to-noise ratio, eye safety, and image quality. Capture volume, residence time, and sensitivity to subject motion are also discussed.

Wheeler et al. [208] describe a prototype "stand-off" iris recognition system designed to work at sensor-to-subject distances of up to 1.5 m. The system uses two wide-field-of-view cameras to perform face location in the scene and an iris camera and illuminator to image the iris. Dong et al. [36] discuss the design of a system to image the iris "at a distance," allowing a stand-off of 3 m. Although current commercial iris biometrics systems all use near-infrared (NIR) illumination, and most research assumes NIR imaging similar to that used in current commercial sensors, Proenca [152] argues for visible wavelength imaging as the more appropriate means to achieve "at a distance" and "on the move" imaging.

Boddeti and Kumar [17] investigate the use of wavefront-coded imagery for iris recognition. This topic has been discussed in the literature before, but Boddeti and Kumar use a larger data set and present experiments to evaluate how different parts of the recognition pipeline (e.g., segmentation, feature extraction) are affected by wavefront coding. They propose using unrestored image outputs from the wavefront-coded camera directly, and test this idea using two different recognition algorithms. They conclude that wavefront coding could help increase the depth of field of an iris recognition system by a factor of four, and that the recognition performance on unrestored images was only slightly worse than the performance on restored images.

There is little published work dealing with imaging the iris under different wavelength illumination. Ross et al. [170] look at imaging the iris with illumination in the 950–1650 nm range, as opposed to the 700–900 nm range typically used in commercial systems. They suggest that it is possible to image different iris structure with different wavelength illumination, raising the possibility of multispectral matching as a means to increased recognition accuracy.

Grabowski et al. [60] describe an approach to iris imaging that is meant to allow characterization of structures in the iris tissue over changes in pupil dilation. They use side-illumination, fixed to glasses frames worn by the subject, with imaging resolution that allows an 800-pixel iris diameter. This is many more "pixels on the iris" than in current commercial sensors.

Chou et al. [31] describe an iris image acquisition system meant to handle off-angle views of the iris and to make iris segmentation easier and more reliable. Their system uses a dual-CCD camera to acquire a color RGB image with one CCD and a near-infrared image with the other. The color image is exploited to improve the reliability of the segmentation. The non-orthogonal-view iris image is rectified to an orthogonal-view iris image using the pupillary boundary.

He et al. [70] design their own iris camera with the goal of being more economical than commercial alternatives, while still acquiring high-quality images. They use a CCD sensor with resolution of 0.48 M pixels, and add a custom glass lens with a fixed focus at 250 mm and NIR-pass filters that transmit wavelengths between 700 and 900 nm. The illumination unit consists of NIR LEDs of 800 nm wavelength, which they arrange to try to minimize specular reflections on the iris.

McCloskey et al. [120] explore a technique termed "flutter shutter" as a means to acquire sharply focused iris images from moving subjects. The idea is that the camera shutter "flutters" between open and closed while the sensor accumulates an image, from which an appropriately designed deblurring algorithm can then recover an in-focus image.

2.2.1 Nonideal Images and Quality Metrics

As mentioned earlier, one important current research emphasis is acquisition of images under less-constrained conditions. As iris images are acquired under less constrained conditions, the issue of image quality becomes more important and complex. Another element of this is the design of algorithms meant to handle "nonideal" or "noisy" images. For our purposes, "nonideal" means something more than just the presence of specular highlights or occlusion by eyelashes or eyelids.

While it is not part of the image acquisition step per se, iris biometric systems typically evaluate the focus quality, and possibly other factors, of each candidate image in order to select usable images. Ren and Xie [167, 168] proposed approaches to evaluating image focus quality that involve finding the iris region before computing the focus value. While iris biometric systems select images based in part on focus quality, there are few publications dealing with deblurring of iris images. Huang et al. [81] investigate image deblurring algorithms that exploit context specific to iris imagery. He et al. [73] estimate the user distance from the sensor in order to estimate the appropriate point spread function (PSF) for image restoration. They measure the distance between two specular highlights on the iris. Using this information, plus knowledge about the positions of the two infrared LEDs, they get the user's distance from the camera without using a special distance sensor. The knowledge of the distance from the sensor is used in estimating the PSF.

Belcher and Du [9] combine percent occlusion, percent dilation, and "feature information" to create an iris image quality metric. To compute "feature information," they calculate the relative entropy of the iris texture when compared with a uniform distribution. To fuse the three types of information into a single score, they first compute an exponential function of occlusion and an exponential function of dilation. The final quality score is the product of the three measures.

Kalka et al. [86] investigate a number of image quality factors, including percent occlusion, defocus, motion blur, gaze deviation, amount of specular reflection on the iris, lighting variation on the iris, and total pixel count on the iris. In evaluating various data sets, they found that the ICE data had more defocused images, the WVU data had more lighting variation, and the CASIA data had more occlusion than the other sets.

Schmid and Nicolo [181] evaluated iris image quality metrics in terms of how well they predict recognition performance. The quality metric is applied to each of a pair of images being matched, and the metrics mapped to a predicted matching score. The metric(s) can then be evaluated by how well the predicted matching score is correlated with the calculated matching score. Schmid and Nicolo experimented with both iris and face image data.

Zhou et al. [218, 219] propose adding four modules to the traditional iris biometrics system in order to handle nonideal images. A "Quality Filter Unit" eliminates images that are too poor quality to be useful. A "Segmentation Evaluation Unit" evaluates the quality of the segmentation. A "Quality Measure Unit" determines if there is sufficient iris area available to generate features. A "Score Fusion Unit" combines a segmentation score and a quality score. Experiments are shown using the MBGC dataset [180] and their own IUPUI near-field iris video dataset.

Zuo and Schmid [221] presented both a global quality metric for selecting individual frames from an iris video or image sequence, and multiple local quality metrics for the iris in a given frame. The global quality metric experiments use the Iris On the Move [119] videos distributed as part of the Multiple Biometric Grand Challenge [145]. The local quality metrics look at segmentation quality, interlacing, illumination contrast, illumination evenness, percent occlusion, pixel count, dilation, off-angle view and blur, and are evaluated using images from the ICE 2005 dataset [19, 146].

Breitenbach and Chawdhry [22] performed experiments looking at quality factors for an image and how they predict performance of face and iris recognition. They synthetically vary image factors such as defocus, contrast, and resolution. They find that the factors considered are better predictors of iris biometric performance than face recognition performance.

Proenca [153] presented an approach to quality assessment of iris images acquired in the visible-light domain. Factors considered in the quality assessment include focus, motion, angle, occlusions, area, pupillary dilation, and levels of iris pigmentation. The claim is that by using the output of the segmentation phase in each assessment, the method is able to handle severely degraded samples.

Phillips and Beveridge [141] presented a challenging view on the topic of using quality metrics in biometric matching. By analogy to AI-completeness in artificial intelligence and completeness in the theory of algorithms, they introduce the concept of biometric-completeness. The idea is that a problem in biometrics is biometric-complete if it can be shown to be equivalent to the biometric recognition problem and "the key result in this paper shows that finding the perfect quality measure for any algorithm is equivalent to finding the perfect verification algorithm."

2.2.2 Image Compression

Daugman and Downing [35] presented a detailed study of the effects of compression of the original iris image on the performance of iris biometrics. They present schemes that combine isolation of the iris region with JPEG and JPEG 2000 compression, evaluate their approach on images from the Iris Challenge Evaluation (ICE) 2005 dataset [19, 146] and conclude that it is "possible to compress iris images to as little as 2000 bytes with minimal impact on recognition performance."

Ives et al. [82] explore the effect of varying levels of JPEG 2000 compression, using the ICE 2005 dataset [19, 146], and find that the false reject rate increases with increasing level of compression, but that the false accept rate is stable.

Konrad et al. [93, 94] aim to compress iris data without degrading matching results. They use JPEG compression on unwrapped polar iris images. They design and compare different quantization tables to use with the JPEG compression. Two of their tested Q-tables are designed to preserve more angular iris texture than radial iris texture (i.e. the horizontal texture in the unwrapped image). The other two Q-tables are derived from the first two through genetic optimization. There is no clear winner among their tested Q-tables, and they conclude that custom Q-tables for iris recognition should be optimized to a specific target bitrate for best performance.

Kostmajer et al. [95] apply compression to the original, rectilinear iris images. They propose custom JPEG quantization tables for iris recognition. Their theory is that the highest and medium frequencies are not essential for iris recognition performance because of the coarse quantization used in template generation. Therefore, they test four custom compression tables, each one with an increasing number of high frequencies suppressed. In most of their tests, their proposed tables outperform the standard JPEG quantization table. Based on their experiments, they conclude that iris compression is not realistic at compression rates greater than 20. On the other hand, their experiments show that compression does not noticeably affect the impostor distribution.

Hämmerle-Uhl et al. [63] use JPEG 2000 compression on original iris images. They aim to improve compression performance using region of interest coding. They detect the iris using edge detection and a Hough transform, then set the ROI to the detected candidate circle with largest radius inside a certain allowed range. They compare compression with and without ROI coding and find that match scores improve and error rates decrease when using the ROI coding.

Carneiro et al. [25] examine the performance of different iris segmentation algorithms in the presence of varying degrees of fractal and JPEG 2000 image compression, using the UBIRIS dataset [154].

2.3 Iris Region Segmentation

Publications related to segmenting the iris region constitute a significant fraction of the published work in iris biometrics. Many of these publications can be grouped as tackling similar versions of the traditional iris segmentation problem; e.g., given one still image, find the pupillary and limbic boundaries. However, there are also a variety of approaches being explored to find occlusion by specular highlights and eyelashes, to segment the iris using less-constrained boundaries, and to refine initial segmentation boundaries.

Iris segmentation algorithms that assume circular boundaries for the iris region continue to appear in some conferences. We have chosen not to cover this subarea of work here, as the current frontier in iris segmentation is generally now focused on removing the assumption of circular boundaries [26, 74, 184] and on refining the segmentation to account for various occlusions and distortions of the iris texture.

Publications also continue to appear that propose iris segmentation techniques that are evaluated on the CASIA version 1 dataset. Again, we have chosen not to cover this subarea of work in this survey. The use of the CASIA v1 dataset to evaluate iris segmentation algorithms is inherently problematic. This is because the images have been edited to have a circular region of constant intensity value for the region of each iris [142]. Therefore, any segmentation algorithm built around the assumption of a circular region of constant dark intensity value should naturally meet with great success on this dataset, even though these conditions are generally not present in the iris region of real images.

A number of researchers have considered various approaches to segmenting the iris with boundaries not constrained to be circles. Wibowo and Maulana [209] evaluated an approach using the CASIA v1 data and their own dataset of 30 visible-light iris images. Labati et al. [99, 100] propose methods to find the pupil center and then to find the inner and outer iris boundaries, presenting experimental results on CASIA v3 and UBIRIS v2 images. Kheirolahy et al. [91] propose a method of finding the pupil in color images, with experiments on the UBIRIS dataset. Chen et al. [29, 30] consider an approach to segmenting the iris region under less-constrained conditions, experimenting with the UBIRIS v2 visible-light iris image dataset, and placing in the top six in the NICE competition. Broussard and Ives [23] trained a neural net to classify pixels in an iris image as either being on an iris boundary or not, selecting the most useful eight features from a pool of 322 possible features. Subjective visual evaluation of results indicates improvement over methods that assume circular boundaries. Zuo and Schmid [222] presented an approach to segmenting the iris using ellipses for the pupillary and the limbic boundaries, with experiments on CASIA, ICE and WVU datasets. Pan et al. [136] detected edge points using "phase congruency analysis" and fit ellipses to the detected edge points. They test their method on CASIA v2 and CASIA v3 twins data sets. Roy and Bhattacharya [173–175] suggested a segmentation method using geometric active contours. They apply opening operators to suppress interference from eyelashes [174]. Next, they approximate elliptical boundaries for the pupil and limbic boundaries. They refine the detected boundary using geometric active contours (i.e., active contours implemented via level set) to a narrow band over the estimated boundary. They fit parabolic curves to the upper and lower eyelids. To isolate the eyelashes, they use 1D Gabor filters and variance of intensity. Roy and Bhattacharya [177] also described a level set style active contour method for finding the pupil and iris boundaries in nonideal iris images, presenting results on the UBIRIS v2, ICE 2005 and WVU nonideal iris datasets.

Ryan et al. [179] present the "starburst method" for segmenting the iris. They preprocessed the image using smoothing and gradient detection, and then they find a pupil location as a starting point for the algorithm. To do so, they set the darkest 5 % of the image to black, and all other pixels to white. Then they create a Chamfer image: the darkest pixel in the Chamfer image is the pixel farthest from any white pixel in a thesholded image. They use the darkest point of the Chamfer image as a starting point. Next, they compute the gradient of the image along rays pointing radially away from the start point. The two highest gradient locations are assumed to be points on the pupillary and limbic boundaries and are used to fit several ellipses using randomly selected subsets of points. An average of the best ellipses was reported as the final boundary. The eyelids were detected using active contours.

Pundlik et al. [155] treat the image as a graph where pixels are nodes and neighboring pixels are joined with edges, Their first goal is to assign a label—either "eyelash" or "non-eyelash"—to each pixel. After removing specular reflections, they use the gradient covariance matrix to find intensity variation in different directions for each pixel. Then they create a probability map, P, that assigns the probability of each pixel having high texture in its neighborhood. The "energy" corresponding to a particular labeling of the images is written as a function of a smoothness term and a data term. The data term is based on a texture probability map. The second goal was to assign each pixel one of four labels: eyelash, pupil, iris, or background. They use a method similar to the initial eyelash segmentation; however, this time they use an alpha-beta swap graph-cut algorithm. Finally, they refine their labels using a geometric algorithm to approximate the iris with an ellipse.

Vatsa et al. [197] improve the speed of active contour segmentation by using a two-level hierarchical approach. First, they find an approximate initial pupil boundary, modeled as an ellipse with five parameters. The parameters are varied in a search for a boundary with maximum intensity change. For each possible parameter combination, the algorithm randomly selects 40 points on the elliptical boundary and calculated total intensity change across the boundary. Once the pupil boundary is found, the algorithm searched for the iris boundary in a similar manner, this time selecting 120 points on the boundary for computing intensity change. The approximate iris boundaries are refined using an active contour approach. The active contour is initialized to the approximate pupil boundary and allowed to vary in a narrow band of $\pm$ 5 pixels. In refining the limbic boundary, the contour is allowed to vary in a band of $\pm$ 10 pixels.

Although there are relatively few papers devoted specifically to this topic, better detection of specular highlights in the iris image is still an area of current research [183, 211]. He et al. [71] acknowledge the difficulty of detecting and removing specular highlights in the iris image and present an interesting multi-sample approach to this problem. They assume that multiple images of the same iris are available, with the specular highlights appearing in different places on the iris in different images. The segmentation of the iris region in the images is simple, and assumes concentric circular boundaries for the pupil and iris. The rectangular iris images from the multiple images are then registered, bright spots detected, and the bright spots replaced with values from a different image.

Liu et al. [110] propose a method for eyelid detection in UBIRIS v2 (visible-light) images. Their method uses a parabolic integro-differential operator similar to the operator described by Daugman for iris localization. They find that their proposed method has lower pixel error compared to algorithms involving the IDO alone, using detected edge pixels alone, or an algorithm using Canny edge detection and a Hough transform.

While most publications assume a single still image as the input to the segmentation stage, Du et al. [39] propose a method of using multiple thresholds on the intensity value in an image to achieve a rough segmentation of the iris in frames of a video sequence. Du et al. [40] also propose an approach to segmentation of iris images obtained in a context in which the subject is not explicitly cooperative. They filter to drop video frames in which the iris is not visible, fit ellipses for the iris boundaries, and develop a method to remove noise in the iris region.

Several researchers have considered the problem of evaluating the quality of an iris segmentation. Kalka et al. [85] tackle the problem of predicting or detecting when iris segmentation has failed, with experiments on the WVU and ICE datasets, and on two iris segmentation algorithms. Li and Savvides [106, 107] present work on taking an existing iris segmentation mask, in principle from any algorithm, and automatically refining it to produce a better segmentation.

Proenca [150, 151] observes that images acquired in the visible wavelength in less-constrained environments tend to have noise that results in severely degraded images. Whereas many iris biometric segmentation algorithms key on the pupil to anchor the segmentation, he proposes to anchor the segmentation on the sclera as much more naturally distinguishable than any other part of the eye. The sclera also provides a useful constraint, in that it must be immediately adjacent on both sides of the iris. One of the differences in iris biometrics processing for visible-light versus near-IR images, is that the pupillary boundary tends to be more distinct in near-IR whereas the limbic boundary appears to be more distinct in visible light.

Lee et al. [102] describe a way to locate and analyze eyes in the MBGC portal videos. They use the Viola-Jones detector that comes with OpenCV and is trained to detect eye pairs. They measure the edge density in an image to determine the focus level and select appropriate frames from the video. The IrisBEE algorithm [144] is used for segmentation and feature extraction. Eyes from the MBGC portal videos are compared to higher quality still iris images. The two-eye detection rate in the videos was 97.7 %. The segmentation rate was 81.5 %, and the matching rate was 56.1 %. This matching rate is low compared to typical iris recognition systems, likely reflecting the low level of iris image quality in the MBGC portal videos.

Munemoto et al. [133] suggest that "it is important to not only exclude the noise region, but also estimate the true texture patterns behind these occlusions. Even though masks are used for comparison of iris features, the features around masks are still affected by noise. This is because the response of filters near the boundary of the mask is affected by the noisy pixels." They used an image-filling algorithm to estimate the texture behind the occlusions. This algorithm iteratively fills 9×9 patches of the occluded region with 9×9 patches from unoccluded regions. It estimates textures at the boundary of the region first, selecting 9×9 source patches from the unoccluded iris that closely match the iris texture near the boundary of the area to be filled.

Thompson and Flynn [195] presented a method of improving the recognition performance of iris biometrics by perturbing parameters of the iris segmentation. The perturbations generate a set of alternate segmentations, and so also alternate iris codes, which effectively result in an improved authentic distribution.

2.4 Texture Coding and Matching

Performing texture analysis to produce a representation of the iris texture, and the matching of such representations, is at the core of any iris biometric system. A large fraction of the publications in iris biometrics deal with this area. It is not necessarily straightforward to organize these publications into well-defined and meaningful categories. Nevertheless, they are grouped here in a way intended to represent important common themes.

2.4.1 Experiments Using the CASIA V1 Dataset

One cluster of publications compares different texture filter formulations and presents experimental results on the CASIA v1 dataset. The issue with the CASIA v1 dataset that was mentioned earlier—artificial, circular, constant intensity pupil regions—does not necessarily compromise the use of this dataset in evaluating the performance of algorithms for texture analysis and matching. However, the small size of the dataset and the many papers in the literature that report near-perfect performance on this dataset make it nearly impossible to use it to document a measurable improvement over the state of the art. Therefore, for space considerations, we do not cover this subarea of publications in this survey. Fatt et al. [48, 49] implement a fairly typical 1D log-Gabor iris biometric system on a digital signal processor (DSP), and show results on CASIA v1 dataset. Showing the relative speed of software versus DSP implementations of an algorithm is an example of a context where using the CASIA v1 dataset may be reasonable.

2.4.2   "Eigen-Iris" Approaches

One group of papers might be characterized, by analogy to "eigen-faces" in face recognition, as using an "eigen-iris" approach. Chowhan and Sihinde [32] proposed using PCA for iris recognition, in an eigen-face style of approach. Moravec et al. [131] also use a PCA-based approach, with color images of 128 irises. Zhiping et al. [217] use a 2-D weighted PCA approach to extracting a feature vector, showing improvement over plain PCA. Chen et al. [28] use 2D PCA and LDA, on UBIRIS images, showing an improvement over PCA or LDA alone. Eskandari and Toygar [46] explored subpattern-based PCA and modular PCA, achieving performance up to 92 % rank-one recognition on the CASIA v3 dataset. Erbilek and Toygar [45] looked at recognition in the presence of occlusions, comparing holistic versus subpattern based approaches, using PCA and subspace LDA for iris matching, with experiments on the CASIA, UPOL, and UBIRIS datasets. Xu and Guo [213] propose to extract iris features from the normalized iris image using a method that they call Complete 2D PCA.

2.4.3   Alternative Texture Filter Formulations

Many researchers have looked at different mathematical formulations of filters to use in analyzing the iris texture. Patil and Patilkulkarni [139] used wavelet analysis to create a texture feature vector, with experiments on the CASIA v2 dataset. Velisavl-jevic [199] experiments with the use of oriented separable wavelet transforms, or directionlets, using the CASIA v3 dataset, and shows that they can give improved performance for a larger size binary iris code. Sun and Tan [188] propose using ordinal features, which represent the relative intensity relationship between regions of the iris image filtered by multi-lobe differential filters. Krichen et al. [96] explore using a normalized phase correlation approach to matching, as an alternative to the standard binary iris code. They compare results to the OSIRIS [14] and Masek [117] algorithms, on the ICE 2005 and the CASIA-BioSecure iris datasets.

Al-Qunaieer and Ghouti [156] used quaternion log-Gabor filters to analyze the texture of images in the UBIRIS color image dataset, and also [56] use a quaternion Fourier Transform and phase correlation to improve performance. Bodade and Talbar [16] used a rotated complex wavelet transform in matching iris textures, with experimental results on the UBIRIS dataset, but do not improve recognition performance over the Gabor wavelet. Tajbakhsh et al. [189] present a method of feature extraction based on Ma et al.'s earlier method of analyzing local intensity variation [114], and propose four improvements to the earlier method to make it work with the noisy images in the UBIRIS data set. Tajbakhsh et al. [190] use a 2-D Discrete Wavelet Transform applied to overlapping 32×32 pixel blocks, and achieve 0.66 % EER on the UBIRIS data.

The motivation behind Miyazawa's proposed method [127] is that Daugman-like, feature-based iris recognition algorithms require many parameters, and that their proposed algorithm should be easier to train. For each comparison using the proposed method, they take two images and select a region that is unoccluded in both images. They take the Discrete Fourier Transform of both valid regions, then apply a phase-only correlation (POC) function. The POC function involves a difference between the phase components from both images. They use band-limited POC to avoid information from high-frequency noise. The proposed algorithm requires only two parameters: one representing the effective horizontal bandwidth for recognition, and the other representing the effective vertical bandwidth. They achieve better results using Phase-Only Correlation than using Masek's 1D log-Gabor algorithm.

2.4.4   Alternative Methods of Texture Analysis

Another group of papers explores texture representation and matching approaches that do not map directly to the typical texture filter framework.

Gray-level cooccurrence matrices (GLCM) can be used to describe texture in an image [66]. A GLCM is formed by counting the cooccurrences of brightness values of pixel pairs in the image at a certain distance and direction. Chen et al. [27] propose a modified GLCM based on looking at triples of pixels instead of pairs. They call their modified method a "3D-GLCM," and use it to describe the texture of iris images in the UBIRIS data set. Using equal error rate, the 2D-GLCM method performs better, but for a FAR of 0 %, the 3D-GLCM performs better.

Kannavara and Bourbakis [90] explored using a local-global graph methodology to generate feature vectors, with experiments on color iris images. Sudha et al. [187] compute a local partial Hausdorff distance based on comparing the edge detected images of two irises, obtaining 98 % rank-one recognition on a UPOL dataset representing 128 irises. Kyaw [98] explores using simple statistical features such as mean, median, mode and variance within concentric bands of the iris, but presents no experimental results. Wu and Wang [210] use intensity surface difference between irises for matching and report relatively low performance on the CASIA v1 dataset. Mehrotra et al. [122] use a Harris corner detector to find interest points, which are paired across images for matching. Tests on Bath, CASIA and IITK datasets indicate that this method does not perform as well as traditional iris code approaches. To avoid aliasing problems from "unwrapping" an iris image, Mehrotra et al. [121] extract features from the annular iris image. They use the SURF algorithm (Speeded Up Robust Features) to identify rotation-invariant features, and report recognition accuracy above 97 % on BATH, CASIA3, and IITK databases. Radhika et al. [158] use continuous dynamic programming to extract iris texture information. They test their method on CASIA v2 and UBIRIS v1 data. Overall, it appears that none of the various different approaches in this category has yet demonstrated any clear performance improvement over the more traditional texture filtering approaches used in iris biometrics.

Patil and Patilkulkarni [137] described a comparison of different texture analysis methods for iris matching. The compare the use of statistical measures (mean, median, mode, variance), lifting wavelet transform, and gray-level cooccurrence matrices for deriving texture features. They perform experiments using the CASIA v2 dataset, and find that the lifting wavelet transform provides the best recognition accuracy. Patil and Patilkulkarni [138] also explored the use of SIFT features for iris biometrics.

Rathgeb and Uhl [162] developed an approach to iris biometrics that uses Contrast Limited Adaptive Histogram Equalization and traces pixel intensity variations along rows of the normalized image (concentric circles of the iris region). These are termed "pixel paths." They achieve an EER on experiments with the CASIA v3 dataset in the range of 1–2 %. They also show how this approach lends itself to cancelable biometrics.

2.4.5   Algorithms that Analyze the Iris in Parts

Several researchers have proposed approaches that analyze the iris region in multiple parts and combine the results. One motivation for this type of approach is to reduce the impact of segmentation errors and noise in the imaging process.

Adam et al. [1] analyze iris texture in eight subregions of the iris and fuse the distances from these local windows, with experiments on data from the CASIA v3 dataset. Bastys et al. [8] divide the iris into sectors and calculate a set number of local extrema in each sector at a number of scales. They achieve perfect separation between genuine and impostor scores for CASIA v1 and CASIA v3 interval, an EER of 0.13 % for the CASIA v2 data, and 0.25 % for the ICE 2005 data. Garg et al. [52] propose a method that uses a grid on the iris image and a vector of the average pixel values in the elements of the grid for representing and matching the iris texture. Eskandari and Toygar [46] explore subpattern-based PCA and modular PCA, achieving performance up to 92 % rank-one recognition on the CASIA v3 dataset. Erbilek and Toygar [45] looked at recognition in the presence of occlusions, comparing holistic versus subpattern based approaches, using PCA and subspace LDA for iris matching, with experiments on the CASIA, UPOL, and UBIRIS datasets. Lin et al. [108] divide the iris area into four local areas and the face into 16 local areas in their approach to iris and face multi-biometrics.

Campos et al. [24] propose an alternative method of feature extraction. They apply histogram equalization and binarization to the unwrapped iris image, and use a self-organizing Map neural network to divide the binary image into nodes. From the topological graph of the image, they compute corresponding Voronoi polygons. Next they calculate the mean, variance, and skewness of the image in each polygonal region. They achieve 99.87 % correct recognition on the Bath University iris data.

Rachubinski [157] presented a method of feature extraction using wavelet coefficients based on a wedgelet dictionary. A wedgelet is a division of a square region into two sections. The wedgelet is parameterized by the distance of the segment from the center of the square, and the angle of the segment dividing the two regions. Rachubinski divided the unwrapped iris image into overlapping local regions of 8×8 pixels, and determines a wedgelet dictionary for each region. The wedgelet angles are quantized to create a binary iris code, and codes are compared using Hamming distances. Rachubinski achieved 100 % rank-one recognition rate (0.15 % EER) on the relatively non-challenging CASIA v1 dataset.

Don et al. [37] present what is termed a "personalized iris matching strategy". A weight map is learned for the features in the image of each given iris, based on training images of that iris. This is conceptually similar to the "fragile bits" work of Hollingsworth. This approach is said to be especially useful in the case of poor quality iris images.

2.4.6 Approaches to Speed Iris Matching

Hao et al. [65] present a technique to speed up the search of a large database of iris codes, with experiments that use over 600,000 iris codes from the ongoing application for border control in the United Arab Emirates. They use a "beacon-guided search" to achieve a "substantial improvement in search speed with a negligible loss of accuracy" in comparison to an exhaustive search.

Gentile et al. [55] experiment with generating a shorter iris code that maintains recognition power, and conclude that it is best to focus on the middle radial bands of the iris, and to sample every n-th band. Gentile et al. [54] also use a short length iris code to index into a large iris dataset to reduce the total number of iris code comparisons to search the dataset, with a small degradation in recognition rate.

Roy and Bhattacharya [172–176] reduced matching time by applying feature selection to choose the most discriminating features. They explore the use of genetic algorithms to select a subset of most useful features for iris matching [172, 176]. In [174] they use Support Vector Machine–Recursive Feature Elimination (SVM-RFE). In [173] they apply a genetic algorithm to select important features, and use an iterative algorithm, called the Contribution-Selection Algorithm, from the field of coalitional game theory, to reduce the feature vector dimension.

Mehrotra et al. [123] propose an indexing algorithm to reduce the search time. They divide each unwrapped iris image into subbands using a multiresolution Discrete Cosine Transform. They create a histogram of transform coefficients for each subband using all the images in the database. They use histograms containing about ten bins each. The algorithm forms a key for each image from noting the bin numbers associated with the subbands of the image. The keys are organized into a search tree. To search for a match to a new image, the algorithm computes the key for the new image, retrieves all irises with matching keys from the database, and compares iris templates from the retrieved set. They achieve a bin miss rate of 1.5 % with a penetration rate of 41 %.

Rathgeb et al. [165] present an approach to "incremental" iris code matching, with the aim of reducing the number of bit comparisons used per recognition result. It is claimed that "the proposed technique offers significant advantages over conventional bit-masking, which would represent binary reliability masks."

2.4.7   Exploiting "fragile" Bits in the Iris Code

Hollingsworth et al. [77] describe the concept of "fragile bits" in the traditional Daugman-style iris code. Bits in the iris code can be fragile due essentially to random variation in the texture filter result, causing them to "flip" between 0 and 1. Recognition performance can be improved by masking an appropriate fraction of the most fragile bits. Dozier et al. [38] use a genetic algorithm to evolve a mask for the iris code that best masks out the "fragile" iris code bits. Hollingsworth et al. [80] describe an approach to averaging the iris image through multiple frames of video, prior to generating the iris code, to improve recognition performance. This approach is effectively reducing the fragility of the bits in the iris code. Hollingsworth et al. [78] also describe an approach to using the spatial coincidence of the fragile bits in the iris code to improve recognition performance.

2.4.8   Use of "Sparse Representation" Techniques

Pillai et al. [147] explore the use of sparse representation techniques for iris biometrics. This approach involves having a number of training images per iris, where the images span the range of different appearances that the iris might have. An unknown iris is then recognized by solving a minimization problem that finds a representation of the unknown image in terms of the training images.

2.5   Multi-biometrics Involving the Iris

The term "multi-biometric" is used to refer to techniques that use more than one biometric sample in making a decision. Often the samples are from different sites on the body; for example, iris and fingerprint. Also they might be from different sensing modalities; for example, 3D and 2D. Or they might be repeated samples from the same sensor and site on the body. The motivation for multi-biometrics is to (a) increase the fraction of the population for which some usable sample can be obtained, and/or (b) increase recognition accuracy, and/or (c) make it more difficult to spoof a biometric system. In India's Unique ID program [169], in many ways the most ambitious biometrics application in the world to date, iris and fingerprint are used primarily, it seems, to increase coverage of the population.

Most multi-biometric work involving the iris has looked at combining iris with some other biometric site, rather than multiple sensing modalities for iris, or repeated iris samples. Papers have been published looking at almost any combination of iris and some other modality that one can imagine. Often the practical motivation for the particular pairing is not clear. The vast majority of this work has used *chimera* subjects; that is, virtual subjects created by pairing together biometric samples from already existing uni-modal datasets. For example, several papers use iris images from a CASIA dataset and face images from the ORL [101] dataset. In general, there is a need for research in this area to progress to using true multi-biometric datasets, to use datasets representing a much larger number of subjects and images than in the ORL face dataset or the CASIA v1 iris dataset, and to compare performance of the multi-biometric approach to performance of state-of-the art algorithms for the individual biometrics. In the summaries below, we have tried to explicitly note the few instances where the dataset used was not chimeric.

Perhaps naturally, the largest cluster of papers in this area deals with the combination of face and iris. This group of publications is multi-biometric both in the sense of combining iris and face, and often also in the sense of using near infrared illumination (for iris) and visible light (for face). Lin et al. [108] generalize the posterior union model (PUM) to perform face and iris multi-biometrics, constructing chimera subjects from the XM2VTS or AR face datasets and the CASIA iris dataset, and dividing the normalized face images into sixteen local areas and the iris area into four local areas. Gan and Liu [51] apply a discrete wavelet transform to face and iris images, and use a kernel Fischer Discriminant analysis, with chimera subjects created from the ORL [101] face database and (apparently) the CASIA v1 iris database. Wang et al. [204, 206] use a complex common vector approach to face and iris, using the ORL and Yale face datasets and the CASIA v1 iris dataset. Liu et al. [109] experiment with a 40-person chimera dataset made from ORL face images and CASIA iris images, with relatively low performance. Wang et al. [205] fuse face and iris information at the feature level. They create a complex feature vector from the real-valued iris feature vector and the real-valued face feature vector. Next, they use complex Fisher discriminate analysis (CFDA) to maximize the between-class scatter with respect to the within-class scatter. They test their algorithm on CASIA v1 iris images and ORL and Yale face images. Wang and Han [201] fuse information from face and iris at the score level. The scores from the two different algorithms are normalized using two sigmoid functions, and then they employ a SVM-based fusion rule to obtain a final score. They test their method using faces from the ORL data set and irises from UBIRIS data set. Breitenbach and Chawdhry [22] perform experiments looking at image quality factors for an image and how they predict performance of face and iris recognition. Rattani and Tistarelli [166] fuse information from face and iris at the feature level. They divide the images into windows, and extract one SIFT feature from each window. They obtain feature vectors of length 128 each from the face, right eye, and left eye images, and find that a fusion of face, right iris and left iris gets better performance than any one or any fusing of two. Morizet and Gilles [132] use data from the FERET face dataset and a CASIA iris dataset in presenting a method that develops a user-specific fusion of scores from the two modalities.

Vatsa et al. [198] consider approaches based on multiple iris samples. They use elements of belief function theory for iris-based multi-biometrics and look at two scenarios: combining results from enrolling one iris with two images and combining results from the left and right iris each enrolled with one image.

A broad variety of other multi-biometric combinations involving the iris have been studied. Several researchers have looked at fingerprint and iris. Baig et al. [5] investigate iris and fingerprint fusion using the Masek algorithm and a SUNY-Buffalo algorithm, respectively, experimenting on a West Virginia University dataset. It is noted that performance is relatively low, due to design for a "small memory footprint realtime system." Ross et al. [171] explore multi-biometric iris and fingerprint where fusion is used only in certain cases within the Doddington Zoo framework, experimenting with a chimera dataset of fingerprints from a WVU dataset and irises from a CASIA dataset. Elmadani [44] presents the "fingerIris" algorithm for combination of iris and fingerprint. The approach is evaluated on a true multi-biometric dataset representing 200 individuals. The system gets 4–5 false reject and/or false accept results on this dataset, depending on the setting of the decision threshold.

Wang et al. [202] explore score-level fusion of iris matching and palmprint matching using an apparently chimera dataset representing 100 persons. Tayal et al. [12, 193, 194] use a wavelets approach to analyze iris texture and speech samples for multi-biometrics. Sheela et al. [185] experiment with iris and signature, using CASIA v2 and MYCT datasets, respectively, but do not focus on multi-biometric combination. Mishra and Pathak [126] explore wavelet analysis of iris and ear images for multi-biometrics on a chimera dataset representing 128 persons.

Poh et al. [149] report on multi-biometric research involving face, iris and fingerprint, carried out as part of the BioSecure project. This project particularly looks at quality-dependent fusion at the score-level and cost-sensitive fusion at the score level. A total of 22 fusion systems were evaluated in this project.

Maltoni et al. [116] discuss pros and cons of fusing multiple biometrics. Generally, fusing more classifiers improves performance if the classifiers are not highly correlated. However, extra classifiers can increase cost and throughput time of the system. Maltoni et al. discuss performing fusion at the image, feature, score, rank, or decision level.

Hollingsworth et al. [79] present an approach that uses multiple iris samples taken using the same sensor, taking advantage of temporal continuity in an iris video to improve matching performance. They select multiple frames from an iris video, unwrap the iris into polar form, and then average multiple frames together. They find that this image-level fusion yield better matching performance than previous multi-gallery score fusion methods.

Conti et al. [33] give an overview of concepts and terminology in multi-biometric systems. They also present an approach to using fuzzy logic methods for score fusion in a multi-biometric system.

Zuo et al. [220] investigate the possibility of matching between a visible-light image and a NIR image of the iris. They formulate a method to estimate the NIR iris image from a color image. It is claimed that this approach "achieves significantly high performance compared to the case when the same NIR image is matched against R (red) channel alone."

2.5.1 Ocular Biometrics

The papers covered in this section deal with "ocular" biometrics as a possible multi-biometric complement to iris. An ocular biometric is one based on features of the region of the face around the eye. Much of this research uses ocular regions cropped from visible-light images, often from the Face Recognition Grand Challenge (FRGC) face image dataset. Xu et al. [212] use local binary pattern (LBP) texture features computed over the ocular region. In experiments with images from the FRGC dataset, they achieve 61 % verification rate at 0.1 % false accept rate. Miller et al. [125] also propose a method using LBP texture features, again using images cropped from the FRGC database. They investigate the effects of image blur, resolution of the periocular region, illumination effects and different color bands. Lyle et al. [113] present an approach to predicting the gender and ethnicity of a person using LBP features and an SVM classifier. In experiments with images from the FRGC dataset, they obtain 93 % accuracy on gender classification and 91 % on Asian/non-Asian ethnicity classification. Bharadwaj et al. [10] present a method of ocular recognition with experiments using the UBIRIS iris images. Their method uses the GIST global descriptor and LBP texture features. Merkow et al. [124] predict the gender of the subject based on features computed from he ocular region, and obtain 85 % correct gender prediction using frontal-view color face images taken from the web.

Hollingsworth et al. [75] study how human observers rate the value of different features of the ocular region for recognition. This study was done with NIR images from the LG 2200 iris sensor. Thus this investigation is more directly relevant to ocular as a complement to iris, and less directly relevant to ocular as a subset of face recognition using visible-light images.

2.6 Privacy and Security

This section includes several somewhat different areas of work. The development of privacy-enhancing techniques generally involves rigorous conceptual or mathematical approaches. More general security techniques look at integrating biometrics into encryption schemes in some way. The study of liveness detection, or spoofing and anti-spoofing, often involves clever exploitation of sensor capabilities.

Ratha [161] gives a broad perspective on security and privacy issues in large-scale biometric systems. Taking a system-level view of biometric authentication, he considers the various possible attack points. He also summarizes the concept of cancelable biometrics as a means to enhance privacy and security. This is a good general article for someone who is not already familiar with basic concepts in this area.

2.6.1   Privacy-Enhancing Techniques

The area of privacy-enhancing techniques for biometrics is challenging and fast-moving. Its importance is perhaps not yet fully understood and appreciated by the field as a whole. One can see the importance of this area by considering what would happen in a biometric-enabled application when a person's biometric template is stolen. The application needs some way to protect each individual's biometric template and/or to be able to revoke an enrollment in the application and reenroll a person.

Several authors have proposed encryption methods to protect the privacy of a biometric template. Luo et al. [112] propose to perform anonymous biometric matching, using encryption to protect the probe biometric. Alghamdi et al. [4] propose using the iris code to generate a key for encryption of the iris image or other data. Moi et al. [129] propose using AES encryption of an enrolled iris code to store the key to encrypted documents.

Li and Du [104, 105] propose watermarking the iris image at the time that it is acquired by the sensor, as a means to later determine the authenticity of the image. This would in principle allow detection of an image that did not originate with the particular sensor.

Tan et al. [192] propose an "image hashing" technique, which converts the iris biometric into a short bit string in a manner that is irreversible. That is, given the short bit string, it is not possible to generate the iris biometric.

Agrawal and Savvides [3] describe an approach to hiding an iris biometric template in a host image. Their steganographic approach is designed to cause imperceptible change in the host image, and to be robust to JPEG artifacts.

Adjedj et al. [2] describe a way to create a biometric identification scheme while storing only encrypted data. Their method uses Symmetric Searchable Encryption which is a technique allowing a server to return all documents containing a particular keyword without learning anything about the keyword. They also use a family of locality sensitive hashes.

Hämmerle-Uhl et al. [62] propose a cancelable biometrics technique for irises. Cancelable biometrics are transformations of the original biometric that can be used for authentication without revealing the original, unaltered biometric, thus improving privacy for the user. In a cancelable biometric system, if a user's biometric is stolen, it can be canceled and reissued. They suggest two types of transformations. One proposed transformation is to randomly re-map blocks of iris texture to create a new signal. A second proposed transformation is to warp the texture along a grid with randomly offset vertices. Färberböck et al. [47] present an approach to transforming rectangular and polar iris images to enable cancelable iris biometrics. They experiment with block re-mapping and texture warping techniques for this purposes, using images from the CASIA v3 iris image dataset. Kanade et al. [87, 88] propose a two-factor approach to cancelable biometrics. Their proposed system uses an iris biometric and a password. In addition, their system uses an error-correcting-code technique and a user-specific shuffling key to increase the separation between the genuine and impostor distributions.

2.6.2 Security

Zhang et al. [215] propose a method to bind cryptographic keys to biometric data. During enrollment, they use Reed-Solomon coding and convolutional coding to add error-correcting data to a random key. They XOR the random key with the iris code, and produce helper data that hides the biometric and the key. During verification, the new iris code is XORed with the helper data, and then Reed-Solomon and Convolutional coding is used to decode the bit string and correct errors, thus unlocking the original cryptographic key. This method is similar to the method proposed by Hao et al. [64].

Rathgeb and Uhl [163] describe how to construct an iris-based fuzzy committment scheme to hide and retrieve a cryptographic key. Like [64], they use Reed-Solomon and Hadamard error-correcting codes. However, they show how to extend this scheme to an arbitrary iris biometrics algorithm.

Rathgeb and Uhl [162] discuss the problem of generating cryptographic keys from iris biometric samples. Their proposed approach uses an interval mapping technique and does not store biometric data in either raw or encrypted form. On experiments with the CASIA v3 dataset they are able to obtain key generation rates as high as 95 % using 5 enrollment samples.

Mahmud et al. [115] present a stream-cipher method that uses an iriscode as an initial input to seed a linear feedback shift register (LFSR). The LFSR is used to implement a stream-cipher. Since biometric templates are not identically repeatable, their system stores the intial biometric key on a smart card, which is programmed to release the key only when a similar biometric template is presented to unlock the smart card. The authors claim that their method is stronger than other ciphers like A5/1 and RC6.

Plaga [148] computes the theoretical maximal achievable information content of biometric keys. A biometric template, such as the iriscode proposed by Daugman, may have a length of 2048 bits. However, there are correlations in the bits, so in actuality, the information content in the template is smaller; for this example, 249 bits. Even so, a cryptographic key must necessarily be even shorter, because some number of bits are required for error correction. The number of bits required for error correction is a function of the number of bit errors between two templates from the same biometric feature. Using numbers provided by Daugman, Plaga determines that the maximum error-free and correlation-free biometric key has length 25 bits. Using numbers from a performance study conducted in the Frankfurt International Airport, Plaga determines that even fewer bits are available for biometric keys derived from face, fingerprint, and iris systems under airport-type operating conditions. Plaga concludes that "current commercial state-of-the-art biometric systems based on a single biometric feature like one finger or iris create templates from which no more than about 30 bits can be derived." Therefore, in order to use biometrics to create keys, either the performance of the systems must be substantially improved, or the systems must employ multi-modal or multi-instance biometrics (e.g., ten-print fingerprints).

Rathgeb and Uhl [164] consider the operation of two-factor authentication systems in which one of the factors is iris biometrics. They illustrate empirically how this helps to increase the separation of the authentic and impostor distributions relative to iris biometrics alone. They point out that the increased recognition accuracy in the two-factor system is based on the assumption "that additional factors are considered to never be stolen, lost, shared or duplicated where in practice the opposite is true" and discuss requirements for performance analysis of two-factor systems where one of the factors is a biometric.

2.6.3   Liveness Detection (anti-Spoofing)

Ruiz-Albacete et al. [178] explore "direct attacks" on an iris biometric system, in which a printed image of an iris is presented to an iris biometric system in an attempt to enroll an iris and/or to match an enrolled iris. They find that with appropriate choice of commercial printer, printer paper, and image processing algorithm, they are able to generate printed iris images that are enrolled and/or matched by the iris biometric system with substantial rates of success. The particular iris biometric system used in the experiments is the LG Iris Access 3000, a model that is no longer marketed. It is not clear that the experience with this system could easily be replicated with current commercial iris biometric systems, as current commercial systems may incorporate some sort of liveness detection that should defeat simple spoof attempts using paper-printed iris images.

Bodade and Talbar [15] propose an approach using multiple images of the same eye to look at variation in pupil dilation in order to detect iris spoofing. Takano and Nakamura [191] describe a neural network approach to iris recognition and to detecting "live" iris versus iris patterns printed on paper with experiments on a limited dataset representing 19 persons.

He et al. [72] aim to detect certain types of spoofs by detecting printed contact lenses. They consider three subregions on the right side of the iris, and three on the left. They analyze texture in each subregion using local binary patterns (LBPs) at multiple scales. Gaussian kernel density estimation is applied to complement the insufficiency of counterfeit iris images. They train an Adaboost classifier and select 85 LBP bins to use in testing. The proposed method achieves lower error rates than previous methods [68, 207].

He et al. [69] research detection of blurry, spoofed images. They note that Daugman's method of computing the FFT [34] can only detect printed contacts with high frequency, but it would fail if the spoofed pattern were partially blurred. He et al. use

wavelet packet decomposition to perform wavelet packet decomposition, and then employ a support vector machine to classify irises as live or spoofed. Their method correctly detects 98.6 % of the spoofed images in their data set.

2.7 Datasets and Evaluations

Datasets and evaluations play a large role in biometrics research. The widespread availability of common datasets has enabled many researchers to enter the field and demonstrate results whose relevance can be more easily understood due to the use of a known dataset. Evaluation programs have given researchers an idea about the current state of the art, and helped to focus and shape research to address the interests of sponsoring agencies.

Proenca et al. [154] describe the UBIRIS v2 dataset of visible-light, color iris images, acquired with four to eight meters distance between subject and sensor, and with subjects in motion. The dataset represents 261 subjects, with over 11,000 iris images. The purpose of the dataset is to support research on visible-light iris images acquired under far from ideal imaging conditions [154].

Johnson et al. [84] describe the "Q-FIRE" dataset of face and iris videos. These videos represent variations in focus blur, off-angle gaze and motion blurb, and are acquired at a range of 5 to 25 ft. This dataset is potentially useful for research in iris, face and multi-biometric face + iris.

Fierrez et al. [50] describe a multi-biometrics dataset acquired as part of the BioSecurID project. The dataset represents 400 persons, with biometric samples for speech, iris, face, handwriting, fingerprints, palmprint, hand contour geometry, and keystroking. The iris images are acquired with an LG Iris Access EOU 3000, and include four samples per eye with subjects not wearing eyeglasses and the presence of contact lenses recorded.

Ortega-Garcia et al. [135] describe a larger and more varied version of the multi-biometrics dataset resulting from the BioSecure Network of Excellence. This version contains biometric data representing more than 600 individuals. The data represents three different scenarios: "(i) over the Internet, (ii) in an office environment with desktop PC, and (iii) in indoor/outdoor environments with mobile portable hardware." Again, the iris part of the dataset was acquired using an LG Iris Access EOU 3000. The total dataset involved the efforts of eleven institutions. The iris portion of the dataset represents 667 persons, with two acquisitions per person, and two images of each iris in each session.

Schmid and Nicolo [182] suggest a method of analyzing the quality of an entire database. They compare the capacity of a recognition system to the capacity of a communication channel. Recognition channel capacity can be thought of as the maximum number of classes that can be successfully recognized. This capacity can also be used as a measure of overall quality of data in a database. The authors evaluate the empirical recognition capacity of biometrics systems that use PCA and ICA. They apply their method to four iris databases and two face databases. They find that the

BATH iris database has a relatively high sample signal-to-noise ratio, followed by CASIA-III, then ICE 2005. WVU had the lowest signal-to-noise ratio.

Krichen et al. [97] gives a brief introduction to the open-source iris recognition system, OSIRIS. They also describe their BioSecure Iris Database, which they combine with the CASIA v2 data to create a database with equal numbers of Asian and European subjects. They test the OSIRIS system on the CASIA-BioSecure data and also on the ICE 2005 data, and show that the OSIRIS system outperforms the Masek open-source system.

Phillips et al. [144] describe the results of the Face Recognition Vendor Test 2006 and the Iris Challenge Evaluation 2006. These evaluations follow on the Face Recognition Grand Challenge and the Iris Challenge Evaluation 2005. The ICE programs resulted in a dataset of over 64,000 iris images from over 350 subjects, acquired using an LG 2200 iris sensor in 2004 and 2005, being made available to the research community [19]. The dataset contains both "ideal" images, and "poor quality" images. The ICE programs also resulted in the source code of a baseline Daugman-like system being made available to the research community.

Petrovska et al. [140] describe the BioSecure benchmarking methodology for evaluating performance of biometric algorithms. The BioSecure reference system provides open-source software, publicly available biometric databases, and evaluation protocols that allow researchers to conduct reproducible research experiments. The book chapter explains the need for a common benchmarking methodology, and summarizes the frameworks. Frameworks for eight different biometric modalities are available: iris, fingerprint, signature, hand geometry, speech, 2D face, 3D face, and talking face.

The U.S. Government has organized a number of biometrics challenge problems and evaluations to motivate advancements in biometric technology. Phillips et al. [180] describe the data available in the Multiple Biometrics Grand Challenge (MBGC). The MBGC includes three different challenge problems, one of which involves iris recognition: the Portal Challenge Problem. The goal of the Portal Challenge Problem is to recognize people from near-infrared and visible-light video as they walk through a portal. Five different types of data are provided as part of the Portal Challenge: (1) still iris images from an LG2200 sensor, (2) video iris images from an LG2200 sensor, (3) medium-resolution, still, frontal face images, (4) high-resolution NIR video acquired from a Sarnoff Iris on the Move (IoM) system, and (5) high-definition, visible-light video acquired at the same time as the IoM videos. MBGC version 1 data was released in May 2008. MBGC version 2 data was released in February 2009.

Newton and Phillips [134] present a meta-analysis of three iris biometric evaluations: the Independent Testing of Iris Recognition Technology performed by the International Biometric Group, the Iris Recognition Study 2006 conducted by Authenti-Corp, and the Iris Challenge Evaluation 2006 conducted by the National Institute of Standards and Technology. The meta-analysis looks at the variation across the three studies in the false non-match rates reported for a false match rate of 1 in 1,000.

2.8 Performance Under Varying Conditions

Some early folklore of the iris biometrics field held that pupil dilation, contact lenses, and template aging do not negatively impact iris biometrics. Bowyer et al. [21] test these assertions. They show that iris biometric performance can be degraded by varying pupil dilation, by wearing non-cosmetic or cosmetic contact lenses, and by time lapse between enrollment and verification. They also show that using a different sensor between enrollment and verification can degrade performance. These factors primarily affect the match distribution, while the non-match distribution remains stable. Thus, for a verification scenario, the false accept rates are unaffected by these factors. For a watchlist scenario however, operators should be aware that suspects may attempt to fool the system by, for example, artificially dilating their eyes or wearing contacts.

Baker et al. [7] look at how contact lenses affect iris recognition, with the conclusion that even normal prescription contacts can cause an increase in the false rejection rate. The size of the increase in the false reject rate varies greatly across different matching algorithms and different types of contact lenses. In general, the effects of contact lenses on iris biometrics accuracy seem not yet fully understood.

Rankin et al. [160] explore effects of pupil dilation using images from three subjects taken over a period of up to 24 weeks under varying pupil dilation conditions, using a biometric slit lamp. Some unusual results are obtained on applying a version of an early Daugman algorithm and Masek's algorithm to these images. However, results generally agree with those of previous researchers that found that pupil dilation increases the false reject rate [61, 76].

Gonzaga and da Costa [57] propose a method to exploit the "consensual reflex" between a person's irises to illuminate one eye with visible light to control the dilation of both pupils, and image the other eye with NIR illumination. In this way, they can compute features of the iris over dilation.

Baker et al. [6] explore the effects of time lapse on iris biometrics. They compare the average Hamming distance between images taken 4 years apart with the average Hamming distance between images taken within a single semester. They find statistically significant evidence that the distance scores between images taken years apart are greater than the distance scores from images taken within a few months of each other. Using the IrisBEE iris matcher, they observe an approximate 0.018 increase in Hamming distance for matches with a 4-year time lapse. The increased false reject rate for the long-time-lapse matches relative to the short-time-lapse matches indicates that a template aging effect exists for iris biometrics. This was the first study to make any rigorous experimental evaluation of the issue of template aging for iris biometrics.

Borgen et al. [18] investigate the effects of common ocular diseases on iris recognition. They use the UBIRISv1 data set and simulate different pathologies. All simulated pathologies were validated by opthalmology and optometry specialists. Changes in iris color, scars from glaucoma surgery, and vessel growths caused only small increases in the false reject rate. Corneal bleaching and scarring caused a false reject rate of 86.8 %. The corneal bleaching caused segmentation of the outer iris boundary to fail in many cases. Central keratitis increased the false reject rate of bright-eyed subjects more than dark-eyed subjects. High-density infiltrates caused more problems with dark-eyed subjects. The authors conclude that iris recognition is robust for some pathologies, but that others—such as corneal bleaching—can unacceptably damage the false reject rate in just three months of disease progression.

2.9 Applications

A small number of publications have appeared which envision the use of iris biometrics in particular application scenarios. One interesting aspect of this group of papers is the very broad range of uses envisioned for biometrics, almost none of which involve national security.

Kadhum et al. propose using iris biometrics to authorize entry through doors to secure areas, an application for which commercial iris biometric systems already exist (e.g., LG Iris). Mondal et al. [130] propose using biometrics for secure access to home appliances over the network. Iris biometrics is used in this paper, but the approach can potential be extended to other biometrics. Garg et al. [53] propose a vision system that will recognize a set of hand gestures to control devices and use iris biometrics to authenticate the user identity. Leonard et al. [103] propose using fingerprint, iris, retina and DNA ("FIRD") to distinctively identify a patient to his or her complete electronic health care record. Mohammadi and Jahanshahi [128] propose an architecture for a secure e-tendering (offering and entering into a contract) system, with iris as the example biometric for identity verification. Wang et al. [203] propose using Daugman-like iris biometrics "to make the large animals be recognizable and traceable from the farm to the slaughterhouse," furthering the goal of food chain safety. Wang et al. [200] propose to use face and iris multi-biometrics as part of a scheme to enforce digital rights management, which would allow only authorized remote users to access content. Hassanien et al. [67] show how an iris template can be embedded in a digital image to prove ownership of the image.

Dutta et al. [41–43] propose embedding the iris code of a person in an audio file as a watermark to prove ownership of the audio file. They apply Haar wavelets at four levels of decomposition to create a feature vector from an iris image. Next, they binarize the feature vector by comparing each element of the vector to the median value in the vector. This process creates a biokey with power evenly distributed throughout the audio spectrum, thus allowing the key to be embedded in the audio signal without affecting listeners. They test their method by embedding biokeys in five different musical samples, then comparing the embedded keys with all iris keys in their database. A high correlation between the embedded key and the stored key is evidence of a match. Their method is robust to various types of attack on the audio signal.

2.9.1 Hardware Implementations

Liu-Jimenez et al. [111] and Rakvic et al. [159] describe the implementation of iris biometric algorithms on FPGAs. Zhao and Xie [216] describe an implementation of an iris biometric system on a DSP. Vandal and Savvides [196] present results of iris matching parallelized for execution on graphics processing units, and report a 14-times speedup relative to state-of-the-art single-core CPUs.

Jang et al. [83] describe the design and implementation of a "portable" or hand-held iris biometric sensor. The heart of the system is an "ultra-mobile personal computer," the Sony model VGN-UX17LP. The system uses a near-infrared illuminator and a CCD camera with a fixed-focus zoom lens. An image restoration algorithm is used to increase the effective capture volume, which is claimed to exceed that of the PIER 2.4 and the HIDE systems.

Kang and Park [89] describe an iris biometrics system implemented to operate on a mobile phone. The system repeatedly takes images of both eyes and performs a quality assessment until at least one image passes the quality assessment check. Then it performs authentication either with one image, or with score-level fusion of two images.

2.10 Theoretical Analyses

There are relatively few studies that might be considered theoretical analyses of fundamental issues in the field. Bhatnagar et al. [11] develop a theoretical model for estimating the probability of random correspondence of two iris codes, and compare this with the analogous value for a pair of palmprints. Kong et al. [92] undertake a theoretical analysis of the Daugman-style iris code representation of iris texture. One interesting element of this is a discussion of the impostor distribution as an instance of the binomial distribution.

Gorodnichy and Hoshino [59] develop a score calibration function that can convert match scores into probability-based confidence scores. They present a theoretical argument and also supporting experimental results to show that this approach results in the best possible detection error tradeoff curves. The calibration that is effected is meant to ensure that "... the statement 'I am 60 % sure that this person is Alice' is correct exactly 60 % of the time."

Yager and Dunstone [214] tested for the existence of "Doddington Zoo" animals in a number of different biometric databases, using a number of biometric algorithms. Each of the animal types was present in some of the experiments and absent in others. The authors note that "The reasons that a particular animal group exist are complex and varied. They depend on a number of factors, including enrollment procedures, feature extraction and matching algorithms, data quality, and intrinsic properties of the user population" [214]. Their analysis also leads the authors to assert that people are rarely "inherently hard to match." Instead, they suggest that matching errors are more likely due to enrollment issues and algorithmic weaknesses rather than intrinsic properties of the users.

Stark et al. [186] conduct experiments in which human observers view iris images and categorized them into groups of similar-appearing texture pattern. The results suggest that there are a small number of generally agreed-upon texture categories. The results also suggest that texture categories may be correlated with ethnicity, although the iris textures in the experiment all represent either Asian or Caucasian ethnicity and so greater variation in ethnicity remains to be examined.

2.11   Discussion

In this section we give eight "recommended reading" suggestions. This is not meant as a best papers list, but rather as a list of papers representing interesting and/or unusual viewpoints and directions in iris biometrics.

Gorodnichy's paper "Evolution and evaluation of biometric systems" [58] is a worthwhile read for those who want to get a sense of how biometric technology is evolving, how the performance of biometric technology is evaluated, and an introduction to much basic biometric terminology. Gorodnichy is Senior Research Scientist with the Canadian Border Services Agency, and so he brings a systems and application-oriented viewpoint to the task of evaluating biometric technology. He particularly makes that point that biometric systems are not fielded in a static context, but that the mix of data and challenges that they must handle naturally evolve over time, and so the biometric technology must evolve as well.

Current commercial iris biometric systems all, to our knowledge, use near-infrared illumination in the 700–900 nm wavelength range. There is also a body of iris biometric research based on visible wavelength images. But there is almost no published work on imaging the iris outside of the 700–900 nm range. For this reason, the paper by Ross et al. [170], "Exploring multispectral iris recognition beyond 900 nm," is unique. It remains to be seen whether or not it will be technically and economically viable to image the iris at multiple wavelengths and/or to match iris texture across wavelengths. For those who are intrigued by the topic, this paper is a good introduction. This is likely an area that will see increased attention in the future.

To our knowledge, the paper by Chou et al. [31], "Non-Orthogonal View Iris Recognition System," is the only system proposed to simultaneously acquire both a visible-light image and a near-infrared image of the iris. They exploit the two images in a complementary manner in the segmentation stage, using the color image to aid in finding the limbic boundary. For anyone interested in multi-biometrics, the relative simplicity of the sensor design and the method of exploiting the two images should be interesting and suggest additional possibilities.

Proenca's paper, "On the Feasibility of the Visible Wavelength, At-a-Distance and On-the-Move Iris Recognition" [152], is interesting because it argues that visible-light imaging is the way to go, especially for imaging "at a distance" and "on the move." This argument runs counter to the approach used by all commercial systems that we are aware of, and also counter to the majority of academic research. However, because it does represent a "contrarian" sort of approach, those interested in the illumination issue for iris biometrics should find this paper worthwhile.

The paper by Pillai et al., "Sparsity inspired selection and recognition of iris images" [147], is the first that we know of to try to transfer the excitement about sparse representation techniques in the face recognition community over to iris recognition. Extraordinary recognition performance has been claimed for face recognition systems using sparse representation techniques. A potential weakness of using a sparse representations approach is the requirement for a large number of training images per iris, and that the images should span the range of different possible appearances. It remains to be seen whether or not sparse representation techniques will revolutionize either face or iris recognition in practice, but this paper is a good starting point for how the concepts could be applied in iris recognition.

The paper by Vatsa et al. [198], "Belief Function Theory Based Biometric Match Score Fusion: Case Studies In Multi-instance and Multi-unit Iris Verification," is interesting as an example for what it terms "multi-instance" and "multi-unit" iris biometrics. Multi-instance refers to using multiple images of the same iris, either to enroll a person in the system, and/or as a probe to be matched for recognition. Multi-unit refers to using an image of both irises rather than a single iris. Early iris biometric systems seem to have all enrolled a person using a single iris biometric template formed from a single image. This paper shows that there are simple ways of increasing recognition performance by using multiple images.

For anyone not already familiar with the concept of cancelable biometrics, the paper by Kanade et al., "Cancelable Iris Biometrics and Using Error-Correcting Codes to Reduce Variability in Biometric Data" [87], should be worth reading. In this particular instance, they propose a two-factor approach to cancelable biometrics. The two factors are the biometric and the password. If needed, a person's current enrollment in a biometric system using this scheme can be canceled, and then the person reenrolled with a new password. This particular proposed system also uses the password to effectively increase the separation between the genuine and impostor distributions.

Zuo and Schmid's paper, "Global and Local Quality Measures for NIR Iris Video" [221], provides a good introduction to the complexity of the problem of evaluating the quality of an iris image. For a single iris image, they compute nine different quality metrics, for segmentation quality, interlacing, illumination contrast, illumination evenness, percent occlusion, pixel count, dilation, off-angle view and blur. Quality metrics concerned with interlacing will presumably not be important in the future, as iris images will be acquired digital rather than digitized from analog video. But the problem is actually even more complex than it appears here. For example, the focus quality of an image is not necessarily even over the entire iris. Also, it is not only the dilation of a single image that is important, but the difference in dilation between two images that are being matched [76].

This group of eight papers that touch on very different topics in the field of iris biometrics research should convey a sense of the breadth of the field. It should also help to convey a sense of the excitement in the field, in that there are many directions being explored that could serve to increase accuracy of, and/or increase the breadth of application of, iris biometrics.

Acknowledgments The authors were supported by the Federal Bureau of Investigation, the Central Intelligence Agency, the Intelligence Advanced Research Projects Activity, the Biometrics Task Force, the Technical Support Working Group under US Army contract W91CRB-08-C-0093, and the Intelligence Community Postdoctoral Fellowship Program.

The opinions, findings, and conclusions or recommendations expressed in this publication are those of the authors and do not necessarily reflect the views of our sponsors. The identification of any commercial product or trade name does not imply endorsement or recommendation by the authors, the University of Notre Dame, or the National Institute of Standards and Technology.

References

1. M. Adam et al., Iris identification based on a local analysis of the iris texture, in *Proceedings of 6th International Symposium on Image and Signal Processing and Analysis (ISPA)*, April, 2009, pp. 523–528
2. M. Adjedj et al., Biometric identification over encrypted data made feasible, in *Information Systems Security*. Lecture Notes in Computer Science, vol, 5905 (2009), pp. 86–100
3. N. Agrawal, M. Savvides, Biometric data hiding: A 3 factor authentication approach to verify identity with a single image using steganography, encryption and matching, in *IEEE Computer Society Conference on Computer Vision and Pattern Recognition Workshops (CVPR Workshops)*, June 2009, pp. 85–92
4. A.S. Alghamdi et al., Bio-chaotic stream cipher-based iris image encryption, in *International Conference on Computational Science and Engineering (CSE '09)*, Aug 2009, pp. 739–744
5. A. Baig et al., Fingerprint-iris fusion based identification system using a single Hamming distance, in *Symposium on Bio-inspired Learning and Intelligent Systems for Security (BLISS '09)*, Aug 2009, pp. 9–12
6. S.E. Baker, K.W. Bowyer, P.J.J.J. Flynn, Empirical evidence for correct iris match score degradation with increased time-lapse between gallery and probe matches, in *Advances in Biometrics*. Lecture Notes in Computer Sciences, vol. 5558 (2009), pp. 1170–1179
7. S.E. Baker et al., Degradation of iris recognition performance due to non-cosmetic prescription contact lenses. Comput. Vis. Image Underst. **114**(9), 1030–1044 (2010)
8. A. Bastys, J. Kranauskas, R. Masiulis, Iris matching by local extremum points of multiscale taylor expansion, in *Advances in Biometrics*. Lecture Notes in Computer Science, vol. 5558 (2009), pp. 1070–1079
9. C. Belcher, Y. Du, A selective feature information approach for iris image-quality measure. IEEE Trans. Inf. Forensics Secur. **3**(3), 572–577 (2008)
10. H. Bharadwaj et al., Periocular biometrics: when iris recognition fails, in *Fourth IEEE International Conference on Biometrics: Theory Applications and Systems (BTAS 10)*, Sept 2010
11. J.R. Bhatnagar, R.K. Patney, B. Lall, An information theoretic approach for formulating probability of random correspondence of biometrics, in *World Congress on Nature & Biologically Inspired Computing (NaBIC)*, Dec 2009, pp. 1184–1189
12. A. Bhattacharjee et al., Decison theory based multimodal biometric authentication system using wavelet transform, in *2009 International Conference on Machine Learning and Cybernetics*, vol. 4, July 2009, pp. 2336–2342

13. D. Bhattacharyya et al., Biometric authentication techniques and its future possibilities, in *Second International Conference on Computer and Electrical Engineering (ICCEE '09)*, vol. 2, Dec 2009, pp. 652–655
14. Biosecure, A biometric reference system for iris OSIRIS version 2.01 (2009)
15. R.M. Bodade, S.N. Talbar, Dynamic iris localisation: a novel approach suitable for fake iris detection, in *International Conference on Ultra Modern Telecommunications & Workshops (ICUMT '09)*, Oct 2009, pp. 1–5
16. R.M. Bodade, S.N. Talbar, Shift invariant Iris feature extraction using rotated complex wavelet and complex wavelet for iris recognition system, in *Seventh International Conference on Advances in Pattern Recognition (ICAPR '09)*, Feb 2009, pp. 449–452
17. V.N. Boddeti, B.V.K.V. Kumar, Extended-depth-of-field iris recognition using unrestored wavefront-coded imagery. IEEE Trans. Syst. Man Cybern. Part A: Syst. Hum. **40**(3), 495–508 (2010)
18. H. Borgen, P. Bours, S. Wolthusen, Simulating the influences of aging and ocular disease on biometric recognition performance, in *Advances in Biometrics*. Lecture Notes in Computer Science, vol. 5558 (2009), pp. 857–867
19. K.W. Bowyer, P.J. Flynn, The ND-IRIS-0405 Iris Image Database
20. K.W. Bowyer, K. Hollingsworth, P. Flynn, Image understanding for Iris biometrics: a survey. Comput. Vis. Image Underst. **110**(2), 281–307 (2008)
21. K.W. Bowyer et al., Factors that degrade the match distribution in iris biometrics, in *Identity in the Information Society*, Dec 2009, pp. 327–343
22. L. Breitenbach, P. Chawdhry, Image quality assessment and performance evaluation for multimodal biometric recognition using face and iris, in *Proceedings of 6th International Symposium on Image and Signal Processing and Analysis (ISPA)*, Sept 2009, pp. 550–555
23. R.P. Broussard, R.W. Ives, Using artificial neural networks and feature saliency to identify iris measurements that contain the most discriminatory information for iris segmentation, in *IEEE Workshop on Computational Intelligence in Biometrics: Theory, Algorithms, and Applications (CIB)*, March 2009, pp. 46–51
24. S. Campos et al., Multimodal algorithm for iris recognition with local topological descriptors, in Progress in *Pattern Recognition, Image Analysis, Computer Vision, and Applications*. Lecture Notes in Computer Science, vol. 5856, 2009, pp. 766–773
25. M. Carneiro et al., Analyzing the performance of algorithms used to localize the iris region in eye images submitted to severely compressed images, in *IEEE International Symposium on Intelligent Signal Processing (WISP)*, Aug 2009, pp. 281–285
26. R. Chen et al., Accurate and fast iris segmentation applied to portable image capture device, in *IEEE International Workshop on Imaging Systems and Techniques (IST '09)*, May 2009, pp. 80–84
27. W. Chen, R. Huang, L. Hsieh, Iris recognition using 3D cooccurrence matrix, in *Advances in Biometrics*. Lecture Notes in Computer Science, vol. 5558 (2009), pp. 1122–1131
28. W.-S. Chen et al., Iris recognition using 2D-LDA + 2D-PCA, in *IEEE International Conference on Acoustics, Speech and Signal Processing (ICASSP)*, April 2009, pp. 869–872
29. Y. Chen et al., A computational efficient iris extraction approach in unconstrained environments, in *IEEE 3rd International Conference on Biometrics: Theory, Applications, and Systems (BTAS 09)*, Sept 2009, pp. 1–7
30. Y. Chen et al., A new unconstrained iris image analysis and segmentation method in biometrics, in *IEEE International Symposium on Biomedical Imaging: From Nano to Macro (ISBI '09)*, June 2009, pp. 13–16
31. C.-T. Chou et al., Non-orthogonal view iris recognition system. IEEE Trans. Circuits Syst. Video Technol. **20**(3), 417–430 (2010)
32. S.S. Chowhan, G.N. Shinde, Evaluation of statistical feature encoding techniques on iris images, in *2009 WRI World Congress on Computer Science and Information Engineering*, vol. 7, Mar 2009, pp. 71–75
33. V. Conti et al., Fuzzy fusion in multimodal biometric systems, in *KES 2007/WIRN 2007*. Lecture Notes in Artificial Intelligence, vol. 4692 (2007), pp. 108–115

34. J. Daugman., Iris recognition and anti-spoofing countermeasures, in *7th International Biometrics Conference*, London, 2004
35. J. Daugman, C. Downing, Effect of Severe Image Compression on Iris Recognition Performance. IEEE Trans. Inf. Forensics Secur. **3**(1), 52–61 (2008)
36. W. Dong, Z. Sun, T. Tan, A design of iris recognition system at a distance, in *Chinese Conference on Pattern Recognition (CCPR)*, Nov 2009, pp. 1–5
37. W. Dong, T. Tan, Z. Sun, Iris matching based on personalized weight map. IEEE Trans. Pattern Anal. Mach. Intell. **33**(9), 1744–1757 (2011)
38. G. Dozier, K. Frederiksen, R. Meeks, Minimizing the number of bits needed for iris recognition via bit inconsistency and GRIT, in *IEEE Workshop on Computational Intelligence in Biometrics: Theory, Algorithms, and Applications, (CIB)*, March 2009, pp. 30–37
39. Y. Du, N.L. Thomas, E. Arslanturk, Multi-level iris video image thresholding, in *IEEE Workshop on Computational Intelligence in Biometrics: Theory, Algorithms, and Applications, (CIB)*, March 2009, pp. 38–45
40. Y. Du et al., Video-based noncooperative iris image segmentation. IEEE Trans. Syst. Man Cybern. Part B: Cybern. **41**(1), 64–74 (2011)
41. M.K. Dutta, P. Gupta, V.K. Pathak, Biometric based watermarking in audio signals, in *International Conference on Multimedia Information Networking and Security (MINES 2009)*, vol. 1, Nov 2009, pp. 10–14
42. M.K. Dutta, P. Gupta, V.K. Pathak, Blind watermarking in audio signals using biometric features in wavelet domain, in *IEEE Region 10 Conference (TENCON)*, Jan 2009, pp. 1–5
43. M. Dutta, P. Gupta, V. Pathak, Biometric based unique key generation for authentic audio watermarking, in *Pattern Recognition and Machine Intelligence*. Lecture Notes in Computer Science, vol. 5909 (2009), pp. 458–463
44. A.B. Elmadani, Human authentication using fingeriris algorithm based on statistical approach, in *Second International Conference on Networked Digital Technologies (NDT 2010)*, 2010, pp. 288–296
45. M. Erbilek, O. Toygar, Recognizing partially occluded irises using subpattern-based approaches, in *24th International Symposium on Computer and Information Sciences (ISCIS)*, Sept 2009, pp. 606–610
46. M. Eskandari, O. Toygar, *Effect of eyelid and eyelash occlusions on iris images using subpattern-based approaches*, in *Fifth International Conference on Soft Computing, Computing with Words and Perceptions in System Analysis, Decision and Control, (ICSCCW)*, Sept 2009, pp. 1–4
47. P. Färberböck et al., Transforming rectangular and polar iris images to enable cancelable biometrics, in *Image Analysis and Recognition*. Lecture Notes in Computer Science, vol. 6112 (2010), pp. 276–286
48. R.Y. Fatt, Y.H. Tay, K.M. Mok, DSP-based implementation and optimization of an iris verification algorithm using textural feature, in *Sixth International Conference on Fuzzy Systems and Knowledge Discovery (FSKD)*, vol. 5, 2009, pp. 374–378
49. R. Fatt, T.Y. Haur, K.M. Mok, iris verification algorithm based on texture analysis and its implementation on DSP, in *International Conference on Signal Acquisition and Processing (ICSAP)*, 2009, pp. 198–202
50. J. Fierrez, J. Galbally, J. Ortega-Garcia, BiosecurID: a multimodal biometric database. Pattern Anal. Appl. **13**, 235–246 (2010)
51. J.-Y. Gan, J.-F. Liu, Fusion and recognition of face and iris feature based on wavelet feature and KFDA, in *International Conference on Wavelet Analysis and Pattern Recognition (ICWAPR)*, July 2009, pp. 47–50
52. R. Garg, V. Gupta, V. Agrawal., Efficient iris recognition method for identification, in *International Conference on Ultra Modern Telecommunications and Workshops, (ICUMT)*, Oct 2009, pp. 1–6
53. R. Garg et al., A biometric security based electronic gadget control using hand gestures, in *International Conference on Ultra Modern Telecommunications & Workshops (ICUMT '09)*, Oct 2009, pp. 1–8

54. J.E. Gentile, N. Ratha, J. Connell, An efficient, two-stage iris recognition system, in *IEEE 3rd International Conference on Biometrics: Theory, Applications, and Systems (BTAS 09)*, Sept 2009
55. J. E. Gentile, N. Ratha, J. Connell, SLIC: short-length iris codes, in *IEEE 3rd International Conference on Biometrics: Theory, Applications, and Systems (BTAS)*, Sept 2009
56. L. Ghouti, F.S. Al-Qunaieer, Color iris recognition using quaternion phase correlation, in *Symposium on Bio-inspired Learning and Intelligent Systems for Security (BLISS '09)*, Aug 2009, pp. 20–25
57. A. Gonzaga, R.M. da Costa, Extraction and selection of dynamic features of the human iris, in *XXII Brazilian Symposium on Computer Graphics and Image Processing (SIBGRAPI)*, Oct 2009, pp. 202–208
58. D.O. Gorodnichy, Evolution and evaluation of biometric systems, in *IEEE Symposium on Computational Intelligence for Security and Defense Applications (CISDA)*, July 2009, pp. 1–8
59. D.O. Gorodnichy, R. Hoshino, Score calibration for optimal biometric identification, in *Advances in Artificial Intelligence*. Lecture Notes in Computer Science, vol. 6085 (2010), pp. 357–361
60. K. Grabowski et al., Iris structure acquisition method, in *16th International Conference Mixed Design of Integrated Circuits and Systems (MIXDES)*, June 2009, pp. 640–643
61. P. Grother et al., IREX I: Performance of iris recognition algorithms on standard images, in *NIST Interagency Report*, vol. 7629 (2009)
62. J. Hämmerle-Uhl, E. Pschernig, A. Uhl, Cancelable iris biometrics using block re-mapping and image warping, in *Information Security*. Lecture Notes in Computer Science, vol. 5735 (2009), pp. 135–142
63. J. Hämmerle-Uhl et al., Improving compressed iris recognition accuracy using JPEG2000 roi coding, in *Advances in Biometrics*. Lecture Notes in Computer Science, vol. 5558 (2009), pp. 1102–1111
64. F. Hao, R. Anderson, J. Daugman, Combining crypto with biometrics effectively. IEEE Trans. Comput. **55**(9), 1081–1088 (2006)
65. F. Hao, J. Daugman, P. Zielinski, A fast search algorithm for a large fuzzy database. IEEE Trans. Inf. Forensics Secur. **3**(2), 203–212 (2008)
66. R. Haralick, K. Shanmugam, L. Dinstein, Textural features for image classification. IEEE Trans. Syst. Man Cybern. **3**(6), 610–621 (1973)
67. A. Hassanien, A. Abraham, C. Grosan, Spiking neural network and wavelets for hiding iris data in digital images. Soft Comput.: Fusion Found. Methodol. Appl. **13**(4), 401–416 (2009)
68. X. He, X. An, P. Shi, Statistical texture analysis based approach for fake iris detection using support vector machine, in *Advances in Biometrics*. Lecture Notes in Computer Science, vol. 4642 (2007), pp. 540–546
69. X. He, Y. Lu, P. Shi, A new fake iris detection method, in *Advances in Biometrics*. Lecture Notes in Computer Science, vol. 5558 (2009), pp. 1132–1139
70. X. He et al., Contactless autofeedback iris capture design. IEEE Trans. Instrum. Meas. **57**(7), 1369–1375 (2008)
71. Y. He, Y.H.H. Yang, H. He, An elimination method of light spot based on iris image fusion. Commun. Comput. Inf. Sci. **15**(12), 415–422 (2008)
72. Z. He et al., Efficient iris spoof detection via boosted local binary patterns, in *Advances in Biometrics*. Lecture Notes in Computer Science, vol. 5558 (2009), pp. 1080–1090
73. Z. He et al., Enhanced usability of iris recognition via efficient user interface and iris image restoration, in *15th IEEE International Conference on Image Processing (ICIP)*, Oct 2008, pp. 261–264
74. Z. He et al., Toward Accurate and Fast Iris Segmentation for Iris Biometrics. IEEE Trans. Pattern Anal. Mach. Intell. **31**(9), 1670–1684 (2009)
75. K.P. Hollingsworth, K.W. Bowyer, P.J. Flynn, Identifying useful features for recognition in near-infrared periocular images, in *Fourth IEEE International Conference on Biometrics: Theory Applications and Systems (BTAS)*, Sept 2010

76. K.P. Hollingsworth, K.W. Bowyer, P.J. Flynn, Pupil dilation degrades iris biometric performance. Comput. Vis. Image Underst. **113**(1), 150–157 (2009)
77. K.P. Hollingsworth, K.W. Bowyer, P.J. Flynn, The Best Bits in an Iris Code. IEEE Trans. Pattern Anal. Mach. Intell. **31**(6), 964–973 (2009)
78. K.P. Hollingsworth, K.W. Bowyer, P.J. Flynn, Using fragile bit coincidence to improve iris recognition, in *IEEE 3rd International Conference on Biometrics: Theory, Applications, and Systems (BTAS)*, Sept 2009, pp. 1–6
79. K. Hollingsworth, K. Bowyer, P.J.J. Flynn, Pupil dilation degrades iris biometric performance. Comput. Vis. Image Underst. **113**(1), 150–157 (2009)
80. K. Hollingsworth et al., Iris Recognition Using Signal-Level Fusion of Frames From Video. IEEE Trans. Inf. Forensics Secur. **4**(4), 837–848 (2009)
81. X. Huang, L. Ren, R. Yang, Image deblurring for less intrusive iris capture, in *IEEE Conference on Computer Vision and Pattern Recognition (CVPR)*, June 2009, pp. 1558–1565
82. R.W. Ives et al., Effects of image compression on iris recognition performance and image quality, in *IEEE Workshop on Computational Intelligence in Biometrics: Theory, Algorithms, and Applications (CIB)*, March 2009, pp. 16–21
83. Y. Jang, B.J. Kang, K.R. Park, A novel portable iris recognition system and usability evaluation. Int. J. Control Autom. Syst. **8**(1), 91–98 (2010)
84. P.A. Johnson et al., Quality in face and iris research ensemble (QFIRE), in *Fourth IEEE International Conference on Biometrics: Theory Applications and Systems (BTAS)*, Sept 2010
85. N. Kalka, N. Bartlow, B. Cukic, An automated method for predicting iris segmentation failures, in *IEEE 3rd International Conference on Biometrics: Theory, Applications, and Systems (BTAS)*, Sept 2009, pp. 1–8
86. N. Kalka et al., Estimating and fusing quality factors for iris biometrics images. IEEE Trans. Syst. Man. Cybern. Part A: Syst. Hum. **40**(3), 509–524 (2010)
87. S. Kanade, D. Petrovska-Delacretaz, B. Dorizzi, Cancelable iris biometrics and using Error Correcting Codes to reduce variability in biometric data, in *IEEE Conference on Computer Vision and Pattern Recognition (CVPR)*, June 2009, pp. 120–127
88. S. Kanade, D. Petrovska-Delacretaz, B. Dorizzi, Multi-biometrics based cryptographic key regeneration scheme, in *IEEE 3rd International Conference on Biometrics: Theory, Applications, and Systems (BTAS)*, Sept 2009
89. B.J. Kang, K.R. Park, A new multi-unit iris authentication based on quality assessment and score level fusion for mobile phones. Mach. Vis. Appl. **21**, 541–553 (2010)
90. R. Kannavara, N. Bourbakis, Iris biometric authentication based on local global graphs: An FPGA implementation, in *IEEE Symposium on Computational Intelligence for Security and Defense Applications (CISDA)*, July 2009, pp. 1–7
91. R. Kheirolahy, H. Ebrahimnezhad, M.H. Sedaaghi, Robust pupil boundary detection by optimized color mapping for iris recognition, in *14th International CSI Computer Conference (CSICC)*, Oct 2009, pp. 170–175
92. A.W.K. Kong, D. Zhang, M.S. Kamel, An analysis of IrisCode. IEEE Trans. Image Process. **19**(2), 522–532 (2010)
93. M. Konrad, H. Stogner, A. Uhl, Custom design of JPEG quantisation tables for compressing iris polar images to improve recognition accuracy, in *Advances in Biometrics*. Lecture Notes in Computer Science, vol. 5558 (2009), pp. 1091–1101
94. M. Konrad, H. Stogner, A. Uhl, Evolutionary optimization of JPEG quantization tables for compressing iris polar images in iris recognition systems, in *Proceedings of 6th International Symposium on Image and Signal Processing and Analysis (ISPA)*, Sept 2009, pp. 534–539
95. G. Kostmajer, H. Stogner, A. Uhl, Custom JPEG quantization for improved iris recognition accuracy, in *Emerging Challenges for Security, Privacy and Trust: IFIP Advances in Information and Communication Technology*, vol. 297 (2009), pp. 76–86
96. E. Krichen, S. Garcia-Salicetti, B. Dorizzi, A new phase-correlation-based iris matching for degraded images. IEEE Trans. Syst. Man Cybern. Part B: Cybern. **39**(4), 924–934 (2009)
97. E. Krichen et al., Iris recognition, in *Guide to Biometric Reference Systems and Performance Evaluation* (Springer, 2009), p. 25

98. K.S.S. Kyaw, Iris recognition system using statistical features for biometric identification, in *International Conference on Electronic Computer Technology*, Feb 2009, pp. 554–556
99. R.D. Labati, V. Piuri, F. Scotti, Agent-based image iris segmentation and multiple views boundary refining, in *IEEE 3rd International Conference on Biometrics: Theory, Applications, and Systems (BTAS)*, Sept 2009, pp. 1–7
100. R.D. Labati, V. Piuri, F. Scotti, Neural-based iterative approach for iris detection in iris recognition systems, in *IEEE Symposium on Computational Intelligence for Security and Defense Applications (CISDA)*, July 2009, pp. 1–6
101. A.C. Laboratories, *The Database of Faces*
102. Y. Lee, P. Phillips, R. Micheals, An automated video-based system for iris recognition, in *Advances in Biometrics*. Lecture Notes in Computer Science, vol. 5558 (2009), pp. 1160–1169
103. D.C. Leonard, A.P. Pons, S.S. Asfour, Realization of a universal patient identifier for electronic medical records through biometric technology. IEEE Trans. Inf Technol. Biomed. **13**(4), 494–500 (2009)
104. Y. Li, S. Du, Biometric watermarking based on affine parameters estimation, in *2nd International Congress on Image and Signal Processing (CISP)*, Oct 2009, pp. 1–6
105. Y. Li, S. Du, Biometric watermarking based on affine parameters estimation, in *International Conference on Multimedia Computing and Systems (ICMCS)*, April 2009, pp. 123–128
106. Y. Li, M. Savvides, A pixel-wise, learning-based approach for occlusion estimation of iris images in polar domain, in *IEEE International Conference on Acoustics, Speech and Signal Processing (ICASSP)*, April 2009, pp. 1357–1360
107. Y. Li, M. Savvides, Automatic iris mask refinement for high performance iris recognition, in *IEEE Workshop on Computational Intelligence in Biometrics: Theory, Algorithms, and Applications (CIB)*, March 2009, pp. 52–58
108. J. Lin et al., Robust person identification with face and iris by modified PUM method, in *International Conference on Apperceiving Computing and Intelligence Analysis (ICACIA)*, Oct 2009, pp. 321–324
109. L. Liu et al., Research on data fusion of multiple biometric features, in *International Conference on Apperceiving Computing and Intelligence Analysis (ICACIA)*, Oct 2009, pp. 112–115
110. X. Liu, P. Li, Q. Song, Eyelid localization in iris images captured in less constrained environment, in *Advances in Biometrics*. Lecture Notes in Computer Science, vol. 5558 (2009), pp. 1140–1149
111. J. Liu-Jimenez, R. Sanchez-Reillo, B. Fernandez-Saavedra, Iris biometrics for embedded systems, in *IEEE Transactions on Very Large Scale Integration (VLSI) Systems*, Feb 2011
112. Y. Luo, S. Cheung, S. Ye, Anonymous biometric access control based on homomorphic encryption, in *IEEE International Conference on Multimedia and Expo (ICME)*, June 2009, pp. 1046–1049
113. J.R. Lyle et al., Soft biometric classification using periocular region features, in *Fourth IEEE International Conference on iometrics: Theory Applications and Systems (BTAS)*, Sept, 2010
114. L. Ma et al., Local intensity variation analysis for iris recognition. Pattern Recogn. **37**(6), 1287–1298 (2004)
115. M. Mahmud, M. K. Khan, K. Alghathbar, Biometric-Gaussian- Stream (BGS) Cipher with new aspect of image encryption (Data Hiding), in *Bio-Science and Bio-Technology* (Springer Berlin Heidelberg, 2009), pp. 97–107
116. D. Maltoni, Biometric fusion, in *Handbook of Fingerprint Recognition* (Springer, 2009)
117. L. Masek, Recognition of human iris patterns for biometric identification. www.csse.uwa.edu.au/pk/studentprojects/libor/LiborMasekThesis.pdf. MA thesis. The University of Western Australia, 2003
118. J.R. Matey, L.R. Kennell, Iris recognition—Beyond one meter, in *Handbook of Remote Biometrics* (2009)
119. J.R. Matey et al., Iris on the move: acquisition of images for iris recognition in less constrained environments. Proc. IEEE **94**(11), 1936–1947 (2006)

120. S. McCloskey, A.W. Au, J. Jelinek, Iris capture from moving subjects using a fluttering shutter, in *Fourth IEEE International Conference on Biometrics: Theory Applications and Systems (BTAS)*, Sept 2010
121. H. Mehrotra, B. Majhi, P. Gupta, Annular Iris recognition using SURF, in *Pattern Recognition and Machine Intelligence*. Lecture Notes in Computer Science, vol. 5909 (2009), pp. 464–469
122. H. Mehrotra et al., An efficient dual stage approach for iris feature extraction using interest point pairing, in *IEEE Workshop on Computational Intelligence in Biometrics: Theory, Algorithms, and Applications (CIB)*, March 2009, pp. 59–62
123. H. Mehrotra et al., Indexing iris biometric database using energy histogram of DCT subbands. Contemp. Comput. **40**(4), 194–204 (2009)
124. J. Merkow, B. Jou, M. Savvides, An exploration of gender identification using only the periocular region, in *Fourth IEEE International Conference on Biometrics: Theory Applications and Systems (BTAS)*, Sept 2010
125. P.E. Miller et al., Performance evaluation of local appearance based periocular recognition, in *Fourth IEEE International Conference on Biometrics: Theory Applications and Systems (BTAS)*, Sept 2010
126. R. Mishra, V. Pathak. Human recognition using fusion of iris and ear data, in *International Conference on Methods and Models in Computer Science (ICM2CS)*, Dec, 2009, pp. 1–5
127. K. Miyazawa et al., An effective approach for iris recognition using phase-based image matching. IEEE Trans. Pattern Anal. Mach. Intell. **30**(10), 1741–1756 (2008)
128. S. Mohammadi, H. Jahanshahi, A secure E-tendering system, in IEEE *International Conference on Electro/Information Technology (EIT)*, June, 2009, pp. 62–67
129. S.H. Moi, N. Rahim, B. Abdul et al., Iris biometric cryptography for identity document, in *International Conference of Soft Computing and Pattern Recognition (SOCPAR)*, Dec 2009, pp. 736–741
130. A. Mondal, K. Roy, P. Bhattacharya, Secure and simplified access to home appliances using iris recognition, in *IEEE Workshop on Computational Intelligence in Biometrics: Theory, Algorithms, and Applications (CIB)*, March 2009, pp. 22–29
131. P. Moravec et al., Normalization impact on SVD-based iris recognition, in *International Conference on Biometrics and Kansei Engineering (ICBAKE)*, June 2009, pp. 60–64
132. N. Morizet, J. Gilles, A new adaptive combination approach to score level fusion for face and iris biometrics combining wavelets and statistical moments, in *Advances in Visual Computing*. Lecture Notes in Computer Science, vol. 5359 (2008), pp. 661–671
133. T. Munemoto, Y.-H. Li, M. Savvides, Hallucinating irises—dealing with partial and occluded iris regions, in *IEEE 2nd International Conference on Biometrics: Theory, Applications, and Systems (BTAS)*, Sept 2008
134. E.M. Newton, P.J. Phillips, Meta-analysis of third-party evaluations of iris recognition. IEEE Trans. Syst. Man Cybern. Part A **39**(1), 4–11 (2009)
135. J. Ortega-Garcia et al., The multi-scenario multi-environment biosecure multimodal database (BMDB). IEEE Trans. Pattern Anal. Mach. Intell. **32**(6), 1097–1111 (2010)
136. L. Pan et al., A robust iris localization model based on phase congruency and least trimmed squares estimation, in *Image Analysis and Processing -ICIAP*. Lecture Notes in Computer Science, vol. 5716 (2009), pp. 682–691
137. C.M. Patil, S. Patilkulkarani, A comparative study of feature extraction approaches for an efficient iris recognition system, in *Information Processing and Management (2010)*, pp. 411–416
138. C.M. Patil, S. Patilkulkarani, An approach to enhance security environment based on sift feature extraction and matching to iris recognition, in *Information Processing and Management*, 2010, pp. 527–530
139. C.M. Patil, S. Patilkulkarani, Iris feature extraction for personal identification using lifting wavelet transform, in *International Conference on Advances in Computing, Control, and Telecommunication Technologies (ACT)*, Dec 2009, pp. 764–766
140. D. Petrovska-Delacretaz, A. Mayoue, B. Dorizzi, The BioSecure benchmarking methodology for biometric performance evaluation, in *Guide to Biometric Reference Systems and Performance Evaluation* (2009)

141. P.J. Phillips, J.R. Beveridge, An introduction to biometriccompleteness: the equivalence of matching and quality, in *IEEE 3rd International Conference on Biometrics: Theory, Applications, and Systems (BTAS)*, Sept 2009, pp. 1–5
142. P.J. Phillips, K.W. Bowyer, P.J. Flynn, Comment on the CASIA version 1.0 iris dataset. IEEE Trans. Pattern Anal. Mach. Intell. **29**(10), 1869–1870 (2007)
143. P.J. Phillips, E.M. Newton, Biometric systems: the rubber meets the road. Proc. IEEE **97**(5), 782–783 (2009)
144. P.J. Phillips et al., FRVT 2006 and ICE 2006 large-scale experimental results. IEEE Trans. Pattern Anal. Mach. Intell., 831–846 (2010)
145. P.J. Phillips et al., Overview of the multiple biometric grand challenge, in *International Conference on Biometrics*. Lecture Notes in Computer Science, vol. 5558 (2009), pp. 705–714
146. P.J. Phillips et al., The iris challenge evaluation 2005, in *2nd IEEE International Conference on Biometrics: Theory, Applications and Systems (BTAS)*, Sept 2008
147. J.K. Pillai, V.M. Patel, R. Chellappa, Sparsity inspired selection and recognition of iris images, in *IEEE 3rd International Conference on Biometrics: Theory, Applications, and Systems (BTAS)*, Sept 2009, pp. 1–6
148. R. Plaga, Biometric keys: suitable use cases and achievable information content. Int. J. Inf. Secur., 447–454 (2009)
149. N. Poh et al., Benchmarking quality-dependent and cost-sensitive score-level multimodal biometric fusion algorithms. IEEE Trans. Inf. Forensics Secur. **4**(4), 849–866 (2009)
150. H. Proenca, Iris recognition: a method to segment visible wavelength iris images acquired on-the-move and at-a-distance, in *Advances in Visual Computing*. Lecture Notes in Computer Science, vol. 5358 (2008), pp. 731–742
151. H. Proenca, Iris recognition: on the segmentation of degraded images acquired in the visible wavelength. IEEE Trans. Pattern Anal. Mach. Intell. **32**(8), 1502–1516 (2010)
152. H. Proenca, On the feasibility of the visible wavelength, at-adistance and on-the-move iris recognition, in *IEEE Workshop on Computational Intelligence in Biometrics: Theory, Algorithms, and Applications (CIB)*, March 2009, pp. 9–15
153. H. Proenca, Quality assessment of degraded iris images acquired in the visible wavelength. IEEE Trans. Inf. Forensics Secur. **6**(1), 82–95 (2011)
154. H. Proenca et al., The UBIRIS.v2: a database of visible wavelength images captured on-the-move and at-a-distance. IEEE Trans. Pattern Anal. Mach. Intell. **32**(8), 1529–1535 (2010)
155. S.J. Pundlik, D.L. Woodard, S.T. Birchfield, Non-ideal iris segmentation using graph cuts, in *IEEE CVPR Workshop on Biometrics*, June 2008
156. F.S. Al-Qunaieer, L. Ghouti, Color iris recognition using hypercomplex gabor wavelets, in *Symposium on Bio-inspired Learning and Intelligent Systems for Security (BLISS '09)*, Aug 2009, pp. 18–19
157. M. Rachubinski, Iris identification using geometrical wavelets, in *Computer Vision and Graphics* (2009)
158. K. Radhika et al., Multi-modal authentication using continuous dynamic programming, in *Biometric ID Management and Multimodal Communication*. Lecture Notes in Computer Science, vol. 5707 (2009), pp. 228–235
159. R.N. Rakvic et al., Parallelizing iris recognition. IEEE Trans. Inf. Forensics Secur. **4**(4), 812–823 (2009)
160. D. Rankin et al., Comparing and improving algorithms for iris recognition, in *13th International Machine Vision and Image Processing Conference (IMVIP)*, Sept 2009, pp. 99–104
161. N.K. Ratha, Privacy protection in high security biometrics applications, in *Ethics and Policy of Biometrics*. Lecture Notes in Computer Science, vol. 6005 (2010), pp. 62–69
162. C. Rathgeb, A. Uhl, Privacy preserving key generation for iris biometrics, in *Communications and Multimedia Security*. Lecture Notes in Computer Science, vol. 6109 (2010), pp. 191–200
163. C. Rathgeb, A. Uhl, Systematic construction of iris-based fuzzy commitment schemes, in *Advances in Biometrics*. Lecture Notes in Computer Science, vol. 5558 (2009), pp. 940–949
164. C. Rathgeb, A. Uhl, Two-factor authentication or how to potentially counterfeit experimental results in biometric systems, in *ICIAR 2010*. Lecture Notes in Computer Science, vol. 6112 (2010), pp. 296–305

165. C. Rathgeb, A. Uhl, P. Wild, Incremental iris recognition: A single-algorithm serial fusion strategy to optimize time complexity, in *Fourth IEEE International Conference on Biometrics: Theory Applications and Systems (BTAS)*, Sept 2010
166. A. Rattani, M. Tistarelli, Robust multi-modal and multi-unit feature level fusion of face and iris biometrics, in *Advances in Biometrics*. Lecture Notes in Computer Science, vol. 5558 (2009), pp. 960–969
167. J. Ren, M. Xie, Evaluation of iris images definition based on pupil's edge kurtosis, in *2nd International Congress on Image and Signal Processing (CISP)*, Oct 2009, pp. 1–4
168. J. Ren, M. Xie, Research on clarity-evaluation-method for iris images, in *Second International Conference on Intelligent Computation Technology and Automation (ICICTA)*, vol. 1, 2009, pp. 682–685
169. K. Ricanek, Dissecting the human identity. Computer, 96–97 (2011)
170. A. Ross, R. Pasula, L. Hornak, Exploring multispectral iris recognition beyond 900 nm, in *IEEE 3rd International Conference on Biometrics: Theory, Applications, and Systems (BTAS)*, Sept 2009
171. A. Ross, A. Rattani, M. Tistarelli, Exploiting the Doddington zoo effect in biometric fusion, in *IEEE 3rd International Conference on Biometrics: Theory, Applications, and Systems (BTAS)*, Sept 2009
172. K. Roy, P. Bhattacharya, Improving features subset selection using genetic algorithms for iris recognition, in *Artificial Neural Networks in Pattern Recognition*. Lecture Notes in Computer Science, vol. 5064 (2008), pp. 292–304
173. K. Roy, P. Bhattacharya, Iris recognition in nonideal situations, in *Information Security*. Lecture Notes in Computer Science, vol. 5735 (2009), pp. 143–150
174. K. Roy, P. Bhattacharya, Level set approaches and adaptive asymmetrical SVMs applied for nonideal iris recognition, in *Image Analysis and Recognition*. Lecture Notes in Computer Science, vol. 5627 (2009), pp. 418–428
175. K. Roy, P. Bhattacharya, Nonideal iris recognition using level set approach and coalitional game theory, in *Computer Vision Systems*. Lecture Notes in Computer Science, vol. 5815 (2009), pp. 394–402
176. K. Roy, P. Bhattacharya, Optimal features subset selection using genetic algorithms for iris recognition, in *Image Analysis and Recognition*. Lecture Notes in Computer Science, vol. 5112 (2008), pp. 894–904
177. K. Roy, P. Bhattacharya, Unideal iris segmentation using region-based active contour model, in *ICIAR*. Lecture Notes in Computer Science, vol. 6112 (2010), pp. 256–265
178. V. Ruiz-Albacete, P. Tome-Gonzalez, F. Alonso-Fernandez, Direct attacks using fake images in iris verification, in *Biometrics and Identity Management*. Lecture Notes in Computer Science, vol. 5372 (2008), pp. 181–190
179. W.J. Ryan et al., Adapting starburst for elliptical iris segmentation, in *IEEE 2nd International Conference on Biometrics: Theory, Applications, and Systems (BTAS)*, Sept 2008
180. J.A. Scallan, S. Weimer, Overview of the multiple biometrics grand challenge, in *Advances in Biometrics*, ed. by M. Tistarelli, M. Nixon, vol. 5558 (Springer, Berlin/Heidelberg, 2009), pp. 705–714
181. N.A. Schmid, F. Nicolo, A method for selecting and ranking quality metrics for optimization of biometric recognition systems, in *Computer Vision and Pattern Recognition Workshops (CVPR Workshops)*, June 2009, pp. 126–133
182. N.A. Schmid, F. Nicolò, On empirical recognition capacity of biometric systems under global PCA and ICA encoding. IEEE Trans. Inf. Forensics Secur. **3**(3), 512–528 (2008)
183. F. Scotti, V. Piuri, Adaptive reflection detection and location in iris biometric images by using computational intelligence techniques. IEEE Trans. Instrum. Meas. **59**(7), 1825–1833 (2010)
184. S. Shah, A. Ross, Iris segmentation using geodesic active contours. IEEE Trans. Inf. Forensics Secur. **4**(4), 824–836 (2009)
185. S. Sheela et al., Iris and signature authentication using continuous dynamic programming, in *2nd International Congress on Image and Signal Processing (CISP)*, Oct 2009, pp. 1–5

186. L. Stark, K.W. Bowyer, S. Siena, Human perceptual categorization of iris texture patterns, in *Fourth IEEE International Conference on Biometrics: Theory Applications and Systems (BTAS)*, Sept 2010
187. N. Sudha et al., Iris recognition on edge maps. IET Comput. Vision **3**(1), 1–7 (2009)
188. Z. Sun, T. Tan, Ordinal measures for iris recognition. IEEE Trans. Pattern Anal. Mach. Intell. **31**(12), 2211–2226 (2009)
189. N. Tajbakhsh, B. Araabi, H. Soltanian-zadeh, Noisy iris verification: a modified version of local intensity variation method, in *Advances in Biometrics*. Lecture Notes in Computer Science, vol. 5558 (2009), pp. 1150–1159
190. N. Tajbakhsh, K. Misaghian, N. Bandari, A region-based iris feature extraction method based on 2D-wavelet transform, in *Biometric ID Management and Multimodal Communication*. Lecture Notes in Computer Science, vol. 5707 (2009), pp. 301–307
191. H. Takano, K. Nakamura, Rotation independent iris recognition by the rotation spreading neural network, in *IEEE 13th International Symposium on Consumer Electronics (ISCE)*, May 2009, pp. 651–654
192. F. Tan et al., Image hashing enabled technique for biometric template protection, in *IEEE Region 10 Conference (TENCON)*, Jan 2009, pp. 1–5
193. A. Tayal et al., A multimodal biometric authentication system using decision theory, iris and speech recognition, in *2nd International Workshop on Nonlinear Dynamics and Synchronization (INDS)*, July 2009, pp. 1–8
194. A. Tayal et al., A multimodal biometric system coupling iris recognition and speaker identification systems through decision theory, in *3rd International Conference on Anti-counterfeiting, Security, and Identification in Communication (ASID)*, Aug 2009, pp. 135–137
195. J.W. Thompson, P.J. Flynn, A segmentation perturbation method for improved iris recognition, in *Fourth IEEE International Conference on Biometrics: Theory Applications and Systems (BTAS)*, Sept 2010
196. N.A. Vandal, M. Savvides, CUDA accelerated iris template matching on Graphics processing units, in *Fourth IEEE International Conference on Biometrics: Theory Applications and Systems (BTAS)*, Sept 2010
197. M. Vatsa, R. Singh, A. Noore, Improving iris recognition performance using segmentation, quality enhancement, match score fusion, and indexing. IEEE Trans. Syst. Man. Cybern. Part B **38**(4), 1021–1035 (2008)
198. M. Vatsa et al., Belief function theory based biometric match score fusion: case studies in multi-instance and multi-unit iris verification, in *Seventh International Conference on Advances in Pattern Recognition (ICAPR)*, Feb 2009, pp. 433–436
199. V. Velisavljevic, Low-complexity iris coding and recognition based on directionlets. IEEE Trans. Inf. Forensics Secur. **4**(3), 410–417 (2009)
200. D. Wang, J. Li, G. Memik, Authentication scheme of DRM system for remote users based on multimodal biometrics, watermarking and smart card, in *WRI Global Congress on Intelligent Systems (GCIS)*, vol. 2, 2009, pp. 530–534
201. F. Wang, J. Han, Multimodal biometric authentication based on score level fusion using support vector machine. Opto-Electron. Rev. **17**, 59–64 (2009)
202. J. Wang et al., Multi-modal biometric authentication fusing iris and palmprint based on GMM, in *IEEE 15th Workshop on Statistical Signal Processing (SSP)*, Aug 2009, pp. 349–352
203. X. Wang, L. Zhao, Q. Kong, Iris recognition system design and development of large animals for tracing source of infection, in *International Joint Conference on Computational Sciences and Optimization (CSO)*, vol. 1, 2009, pp. 610–613
204. Z.F. Wang et al., Complex common vector for multimodal biometric recognition. Electron. Lett. **45**(10), 495–496 (2009)
205. Z. Wang et al., Feature-level fusion of iris and face for personal identification, in *Advances in Neural Networks—ISNN 2009*. Lecture Notes in Computer Science, vol. 5553, 2009, pp. 356–364
206. Z. Wang et al., Multimodal biometric recognition based on complex KFDA, in *Fifth International Conference on Information Assurance and Security (IAS)*, vol. 2, 2009, pp. 177–180

207. Z. Wei et al., Counterfeit iris detection based on texture analysis, in *19th International Conference on Pattern Recognition* (2008)
208. F.W. Wheeler et al., Stand-off iris recognition system, in *IEEE 2nd International Conference on Biometrics: Theory, Applications, and Systems (BTAS)*, Sept 2008
209. E.P. Wibowo, W.S. Maulana, Real-time iris recognition system using a proposed method, in *International Conference on Signal Processing Systems*, May 2009, pp. 98–102
210. D.-M. Wu, J.-N. Wang, An improved iris recognition method based on gray surface matching, in *Fifth International Conference on Information Assurance and Security (IAS)*, vol. 1, 2009, pp. 247–249
211. Z. Xiangde et al., Noise detection of iris image based on texture analysis, in *Chinese Control and Decision Conference (CCDC)*, June 2009, pp. 2366–2370
212. J. Xu et al., Robust local binary pattern feature sets for periocular biometric identification, in *Fourth IEEE International Conference on Biometrics: Theory Applications and Systems (BTAS)*, Sept 2010
213. X. Xu, P. Guo, Iris feature extraction based on the complete 2DPCA, in *Advances in Neural Networks*. Lecture Notes in Computer Science, vol. 5552 (2009), pp. 950–958
214. N. Yager, T. Dunstone, The biometric menagerie. IEEE Trans. Pattern Anal. Mach. Intell. **32**(2), 220–230 (2010)
215. L. Zhang et al., Robust biometric key extraction based on iris cryptosystem, in *Advances in Biometrics*. Lecture Notes in Computer Science, vol. 5558 (2009)
216. X. Zhao, M. Xie, A practical design of iris recognition system based on DSP, in *International Conference on Intelligent Human-Machine Systems and Cybernetics (IHMSC)*, vol. 1, 2009, pp. 66–70
217. Z. Zhiping, H. Maomao, S. Ziwen, An iris recognition method based on 2DWPCA and neural network, in *Chinese Control and Decision Conference (CCDC)*, June 2009, pp. 2357–2360
218. Z. Zhou, Y. Du, C. Belcher, Transforming traditional iris recognition systems to work in nonideal situations. IEEE Trans. Ind. Electron. **56**(8), 3203–3213 (2009)
219. Z. Zhou, Y. Du, C. Belcher, Transforming traditional iris recognition systems to work on nonideal situations, in *IEEE Workshop on Computational Intelligence in Biometrics: Theory, Algorithms, and Applications (CIB)*, March 2009, pp. 1–8
220. J. Zuo, F. Nicolo, N.A. Schmid, Cross spectral iris matching based on predictive image mapping, in *Fourth IEEE International Conference on Biometrics: Theory Applications and Systems (BTAS)*, Sept 2010
221. J. Zuo, N.A. Schmid, Global and local quality measures for NIR iris video, in *Computer Vision and Pattern Recognition Workshops (CVPRW)*, June 2009, pp. 120–125
222. J. Zuo, N.A. Schmid, On a Methodology for Robust Segmentation of Nonideal Iris Images. IEEE Transactions on Systems, Man, and Cybernetics, Part B: Cybernetics **40**(3), 703–718 (2010)

Chapter 3
Optics of Iris Imaging Systems

David Ackerman

Abstract Iris imaging systems must capture iris images of sufficient quality to populate an enrollment database or to provide probe images that reliably match to existing enrollment images. From whatever distance they are taken, the iris images must therefore resolve information from the iris sufficient for the task of recognition. This chapter reviews concepts of optics and photography needed to specify requirements on the image acquisition components of systems which create iris images for the purpose of recognition. We consider fundamental and practical limitations of components of such systems and consider as examples, iris imaging systems that operate at 0.3 and 3 m on constrained and relatively unconstrained subjects.

3.1 Introduction

The goal of this chapter is to understand the optics of an iris imaging system. An iris imaging system captures a single or dual iris image at a given distance using illumination over a prescribed wavelength band. Design of an imaging system or camera to accomplish this task requires an understanding of the fundamental and practical capabilities and limitations of the camera components such as the lens and image sensor. The resulting iris image must satisfy requirements, for example, on spatial resolution and signal-to-noise ratio, so that it can adequately serve as an enrollment image to be encoded and stored in a database or as an identification image to be encoded and compared with database iris codes for verification or identification. We will refer to the overall system that combines an iris imager and a means to identify an iris image as an iris recognition system.

We start by listing assumptions about a typical iris that we intend to image. An iris, the colored portion of an eye surrounding the pupil, is about 11 ± 1.5 mm in diameter [9] and sits behind the partially reflective cornea. We note that the diffuse reflectivity of an iris, referred to as its albedo, is dependent on illumination wavelength and

D. Ackerman (✉)
SRI, Princeton, NJ, USA
e-mail: david.ackerman@sri.com

© Springer-Verlag London 2016
K.W. Bowyer and M.J. Burge (eds.), *Handbook of Iris Recognition*,
Advances in Computer Vision and Pattern Recognition,
DOI 10.1007/978-1-4471-6784-6_3

is typically low, around 10 %, in the near-infrared (NIR) band. In the NIR band of 700–900 nm throughout which most iris imagery is acquired, the spatial variation in iris reflectivity which gives each iris its unique appearance results from subtle shadings of a few percent in contrast over a range of length scales from microns to millimeters.

The level of fidelity of an iris image needed to distinguish it from other irises is a topic of great interest to manufacturers and users of iris recognition systems. In this chapter, we will not recommend specific image requirements or threshold values for image metrics. Requirements on iris images are listed in ISO/IEC standards and are, at the time of this writing, undergoing careful scrutiny and revision [1]. We will, however, describe a framework for understanding the connection between components of an iris imaging system and measurable attributes of the images expected from such a system. In Sect. 3.4, we will briefly discuss the relationship of an imaging system and the algorithm used to analyze its images, that is, to segment or isolate irises from the larger image, to encode them, and to match the resulting numerical templates to those of other irises.

Finally, we will list some attributes of typical iris imaging systems that form the recipe for most of the successful instruments that are available today. Currently, available iris cameras that operate at approximately 30 cm or less from the subject typically resolve at least 200 pixels across an iris diameter. Those few systems operating at longer distances do not all utilize this level of spatial resolution. Most iris imaging systems use near-infrared illumination between 700 and 900 nm in order to minimize absorption by pigmentation on the front surface of the iris but enable the use of silicon imagers with reasonable sensitivity to image the structural component of the iris that becomes visible in NIR behind the front surface [10]. All iris imaging systems conform to accepted eye-safety standards [2] which limit the irradiance and radiance of near-infrared illumination upon subjects' eyes, whether continuous or pulsed.

While most iris imaging systems share common elements, each system is optimized for particular use conditions according to constraints on size, weight, power, operating distance, ambient conditions, and the expected behavior of subjects. In the next section, we will discuss some basic photographic concepts that will allow us to connect intended use conditions to requirements on iris images in order to design the imaging parts of an iris recognition system.

3.2 Review of Photographic Concepts

In this section, we discuss the interaction of light with the optical components of an iris imaging system or camera. We will treat light using a variety of equally valid models.

3.2.1 Geometrical Optics

Light can be modeled as massless particles, that is, photons, waves, or rays. Geometrical optics builds upon a ray model in order to understand the propagation of light from an illuminated object through an optical system to an image sensor such as in a camera. We next consider some simple concepts of geometrical optics that will facilitate our examination of iris imaging systems. While commercially available ray-tracing programs can predict the performance of complicated lens arrays, we will use the simplest thin lens approximations to obtain predictions of lens behavior. These predictions based on simple approximations that model complex multielement lenses as single thin lenses are still useful.

3.2.1.1 Focal Length of a Lens

A lens is specified by a number of parameters; we will start by using only a focal length, defined as the distance from the plane of a thin lens to the point of convergence of parallel rays through the lens. Figure 3.1 shows a thin lens focusing an object onto an image plane. Two important rays are traced by dashed lines. A marginal ray leaves the object approaching the lens in a direction parallel to the optical axis. When the marginal ray crosses the plane of the thin lens, it is refracted so that it crosses the optical axis at a distance from the lens equal to the focal length of the lens. A chief ray leaves the object in the direction of the center of the thin lens, emerging on the opposite side of the lens with its direction unchanged. Both rays carry information about the object as they converge at the focused image.

When an object at distance d_o creates a focused image at distance d_i through a lens of focal length f as shown in Fig. 3.1, the geometry of similar triangles yields the lensmaker's formula:

$$\frac{1}{f} = \frac{1}{d_o} + \frac{1}{d_i} \tag{3.1}$$

The magnification of an imaging system is the ratio of the size of the image h_i to the size of the object h_o, which can be rewritten in terms of the image and object

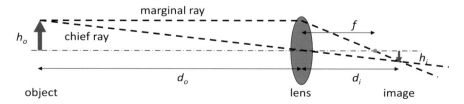

Fig. 3.1 An object (*blue arrow* on *left*, d_o from the lens) is imaged onto an image plane (as *inverted blue arrow* on *right*, d_i from the lens.) The so-called marginal and chief rays converge in the image plane and, in this case, predict the position of the tip of the image *arrow*

distances, $M = d_i/d_o$ Starting with d_o and f and using the lensmaker's formula (3.1), we find

$$M \equiv \frac{h_i}{h_o} = \frac{d_i}{d_o} = \frac{f}{d_o - f} \qquad (3.2)$$

In a typical camera setup, the numerical value of M is most often less than one, while in a microscope M is typically greater than one. For the setup shown in Fig. 3.1, when the object distance is much greater than the focal length of the lens, $M \sim f/d_o$. In other words, M is roughly the reciprocal of the number of focal lengths between the object and the camera.

3.2.1.2 Object-Referred Pixel Size and Field of View

The digital image sensor of a camera is made from an array of photosensitive picture elements or pixels. Thus, an image in a digital camera is cast upon a typically square array of elements which convert the image light intensity to photo-induced charge which is then converted to voltage and measured for each pixel in order to record the image. A useful concept in comparing the size of features in an image to the corresponding features of the object is the object-referred pixel size L_{orp}, defined as the dimension on the object which is imaged onto a single pixel on the imager. If the size of a single square pixel is L_p, then

$$L_{orp} = \frac{L_p}{M} \sim \frac{L_p \cdot d_o}{f} \qquad (3.3)$$

in which the second expression for L_{orp} applies to cases in which $d_o \gg f$. For example, if an image sensor with $6\,\mu m$ pixels receives a focused image of a 2 m distant object using a 100-mm focal length lens, $L_{orp} \sim 120\,\mu m$. In the spirit of geometrical optics, this means that square blocks of the object $120\,\mu m$ on a side are imaged onto single pixels as shown in Fig. 3.2 in which an iris (object) is imaged onto an image sensor.

The field of view of a digital camera is determined by the size of the image sensor assuming that the optical system is designed to create an image that covers the sensor. If the sensor in Fig. 3.2 is made of N_h pixels in the horizontal direction and N_v pixels in the vertical direction, then the dimensions of the region on the object that can be imaged by the sensor are determined by the magnification of the optics and the pixel count:

$$\mathrm{FOV}_j = N_j \cdot L_{orp} \qquad \text{where} \quad j = h, v \qquad (3.4)$$

Thus, in our previous example in which $L_{orp} \sim 120\,\mu m$, an image sensor with $1{,}280 \times 960$ pixels will provide a field of view of $14.6 \times 10.9\,cm$. A sensor with more pixels will create a larger field of view as will an optical system with lower magnification, for example, shorter focal length lens and/or greater object distance.

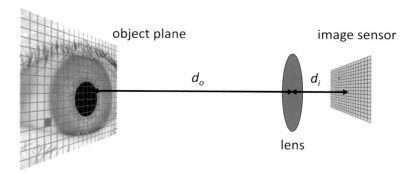

Fig. 3.2 An object (*left*, d_o from the lens) is imaged onto an image plane (*right*, d_i from the lens.) The portion of object shown by the *red square* is imaged onto a single pixel shown as another *red square* on the image plane

Sometimes, it is useful to consider the field of view in terms of angle rather than area. In this case, we simply convert the horizontal and vertical dimensions of the field of view to angles subtended by the field of view with respect to the optical axis. For angular field of view, Eq. (3.4) becomes

$$\text{Angular FOV}_j = 2 \arctan\left(\frac{N_j \cdot L_{\text{orp}}}{2}\right); \quad \text{where} \quad j = h, v; \quad \text{units of radians} \tag{3.5}$$

3.2.1.3   F-Number and Lens Aperture

In addition to focal length, camera lenses are often characterized by their so-called F-number, where F is defined by Eq. (3.6) in terms of focal length f and lens aperture D and illustrated in Fig. 3.3.

$$F = \frac{f}{D} \tag{3.6}$$

Fig. 3.3 Schematic of a thin lens of focal length f and aperture diameter D which would then have $F = f/D$

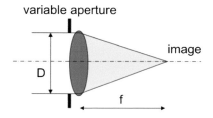

Thus, a lens with 100-mm focal length and a 25-mm diameter clear aperture for gathering light would be conventionally labeled $F/4$ and spoken as "$F4$." Many lenses have variable apertures and thus variable F-number. Changing the diameter of the lens aperture varies the amount of light collected so that in dim lighting, a low F-number would gather light at a greater rate and necessitate a shorter exposure than at high F-number. In the days of film cameras, a lens with a larger aperture that would admit more light than a lens of the same focal length with a smaller aperture was referred to as a "fast" lens since the rate at which the film would be exposed was relatively fast. A lens with comparatively smaller aperture was referred to as a "slow" lens.

3.2.1.4   Depth of Field

Aperture size affects the photographic depth of field of an imaging system. Depth of field refers to a range in object distance that an object can occupy for a given lens and given image distance that results in an in-focus image. It is the subjective judgment of focus quality that makes depth of field a subjective quantity. To quantify depth of field requires specifying the dimension of a blur spot in the image plane beyond which a point image is judged out of focus. The size of such a blur spot is referred to as the "circle of confusion" in the context of depth of field. Figure 3.4 schematically shows three objects spread out in object distance along the optical axis. Only the middle object is placed at an object distance that is focused for the lens and image distance, that is, the object distance of the middle object together with the image distance and satisfy the lensmaker Eq. (3.2).

Figure 3.4 illustrates the cases of large and small aperture lenses and graphically illustrates why a lens set to larger aperture exhibits relatively shallow depth of field compared to the same lens set to a smaller aperture. In the insets of Fig. 3.4, the low F-number case (top) creates images using rays, some of which impinge on the image sensor at steeper angles than in the case of higher F-number (bottom). An imaging system with high F-number (small aperture) has a larger range in object positions for a given circle of confusion because the rays from the various positions on the object plane approach the imager at relatively shallow angles and diverge more gradually in the vicinity of the image plane. The effect of F-number on image focus is shown dramatically in Fig. 3.5 for two cases that feature objects spread out in object distance.

The ray geometry of Fig. 3.4 provides an expression for depth of field (DoF) that is presented in (3.5) and which can be approximated by Eq. (3.7):

$$\text{DoF} \approx 2C \cdot F \cdot \left(\frac{d}{f}\right)^2 \tag{3.7}$$

in which d is object distance, f is lens focal length, F is lens F-number, and C is the subjective quantity circle of confusion. As an example, if we pick circle of

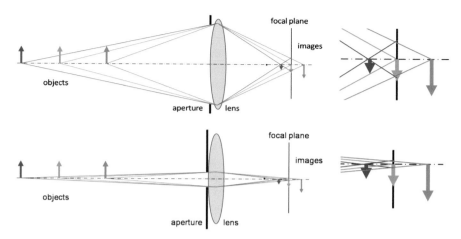

Fig. 3.4 Three objects (*blue, green,* and *red arrows*) at three different object distances create images at corresponding image distances. The image distance of only the middle object (*green arrow*) corresponds to the position of the focal plane at which the image sensor is placed. Thus, only the *green arrow* is in focus. The *upper figures* show the case of a large aperture (low F-number) in which rays from the base of the *arrows* impinge on the image sensor at relatively large angles. Thus, as shown in the *upper right inset*, the *blue arrow* is blurred because rays from its base cross in front of the imager and have diverged at the position of the sensor. Similarly, rays from the base of the *red arrow* are yet to converge as they hit the image sensor and so the *red arrow* is also out of focus. The *lower figures* show the case of small aperture (high F-number) in which rays from the base of the *arrows* impinge upon the imager at relatively low angles. In this case, although the *blue* and *red arrows* are also out of focus, the degree of blur is smaller. A larger aperture results in shallow depth of field, whereas smaller aperture creates relatively larger depth of field

Fig. 3.5 Example of a scene that extends over a wide range in object distance photographed with shallow (*left*) and large (*right*) depth of field. The focal plane is set at the labeled bottle. While the bottle is in focus in both scenes, the foreground and background objects on the *left* are out of focus as imaged with aperture set to *F*/2.8 while the same features are sharper on the *right* as imaged with aperture set to *F*/16

confusion C to equal 1 pixel dimension $= 6\,\mu m$, (certainly, C cannot be less than 1 pixel) and if $d = 2\,m$, $f = 100\,mm$, and $F = 4$, we find DoF $\approx 2\,cm$. Specifically, DoF represents the distance measured along the optical axis of the camera from the nearest to the furthest in-focus object position. In this particular case, the DoF is approximately 1 % of the object distance. Changing the F-number of the lens from $F/4$ to $F/8$ by decreasing the lens aperture by a factor of two increases the DoF by a factor of 2 to about 4 cm. If we accept as focused an image with a blur spot in the image plane of two pixels instead of one, DoF would double. (This might be the case with a color image in which each individual color is interpolated over ~ 2 pixels.) Changing object distance or lens focal length by a factor of 2 would change DoF by a factor of 4.

Geometrical optics that we have presented so far predicts a field of view determined by lens and image sensor characteristics and a depth of field set by the lens focal length and aperture for a given object distance. Together, a volume with lateral dimensions (measured perpendicular to the optical axis) equal to that of the field of view and with axial dimension (measured along the optical axis) equal to that of the depth of field defines a capture volume. Inside the capture volume, an in-focus object is imaged onto the sensor. We will use the concept of capture volume in designing an iris imager in Sect. 3.3.

3.2.2 Spatial Resolution

Spatial resolution measures the response of an image capture device to the spectrum of spatial frequencies that comprise an object. Spatial resolution of an imaging system is a function of spatial frequency (pitch and orientation) as well as lens- and image sensor-related parameters including position in the field of view(lens-related), illumination spectrum (lens- and sensor-related), object distance (lens-related), and brightness (sensor-related). Because spatial resolution is fundamentally limited by the wave phenomenon of, we will start the discussion of spatial resolution using a wave model of light rather than the ray model of geometrical optics. We will then use ray tracing to consider aberrations due to imperfect lenses which further degrade spatial resolution. Finally, we will consider quality of focus as it affects spatial resolution.

Ultimately, the spatial resolution of an entire system determines the fidelity with which an iris imaging system renders the large and small features of an iris. However, looking ahead to Sect. 3.4, it is important to keep in mind that a given algorithm exploits a particular subset of the iris information, determined by its own spatial frequency response. Therefore, accurate prediction of biometric performance of an iris recognition system requires knowledge of both the spatial resolution of the capture device and spatial frequency bandwidth of the matching algorithm.

3.2.2.1 Diffraction Fundamentally Limits Spatial Resolution

A measure of spatial resolution of an imaging system is its point spread function (PSF), the image of a point object. Observing a small LED pilot light across a darkened room without corrective lenses provides a view of the PSF of the observer's eyes at the LED wavelength. Crudely, the PSF is a blur spot of size that characterizes the smallest feature resolvable by an imaging system. An ideal image convolved with the system PSF produces the actual captured image (allowing for variation of PSF over the field of view). Diffraction fundamentally limits the PSF, dependent upon the size (and shape) of the aperture of the collecting lens, the object distance, and the illumination wavelength.

Loosely speaking, diffraction results from the interaction of waves with an object illuminated by these waves. In this sense, water waves, sound waves, and light waves behave similarly with an interaction characterized by the ratio of object size to wavelength. A clear example of diffraction of water waves is shown in Fig. 3.6. The wavelength of near-infrared light is about seven orders of magnitude shorter than that of ocean waves of Fig. 3.6, but diffraction of light nevertheless bears a close resemblance to that of water or sound waves. To the extent that we can approximate the diffraction of light as a scalar phenomenon, thereby ignoring the vector nature of electromagnetic waves, diffraction of light can be computed relatively easily. In the so-called Fraunhofer approximation [4], in which the object size must be comparable to or greater than the wavelength of light but must also be much smaller than the distance between the object and viewer and the field of view, we find that the distribution of light diffracted by an object closely approximates a scaled Fourier transform of the object, where the scaling relates to the optical wavelength. A mathematical description of scalar diffraction theory that underlies the Fraunhofer approximation is given in Refs. [7, 11].

Fig. 3.6 Image of water waves interacting with a breakwater taken from Ref. [11]

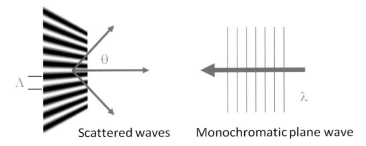

Scattered waves   Monochromatic plane wave

Fig. 3.7 Monochromatic plane waves of wavelength λ impinge normally on a grating of spatial wavelength Λ from the *right*. The grating scatters the waves along three directions described in terms of their angle θ from the normal

Reference [11] provides an approximate mathematical description of diffraction, from which we can gain an intuitive understanding of the diffraction phenomenon in the Fraunhofer diffraction regime by thinking of objects that diffract light in terms of the effects upon light waves of each of the individual spatial frequency components of an object. A simple object to start with is a sinusoidal grating of the type found in an optical spectrometer, manufactured holographically and illustrated schematically in Fig. 3.7.

Light normally incident on the grating (from the front in the case of a reflective grating or the back in the case of a transmissive grating) is scattered by each line in the grating. The scattered light constructively interferes as it radiates from the grating with its energy concentrated in three directions, one normal to the grating and two at equal and opposite directions relative to the normal direction. The directions, in terms of angle θ from the normal direction, are given by the formula

$$n\lambda = \Lambda \sin \theta \tag{3.8}$$

where λ = wavelength of light, Λ = wavelength of grating, and $n = -1, 0,$ and 1. Each angle corresponds to a direction of constructive interference that can be assigned to a spatial frequency of the grating: $n = \pm 1$ for the two sine waves of wavelengths $\pm \Lambda$ that combine to create a standing wave of the proper wavelength and phase, and $n = 0$ for an average value that simply offsets the standing wave. Here, we avoid the issue of the finite extent of the grating and think of it as very large, containing many lines. In this approximation, we can say that the sinusoidal grating diffracts light in three discrete directions. Note that the ± 1 order diffraction angle increases with λ / Λ, that is, with longer wavelength light or shorter wavelength (higher spatial frequency) grating. Because we can regard any object as a sum of its spatial frequency components, we can analyze Fraunhofer diffraction as the net effect of diffraction from the set of individual gratings that comprise an object, each with a particular grating period, phase, amplitude, and orientation. Objects with small features possess high

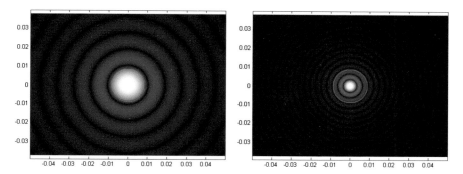

Fig. 3.8 Diffraction patterns created by 850-nm light on a screen placed 2 m in front of circular apertures of different sizes, 200-μm diameter (*left*) and 600-μm diameter (*right*). The *red circles* suggest the clear opening of a lens (in this example, 70-mm focal length set to *F*/4) that could receive the diffracted light and reimage it on a sensor

spatial frequencies which diffract light at large angles. Objects that are comprised of comparatively lower spatial frequencies will diffract light at smaller angles.

An illustration of Fraunhofer diffraction from two similar objects appears in Fig. 3.8. Here, light strikes circular apertures from the back and diffracts forward where it hits screens in front of the apertures. In the case of a small aperture, comprised of relatively high spatial frequencies, the diffraction pattern is coarse and spreads over a relatively large area because the diffraction due to its high spatial frequencies occurs at large angles. In comparison, the diffracted pattern appearing on the screen due to the larger aperture is concentrated over a relatively smaller area. The larger aperture contains relatively lower spatial frequency content which diffracts light of a given wavelength at smaller angles. The key concept is that small or sharp features, made of high spatial frequencies, diffract light at larger angles relative to the normal direction. In fact, we can regard the diffraction pattern in the Fraunhofer regime as a scaled Fourier transform of the object with the lowest spatial frequency components traveling straight to the screen and the higher spatial frequency components diffracted at angles away from the center of the diffraction pattern.

A direct consequence of diffraction is illustrated by the red circles in Fig. 3.8, which represent the input clear apertures of camera lenses that might be used to focus on and create images of the two illuminated circular apertures that are diffracting the illumination. Because a lens cannot admit light beyond its clear opening, it cannot use rejected light to rebuild the image of the object. Since the higher spatial frequencies of an object result in larger angle diffraction, the red circles represent a cutoff that effectively low-pass filters the spatial frequency spectrum of the object. For different lens apertures, as shown in Fig. 3.9, the same object imaged through a smaller aperture suffers more filtering than imaged through a larger aperture. The effects of the filtering can be visualized at the image plane of the lens where the spatial frequency components are reconstituted into a filtered representation of the

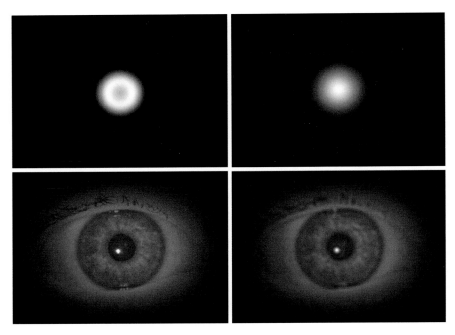

Fig. 3.9 *Top row* Images of 600-μm aperture with simulated diffraction due to 850-nm illumination, 2.5 m object distance, 70-mm focal length lens set to *F*/4 (17.5-mm clear lens aperture, *left*) and *F*/11 (6.4-mm clear lens aperture, *right*) showing increasing diffraction effects with smaller aperture. *Lower row* Images of human iris with simulated diffraction under same imaging conditions with 70-mm lens set at *F*/4 (*left*) and *F*/11 (*right*)

original object. The more of the original components that are included in the image, the more faithfully the image represents the original. In Fig. 3.9, we simulate the 600-μm aperture shown in Fig. 3.8, filtered by *F*/4 and *F*/11 apertures. The larger aperture (*F*/4) produces a sharper image. In a second example using a human iris as an object, the same effect of (simulated) diffraction is illustrated in lower row of Fig. 3.9 with aperture also set to *F*/4 and *F*/11. Realistic loss of resolution of the fine iris details due to diffraction is visible in the *F*/11 iris image.

Diffraction limits the size of the smallest object that can be imaged by an optical system. The diffraction limit can be derived in the Fraunhofer approximation (3.4) and (3.8) and simply stated as follows:

$$\Delta x_d \cong \frac{\lambda d}{D} \tag{3.9}$$

in which Δx_d = the diameter (full width at half max, FWHM) of the smallest spot that can be resolved in the object plane, λ = illumination wavelength, d = object distance, and D = aperture diameter. Spots that are smaller than the diffraction limit are blurred to the diffraction-limited spot size. We can use Eqs. (3.2) and (3.6) to convert the diffraction-limited spot size in the object plane to that appearing in the image plane (indicated with a prime) from which we get

$$\Delta x'_d \approx \frac{\lambda \cdot d_o}{D} \cdot M \approx \frac{\lambda \cdot d_o}{D} \cdot \frac{f}{d_o} = \lambda \cdot F \qquad (3.10)$$

in which F = F-number of the lens.

Equation (3.10) relates the image plane blur spot to the F-number of the lens for a given illumination wavelength so that, for example, with a wavelength of 850 nm typical of near-infrared light and an $F/4$ lens, we would expect an image plane blur spot of approximately $\Delta x'_d \approx 3.4\,\mu$m. It is instructive to compare the image plane blur spot size to that of the pixel pitch of the imager as pictured schematically in Fig. 3.10. The ratio of image plane spot size to pixel pitch is simply $\Delta x' d / L_p \approx (\lambda / L_p) \cdot F$, which is "tuned" by F. A large value of F (small aperture, strong diffraction-related filtering) creates a blur spot on the imager that is larger than a pixel dimension, while a small value of F (large aperture, weak diffraction filtering) creates a blur spot that is smaller than a pixel dimension. Figure 3.10 illustrates both of these cases and the intermediate case in which $F \approx L_p / \lambda$ which matches the blur spot and pixel dimension.

In the case of a very small blur spot, the image resolution is pixel limited. In other words, the smallest image feature is determined by the spatial quantization of the image into chunks corresponding to individual pixels. In this case, the lens resolution (and cost!) exceeds the capabilities of the image sensor. The opposite case in which the diffraction-induced blur spot size covers many pixels creates a diffraction-limited image. In this case, the sampling density (and cost!) of the pixel array on the image sensor exceeds the capability of the lens. A practical design optimizes performance bearing in mind the cost of components. By such reasoning, the intermediate case in which F-number, pixel dimension, and illumination wavelength are arranged to match the image plane blur spot to the pixel dimension is optimal. As an example, for 6-μm pixels and 850-nm illumination, $F/7$ provides an optimal match. For the same illumination but with smaller pixels $\sim 2\,\mu$m, as would be found in cell phone imagers, $F/2.4$ is required to optimize performance. From the previous discussion of depth of

Fig. 3.10 Diffraction blur spots on an image sensor showing pixel grid. Large blur spot (*right*) results in diffraction-limited resolution while small blur spot (*left*) results in pixel-limited resolution. Center blur spot is match to pixel pitch

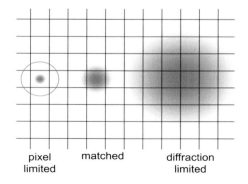

pixel limited   matched   diffraction limited

field, we see that optimizing blur spot size for smaller pixels (for a given illumination wavelength) forces use of a lower F-number which reduces DoF. Balancing design considerations of image resolution, depth of field with practical considerations of system performance and cost involves trade-offs that are the basis of camera design. As we shall see, system performance criteria are determined by the end use of the camera, be it for wedding photography, aerial surveillance, or iris recognition. In any design, however, the fundamental (unavoidable) effects of diffraction must be considered.

3.2.2.2 Lens Quality Practically Limits Spatial Resolution

Fundamental limitations such as diffraction are compounded by practical limitations related to lens quality. A mass-produced molded plastic lens might be lower in cost compared to a diffraction-limited multielement aspheric glass lens, but it might also produce a poorer quality image. Careful ray-tracing programs follow the trajectory of light through any arrangement of refracting materials and can determine parameters such as the quality of focus. Sacrifices in design and materials can result in lens aberrations that compromise performance as illustrated [12] in the ray tracing of Fig. 3.11. Pictured in Fig. 3.11 is a thin lens that creates a sharp focus. Close inspection of the focus reveals that parallel rays, especially those entering the lens at its periphery do not cross at a single point. This phenomenon is graphed as a scatter pattern thereby quantitatively connecting the lens design to a measure of spatial resolution. Certainly, we cannot expect to create a blur spot that is smaller than the scatter of rays at a point of best focus. By means of ray tracing, we discover a level of spatial resolution that can achieve the diffraction limit in the case of high-quality lenses but for other lenses can be considerably poorer in spatial resolution than predicted by the fundamental diffraction limit.

Referring back to Fig. 3.10, we see that opening the aperture in an attempt to achieve pixel-limited spatial resolution might result in aberration-limited resolution as suggested by the red circle created by a collection of rays such as shown in

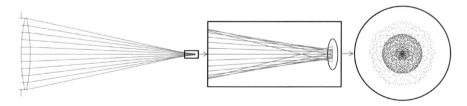

Fig. 3.11 Parallel rays impinging on a lens (*left*) are refracted to a focus within the *black rectangle*. An expanded view of the area within the rectangle shows that rays do not all focus to the same point due to lens aberration which is most apparent in rays passing through the outer portions of the lens. A collection of points corresponding to rays in the image plane is plotted (*right*) showing the scatter which produces a blurred focus in the image plane

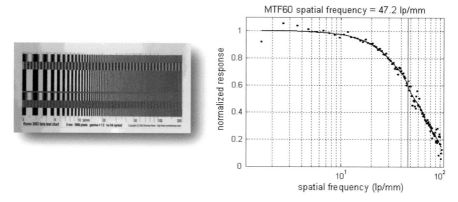

Fig. 3.12 A test target due to Ref. [8] (*left*) features sine and square waves of decreasing spatial frequency which can be imaged resulting in contrast (normalized peak to valley variation) which is plotted as a function of image plane spatial frequency (*right*). *Red line* indicates image plane spatial frequency at which contrast drops to 60 % in keeping with ISO/IEC image quality specification of Ref. [1]

Fig. 3.11 that is larger than the theoretically achievable diffraction-limited spot. In practice, there is an optimum aperture size for a given lens to achieve best spatial resolution. Spatial resolution can be measured by a number of techniques and can be characterized in terms of modulation transfer function (MTF) which is the Fourier transform of the point spread function. One technique for measuring MTF uses a grating with increasing pitch and uniform contrast, as illustrated in Fig. 3.12 and detailed in Ref. [8].

Roughly speaking, it takes a distance equal to that of four blur spots to discern a single line pair (or sinusoidal cycle) at the limit of resolution, for example, when contrast in the perceived modulation pattern has dropped to half of its original value. By such a measure, the data of Fig. 3.13 indicate that at $F/5.6$, the lens under test

Fig. 3.13 MTF_{60} as a function of F-number for a 70-mm lens showing a peak at around $F/5.6$ at which spatial resolution is an optimum trade-off of aberration and diffraction

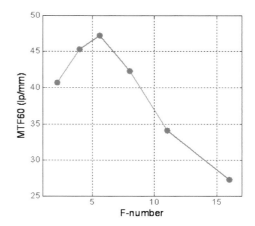

should be producing a blur spot at 850 nm of approximately $(1/\text{MTF}_{50})/4 \sim 4.5\,\mu\text{m}$. The image plane diffraction-limited spot for this particularly high-quality lens is approximately $\Delta x_d \approx F \cdot \lambda \sim 4.8\,\mu\text{m}$, in good agreement within the spirit of the approximations used. If we measure MTF as a function of F-number, we trace out a lens performance curve that conforms to the suggestion of Fig. 3.10, namely, that high F-number performance suffers due to diffraction and low F-number performance suffers due to lens aberration. Performance of the lens under test peaks at $F/5.6$. Thus, we have combined the wave concept of diffraction and the ray concepts that describe lenses to get a picture of how lenses and image sensors work together to provide spatial resolution.

For concreteness, we approximate the measured MTF of a lens at a particular wavelength and F-number such as that represented in Fig. 3.12 with a Gaussian profile and 50 % contrast point which we will call MTF_{50}. We assume that the effects of diffraction and aberration contribute independently to the measured MTF curve. (With a perfect lens, we would measure the effects of diffraction only.) The width of the PSF due to diffraction and aberration can be approximated by Eq. (3.11) which assumes that the PSF, of diameter $x'_{1/2}$, is due to independent Gaussian contributions of diffraction and aberration. In Eq. (3.11), the broadening due to aberration $\Delta x'_{ab}$ and that due to diffraction λF adds in quadrature.

$$x'_{\left(\frac{1}{2}\right)} = \sqrt{(\Delta x'\, ab)^2 + (\lambda \cdot F)^2} \tag{3.11}$$

Finally, we can account for defocus by further broadening the PSF diameter. The details of defocus broadening relate to the size and shape of the lens aperture. To avoid incurring defocus broadening, we must ensure that an object remains within the depth of field, that is, remains in the capture volume.

3.2.3 Signal and Noise

Thus far, we have discussed light in terms of waves and rays. Now, we switch to a photon description of light as a particle similar to a drop of rain or a billiard ball. This picture is valuable in discussing light as it hits an image sensor and is transformed into electrical charge which is counted in order to profile intensity as a function of position in an image. Figure 3.14 shows a schematic camera with lens,

Fig. 3.14 Schematic lens, aperture, and image sensor

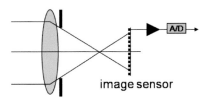

image sensor

Fig. 3.15 Analogous representation of image sensor pixels and light particles as buckets catching rain. A given bucket catches, on average, S photons. The bucket-to-bucket variance in photon number due to shot noise is also S

aperture, image sensor, and transducer that creates a digital representation of an image. A row of pixels from the image sensor, represented as buckets,[1] is shown in Fig. 3.15. Photons from a flat field image (spatially uniform intensity) impinge upon the lens and are imaged onto the sensor. After an exposure time when the shutter is closed and the sensor is no longer exposed to light, each bucket or pixel holds a certain number of photoelectrons, each resulting from a photon. In the case of a flat field image, the number of photons in the buckets would be expected to be uniform since the object that fills the field of view is itself uniformly irradiated with light. However, experiments show that the photoelectron number varies from pixel to pixel due to the random rate of photons arriving from the object. The variance of the photoelectron number across the imager is equal to the average number of photons when the variation of photon rate is determined only by the random rate of photon arrival. The process that determines the variance of photon number is known as shot noise and is a consequence quantum mechanics.

The result is that after an exposure time, the jth pixel (bucket) contains S_j photoelectrons with an average over all pixels of $\langle S_j \rangle$. In the case of shot noise, the variance in S_j is equal to $\langle S_j \rangle$ and, therefore, the standard deviation in the photon count in the buckets is $\sqrt{\langle S_j \rangle}$. If we consider an image with dim and bright regions, we find that the signal-to-noise ratio (SNR), defined as the ratio of the average photoelectron number to the standard deviation in photoelectron number, becomes

$$\text{SNR} = \frac{\langle S_j \rangle}{\sqrt{\langle S_j \rangle}} = \sqrt{\langle S_j \rangle} \qquad (3.12)$$

In a dim region in which the average photoelectron count is 100, SNR $= 10$ while in a bright region in which average photoelectron count is 10,000, SNR $= 100$ as shown schematically in Fig. 3.16 in which the noise in the dim region is fractionally higher than in the brighter region due to shot noise.

Other sources of noise can contribute to variation in photoelectron count in a given pixel including read noise, a variation occurring in the transformation of charge to

---

[1] In this discussion, we assume that photons that end up in one bucket remain in that bucket. In reality, we need to consider the possibility of photons finding their way into neighboring buckets, an effect that would further degrade spatial resolution.

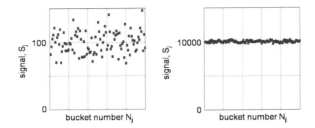

Fig. 3.16 Number of photoelectrons captured as a function of pixel (bucket) number in an area of an image exposed to a low light level (*left*) and higher light level (*right*). At higher light level, the absolute noise level is relatively higher, but its fractional effect on the image is less than in the lower light portion of the image. We can say that the SNR of the brighter part of the image is higher than the dimmer part of the image

voltage, and dark current which creates photoelectrons in the absence of signal from an object. Processes beyond fundamental shot noise contribute independently to the total noise which is computed as the square root of the sum of the squares of each independent contribution. As an example, SNR in the presence of read noise N_r becomes

$$\text{SNR} = \frac{\langle S_j \rangle}{\sqrt{\langle S_j \rangle + N_r^2}} = \sqrt{\langle S_j \rangle} \cdot \frac{1}{\sqrt{1 + \frac{N_r^2}{\langle S_j \rangle}}} \qquad (3.13)$$

from which it is clear that SNR reduces to that shown by Eq. (3.12) when read noise is insignificant. However, in the case of very dim images, read noise and other contributions become lower bounds on noise and decrease SNR.

We now estimate SNR for an imaging system starting with an object that is illuminated at wavelength λ by a level of irradiance (power/area) of I. We assume that the light scatters from the object in a Lambertian pattern, that is, with an angular distribution proportional to the cosine of the angle between the normal and the object and the angle of scattering and with a diffuse reflection coefficient or albedo of a. A Lambertian model is reasonable for a wide class of non-shiny materials including the human iris. Next, we assume an optical system with an aperture and lens which creates an image on a sensor with individual pixels. For simplicity, we assume that we are in the shot noise regime in which contributions to noise other than shot noise are insignificant due to adequate illumination. Finally, we assume that the sensor has a quantum efficiency QE (ratio of photoelectrons created to incident photons) and that the exposure time is τ_{exp}. The imaging system is shown in Fig. 3.17.

The number of photoelectrons per pixel per exposure time is given by Eq. (3.14), using Eqs. (3.2) and (3.6), in terms of pixel dimension L_p, magnification M, albedo α, collection cone half-angle θ, exposure time τ_{exp}, quantum efficiency QE, photon energy $E_\gamma = hc/\lambda$, F-number F, and wavelength λ, as well as fundamental constants, h and c.

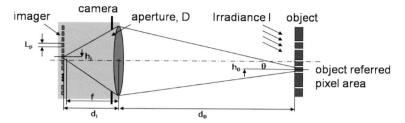

Fig. 3.17 Schematic view of imaging system showing object (*right*), a distance d_o from the lens and aperture. Pixels from the imager located a distance d_i from the lens, are projected onto the object and appear with size L_{orp}

$$S = I \cdot \left(\frac{L_p}{M}\right)^2 \cdot a \cdot \sin^2\theta \cdot \frac{\tau_{exp} \cdot QE}{E_\gamma} = I \cdot \left(\frac{L_p}{2F}\right)^2 \cdot a \cdot \frac{\tau_{exp} \cdot QE \cdot \lambda}{hc} \quad (3.14)$$

Equation (3.15) gives an expression for signal-to-noise ratio SNR for the imaging system as

$$\text{SNR} = \left(\frac{L_p}{2F}\right) \cdot \sqrt{\frac{I \cdot a \cdot \tau_{exp} \cdot QE \cdot \lambda}{hc}} \quad (3.15)$$

Notably, lens' focal length and object distance do not appear in Eq. 3.11. SNR is proportional to pixel size and inversely proportional to F-number; larger pixels and a faster lens improve SNR. In addition, SNR is proportion to the square root of a factor that relates to photoelectron collection. Increased irradiance on target, higher target albedo, longer exposures, and higher sensor quantum efficiency all improve SNR (but only proportional to the square root of the increase).

It should be noted that on some digital still cameras, a setting labeled as ISO (from the International Standards Organization) produces higher sensitivity to light. The equivalent video camera setting is more aptly labeled signal gain. In both digital still and video cameras, increasing the ISO or gain settings boosts the transduction ratio of charge to voltage and therefore does not increase SNR. If fact, charge-to-voltage amplification noise typically increases at higher gain settings so that high ISO or gain might reduce SNR.

3.2.4   Trade-Offs and Constraints

Camera design requirements often lead to trade-offs which produce design constraints. If illumination is dim and long exposures are impractical due to subject motion, a large aperture can be used at the expense of shallow depth of field and increased susceptibility to lens aberration. Alternatively, high signal gain can be used at the expense of SNR. If a large depth of field is required, then a small lens aperture might reduce spatial resolution due to diffraction, in which case a reduced cost lens might do just as good a job as an expensive one. Some design trade-offs are fairly obvious, such as exposure time and signal-to-noise ratio. However, under some situations, design trades produce interesting and nonobvious design constraints. Such is the case with depth of field under the constraint that matches the diffraction-limited spot size to a pixel dimension as is practical for high spatial resolution iris imaging.

We start by considering Eq. (3.7) in which circle of confusion C matches a single pixel dimension L_p. In other words, while the blur in the image plane due to defocus is comparable to the size of one pixel, we consider the object to be in focus. Furthermore, using Eq. (3.10), we match the diffraction-limited blur to the size of one pixel, which, given the illumination wavelength λ and the pixel pitch, sets the F-number of the lens. Finally, we recognize that the quantity (d/f) in Eq. (3.7) is approximately the inverse magnification given in Eq. (3.2) for $d \gg f$, which can be written as $(d/f) \sim M^{-1} \sim L_{\mathrm{orp}}/L_p$. Putting these pieces together, we get Eq. (3.16), which predicts depth of field under the conditions that (1) we maintain the diffraction-limited blur spot comparable to a pixel size and (2) we maintain object-referred pixel size at a given value dictated by the imaging application, both quite reasonable for an iris imaging system.

$$\mathrm{DoF} \approx 2C \cdot F \cdot \left(\frac{d}{f}\right)^2 \sim 2L_p \cdot \frac{L_p}{\lambda} \cdot \left(\frac{L_{\mathrm{orp}}}{L_p}\right)^2 = 2\frac{L_{\mathrm{orp}}^2}{\lambda} \qquad (3.16)$$

Equation (3.16) yields a constraint, namely, that under the given conditions, depth of field is approximately constant, independent of object distance.

If $L_{\mathrm{orp}} = 100\,\mathrm{mm}$ and $\lambda = 850\,\mathrm{nm}$, DoF $\sim 3\,\mathrm{cm}$. (This is, of course, because lens focal length must increase with object distance to maintain constant L_{orp}.) Nevertheless, Eq. (3.16) suggests that an ordinary iris recognition camera working at 30 cm, using a diffraction-limited 10-mm lens and a 30-m long-distance iris recognition system using a high-quality 1-m focal length telescope will have comparable depths of field. Equation (3.16) also is useful in determining whether an autofocus mechanism is needed for an iris imaging system or whether a fixed focus imager, for which the subject or operator adjusts the subject-to-camera distance, is adequate.

Another interesting case that arises under similar conditions predicts signal-to-noise ratio when lens aperture is chosen to match diffraction blur to a pixel dimension. In this case, Eq. (3.15) yields

$$\mathrm{SNR} = \left(\frac{L_p}{2F}\right) \cdot \sqrt{\frac{I \cdot a \cdot \tau_{\exp} \cdot \mathrm{QE} \cdot \lambda}{hc}} \sim \sqrt{\frac{I \cdot a \cdot \tau_{\exp} \cdot \mathrm{QE} \cdot \lambda^3}{4hc}} \qquad (3.17)$$

independent of lens parameters and object distance (assuming that irradiance on target is a constant). Assuming that the irradiance is limited by eye-safety considerations, that the exposure time is limited by subject motion considerations, and that QE is typically 0.1–0.2, Eq. (3.17) can be used to predict an upper bound on SNR in a given application. Equations (3.16) and (3.17) express design constraints that arise from reasonable conditions encountered in design of an iris imaging system.

3.3 Camera Design

The previous section reviewed photographic concepts and laid the groundwork for design of an iris imaging system. In this section, we will use the concepts to design two iris cameras that work in different scenarios. The first is more typical of iris cameras available at the time this chapter was written, working at around 0.3 m. Such systems include wall-mounted and handheld units, some of which capture a single iris and some of which capture dual iris images, often with multiple cameras. The second iris camera captures images from ten times further, 3 m, and is useful in applications with fewer subject constraints. As such, the second system must allow for position and motion of the subjects. In both systems, we will assume that illumination operates with an approximate wavelength of 850 nm at an eye-safe level. Eye safety is a primary concern for active illumination systems. A full discussion of eye safety is out of the scope of this chapter; the reader is referred to Ref. [2]. One important aspect of eye safety is worth mentioning, however. In the near-infrared wavelength band, shorter duration exposures are safer than longer ones with the threshold level of irradiance given in Ref. [2] by Eq. (3.18):

$$I_{\text{TLV}} = \frac{1,800}{t^{0.75}} \quad \text{in units of mW/cm}^2 \tag{3.18}$$

The implication is that higher irradiance exposure is safe in short doses. If short pulse illumination coordinated with an equally short camera exposure times can supply enough photons to meet SNR requirements while remaining eye safe, it can address the problem of motion blur. On the other hand, continuous and less bright illumination can avoid the complexity of pulsed illuminators at the expense of lower motion tolerance.

3.3.1 0.3-m Iris Imaging System

Design of a $d_o = 0.3$ m iris imaging system optimizes spatial resolution and signal-to-noise ratio for the prescribed use, in this case assuming a cooperative and motionless subject aligned with the field of view. For concreteness, let FoV = 0.13 m in width which allows for capture of two irises in one image and let illumination wavelength $\lambda = 850$ nm, ideal for penetrating dark iris pigmentation but still detectable by a silicon image sensor [5].

We shop for image sensors with several factors in mind. First, we want good quantum efficiency at 850 nm. At 850 nm at the time of this writing, 10 % QE is good for a front-illuminated silicon image sensor and 20 % would be excellent. Next, we want enough pixels to give adequate resolution across an iris since we do not want to be pixel limited at a resolution that is inadequate for iris recognition. At the time of writing this chapter, the ISO/IEC standard body has yet to finalize what resolution is adequate for iris recognition with proposals ranging from 7 to 20 samples per mm

in the object plane. Finally, we want enough pixels in the imager to cover the field
of view at the chosen sample density. As an example, we choose an object-referred
pixel size L_{orp} of $100\,\mu$m which gives 10 samples/mm and roughly 100 pixels across
an iris (3.2). Knowing L_{orp} and knowing the width of the FoV dictates the number of
pixels across the image sensor, in this case, $0.13\,\mathrm{m}/100\,\mu$ m $= 1,300$. This particular
example would suggest a 1.3-Mpixel imager with $1,300 \times 1,000$ pixels. (Of course,
the imager could have more pixels so long as we could read images from it fast
enough and could afford its cost.)

With an image sensor in mind, specifically one that has 1.3 MPx, adequate QE
and operates with a global shutter to avoid image shearing, we shop for a lens,
preferably one with good transmission and MTF at the illumination wavelength. A
current ISO/IEC proposal for MTF of an iris imaging system suggests a minimum
of 2 line pairs/mm on an object with at least 60 % contrast. If we assume about
4 pixels per line/pair, 2 lp/mm translates to 8 pixels/mm which, for a conservative
design, we round up to a pixel density of 10 px/mm on the object plane. L_{orp} is
therefore $100\,\mu$m consistent with our sensor plans from above. Given the pixel size
on the chosen imager, say $3.5\,\mu$m, and the object sampling density given by L_{orp}, we
immediately know the required magnification $M = L_{\mathrm{p}}/L_{\mathrm{orp}} = 3.5/100$. Given the
object distance d_{o}, M, and Eq. (3.2), we calculate the required lens focal length. In
this case, we manipulate Eq. (3.2) to give

$$f = d_{\mathrm{o}} \cdot \frac{1}{M^{-1} + 1} \tag{3.19}$$

which, for $d_{\mathrm{o}} = 0.3\,$m and $M = 0.035$, requires a 10-mm focal length lens.

The required MTF at the image plane is given by the ISO/IEC MTF standard for
the object plane converted using magnification from 2 lp/mm to $(2\,\mathrm{lp/mm} \times M^{-1})$
$= 58\,$lp/mm. If the chosen 10-mm focal length lens can far outperform this level of
spatial resolution, we can regard the lens as diffraction limited. Two subtleties are
worth mentioning. First, manufacturers' MTF specifications are frequently stated
as a single number, for example, 100 lp/mm. In this case, the specification typically
refers to the peak performance (see Fig. 3.13) in visible light. Since we are concerned
with a near-infrared wavelength, we must use caution in accepting the manufacturer's
specification. However, it is possible that the specification is overly conservative if
it averages over a broad spectrum. The second consideration is lens transmission
which is often tuned using lens coatings for visible light at the expense of near-
infrared performance. We do not want a lens with elements coated in such a way to
reduce contrast or transmit only 40 % of 850-nm light! It is always best to measure
the MTF of a candidate lens. We will proceed by assuming a diffraction-limited lens
for our design.

Since it is cost-efficient to match the blur spot of the lens to the pixel size, assuming
that the lens is diffraction limited or at least close, we use Eq. (3.10) to calculate the F-
number for the desired "matched" condition, in this case $F = 3.5\,\mu\mathrm{m}/850\,\mathrm{nm} = 4.1$.
With an $F/4$, 10-mm lens at an object distance of 0.3 m, we can compute the depth
of field assuming a value of circle of confusion C. For now, we will take $C = 1$

pixel $= 3.5\,\mu$m. Using Eq. (3.7) gives DoF $= 2.5$ cm, quite close to the estimate of Eq. (3.16), representing approximately 10 % of the object distance and requiring careful focusing. If we allow images to be taken outside the DoF, defocus will degrade spatial resolution so this might be a situation that would benefit from an autofocus mechanism, despite its complexity and cost.

With a depth of field and field of view, we can consider the "capture volume" of the camera as a volume in object space inside of which any object will appear in focus. Simplistically, we consider the capture volume to be the field of view 13×10 cm in directions perpendicular to the optical axis $\times$ depth of field $= 2.5$ cm along the optical axis.

Finally, we calculate the SNR for the imaging system by assuming a given level of irradiance on the object, an object albedo, and an exposure time. The irradiance is determined by the available light from all sources of 850-nm illumination. These might include the sun but most commonly include one or more light-emitting diodes (LEDs) tuned to the desired wavelength. Iris albedo is roughly 10 %. Exposure time is determined by the motion of the object. Sports photography requires very short exposures to capture rapidly moving subjects while avoiding motion blur. Astrophotography requires long exposures for its dim subjects that move slowly and predictably. For iris photography, we can arrange that subjects remain fixed in place by providing chin or forehead rests. If we allow freestanding, nominally stationary subjects, we must account for postural sway. For this example, we choose an exposure time of 30 ms. A subject moving a few $\times L_{\text{orp}}$ in an exposure time will produce a motion-smeared image. In this case, subject motion perpendicular to the optical axis must remain below $\sim 100\,\mu$m/0.03 s ~ 0.5 cm/s which is quite still.

Assuming a safe and readily attainable level of irradiance of $50\,$W/m^2 and an image sensor QE $= 0.1$, we use Eq. (3.15) to predict a value of SNR $= 110$. An acceptable value of SNR for iris recognition is not well established with a provisional ISO/IEC recommendation of ~ 100 (3.2). Note that SNR is often quoted in units of dB. However, this unit is ambiguous since some disciplines use $20 \times \log_{10}(R)$ while others use $10 \times \log_{10}(R)$ to convert the dimensionless number R to dB—it is unambiguous to use dimensionless signal-to-noise ratio R.

The example camera design will work well for a stationary subject, capturing both irises at once with adequate spatial resolution and signal-to-noise ratio. In the next section, we consider requirements of an iris imaging system used to capture irises at 3 m. Some of the requirements need to change while others stay fixed.

3.3.2 3-m Iris Imaging System

With an iris imaging system at 3 m from the subject, we can imagine a less constrained capture scenario. Therefore, as an added requirement, we specify that a subject may be approaching the system at 1 m/s with a component of velocity perpendicular to the optical axis of up to 0.1 m/s.

Again, we address illumination with an emphasis on eye safety. Placing the illuminators closer to the subject than 3 m allows lower power to be used which reduces the risk of approaching an unsafe level of irradiance or radiance. Whether at 3 m or closer, we will assume that illuminators are distributed in such a way to provide uniform lighting for all subject positions and heights required for the system without detailing the mechanism. Indeed, lighting is an important part of an iris imaging system but for now, we will simply stipulate that over the capture volume, we have an illuminator design that provides $50 \, W/m^2$ for all subject heights and positions. Examples of manufacturers who have addressed the issue of illumination at a distance include those of Refs. [3, 6].

In a similar fashion to designing the 0.3 m system in Sect. 3.3.1, we start by assuming $L_{orp} = 100 \, \mu m$. However, because of the less constrained scenario, we demand a field of view that is larger than the 0.3 m system, in this case, 25-cm wide and 20-cm high, necessitating an image sensor with a $2,500 \times 2,000$ pixel count. Such a 5-MPx image sensor will cost more than the 1.3-MPx sensor used in the 0.3-m system, but the larger FoV enables more tolerant alignment of the camera to the user. We again use an image sensor with 3.5-μm pixel pitch.

At 3 m, the focal length of the lens, given by Eq. (3.19), is approximately ten times longer or 100 mm since the only parameter in Eq. (3.19) that has changed is d_o. Similarly, we specify the same $F/4$ aperture since we are working with the same illumination wavelength and pixel pitch as in the 0.3 m system. We also note that in accord with the prediction of Eqs. (3.7), (3.16) gives a very similar DoF = 2.5 cm for the 3 m iris imaging system. Even if we allow for a larger circle of confusion equal to $3 \times L_p$ and close the aperture from $F/4$ to $F/5$, the DoF barely reaches 10 cm. A subject approaching the imaging system at 1 m/s passes through the DoF in 30–100 ms depending on the subjective definition of DoF that is applied. In any case, catching an in-focus image is a challenge for such a system. To address this challenge, we must either use a form of tracking autofocus or capture images fast enough to ensure that some subset of captured images are adequately focused for the purpose of iris recognition. Assuming that the imager can be run at a video rate of 30 frames per second, we obtain an image every 33 ms, which is adequate to capture a few in-focus images for a DoF of 3–10 cm and a 1 m/s approach speed.

However, we must also account of a transverse motion (perpendicular to the optical axis) of 0.1 m/s. At this speed, a subject traverses a distance of one L_{orp} in 1 ms. If we can apply a 1-ms optical pulse coordinated with a 1-ms camera shutter exposure, the transverse subject motion can be effectively frozen. The combination of short pulse and fast video frame rate is required for a system that operates at 3 m with a fixed capture volume and the reduced constraints of an approaching subject. An altogether different system which uses predictive tracking autofocus could address the challenges differently by translating the capture volume along with the subject while operating with continuous illumination and lower frame rate. The decision between a fixed capture volume with pulsed illumination and high video frame rate or tracking autofocus with lower frame rate and continuous illumination is clearly a difficult one with different manufacturers taking different approaches.

In the case of fixed capture volume, Eq. (3.15) predicts a low SNR with the same irradiance as the 0.3-m system and a short 1-ms exposure time. As a consequence, the fixed capture volume 3-m system must use a higher irradiance for a shorter time, consistent with the need to suppress motion smear and remain eye safe. Pressured to capture as many photoelectrons in the short exposure as possible, we seek a sensor with higher QE of 0.2, extend the exposure to 1.5 ms, and increase irradiance to $600 \, \text{W/m}^2$ on the subject, ultimately yielding SNR ~ 100. Tuning such a camera to capture in-focus images of moving subjects demonstrates the engineering compromises of a 3-m iris imager design.

3.4   Epilogue: Requirements of an Iris Recognition System

So far, we have discussed principles of optics and designed iris imaging systems without reference to the segmenting (isolating the iris from a large field of view), encoding, and matching algorithms that perform the actual iris recognition functions. The design rules that we have used are photographic in nature and equally applicable to wedding photography as they are to aerial photography where requirements upon spatial resolution and SNR are deeply understood.

In this last section, we ask a series of questions without answering them: What are the actual spatial resolution and SNR requirements for iris recognition? How do these requirements depend on the use case, for example, number of subjects in the database? How do they depend on the specific algorithm used to perform the matching? If the requirements are algorithm specific, is it advantageous to co-optimize the imaging system with the algorithm to achieve the best overall system performance? Or is a fixed standard to which all iris imaging systems must comply a better strategy? Certainly, application of standards affects iris imaging device manufacturers, iris matching algorithm developers, and the customers who buy iris recognition systems comprising both components so the question is not simply academic.

Questions of iris imaging system requirements divide the user community into two segments. In the first segment are iris recognition system users who rate either high performance or low cost as their top priority. A high-performance system, for example, would operate in a high-security environment with stringent standards upon failure to enroll and especially on false non-match rates. A low-cost system would, for example, enable cost-effective proliferation through a low-security infrastructure such as an enterprise time-in-attendance or a national entitlement system. A second segment of users places lifetime maintenance of an iris recognition system as the top priority. For the second set of users, multiple sourcing, interoperability, and forward/backward compatibility trump purchase cost and performance.

It is the second segment of users who drive the application of a single standard on iris imaging systems. For purchase of iris imaging systems across multiple branches of government, for example, the value of a single standard by which equipment is qualified ensures that competitive bidding, replacing, and upgrading can occur without reliance on a single supplier or a narrowly available system. By the same token, for cost-driven commercial installations, a single standard on iris imaging systems might preclude a low-cost alternative, with adequate performance that fits a budget. In this case, a single standard might keep a potential user from choosing iris recognition to fit their needs. A single standard on iris imagers might also reduce the incentive to develop a high-performance system based on an integrated sensor/algorithm approach.

Sections 3.2 and 3.3 of this chapter provide the basic design tools needed to create an iris imager to meet the imaging requirements of any user. The future of iris imaging systems will be driven by the use cases, cost constraints, and algorithms that motivate their design. As iris imaging requirements evolve, the design principles outlined herein will provide the basis of understanding the optics of iris imaging systems.

References

1. I. 2.-6. A. A, *Iris Image Quality Standard SC 37N 3331* (2009)
2. ACGIH, Threshold limit value for chemical substances and physical agents and biological exposure indices (2002)
3. AOptix, *Insigth VM*
4. M. Born, E. Wolf, *Principals of optics*, vol.7 (Cambridge University Press, 1999), p. 8.3.3
5. M.J. Burge, M.K. Monaco, Multispectral iris fusion for enhancement, interoperability, and cross wavelength matching, in *SPIE Defense, Security, and Sensing. International Society for Optics and Photonics* (2009), pp. 73341D–73341D
6. S. International, *Iris on the move* (2011)
7. J.D. Jackson, *Classical electrodynamics*, vol. 3 (Wiley, New York, 1962)
8. N. Koren, *Understanding image sharpness part 5: lens testing* (2003)
9. A. Lefohn et al., An ocularist's approach to human iris synthesis. IEEE Comput. Graph. Appl. **23**(6), 70–75 (2003)
10. A. Muroó et al., *The human iris structure and its usages*, vol. 39 (2000), pp. 87–95
11. R. Trebino, *Diffraction and the Fourier Transform* (2008)
12. Zemax, *Software for Optical System Design*

Chapter 4
Standard Iris Storage Formats

George Quinn, Patrick Grother and Elham Tabassi

Abstract Iris recognition standards are open specifications for iris cameras, iris image properties, and iris image records. Biometric data standards are a necessity for applications in which a consumer of a data record must process biometric input from an arbitrary producer. The archetype for standard iris storage formats has been the flight of standards already developed for the storage of biometric data on electronic passports.

4.1 Introduction

Iris recognition standards are open specifications for iris cameras, iris image properties, and iris image records. Biometric data standards are a necessity for applications in which a consumer of a data record must process biometric input from an arbitrary producer. The archetype for standard iris storage formats has been the flight of standards already developed for the storage of biometric data on electronic passports. The most widely implemented of these is the ISO/IEC 19794-5 [5], which specifies the format requirements for the storage of facial images in the Data Group (DG2) container of the smart card chip.[1] In this case the producer of the record, a national passport issuer, is tasked with collecting and preparing a facial image conformant

---

[1] For iris recognition, the electronic passport's logical data structure specification includes an analogous container, DG4, that will hold an ISO/IEC 19794-6 iris image record. To date this has not been widely utilized.

G. Quinn (✉) · P. Grother · E. Tabassi
National Institute of Standards and Technology, Gaithersburg, MD, USA
e-mail: gw@nist.gov

P. Grother
e-mail: gw@nist.gov

E. Tabassi
e-mail: gw@nist.gov

© Springer-Verlag London 2016
K.W. Bowyer and M.J. Burge (eds.), *Handbook of Iris Recognition*,
Advances in Computer Vision and Pattern Recognition,
DOI 10.1007/978-1-4471-6784-6_4

89

to the standard. An immigration checkpoint is later tasked with reading and using that image. The extent to which such exchanges are successful is quantified in terms of performance metrics for identification, verification, and enrollment. To this end, formal, open, and widely implemented documentary standards are critical elements.

4.2 Role and Importance of Iris Standards

Image data interchange standards define parseable records that allow syntactic interoperability. This is a foundational element for a marketplace of off-the-shelf products and is a necessary condition to achieve supplier independence and to prevent vendor lock-in. It is perhaps surprising that while many raster image formats are open and standardized [20–22], it remains common to store images in fully proprietary (i.e., unpublished) formats. Such practices may be acceptable *within* an application, but are fatal once cross-organizational interchange of data is required. Data format standards allow modular integration of products without compromising architectural scope. Additionally, they facilitate the upgrade process thereby preventing obsolescence.

There are several business implications of standards development. A well-structured and widely implemented standard can create entirely new markets for companies (e.g., e-Passports can include face, finger and iris records). On the other hand, robust standards also promote competition, which leads to reduced profit margins. This process, commoditization, is an inhibitory factor for many technology companies that balance the promise of new or expanded marketplaces against reduced barriers to entry for competitors. The decision to enter the marketplace is influenced by the amount of intellectual property that a standard allows suppliers to hide behind their implementations. From the users perspective, standards serve to promote competition, which leads to enhanced performance. For example, the National Institute of Standards and Technology (NIST) conducted the Iris Exchange test (IREX I [6]), to offer quantitative support to iris recognition standards. Ten providers implemented the software modules necessary to create a standard record and to recognize it. This commercial support constituted an order of magnitude expansion of the iris recognition industry compared to five years earlier.

Standards do not in and of themselves assure interoperability. Specifically, when a standard is not fully prescriptive or does not allow for optional content, multiple implementations of the standard may still lack interoperability with one another. This problem can be averted by applying further constraints on the application of the standard. "Application profile" standards identify the needed base standards and refine their optional content and interpretations. This was done recently by the US Government for its PIV employee credential [16].

Iris interoperabilityrequires that data records are both syntactically and semantically understood by the receiving system. The syntactic requirements of a standard allow parsing software to find the correct information. The semantic requirements are present to regulate the appearance of the iris image (i.e., the array of pixel values) so that an iris recognition algorithm is able to *accurately* compare or identify the input image. For example, a blurred image will often not be recognizable. The notion that syntactic correctness is not in itself sufficient for interoperability is an important aspect of biometrics that is not always present in other fields.

4.3   History of Iris Standardization

The current iris standards descend from standardization efforts beginning around 2002. At that time, the only commercial entity in the field, Iridian, maintained a certification program for iris camera manufacturers to establish minimum standards for image quality and functionality. While some cameras produced an image, the closed-format IrisCode template was effectively the data interchange format because the only recognition provider was Iridian. After the September 11 attack, there was considerable impetus behind secure credentialling in a number of applications. Foremost of these was border management, and the International Civil Aviation Organization's (ICAO's) standardization of the electronic passport was paralleled by the development of biometric data interchange standards in the newly formed ISO/IEC JTC 1 Subcommittee 37 for Biometrics [17]. The iris recognition industry at the time, essentially the Iridian company, volunteered the first draft of a data interchange record format, which was progressed in parallel efforts in the United States and internationally. The results, respectively, were INCITS 379 and the almost identical international standard ISO/IEC 19794-6 [18] (see Table 4.1). Both standards included essentially two iris image formats. The first was a generic rectilinear format (see Fig. 4.1) and the second was a polar-sampled version of the iris texture lying between non-concentric limbic and pupil circles. The latter format was intended to support the compact storage of iris imagery on identity credentials.

Table 4.1 The evolution of contemporary iris image standards

Date	Title of standard
05/2004	INCITS 379—Iris Image Interchange Format
06/2005	ISO/IEC 19794—Biometric data interchange formats—Part 6: Iris image data
04/2007	ANSI/NIST-ITL 1-2007 Data Format for the Interchange of Fingerprint, Facial, & Other Biometric Information Type 17
–/2011	ISO/IEC 19794—Biometric data interchange formats—Part 6: Iris image data, second edition
–/2011	ANSI/NIST-ITL 1-2007 Data Format for the Interchange of Fingerprint, Facial, & Other Biometric Information Type 17, second edition
–/2013	ISO/IEC 29794—Biometric sample quality—Part 6: Iris image data
–/2013	ISO/IEC 29109—Conformance testing methodology for biometric data interchange & formats defined in ISO/IEC 19794—Part 6: Iris image data

(a)

(b)

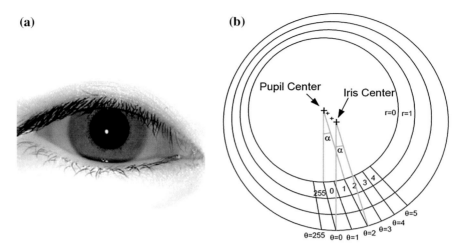

Fig. 4.1 ISO/IEC 19794-6 supports both rectilinear and polar storage formats. The *right figure* illustrates how pixels are sampled in the polar format. **a** Rectilinear. **b** Polar

The rectilinear version of the ISO standard was adopted by the law enforcement community in the ANSI/NIST Type 17 record. The polar format was not considered because compact size was not an imperative. This decision was fortuitous in light of subsequent technical contributions to SC37 Working Group 3 [Germany, N2059; Great Britain, N2124] that asserted the accuracy of the polar format is critically sensitive to the consistency of localization and subject to sampling problems [12]. The two documents advocated removal of the polar format from the standard. A useful GB contribution [3] suggested the compact size of the polar format (around 2 kbytes) could alternatively be achieved via cropping and compression of the rectilinear format. While interoperability problems were never formally demonstrated, the SC37 working group solicited quantitative evidence for the newly proposed formats. In the United States, the National Institute of Standards and Technology (NIST) was concurrently interested in establishing a set of specifications for the efficient transmission of iris images across networks and for storage on ISO/IEC 7816 crypto-tokens [7]. To this end, NIST initiated the IREX study to evaluate the proposed image formats. The results of the IREX I evaluation lead to the adoption of compact iris storage formats in the ISO/IEC 19794-6 standard. The same formats were subsequently incorporated into the ANSI/NIST-ITL 1-2007 standard for law enforcement due to their potential for supporting network-based and mobile identification.

In 2009, NIST initiated the IREX II Iris Quality Calibration and Evaluation (IQCE) to support the development of a standard addressing iris image quality. Prior studies on the iris biometric [1, 10, 15] revealed that problems such as poor focus, motion blur, occlusion by eyelids, and off-angle gazes negatively impact recognition accuracy. The new standard, ISO/IEC 29794-6: Iris Image Quality [19], formally defines a vector of quality components for iris images, where each component is a quantitative measure of a subject-specific or image-specific covariate. The evaluation also aims to promote the development of automated quality assessment algorithms. The ability to identify poor quality images quickly and effectively is particularly useful for acquisition systems that are tasked with identifying the best quality iris image among several potential candidates.

4.4   Storage Size Constraints

Many biometric systems operate with restrictions on the size of stored samples. For example, smart-cards typically have a maximum storage capacity for their biometric samples. Additionally, smaller samples reduce the to-card and from-card transfer times, which can influence the selection of modality (e.g., fingerprint, iris) as well as the number of instances (e.g., two fingers, two irises). Centralized systems operating over limited bandwidth connections would also experience a benefit from reduced transfer times. Figure 4.2 depicts a network-centric application where field units (at left) pass compact KIND 3 and KIND 7 iris records across narrow bandwidth connections to a central server for enrollment. Compact iris records would transfer more quickly and require less storage space on the central server.

Broadly, there are two operational scenarios where compact storage formats are advantageous:

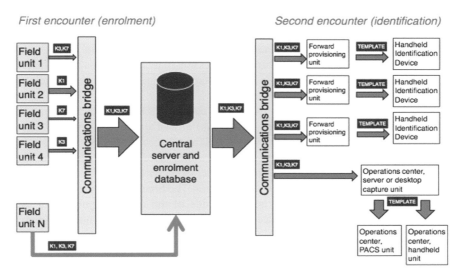

Fig. 4.2 Example of a network-centric application where standardized iris data is stored centrally and in the field. The *left*-to-*right* data flow represents the temporal sequence of enrollment followed by identification

- Identity credential: A compressed standard iris image is stored on, for example, an ISO/IEC 7816 smart card, and is compared during authentication against a newly collected uncompressed sample. This scenario is representative of cooperative physical or logical access control situations in which the first sample is collected and prepared in an attended formal enrollment session, and the authentication sample exists only for the duration of the attempt. In this scenario, matching is performed between uncompressed verification samples and compressed enrollment samples.
- Central matching facility: Compressed standard samples are submitted to a central dataset. These are the first-encounter "enrollment" samples. Subsequently, compressed samples are transmitted to the central facility and are matched against the enrollments. Compression is implied by operational network bandwidth constraints. This scenario is typical in open-universe one-to-many applications such as visa fraud detection and watchlists. In this case, compression is applied to both authentication and enrollment samples.

4.5 Standard Storage Formats

Standardized iris images (i.e., iris records), are not iris templates. Rather, they are specialized interoperable images designed for the efficient storage and transmission of iris data. Templates contain proprietary "black box" feature representations that are typically specific to only a particular provider's matching algorithm. As such, their content is nonstandard, non-interoperable and not suitable for cross-agency exchange of iris data. The role of standardized images is depicted in Fig. 4.3. Iris segmentation precedes the second stage of processing in which features are extracted from iris records to form a template. The last stage, recognition, involves matching of templates to produce comparison scores.

   IREX I evaluated three potential storage formats for iris images. Each is depicted in Fig. 4.4. Conversion of a raw iris image into any of the record types requires localization of iris features. Preparation of a KIND 3 record requires detection of the iris center and limbus boundary, which are then used to crop and center the iris. A KIND 7 record undergoes similar processing with the additional step of detecting the iris-eyelid and iris-sclera boundaries. The boundaries are used to apply a pixel masking operation to the regions outside of the iris. The purpose of the masking operation is to make it easier to compress the image to smaller storage

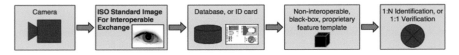

Fig. 4.3 Role of standardized imagery in a typical iris recognition system

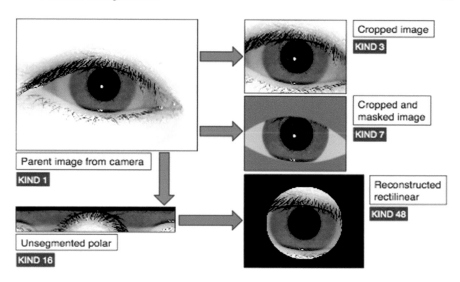

Fig. 4.4 Iris record formats tested in IREX I

sizes. For either format, the part of the image containing the iris features is left unchanged. A KIND 16 record stores the iris image in a polar format. Preparation of this record type involves defining concentric circles inside the pupil and outside the iris followed by a rectilinear-to-polar mapping. The polar format stores a fixed number of circumferential pixels at each radial distance, which effectively stores the inner part of the iris at a higher sampling rate (see Fig. 4.1b).

4.6   Compression Formats

Compression is applied to images to reduce their storage size and transmission times. Compression algorithms are either lossless or lossy. Lossless compression maintains perfect fidelity to the original data. Lossy compression, on the other hand, discards some of the information, usually to achieve higher compression. When lossy compression is applied to an iris image, it alters the pixel values within the iris region. At low compression, the changes are inconsequential, but when compression is applied with sufficient severity, visible artifacts appear that can lead to recognition errors.

The ISO/IEC 19794-6 standard includes support for two methods of lossy image compression. The first, JPEG [14], is a popular and widely supported lossy storage format that uses a variety of methods to compress the image. Although optimized for digital photography, JPEG has proven useful for storing biometric samples for a range of modalities [4, 5, 11]. The second, JPEG 2000 [21], was developed to supersede JPEG and uses newly designed wavelet-based technology. Although less

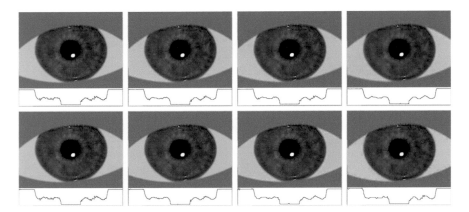

Fig. 4.5 A single iris record compressed to different file sizes. From *left*, to *right*, the image is uncompressed, and compressed to 4, 3, and 2 K. JPEG 2000 is applied to the *top* row images, and JPEG to the *bottom*. Beneath each image is a horizontal scanline of pixel intensities across the center of the image

widely supported than its predecessor, JPEG 2000 has been generally shown to achieve superior compression [2, 9]. Figure 4.5 illustrates the types of artifacts that are introduced when iris images are heavily compressed. JPEG compression artifacts manifest as "macroblocking" and "mosquito noise", while JPEG 2000 compression artifacts manifest as blurring and ringing around areas of sharp contrast.

Certain properties of an iris image determine how well it compresses to a particular storage size. Generally speaking, images with a lot of high gradient information are more difficult to compress since they tend to lack the redundancy that compression algorithms exploit. Some of these high gradient features are irrelevant for the purposes of matching (e.g., eyelashes and skin texture) and can be discarded. The KIND 7 format was specifically formulated to improve the efficiency of compression by replacing the sclera, eyelids, and eyelashes with a uniform color, since regions of uniform color contribute minimally to the encoding space. A disadvantage of the KIND 7 format is that it requires additional processing and localization of a greater number of features around the iris.

4.7 Effect of Compression on Matching Accuracy

Several studies have investigated the effect of image compression on iris recognition accuracy. Ives et al. [8] applied JPEG 2000 compression to iris images and found that a compression ratio of 20 to 1 was possible without a discernible effect on impostor scores and only a minimal effect on genuine scores when using the Masek algorithm. Rakshit et al. [13] also applied JPEG 2000 compression to iris images and concluded that compressing the images to 0.5 bits-per-pixel actually improves ROC performance through noise reduction. This result could not be confirmed in IREX I. The authors also concluded that compressing the images using JPEG 2000 is generally preferable to downsampling to lower resolutions. Daugman [2] tested both JPEG and JPEG 2000 compression and found that, with the appropriate adjustments and compression parameters, samples could be reduced to as little as 2000 bytes with little impact on accuracy. The conclusions from these studies are based on data collected from one or two matching algorithms run over relatively small datasets. IREX I sought to verify some of the key results of these studies over much larger datasets and with matching algorithms from several providers.

IREX I explored the effect of compression on iris impostor comparisons. The evaluation found that the impostor distribution is generally invariant to JPEG 2000 compression for most algorithms. This is a desirable property since iris recognition systems can be easily calibrated to operate at known false match rates, even in the presence of varying amounts of compression. Indeed, a strength of the well-known IrisCode matching algorithm is that it has been shown to produce a stable and predictable impostor distribution under a variety of circumstances. For some algorithms JPEG compression caused an increase in impostor scores. Although this typically only occurred at sample sizes below 2000 bytes, it contraindicates the use of JPEG compression.

When the impostor distribution is stable, variations in matching accuracy are reflected in the genuine distribution. Results of the IREX evaluation demonstrate that compressed iris images are more likely to cause false non-matches. Figure 4.6 shows how progressively greater amounts of compression adversely affect the impostor

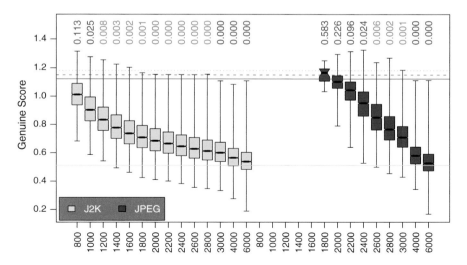

Fig. 4.6 Distribution of genuine scores for a matching algorithm when KIND 7 enrollment records were compressed to specific file sizes (specified along the vertical axis in bytes). The three *blue lines* correspond, from the *top*, to FMR's of $10^{(-2,-3,-4)}$, while the *gray line* refers to the median score for uncompressed images

distribution for one algorithm submitted to IREX I. Only enrollment images were compressed (as in the identity credential scenario). Typically, matching accuracy begins to degrade around 6000 bytes and occurs more rapidly for JPEG compression. At higher compression ratios the distribution becomes more long tailed, indicating the median genuine score alone does not fully capture possible changes in matching accuracy.

4.8 Compression Guildelines

Iris images can be compressed to as little as 2 kbytes, making them suitable for storage on ISO/IEC 7816 integrated circuit "smart card" identification tokens. However, the high amount of compression leads to a reduction in matching accuracy. IREX I provides guidance for the effective usage of standard iris storage formats. Application-specific recommendations on compression and format based on the storage limitations of the system are presented in Fig. 4.7. The evaluation also makes the following general recommendations and observations:

• JPEG 2000 is generally superior at compressing iris images than JPEG. When matching accuracy is paramount and storage space is limited to 20 kbytes or less, JPEG 2000 should be used.
• The cropped-and-masked KIND 7 image format should be retained and advanced as the primary format for the exchange of compact iris images smaller than 3KB.

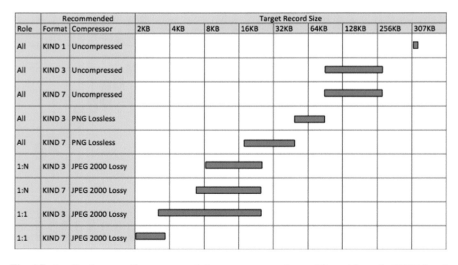

Fig. 4.7 Application-specific recommendations on compression and format from the IREX I evaluation

At larger sizes or lower compression ratios, the KIND 3 format should be used since it is more easily and safely instantiated.

- Recognition error rates associated with the KIND 16 unsegmented polar format are much larger than those attained with the rectilinear formats. For this reason, IREX I recommended that the polar format be rejected from inclusion in the ISO/IEC 19794-6 standard.
- The KIND 7 format is best at preserving the iris texture when the image must be compressed to a small target record size. However, if storage space and network bandwidth are not limiting factors, the additional masking step required to convert an iris image to a KIND 7 record is unnecessary and can introduce problems if the eyelids are not correctly localized.

4.9 Summary

Biometric data standards define interchange formats for the storage and transmission of biometric data. Well-structured and widely implemented biometric data standards serve to facilitate the exchange of biometric data across different agencies and organizations and help promote fair competition in the marketplace. Both INCITS 379 and ISO/IEC 19794-6 define two rectilinear formats and one polar format for iris images. In 2009, NIST initiated the IREX I evaluation to develop and test compact iris storage formats. Such formats are important for applications where network bandwidth is limited or when iris records must be stored on smart card chips that have limited storage capacities. The evaluation determined that iris images can be compressed to as little as 2 kbytes, making them suitable for storage on ISO/IEC 7816 integrated circuit smart card identification tokens. If storage space is extremely limited ($<$3 kbytes per image), iris images should be stored as KIND 7 records using JPEG 2000 compression. When storage constraints are more relaxed, KIND 3 records are preferred since they are easier and safer to instantiate.

References

1. A. Abhyankar, S. Schuckers, Iris quality assessment and biorthogonal wavelet based encoding for recognition. Pattern Recogn. **42**(9), 1878–1894 (2009)
2. J. Daugman, Biometric decision landscapes. Technical Report TR482. University of Cambridge Computer Laboratory (2000)
3. J. Daugman, C. Downing, Effect of severe image compression on iris recognition performance. Technical report. University of Cambridge, Computer Laboratory (2007)
4. Finger image-based data interchange format. ANSI-INCITS 381-2004, Washington (2004)
5. P. Griffin, Face recognition format for data interchange. Committee Draft ISO/IEC 19794-5 SC37 M1/03-0494 SC37 Document 342. Identix Corporate Research Center (2003)
6. P. Grother et al., Performance of iris recognition algorithms on standard images. Technical report. National Institute of Standards and Technology (2009)
7. ISO/IEC 7816-15. International Standard. JTC1::SC17 (2004)

8. R.W. Ives et al., Effects of image compression on iris recognition system performance. J. Electron. Imaging **17** (2008)
9. A. Mascher-Kampfer, H. Stögner, A. Uhl, Comparison of compression algorithms' impact on fingerprint and face recognition accuracy, in *Proceedings of the SPIE*, vol. 6508, 2007, pp. 650810.1–650810.12
10. J. Matey et al., Iris on the move: acquisition of images for iris recognition in less constrained environments. Proc. IEEE **94**(11), 1936–947 (2006)
11. R. Onyshczak, A. Youssef, *Automatic Fingerprint Recognition Systems* (Cambridge University Press, Cambridge, 2004), Chap. 19
12. H. Proença, L.A. Alex, Iris recognition: an analysis of the aliasing problem in the iris normalization stage, in *International Conference on Computational Intelligence and Security*, vol. 2, 2006, pp. 1771–1774
13. S. Rakshit, D.M. Monro, An evaluation of image sampling and compression for human iris recognition. IEEE Trans. Inf. Forensics Secur. **2**(3–2), 605–612 (2007)
14. G.K. Wallace, The JPEG still picture compression standard. Commun. ACM **34**(4), 30–44 (1991)
15. Z. Wei et al., Robust and fast assessment of iris image quality, in *Advances in Biometrics* (2005), pp. 464–471
16. C. Wilson, P. Grother, R. Chandramouli, Biometric data sepcificaiton for personal identity verification. Technical report. NIST Special Publication 800-76-1. National Institute of Standards and Technology (2007). http://csrc.nist.gov/publications/nistpubs/800-76-1/SP800-76-1_012407.pdf
17. W. G. 3. ISO/IEC 19794 Biometric Data Interchange Formats (2005)
18. W. G. 3. ISO/IEC CD 19794-6 Information Technology—Biometric Data Interchange Formats – part 6: Iris Image Data. International Standard. JTC1::SC37 (2006)
19. W. G. 3. ISO/IEC CD 29794-6 Information Technology—Biometric Sample Quality – part 6: Iris Image Data. International Standard (2015)
20. W. G. 5. ISO/IEC 10918-1 Digital compression and coding of cintuniuoustone still images: Requirements and guidelines. International Standard.JTC1::SC29 (1994)
21. W. G. 5. ISO/IEC 15444-1 JPEG 20000 image coding system: Core cording system. International Standard. JTC1::SC29 (2004)
22. W. G. 5. ISO/IEC 15948 Protable Network Graphics (PNG): Functional specification. International Standard. JTC1::SC24 (2004)

Chapter 5
Iris Quality Metrics for Adaptive Authentication

N. Schmid, J. Zuo, F. Nicolo and H. Wechsler

Abstract Iris sample quality has a number of important applications. It can be used at a variety of processing levels in iris recognition systems, for example, at the acquisition stage, at image enhancement stage, or at matching and fusion stage. Metrics designed to evaluate iris sample quality are used as figures of merit to quantify degradations in iris images due to environmental conditions, unconstrained presentation of individuals or due to postprocessing that can reduce iris information in the data. This chapter presents a short summary of quality factors traditionally used in iris recognition systems. It further introduces new metrics that can be used to evaluate iris image quality. The performance of the individual quality measures is analyzed, and their adaptive inclusion into iris recognition systems is demonstrated. Three methods to improve the performance of biometric matchers based on vectors of quality measures are described. For all the three methods, the reported experimental results show significant performance improvement when applied to iris biometrics. This confirms that the newly proposed quality measures are informative in the sense that their involvement results in improved iris recognition performance.

N. Schmid (✉)
West Virginia University, Morgantown, WV, USA
e-mail: Natalia.Schmid@mail.wvu.edu

J. Zuo
Symantec Corp, San Francisco, CA, USA
e-mail: jingce.zuo@gmail.com

F. Nicolo
ZOLL Medical Corporation, Pittsburgh, PA, USA
e-mail: nicolofrancesco@gmail.com

H. Wechsler
George Mason University, Fairfax, VA, USA
e-mail: wechsler@cs.gmu.edu

© Springer-Verlag London 2016
K.W. Bowyer and M.J. Burge (eds.), *Handbook of Iris Recognition*,
Advances in Computer Vision and Pattern Recognition,
DOI 10.1007/978-1-4471-6784-6_5

5.1 Introduction

Assessment of iris image quality is one of the important research venues recently identified in the field of iris biometrics [2, 13, 14]. Iris quality is evaluated by means of quality metrics. The main role of these metrics is to quantify, at the stage of data acquisition or at a later processing stage, what information an iris image contains to discriminate the iris class, which it represents, from all other iris classes in a database. In many cases, the quality metrics are used to decide if the image should be discarded or should be further processed by iris recognition system.

Quality of iris images is determined by many factors that can be broadly divided into two groups: (a) environmental and camera effects and (b) unconstrained presentation of a subject. As an example, images can be of low quality due to insufficient lighting, defocus blur, off-angle presentation, and heavy occlusion. These factors affect iris segmentation and later encoding and matching.

Previous works on iris image quality can be placed into two categories: local and global analysis. Zhu et al. [16] evaluated quality by analyzing the coefficients of particular areas of iris texture by employing discrete wavelet decomposition. Chen et al. [3] classified iris quality by measuring the energy of concentric iris bands obtained from 2-D wavelets. Ma et al. [11] analyzed the Fourier spectra of local iris regions to characterize out-of-focus and motion blur and occlusions. Zhang and Salganicaff examined the sharpness of the region between the pupil and the iris. Daugman [4] and Kang and Park [8] characterized quality by quantifying the energy of high spatial frequencies over the entire image region. Belcher and Du [1] proposed a clarity measure by comparing the sharpness loss within various iris image regions against the blurred version of the same regions. The major feature of these approaches is that the evaluation of iris image quality is reduced to the estimation of a single [3, 4, 8] or a pair of factors [11], such as out-of-focus blur, motion blur, and occlusion. A more comprehensive set of quality factors was introduced by Kalka et al. [6, 7], where 7 factors that can affect iris image quality were identified: out-of-focus and motion blur, occlusion, specular reflection, illumination, off-angle, and pixel count. Recently, National Institute of Standards and Technology (NIST) identified 16 iris image properties that influence the recognition accuracy in Iris Exchange (IREX) II Iris Quality Calibration and Evaluation (IQCE) [15].

The components of a vector of quality measures, however, rarely carry equal weight in terms of their relationship to the performance of the matcher. In practical applications (such as US Visit program), it is required to keep a single biometric quality measure in order to decide if biometric samples are suitable for further processing and matching. Research questions should thus be concerned with (5.1) what quality measures to use; (5.2) how to combine multiple quality measures into a single quality index without losing the information that the vector of quality measures contains; and (5.3) how to use this vector to improve performance of biometric systems?

Most of the quality-based matchers described in the literature involve biometric sample quality at the matching stage by concatenating matching scores due to the original matcher and quality measures. These matchers are known as Q-stack classifiers [9, 12]. In spite of the fundamental theory presented in these works in support of Q-stack classifiers, the improvement of performance is marginal, if at all (see [5, 9]). More noticeable improvements are reported for Q-stack classifiers operating on multiple algorithms or multiple matchers [5, 12].

This chapter suggests several methods on the use of biometric sample quality to improve the performance of a single matcher. It targets two main applications for quality measures: (5.1) to improve performance of a matcher by predicting its Quality of Sample (QS) index or Confidence in Score (CS) and using them to decide if the underlying biometric sample should be retained or discarded (5.2) to design a nonlinear matcher that treats a vector of quality measures as a set of weak features.

The remainder of the chapter is organized as follows. Section 5.2 introduces 10 new quality factors for a segmented iris template. Section 5.3 evaluates performance of metrics summarized in Sect. 5.2. Section 5.4 describes three proposed methods to boost the performance using the estimated quality factors. Section 5.5 concludes this chapter.

5.2   Quality Evaluation

A traditional iris recognition system processes, segments, and encodes iris images sequentially. Simultaneously, local iris quality factors are evaluated. These quality factors can be later used to enhance performance of an iris recognition system alone or of a multimodal system with iris being one of the modalities. In the following subsections, new individual iris quality factors are introduced, and procedures to evaluate them are described. The factors are segmentation scores, interlacing, illumination, lighting, occlusion, pixel count, dilation, off-angle, and blur. The subsections below present a summary of the development, while detailed description is provided in [18–20].

5.2.1   Iris Segmentation Scores

Since most of local iris quality measures are applied to segmented iris images, the metrics evaluating the precision of the segmentation should be given a higher priority compared to other factors. Two segmentation scores Q_{p_seg} and Q_{i_seg} introduced in [17] can be used as two distinct quality metrics related to the segmentation itself. These metrics analyze the gradient values along the pupil and limbic boundaries. Larger value of the metrics indicates more precise segmentation.

To evaluate the cumulative intensity gradient along the estimated pupil and iris boundaries, the iris image (Fig. 5.1a) is unwrapped to the template (Fig. 5.1b) and its corresponding noise mask (Fig. 5.1c). First, a band covering the estimated pupil boundary (Fig. 5.1d) is analyzed. For each horizontal pixel in unwrapped image, we evaluate the intensity gradient along the vertical direction. If a gradient value for one of vertical pixels exceeds a specified threshold, we will say that at this location (horizontal location) the boundary is detected (Fig. 5.1e). We further count

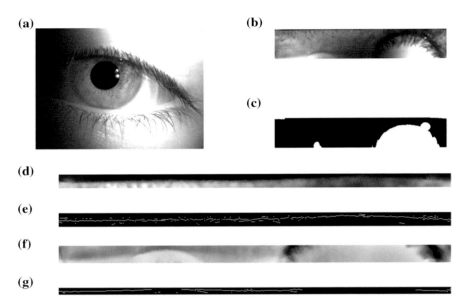

Fig. 5.1 The steps performed by the automatic algorithm for evaluation of precision of iris segmentation: **a** the original image, **b** the unwrapped template, **c** the unwrapped mask, **d** the extended portion of unwrapped iris on the pupil side, **e** the result of the edge detection on the pupil side, **f** the extended portion of unwrapped iris on the sclera side, **g** the result of the edge detection on the sclera side

the number of horizontal locations with the gradient exceeding the threshold and divide by the total number of horizontal pixels in the unwrapped iris. A similar evaluation is performed for the iris boundary (Fig. 5.1f). Since in majority of cases the limbic boundary is not sufficiently sharp, a vertically compressed version is used in place of the original unwrapped image to detect the edge (Fig. 5.1g). Denote by Q_{p_seg} and Q_{i_seg} the percentage of horizontal pixels with the gradient exceeding the prespecified threshold where Q_{p_seg} is for the pupil boundary and Q_{i_seg} is for the limbic boundary. However, occluded parts will not be taken into account. The larger the values of these parameters, the better are the estimates of the boundaries.

5.2.2 Interlacing

Poor interlacing is a disturbing artifact. Interestingly, a poorly interlaced image may result in a high focus score in spite of strong defocus of either even or odd lines. These artifacts should be detected. If there is a large difference between odd and even lines then there must be a clear motion related interlacing effect. The image may be either discarded, or divided to two sub-images: odd rows and even rows. The difference between odd rows and even rows $Inter_l$ can be calculated as

$$\text{Inter}_1 = \frac{\sum\limits_{i=1:2:m-1} 2 \sum\limits_{j=1}^{n} |I_{i,j} - I_{i+1,j}|}{m \times n} \tag{5.1}$$

for an image I with m rows and n columns. The function must be normalized by subtracting Inter_2 calculated using odd or even rows only

$$\text{Inter}_2 = \frac{\sum\limits_{i=1}^{m-2} \sum\limits_{j=1}^{n} |I_{i,j} - I_{i+2,j}|}{(m-2) \times n} \tag{5.2}$$

resulting in

$$Q_{\text{interlacing}} = \text{Inter}_1 - \text{Inter}_2. \tag{5.3}$$

Note that the high values of $Q_{\text{interlacing}}$ indicate poor interlacing.

5.2.3   Illumination

The contrast of the image is mainly determined by the level and strength of the illumination. The illumination level is the mean intensity value of the iris area:

$$Q_{\text{illumination}} = \frac{\sum\limits_{\text{unaffected iris area}} I_{i,j}}{\sum\limits_{\text{unaffected iris area}} 1}. \tag{5.4}$$

To get a more precise estimation of this factor, only unaffected (by occlusion or specular reflections) area is considered. The value that $Q_{\text{illumination}}$ can take ranges from 0 to 255. This factor can be affected by the color of the iris. Large values of the measure indicate high illumination value.

5.2.4   Lighting

Sided or uneven illumination of the iris often results in performance degradation. Illumination pattern can be treated as a low frequency signal that distorts encoded iris images. The variance of the mean intensity evaluated over small blocks is proposed as a measure of the uneven illumination. The calculation of the lighting factor is similar to the procedure described in [7], but without normalization to [0, 1]. Note that bad lighting condition is characterized by a large value of the metric.

5.2.5 Occlusion

This attribute measures the fraction of the iris area occluded by other objects such as eyelids, eyelashes and specular reflections. The proposed metric evaluates the percentage of the unoccluded area in the unwrapped template. Denote by M the binary occlusion mask of the unwrapped iris template. The value "1" at location (i, j) in the mask indicates that it is a point of occlusion. Then the occlusion metric is

$$Q_{\text{ocllusion}} = \frac{\sum\limits_{\{(i,j):\, M_{i,j}=0\}} 1}{\sum\limits_{\{(i,j):\, M_{i,j}\geq 0\}} 1} \tag{5.5}$$

The usage of the percentage can reduce the correlation between this quality factor and the resolution factor. This quality factor is similar to the pixel count factor in [7]. Large values of the metric indicate smaller occlusions.

5.2.6 Pixel Count

To distinct it from the occlusion factor, pixel count finds the total iris area including its occluded area

$$Q_{\text{pixel count}} = \sum\limits_{\text{iris area}} 1. \tag{5.6}$$

Large values of the metric correspond to high pixel counts.

5.2.7 Dilation

The dilation factor measures the degree of the pupil dilation. The value of the dilation factor is calculated by taking the ratio of $Q_{\text{pixel count}}$ to the total iris and pupil area:

$$Q_{\text{dilation}} = \frac{\sum\limits_{\text{iris area}} 1}{\sum\limits_{\text{iris area}} 1 + \sum\limits_{\text{pupil area}} 1}. \tag{5.7}$$

The metric Q_{dilation} takes values between 0 and 1. This factor also affects pixel count. Note that small pupil dilations are characterized by large values of the metric.

5.2.8 Off-Angle

This factor measures the relative orientation of the iris with respect to the camera. Assuming that the frontal view iris has a circular shape, the off-angle view becomes an ellipse. The off-angle quality factor is a ratio of the two main axes of the ellipse fitted into the iris boundary:

$$Q_{\text{offangle}} = \frac{b}{a}, \tag{5.8}$$

where b is the minor axis and a is the major axis of an ellipse. These values are obtained after the iris has been segmented. Note that the large values of the metric indicate that the image is close to frontal view.

5.2.9 Blur

Both motion and defocus blurs are treated simultaneously. This method uses spectral components of an iris image and involves a number of preprocessing steps.

First, the area of interest (iris region) is segmented, and an ellipse with the center at (x_i, y_i) and the major axes a and b is fitted into the iris region. We then expand the image around the area of interest by 250 % along the major axis a and choose the iris center (x_i, y_i) as the center of the expanded image.

A small median filter is then applied to denoise the image. To compensate the difference in resolution, the area of interest is normalized to the size 151×151. This selection is due to resolution requirement imposed by standards: 120 or more pixels across the iris. A 2D FFT transform is applied to normalized image in order to extract the frequency information denoted here by P:

$$P = log_{10} \left| FFT(I_{\text{crop}}) \right|, \tag{5.9}$$

where I_{crop} is the cropped iris area after normalization.

The power distribution of P is analyzed, and its central area is used to calculate a decision threshold. Here the threshold is empirically selected. We select the average power of a centered 13 pixel diamond shaped area as the value of the threshold γ :

$$\gamma = \frac{\displaystyle\sum_{\{(i,j):\ (i-76)^2+(j-76)^2<16\}} P_{i,j}}{13 \times 1.5}. \tag{5.10}$$

Then the number of pixels with the power exceeding the threshold value is counted. This number is scaled by a coefficient involving the dilation information. The final expression for the Q_{blur} becomes:

$$Q_{\text{blur}} = (1 + Q_{\text{dilation}}^6) \sum_{P_{i,j}>\gamma} 1. \tag{5.11}$$

(a)   **(b)**   **(c)**

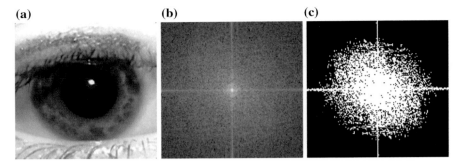

Fig. 5.2 Example of blur estimation **a** the cropped area, **b** the power spectrum and **c** the results of thresholding

Steps illustrating the evaluation of the blur quality score are shown in Fig. 5.2. This specific image has the blur score equal to 5953.6.

Note that larger values of the metric correspond to a smaller amount of blur.

In the following two sections the application of the designed quality measures is a twofold: (5.1) we show that good quality images can be separated from poor quality images by involving the proposed quality measures and (5.2) we use quality measures to design quality-based adaptive iris authentication systems.

5.3 Performance of Quality Metrics

All experiments are performed using ICE 2005 dataset [10]. The enhancement, encoding and matching procedures follow Daugman's implementation.

We perform a number of experiments. For each individual factor, the ICE 2005 dataset is used to form three subsets of images. The first subset is composed of the entire ICE dataset. To form the second and the third subsets, we involve the distribution of values of a selected quality factor. The second set includes all images with the value of selected quality factor exceeding 0.75th qauntile. The third set is composed of all images with the value of selected quality factors exceeding 0.9th quantile.

The panels in Figs. 5.3 and 5.4 each displays three Receiver Operating Characteristic (ROC) sets obtained using data in subsets 1, 2, and 3. Note that all results can be placed into those based on a relative quality score (in our case, it is the difference of two quality values for two distinct images) and those based on an absolute measure. Examples of relative measures include interlacing, illumination, pixel count and off-angle (Fig. 5.4). The other measures are used as absolute.

From Figs. 5.3 and 5.4 regardless of the type of the measure, the difference between ROCs formed from the three subsets of ICE 2005 dataset are quite noticeable. This

Fig. 5.3 ROC curves for
ICE2005 dataset **a** selecting
images using pupil
segmentation score;
b selecting images using
dilation measure; and
c selecting images using
minus blur measure

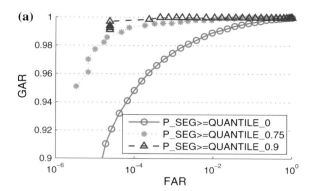

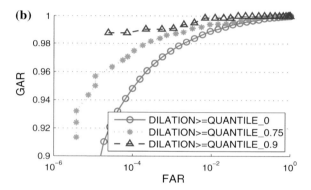

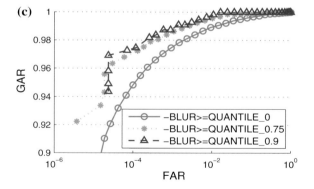

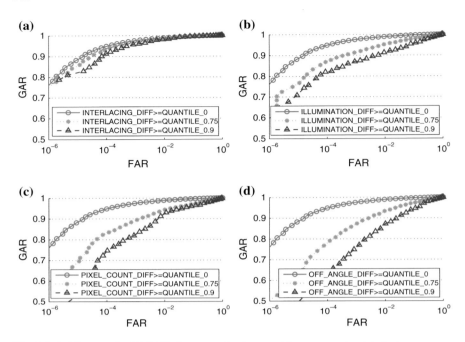

Fig. 5.4 ROC curves for ICE2005 dataset **a** selecting matching scores using interlacing measure; **b** selecting matching scores using illumination measure; **c** selecting matching scores using pixel count measure; and **d** selecting images using off-angle measure

indicates that each individual factor proposed in this work does influence recognition performance of a Gabor filter-based system.

5.4 Quality-Based Adaptive Authentication

This section suggests another use of quality factors. Three different methods to enhance performance of biometric systems due to quality factors are presented. In the first two methods the quality factors are combined to produce a single metric either characterizing the overall quality of an iris image or characterizing the confidence level of a matching score. The third method treats quality factors as additional weak features that improve performance of the matcher. In each of the three methods, the functional relationship between vectors of quality measures and the predicted (estimated) measures is not known. The problem of estimating this relationship is stated as a multivariate regression problem:

$$Y = f(X_1, \ldots, X_K), \tag{5.12}$$

where f is a multivariate adaptive mapping, variable Y is the output variable, and $X_1, \ldots, X_K$ is a vector of K input variables. To estimate $f(\cdot)$ we involve a set of labeled training data. The multivariate adaptive mapping $f(\cdot)$ can be implemented using a variety of multivariate functions and systems. The results reported below are obtained using a feed forward neural network (FFNN). Once the function $f(\cdot)$ is estimated, it is used to predict the output variable from unlabeled input data.

5.4.1 Quality of Sample

Here the vector of quality factors introduced in Sect. 5.2 is used to generate a single quality index by fusing the entries of the vector. Since the index has to be indicative of the performance of iris matcher, we propose to use d-prime index as the combined quality index. This simple single value performance measure requires only a small amount of labeled data per iris class to estimate it. Denote by QS_A the overall quality index of sample A. Then the expression for QS_A is given by

$$QS_A = \frac{|m(\text{Imp. Scores})_A - m(\text{Gen. Scores})_A|}{\sqrt{var(\text{Imp. Scores})_A + var(\text{Gen. Scores})_A}}, \qquad (5.13)$$

where $m(\cdot)_A$ and $var(\cdot)_A$ are the sample mean and sample variance of genuine and imposter scores formed by involving the sample A.

Using the labeled training set QS is estimated for every biometric sample. This requires that a set of genuine matching scores and a set of imposter matching scores involving the same biometric sample be formed. For unlabeled biometric samples this task becomes almost impossible. However, having quality vectors associated with each biometric sample makes it possible to *predict* the QS of unlabeled data. The QS of an unlabeled sample can be obtained as the output parameter of a nonlinear multivariate adaptive mapping applied to a vector of quality measures from the same sample. Let $\mathbf{Q}_A = [Q_{A,1}, \ldots, Q_{A,K}]^T$ be a vector of K quality measures characterizing a biometric sample A. The superscript T indicates the transpose operation. Let $f_{QS}(\cdot)$ be a nonlinear multivariate adaptive mapping that maps a vector of quality measure $\mathbf{Q}_A$ into the quality index QS_A. Let $\hat{f}_{QS}(\cdot)$ be its estimated version. Then QS_A is predicted as $QS_A = \hat{f}_{QS}(\mathbf{Q}_A)$. The predicted value of QS can be then used to decide if the underlying biometric sample should be retained or discarded to improve the performance of the original matcher.

5.4.2 Confidence in Scores

The second method evaluates the confidence level assigned to matching scores associated with a pair of biometric samples. The confidence in genuine and imposter

Fig. 5.5 Illustration of the
confidence in scores (CS)

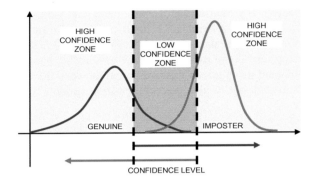

scores (CS) is defined as follows:

$$CS_G = \begin{cases} 0, & HD_G < Q(HD_G)_x, \\ -\frac{HD_G - Q(HD_G)_x}{Q(HD_G)_y - Q(HD_G)_x}, & \text{otherwise,} \end{cases} \qquad (5.14)$$

$$CS_I = \begin{cases} 0, & HD_I > Q(HD_I)_{1-x}, \\ -\frac{Q(HD_I)_{1-x} - HD_I}{Q(HD_I)_{1-x} - Q(HD_I)_{1-y}}, & \text{otherwise,} \end{cases} \qquad (5.15)$$

where $Q(HD_G)_x$ and $Q(HD_I)_y$ are the quantile points at the quantile x and y for
genuine and imposter scores, respectively. The levels of the quantiles were optimized
empirically. The values resulting in significantly improved verification performance
are $x = 0.7$ and $y = 0.9$. Figure 5.5 illustrates genuine and imposter distributions
typical for Hamming Distances (HDs).

The CS of an unlabeled biometric sample is predicted using a nonlinear adaptive
mapping and a vector of quality measures (input parameters). The nonlinear adaptive
mapping is trained using a set of labeled data in the form of vectors of quality
measures and the corresponding CS values obtained using Eqs. (5.14) and (5.15). At
the testing stage the CS value is predicted based on a vector of quality measures only.
This information is used to keep or discard the corresponding matching score. The
procedure of predicting the CS of matching scores between two biometric samples
A and B is $CS_{AB} = \hat{f}_{CS}(\mathbf{Q}_A, \mathbf{Q}_B)$, where $\hat{f}_{CS}(\cdot)$ is a multivariate adaptive mapping
(FFNN in our case) estimated using training data.

5.4.3 Quality Sample and Template Features

The third method suggests to treat quality vectors as weak features that can be
combined with biometric template features. Let $\mathbf{Q}_A$ and $\mathbf{C}_A$ be a vector of K quality
measures and a template vector associated with a biometric sample A. Then the
extended template, denote it by $\mathbf{F}_A$, of the sample A is the vector $\mathbf{F}_A = [\mathbf{Q}_A^T, \mathbf{C}_A^T]^T$.

Fig. 5.6 Combining quality vectors and templates

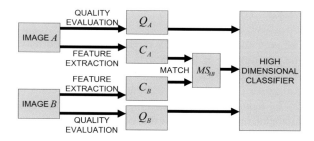

When two biometric samples A and B are compared, the distance (or similarity) between $\mathbf{C}_A$ and $\mathbf{C}_B$ will be saved as MS_{AB}, while the quality vectors $\mathbf{Q}_A$ and $\mathbf{Q}_B$ will be treated as extra dimensions that may improve performance of the original matcher, provided these dimensions contain sufficient discriminative information.

A block diagram of the proposed quality enhanced matcher is shown in Fig. 5.6. The input to the high dimensional classifier is a vector $[\mathbf{Q}_A^T, \mathbf{Q}_B^T, MS_{AB}]^T$. The output of the classifier is a decision made by the classifier. The decision is a binary valued variable corresponding to $\{Genuine, Imposter\}$. The high dimensional classifier is implemented using a nonlinear adaptive mapping. Denote $\eta_{A,B}$ as the output variable predicted using vectors of the quality measures and the matching score of the biometric samples A and B. Then the prediction procedure is described as $\eta_{A,B} = \hat{f}_{QST}\left(\mathbf{Q}_A^T, \mathbf{Q}_B^T, MS_{AB}\right)$, where $\hat{f}_{QST}$ is an estimated version of f_{QST}.

5.4.4 Experimental Results

All experiments were performed using ICE 2005 dataset and processing steps described in Sect. 5.3. We generated $26,867$ genuine matching scores and $4,331,761$ imposter matching scores from $2,953$ iris biometric samples.

5.4.4.1 Neural Network

The nonlinear mapping is implemented using Feed Forward Neural Network (FFNN). Training data are assigned labels according to the functional use of the mapping and a set of input and output parameters. The final design is achieved by trading off the complexity and the performance of the network with two hidden layers. For the iris experiments, the first hidden layer of the FFNN is composed of 16 neurons while the second layer is composed of 2 neurons. The training data are divided randomly in two subsets: a learning subset composed of 60 % of training data and a validation subset made of remaining 40 % of data. The training process stops when the mean square error drops below 10^{-4}. The experimental results described below are obtained using codes from the Neural Network Toolbox in *MATLAB*^{TM}.

5.4.4.2   QS Evaluation

The performance of the QS method is evaluated by randomly selecting 1, 500 iris images from the ICE 2005 dataset to form the training set. The remaining 1, 453 iris images are used to form the testing set. The QS of unlabeled images from the testing set is predicted based on the quality vector (quality factors 1 through 10) and by using a FFNN trained on labeled samples. During performance evaluation, unlabeled images with the value of predicted QS above a preset quantile are retained. Figure 5.7 displays three Receiver Operating Characteristic (ROC) curves parameterized by zero, 10 and 40 % quantile levels. The ROC curve marked as "original" is parameterized by zero quantile level, which means that no poor quality biometric samples were discarded. Note that by discarding only 10 % of iris images with the low predicted QS index, a considerable performance improvement can be achieved. Figure 5.8 displays a box plot of the Equal Error Rate (EER) as a function of the quantile used to select iris samples with high QS value. It is a summary of ten independent trials, where training and testing data are sampled at random. It can be observed that regardless of the composition of training and testing data, removing iris images characterized by low predicted QS improves matching performance of the original matcher. The higher the value of QS is, the better the performance is.

Fig. 5.7 Performance improvement achieved by selecting only images with high QS values

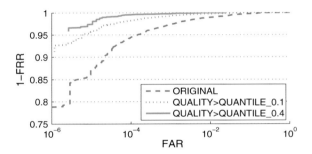

Fig. 5.8 Performance improvement by selecting only images with a quality value larger than a certain quantile

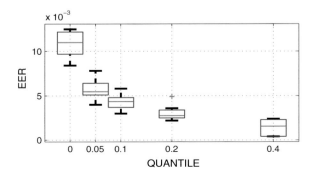

5.4.4.3 CS Evaluation

To assess the performance of the CS method, 20,000 genuine matching scores, 200,000 matching imposter scores and the vectors of quality measures associated with iris images were used to train a FFNN. The remaining data were used for testing. The matcher was designed to be symmetric with respect to quality vectors, that is, if $\mathbf{Q}_A$ and $\mathbf{Q}_B$ are two vectors of quality measures associated with iris image A and B, training included both the pair $(\mathbf{Q}_A, \mathbf{Q}_B)$ and the pair $(\mathbf{Q}_B, \mathbf{Q}_A)$ and the associated matching score. The testing experiment is similar to the experiment of the previous subsection with the difference that pairs of quality vectors are used to predict the *CS* values.

Figure 5.9 shows three ROC curves: the original curve, the curve formed from iris data with the predicted CS values exceeding 20 % quantile and the curve formed from iris data with the predicted CS values exceeding 50 % quantile. Performance improves when low confidence matching scores are discarded. Figure 5.10 summarizes the results of ten trials. Again, training set is formed by randomly sampling iris images from a larger set. The trends and results are consistent.

Fig. 5.9 Performance improvement achieved by selecting only matching scores with high CS values

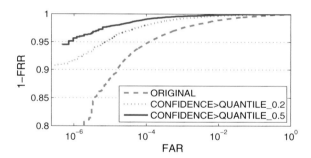

Fig. 5.10 Performance improvement by selecting only matching scores with a confidence level higher than a certain quantile

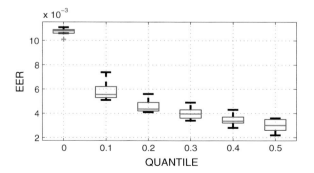

Table 5.1 Performance with/without quality factors

	Original EER	New EER	Original FRR at 0.001 FAR	New FRR at 0.001 FAR
Trial 1	0.0107	0.0065	0.0251	0.0197
Trial 2	0.0110	0.0076	0.0246	0.0186
Trial 3	0.0109	0.0072	0.0251	0.0192
Trial 4	0.0109	0.0068	0.0249	0.0193
Trial 5	0.0106	0.0086	0.0244	0.0229

5.4.4.4   QST Evaluation

The matcher is now a FFNN trained and tested as follows. During training the label "1" is assigned to all genuine vectors on the input and the label "−1" is assigned to all imposter vectors on the input to the neural network. During testing the output label is predicted based on the input vector of quality metrics and the original matching score. The output label in this case is a real number. The high dimensional classifier makes decision in favor of Genuine class if the output label is close to 1. It decides in favor of Imposter, if the output label is closer to −1. When the decision threshold varies, the performance of the high dimensional classifier is characterized by the ROC curve.

To assess the performance of the QST method 20,000 genuine scores and 200,000 imposter scores and associated quality vectors were involved in training. The remaining vector triplets were used for testing. The success of the QST method depends on the data selected for training and testing. A single trial out of set of 20 trials resulted in a perfect separation of genuine and imposter matching scores. In the other cases the % improvement was between 20 and 35 %. The results of five first trials are shown in Table 5.1. In columns 2 and 3 it displays the values of *EER* without/with quality factors. In columns 3 and 4 the table displays the values of False Reject Rate (FRR) evaluated at 0.001 False Accept Rate (FAR).

5.5   Conclusions

This chapter introduced a number of new absolute and relative (global and local) quality factors for iris images. The performance of the proposed measures was evaluated by analyzing the relationship between the quality of iris images and verification performance of the system (in terms of ROC curves). These relationships indicate that proposed quality measures have good selectivity in terms of recognition performance.

Using quality factors as a means to characterize the overall iris image quality, the confidence in matching score or to treat them as weak features is an alternative application of the quality factors. Three methods for matching iris biometrics using quality metrics are presented. The methods are adaptive and use nonlinear mappings for making predictions on quality measures and corresponding verification scores. The reported experimental results illustrate the importance of predictive and selective integration of quality measures for biometric authentication and show significant advantages compared to existing methods.

References

1. C. Belcher, Y. Du, Information distance based selective feature clarity measure for iris recognition, in *Proceedings of the SPIE Symposium on Defense and Security Conference on Human Identification Technology IV*, vol. 6494. Orlando, FL, 2007
2. K.W. Bowyer et al., Image understanding for iris biometrics: a survey. J. Comput. Vis. Image Underst. **110**, 281–307 (2008)
3. Y. Chen et al., Localized iris image quality using 2-D wavelets, in *Proceedings of International Conference on Biometrics (ICB'06)*, Hong Kong, China, Jan 2006, pp. 373–381
4. J. Daugman, How iris recognition works. IEEE Trans. Circuits Syst. Video Technol. **14.1**, 21–30 (2004)
5. H. Fronthaler et al., Fingerprint image-quality estimation and its application to multialgorithm verification. IEEE Trans. IFS **3**(2), 331–338 (2008)
6. N.D. Kalka, Image quality assessment for iris biometric. MA thesis. West Virginia University, Morgantown, WV, USA (2005)
7. N.D. Kalka et al., Image quality assessment for iris biometric, in *SPIE 6202: Biometric Technology for Human Identification III*, vol. 6202. April 2006, pp. D1–D11
8. B.J. Kang, K.R. Park, A study on iris image restoration, in *International Conference on Audio- and Video-Based Biometric Person Authentication*, Rye Brook, NY, July 2005, pp. 31–40
9. K. Kryszczuk, A. Drygajlo, Improving classification with class- independent quality measures: Q-stack in face verification, in *Proceedings of ICB 2007* (Korea University, Seoul, Korea, 2007), pp. 1124–1133
10. X. Liu et al., Experiments with an improved iris segmentation algorithm, in *Fourth IEEE Workshop on Automatic Identification Technologies (AutoID)*, Buffalo, NY, Oct 2005, pp. 118–123
11. L. Ma et al., Personal identification based on iris texture analysis. Pattern Recogn. **25**(12), 1519–1533 (2003)
12. K. Nandakumar et al., Likelihood ratio-based biometric score fusion. IEEE Trans. PAMI **30**(2), 342–347 (2008)
13. National Institute of Standards and Technology (NIST), *Biometric Quality Workshop* (2006)
14. National Institute of Standards and Technology (NIST), *Biometric Quality Workshop II* (2007)
15. National Institute of Standards and Technology (NIST), *Iris Exchange (IREX) II: Iris Quality Calibration and Evaluation (IQCE)* (2011)
16. X. Zhu et al., A quality evaluation method of iris images sequence based on wavelet coefficients in "Region of Interest", in *Proceedings of the The Fourth International Conference on Computer and Information Technology (CIT'04)* (IEEE Computer Society, Washington, DC, USA, 2004), pp. 24–27
17. J. Zuo, N.A. Schmid, An automatic algorithm for evaluating the precision of iris segmentation, in *International Conference on Biometrics: Theory, Applications, and Systems (BTAS'08)*, Washington, DC, USA, Sept 2008

18. J. Zuo, N.A. Schmid, Global and local quality measures for NIR iris video, in *Proceedings of the 2009 IEEE CVPR Workshops*, Miami, FL, USA, June 2009, pp. 1–6
19. J. Zuo, N.A. Schmid, On a methodology for robust segmentation of nonideal iris images. IEEE Trans. Syst. Man Cybern. Part B: Cybern. **40**(3), 703–718 (2010)
20. J. Zuo et al., Adaptive biometric authentication using nonlinear mappings on quality measures and verification scores, in *17th IEEE International Conference on Image Processing (ICIP'10)*, Hong Kong, China, Sept 2010, pp. 4077–4080

Chapter 6
Quality and Demographic Investigation of ICE 2006

P. Jonathon Phillips and Patrick J. Flynn

Abstract There have been four major experimental evaluations of iris recognition technology in recent years: the ITIRT evaluation conducted by the International Biometric Group, the Iris '06 evaluation conducted by Authenti-Corp, and the Iris Challenge Evaluation (ICE) 2006 and Iris Exchange (IREX) conducted by the National Institute of Standards and Technology. These experimental evaluations employed different vendor technologies and experimental specifications, but yield consistent results in the areas where the specifications intersect. In the ICE 2006, participants were allowed to submit quality measures. We investigate the properties of their quality submissions.

6.1 Introduction

There have been four major experimental evaluations of iris recognition technology in recent years: the ITIRT evaluation conducted by the International Biometric Group, the Iris '06 evaluation conducted by Authenti-Corp, and the Iris Challenge Evaluation (ICE) 2006 and Iris Exchange (IREX) conducted by the National Institute of Standards and Technology. These experimental evaluations employed different vendor technologies and experimental specifications, but yield consistent results in the areas where the specifications intersect. Thus, these studies jointly established an overall performance level for iris recognition [1, 4–6, 8]. Overall performance on a dataset does not give a complete characterization of performance. For real-world applications, scientific knowledge, and technology advancement it is necessary to have a finer grained characterization of performance.

P.J. Phillips
National Institute of Standards and Technology, Gaithersburg, MD, USA
e-mail: jonathon@nist.gov

P.J. Flynn (✉)
University of Notre Dame, Notre Dame, IN, USA
e-mail: flynn@nd.edu

© Springer-Verlag London 2016

K.W. Bowyer and M.J. Burge (eds.), *Handbook of Iris Recognition*,
Advances in Computer Vision and Pattern Recognition,
DOI 10.1007/978-1-4471-6784-6_6

Formally speaking, a covariate is a variable that is potentially predictive of an outcome. A focus of this study is the effect of quality measurements (covariates) on iris recognition system performance (the outcome). In this context, covariates that can affect performance fall into two categories. The first category is subject covariates. These are properties of an individual or of an iris. Examples are sex, race, eye color, the presence/absence, and type of corrective lenses worn during acquisition, and the eye (left or right). The second category of covariates contains image covariates. These are properties of the image of the iris and can vary from image to image of the same iris. Examples of these covariates include iris size (e.g., diameter in pixels), iris dilation (e.g., radius of pupil in pixels), degree of occlusion by eyelids or eyelashes, and focus quality.

Quality metrics have a special place in iris recognition. Iris sensors employ embedded algorithms for quality assessment that are used to discard images and (if necessary) trigger reacquisition. The precise nature of the quality metrics used is unknown. This quality metric is often used to prescreen iris images and trigger reacquisition in the event that quality is judged to be poor. One can identify and casually define several potential degradations to the subjective quality of an iris image, such as defocus, motion blur, strong occlusion, large pupil size, off-axis eye pose (i.e., nonzero gaze angle relative to the optical axis), the presence of corrective lenses and lens reflections, contact lens registration marks or brands, refractive artifacts from corrective lenses, spoofing attempts using cosmetic lenses, surgical consequences such as deformed irises, pathological conditions such as cataracts, iris nevi (sometimes presenting as eye carcinoma), aniridia (lack of irises) or albinism (melanin deficiency), etc. Not all of these conditions have been studied at length in the literature; few are amenable to rigorous analysis today due to the paucity of data presenting the conditions involved. Although one can subjectively judge iris image quality and perhaps implement software that parallels a human judgement, it does not follow that iris recognition system performance on such data will degrade in tandem with the subjective judgement.

In the ICE 2006, participants were allowed to submit quality measures. For the three iris algorithm reported in Phillips et al. [8], we investigate the properties of their quality submissions. To look at the question of "are the three quality measures the same thing?"—we looked at the correlation among the three quality measures. We investigated the effect of demographics on the quality measures. Finally, we investigated the ability of the quality measures to predict performance. For numerous applications, this is the acid test of the effectiveness of quality measures.

6.2 ICE 2006: Methodology

6.2.1 Data

The ICE 2006 data was collected at the University of Notre Dame as part of a larger multiple biometric data collection effort [8]. The images were acquired between

January 2004 and May 2005. The iris images were collected with a LG EOU 2200 that allowed for the collection of images with a broader range of quality than the sensor would normally acquire. This includes iris images that did not pass the quality control software embedded in the LG EOU 2200. The LG EOU 2200 is a complete acquisition system and has automatic image quality control checks.

The image quality software embedded in the LG EOU 2200 is one of numerous iris quality measures. Prior to the start of the data collection, an arrangement was made to minimize the effect of the LG EOU 2200 quality screening software on the data collection. By agreement between U. of Notre Dame and Iridian, a modified version of the acquisition software was provided. The modified software allowed all images from the sensor to be saved under certain conditions, as explained below.

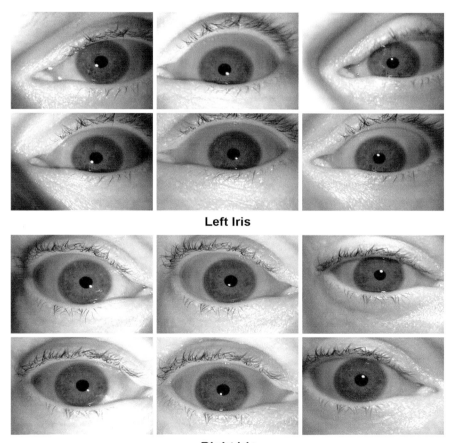

Left Iris

Right Iris

Fig. 6.1 Example of iris images from an acquisition session

The iris images are 640 (width) by 480 (height) pixels in resolution. For most "good" iris images, the diameter of the iris in the image exceeds 200 pixels. The images are stored with 8 bits of intensity, but every third intensity level is unused. This is the result of a contrast stretching automatically applied within the LG EOU 2200 system. The iris images were digitized from NTSC video and the iris images may have interlace artifacts due to motion of the subjects.

In our acquisitions, subjects were seated in front of the system. The system provided recorded voice prompts to aid the subject in positioning their eye at the appropriate distance from the sensor. The system took images in "shots" of three. Each image was illuminated by one of three near infrared light-emitting diodes (LEDs).

For a given subject at a given iris acquisition session, two "shots" of three images were taken for each eye, for a total of 12 images; see Fig. 6.1 for example, set of images from an acquisition session. Figure 6.2 shows examples of "lower" quality iris images. The system provided a feedback sound when an acceptable shot of images was taken. An acceptable shot had one or more images that passed the LG EOU 2200s built-in quality checks, but all three images were saved. If none of the three images passed the built-in quality checks, then none of the three images were saved. At least one third of the iris images did pass the Iridian quality control checks, and up to two thirds did not pass. A manual quality control step was performed at Notre Dame to remove images in which, for example, the eye was not visible at all due to the subject having turned their head.

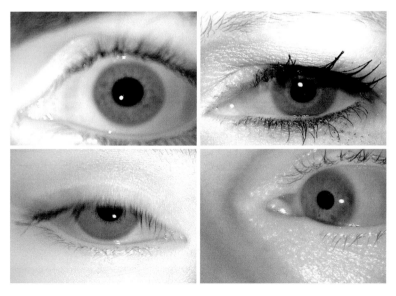

Fig. 6.2 Examples of "lower" quality iris images in the ICE 2006 dataset

Table 6.1   The list of recognition and quality algorithms covered in this chapter

Group	Iris recognition algorithm	Iris quality algorithm
U. of Cambridge	CAM-2	CAM-2-Q
Iritech	IRTCH-2	IRTCH-2-Q
Sagem-Iridian	SI-2	SI-2-Q

Column headings identify each participant group. The organization that submitted an algorithm is listed in the group column. The abbreviations used in this chapter are presented in the Iris recognition algorithm and Iris quality algorithm columns

6.2.2   Protocol

The ICE 2006 evaluated algorithms. Participants had to deliver executable versions of their algorithms to NIST. The executables had to be received by NIST by 15 June 2006. The ICE 2006 was open to academia, industry, and research laboratories. Participants could submit multiple algorithms.

The format for submissions was binary executables that could be run independently on the test server. All submitted executables had to run using a specified set of command line arguments. The command line arguments included an experiment parameter file, files that contained the sets of biometric samples to be matched, and name of the output similarity file.

The ICE 2006 had an optional iris image quality task. For the quality task, executables gave a quality score for each iris image. The quality score had to be an integer in the range between 0 and 100, with 100 being the highest quality. A quality score is a number that rates an image's utility to a recognition system and should be predictive of performance [3].

The test system hardware for the ICE 2006 was a Dell PowerEdge 850 server with a single Intel Pentium 4 3.6GHz 660 processor and 2MB of 800Mhz cache. All systems had 4GB of 533MHz DDR2 RAM. At no time did the test system have access to the Internet. The ICE 2006 allowed executables that would run under Windows Server 2003 (standard edition) and Linux Fedora Core 3 operating systems.

Table 6.1 lists the ICE 2006 algorithms whose results are presented in this chapter. These are the same algorithms reported in Phillips et al [8]. All three of these submissions included a quality measure. All three matching algorithms and their quality algorithms were fully automatic.

6.3   Overview of the ICE 2006 Algorithm Performance Results

In this section we summarize the ICE 2006 results that were published in Phillips et al. [8].

The images for the ICE 2006 were collected over three academic semesters: Spring 2004, Fall 2004, and Spring 2005. In computing performance, all similarity scores

Fig. 6.3 Summary of the
performance of the ICE
2006. Results are presented
for three groups: Cambridge
(Cam-2), Iritech (IrTch-2),
and Sagem-Iridian (SI-2).
Performance is broken out by
right and *left* eyes. The false
reject rate (FRR) at a false
accept rate (FAR) of 0.001 is
reported. Performance is
reported for 29,056 *right* and
30,502 *left* iris images from
240 subjects with 30
partitions for each eye. This
figure is from Phillips
et al. [8]

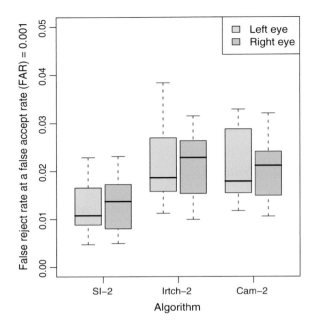

are cross semesters; i.e., iris images taken in the same semester were not compared.
There were 30 partitions for the left eye and 30 partitions for the right eye. For
each algorithm, the false reject rate (FRR) at a false accept rate (FAR) of 0.001 was
computed independently for each partition. The performance for each eye at a FAR
of 0.001 was characterized by 30 FRRs which were summarized by a boxplot.

Performance for the ICE 2006 benchmark is presented in Fig. 6.3 for algorithms from three groups: Sagem-Iridian (SI-2), Iritech (IRTCH-2), and Cambridge
(CAM-2). The interquartile range for all three algorithms overlaps, with the largest
amount of overlap between Iritech (IRTCH-2), and Cambridge (CAM-2).

6.4   Quality Scores for ICE 2006

The ICE 2006 protocol allowed for algorithms to report a quality measure for each
iris image. Because the input to the quality module was an iris image, by their nature,
the quality metrics are image-based. Quality scores were required to be reported as an
integer between 0 and 100, with 100 being the highest quality. Figure 6.4 shows the
histograms of quality scores for Sagem-Iridian (SI-2-Q), Iritech (IRTCH-2-Q), and
Cambridge (CAM-2-Q). The quality score distribution for Sagem-Iridian is bimodal
with modes at 0 and 100.

Fig. 6.4 Histogram of the
quality scores for **a**
Sagem-Iridian (SI-2-Q),
b Cambridge (Cam-2-Q),
and **c** Iritech (Irtch-2-Q)

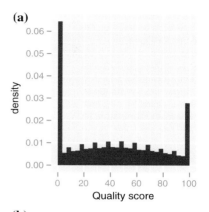

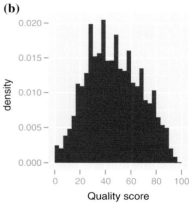

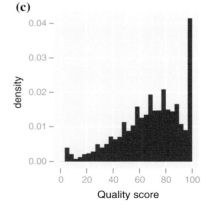

Fig. 6.5 Scatterplot and
correlation between quality
scores for the quality
submissions to the ICE 2006.
a Shows the correlation be
Cam-2-Q and SI-2-Q,
b Shows the correlation be
Irtch-2-Q and SI-2-Q, and
c Shows the correlation be
Irtch-2-Q and Cam-2-Q

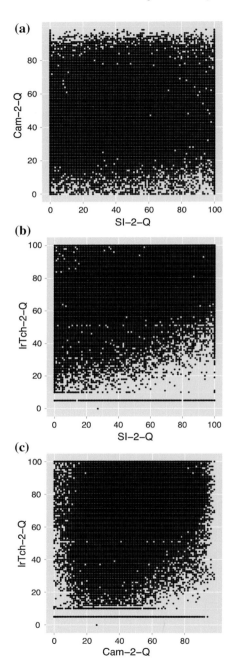

Table 6.2 Correlation between quality scores

Quality scores	Pearson's r	Spearman's ρ
SI-2-Q versus CAM-2-Q	0.122	0.131
SI-2-Q versus IRTCH-2-Q	0.349	0.348
CAM-2-Q versus IRTCH-2-Q	0.120	0.108

Correlation coefficients are given for Pearson's r and Spearman's ρ

6.4.1   Quality Score Correlation Study

Intuitively, one would expect that quality scores measure generic iris image properties, such as amount of occlusion, in-focus measure, or amount of motion blur. While
high correlation between quality measures might not be expected, some correlation
is to be expected. This is especially true if a quality metric is intended to generalize to multiple algorithm approaches. Our first experiment explored the correlation
among the quality scores returned by Sagem-Iridian (SI-2-Q), Iritech (IRTCH-2-Q),
and Cambridge (CAM-2-Q). Scatterplots for comparing the quality measures is given
in Fig. 6.5. Each point in a scatterplot is an iris image with coordinates being the quality score for two participants. In each scatterplot there are 59,558 points, one for each
iris image in the ICE 2006 data set.

The corresponding Pearson and Spearman correlation coefficients calculated for
pairs of participant quality scores are given in Table 6.2. These coefficients reflect
little correlation between quality scores for the different participants.

6.4.2   Correlation Between Right and Left Irises

One of the open questions in biometrics is whether or not there exists correlations
between the left and right irises of a person. Analysis performed on the ICE 2005
results showed that for submitted quality scores there was a correlation between the
left and right irises of a person [9]. This analysis is repeated for the quality scores
for the ICE 2006.

The first step computes the average quality score for each person for both
the left and right iris images. The average quality score for all the left irises
for person i is denoted by $\rho_L(i)$, and the corresponding average for the right iris
images is $\rho_R(i)$. Figure 6.6 shows scatterplots for $\rho_L(i)$ versus $\rho_R(i)$ for each of the
three quality measures Sagem-Iridian (SI-2-Q), Iritech (IRTCH-2-Q), and Cambridge
(CAM-2-Q). Each point in the scatterplot is a subject and the coordinates of the point
are $(\rho_L(i), \rho_R(i))$. Quality scores from left and right irises from 240 subjects were
included in this analysis. Included in Fig. 6.6 is the regression line for $\rho_L(i)$ versus
$\rho_R(i)$. Table 6.3 lists the Pearson's r and Spearman's ρ correlation coefficients for
mean subject quality scores for the left and right irises, $\rho_L(i)$ versus $\rho_R(i)$.

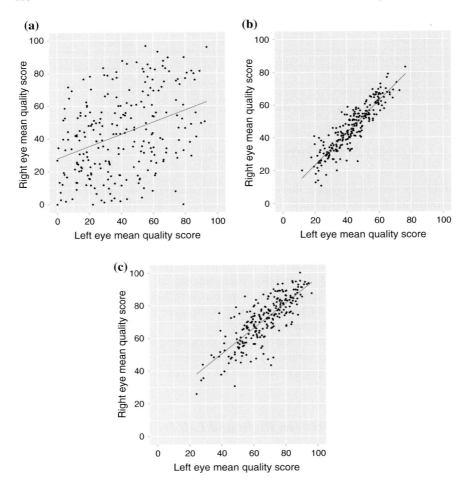

Fig. 6.6 Scatterplot and correlation between subjects' mean quality score for the left and right eyes. The scatterplots are for quality modules **a** SI-2-Q, **b** Cam-2-Q, and **c** IrTch-2-Q

Table 6.3 Correlation coefficients between mean quality scores for the left and right irises

Quality score	Pearson's r	Spearman's ρ
SI-2	0.362	0.347
CAM-2	0.896	0.896
IRTCH-2	0.790	0.781

Correlation coefficients are given for Pearson's r and Spearman's ρ

The results show that the average left and right quality measure are highly correlated for Cambridge and Iritech. The lower amount of correlation between the left
and right irises for Sagem-Iridian SI-2-Q module maybe due to the bimodal nature
of the module's quality score distribution, as shown in Fig. 6.4.

6.4.3 Demographics and Quality Scores

In face recognition the sex, race, age, and other subject covariates effect performance [2, 7]. It has been suggested that eye color and race effect the performance
of iris recognition systems.

The two largest demographic groups in the ICE 2006 data set are Caucasians and
East Asians. The eye color for the East Asians was uniformly labeled dark. However,
for the Caucasian subject had a full range of eye colors including green, blue, hazel,
and brown. The Caucasian eye colors were grouped into light and dark to ensure that
there were sufficient number of subjects in each category. The light eyes consisted
of green and blues eyes and the dark colors consisted of hazel and brown eyes. Since
race and eye color are not independent factors, for our analysis on the effect of race
and eye color, we combine these factors into one factor with three levels: Caucasian
with light irises, Caucasian with dark irises, and East Asians.

Since the quality scores from the three quality algorithms have different distributions, for the analysis in this section the quality scores were normalized. The first step
in the normalization process was to compute the empirical cumulative distribution
function $\hat{F}$. The normalized quality scores are then computed by $q' = \hat{F}^{-1}(q)$ for
the original quality score q. The normalized quality scores q' are between 0.0 and
1.0, and have an approximately uniform distribution. (Note: because the distribution
of the Sagem-Iridian quality scores has peaks at 0 and 100, the normalized quality
scores do not have an uniform distribution.)

Figure 6.7 shows boxplots of the normalized quality for broken out by East Asian,
Caucasian with dark irises, and Caucasian with light irises. Results are reported for
Sagem-Iridian (SI-2-Q), Iritech (IRTCH-2-Q), and Cambridge (CAM-2-Q).

The plots in Fig. 6.7 clearly show that the quality measures are sensitive to race
and eye color. For Sagem-Iridian and Iritech, the median quality scores are ordered
by East Asian, Caucasians with dark colored irises, and then Caucasians with light
colored irises. For the Cambridge quality module, the ordering of the median of the
quality scores is the opposite. Figure 6.7 shows that the quality modules respond
qualitatively different to race and eye color.

We looked at the effect of the sex of the subject on the distribution of quality
scores. For the ICE 2006 submissions, the results of our analysis showed that the sex
of the subject did not affect the distribution of the quality scores.

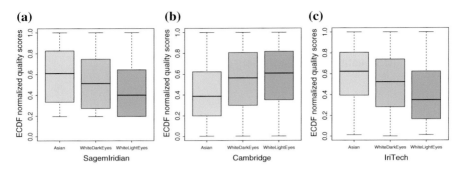

Fig. 6.7 Boxplots of quality score broken out by East Asian, Caucasians' with *dark* iris color, and Caucasians' with *light* iris color. Results are reported for **a** the Sagem-Iridian (SI-2-Q), **b** Iritech (IRTCH-2-Q), and **c** Cambridge (CAM-2-Q) quality modules

6.5 Quality Scores and Performance

Quality scores are computed independently for each iris image. The underlying assumption is that quality scores are predictive of performance. If two iris images have "high" quality scores, then when they are compared the matching algorithm is likely to give the correct answer. The obvious use of quality scores is to exclude "low" quality iris images from the matching step. This is a sensible operational step for enrollment (population of the gallery set), since additional images are relatively easy to acquire from a cooperative subject at enrollment. Some scenarios may also allow multiple images to be acquired online, then selecting the highest quality image for enrollment. Our analysis models the above scenario where the quality controls are at the points of enrollment and acquisition. In this model, when two iris images are compared, both iris images independently meet the quality standard for the system. In the analysis in this section, we systematically vary the quality threshold and assess its impact on performance.

One of the goals in quality research is the development of quality measures that are effective for multiple algorithms. This property is sometimes referred to as universality of quality metrics. To investigate universality, explored the effectiveness of each quality measures against each of the three matching algorithms.

6.5.1 Measuring Performance of Quality Measures

It is well established in biometrics that performance of an algorithm needs to report both type I and type II errors, with FRR and FAR as the basis for our analysis. In this section we extend the traditional FRR and FAR trade-off to include quality measures, which follows [3]. Computation of FRR and FAR is based on similarity scores that results from comparing two iris images. The first step takes quality scores for an iris

image and creates a quality score for a pair of iris images. The second step plots the
trade-off in performance among FRR, FAR, and quality scores.

The first step is to compute image quality scores for each image in both the target
and query sets. The quality for an iris image q is denoted by $r(q)$.

The next step is to define a quality measure for a pair of iris images q and t.
Computing a quality measure $r(t, q)$ for a pair of iris images makes it possible to
associate each similarity score $s(i, j)$ with a quality score. For the analysis in this
chapter, the quality measure $r(t, q) = \min(r(t), r(q))$. The selection of the min function models the situation where the target and query images are acquired separately
and both images must have a minimum quality score to be saved. In computing $r(q, t)$,
other possible functions include average and weighted average. The selection of the
appropriate function depends on the scenario being modeled.

The last step is to extend the characterization of verification performance to include
quality scores. Whereas, the traditional characterization of verification performance
is traded-off between FRR and FAR, the extended version shows the trade-off among
FRR, FAR, and quality rate (QR). For the quality performance analysis in this chapter,
we need a decision threshold and the quality range. In the quality analysis, a decision
threshold λ serves the same purpose as in traditional signal detection analysis. Image
quality is characterized by a quality rate which is defined as

$$QR(\tau_l, \tau_u) = \frac{|\tau_l \le r(t), r(q) \le \tau_u|}{|\mathcal{T}| + |\mathcal{Q}|}.$$

The QR gives the fraction of iris images that fall within the quality range. For each
image quality threshold τ, FRR and FAR are computed from the similarity scores
that have a quality score above τ. Formally $FRR(\tau_l, \tau_u, \lambda)$ and $FAR(\tau_l, \tau_u, \lambda)$ are

$$FRR(\tau_l, \tau_u, \lambda) = \frac{|s(t, q) \le \lambda, \text{ where } (t, q) \text{ is match and } \tau_l \le r(t), r(q) \le \tau_u||}{|(t, q) \text{ are matches and } \tau_l \le r(t), r(q) \le \tau_u|},$$

and

$$FAR(\tau_l, \tau_u, \lambda) = \frac{|s(t, q) \ge \lambda, \text{ where } (t, q) \text{ is nonmatch and } \tau_l \le r(t), r(q) \le \tau_u|}{|(t, q) \text{ are nonmatches and } \tau_l \le r(t), r(q) \le \tau_u|}.$$

For each experiment in this chapter, the same base decision threshold λ_0 was
selected for each algorithm. The decision threshold λ_0 corresponds to a FAR of
0.001 computed the entire ICE 2006 experiment as described in Sect. 6.3. Given
this threshold λ_0, the quality performance statistics $QR(\tau_l, \tau_u)$, $FRR(\tau_l, \tau_u, \lambda_0)$, and
$FAR(\tau_l, \tau_u, \lambda_0)$ are computed for different values of the quality thresholds τ_l and τ_u.
For the analysis in this chapter, the selection criteria fall into two categories. In the
first, the upper threshold τ_u is set to the maximum quality score ($\tau_u = 100$), and
τ_l is varied. This selection criteria computes performance when the quality scores
are above a threshold set by τ_l. This method measures the trade-off among QR,
FRR, and FAR as the quality of iris images increases. In the second category, the

lower threshold τ_l is set to the minimum quality score ($\tau_l = 0$), and τ_u is varied. This selection criteria computes performance when the quality scores are below the threshold set by τ_u. This method measures the trade-off among QR, FRR, and FAR on lower quality images.

6.5.2 Effect of Quality Scores on Performance

The underlying premise for quality measures is that they are predictive of performance. In addition, a desirable property of quality measures is that they are universal. A quality measure is universal if it is predictive of performance for a class of algorithms.

In this experiment, we test the predictive property of the quality measures in the ICE 2006 and their universality. To test predictive property of the ICE 2006 quality measures, performance is computed as the minimum threshold of quality scores is increased. For this analysis the upper threshold τ_u is set to the maximum value of 100. Then QR, FRR, and FAR are computed for twenty increasing values of the lower threshold. The values for τ_l are 0, 5, 10, ..., 95. The case when $\tau_l = 0$ corresponds to no pruning by quality. The lower thresholds of 5, 10, ..., 95 correspond to requiring increasing levels of quality of the target and query images.

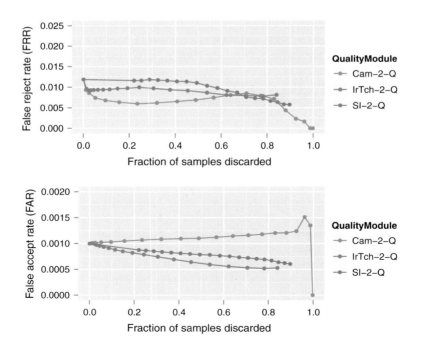

Fig. 6.8 Effect of all three quality measures on matcher SI-2

The analysis in this chapter presents results for three matching algorithms. Each of these groups also submitted a quality algorithm. To test universality, we measured the predictive power of each quality measure against all three matching algorithms.

To show the trade-off among QR, FRR, and FAR, we plot QR versus FRR and QR versus FAR. In plots of QR versus FRR, the horizontal axis is $QR(\tau_l, 100)$ and the vertical axis is $FRR(\lambda_0, \tau_l, 100)$. When $\tau_l = 0$, $QR(\tau_l, 100) = 1$, and $FRR(\lambda_0, \tau_l, 100) = FRR(\lambda_0)$, which is the FRR at a FAR of 0.001. In plots of QR versus FAR, the horizontal axis is $QR(\tau_l, 100)$ and the vertical axis is $FAR(\lambda_0, \tau_l, 100)$. When $\tau_l = 0$, $FAR(\lambda_0, \tau_l, 100) = 0.001$.

If this premise is true, then as lower quality biometric samples are removed, performance should improve. It is desirable that quality scores are predictive of performance for multiple algorithms.

Figures 6.8, 6.9, and 6.10 present the performance triplet values by matching algorithm, by triplet element, by quality scorer, and by quality pruning threshold. Figure 6.8 contains results for matcher SI-2, Fig. 6.9 contains results for matcher IRTCH-2, and Fig. 6.10 contains results for matcher CAM-2. In each figure, the top plot contains FRR curves for each of the three quality scorers SI-2-Q, IRTCH-2-Q, and CAM-2-Q, (plotted in different colors), and the bottom plot shows FAR curves. The points in each plot indicate the components of the operating point triplet for quality pruning thresholds proceeding from 0.0 at the left edge to 1.0 at the right edge. The

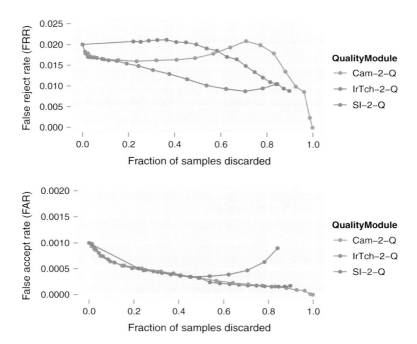

Fig. 6.9 Effect of all three quality measures on matcher Irtch-2

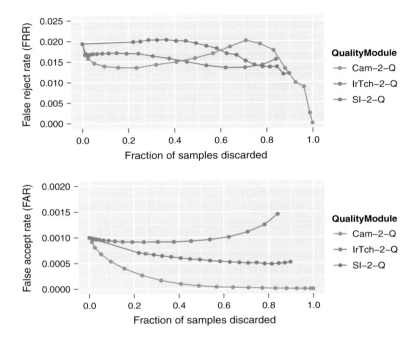

Fig. 6.10 Effect of all three quality measures on matcher CAM-2

horizontal axis measures the percentage of iris-pairs discarded by the quality pruning threshold for each curve.

In Fig. 6.8, the red curve in the bottom plot shows the values of FAR for the SI-2 matcher as iris samples are discarded using quality module CAM-2-Q. With no quality-based pruning at the left, the FAR = 0.001. As more images are pruned by the quality module CAM-2-Q, the FAR increase under the fraction pruned is about 0.9. For the other two quality modules, FAR decreases with quality-based pruning.

6.6 Discussions and Conclusions

The core experiments in this analysis looked at the universality of the ICE 2006 quality measures. The first study looked at the correlation among the three quality measures. Spearman's correlation coefficient ranged from 0.108 to 0.348. This showed minimal correlation among the quality measures.

One study looked at the effect of eye color and race on the quality measures. For the SI-2-Q and IRTECH-2-Q measures, the median quality measures were ordered Asian, Caucasian with light colored eyes, and Caucasian with dark colored eyes (from highest to lowest). For the CAM-2-Q measure, the median quality measures had the reverse order (Caucasian with dark colored eyes, Caucasian with light colored eyes, and Asian). This showed that the quality measures were sensitive to the combination of eye color and race. In addition, the sensitivity varied by quality measures.

In the final experiment, we looked at the ability of the quality measures to predict performance. The results showed that none of the three quality measures could universally predict performance.

These three core experiments suggest that the three quality modules are measuring different properties of an iris. Also, the three matchers respond differently to these properties.

Since the ICE 2006 conducted, research in quality measures for iris images has continued. The IREX II Iris Quality Calibration and Evaluation (IQCE) will measure progress in the development of iris quality algorithms.[1]

Acknowledgments We acknowledge the support of Department of Homeland Security's Science and Technology Department and Transportation Security Administration (TSA), the Director of National Intelligence's Information Technology Innovation Center, the Federal Bureau of Investigation (FBI), the National Institute of Justice, and the Technical Support Working Group (TSWG). This work was undertaken during PJF's sabbatical leave at NIST. The support of NIST is gratefully acknowledged. Biometrics research at the University of Notre Dame is supported by the National Science Foundation under grant CNS01-30839, by the US Department of Justice, and by UNISYS Corp. The identification of any commercial product or trade name does not imply endorsement or recommendation by the National Institute of Standards and Technology or the U. of Notre Dame.

References

1. Authenti-Corp, Iris recognition study 2006 (IRIS06). Technical report. Version 0.40. Authenti-Corp (2007)
2. J.R. Beveridge et al., Factors that influence algorithm performance in the Face Recognition Grand Challenge. Comput. Vis. Image Underst. **113**, 750–762 (2009)
3. P. Grother, E. Tabassi, Performance of biometric quality measures. IEEE Trans. PAMI **29**, 531–543 (2007)
4. P.J. Grother et al., IREX I Performance of iris recognition algorithms on standard images. Technical report. NISTIR 7629. National Institute of Standards and Technology (2009)
5. International Biometric Group, Independent Testing of Iris Recognition Technology. Technical report. International Biometric Group (2005)
6. E.M. Newton, P.J. Phillips, Meta-analysis of third-party evaluations of iris recognition. IEEE Trans. SMC-A **39**(1), 4–11 (2009)
7. P.J. Phillips et al., Face recognition vendor test 2002: evaluation report. Technical report. NISTIR 6965. National Institute of Standards and Technology (2003). http://www.frvt.org
8. P.J. Phillips et al., FRVT 2006 and ICE 2006 large-scale results. IEEE Trans. PAMI **32**(5), 831–846 (2010)
9. P. Phillips et al., The iris challenge evaluation 2005, in *Second IEEE International Conference on Biometrics: Theory, Applications, and Systems* (2008)

---

[1]For details on IREX II IQCE see http://iris.nist.gov.

Chapter 7
Methods for Iris Segmentation

Raghavender Jillela and Arun A. Ross

Abstract Under ideal image acquisition conditions, the iris biometric has been observed to provide high recognition performance compared to other biometric traits. Such a performance is possible by accurately segmenting the iris region from the given ocular image. This chapter discusses the challenges associated with the segmentation process, along with some of the prominent iris segmentation techniques proposed in the literature. The methods are presented according to their suitability for segmenting iris images acquired under different wavelengths of illumination. Furthermore, methods to refine and evaluate the output of the iris segmentation routine are presented. The goal of this chapter is to provide a brief overview of the progress made in iris segmentation.

7.1 Introduction

An iris acquisition system typically captures an image of the eye that, besides the iris, includes the pupil, eyelids, eyelashes, and sclera. The process of locating and isolating the iris from such an image is known as iris *localization* or *segmentation*. The primary task of segmentation is to determine the pixels in a given image that correspond to the iris region. In Fig. 7.1, the pupillary boundary refers to the boundary separating the pupil (the black region in the center of the eye) from the iris (the textured region surrounding the pupil) while the limbus boundary refers to the boundary separating the iris from the sclera (the white of the eye). Typically, segmentation is accomplished by detecting the pupillary and limbus boundaries as well as the eyelids and eyelashes that can interrupt the contour of the limbus boundary. Iris segmentation is considered

R. Jillela
Digital Signal Corporation, Chantilly, VA, USA

A.A. Ross (✉)
Integrated Pattern Recognition and Biometrics Lab (i-PRoBe), Michigan State University, East Lansing, MI, USA
e-mail: rossarun@cse.msu.edu

© Springer-Verlag London 2016
K.W. Bowyer and M.J. Burge (eds.), *Handbook of Iris Recognition*,
Advances in Computer Vision and Pattern Recognition,
DOI 10.1007/978-1-4471-6784-6_7

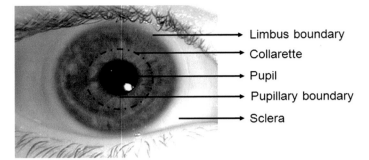

Limbus boundary
Collarette
Pupil
Pupillary boundary
Sclera

Fig. 7.1 The anterior surface anatomy of a human iris. Note that some of the artifacts are caused by the clear contact lens worn by the subject

to be a critical component of any iris biometric system. Inaccuracies in localizing the iris can severely impact the matching accuracy of the system, thereby undermining its utility.

To provide an accurate output, an iris segmentation algorithm is required to consider the following characteristics of the iris boundaries[1]:

1. *Circularity of the iris boundaries*: Some of the earliest iris segmentation algorithms [9, 51] operated under the assumption that the iris boundaries are circular. However, the iris boundaries may not always be circular. Figure 7.2 shows a sample iris image in which the pupillary boundary is elliptical in shape. A wide number of recently proposed segmentation algorithms [10, 42] aim to accommodate noncircular (or even non-conic) boundaries.

2. *Nasal inclination of the pupil*: In most cases, the pupil has been observed to be nasally inclined. Therefore, the center (or centroid) of the pupillary boundary may not always coincide with that of the limbus boundary. Figure 7.3 shows an iris image with non-concentric iris boundaries.

3. *Difference in the variation of pixel intensities at the boundaries*: Typically, the variation in pixel intensities across the pupillary boundary is much stronger than the variation across the limbus boundary.[2] This property lends to the fact that, in most cases, the pupillary boundary can be easily detected using intensity thresholding operation. On the other hand, determining the limbus boundary can be a relatively difficult task.

---

[1]The term "iris boundaries" is used in this chapter to collectively refer to both the pupillary and limbus boundaries.

[2]This is true for images obtained in the near-infrared spectrum.

(a) **(b)** **(c)**

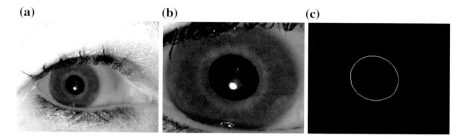

Fig. 7.2 **a** Input iris image. **b** Close-up view of the iris. **c** Contour indicating the pupillary boundary. Notice that the pupillary boundary is elliptical, and not circular

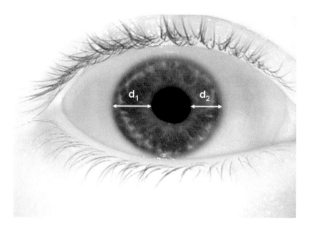

Fig. 7.3 An image showing the *right* eye of an individual. Notice that the pupil is slightly inclined toward the subject's nose (on the *right side* of the image). The distance from the pupillary boundary to the limbus boundary on the *left side* of the image, d_1, is greater than the distance on the *right side*, d_2. Note that the image has been processed for clarity purposes (specular reflections removed in the pupil region)

7.2 Role of Image Acquisition in Iris Segmentation

The choice and performance of an iris segmentation algorithm typically depend on the image acquisition conditions [54]. This is because the appearance and image-level characteristics of the iris boundaries can differ under varying image acquisition protocols. Two major image acquisition factors that can impact iris segmentation are:

1. *Imaging wavelengths*: The appearance of the iris boundaries can vary depending on the wavelength (i.e., spectral band) used to acquire the image. This is caused by the response of melanin, a color-inducing pigment, to the varying illumination wavelengths. Sample iris images acquired under varying wavelengths of sillumination are provided in Fig. 7.4.

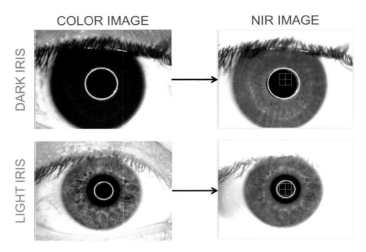

Fig. 7.4 Corresponding pairs of iris images acquired in the visible (color) and near-infrared (NIR) spectral bands. Notice that the pupil and limbic boundaries are well discerned in NIR images. Image taken from [6]

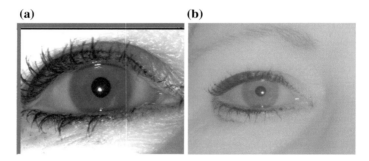

Fig. 7.5 Iris images of a subject acquired using two different sensors

2. *Type of sensor*: The appearance of iris boundaries in an image can also depend on: (a) the characteristics of sensor used (e.g., image resolution, focal length, depth of field, wavelength and configuration of the illuminating source, optics and polarizing filters used, stand-off distance,[3] etc.) and (b) type of sensor used (e.g., wall-mounted, portable, walk-through sensors, etc.). Figure 7.5 shows iris images of a subject acquired using two different sensors.

Figure 7.6 illustrates the impact of image acquisition on iris segmentation. It can be observed that the iris segmentation output can differ when applied on images of a given subject acquired using different sensors.

---

[3]Distance between the user and the sensor.

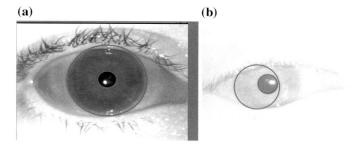

Fig. 7.6 Output obtained using an iris segmentation algorithm on images of a subject acquired using two different sensors. Notice that the output is incorrect in (**b**) due to different gain and exposure settings of the sensor

7.2.1   On NIR Versus VIS Imaging

The image acquisition protocols are determined by the application in which an iris recognition system is deployed. Iris recognition systems typically operate in the near-infrared (NIR) spectrum. This is because the NIR spectrum ensures that the acquired image reveals information related to the texture of the iris, rather than its pigmentation. This property in turn contributes to the high recognition performance of iris imaged in the NIR spectrum. Images acquired under the visible (VIS) spectrum have also been used for iris recognition. This is because VIS iris recognition could facilitate recognition at larger distances, and with greater user convenience.

NIR iris images typically outperform VIS iris images from a matching accuracy perspective since the richness of iris texture is not always well captured in a VIS image. In this chapter, some of the well-known approaches used for both NIR and VIS iris segmentation images are discussed. A review of techniques useful for VIS iris segmentation under challenging conditions can be found in [24].

7.3   Challenges in Iris Segmentation

A majority of iris recognition systems require a significant amount of user cooperation during image acquisition to provide good recognition performance. For an iris image acquired under near-ideal conditions (e.g., good illumination, cooperative subject, unoccluded iris, etc.), iris segmentation can be accomplished using simple image-processing techniques. This is based on the observation that both the iris boundaries show significant variation in pixel intensities across their contours (e.g., iris versus the pupil, and iris versus the sclera). However, when an iris image is acquired under non-ideal conditions, segmentation becomes a challenging task. Some of the factors that render iris segmentation challenging are listed below.

1. **Occlusions caused by the anatomical features of the eye**: One of the most
   common and significant challenge faced during iris segmentation is the occlusion
   caused by the eyelids and/or the eyelashes.

   - *Eyelids*: The eyelids are thin folds of skin that cover and protect the eye
     from foreign bodies and extreme lighting. The movement of eyelids can be
     both voluntary (e.g., closing eyelids when tired), or involuntary (e.g., blink
     caused by a reflex). To obtain an unoccluded image of the iris, the user is
     required to hold the eyelids wide open for a brief period of time during image
     acquisition. However, under normal conditions, a minor portion of the human
     eye is typically occluded on the top and the bottom, by the upper and the
     lower eyelid, respectively. Figure 7.7 shows an iris image exhibiting eyelid
     occlusion. In such cases, the contour of the limbus boundary is no longer
     circular or elliptical.
   - *Eyelashes*: Eyelashes are the hair at the end of the eyelids. Like eyelids, eye-
     lashes also provide protection to the eye from external debris. Although the
     occlusions caused by eyelashes are minimal, accurate detection of the limbus
     boundary becomes very difficult in the presence of eyelashes. This is due to
     the fact that eyelashes can cause uneven interruptions at the limbus bound-
     ary. Empirical observations reveal that eyelash occlusion is typically more
     pronounced in Asian subjects, due to the presence of the epicanthic fold.
     Figure 7.8 shows an iris image with eyelash occlusions.

2. **Illumination**: The level and the type of illumination (lighting) used, along with
   the eye region on which it is focussed, play an important role in the quality of an
   iris image.

   - *Poor illumination*: Segmenting an iris image acquired under poor illumination
     is extremely difficult because the image may offer minimal or no information
     about the boundaries of the iris. Furthermore, the texture of the iris in such
     images may not be adequately highlighted, resulting in poor recognition per-
     formance. Figure 7.9 shows an iris image acquired under poor illumination
     conditions.

Fig. 7.7 An iris image
showing occlusions caused
by the eyelids

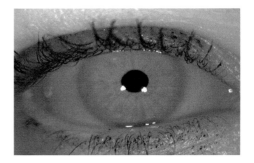

Fig. 7.8 An iris image showing occlusions due to eyelashes

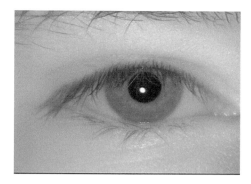

Fig. 7.9 An iris image acquired under poor illumination conditions. Although the iris boundaries can be distinguished by humans, automatic segmentation of such images is extremely difficult

Fig. 7.10 An iris image containing specular reflections on the pupillary boundary

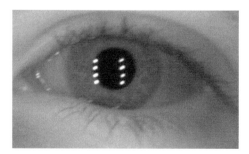

- *Specular reflections*: Specular reflections are small regions in an iris image characterized by pixels of high intensity values that are typically caused by improper focusing of the light source. If specular reflections are present on (or even close to) the iris boundaries, iris segmentation becomes difficult. Figure 7.10 shows an iris image with specular reflections on the pupillary boundary.

3. **User cooperation**: Most iris image acquisition systems require a considerable amount of user cooperation to record a good quality image. In cases where the user cooperation is low, the acquired images can be of poor quality, thereby affecting the segmentation performance.

Fig. 7.11 An off-angle iris
image

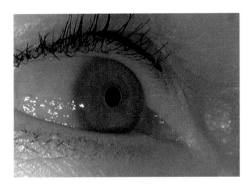

Fig. 7.12 An iris image
containing motion blur

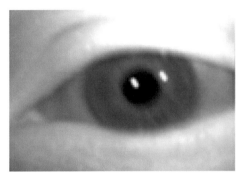

- *Off-angle iris*: Off-angle iris images are caused when the sensor is not orthogonal to the plane of the iris. In such cases, the surface area of the iris is reduced, and the detection of the boundaries becomes difficult. Off-angle iris images are typically caused in situations where the image acquisition is non-ideal, i.e., when the subject is in motion, or not aware of the image acquisition process. Figure 7.11 shows an off-angle iris image.
- *Motion blur*: Motion blur in iris images can occur mainly due to three reasons: (a) when the image is acquired from a moving subject, (b) movement of the camera, and (c) movement of the subject's eye while adjusting to the device and the environment. In images containing motion blur, the intensity variations across the iris boundaries may be reduced, thereby impacting segmentation. Figure 7.12 shows an image containing motion blur.
- *Eye glasses or contact lenses*: If a user wears an eye glass or contact lens, the acquired iris images may suffer from additional reflection artifacts due to these entities. In a cooperative iris recognition system, this problem can be minimized by requesting the user to avoid wearing eye glasses during image acquisition. However, if a subject wears contact lenses (cosmetic/noncosmetic), it may not be convenient for the user to remove them, even in a cooperative iris recognition system. Research has shown that contact lenses can impact the

Fig. 7.13 Iris image of a subject wearing a non-cosmetic, hard contact lens. An automated segmentation scheme may fail to distinguish the iris boundaries from the lens boundary. Image source: Baker et al. [3] ©Elsevier

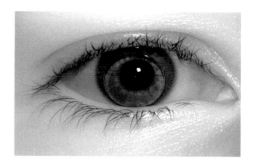

Fig. 7.14 Close-up of an iris image acquired at a large stand-off distance

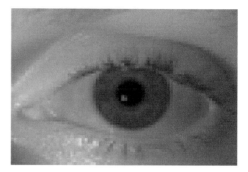

performance of iris segmentation and recognition [3]. Figure 7.13 shows the iris image of a user wearing a contact lens (non-cosmetic, hard lens).

4. **External factors**: Some external factors play a major role in the quality of the input iris images, thereby impacting the segmentation performance.

   - *Stand-off distance*: Stand-off distance refers to the distance of the camera from the subject. If the stand-off distance is large, the resolution (number of pixels occupied by the iris region in an image) can be low. In such cases, the iris boundaries may not be clearly distinguishable. Figure 7.14 shows an iris image acquired at a large stand-off distance.
   - *Image sensors*: The following factors related to image sensors play a significant role in acquiring a good quality iris image:
     a. Resolution of the sensor: A high-resolution sensor that can capture iris images with a minimum diameter of 200 pixels are preferred over other low resolution sensors.
     b. Positioning of the sensor: The positioning of the sensor plays an important role in acquiring an iris image of good quality. For example, if the iris sensor is placed above or below the eye level of a subject, the acquired image may contain an off-angle iris.
     c. Sensor noise: Although not seen as a major factor, sensor noise can produce artifacts in an image, thereby affecting iris segmentation.

(a)   **(b)**

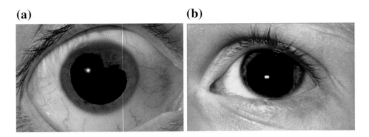

Fig. 7.15 Iris images of subjects suffering from congenital iris abnormalities. Notice that the pupil boundary is neither circular nor elliptical. Image sources: http://scienceroll.files. wordpress.com/2007/06/congenitalirisabnorm.jpg and https://www.studyblue.com/notes/note/n/ iris/deck/7866392

- *Nature of the interacting population*: To acquire a good quality iris image, it is required for the target population to be cooperative and habituated with the iris image acquisition system.
- *Outliers*: In very rare cases, abnormalities in the shape of the iris can cause problems with segmentation. Examples of subjects suffering from congenital iris abnormalities are shown in Fig. 7.15. In such cases, it can be noticed that the iris boundaries are neither circular nor elliptical.

7.4   Classical Iris Segmentation Algorithms

7.4.1   Integro-Differential Operator

The technique proposed by Daugman [9] in the early 1990s is considered to be the pioneering work in the field of automated iris recognition. A vast majority of commercial iris recognition systems worldwide, employ Daugman's approach. In this approach, iris segmentation is carried out using an integro-differential operator. The segmentation process is performed by approximating the iris boundaries as perfect circles.

Given an iris image $I(x, y)$, it is first convolved with an image smoothing function (e.g., a Gaussian filter). This process of smoothening the image helps in (a) attenuating the effect of noise (e.g., sensor noise) in the image, and (b) eliminating undesired weak edges (e.g., boundaries within the iris), while retaining the desired strong edges (e.g., iris boundaries, eyelid boundaries, etc.). An integro-differential operator is then used to search for the maximum value of a normalized integral along circular contours of varying radii and center coordinates. The search process over the image domain (x, y) using an integro-differential operator can be mathematically expressed as:

$$\mathbf{max}(r, x_0, y_0) \left| G_\sigma(r) * \frac{\partial}{\partial r} \oint_{r, x_0, y_0} \frac{I(x, y)}{2\pi r} ds \right|, \tag{7.1}$$

where

$$G_\sigma(r) = \frac{1}{\sqrt{2\pi}\sigma} \exp^{-\left(\frac{(r-r_0)^2}{2\sigma^2}\right)} \tag{7.2}$$

represents the radial Gaussian with a center r_0 and standard deviation (scale) σ, which is used for image smoothing. The symbol $*$ denotes the convolution operation, and r represents the radius of the circular arc ds, centered at the location (x_0, y_0). The division by a factor of $2\pi r$ normalizes the circular integral with respect to its perimeter. In other words, the integro-differential operator behaves as a circular edge detector, that searches iteratively for the maximum response of a contour path defined by the parameters (x_0, y_0, r). Depending on the values of the radii considered, the optimal parameters of the integro-differential operator are treated as either the pupillary or limbus boundaries. Figure 7.16 illustrates the search process using an integro-differential operator.

The value of σ, which controls the amount of blurring of the iris image, can be varied when searching for the pupillary and the limbus boundaries. As the pixel intensity variation across the pupillary boundary is more pronounced, the σ value can be set for a coarse scale of convolution. On the other hand, when the search process is carried out for the limbus boundary, the σ value is set for a finer convolution scale. This is due to the nominal variation of the pixel intensities across the limbus boundary.

In an iris image acquired under near-ideal conditions from a cooperative subject, both the iris boundaries can be easily detected using the integro-differential operator. However, in an image acquired under nonideal conditions, the limbus boundary may not be completely circular due to the occlusions caused by the eyelids. Therefore, when searching for the limbus boundary, the angular arc of integration, ds, is often restricted to the left and right quadrants (i.e., near the vertical edges of the iris). When searching for the pupillary boundary, this arc can be extended over a wider range, as the eyelid occlusions are relatively small. Once both the iris boundaries are

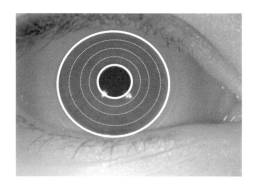

Fig. 7.16 Iris segmentation using the integro-differential operator

Fig. 7.17 Output obtained
by applying an
integro-differential operator
to detect both the iris and
eyebrow boundaries

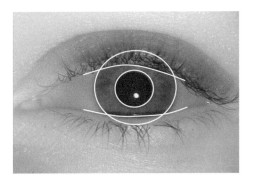

detected, the boundaries of the eyelids can be detected by changing the integration
path of the operator from circular to arcuate. Figure 7.17 shows the output of the
integro-differential operator when used to detect both the iris boundaries and the
eyebrows.

Despite successfully determining the iris boundaries using an integro-differential
operator, the localized iris may be further occluded by other noisy regions such as
eyelashes, shadows, or specular reflections. Therefore, a noise mask[4] that records
the locations of these undesired occlusions is correspondingly generated. This mask
is later used during the matching stage to mitigate the effect of noisy pixels.

7.4.2 Hough Transform

Another widely used classical iris segmentation algorithm was proposed by Wildes et
al. [50, 51]. To detect each iris boundary, the algorithm relies on the Hough transform:
a histogram-based model-fitting approach. First, an edge map of the input image is
generated using a gradient-based edge detector. A voting procedure is then applied
on the thresholded edge map, to determine the parameter values for a contour that
best fits a circle.

Given an iris image $I(x, y)$, the edge map of an input image can be highlighted
by thresholding the magnitude of the image intensity gradient. This operation can be
mathematically expressed as:

$$| \bigtriangledown G(x, y) * I(x, y) | \geq th, \tag{7.3}$$

where $\bigtriangledown \equiv (\partial/\partial x, \partial/\partial y)$, and th denotes an empirically chosen intensity threshold.
$G(x, y)$ represents a two dimensional Gaussian with center, (x_0, y_0), and standard

---

[4]The process of generating a noise mask, and the subsequent schemes for iris normalization and
matching are very similar in a majority of iris recognition algorithms. However, as the chapter
focuses only on iris segmentation, these details are not discussed. The reader is directed to the
original publication by Daugman [9] for further information.

deviation, σ, used for smoothing the image. The purpose of image smoothing is to (a) select the spatial scale of edges under consideration, and (b) reduce the effect of noise on the thresholding process. The mathematical expression for the Gaussian is:

$$G(x, y) = \frac{1}{2\pi\sigma^2} \exp^{-\frac{(x-x_0)^2+(y-y_0)^2}{2\sigma^2}}. \tag{7.4}$$

The image thresholding operation yields an approximate edge map consisting of the iris boundary (along with other prominent edges). In most cases, such an output would consist of noncontinuous, noncircular contours. Therefore, the edge map is thinned using a morphological operation, and a voting procedure is used to determine the parameters of the iris boundaries. Hough transform [21], a standard machine vision technique for fitting simple contour models to images, is typically used during the voting process.

When searching for the limbus boundary contour, the image intensity derivatives corresponding to vertical edges are weighted more during the voting process. This directional selectivity grants preference to the left and right portions of the limbus boundary over its upper and lower portions. Therefore, even if the upper and lower portions of the limbus boundary are occluded by eyelids, the left and right portions remain clearly visible and oriented (assuming the head is in an upright position).

Consider a set of edge points (x_j, y_j), $j = \{1, 2, \ldots, n\}$, obtained by the image thresholding operation. The goal is to determine if a subset of these points are associated with the contour of a circle. A circle can be parameterized as (x_c, y_c, r) where (x_c, y_c) denotes its center and r denotes its radius. The Hough transform detects circular contours in the edge image by defining an accumulator array, H, whose entries $H(x_c, y_c, r)$ are computed as follows:

$$H(x_c, y_c, r) = \sum_{j=1}^{n} h(x_j, y_j, x_c, y_c, r) \tag{7.5}$$

where

$$h(x_j, y_j, x_c, y_c, r) = \begin{cases} 1, & \text{if } g(x_j, y_j, x_c, y_c, r) = 0 \\ 0, & \text{otherwise.} \end{cases} \tag{7.6}$$

and

$$g(x_j, y_j, x_c, y_c, r) = (x_j - x_c)^2 + (y_j - y_c^2) - r^2. \tag{7.7}$$

For each edge point (x_j, y_j), $g(x_j, y_j, x_c, y_c, r)$ is set to 0 if the parameter triplet (x_c, y_c, r) represents a circle through that point. The parameter triplet that maximizes H is considered to be a reasonable choice to represent the contour of interest. The maximizing parameter triplet is determined by first building $H(x_c, y_c, r)$ as an array (indexed by discretized values for x_c, y_c, and r), and then scanning for the triplet that corresponds to the largest value in the array.

The same process (consisting of thresholding and voting) is used to determine the pupillary boundary, but with the following minor modifications:

1. The image is filtered with a gradient-based edge detector that is *not* directionally tuned. This is due to the fact that the pupillary boundary is less prone to occlusion from the eyelids.
2. The permissible parameter values (x_c, y_c, r) are constrained to lie within the circle that describes the limbus boundary.

Once both the iris boundaries are detected, it is necessary to determine the locations of the upper and lower eyelids that may occlude the iris. To perform this operation, a gradient-based edge detector that is tuned to favor horizontal edges is used. This is based on the fact that the contour of the upper and lower eyelids within the limbus boundary would be nearly horizontal (under the assumption that the subject's head is in an upright position). The upper and lower eyelids are modeled as two separate parabolic arcs of the form $x(t) = a_x t^2 + b_x t + c_x$, and $y(t) = a_y t^2 + b_y t + c_y$ with $0 \leq t \leq 1$. The parameters a_x, b_x, c_x, a_y, b_y, and c_y, are once again determined using the same histogram-based model-fitting approach.

7.5 Other Prominent Approaches

Both the aforementioned techniques approximate an iris boundary with a circle or an ellipse. However, such an approximation may not be always suitable. Iris recognition performance can be improved by determining the precise boundaries of the iris, rather than their approximations. Determining the precise boundaries of the iris reduces the noise from occlusions, especially those caused by eyelashes. Figure 7.18 shows the difference between an approximated and a precisely determined iris boundary.

Methods that use curve evolution processes (e.g., Geodesic Active Contours, level sets, etc.) could be extremely beneficial in determining the precise boundaries of an iris. In this section, some such techniques are discussed.

(a)   **(b)**   **(c)**

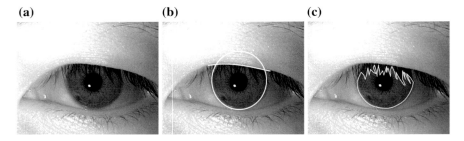

Fig. 7.18 a An eye image in which the limbus boundary is occluded by the eyelashes. **b** Approximate limbus boundary obtained using Daugman's integro-differential operator. **c** Precise limbus boundary obtained by a curve evolution technique. Notice that the precise segmentation helps in avoiding the noise caused by eyelash occlusion

7.5.1 Geodesic Active Contours

This approach, proposed by Shah and Ross [45], is based on the relation between active contours and the computation of geodesics (minimal length curves). The strategy is to evolve an arbitrarily initialized curve from within the iris under the influence of geometric properties of the iris boundary. GACs combine the energy minimization approach of the classical "snakes" and the geometric active contours based on curve evolution.

Let $\gamma(t)$ be the curve, that has to gravitate toward the outer boundary of the iris, at a particular time t. The time t corresponds to the iteration number. Let ψ be a function measuring the signed distance from the curve $\gamma(t)$. That is, $\psi(x, y) =$ distance of point (x, y) to the curve $\gamma(t)$.

$$\psi(x, y) = \begin{cases} 0 & \text{if } (x,y) \text{ is on the curve;} \\ < 0 & \text{if } (x,y) \text{ is inside the curve;} \\ > 0 & \text{if } (x,y) \text{ is outside the curve.} \end{cases} \tag{7.8}$$

Here, ψ is of the same dimension as that of the eye image $I(x, y)$. The curve $\gamma(t)$ is called the level set of the function ψ. Level sets are the set of all points in ψ where ψ is some constant. Thus $\psi = 0$ is the zeroth level set, $\psi = 1$ is the first level set, and so on. ψ is the implicit representation of the curve $\gamma(t)$ and is called the embedding function since it embeds the evolution of $\gamma(t)$. The embedding function evolves under the influence of image gradients and the region's characteristics so that the curve $\gamma(t)$ approaches the desired boundary of the iris. The initial curve $\gamma(t)$ is assumed to be a circle of radius r just beyond the pupillary boundary. Let the curve $\gamma(t)$ be the zeroth level set of the embedding function. This implies that

$$\frac{d\psi}{dt} = 0.$$

By the chain rule,

$$\frac{d\psi}{dt} = \frac{\partial \psi}{\partial x}\frac{dx}{dt} + \frac{\partial \psi}{\partial y}\frac{dy}{dt} + \frac{\partial \psi}{\partial t},$$

i.e.,

$$\frac{\partial \psi}{\partial t} = -\nabla\psi.\gamma'(t).$$

Splitting the $\gamma'(t)$ in the normal $(N(t))$ and tangential $(T(t))$ directions,

$$\frac{\partial \psi}{\partial t} = -\nabla\psi.(v_N N(t) + v_T T(t)).$$

Now, since $\nabla \psi$ is perpendicular to the tangent to $\gamma(t)$,

$$\frac{\partial \psi}{\partial t} = -\nabla \psi . (v_N N(t)). \tag{7.9}$$

The normal component is given by

$$N = \frac{\nabla \psi}{\|\nabla \psi\|}.$$

Substituting this in Eq. (7.9),

$$\frac{\partial \psi}{\partial t} = -v_N \|\nabla \psi\|.$$

Let v_N be a function of the curvature of the curve κ, stopping function K (to stop the evolution of the curve) and the inflation force c (to evolve the curve in the outward direction) such that,

$$\frac{\partial \psi}{\partial t} = -(div(K \frac{\nabla \psi}{\|\nabla \psi\|}) + cK)\|\nabla \psi\|.$$

Thus, the evolution equation for $\psi_t{}^5$ such that $\gamma(t)$ remains the zeroth level set is given by

$$\psi_t = -K(c + \epsilon \kappa)\|\nabla \psi\| + \nabla \psi . \nabla K, \tag{7.10}$$

where, K, the stopping term for the evolution, is an image dependent force and is used to decelerate the evolution near the boundary; c is the velocity of the evolution; ϵ indicates the degree of smoothness of the level sets; and κ is the curvature of the level sets computed as

$$\kappa = -\frac{\psi_{xx}\psi_y^2 - 2\psi_x\psi_y\psi_{xy} + \psi_{yy}\psi_x^2}{(\psi_x^2 + \psi_y^2)^{\frac{3}{2}}}.$$

Here, ψ_x is the gradient of the image in the x direction; ψ_y is the gradient in the y direction; ψ_{xx} is the 2nd order gradient in the x direction; ψ_{yy} is the 2nd order gradient in the y direction; and ψ_{xy} is the 2nd order gradient, first in the x direction and then in the y direction. Equation (7.10) is the level set representation of the geodesic active contour model. This means that the level set C of ψ is evolving according to

$$C_t = K(c + \epsilon \kappa)\mathbf{N} - (\nabla K . \mathbf{N})\mathbf{N} \tag{7.11}$$

where N is the normal to the curve. The term $\kappa \mathbf{N}$ provides the smoothing constraints on the level sets by reducing their total curvature. The term $c\mathbf{N}$ acts like a balloon force

---

[5] The subscript t denotes the iteration number.

and it pushes the curve outward toward the object boundary. The goal of the stopping function is to slow down the evolution when it reaches the boundary. However, the evolution of the curve will terminate only when $K = 0$, i.e., near an ideal edge. In most images, the gradient values will be different along the edge, thus requiring the use of different K values. In order to circumvent this issue, the third geodesic term $((\nabla K . \mathbf{N}))$ is necessary so that the curve is attracted toward the boundary (∇K points toward the middle of the boundary). This term makes it possible to terminate the evolution process even if (a) the stopping function has different values along the edges, and (b) gaps are present in the stopping function.

The stopping term used for the evolution of level sets is given by

$$K(x, y) = \frac{1}{1 + (\frac{\|\nabla(G(x,y) \star I(x,y))\|}{k})^{\alpha}} \tag{7.12}$$

where $I(x, y)$ is the image to be segmented, $G(x,y)$ is a Gaussian filter, and k and α are constants. As can be seen, $K(x, y)$ is not a function of t.

Consider an iris image to be segmented as shown in Fig. 7.19a. The stopping function K obtained from this image is shown in Fig. 7.19b (for $k = 2.8$ and $\alpha = 8$). Assuming that the inner iris boundary (i.e., the pupillary boundary) has

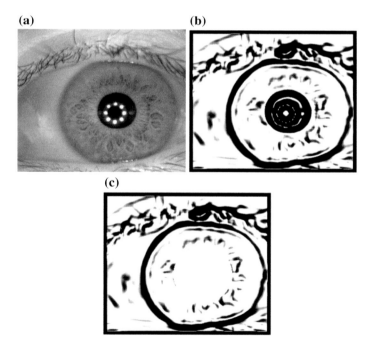

Fig. 7.19 Stopping function for the geodesic active contours. **a** Original iris image, **b** stopping function K, and **c** modified stopping function K'

(a)   **(b)**

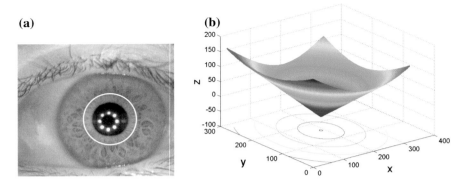

Fig. 7.20 Contour initialization for iris segmentation using GAC. **a** Zeroth level set (initial contour), **b** mesh plot denoting the signed distance function ψ

already been detected, the stopping function K is modified by deleting the circular edges corresponding to the pupillary boundary, resulting in a new stopping function K'. This ensures that the evolving level set is not terminated by the edges of the pupillary boundary (Fig. 7.19c).

A contour is first initialized near the pupil (Fig. 7.20a). The embedding function ψ is initialized as a signed distance function to $\gamma(t = 0)$ which looks like a cone (Fig. 7.20b). Discretizing Eq. 7.10 leads to the following equation:

$$\frac{\psi_{i,j}^{t+1} - \psi_{i,j}^{t}}{\Delta t} = -cK'_{i,j}\|\nabla\psi^{t}\| - K'_{i,j}(\epsilon\kappa_{i,j}^{t}\|\nabla\psi^{t}\|) + \nabla\psi_{i,j}^{t}.\nabla K'^{t}_{i,j}, \qquad (7.13)$$

where Δt is the time step (e.g., Δt can be set to 0.05). The first term $(cK'_{i,j}\|\nabla\psi^{t}\|)$ on the right hand side of the above equation is the velocity term (advection term) and, in the case of iris segmentation, acts as an inflation force. This term can lead to singularities and hence is discretized using upwind finite differences. The upwind scheme for approximating $\|\nabla\psi\|$ is given by:

$$\|\nabla\psi\| = \sqrt{A},$$
$$A = min(D_x^{-} \ \psi_{i,j}, 0)^2 + max(D_x^{+} \ \psi_{i,j}, 0)^2$$
$$+ min(D_y^{-} \ \psi_{i,j}, 0)^2 + min(D_y^{+} \ \psi_{i,j}, 0)^2.$$

where $D_x^{-} \ \psi$ is the first order backward difference of ψ in the x-direction; $D_x^{+} \ \psi$ is the first order forward difference of ψ in the x-direction; $D_y^{-} \ \psi$ is the first order backward difference of ψ in the y-direction; and $D_y^{+} \ \psi$ is the first order forward difference of ψ in the y-direction. The second term $(K'_{i,j}(\epsilon\kappa_{i,j}^{t}\|\nabla\psi^{t}\|))$ is a curvature based smoothing term and can be discretized using central differences. In our implementation, $c = 0.65$ and $\epsilon = 1$ for all iris images. The third geodesic term $(\nabla\psi_{i,j}^{t}.\nabla K'^{t}_{i,j})$ is also discretized using the central differences.

After evolving the embedding function ψ according to Equation (7.13), the curve begins to grow until it satisfies the stopping criterion defined by the stopping function K'. But at times, the contour continues to evolve in a local region of the image where the stopping criterion is not strong. This leads to overevolution of the contour. This can be avoided by minimizing the thin plate spline energy of the contour. By computing the difference in energy between two successive contours, the evolution scheme can be regulated. If the difference between the contours is less than a threshold (indicating that the contour evolution has stopped at most places), then the contour evolution process is terminated. The evolution of the curve and the corresponding embedding functions are illustrated in Fig. 7.21.

Since the radial fibers may be thick in certain portions of the iris, or the crypts present in the ciliary region may be unusually dark, this can lead to prominent edges in the stopping function. If the segmentation technique is based on parametric curves, then the evolution of the curve might terminate at these local minima. However, geodesic active contours are able to split at such local minima are able to split at such local minima and merge again. Thus, they are able to effectively deal with the problems of local minima, thereby ensuring that the final contour corresponds to the true limbus boundary (Fig. 7.22).

7.5.2   Variational Level Sets

Another approach that can be used to precisely determine the iris boundaries is based on variational level sets [42, 43]. This approach uses partial differential equations (PDE) to numerically solve the evolution of the curves that define the iris boundaries. The iris boundaries are first approximated using elliptical models, which are then refined using geometric active contours with variational formulation.

Given an iris image, first an elliptical model with parameters $(p_1, p_2, r_1, r_2, \varphi)$ is used to roughly determine the pupillary boundary. Here, (p_1, p_2) represents the center of the ellipse; r_1, r_2, denote the semimajor axis and semiminor axis, respectively; and φ denotes the orientation of the ellipse. By limiting the values of the semimajor and semiminor axes to a specified range, the other parameters are iteratively varied with a small step size of three pixels to increase the size of the ellipse. At every iteration, a fixed number of points are randomly chosen on the circumference of the ellipse, and the total intensity difference between the chosen points and the center of the ellipse is computed. The boundary with the maximum intensity variation is chosen as the pupillary boundary. A rough contour of the limbus boundary is also determined in the same manner, with a different set of parameters for the semimajor and semiminor axes. Figure 7.23 shows an iris image with the rough contours of the pupillary and limbus boundaries obtained using the elliptical model.

Once the rough contours of the iris boundaries are obtained, the level set approach is applied to determine the precise contours. In the level set approach, the rough contour determined using the elliptical model is used as an active contour C, which can be represented as the zero level set $C(t) = \{(x, y) \mid \phi(t, x, y) = 0\}$ of a level set

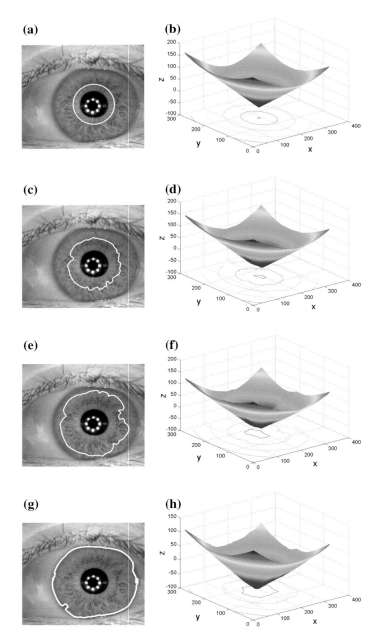

Fig. 7.21 Evolution of the geodesic active contour during iris segmentation. **a** Iris image with initial contour, **b** embedding function ψ (X and Y axes correspond to the spatial extent of the eye image and the Z axis represents different level sets), **c, d, e, f** contours after 600 and 1400 iterations, and their corresponding embedding functions, and **g, h** Final contour after 1800 iterations (contours shown in *white*)

(a)   **(b)**

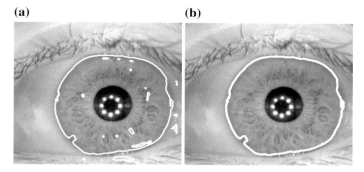

Fig. 7.22 The final contour obtained when segmenting the iris using the GAC scheme. **a** Example of a geodesic contour splitting at various local minima, **b** final contour (contours shown in *white*)

Fig. 7.23 Rough contours of the pupillary and limbus boundaries obtained using the elliptical model. Notice that the rough contours do not precisely match the true iris boundaries. Image source: Roy et al. [43] ©Elsevier

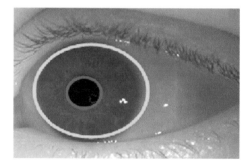

function $\phi(t, x, y)$. The objective of the level set approach is to determine a curve within the level set function, such that the total energy of the curve is minimum. The total energy of the curve is defined by the equation:

$$\varepsilon(\phi) = \mu\rho(\phi) + \varepsilon_{g,\lambda,\nu}(\phi), \tag{7.14}$$

where the parameters $\varepsilon_{g,\lambda,\nu}(\phi)$ and $\rho(\phi)$ denote the external, and the internal energies of the curve, respectively, and $\mu > 0$. The external energy parameter depends on the image data, and drives the zero level set toward the boundary of the desired contour. On the other hand, the internal energy parameter helps in penalizing the deviation of the level set function, ϕ, from the signed distance function during the evolution of the curve.

The internal energy term in the above equation is further defined as:

$$\rho(\phi) = \int_{\Omega} \frac{1}{2}(|\nabla\phi| - 1)^2 dxdy, \tag{7.15}$$

where Ω represents the image domain.

Similarly, the external energy term $\varepsilon_{g,\lambda,\nu}(\phi)$ can be further defined as:

$$\varepsilon_{g,\lambda,\nu}(\phi) = \lambda L_g(\phi) + \nu A_g(\phi), \tag{7.16}$$

where $\lambda > 0$, and ν are constants. The term g denotes an edge detector function, and is defined as:

$$g = \frac{1}{1 + |\nabla G_\sigma * I|^2}, \tag{7.17}$$

where G_σ denotes the Gaussian kernel with a standard deviation of σ, and I denotes the image. The term $L_g(\phi)$ is used to measure the length of the zero level set curve of ϕ, and is given by:

$$L_g(\phi) = \int_\Omega g\delta(\phi) |\nabla \phi| \, dxdy, \tag{7.18}$$

where δ is the univariate Dirac function. The term $A_g(\phi)$ is used to speed up the curve evolution, and is defined as:

$$A_g(\phi) = \int_\Omega gH(-\phi)dxdy, \tag{7.19}$$

where H is the Heaviside function.

The desired evolution equation of the level set function can be obtained by determining the value of $\frac{\partial \phi}{\partial t}$, using the following equation:

$$\frac{\partial \phi}{\partial t} = -\frac{\partial \varepsilon}{\partial \phi}, \tag{7.20}$$

where $\frac{\partial \varepsilon}{\partial \phi}$ represents the Gateaux derivative of ϵ. The value of ϕ that minimizes the total energy function can be determined by satisfying the Euler–Lagrange equation, $\frac{\partial \varepsilon}{\partial \phi} = 0$. The Gateaux derivative of the functional ε can be written as follows:

$$\frac{\partial \varepsilon}{\partial \phi} = -\mu\left[\Delta\phi - div(\frac{\nabla\phi}{|\nabla\phi|})\right] - \lambda\delta(\phi)div(g\frac{\nabla\phi}{|\nabla\phi|}) - \nu g\delta(\phi)). \tag{7.21}$$

Thus, the desired equation of the level set function can be defined as:

$$\frac{\partial \phi}{\partial t} = \mu\left[\Delta\phi - div(\frac{\nabla\phi}{|\nabla\phi|})\right] + \lambda\delta(\phi)div(g\frac{\nabla\phi}{|\nabla\phi|}) + \nu g\delta(\phi)). \tag{7.22}$$

The last two terms on the right hand side of the above equation represent the gradient flows of the energy functional. These terms help in driving the zero level curve toward the boundaries of the required surface. The Dirac function $\delta(x)$ in the above equation is defined as:

Fig. 7.24 Final output
obtained using the
variational level set
approach, where both the iris
boundaries are precisely
determined. Image source:
Roy et al. [43] ©Elsevier

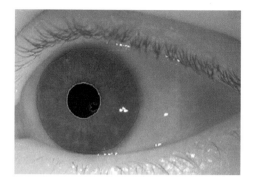

$$\delta_\varepsilon(x) = \begin{cases} 0, & |x| > \epsilon \\ \frac{1}{2\epsilon}\left[1 + \cos(\frac{\pi x}{\epsilon})\right], & |x| \le \epsilon. \end{cases} \tag{7.23}$$

For the active contour ϕ, the curve evolution process for the pupillary boundary is carried out within a small range of ± 10 pixels from the rough contour. For the limbus boundary, this range is increased to ± 20 pixels. The curve evolution process is carried out from the outside of the approximated pupil boundary to avoid the effect of specular reflections. On the other hand, the process is carried out from the inside of the approximated limbus boundary to reduce the effect of eyelids and the eyelashes. Figure 7.24 shows the final output obtained by the variational level set approach, in which both the iris boundaries are precisely detected. Figure 7.25 shows the output of iris segmentation using the variational level set approach on some nonideal iris images.

7.5.3 Fourier-Based Approximation

Daugman [10] suggested the use of the Fourier series approximation in order to deduce the boundaries of the iris. The benefit of such an approximation is that the resulting output satisfies the following expectations:

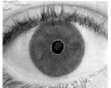   

Fig. 7.25 Output of iris segmentation scheme using variational level set approach on some nonideal iris images from the UBIRIS Version 1 dataset. Notice that the segmentation results are fairly precise. Image source: Roy et al. [43] ©Elsevier

1. *Completeness*: An iris image may exhibit interruptions in its boundaries (e.g.,
   interruptions caused by the specular reflections and eyelids to the pupillary and
   limbus boundaries, respectively). Therefore, the boundary detected by the segmentation algorithm must be robust to such interruptions.
2. *Closure*: Both the iris boundaries detected by the segmentation algorithm are
   expected to continue their trajectory across the interruptions on a principled basis,
   and form closed curves.

In this technique, given an image I, the coarse contour of the iris boundary is
determined using active contours. Let the coarse iris contour be represented by N
regularly spaced angular samples, given by $\{r_\theta\}$, $\theta = 0$ to $\theta = N - 1$. From this
coarse contour, the corresponding iris boundary $\{R_\theta\}$, $\theta = 0$ to $\theta = N - 1$, that satisfies the above two conditions has to be determined. This can be achieved by the
Fourier series approximation of the coarse contour data, expressed as follows:

$$R_\theta = \frac{1}{N} \sum_{k=0}^{M-1} C_k \exp^{2\pi i k \theta / N}, \tag{7.24}$$

where $\{C_k\}$ represents a set of M discrete Fourier coefficients, for $k = 0$ to $k = M - 1$,
determined by the following equation:

$$C_k = \sum_{\theta=0}^{N-1} r_\theta \exp^{-2\pi i k \theta / N}. \tag{7.25}$$

Generally, the zeroth-order Fourier coefficient (or the DC term C_0) describes the
average curvature of the obtained boundary. Since this technique is used for determining the iris boundaries, the zeroth-order coefficient determines the approximate
radius of the output contour.

The value of M represents the number of active Fourier coefficients that are used in
the approximation process. This value represents the number of degrees of freedom
for the shape model of the boundary. In the simplest scenario, i.e., $M = 1$, the model
of the boundary will be circular. The value of M also acts as a trade-off between the
preciseness of the shape versus the strictness of the constraints (which corresponds
to the complexity of the model). A strict set of constraints leads to a complex model,
while a weak set of constraints leads to a simple model. Daugman suggests that
$M = 17$ is a good choice for the pupillary boundary, and $M = 5$ for the limbus
boundary. The two different choices for M are supported by the computer vision
principle that strong data may be modeled with only weak constraints, while weak
data should be modeled with strong constraints. The limbus boundary is considered
as weak data because the occlusions caused by the eyelids and eyelashes are generally
high. On the other hand, the pupillary boundary is considered as stronger data because
the interruptions caused by the specular reflections are relatively minimal.

Figure 7.26 shows the segmentation output obtained using the Fourier-based
approximation. The lower left corner of the image shows a *snake* that corresponds

Fig. 7.26 Iris segmentation
using Daugman's Fourier
approximation approach.
Image source: Daugman [10]
©IEEE. Image has been
edited for clarity

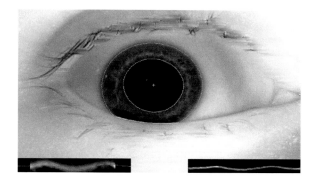

to the limbus boundary. The *snake* on the lower right corner of the image corresponds to the pupillary boundary. Both the snakes consist of two components: (a) a fuzzy ribbon-like data distribution that corresponds to the coarse contour, r_θ, and (b) a dotted curve that corresponds to the Fourier series approximation, R_θ. The characteristics of these snakes can be listed as follows:

1. The endpoints for both the snakes meet at the six o'clock position.
2. The thickness of each snake roughly corresponds to the sharpness of the corresponding edge.
3. The more uninterrupted an iris boundary is, the flatter and straighter the snake will be.

From the lower right corner of the figure, it can be noticed that the curve r_θ corresponding to the limbus boundary exhibits interruptions caused by the eyelid. However, the curve R_θ continues its trajectory even across the interruptions, proving the effectiveness of the approach.

7.6 Visible Wavelength Iris Segmentation

7.6.1 Color Component Features

As mentioned in Sect. 7.2.1, a majority of existing segmentation techniques use near infrared images as their input. Such images typically exhibit higher contrast between the pupil and the iris regions, and induce the usual option of determining the pupillary border. In contrast, visible wavelength images usually exhibit less contrast between the pupil and the iris. This supports the inversion of the order in which the iris boundaries are segmented for visible images. An iris image acquired using a sensor that operates under visible wavelength is shown in Fig. 7.27.

Proenca suggests an approach [37, 38] to perform automatic segmentation of the iris images acquired in the visible wavelength. Furthermore, the approach can

Fig. 7.27 An iris image
acquired in the visible
wavelength. Notice that the
intensity contrast between
the pupil and the iris is low

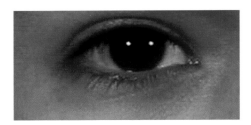

perform iris segmentation on images that are acquired at a large imaging distance
(4–8 m), on the move, and under varying lighting. From the input image, the proposed
technique first detects the sclera, as it is the most distinguishable region even under
varying lighting conditions. Then, the fact that sclera mandatorily lies next to the iris
is taken into account, and the iris regions are detected. A neural pattern recognition
approach is later used to perform the segmentation.

The entire process can be broken down into three stages: detection of the regions
that correspond to the iris; segmentation of the iris; and detection and elimination
of the noisy regions. Given an image I, the sclera region is first detected. This is
because in some images, iris detection is rather difficult. However, due to the naturally
distinguishable appearance (color) of the sclera, it can be detected first by an approach
which analyzes the color spaces of the image. Based on an empirical analysis, the
author suggests three color components: hue (h), blue (cb), and red chroma (cr), that
can characterize information about the sclera. The contrast between the sclera and
the remaining parts of the eye can be maximized using these three color components.

Given an iris image I, a 20-dimensional feature vector is constructed for each
pixel, which can be denoted by the following expression:

$$\{x, y, h_{0,3,7}^{\mu,\sigma}(x, y), cb_{0,3,7}^{\mu,\sigma}(x, y), cr_{0,3,7}^{\mu,\sigma}(x, y)\} \tag{7.26}$$

where x and y denote the position of the pixel, and $h()$, $cb()$, and $cr()$ denote the hue,
blue, and red chroma components of the image at that pixel. The subscript denotes
the radii of the circle that is centered at the pixel. The parameters μ, and σ, denote the
mean, and the standard deviation, respectively, of the set of pixels which fall within
those circular regions. For example, the term $cb_{0,3,7}^{\mu,\sigma}(x, y)$ means that six features
were extracted from regions of the blue color component: three averages and three
standard deviations, computed locally within regions of circles with radii 0, 3 and
7, centered at the considered pixel (x, y). Once the feature vectors for all the image
pixels are calculated for all the images, a neural network classifier is used to obtain
the sclera map. This map indicates the location of sclera in the image.

To detect the iris, the information obtained using the sclera map is used. The author
suggests that a pixel which lies within iris boundaries, when frontally imaged, will
have similar number of sclera pixels on both sides. On the other hand, if the iris is off-
angle, then the number of pixels of sclera on one side will be more than the number of
pixels on the other side. To detect the iris pixels, another feature vector is generated.

The data obtained from the sclera detection stage is used to obtain a new feature, referred to as "proportion of sclera" $p(x, y)$, for each image pixel. This feature helps in measuring the proportion of pixels that belong to the sclera in a direction d, with respect to the pixel at location (x, y). The notation used for the directions are $\uparrow$ for north, $\downarrow$ for south, $\leftarrow$ for east and $\rightarrow$ for west. The feature vectors for each pixel are generated using the proportion of sclera information as follows:

$$p_{\leftarrow}(x, y) = \mu(sc((1, y - 1), (x, y))), \tag{7.27}$$

$$p_{\rightarrow}(x, y) = \mu(sc((x, y - 1), (w, y))), \tag{7.28}$$

$$p_{\uparrow}(x, y) = \mu(sc((x - 1, 1), (x, y))), \tag{7.29}$$

$$p_{\downarrow}(x, y) = \mu(sc((x - 1, y), (x, h))), \tag{7.30}$$

where $sc((., .), (., .))$ denotes the regions of the image cropped from the detected sclera, delimited by the top-left and bottom-right corner coordinates. w and h denote the width and height, respectively. The value of $p()$ is set to 0 for all sclera pixels. The "proportion of sclera" values, pixel positions, local image saturation, and blue chrominance are then used to form a new feature vector represented as:

$$\{x, y, s_{0,3,7}^{\mu,\sigma}(x, y), cb_{0,3,7}^{\mu,\sigma}(x, y), p_{\leftarrow,\rightarrow,\uparrow,\downarrow}(x, y)\} \tag{7.31}$$

where $s()$ and $cb()$ denote saturation and blue chrominance. Once again, the choice of color components is based on empirical evaluation.

Multilayered perceptron feed forward neural networks with one hidden layer are used by both classification stages. The neural network is trained using sample images and its output on a test image is considered to effectively decide the boundaries of the iris. Once the set of image pixels that correspond to a noise-free iris are identified, the goal is to determine the contours of the pupil and sclera of the iris. For this purpose, shape parameterization techniques are used.

7.6.2 Zernike Moments

Tan and Kumar proposed a segmentation approach [46] that is similar to that of Proenca [38], in which the iris is localized by first determining the sclera regions. Given an iris image I, the sclera feature vector at a given location (x, y) is computed as:

$$\{x, y, S_r^{\mu\sigma}, nb_r^{\mu\sigma}, d_{cr-cb(r)}^{\mu\sigma}, d_{RGB}(x_1, x_2), \mu_{RGB}(x, y)\}, \tag{7.32}$$

where S, nb, d_{cr-cb}, d_{RGB} and μ_c denote the saturation, normalized blue, difference of chroma red (cr) and chroma blue (cb), and the mean value of the R, G, B channels, at (x, y) respectively. The term r denotes the radius of the region of interest (ROI) circle centered at (x, y). The superscripts μ and σ indicate the mean and the standard deviation of the considered features within the ROI. The saturation and normalized blue values (i.e., S and nb) are considered after subtracting their mean values within the ROI. The terms d_{cr-cb}, d_{RGB}, and μ_c are computed as follows:

$$d_{cr-cb}(x, y) = cr(x, y) - cb(x, y), \tag{7.33}$$

$$d_{RGB}(x, y) = 2I_R(x, y) - I_G(x, y) - I_B(x, y), \tag{7.34}$$

$$\mu_{RGB}(x, y) = \frac{1}{N} \sum_{c\{R,G,B\}} I_c(x, y). \tag{7.35}$$

The term N represents the total number of color channels in the given image ($N = 3$), and acts as a normalizing factor. Sample images corresponding to various features used in this method are shown in Fig. 7.28. The final feature vectors are then provided as input to an SVM classifier which distinguishes the sclera from non-sclera regions. The iris feature vectors are computed using the localized Zernike moments and sclera information (determined in the previous stage) as follows:

$$\{x, y, I_R(x, y), Z_{mn}^r(I), p_{w,e,n,s}(x, y)\}, \tag{7.36}$$

where I_R represents the red channel of the input image. The term Z represents a function that computes the Zernike moments of I within a circular ROI of radius r, centered at (x, y), given as:

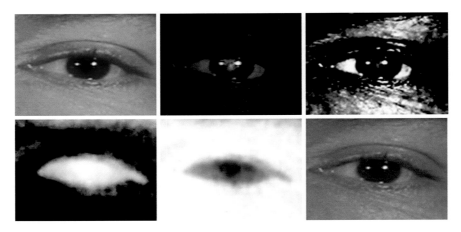

Fig. 7.28 *Top row* (*left* to *right*) Given VIS iris image, saturation component, and normalized blue component, respectively. *Bottom row* (*left* to *right*) Difference of chroma red (*cr*) and chroma blue (*cb*) components, difference of *RGB*, and mean component of *RGB*, respectively. Image taken from [46]

$$Z_{mn} = \frac{m+1}{\pi} \sum_x \sum_y f(x, y)[V_{mn}(x, y)] * dxdy. \qquad (7.37)$$

The subscripts m and n denote the order and angular dependence of the Zernike moments. The term $f(x, y)$ denotes the ROI under consideration and V_{mn} is the Zernike polynomial []. The terms $p_{w,e,n,s}(x, y)$ denote the proportion of sclera in the west (w), east (e), north (n), and south (s) directions, respectively. The values of $p_{w,e,n,s}(x, y)$ can be computed using Eqs. (7.27), (7.28), (7.29), (7.30), respectively. A different SVM classifier is then used to classify image pixels into iris and non-iris regions. The edge maps obtained from this stage are refined to accurately determine the limbus and pupillary boundaries.

7.6.3   Boundary Regularization

The approach proposed by Labati and Scotti performs iris segmentation on *RGB* images by first converting them to gray scale [27]. The segmentation process is divided into multiple stages. Given an iris image I, an Integro-Differential Operator (IDO) is used to determine the rough locations of the pupillary and limbus boundaries [12]. Let the output of this step be denoted by $\{x_p, y_p, r_p\}$ and $\{x_l, y_l, r_l\}$, where (x_p, y_p) and (x_l, y_l) represent the pupillary and limbus boundary centers, and r_p and r_l are their corresponding radii, respectively.

In the next stage, radial *strips* of fixed sizes around both the boundaries are extracted from the gradient image of I. These strips can be perceived as regions encompassed between concentric circles of specific radii around the limbus and pupillary boundaries. A Sobel edge filter is convolved with the iris image I. Let the magnitude and phase of the convolution output be denoted by $G(x, y)$ and $\theta(x, y)$, respectively. A gradient image, $R(x, y)$, with respect to a reference point (x_0, y_0), denoted by $R(x, y)|_{x_0, y_0}$, can then be computed as:

$$R(x, y)|_{x_0, y_0} = G(x, y) \cos(\theta(x, y) - \Omega(x, y, x_0, y_0)), \qquad (7.38)$$

where Ω represents the *angle* image, computed using the following equation:

$$\Omega(x, y, x_0, y_0) = \tan^{-1}[(y - y_0)/(x - x_0)]. \qquad (7.39)$$

The radial strip image corresponding to the pupillary boundary (x_p, y_p) is computed using the equation:

$$R_p(x, y) = \begin{cases} R(x, y)|_{x_p, y_p}, \ \text{if} \ r_p(1 - \alpha) \leq \dots \\ \dots \sqrt{((x - x_p)^2 + (y - y_p)^2)} \leq r_p(1 + \alpha); \\ 0, \ \text{otherwise}. \end{cases} \qquad (7.40)$$

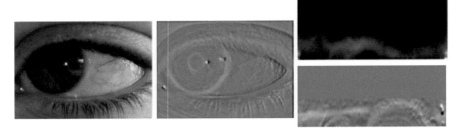

Fig. 7.29 *Left* Given VIS iris image. *Middle* Corresponding gradient image obtained by Sobel edge filtering. *Right top* and *bottom* Radial strip images corresponding to the pupillary and limbic boundaries, respectively. Image taken from [27]

Similarly, the radial strip image corresponding to the limbus boundary (x_l, y_l) is computed using the equation:

$$R_l(x, y) = \begin{cases} R(x, y)\,|_{x_l,y_l}, \text{ if } r_l(1 - \alpha) \leq \ldots \\ \ldots \sqrt{((x - x_l)^2 + (y - y_l)^2)} \leq r_l(1 + \alpha); \\ 0, \text{ otherwise .} \end{cases} \qquad (7.41)$$

The value of α is determined empirically based on a training dataset. The radial strip images, $R_p(x, y)$ and $R_l(x, y)$, in Cartesian coordinates are then unwrapped using Daugman's approach [12] into pseudopolar coordinates, yielding $R_p(\rho, \theta)$ and $R_l(\rho, \theta)$, respectively. Sample radial strip images extracted from a gradient image are shown in Fig. 7.29.

The next step of the algorithm attempts to determine the accurate locations of the limbus and pupillary boundaries from the corresponding unwrapped $R_l(\rho, \theta)$ and $R_p(\rho, \theta)$ images, respectively. To this end, the local maxima along the columns (ρ axis) of the images are computed. This is based on the observation that an iris boundary exhibits high values within the localized radial gradient image. The first approximation of the limbus and pupillary boundaries, $b_p(\theta)$ and $b_l(\theta)$, are computed from $R_p(\rho, \theta)$ and $R_l(\rho, \theta)$, as:

$$b_p(\theta) = \max_{r_p(1-\alpha) \leq \rho \leq r_p(1+\alpha)} R_p(\rho, \theta), \qquad (7.42)$$

and

$$b_l(\theta) = \max_{r_l(1-\alpha) \leq \rho \leq r_l(1+\alpha)} R_l(\rho, \theta), \qquad (7.43)$$

respectively. It is possible that the obtained boundary approximations suffer from abrupt variations in their shape and continuity due to occlusions from eyelashes or eyelids. This is mitigated by applying boundary regularization based on empirical observations. A reliable estimate of pupillary boundary, B_θ, can be obtained from its corresponding approximation $b_p(\theta)$ as follows:

1. Starting from an angle θ_i, all the values of $b_p(\theta)$ that satisfy the inequality $\mid b_p(\theta_i) - b_p(\theta_j) \mid < t_1$ are collected. The term t_1 denotes an empirical threshold, $(i < j)$, and $i = 1 : 1 : N$ where N is the angular resolution of the analysis and is set to $360/N°$. This step helps in identifying the continuous segments.
2. To ensure polar continuity, two segments are merged if the first point of the first segment and the last point of the last segment satisfy previous condition.
3. If $(j - i) > t_2$, the segment is considered to be continuous, and the values $\{b_p(\theta_i), b_p(\theta_{i=1}), \ldots b_p(\theta_j)\}$ are stacked in the vector B. Otherwise, the segment is considered to be discontinues and $(j - i)$ zeros are stacked in B.
4. The above steps are repeated until all the available points within the approximated boundary are processed.

The same procedure is applied on the approximate limbus boundary, $b_l(\theta)$, to determine its corresponding reliable estimate, $B_l(\theta)$. Both $B_p(\theta)$ and $B_l(\theta)$ can exhibit sharp variations in their contours (potentially caused by eyelashes, eyelids, etc.). To this end, boundary smoothing is performed using the Fourier coefficients method suggested by Daugman [10]. In this method, a given iris boundary $B(\theta)$ is expressed in terms of the set of coefficients corresponding to the Fourier Series as:

$$C_k = \sum_{\theta=0}^{N-1} B(\theta) \exp(-j(2\pi/N)k\theta). \tag{7.44}$$

To obtain the smoothing effect, the boundary is expressed using only the first M (instead of N) Fourier coefficients as:

$$\hat{b}(\theta) = \frac{1}{N} \sum_{i=0}^{M-1} C_k \exp(-j(2\pi/N)k\theta), \tag{7.45}$$

where $M < N$. The choice of M regulates the smoothness of the boundary and is determined based on empirical evaluations. A sample iris segmentation output obtained by the regularization process is shown in Fig. 7.30.

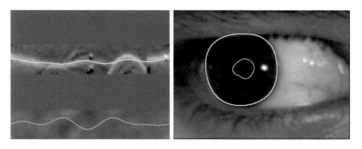

Fig. 7.30 *Left* Regularization output obtained by the segmentation approach. *Right* Segmentation output overlaid on the gray scale version of the input VIS iris image. Image taken from [27]

7.7   Iris Segmentation Approaches Suitable for Varying User Constraints

As mentioned in Sect. 7.2, image acquisition plays an important role in the performance of an iris recognition system. Early iris recognition systems required significant cooperation from the subjects during image acquisition. This helped in acquiring good quality iris images, with minimal or no occlusions. As a trade-off, algorithms with low computational complexity [13, 50] were sufficient for the task of iris segmentation. With an increased demand for accurate iris recognition under practical scenarios (e.g., from a distance, under covert conditions, etc.), the requirements imposed during image acquisition are being relaxed. While this can impart flexibility to the image acquisition process, the quality of the acquired images can reduce drastically. In such cases, complex algorithms may be required to perform segmentation while being robust to the factors mentioned in Sect. 7.3. This section discusses some iris segmentation algorithms, grouped according to the image acquisition conditions they are designed for.

7.7.1   Stationary Subjects, Highly Constrained Conditions

Images acquired under constrained conditions are often expected to be of high quality. This is because the user is typically still and cooperatively offers the iris images. Figure 7.31 shows an image acquisition system which requires significant user cooperation. In such scenarios, the classical algorithms described in Sect. 7.4 have been observed to provide good segmentation performance.

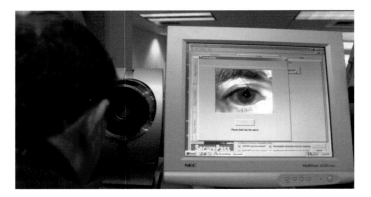

Fig. 7.31 Conventional iris image acquisition system requiring considerable user cooperation. Image source: http://www.life.com/image/1668585

7.7.2 Stationary Subjects, Less Constrained Conditions

The public usage iris recognition system proposed by Negin et al. [35] may be considered to be one of the first systems that attempted to relax the image acquisition conditions. While other iris recognition systems prior to this work required the user to be in close proximity to the sensor, the proposed system allowed a stand-off distance of up to 3 feet. Furthermore, the proposed system allowed for an easy *public setup*, compared to its counterparts. An example of such a public setup could be the use of iris recognition technology to access an Automated Teller Machine (ATM). Even if the user at the ATM does not stand completely still, the system would be able to perform iris recognition during the transaction.

To use the system, the user was required to be reasonably cooperative and focus their gaze toward the system camera. The system would provide feedback to facilitate easy image acquisition of the user's eye. A high-resolution video image of one eye of the user would be captured and used for recognition purposes. The image acquisition setup of the system is shown in Fig. 7.32.

The various steps involved in the working of this system, along with the functioning of the individual components, are provided below:

1. The user stands in front of the system, with a maximum allowable stand-off distance of 3 feet.
2. A wide field of view (WFOV) camera pair is used to capture an image of the user's torso, as shown in Fig. 7.33. The system then applies an image-processing algorithm to locate the eyes of the user.

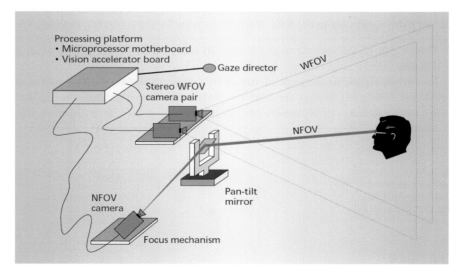

Fig. 7.32 Image acquisition setup for the public use iris recognition system. Image source: Negin et al. [35] ©IEEE

Fig. 7.33 Image of a user's
torso acquired by the WFOV
camera. Image source: Negin
et al. [35] ©IEEE

3. A narrow field of view (NFOV) camera pair is separately used to focus on the
   eye region. The system controls a gaze director to aid the user to look toward
   the camera. A pan–tilt mirror is simultaneously used to direct the optical axis
   of the NFOV camera pair to ensure that the user's eye is focussed properly. As
   infrared illuminators are used during image acquisition, the system could operate
   even if the subject wore eyeglasses, contact lenses, or in a nighttime environment.
   Figure 7.34 shows a sample image acquired at this stage.
4. A circular grid was used as a guide by the system to localize the iris region in the
   image acquired by the NFOV camera. The use of a circular grid simultaneously
   allowed for the exclusion of noisy regions such as the pupil, sclera, and the eyelids.
   The region lying within the grid was used for encoding and recognition. A sample
   image showing the circular grid for localizing the iris region is shown in Fig. 7.35.

While this system relaxed the acquisition conditions only moderately, it is considered to be significant in the field of iris biometrics for the following reasons:

1. This is one of the earliest works related to successful iris recognition from a
   distance.
2. This work highlights the dependency of iris segmentation on the eye detection
   scheme. When iris images are acquired from a distance, it has to be noted that
   eye detection has to be accurately performed to obtain good segmentation performance.

Fig. 7.34 Image of the
user's eye, acquired by the
NFOV camera. Image
source: Negin et al. [35]
©IEEE

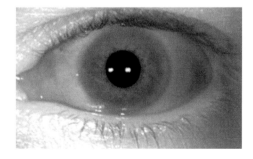

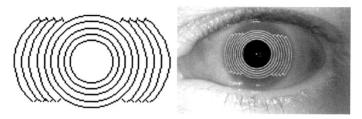

Fig. 7.35 *Left* Circular grid used for iris localization. *Right* Iris image with the circular grid overlaid. Image source: Negin et al. [35] ©IEEE

7.7.3 Moving Subjects Through Portals: Iris on the Move (IOM) Systems

The "Iris On the Move" (IOM) system developed by Matey et al. [34] is considered to be another major development in the field of iris recognition from a distance. The IOM system significantly reduces the constraints on the position and the motion of a user during image acquisition. Such a flexibility is made possible by using an improved image acquisition system, that uses high-resolution cameras and video-synchronized illumination mounted on a minimally confining portal.

The setup of the IOM system consists of a walk-through portal, similar to a metal detector. Near Infrared (NIR) illumination sources, and high-resolution image sensors are fixed to the portal. Images are acquired when a user walks through the portal at a normal walking speed (<1 ms). Stand-off distances up to 3 meters is possible, with a minimum requirement that the user be moderately cooperative. The system can acquire images even when a user wears eyeglasses or contact lenses, but cannot see through sunglasses. The camera used in the IOM system was Securimetrics PIER 2.3, which can acquire iris images with an approximate diameter of 200 pixels. As the heights of subjects can vary by a large factor, the system uses a set of cameras instead of one single camera. The setup of an IOM system is shown in Fig. 7.36.

Fig. 7.36 Image acquisition setup for the iris on the move system. Image source: Matey et al. [34] ©IEEE

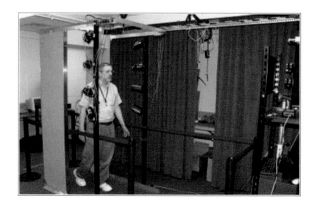

Fig. 7.37 Image acquired
using the IOM system,
exhibiting a specular
reflection pattern that
corresponds to the
illuminator pattern. Image
source: Matey et al. [34]
©IEEE

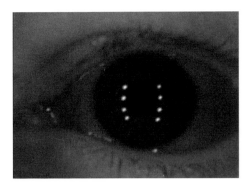

The raw data acquired by the IOM system is typically a set of high-resolution facial images (2048 × 2048 pixels). This is possible due to the high-resolution and wide field of view of the cameras involved. The key requirement of the IOM system is that it should perform image acquisition, segmentation, and recognition in real time. The IOM system is considered to be an industrial application of the iris recognition technology that is expected to serve a large volume of people in short time. To reduce the computational time and processing speed of the system, the authors suggest a segmentation routine which is significantly different from the other segmentation schemes in the literature.

An iris image acquired by the IOM system typically exhibits a pattern of specular reflections on the iris. These specular reflections are caused by the Near Infrared (NIR) illumination system used during image acquisition. The pattern of the specular reflections is strongly dependent on the pattern in which the illuminators are arranged. Figure 7.37 shows a sample NIR image exhibiting the specular reflections that correspond to the illumination pattern.

Instead of ignoring specular reflections as noise, the segmentation scheme in the IOM system, in fact makes effective use of the pattern. A match filter is applied to the captured image producing the highest responses on the in-focus specularities. Once the specularities are detected, a thresholding scheme is used to binarize the image. This process yields an image showing only the locations of the specularities. The border, width, height and center of each specularity is determined in the binary image. As the illuminator pattern is predetermined, specularity patterns that are inconsistent with the illuminator pattern (or those that are oddly shaped) are ignored. For the images that have strong correspondence between the specular reflection and the illuminator patterns, the iris regions around the specular reflections are extracted. Figure 7.38 shows an iris image in which segmentation is performed using the specular reflection patterns.

The contribution of the IOM system in the field of iris recognition is significant for the following reasons:

Fig. 7.38 Iris segmentation using the specular reflection pattern in the image. Once the specular reflection pattern is detected, a specified area around the pattern is used for unwrapping and feature extraction. Image source: Matey et al. [34] ©IEEE

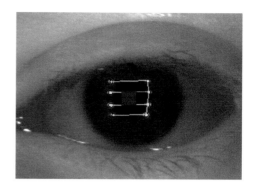

1. IOM is the first image acquisition and recognition system that can work on iris images obtained from users walking at a normal pace.
2. The system allows for real-time recognition while relaxing the constraints imposed on the user, compared to its predecessors.

7.7.4 Unconstrained Conditions

Iris images acquired under unconstrained conditions are often considered to be non-ideal for performing segmentation. This is because of their poor quality, caused by factors such as specular reflections, motion blur, occlusion, off-angle, etc. A relevant scenario that describes such conditions is iris segmentation in images acquired using mobile systems. Recent developments in mobile-based iris recognition indicate the usage of a separate NIR illuminator for image acquisition [8]. However, there has been an increasing interest in performing iris segmentation in VIS images acquired using mobile devices.

7.8 Approaches to Refine Iris Segmentation

One of the major concerns in iris segmentation is the over- or undersegmentation of the iris boundaries. Over segmentation refers to the situation where the radius of the detected iris boundary is larger than that of the actual boundary. On the other hand, under segmentation refers to the situation where the radius of the detected iris boundary is smaller than the actual boundary. Figure 7.39 shows a sample image for each case.

In both cases, the offset between the actual iris boundary and the detected iris boundary is not large. However, such minor offsets can significantly lower iris recognition performance. This is due to the inclusion of noise or regions that do not contain

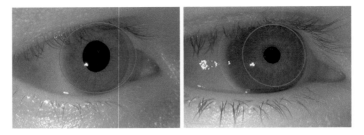

Fig. 7.39 *Left* Oversegmented limbus boundary. *Right* Under segmented limbus boundary

discriminatory texture information (e.g., sclera, eyelashes, etc.). In this section, some approaches are discussed that attempt to refine segmentation by operating on finer details in the vicinity of the iris.

7.8.1 Eyelash Removal in Iris Images

One of the many factors that affect iris recognition performance is the occlusion caused by eyelashes. While some approaches ignore the iris regions occluded by eyelashes [32], others detect the eyelashes and mask them while encoding [11]. On the contrary, the technique proposed by Zhang et al. [53] attempts to restore the iris regions that are occluded by the eyelashes. A nonlinear conditional directional filtering approach is used to perform the restoration. The proposed technique is an iterative approach involving the following steps: (a) detecting the pixels that correspond to eyelash occlusion, (b) detecting the direction of the eyelash that causes the occlusion, (c) local filtering of occlusion region in the direction that is perpendicular to the eyelash, (d) restoring the pixel intensity by using a 1D median filter.

The proposed technique is more suited for unwrapped or normalized iris images, rather than the original iris images. The unwrapped iris images in this work are of size 512×80 pixels, and the top 48 rows of pixels nearest to the pupil are used by the eyelash removal technique. Figure 7.40 shows eyelash occlusion in an unwrapped iris image.

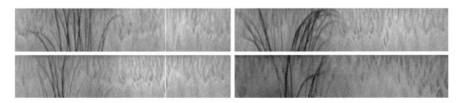

Fig. 7.40 Unwrapped iris images containing eyelash occlusion. Image source: Zhang et al. [53] ©IEEE

-1	-2	-1	z_1	z_2	z_3	-1	0	1
0	0	0	z_4	z_5	z_6	-2	0	2
1	2	1	z_7	z_8	z_9	-1	0	1

Fig. 7.41 *Left* x derivative for a Sobel Edge filter. *Center* image region under consideration. *Right* y derivative for a Sobel edge filter

An eyelash is expected to cause a discontinuity along its edges. Therefore, given an unwrapped iris image I, an eyelash is detected, and its direction is estimated by using an edge filter. For this purpose, a 3×3 Sobel edge filter is applied on the image. A Sobel edge filter is shown in Fig. 7.41.

For each pixel, the gradients in the x and y directions $[G_x, G_y]$ can be determined by the following equations:

$$G_x = (z_7 + 2z_8 + z_9) - (z_1 + 2z_2 + z_3) \tag{7.46}$$

$$G_y = (z_3 + 2z_6 + z_9) - (z_1 + 2z_4 + z_7) \tag{7.47}$$

Similarly, the magnitude of the gradient at the center of the mask, *Grad*, is computed as:

$$Grad = \sqrt{(G_x^2 + G_y^2)}. \tag{7.48}$$

The local gradient direction that is perpendicular to the edge can then be determined by:

$$\theta = \arctan\left(G_y/G_x\right). \tag{7.49}$$

To determine if a pixel is occluded or not, a window of size $m \times n$ is centered at a pixel, and the gradient direction variance for the r pixels that lie within the window and have a *Grad* value above a specific threshold is computed as follows:

$$Var\_Grad = \frac{1}{r-1} \sum_{i=1}^{r} (\theta_i - \overline{\theta})^2. \tag{7.50}$$

A strong edge is indicated if the gradient direction has a small variance, and the pixel is classified as being affected by an eyelash. To restore such a pixel, a 1D median filter of length L is applied along the direction θ. This process outputs an estimate of the value of the image with the eyelash removed.

To avoid incorrectly filtering non-eyelash pixels, pixel alteration is carried out only if the change in the pixel exceeds a certain threshold, related to the total variance of the image. For this purpose, a parameter *Recover* is computed as follows:

$$Recover = Diff - k * Var(Image) \tag{7.51}$$

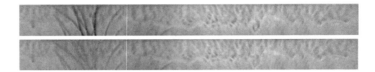

Fig. 7.42 *Top* Image affected by eyelash occlusion. *Bottom* Output obtained by applying the eyelash removal technique. Image source: Zhang et al. [53] ©IEEE

where *Diff* represents the difference in the intensity between the filtered and the unfiltered pixel, $Var(Image)$ represents the intensity variance of the whole unfiltered image, k denotes parameter used to tune the threshold. The pixel is replaced by the filtered value, only if *Recover* is positive. By using this approach, the visual appearance is not significantly changed, but the recognition performance is improved. Figure 7.42 shows an unwrapped iris image before and after applying the approach.

7.8.2 Improving Daugman's Classical Segmentation Algorithm

Libor Masek's MATLAB package [33] is one of the most widely used open source implementations for iris segmentation. For good quality iris images acquired under regular imaging conditions, Libor Masek's implementation results in good segmentation performance. However, Liu et al. [30] showed that the segmentation performance can be further improved by incorporating minor modifications to Libor Masek's implementation. The two most significant modifications that were used to improve the segmentation performance of Libor Masek's implementation are as follows:

1. Reversal of the detection order of the iris boundaries: In Masek's implementation, the limbus boundary is detected first, followed by the pupillary boundary. However, by reversing the detection order, slightly better segmentation performance can be observed. This is based on the fact that the pupillary boundary exhibits strong intensity variation at its boundary, when compared to that of the limbus boundary. By reversing the order, the dependency problem can be minimized.
2. Eyelid detection: Libor Masek's implementation models the eyelids as two horizontal lines. As a result of such an approximation, some of the iris texture can be occluded. The authors suggest splitting the top and bottom eyelid regions into two different portions each as shown in Fig. 7.43, and then performing eyelid detection. As a result of this, the eyelids will no longer be approximated as straight lines but will appear curvy. This modification avoids unnecessary occlusion of the iris during eyelid estimation. Figure 7.44 shows the difference observed in eyelid detection using the proposed modification.

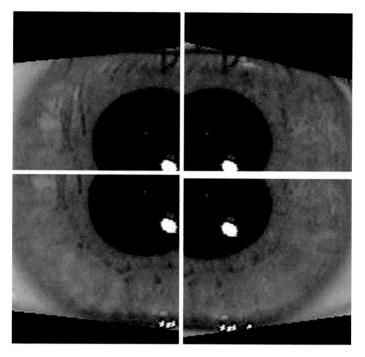

Fig. 7.43 Splitting of the eyelid into four portions to allow better detection of eyelid. Image source: Liu et al. [30] ©IEEE

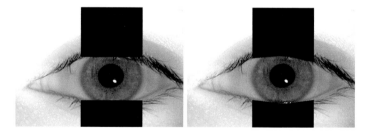

Fig. 7.44 *Left* Eyelid detection using Libor Masek's approach. *Right* Improved eyelid detection using the proposed modifications. Image source: Liu et al. [30] ©IEEE

7.9   Predicting Errors in Iris Segmentation

The performance of an iris recognition system is highly dependent on the output of iris segmentation. If an incorrectly segmented region is used for recognition, the lack of rich distinctive texture can reduce recognition performance. Thus, designing an algorithm that can examine the input image and predict in advance if segmentation is likely to fail or not would be beneficial. Such a scheme can be used to provide feedback during image acquisition, requiring the user to provide a better, more useful image. When acquiring a new image is not a possibility, the image can at least be flagged to avoid being used for recognition purposes. Manual segmentation could then be used to further process such an image. Another possibility is to design an algorithm that can evaluate the output of the segmentation routine and determine if the segmentation has failed or not.

Some algorithms [7, 25] compute the quality of the iris region using local image analysis. However, such algorithms require at least a coarsely segmented iris. If the segmentation is improper, the quality estimate will be incorrect, thus defeating the motive for such an exercise.

Kalka et al. [26] propose an algorithm which evaluates the output of the pupil and iris segmentation routines. The algorithm is based on combining probabilistic intensity features with geometric features to generate scores that indicate the success of segmentation. A decision tree-based machine learning approach is used to render a binary decision: success or failure. The proposed method, therefore, predicts whether the output of segmentation is good (both the pupil and iris boundaries were correctly estimated) or bad (at least one of the boundaries was incorrectly estimated).

The following measures are taken into account:

1. Pupil segmentation measure: One of the major concerns here is related to the over- or undersegmentation of the pupil. To take into account such problems, a probabilistic model is used to fit the segmentation output for the pupil. The output of the model is then used to generate an oversegmentation or undersegmentation score.

2. Geometric iris measure: This is based on the fact that the limbus and pupillary boundaries are actually concentric (circles or ellipses) when they are frontally imaged. Therefore, a measure based on eccentricity and concentricity of the boundaries is taken into account.

Given an iris image segmentation output, the goal is to assign a score to that output, which indicates the "goodness" of segmentation based on the above factors. First, the pupil boundary is checked to establish whether it is over- or undersegmented. For this, consider an image I, and let its pupillary contour be represented as $\bar{x}$. The task is to decide whether the pixels lying within the boundary $\bar{x}$ actually belong to the pupil or not. To this end, a probabilistic model is associated with $\bar{x}$, which formulates a likelihood ratio test, $\Lambda(\bar{x})$, as follows:

$$\Lambda(\bar{x}) = \frac{P(\bar{x} \mid H_1)}{P(\bar{x} \mid H_0)} \geq \eta \tag{7.52}$$

where $H_1 : \bar{x}$ corresponds to a pupil pixel and $H_0 : \bar{x}$ corresponds to a non-pupil pixel. Based on empirical evaluation, the authors use a Gamma distribution $\Gamma(k, \Theta)$, for $P(\bar{x} \mid H_1)$, and a Gaussian distribution $N(\mu, \sigma^2)$ for $P(\bar{x} \mid H_1)$, respectively. The value of the shape parameter k is fixed to 1. To obtain the scale parameter value Θ, the spatial histogram of the image intensities in the region of interest is computed. From the histogram, the scale parameter is estimated as:

$$\hat{\Theta} = \sum_{i=0}^{Bin(P_t)} x_i w_i \qquad (7.53)$$

where P_t) denotes the threshold used to constrain the size of the pupil region, x_i is a gray level bin from the histogram of the region of interest, and w_i is the weight associated with bin x_i. In other words, Θ is obtained by summing the product of the gray level bins and the associated weights until the bin corresponding to P_t is reached. The parameters of the Gaussian are estimated using the following equations:

$$\hat{\mu} = \sum_{i=Bin(P_t)+1}^{Bin(I_t)} x_i w_i \qquad (7.54)$$

$$\hat{\sigma}^2 = \sum_{i=Bin(P_t)+1}^{Bin(I_t)} w_i (x_i - \hat{\mu})^2 \qquad (7.55)$$

where I_t is a threshold used to constrain the size of the iris region, x_i is the gray level bin in the histogram corresponding to the region of interest, and w_i is the weight associated with bin x_i. Thresholds P_t and I_t are determined experimentally. Every pixel within the pupil boundary is assigned a 0 or 1, based on the likelihood ratio test. Once values are assigned to all pixels in the region of interest, the oversegmentation measure P_{over} is computed as the ratio of the number of 0's to that of 1's.

To measure the undersegmentation of the pupil boundary, an iterative approach is employed where the estimated pupil radius (or major and minor axes in case of an ellipse) is increased and it is determined whether the pixels inside the expanded region are pupil pixels by the same approach as above. This process is continued until the pupil radius reaches the size of the iris radius, or the ratio of pupil to non-pupil pixels is less than 20 %. The use of a threshold prevents the influence of heterogenous factors such as dark eyelashes/eyelids and reduces unnecessary computations. The final under segmentation score is defined as follows:

$$P_{under} = \frac{P_{over}}{P_{over} + P_{est\_under}} \qquad (7.56)$$

P_{est_under} is the total number of estimated pupil pixels over all iterations.

To obtain yet another score value for the accuracy of segmentation, the concentricity and eccentricity of the iris and pupil boundaries are used. These values are measured using the following equations:

$$I_C = \sqrt{(p_x - i_x)^2 + (p_y - i_y)^2} \qquad (7.57)$$

$$I_E = \sqrt{(p_x - i_x)^2 + (p_y - i_y)^2} + \arccos\left(\frac{b_i}{a_i}\right) * 100 + \arccos\left(\frac{b_p}{a_p}\right) * 100 \qquad (7.58)$$

Fig. 7.45 Noisy iris images acquired under nonideal conditions which render iris segmentation very challenging. Note that due to poor quality of the image, a high recognition accuracy may not be guaranteed even with an accurate iris segmentation

where (p_x, p_y) are the pupil center coordinates, (i_x, i_y) are the iris center coordinates, b_i and a_i are the semiminor and semimajor axes for the iris ellipse, respectively, and b_p and a_p are the semiminor and semimajor axes for the pupil ellipse, respectively.

Once both the pupil segmentation score and the iris segmentation scores are available, a Naive Bayes tree classifier is used to generate a final score. This final score is binarized to indicate the performance of iris segmentation.

7.10 On the Use of Ocular Information

Iris segmentation can be computationally expensive in the iris recognition pipeline. Complex approaches and subroutines have been increasingly used to accommodate iris recognition using noisy iris images. However, under nonideal conditions, iris segmentation may not always be effective due to the poor quality of the images. Additionally, in such images, a high recognition rate may not be guaranteed even with an accurate segmentation output. Figure 7.45 illustrates some iris images acquired under highly nonideal conditions. Under such conditions, the ocular region (surrounding regions of the eye) may be helpful in improving the recognition performance. A detailed overview of ocular recognition and relevant approaches can be found in [23].

7.11 Conclusion

Segmentation plays a significant role in the recognition performance of an iris biometric system. A majority of algorithms proposed in the literature assume that the input image of the eye is of good quality. However, with an increasing need for faster and accurate recognition systems, the conditions imposed during image acquisition have been relaxed. As a result, the quality of images may be reduced, forcing the need for robust segmentation algorithms that can tolerate a wide variety of image degradations (see Table 7.1). A number of iris segmentation algorithms were discussed

Table 7.1 Well-known iris segmentation techniques proposed in the literature

Author(s)	(Wavelength) Segmentation technique
Daugman [12]	(NIR) Integro-differential operator
Wildes [50]	(NIR) Edge detection and Hough transform
Bole [5]	(NIR) Edge and contour detection
Masek [33]	(NIR) Edge detection and Hough transform
Ma et al. [31]	(NIR) Edge detection and Hough transform
Lim et al. [29]	(NIR) Edge detection and Hough transform
Ma et al. [32]	(NIR) Edge detection and Hough transform
Huang et al. [20]	(NIR) Edge detection and Hough transform
Huang et al. [19]	(NIR) Phase congruency and Hough transform
Yuan et al. [52]	(NIR) Edge detection and Hough transform
Dorairaj et al. [14]	(NIR) Integro-differential operator
Thornton et al. [48]	(NIR) Hough transform
Abhyankar [1]	(NIR) Active Shape Models
Du et al. [15]	(NIR) Scale Invariant Feature Transform
Pundlik et al. [40]	(NIR) Graph cuts
Shah [45]	(NIR) Geodesic Active Contours
Daugman [10]	(NIR) Fourier-based approximation
Roy et al. [42]	(NIR) Variational Level Sets
Zuo [55]	(NIR) Ellipse fitting
He et al. [17]	(NIR) Pulling and pushing model
Boddeti [4]	(NIR) Texture statistics
Hu et al. [18]	(NIR) Iterative directional ray approximation
Proenca [38]	(VIS) Color component analysis
Kumar [46]	(VIS) Zernike moments
Sankowski [44]	(VIS) Edge presence and sclera intensity measurement
Labatti [27]	(VIS) Boundary regularization
Tan et al. [47]	(VIS) Clustering, semantic rules, and Integro-Differential Operator
Almeida [2]	(VIS) Knowledge based successive decision rules
Proenca [39]	(VIS) Color and shape descriptor fusion
Raffei et al. [41]	(VIS) Multiscale sparse representation of local Radon transform
Oroz et al. [36]	(VIS) Mathematical morphology
Frucci et al. [16]	(VIS) Watershed algorithm
Li et al. [28]	(VIS) K-means clustering of gray-level co-occurrence histograms
Jeong et al. [22]	(VIS) Adaboost and color segmentation
Uhl [49]	(VIS) Iterative refinement approach

in this chapter. From this discussion, it is evident that (a) iris segmentation is an important problem; (b) substantial effort has been invested by researchers in solving the problem of iris segmentation under different scenarios; (c) the performance of an iris segmentation algorithm depends upon a number of intrinsic image characteristics including the wavelength of illumination, spatial resolution of the iris, and degree of occlusion; (d) the methodology and computational demands of different iris segmentation algorithms can vary considerably; and (e) evaluating the output of an iris segmentation routine and combining the outputs of multiple iris segmentation methods are ongoing activities in the iris biometric community.

References

1. A. Abhyankar, S. Schuckers, Active shape models for effective iris segmentation, in *Proceedings of SPIE Conference on Biometric Technology for Human Identification III*, vol. 6202, Apr 2006, pp. 1–62020
2. P. Almeida, A Knowledge-based approach to the Iris segmentation problem. Image Vis. Comput. **28**(2), 238–245 (2010)
3. S. Baker et al., Degradation of iris recognition performance due to non-cosmetic prescription contact lenses. Comput. Vis. Image Underst. (2010)
4. V. Boddeti, B.V.K.V. Kumar, K. Ramkumar, Improved iris segmentation based on local texture statistics, in *Asilomar Conference on Signals, Systems and Computers (ASILOMAR)* Nov 2011, pp. 2147–2151
5. W.W. Boles, B. Boashash, A human identification technique using images of the iris and wavelet transform. IEEE Trans. Signal Process. **46**(4), 1185–1188 (1998)
6. C. Boyce et al., in *Multispectral Iris Analysis: A Preliminary Study, Computer Vision and Pattern Recognition Workshop on Biometrics*
7. Y. Chen, S. Dass, A. Jain, Fingerprint quality indices for predicting authentication performance, in *Procedings of the Audioand Video-based Biometric Person Authentication (AVBPA)*, July 2005, pp. 160–170
8. D.M.I.R. Company (2015)
9. J. Daugman, How iris recognition works, in vol. 1 (2002)
10. J. Daugman, New methods in iris recognition. IEEE Trans. Syst. Man Cybern. Part B: Cybern. **37**(5), 1167–1175 (2007)
11. J. Daugman, The importance of being random. Pattern Recognit. **36**(2), 279–291 (2003)
12. J.G. Daugman, High confidence visual recognition of persons by a test of statistical independence. IEEE Trans. Pattern Anal. Mach. Intell. **15**(11), 1148–1160 (1993)
13. J. Daugman, How iris recognition works. IEEE Trans. Circuits Syst. Video Technol. **14**(1), 21–30 (2004)
14. V. Dorairaj, N.A. Schmid, G. Fahmy, Performance evaluation of iris based recognition system implementing PCA and ICA encoding techniques, in *Proceedings of SPIE Conference on Biometric Technology for Human Identification III*, April 2005
15. Y. Du, C. Belcher, Z. Zhou, Scale invariant Gabor descriptor-based noncooperative iris recognition. EURASIP J. Adv. Signal Process. **2010** (2010)
16. M. Frucci, M. Nappi, D. Riccio, Watershed based iris segmentation, in *Lecture Notes in Computer Science* (Springer, Berlin, 2013), pp. 204–212
17. Z. He et al., Boosting ordinal features for accurate and fast iris recognition, in *IEEE Conference on Computer Vision and Pattern Recognition* (2008), pp. 1–8
18. X. Hu, V. Pauca, R. Plemmons, Iterative directional ray based iris segmentation for challenging periocular images, in *Biometric Recognition, Lecture Notes in Computer Science*, vol. 7098 (Springer, Berlin, 2011), pp. 91–99

19. J. Huang et al., A new iris segmentation method for recognition. in *Proceedings of the 17th International Conference on Pattern Recognition (ICPR)*, vol. 3, Aug 2004, pp. 23–26

20. J. Huang et al., Iris model based on local orientation description, in *Proceedings of Asian Conference on Computer Vision*, Apr 2004, pp. 954–959

21. J. Illingworth, J. Kittler, A survey of the Hough transform. Comput. Vis. Graph. Image Process. **44**(1), 87–116 (1988)

22. D. Jeong et al., A new iris segmentation method for non-ideal iris images. Image Vis. Comput. **28**(2), 254–260 (2010)

23. R. Jillela, Techniques for Ocular Biometric Recognition under Non-ideal Conditions. West Virginia University: Ph.D. Dissertation (2013)

24. R. Jillela, A. Ross, Segmenting iris images in the visible spectrum with applications in mobile biometrics. Pattern Recognit. Lett. **57**, 4–16 (2015)

25. N.D. Kalka et al., Proceedings of the SPIE conference on biometric technologies for human identification III, in *Image Quality Assessment for Iris Biometric* (2006), pp. 1–11

26. N. Kalka, N. Bartlow, B. Cukic, An automated method for predicting iris segmentation failures, in Sept 2009, pp. 1–8

27. R. Labati, F. Scotti, Noisy iris segmentation with boundary regularization and reflections removal. Image Vis. Comput. (IVC) **28**(2), 270–277 (2010)

28. P. Li et al., Robust and accurate iris segmentation in very noisy iris images. Image Vis. Comput. **28**(2), 246–253 (2010)

29. S. Lim et al., Efficient iris recognition through improvement of feature vector and classifier. J. Electron. Telecommun. Res. Inst. **33**(2), 61–70 (2001)

30. X. Liu, K. Bowyer, P.J. Flynn, Experiments with an improved iris segmentation algorithm, in Oct 2005, pp. 118–123

31. L. Ma, Y. Wang, T. Tan, Iris recognition using circular symmetric filters, in *Proceedings of the 16th International Conference on Pattern Recognition (ICPR)*, vol. 2, Aug 2002, pp. 805–808

32. L. Ma et al., Efficient iris recognition by characterizing key local variations. IEEE Trans. Image Process. **13**(6), 739–750 (2004)

33. L. Masek, P. Kovesi, MATLAB Source Code for a Biometric Identification System Based on Iris Patterns. Tech. rep. The School of Computer Science and Software Engineering, The University of Western Australia (2003)

34. J. Matey et al., Iris on the move: acquisition of images for iris recognition in less constrained environments. Proc. IEEE **94**(11), 1936–1947 (2006)

35. M. Negin et al., An iris biometric system for public and personal use. Computer **33**(2), 70–75 (2000)

36. M. Oroz, E. Faure, J. Angulo, Robust iris segmentation on uncalibrated noisy images using mathematical morphology. Image Vis. Comput. **28**(2), 278–284 (2010)

37. H. Proenca, Iris recognition: a method to segment visible wavelength iris images acquired on-the-move and at-a-distance, in *ISVC 2008: 4th International Symposium on Visual Computing*, vol. 1, Dec 2008, pp. 731–742

38. H. Proenca, Iris recognition: on the segmentation of degraded images acquired in the visible wavelength. IEEE Trans. Pattern Anal. Mach. Intell. **32**(8), 1502–1516 (2010)

39. H. Proenca, G. Santos, Fusing color and shape descriptors in the recognition of degraded iris images acquired at visible wavelengths. Comput. Vis. Image Underst. **116**(2), 167–178 (2012)

40. S.J. Pundlik, D.L. Woodard, S.T. Birchfield, Non-ideal iris segmentation using graph cuts, in *IEEE Computer Society Conference on Computer Vision and Pattern Recognition Workshops*, June 2008, pp. 1–6

41. A. Raffei et al., Feature extraction for different distances of visible reflection iris using multiscale sparse representation of local radon transform. Pattern Recognit. **46**(10), 2622–2633 (2013)

42. K. Roy, P. Bhattacharya, Variational level set method and game theory applied for nonideal iris recognition, in *Proceedings of the International Conference on Image Processing (ICIP)* (2009), pp. 2721–2724

43. K. Roy, P. Bhattacharya, C.Y. Suen, Iris segmentation using variational level set method. Optics Lasers Eng. **49**(4), 578–588 (2011)
44. W. Sankowski et al., Reliable algorithm for iris segmentation in eye image. Image Vis. Comput. **28**(2), 231–237 (2010)
45. S. Shah, A. Ross, Iris segmentation using geodesic active contours. IEEE Trans. Inf. Forensics Secur. (TIFS) **4**(4), 824–836 (2009)
46. C. Tan, A. Kumar, Automated segmentation of iris images using visible wavelength face images, in *IEEE Computer Society Conference on Computer Vision and Pattern Recognition Workshops (CVPRW)*, June 2011, pp. 9–14
47. T. Tan, Z. He, Z. Sun, Efficient and robust segmentation of noisy iris images for non-cooperative iris recognition. Image Vis. Comput. **28**(2), 223–230 (2010)
48. J. Thornton, M. Savvides, B.V.K.V. Kumar, Robust iris recognition using advanced correlation techniques, in *Conference on Image Analysis and Recognition (ICIAR)*, vol. 3656, Sept 2005, pp. 1098–1105
49. A. Uhl, P. Wild, Multi-stage visible wavelength and near infrared iris segmentation framework, in *Image Analysis and Recognition, Lecture Notes in Computer Science*, vol. 7325 (2012), pp. 1–10
50. R. Wildes, Iris recognition: an emerging biometric technology. Proc. IEEE **85**(9), 1348–1363 (1997)
51. R. Wildes et al., A system for automated iris recognition, in *Proceedings of the Second IEEE Workshop on Applications of Computer Vision*, Dec 1994, pp. 121–128
52. X. Yuan, P. Shi, Iris feature extraction using 2D phase congruency, in *Third International Conference on Information Technology and Applications (ICITA)*, vol. 33, July 2005, pp. 437–441
53. D. Zhang, D. Monro, S. Rakshit, Eyelash removal method for human iris recognition, in *ICIP06* (2006), pp. 285–288
54. J. Zuo, N. Kalka, N. Schmid, A robust IRIS segmentation procedure for unconstrained subject presentation, in Aug 2006, pp. 1–6
55. J. Zuo, N. Schmid, On a methodology for robust segmentation of nonideal iris images. IEEE Trans. Syst. Man Cybern. Part B: Cybern. **40**(3), 703–718 (2010)

Chapter 8
Iris Recognition with Taylor Expansion Features

Algirdas Bastys, Justas Kranauskas and Volker Krüger

Abstract The random distribution of features in an iris image texture allows to perform iris-based personal authentication with high confidence. In this chapter we describe three iris representations. The first one is a phase-based iris texture representation which is based on a binarized multi-scale Taylor expansion. The second one describes the iris by using the most significant local extremum points of the first two Taylor expansion coefficients. The third method is a combination of the first two representations. For all methods we provide efficient similarity measures which are robust to moderate iris segmentation inaccuracies. Using three public iris datasets, we show (a) the compact template size of the first two representations and (b) their effectiveness: the first two representations alone perform well already, but in combination, they outperform state-of-the-art iris recognition approaches significantly.

8.1   Introduction

Iris images have a complex texture of visible particles of different sizes. The particles come from freckles, furrows, stripes, coronas, occluding eyelashes, etc. The distribution of these particles on the iris in terms of their locations, shapes, and sizes is random and differs from eye to eye which is the reason why iris images are such an effective biometric for verification and identification.

Generally, there are three different types of approaches to capture the individual distribution of particles on the iris: phase-based techniques [7–10, 20], techniques based on zero-crossings [4, 21, 27, 28], and more intuitive iris texture descriptors [15, 23, 29–31, 33]. Despite the seeming differences in phase, zero-crossing, and texture-based iris descriptors the approaches are all closely related. For example, all

A. Bastys · J. Kranauskas
Vilnius University, Vilnius, Lithuania
e-mail: algirdas.bastys@mif.vu.lt

V. Krüger (✉)
Aalborg University, Aalborg, Denmark
e-mail: vok@rvmi.aau.dk

© Springer-Verlag London 2016
K.W. Bowyer and M.J. Burge (eds.), *Handbook of Iris Recognition*,
Advances in Computer Vision and Pattern Recognition,
DOI 10.1007/978-1-4471-6784-6_8

three iris descriptions preserve information about the original image texture with a large likelihood.

In this book chapter, we present results of using a multi-scale Taylor expansion of the iris pattern [3] from which we are computing local extrema and phase information.

Phase-based iris recognition algorithms are the most popular ones and show good speed and verification performances (see [7–10, 20]). Our phase-based iris representation uses features that are computed from a binarized multi-scale Taylor expansion. Our phase information is an iris code in which 0 codes a negative and 1 codes a positive sign of the expansions [3].

Local extrema of wavelet, Gabor, or other expansions for iris recognition were used earlier [1, 16, 17]. But, e.g., unlike the 1D local extrema as used in [16], we use 2D local extrema points of the multi-scale expansion. Such an approach reduces the size of the iris template which is important for efficient processing in large-scale applications, and it eliminates correlations of the local extrema points along the radial direction which improves reliability. Furthermore, the first two coefficients of the multi-scale Taylor expansion have a transparent interpretation and they can be computed very efficiently. Our local extrema are computed from approximations of the first- and second- order Taylor coefficients of the multi-scale Taylor expansion [2, 3], averaged over different scales. The most significant local extrema of the Taylor expansions define the most significant iris texture variations.

As we will show in our experiments, the 2D local extrema and the phase-based approaches alone reach very good results already, but, interestingly, their combination reaches one of the highest recognition rate on the databases Casia2.0, ICE-1 and MBGC-3l.

For all methods, we employ efficient and elastic iris template matching schemes [13, 26] that allow to compensate for slight segmentation and localization errors of the iris features and assure efficient processing.

The chapter is structured as follows: we will briefly discuss the automatic segmentation used for preprocessing of the database images in Sect. 8.2. In Sects. 8.3, 8.3.2 and 8.3.3 we discuss the binary and the local extrema-based iris representations. In Sect. 8.3.4 we discuss the elastic matching scheme for the phase-based approach and the efficient matching scheme for the local extrema-based approach. The joint distance measure is a combination of the phase-based and the local extrema-based distance measures and it is discussed in Sect. 8.4. The thorough evaluation for all three approaches is provided in Sect. 8.4. We conclude with final remarks in Sect. 8.5.

8.2 Segmentation

The iris segmentation process consists of mainly three steps [2, 3]: (1) localizing the inner and outer boundaries of the iris, (2) the optional detection of occluding upper and lower eyelids, and (3) the detection and removal of reflections on the cornea or the eyeglasses. For iris segmentation, we use standard state-of-the-art image processing techniques (see also [11] for a general overview on eye detection.).

Fig. 8.1 Approximation of
the inner and outer iris
boundaries by convex
contours. The iris image is
taken from the Casia V3
interval database. Figure
reproduced with permission
from [3]

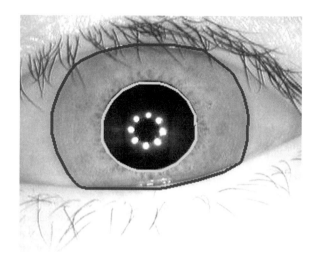

Figure 8.1 illustrates a typical segmentation result, the contours are approximated by short Fourier series.

8.3   Iris Features from Multi-scale Taylor Expansion

In this section we discuss the two Taylor-based approaches in detail. For both the approaches, we use the first two coefficients of the Taylor expansion that models the iris at different radii and scales. We compute the binary features by thresholding and binarizing the first two Taylor coefficients. For the local extrema approach, we use the local extrema points of the first two Taylor coefficients on different scales.

In the following, we give a brief overview of the Taylor expansion as far as we need it for understanding the later discussions. In Sect. 8.3.2, we discuss the binary features and Sect. 8.3.3 goes into the details of the local extrema-based features.

8.3.1   Brief Introduction to the Taylor Expansion

Consider the one-dimensional iris pattern at a specific pseudo-polar radius $r = const$ as an analytic one-dimensional signal $u = u(x)$ where x denotes the pseudo-polar angle. Then, we are able to express the iris pattern using a classic Taylor series expansion centered on any fixed point $x = x_i$. The zero coefficient of the expansion, given by $u(x_i)$, is strongly illumination dependent and will not use it. The first- and second-order coefficients are given as $\frac{u'(x_i)}{1!}$ and $\frac{u''(x_i)}{2!}$. The first derivative $u'(x)$ measures the transition rate of the signal around point x, i.e., a big positive value of $u'(x)$ reflects a fast increasing transition of the signal around point x and a big negative $u'(x)$ reflects a fast decay around the same point. The sign of the second derivative $u''(x)$ provides information about the type of concavity of a graph $\{x, u(x)\}$ around x, i.e., if $u''(x) > 0$ then $\{x, u(x)\}$ is concave upward and if $u''(x) < 0$ then the graph $\{x, u(x)\}$ is concave downward around point x.

At a local negative minimum or positive maximum of the first derivative, the second derivative will have a zero-crossing. Note that the derivatives $u'(x)$ and $u''(x)$ can be estimated only numerically and therefore results of the approximations significantly depend on the scale at which variations of the signal are estimated. As pointed out above, we neglect the 0-th order Taylor coefficients of $u(x_i)$ because of their illumination dependency. The first two terms of the Taylor series expansion define the local linear and the quadratic behavior of u around the point of the expansion. Extrema of the first derivative indicate points where the signal u has its greatest local asymmetry. Similarly, extrema of second derivative indicate points of great local symmetry of u. It is interesting to note that the real part of the familiar Gabor response at a point x is similar to the second-order Taylor coefficient centered at the point x, and imaginary part the Gabor response is alike to the first- order Taylor coefficient.

Let us give a formal definitions. The well-known Taylor series expansion

$$u(x) = \sum_{n=0}^{\infty} \frac{u^{(n)}(a)}{n!}(x-a)^n \tag{8.1}$$

assures us that a sufficiently regular function u can be reconstructed from its Taylor coefficients $\frac{u^{(n)}(a)}{n!}$. In theory, Taylor coefficients can be derived from the $u(x)$ values known at any narrow surrounding of the center point $x = a$. Let us consider some details of the estimation at different scales of the first two derivatives of the iris texture. The estimation technique of the derivatives at different scales is similar to the wavelet multi-resolution analysis. Let us consider some even smooth density $p = p(x) \geq 0$ that has its maximum at $x = 0$ and a normalized L_1 energy

$$\int_{-\infty}^{\infty} p(x)\,dx = 1 . \tag{8.2}$$

Let us fix some scale $\sigma > 0$ and consider the convolutions

$$(u' * D_\sigma p)(x) = 1/\sigma \int_{-\infty}^{\infty} p(\xi/\sigma)u'(\xi - x)\,d\xi \tag{8.3}$$

and

$$(u'' * D_\sigma p)(x) = 1/\sigma \int_{-\infty}^{\infty} p(\xi/\sigma)u''(\xi - x)\,d\xi , \tag{8.4}$$

where D_σ is the dilation operator for a given scale σ. We can observe that for a larger scale σ the blurring of the signals $u'(x)$ and $u''(x)$ increases. If σ vanishes, then $(u' * D_\sigma p)(x)$ and $(u'' * D_\sigma p)(x)$ converge to $u'(x)$ and $u''(x)$, respectively.

The density $p = p(x)$ defines the rule for averaging the derivatives. A function meeting the requirements of p is $\mathrm{sech}(x) = 2/(e^x + e^{-x})$: It has the required symmetry, tends exponentially to zero at infinity and its L_1 norm equals to π. Therefore, we use the following density function

$$p(x) = \frac{\mathrm{sech}(x)}{\pi} .$$ (8.5)

The iris texture along the angular direction can be described as a discrete periodic sequence $u_i = u(i)$ of some length NX. Defining $u(x)$ through linear interpolation $u(x) = u_i + (x - i)(u_{i+1} - u_i)$, $x \in [i, i + 1)$, we have

$$u''(x) = \sum_{i=-\infty}^{\infty} (u_{i+1} - 2u_i + u_{i-1})\delta(x - i)$$ (8.6)

and

$$\begin{aligned}
(u'' * D_\sigma p)(x) &= \frac{1}{\sigma} \sum_{i=-\infty}^{\infty} (u_{i+1} - 2u_i + u_{i-1}) p(\frac{x+i}{\sigma}) \\
&= \sum_{i=0}^{NX-1} \Delta u_i p_\sigma^{NX}(x + i) \\
&= \sum_{i=0}^{NX-1} u_i \Delta p_\sigma^{NX}(x + i).
\end{aligned}$$ (8.7)

Here, $\delta(x)$ is Dirac's delta function,

$$\Delta u_i = u(i + 1) - 2u(i) + u(i - 1),$$ (8.8)

and

$$p_\sigma^{NX}(x) = \frac{\sum_{i=-\infty}^{\infty} p(\frac{x+i*NX}{\sigma})}{\sigma}.$$ (8.9)

Similarly, for the first derivative we have

$$(u' * D_\sigma p)(j) = - \sum_{i=0}^{NX-1} \Delta u_i q^{NX} \sigma(j + i),$$

$$q_\sigma^{NX}(x) = \sum_{i=-\infty}^{\infty} 2 \arctan(\frac{x + i * NX}{\sigma}).$$ (8.10)

Table 8.1 Derivatives and averaging parameters used in derivation of multi-scale Taylor expansion and local features

Scale and filter type index s	Blurred derivative	$\sigma_x = \sigma$ of horizontal direction	$\sigma_y = \sigma$ of vertical direction
0	u_x	$\frac{6}{8}$	$\frac{1}{2}$
1	u_x	$\frac{9}{8}$	$\frac{1}{2}$
2	u_x	$\frac{15}{8}$	$\frac{1}{2}$
3	u_{xx}	$\frac{9}{8}$	$\frac{1}{2}$
4	u_{xx}	$\frac{15}{8}$	$\frac{1}{2}$
5	u_{xx}	$\frac{24}{8}$	$\frac{1}{2}$
6	u_y	$\frac{1}{2}$	$\frac{9}{8}$
7	u_{yy}	$\frac{1}{2}$	$\frac{15}{8}$

Due to the symmetry of the density function (8.5), Eq. (8.7) defines a filtration of the 1D data $\{u_i\}$ by an even-symmetric filter and (8.10) defines an odd-symmetric filter. In wavelet terminology the even and odd filters have two and one vanishing moments, respectively. The proposed filters have more freedom in choosing the basic function $p^\sigma = p^\sigma(x)$ than the dyadic wavelet filtration, and they do not have dyadic restrictions for the scale σ. To regularize the filtration results that approximate second- (even filters) or first (odd filters)-order derivatives at different scales σ, we apply smoothing in the orthogonal direction by using the same density $p^\sigma = p^\sigma(y)$ but with a smaller scale value σ'.

Table 8.1 summarizes the scales, type of symmetries, and directions that we have used to calculate the differences. The differences calculated along the x and y axis correspond to horizontal and vertical type filters. Derivatives in x direction were estimated at 3 different scales while derivatives in y direction were estimated only at 1 scale. The number of derivatives along angular and radial directions were chosen experimentally. It seems that derivatives along radial (y) direction are less useful since sometimes they enhance the edges from undetected eyelids or pupil/iris boundary. These segmentation errors lead to increased interclass similarity.

8.3.2 Binary Features as Local Iris Features

Following Daugman's traditions, we define the iris binary features simply by binarizing the blurred first- and second-order Taylor coefficients u_x, u_{xx}, u_y, and u_{yy}. To be precise, consider the points (i, j) belonging to the iris region bounded by the two convex iris contours. If after blurring with scales σ_x and σ_y, we have $u_x(i, j) > 0$ at a point (i, j) then we set the binary feature $(u_x)_{i,j} = 1$. If we have for the same conditions $u_x(i, j) < 0$, then the binary feature is set to $(u_x)_{i,j} = 0$. Finally, if the point (i, j) does not belong to the iris region bounded by two convex contours or if $u_x(i, j) = 0$, then the binary feature $(u_x)_{i,j}$ is chosen randomly with equal probability.

Different from binary features that are used to describe the phase of Gabor responses, our binary features have a transparent interpretation. For example, if u_x has the value $(u_x)_{i,j} = 1$ when blurred at scales σ_x and σ_y it means that the iris texture at scale σ_x and σ_y increases along angular direction around (i, j) point. If, on the other hand, $(u_{yy})_{i,j} = 0$, one can state that the iris texture is concave along radial direction around (i, j) point. A random definition of binary features occurs at points that correspond to regions of iris texture that is occluded by eyelids or that are located in areas with constant gray values. For example, in specular reflection regions one can have $u(x, y) \equiv 255$ that leads to $u_x(x, y) \equiv 0$ and $u_y(x, y) \equiv 0$. The random definition of binary features at problematic iris regions reduces iris interclass similarity variation and avoids iris similarity scores normalization problem that arises when binary features corresponding to eyelids and eyelashes are ignored in similarity evaluation (Fig. 8.2).

Since we are using eight different continuous two-dimensional multi-scale Taylor expansion coefficients (see Table 8.1) we are obtaining eight binary maps after binarization. Figure 8.3, top, illustrates 240861.tiff and 243395.tiff iris images of NIST ICE2005 iris dataset and their unwrapped versions (Fig. 8.3, bottom). These two images constitute a genuine pair. Figure 8.4 shows the eight binary maps of the multi-scale Taylor features of the two unwrapped iris images from Fig. 8.3. The white and black pixels indicate locations of positive and negative averaged first- and second-order Taylor coefficients, respectively. Combining at any fixed location (i, j) eight bits of binary features we form a byte type feature

$$\mathbf{f}[i][j] = \sum_{k=0}^{7} \{\text{feature bit of k-th binary map at position } (i, j)\}2^k. \qquad (8.11)$$

Fig. 8.2 The iris is divided into the different sectors 0 . . . 15. Figure reproduced with permission from [3]

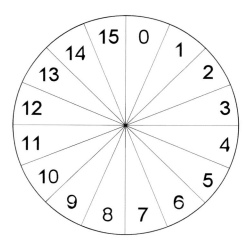

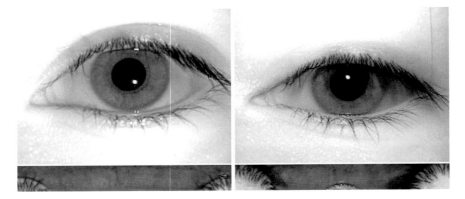

Fig. 8.3 240861 and 243395 iris images from the NIST ICE2005 dataset (*above*). Unwrapped 240861 and 243395 iris images (*below*). Figure reproduced with permission from [3]

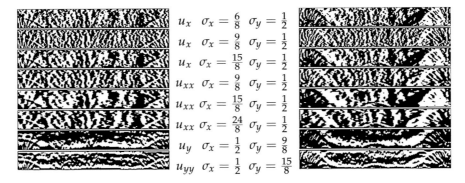

$$u_x \quad \sigma_x = \tfrac{6}{8} \quad \sigma_y = \tfrac{1}{2}$$
$$u_x \quad \sigma_x = \tfrac{9}{8} \quad \sigma_y = \tfrac{1}{2}$$
$$u_x \quad \sigma_x = \tfrac{15}{8} \quad \sigma_y = \tfrac{1}{2}$$
$$u_{xx} \quad \sigma_x = \tfrac{9}{8} \quad \sigma_y = \tfrac{1}{2}$$
$$u_{xx} \quad \sigma_x = \tfrac{15}{8} \quad \sigma_y = \tfrac{1}{2}$$
$$u_{xx} \quad \sigma_x = \tfrac{24}{8} \quad \sigma_y = \tfrac{1}{2}$$
$$u_y \quad \sigma_x = \tfrac{1}{2} \quad \sigma_y = \tfrac{9}{8}$$
$$u_{yy} \quad \sigma_x = \tfrac{1}{2} \quad \sigma_y = \tfrac{15}{8}$$

Fig. 8.4 Eight binary maps of multi-scale Taylor expansion of unwrapped 240861 and 243395 iris images. *White* pixels correspond to binary one and *black pixels* to binary zero. Figure reproduced with permission from [3]

Here, indexes i and j correspond to the unwrapped angular and radial positions. After some experimentation, we found that an iris template size of 256×32 gives the best compromise between speed and accuracy for the iris template matching. We will assume this iris template size ($256 \times 32 = 8192$ [byte]) in the description of iris template matching technique in Sect. 8.3.4.

8.3.3 Local Extrema as Iris Features

It is the coefficients with largest squared values in the Taylor expansion and in the wavelet transform that give the main contribution for the approximation of the original signal. Thus, we use local extrema (positive local maxima and negative local minima) of blurred derivatives as local descriptors of the iris texture. To assure a better stability an extremum is used as a feature only if (a) the local extrema at a particular scale σ_0 exceeds the same derivative at the same position but with larger scales $\sigma > \sigma_0$ and (b) if its magnitude is large enough. However, to avoid thresholding the magnitude at this stage we chose the best extrema points in the following way:

1. subdivide the iris texture along the polar angle direction into 16 equal sectors,
2. enumerate sectors clockwise according to Fig. 8.2,
3. ignore sectors 0, 1, 2, 7,7, 13, 14, and 15 because the iris texture in these sectors is likely to be occluded by the upper and lower lids,
4. choose no more than K biggest local extrema from each scale and each of the remaining sector for some predefined K. For the reminder of the paper, we will refer to the remaining sectors as *active sectors*.

   Figure 8.5 illustrates local extrema points that were found in the active sectors for the 242116.tiff and 241643.tiff iris images from the NIST ICE2005 iris dataset. These two images constitute genuine pairs. The two presented derivatives u_{xx} and u_{yy} are calculated using the averaging parameters defined by the 6th ($s = 5$) and 8th ($s = 7$) row of the Table 8.1. The "+" and "−" mark local maxima and minima points of the averaged Taylor expansion. The presented iris texture has no clearly expressed freckles, furrows, stripes, or coronas in the active sectors. However, there are blurred dark and bright blobs where local maxima and minima indicate the blobs of the size that resonates with the averaging scale σ.

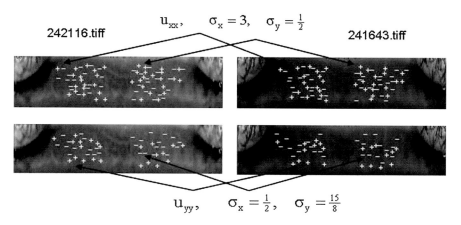

Fig. 8.5 Unwrapped 242116 and 241643 iris images from the NIST ICE2005 dataset. "+" and "−" mark local maxima and minima of the averaged u_{xx} and u_{yy} derivatives (u_{xx}—above, u_{yy}—below). *Arrows* points to the examples of extrema points that have correspondences in both images. Figure reproduced with permission from [3]

8.3.4 Elastic Similarity Metric for Comparison of Binary Feature Maps

Let $\mathbf{f}^A[i][j]$ and $\mathbf{f}^B[i][j]$, $(i, j) \in \{256 \times 32\}$ be two sets of binary features formed from the multi-scale Taylor expansions of iris images A and B. The traditional Daugman approach of matching two binary iris templates consists of calculating the Hamming distance for different angular shifts and the final distance is the minimum of all calculated distances. To be more consistent with our local extrema- based iris matching technique (see [3]), we will construct a similarity metric instead of a distance measure. A similarity measure of a pair of iris images can be defined simply by the maximal number of matched bits of their binary features maps where the maximization is performed over a fixed number of angular shifts, i.e.,

$$\text{similarity}(A, B) = \max_{\alpha} \sum_{i,j} \#_0(\mathbf{f}^A[i][j] \hat{\ } \mathbf{f}^B[i + \alpha][j]). \tag{8.12}$$

Here, $\hat{\ }$ denotes bit-wise XOR operation of two bytes and $\#_0(\mathbf{b})$ is number of zero bits in byte $\mathbf{b}$. However, such a Daugman type similarity measure (8.12) underestimates the similarity of genuine pairs that have slight segmentation inaccuracies or nonlinearly deformed texture. To make the iris similarity measure more robust for such deformations and to have the possibility to control the eyelids and eyelashes influences, we again subdivided the unwrapped iris into sectors as done above in Sect. 8.3.3 and Fig. 8.2.

Let $k \in \{3, 4, 5, 6, 9, 10, 11, 12\}$ be a sector number and α and β two shifts in the angular and radial direction. The similarity of two shifted k sectors is computed as

$$\text{score}_k(A, B; \alpha, \beta) =$$

$$\sum_{i=k*16}^{(k+1)*16-1} \sum_{j=0}^{31} \#_0(\mathbf{f}^A[i][j] \hat{\ } \mathbf{f}^B[i + \alpha][j + \beta]) . \tag{8.13}$$

Because of the angular periodicity of the iris texture and the size of 256×32 (see Sect. 8.3.2) we assume 256 periodicity of $\mathbf{f}^B[i + \alpha][j + \beta]$ in the first variable i. Similarly, in order to properly define $\mathbf{f}^B[i + \alpha][j + \beta]$ for all $[j + \beta]$ we assumed 32 periodicity in the second variable, but this assumption does not have a natural interpretation. Maximizing Eq. (8.13) over the angular shifts α compensates possible iris rotations, maximizing over the radial shifts β allows to reduce possible influences of slight segmentation inaccuracies.

By allowing α_k and β_k to maximize the accumulative similarity scores of the two k sectors independently for different sectors k, we are able to compensate for nonlinear deformations of the iris texture. Unfortunately, such degree of freedom undesirably increases also impostor pairs similarity variation. To reach a compromise between the increase of genuine pair average similarity and a rise of variation of impostor pairs similarity, we define the elastic iris similarity measure as follows:

Definition 8.1 Let A and B be two iris images templates formed from binary maps of the Taylor multi-scale expansion features. Then, their elastic similarity is

$$\widetilde{score}^*(A, B) = \max_{\{\alpha_k, \beta_k\}_{k=3}^{12} \in T} \sum_{k=3}^{12} score_k(A, B; \alpha_k, \beta_k), \qquad (8.14)$$

$$T = \Big\{ \{\alpha_k, \beta_k\}_{k=3}^{12} : |\alpha_k - \alpha_{k-1}| \leq 1, |\beta_k - \beta_{k-1}| \leq 1, k = 4, \ldots, 12;$$

$$|\alpha_k| \leq KX, |\beta_k| \leq KY, k = 3, 4, \ldots, 12 \Big\}. \qquad (8.15)$$

Here, KX and KY are integer parameters defining $2KX + 1$ rotations and $2KY + 1$ radial shifts under which the similarity scores of shifted and rotated iris templates are evaluated.

The concrete choice of KX and KY values can be adjusted to iris database and magnitude of segmentation inaccuracies. In our experimentations the average used values are $KX = 10$ and $KY = 2$. The set T defines the admissible shifts $\{\alpha_k, \beta_k\}_{k=3}^{12}$ under which the similarity scores are maximized. The $|\alpha_k| \leq KX$ and $|\beta_k| \leq KY$ conditions restrict the maximal admissible shifts. The $|\alpha_k - \alpha_{k-1}| \leq 1$ and $|\beta_k - \beta_{k-1}| \leq 1$ inequalities ensure the continuity of admissible deformations in the iris matching routine. The sum $\sum_{k=3}^{12} score_k(A, B; \alpha_k, \beta_k)$ includes the similarity of the sectors with indices $k = 7$ and $k = 8$ that we proposed to avoid because the iris texture in these sectors is likely to be occluded by lower lid. Therefore in the calculation of (8.14) we put $score_7(A, B; \alpha_7, \beta_7) = score_8(A, B; \alpha_8, \beta_8) = 0$. However, values of $\alpha_7, \beta_7, \alpha_8$ and β_8 influence the accumulative elastic similarity scores through the set T that defines all the admissible shifts.

Direct maximization of the elastic similarity scores over the set T would require the evaluation of $4KXKY9^9$ accumulated similarity scores. In the following, we provide a dynamic programming approach for calculating (8.14) that reduces the maximization complexity to $4KXKY9$ arithmetic operations. In the reminder of this section we will skip, for better readability, the explicit reference to the iris images A and B in the notation. For example instead of $score_k(A, B; \alpha, \beta)$ we will write $score_k(\alpha, \beta)$.

Proposition 8.1 *Let the initial values of* $(2KX + 1) \times (2KY + 1)$ *of accumulative scores be set to*

$$\widetilde{sum}_3(\alpha, \beta) = score_3(\alpha, \beta), \ |\alpha| \leq KX, |\beta| \leq KY . \qquad (8.16)$$

For $k = 4, 5, \ldots, 12$ *the accumulative scores are calculated using the following dynamic programming rule:*

$$\widetilde{sum}_k(\alpha, \beta) = score_k(\alpha, \beta) + \max_{\substack{i,j=-1,0,1: \\ |\alpha+i| \le KX \\ |\beta+j| \le KY}} \widetilde{sum}_{k-1}(\alpha + i, \beta + j) \ . \qquad (8.17)$$

Then, the maximum of $\widetilde{sum}_{12}$ gives the final elastic similarity scores (8.14), i.e.,

$$\widetilde{score}^*(A, B) = \max_{\substack{|\alpha| \le KX \\ |\beta| \le KY}} \widetilde{sum}_{12}(\alpha, \beta). \qquad (8.18)$$

Proof Let

$$\max_{\substack{|\alpha| \le KX \\ |\beta| \le KY}} \widetilde{sum}_{12}(\alpha, \beta) = \widetilde{sum}_{12}(\alpha_{12}^*, \beta_{12}^*) \ .$$

Then, using repeatedly (8.17) we have

$$\widetilde{sum}_k(\alpha_k^*, \beta_k^*) = score_k(\alpha_k^*, \beta_k^*) + \widetilde{sum}_{k-1}(\alpha_{k-1}^*, \beta_{k-1}^*), \ k = 12, 11, \ldots, 4,$$

where for all $k = 12, 11, \ldots, 3$ the following inequalities hold true:

$$|\alpha_k^*| \le KX, |\beta_k^*| \le KY,$$

and for $k > 3$

$$|\alpha_k^* - \alpha_{k-1}^*| \le 1, |\beta_k^* - \beta_{k-1}^*| \le 1.$$

Therefore, we have a set of shifts $\{\alpha_k^*, \beta_k^*\}_{k=3}^{12} \in T$ and

$$\widetilde{sum}_{12}(\alpha_{12}^*, \beta_{12}^*) = \sum_{k=3}^{12} score_k(\alpha_k^*, \beta_k^*)$$

$$\le \max_{\{\alpha_k, \beta_k\}_{k=3}^{12} \in T} \sum_{k=3}^{12} score_k(\alpha_k, \beta_k) = \widetilde{score}^*(A, B). \qquad (8.19)$$

On the other hand let a set $\{^*\alpha_k, {}^*\beta_k\}_{k=3}^{12}$ result in a maximum of Eq. (8.14), i.e., the set is admissible (belongs to T) and

$$\max_{\{\alpha_k, \beta_k\}_{k=3}^{12} \in T} \sum_{k=3}^{12} score_k(\alpha_k, \beta_k) = \sum_{k=3}^{12} score_k(^*\alpha_k, {}^*\beta_k).$$

We will show that for this set we have

$$\widetilde{sum}_3(^*\alpha_3, {}^*\beta_3) = score_k(^*\alpha_3, {}^*\beta_3) \qquad (8.20)$$

and

$$\widetilde{sum}_k(^*\alpha_k, {^*}\beta_k) = score_k(^*\alpha_k, {^*}\beta_k) + \widetilde{sum}_{k-1}(^*\alpha_{k-1}, {^*}\beta_{k-1}), \; k = 4, 5, \dots 12 \; .$$
$$(8.21)$$

The equality (8.20) holds true simply by the definition in (8.16). Let us suppose that for some k Eq. (8.21) fails. Then, for this k using (8.17) we will have

$$\widetilde{sum}_{k-1}(^*\alpha_{k-1}, {^*}\beta_{k-1}) < \widetilde{sum}_{k-1}(^*\alpha_k + i, {^*}\beta_k + j),$$

where $|i| \leq 1, |j| \leq 1, |^*\alpha_k + i| = |\overline{\alpha}_{k-1}| \leq KX$, and $|^*\beta_k + j| = |\overline{\beta}_{k-1}| \leq KY$. The last inequality gives that there exists a shift set $\{\overline{\alpha}_3, \overline{\beta}_3, \dots, \overline{\alpha}_{k-1}, \overline{\beta}_{k-1}, {^*}\alpha_k,$ ${^*}\beta_k, \dots, {^*}\alpha_{12}, {^*}\beta_{12}\} \in T$ such that

$$\sum_{i=3}^{12} score_i(^*\alpha_i, {^*}\beta_i) = \sum_{i=3}^{k-1} score_i(^*\alpha_i, {^*}\beta_i) + \sum_{i=k}^{12} score_i(^*\alpha_i, {^*}\beta_i)$$

$$< \sum_{i=3}^{k-1} score_i(\overline{\alpha}_i, \overline{\beta}_i) + \sum_{i=k}^{12} score_i(^*\alpha_i, {^*}\beta_i) \; ,$$
$$(8.22)$$

which contradicts to the assumption that the set $\{^*\alpha_k, {^*}\beta_k\}_{k=3}^{12}$ is a maximum of (8.14). The obtained contradiction proves Eq. (8.21). Therefore,

$$\widetilde{sum}_{12}(\alpha_{12}^*, \beta_{12}^*) = \max_{|\alpha| \leq KX, |\beta| \leq KY} \widetilde{sum}_{12}(\alpha, \beta)$$

$$\geq \widetilde{sum}_{12}(^*\alpha_{12}, {^*}\beta_{12}) = \widetilde{score}^*(A, B).$$
$$(8.23)$$

By combining (8.19) and (8.23) inequalities we get (8.18).

Table 8.2 illustrates ordinary and elastic similarity scores. For short only similarity scores of sections 6, 7, 8, and 9 for ICE 240861 and 243395 iris images are presented. The scores are represented as percentage of alike bits of shifted sectors. For this example ordinary similarity scores are $score^*(A, B) = \max_{\alpha,\beta} sum_9(\alpha, \beta) = sum_9(1, 0) = 255 = 255/4 \; [\%] = 64 \; [\%]$. The elastic similarity scores are $\widetilde{score}^*(A, B) = \max_{\alpha,\beta} \widetilde{sum}_9(\alpha, \beta) = \widetilde{sum}_9(-1, 0) = 291 = 291/4 \; [\%] = 73 \; [\%]$. The admissible shifts optimal set is the following: $(\alpha_6^*, \beta_6^*) = (2, 0), (\alpha_7^*, \beta_7^*) = (1, 0),$ $(\alpha_8^*, \beta_8^*) = (0, -1), (\alpha_9^*, \beta_9^*) = (-1, 0)$. The ICE (240861,243395) is a genuine pair and for this pair the elastic versus ordinary measure gives a significant increase of similarity scores.

Table 8.2 An example of similarity scores $score_k$ for sections $k = 6, 7, 8,$ and 9 of ICE 240861 and 243395 iris images with horizontal and vertical translations: $\alpha = -2, -1, 0, 1, 2, beta = -1, 0, 1$

Section score $score_6(\alpha,\beta)$						Accumulative scores $sum_6(\alpha,\beta)$						Elastic score $\widetilde{sum}_6(\alpha,\beta)$					
$\frac{\alpha}{\beta}$	−2	−1	0	1	2	$\frac{\alpha}{\beta}$	−2	−1	0	1	2	$\frac{\alpha}{\beta}$	−2	−1	0	1	2
−1	38	38	45	57	73	−1	38	38	45	57	73	−1	38	38	45	57	73
0	38	40	48	62	75	0	38	40	48	**62**	75	0	38	40	48	62	**75**
1	40	45	53	64	69	1	40	45	53	64	69	1	40	45	53	64	69

$score_7(\alpha,\beta)$						$sum_7(\alpha,\beta)$						$\widetilde{sum}_7(\alpha,\beta)$					
$\frac{\alpha}{\beta}$	−2	−1	0	1	2	$\frac{\alpha}{\beta}$	−2	−1	0	1	2	$\frac{\alpha}{\beta}$	−2	−1	0	1	2
−1	41	44	54	68	72	−1	79	82	99	125	145	−1	81	92	116	143	147
0	39	44	57	71	72	0	77	84	105	**133**	147	0	84	97	121	**146**	147
1	44	50	58	67	63	1	84	95	111	131	132	1	89	103	122	142	138

$score_8(\alpha,\beta)$						$sum_8(\alpha,\beta)$						$\widetilde{sum}_8(\alpha,\beta)$					
$\frac{\alpha}{\beta}$	−2	−1	0	1	2	$\frac{\alpha}{\beta}$	−2	−1	0	1	2	$\frac{\alpha}{\beta}$	−2	−1	0	1	2
−1	48	61	74	73	59	−1	127	143	173	198	204	−1	145	182	**220**	220	206
0	47	60	73	74	60	0	124	144	178	**207**	207	0	150	182	219	221	207
1	48	60	68	69	57	1	132	155	179	200	189	1	151	182	214	216	204

$score_9(\alpha,\beta)$						$sum_9(\alpha,\beta)$						$\widetilde{sum}_9(\alpha,\beta)$					
$\frac{\alpha}{\beta}$	−2	−1	0	1	2	$\frac{\alpha}{\beta}$	−2	−1	0	1	2	$\frac{\alpha}{\beta}$	−2	−1	0	1	2
−1	60	68	64	49	38	−1	187	211	237	247	242	−1	242	288	285	270	259
0	64	71	65	48	36	0	188	215	243	**255**	243	0	246	**291**	286	269	257
1	60	66	61	50	41	1	192	221	240	250	230	1	242	285	282	271	262

sum_k give accumulated similarity scores and $\widetilde{sum}_k$ corresponding elastic sums

8.3.5 Similarity Metric for Comparison of Local Feature Maps

In this and the next subsections, we present a highly efficient similarity metric for the local extrema features.

Let A and B be sets of local features formed from our Taylor local extrema estimated at different scales. A particular feature $f_i = \{x_i, y_i, s_i, z_i\}$ has the following attributes:

- (x_i, y_i)—local extremum position defined by two integer numbers x_i and y_i.
- $s_i \in \{0, 1, \cdots, 7\}$—scale and filter type index (see Table 8.1 for details).
- $z_i \in \{0, 1\}$—extremum type marker. 0 was used for local maximum points and 1 for local minimum points.

The similarity metric between two local feature sets is defined by a normalized sum of similarity scores of feature pairs. A particular feature pair (f_i^A, f_j^B) can gain nonzero similarity scores only if f_i^A and f_j^B correspond to the same filter and extremum type. In the following we will call such features *congeneric*:

Definition 8.2 Two local features $f_i^A = \{x_i^A, y_i^A, s_i^A, z_i^A\}$ and $f_j^B = \{x_j^B, y_j^B, s_j^B, z_j^B\}$ are *congeneric* if they (a) appear at the same scale, i.e., $s_i^A = s_j^B$, and (b) correspond to the same type of extremum, i.e., $z_i^A = z_j^B$.

Two congeneric features can gain a positive similarity only if their positions are close. The distance between two affine (x_i^A, y_i^A) and (x_j^B, y_j^B) points is estimated again by considering a possible alignment of the two irises by means of an angular rotation and radial translation. Angular rotation and radial translation correspond to some shift along x and y directions, respectively.[1] With fixed α and β shifts in x and y direction we use the following score similarity expression:

$$s(f_i^A, f_j^B; \alpha, \beta) = \begin{cases} 0 & \text{if } s_i^A \neq s_j^B \text{ or } z_i^A \neq z_j^B; \\ |DX - |x_i^A - x_j^B - \alpha||_+ \times |DY - |y_i^A - y_j^B - \beta||_+ & \text{otherwise.} \end{cases}$$

$$(8.24)$$

Here, DX and DY are two positive integer parameters that define maximal acceptable distance along x and y directions, and

$$|a|_+ = \begin{cases} a & \text{if } a > 0, \\ 0 & \text{otherwise.} \end{cases} \qquad (8.25)$$

For fixed angular and radial shifts α and β the proposed expression allocates maximum similarity for the positions (x_i^A, y_i^A) and (x_j^B, y_j^B) that coincide after α and β shifts. The relative decay of the similarity is controlled by constants DX and DY (respectively in x and y directions). Greater DX and DY values mean that more intraclass variation of positions is tolerated. Note that the defined similarity measure is a piecewise bilinear function with respect to the angular and radial shifts. We will utilize this later for fast calculation of similarity scores.

The similarity scores between the feature set A and an α rotated and β radially shifted feature set B is defined as the sum of the similarity scores of local features pairs, i.e.,

$$score(A, B; \alpha, \beta) = \sum_{i=1}^{NA} \sum_{j=1}^{NB} s(f_i^A, f_j^B; \alpha, \beta) , \qquad (8.26)$$

where NA and NB are given by the number of features in A and in B, respectively. The final similarity score between feature sets A and B is then defined by the following maximum:

$$score^*(A, B) = q(NA, NB) \max_{\substack{-KX \leq \alpha \leq KX \\ -KY \leq \beta \leq KY}} score(A, B; \alpha, \beta) , \qquad (8.27)$$

with KX and KY as defined in the previous section, and $q(NA, NB) = \frac{1}{\min(NA, NB)}$ is a normalization factor.

---

[1] Shift along the x direction inherits angular periodicity.

8.3.6   Efficient Calculation of Similarity Scores for Local Features Maps

The intuitive approach for calculating the similarity scores as defined by Eqs. (8.24)–(8.27) requires $\mathcal{O}((2KX+1) \times (2KY+1) \times NA \times NB)$ arithmetic operations. We will now provide a more efficient method for calculating the $(2KX+1) \times (2KY+1)$ score matrix elements $score(A, B; \alpha, \beta)$ with at most $\mathcal{O}((2KX+1) \times (2KY+1)) + \mathcal{O}(NA \times NB)$ arithmetic operations. The idea is based on the observation that $score(\alpha, \beta)$, as defined in (8.26) and (8.27), is piecewise bilinear with respect to α and β and that it consists of $|DX - |\alpha - a||_+ \times |DY - |\beta - b||_+$ terms. Thus, the numerical derivatives

$$s(\alpha, \beta)_{\alpha\alpha,\beta\beta} = s(\alpha+1, \beta)_{\beta\beta} - 2s(\alpha, \beta)_{\beta\beta} + s(\alpha-1, \beta)_{\beta\beta},$$
$$s(\alpha, \beta)_{\beta\beta} = s(\alpha, \beta+1) - 2s(\alpha, \beta) + s(\alpha, \beta-1), \tag{8.28}$$

are equal to zero at linear pieces. Here, and occasionally later we use the short notation

$$s(\alpha, \beta) = score(A, B; \alpha, \beta). \tag{8.29}$$

The piecewise bilinearity of $score(A, B; \alpha, \beta)$ allows us to show the following Lemma:

Proposition 8.2 *Let $A = \{f_i^A = (x_i^A, y_i^A, s_i^A, z_i^A\}_{i=1}^{NA}$ and $B = \{f_j^B = (x_j^B, y_j^B, s_j^B, z_j^B\}_{j=1}^{NB}$ be local features sets, $s(\alpha, \beta) = score(A, B; \alpha, \beta)$ and*

$$hits(\alpha, \beta) = \#\big\{(i, j) : s_i^A = s_j^B, z_i^A = z_j^B, x_i^A - x_j^B = \alpha, y_i^A - y_j^B = \beta\big\} \tag{8.30}$$

is the counting function of pairs of congeneric features that can be superpositioned by the α and β shifts along x and y directions. Then, the following equation is satisfied:

$$s(\alpha, \beta)_{\alpha\alpha,\beta\beta} = \sum_{i=-1}^{1} \sum_{j=-1}^{1} \gamma_{i,j} hits(\alpha + iDX, \beta + jDY) \tag{8.31}$$

with

$$\left|\gamma_{i,j}\right|_{i,j=-1}^{1} = \begin{vmatrix} 1 & -2 & 1 \\ -2 & 4 & -2 \\ 1 & -2 & 1 \end{vmatrix}. \tag{8.32}$$

Proof Direct calculation of $\delta(\alpha, \beta) = (|DX - |\alpha - a||_+ |DY - |\beta - b||_+)_{\alpha\alpha,\beta\beta}$ for all integer $DX, DY, a = x_i^A - x_j^B$, and $b = y_i^A - y_j^B$, gives

$$\delta(\alpha, \beta) = \begin{cases} 4 & \text{if } \alpha = a, \beta = b, \\ -2 & \text{if } \alpha = a, \beta = b \pm DY \text{ or } \alpha = a \pm DX, \beta = b, \\ 1 & \text{if } \alpha = a \pm DX, \beta = b \pm DY, \\ 0 & \text{otherwise.} \end{cases} \tag{8.33}$$

Successive application of this formula to (8.27) and (8.26) yields (8.31).

Direct calculation of the counting matrix $\{hits(\alpha, \beta)\}$, with $\alpha = -KX..KX$ and $\beta = -KY..KY$, requires $\mathcal{O}(NA \times NB)$ arithmetic operations. However, using the precalculated tables

$$index^A(x, y; s, z) = \{i : s_i^A = s, z_i^A = z, x = x_i^A - \alpha, y = y_i^A - \beta, |\alpha| \leq KX, |\beta| \leq KY\},$$
$$x = 0, 1, \ldots, W - 1, y = 0, 1, \ldots, H - 1,$$

the *hits* counting algorithm

$$for(j = 1; j \leq NB; ++j)$$
$$for(i \in index^A(x_j^B, y_j^B; s_j^B, z_j^B))$$
$$++hits(x_i^A - x_j^B, y_i^A - y_j^B)$$

would require only $\mathcal{O}(NA \times NB \times KX \times KY/(W \times H))$ arithmetic operations. Here, W and H denote width and height of the unwrapped iris image and it is assumed that local extrema points are uniformly distributed within the unwrapped rectangular area of the iris image. In our experimentations with real iris data, we had the following settings: NA and NB were in the order of 300, $KX = 10$, $KY = 2$, $W = 256$, and $H = 32$. With these the $\mathcal{O}(NA \times NB \times KX \times KY/(W \times H))$ complexity is significantly lower than $\mathcal{O}(NA \times NB)$.

For identification, the precalculation cost of the index tables is not significant. However, precalculation may slow down the proposed *hits* counting algorithm in the verification case.

The fast computation of the *hits* function leads to fast calculation of the right-hand side of the (8.31). To efficiently compute the similarity score matrix $\{s(\alpha, \beta)\}_{\alpha=-KX, \beta=-KY}^{KX, KY}$, we require a fast inversion of $s_{\alpha\alpha, \beta\beta}$. Let us consider first the inversion problem in the one-dimensional case with the second-order integer numerical derivative

$$s_{\alpha\alpha}(\alpha) = s(\alpha - 1) - 2s(\alpha) + s(\alpha + 1), \tag{8.34}$$

with the initial condition

$$s(\alpha) \equiv 0 \text{ for all } \alpha \leq 0 . \tag{8.35}$$

We are looking for the values $s(\alpha)$. Numerical integration for $s(\alpha)$ gives

$$Is_{\alpha\alpha}(\alpha) = \sum_{i<\alpha} s_{\alpha\alpha}(\alpha) = \sum_{i<\alpha}(s(i+1) - s(i) - (s(i) - s(i-1)))$$

$$= s(\alpha) - s(\alpha - 1) \ . \tag{8.36}$$

Applying numerical integration and the initial conditions $s(\alpha) \equiv 0, \forall \alpha \le 0$ for the second time, we get

$$I^2 s_{\alpha\alpha}(\alpha) = \sum_{i \le \alpha} I s_{\alpha\alpha}(\alpha) = \sum_{i \le \alpha}(s(i) - s(i-1))$$

$$= \sum_{i \le \alpha} s(i) - \sum_{i \le \alpha-1} s(i) = s(\alpha) \ . \tag{8.37}$$

Notice that generally the double numerical integration is computationally unstable. However, under our assumptions where we are dealing with integer values $s(\alpha - 1) - 2s(\alpha) + s(\alpha + 1)$ and $s(\alpha) \equiv 0, \forall \alpha \le 0$, the double numerical integration uses only integer arithmetics which is computationally stable.

In the two-dimensional case, if $s(\alpha, \beta) = 0$ for all $\alpha \le 0$ and $\beta \le 0$, we have

$$I^{2,1} s_{\alpha\alpha,\beta\beta}(\alpha, \beta) = \sum_{j<\beta} I^{2,0} s_{\alpha\alpha,\beta\beta}(\alpha, \beta) = \sum_{j<\beta}(s(\alpha, j+1) - 2s(\alpha, j) + s(\alpha, j-1)$$

$$= s(\alpha, \beta) - s(\alpha, \beta - 1) \tag{8.38}$$

and

$$I^{2,2} s_{\alpha\alpha,\beta\beta}(\alpha, \beta) = \sum_{j \le \beta} I^{2,1} s_{\alpha\alpha,\beta\beta}(\alpha, \beta) = \sum_{j \le \beta}(s(\alpha, \beta) - s(\alpha, \beta - 1))$$

$$= s(\alpha, \beta). \tag{8.39}$$

Thus, repeated summations allow to compute the inverse of $s_{\alpha\alpha,\beta\beta}$.

To summarize

Proposition 8.3 *Let*

$$u(\alpha, \beta) = 0 \ \textit{for all sufficient small } \alpha \ \textit{or} \ \beta,$$

$$I^{0,0} u(\alpha, \beta) = u(\alpha, \beta),$$

$$I^{n,m} u(\alpha, \beta) = \sum_{i \le \alpha - n \% 2} I^{n-1,m} u(i, \beta), n > 0, m \ge 0,$$

$$I^{n,m} u(\alpha, \beta) = \sum_{j \le \beta - m \% 2} I^{n,m-1} u(\alpha, j), n \ge 0, m > 0,$$

and coefficients $\{\gamma\}_{i,j=-1}^{1}$ *are defined by (8.32). Then* $\forall \ |\alpha| \leq KX, \ |\beta| \leq KY,$

$$score(A, B; \alpha, \beta) = \sum_{i=-1}^{1} \sum_{j=-1}^{1} \gamma_{i,j} I^{2,2} hits(\alpha + iDX, \beta + jDY). \qquad (8.40)$$

8.4 Experimental Results

In this section, we document our experiments with the three approaches. For the experiments, we have used three publicly available iris databases in all experiments: the Chinese Academy of Sciences Casia 2.0 (device1) [6], the US National Institute of Standards and Technology (NIST) "Iris Challenge Evaluation", experiment 1 (right eye), (ICE-1) [22], and the NIST "Multiple Biometric Grand Challenge" (MBGC), Portal Challenge, experiment 3, left eye (MBGC-3l) [24].

Initial iris segmentation was performed fully automatic for all iris images in the datasets ICE-1 and Casia 2.0 using the methods in Sect. 8.2. For an automatic segmentation of the MBGC-3l dataset, the methods in Sect. 8.2 were slightly enhanced. The MBGC Portal Challenge MBGC-3l dataset contains a gallery set with 571 high-resolution (2048 × 2048) near-infrared (NIR) videos of faces that were acquired from a Sarnoff Iris on the Move (IoM) system [18]. The IoM system was designed to capture iris imagery as a person walks through the portal. We observed that our iris segmentation algorithm from Sect. 8.2 works slowly and unreliably for the high-resolution video data that contains almost a full face image. To improve the iris segmentation performance, we used an approach which detects reflections of portal illumination system. The reflections form patterns of eight bright spots, which are usually situated on the iris or even the pupil. When reflection patterns of the left or right eye are detected, a rectangle, centered by the average position of reflections, is cropped. This cropped image contains the iris in the usual proportions so that it can be reliably handled by our original segmentation algorithm [2].

8.4.1 Size of Template

Different irises have each a distinct number of local sharp variations, so the template size for different irises using our proposed features is variable. The average template size can be controlled by the parameter K, which defines the upper limit of the number of *congeneric* local features in one sector (see Fig. 8.2). In all our experiments we used the 8 sectors {3, 4, 5, 6, 9, 10, 11, 12}.

Each sector in an unwrapped rectangular iris image (of width $W = 256$ and height $H = 32$) has 16×32 pixels. Congeneric features of one sector are written to the template in the following order: $\{N, x'_1, y_1, x'_2, y_2, \ldots, x'_N, y_N\}$, where N is number of congeneric features, with $(x'_n, y_n), n = 1, \ldots, N$ being the positions of local features

Table 8.3 Dependency of average size (in bytes) of one template and their standard deviations on iris databases and maximum allowable local extrema amount in one section (number K)

K	Casia 2.0	ICE-1	MBGC-3l
1	190 ± 6	177 ± 7	191 ± 3
2	328 ± 13	288 ± 15	330 ± 9
3	452 ± 20	379 ± 24	457 ± 18
5	619 ± 34	498 ± 42	637 ± 43
7	679 ± 44	540 ± 51	710 ± 62

in a sector. We assumed that $K \leq 7$. Thus, $0 \leq n \leq 8, 0 \leq x_i' \leq 16$, and $0 \leq y_i \leq 32$ can be represented in 3, 4, and 5 bits, respectively. Therefore, the maximal number of bytes in one template is at most $(bitsForN + (bitsForX_i' + bitsForY_i) * K) * (\# \text{ of used sectors}) * (\# \text{ of different congeneric classes}))/8) = (3 + (4 + 5) * 7) * 8 * 16)/8 = 1056$. Table 8.3 shows the real average iris template sizes for the three different databases corresponding to maximal allowable local extrema number K per sector. The average template size in Casia 2.0, ICE-1, and MBGC-3l is 643 bytes which constitutes 61 % of the possible maximal template size for maximum value $K = 7$. For $K = 5$ the average template size is comparable to the size of Daugman's iriscode [7]. Furthermore, we can observe clusters of local extrema at the same (x_i', y_i) locations but at different scales. These clusters can be used to compress the iris templates even more, however a further analysis of such compressibility was not performed.

8.4.2 Verification Performance

We use Detection Error Tradeoff (DET) curves [19] to document the quality of our approaches. The DET curves plot the False Acceptance Rate (FAR) versus the False Rejection Rate (FRR) along the log–log axes' for differentsimilarities or distance threshold values. Our experiments show that the verification quality as expected increases with increasing maximum number K of congeneric features per sector. The results presented in this section were achieved with $K = 7$.

In the following, we present the results for

1. matching two local maxima feature sets A and B, $\widetilde{score}^*_{local\ extr.}(A, B)$,
2. for matching two binary feature sets A and B, $\widetilde{score}^*_{phase}(A, B)$.
3. After proper normalization these two elastic similarities are combined to define the joint feature

$$\widetilde{score}^*_{local\ extr.\ +\ phase}(A, B) = \frac{\widetilde{score}^*_{local\ extr.}(A, B) + \widetilde{score}^*_{phase}(A, B)}{2}.$$

(8.41)

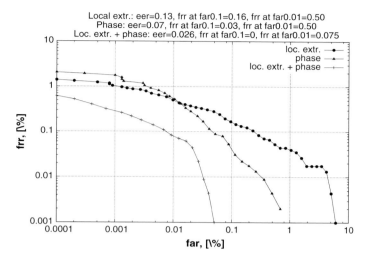

Fig. 8.6 DET curves for Casia 2.0 (device 1) iris database. Figure reproduced with permission from [3]

For Casia 2.0 (device 1) iris database, we have evaluated $_{20}C_2 \times 60 = 11400$ genuine and $_{60}C_2 \times 20^2 = 708000$ impostor similarity scores. It is recognized that Casia 2.0 iris database has lower quality than Casia 1.0 [20] images. The best result that can be found in the literature is $EER = 0.58\%$ [20]. In our experiments, we already obtained considerably better results for the proposed local extrema features of the multi-scale Taylor expansion coefficients $EER = 0.13\%$, $ZeroFAR = 1.63\%$, and $ZeroFRR = 5.52\%$. The corresponding verification performance based solely on the elastic phase-based metric is with $EER = 0.07\%$, $ZeroFAR = 2.1\%$, and $ZeroFRR = 0.49\%$ similar. The similarity measure for the joint features $\widetilde{score}^*_{local\ extr.+phase}$ gives even considerably better results: $EER = 0.026\%$, $ZeroFAR = 0.65\%$, and $ZeroFRR = 0.044\%$. In Fig. 8.6 the DET curves for Casia 2.0 iris database are shown. In this and all following DET curves the results based on local maxima features are marked with filled circles, the results for the binarized phase-based features are marked by filled triangles, and the joint features are marked by + signs.

For the NIST "Iris Challenge Evaluation", experiment 1, (ICE-1) iris database local extrema-based verification algorithm relatively produced the worst results. The image database contains very difficult and corrupted examples, sometimes with big eyelid occlusion, off-angle or with an iris partly outside the image frame. Poor focus of a part of the iris images especially degrades the quality of the verification results, out of focus iris images lose all subtle details of the iris texture, which results in a significant decay of number of Taylor decomposition local extrema at tiny scales. For the ICE-1 iris database we have evaluated 12214 genuine and 1002386 impostor similarity scores. We obtained for the local maxima features $EER = 0.25\%$, $frr@far0.1 = 0.42\%$, $frr@far0.01 = 0.83\%$, the

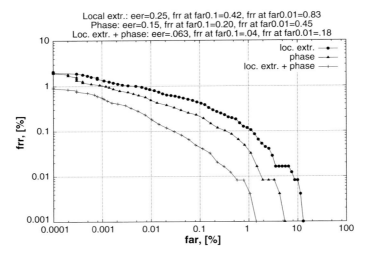

Fig. 8.7 DET curves for ICE1 iris database. Figure reproduced with permission from [3]

binarized phase features showed better results than the ones of the local extrema features: $EER = 0.15\,\%$, $frr@far0.1 = 0.20\,\%$, $frr@far0.01 = 0.45\,\%$. This is slightly worse than the best reported results of a newer Daugman algorithm [10]: $EER = 0.11\,\%$, $frr@far0.1 = 0.12\,\%$, $frr@far0.01 = 0.30\,\%$. Daugman's algorithm concentrates on segmentation improvements, which tolerate off-angle and deformed iris inner and outer boundaries, which are present in the ICE-1 iris database. The iris features and matching routines in [10] still remain phase based. Using the $\widetilde{score}^*_{local\ extr.+phase}$ similarity measure gives $EER = 0.063\,\%$, $frr@far0.1 = 0.04\,\%$, $frr@far0.01 = 0.18\,\%$, and considerably outperforms the ones of [10] (Fig. 8.7).

The design of MBGC problem was conditioned by a number of new iris recognition systems which should allow to perform human iris identification at a distance and on the move. The following iris data were collected for this challenge:

- Still iris images were collected with an LG2200 iris camera with intentionally degraded quality as described in [5].
- Iris video sequences were collected with the same LG2200 iris camera, digitized and transcoded to MPEG-4 format with high bit rate allowance, thus yielding near-lossless encoding.
- Very high-resolution near-infrared (NIR) video of faces were acquired from a Sarnoff Iris on the Move (IoM) system [18]. The IoM system was designed to capture iris imagery as a person walks through the portal. One frame of NIR video has 2048×2048 pixels and average diameter of one iris is approximately 140 pixels.

Twelve experiments in five different categories were defined in this challenge. We chose experiment MBGC-3l in which NIR video data is compared with left iris still image. Following the decision of NIST, we skipped MBGC-3r experiment for right irises, since right irises were missing in 25 out of 571 videos.

The DET curve for MBGC-3l experiment was calculated following the MBGC protocol. The protocol allowed normalization of similarity scores and we used z-score normalization for this purpose. Following the MBGC protocol, 27671 genuine and 603021 impostor similarity scores were evaluated. Because of pure iris resolution (only about 140 pixels in iris diameter) and different data acquisition conditions (video vs. still iris images) it is hard to expect very high verification results. We achieve with the local maxima features $EER = 2.27\,\%$, $ZeroFAR = 28\,\%$, $frr@far1 = 2.93\,\%$, and $frr@far0.1 = 6.4\,\%$. Only a small amount of work on iris recognition using the MBGC data has been published so far. Some preliminary results of mainly commercial systems were presented at a workshop [25]. In [12], Hollingsworth et al. proposed an improvement and speedup of iris recognition using a signal-level fusion of iris frames from video. Their paper presents some experimental results, where MBGC videos for both gallery and probe sets were used. In [14], methods to detect eyes in the MBGC portal videos and to measure the quality of the extracted eye images were presented. They achieved a false rejection rate of 43.90 % at a false acceptance rate of 0.80 %. In [32], Zhou et al. suggest to add some additional steps to the traditional iris system in order to improve the performance. After inclusion of four additional steps, they received $frr@far0.1 = 28.6\,\%$ and $frr@far0.01 = 42.7\,\%$ for the MBGC-3l dataset. For the joint similarity measure $\widetilde{score}^{*}_{local\ extr.+phase}$ we reach an error rate of $EER = 1.21\,\%$, $ZeroFAR = 12.6\,\%$, $frr@far1 = 1.27\,\%$, and $frr@far0.1 = 2.98\,\%$. Analysis of DET curves of the three different algorithms (see Fig. 8.8) indicates that for the MBGC iris dataset

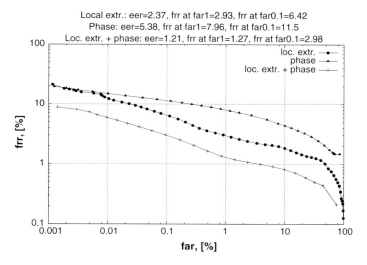

Fig. 8.8 DET curves for MBGC, Portal Challenge, experiment 3L, iris database. Figure reproduced with permission from [3]

algorithm based on local extrema outperforms the phase-based algorithm. This can be caused by local extrema being more robust to different lightning conditions and low resolution of iris video images.

8.5   Summary and Conclusions

It is interesting to note that despite the intuitive similarity to the Gabor features, the Taylor's coefficients have greater localization in the space domain. The localization is gathered at the expense of poor feature resolution in the frequency domain. Such proportion of localization in space and frequency domains is natural for the iris where local objects as freckles, furrows, stripes, coronas dominate the texture, and where periodic texture patterns that are well localized in frequency domain are rare.

The local maxima and the binary features seem to be complementing each other so that their fusion gives a verification performance that is among the best verification results published so far in academic papers. Despite the noticeable improvement of the iris verification quality due to the fusion of the similarity scores, we should mention that our binarized phase matrix increases the template size by 2048 bytes and significantly decreases the matching speed. The matching speed decreases because of the warped similarity calculation. Using only a 3.2 GHz Pentium 4 processor, we were able to compare $\approx$5000 iris templates per second. It is likely, however, that more accurate iris segmentation as done in [10] can eliminate the necessity to search for optimal shifts along radial direction.

References

1. K. Bae, S. Noh, J. Kim, Iris Feature Extraction Using Independent Component Analysis (2003), pp. 838–844
2. A. Bastys, J. Kranauskas, R. Masiulis, Iris recognition by local extremum points of multiscale Taylor expansion. Pattern Recognit. **42**(9), 1869–1877 (2009)
3. A. Bastys, J. Kranauskas, V. Krüger, Iris recognition by fusing different representations of multi-scale Taylor expansion. Comput. Vis. Image Underst. **115**(6), 804–816 (2011)
4. W. Boles, B. Boashash, A human identification technique using images of the iris and wavelet transform. IEEE Trans. Signal Process. **46**, 1185–1188 (1998)
5. K.W. Bowyer et al., Factors that degrade the match distribution in iris biometrics, in *Identity in the Information Society* (2009), p. 17
6. Chinese Academy of Sciences—Institute of Automation Iris Database 1.0 (2003)
7. J. Daugman, High confidence visual recognition of persons by a test of statistical independence. IEEE Trans. Pattern Anal. Mach. Intell. **15**(11), 1148–1161 (1993)
8. J. Daugman, Statistical richness of visual phase information: update on recognizing persons by iris patterns. Int. J. Comput. Vis. **45**(1), 25–38 (2001)
9. J. Daugman, Demodulation by complex-valued wavelets for stochastic pattern recognition. Int. J. Wavelets Multiresolut. Inf. Process. **1**(1), 1–17 (2003)
10. J. Daugman, New methods in iris recognition. IEEE Trans. Syst. Man Cybern. **37**(5), 1167–1175 (2007)

11. D.W. Hansen, Q. Ji, In the eye of the beholder: a survey of models for eyes and gaze. IEEE Trans. Pattern Anal. Mach. Intell. **32**(3), 478–500 (2010)
12. K. Hollingsworth et al., Iris recognition using signal-level fusion of frames from video. IEEE Trans. Inf. Forensics Secur. **4**(4), 837–848 (2009)
13. J.B. Kruskal, M. Liberman, in *The Symmetric Time-Warping Problem: From Continuous to Discrete* (Addison-Wesley, Reading, 1983)
14. Y.Y. Lee, P.J. Phillips, R.J. Micheals, An Automated Video-Based System for Iris Recognition (2009), pp. 1160–1169
15. S. Lim et al., Efficient iris recognition through improvement of feature vector and classifier. ETRI J. **23**(2), 1–70 (2001)
16. L. Ma et al., Efficient iris recognition by characterizing key local variations. IEEE Trans. Image Process. **13**(6) (2004)
17. L. Ma, Person identification based on iris recognition, in Ph.D dissertation, Inst. Automation, Chinese Academy of Sciences (2003)
18. J.R. Matey et al., Iris on the move: acquisition of images for iris recognition in less constrained environments. Proc. IEEE **94**(11), 1936–1946 (2009)
19. C.E. Metz, Basic principles of ROC analysis. Semin. Nucl. Med. **8**, 283–298 (1978)
20. K. Miyazawa et al., A phase-based iris recognition algorithm. Lect. J. Comput. Sci. (2005)
21. D.M. Monro, S. Rakshit, D. Zhang, DCT-based iris recognition. IEEE Trans. Pattern Anal. Mach. Intell. **29**(4), 586–595 (2007)
22. National Institute of Standards and Technology (NIST), Iris Challenge Evaluation (ICE) (2009)
23. C. Park et al., Iris-Based Personal Authentication Using a Normalized Directional Energy Feature (2003), pp. 224–232
24. P. Phillips et al., Overview of the multiple biometrics grand challenge, in *Advances in Biometrics* (2009), pp. 705–714
25. P.J. Phillips, MBGC Presentations and Publications (2009)
26. H. Sahbi, N. Boujemaa, Robust Matching by Dynamic Space Warping for Accurate Face Recognition, vol. 1 (2001), pp. 1010–1013
27. C. Sanchez-Avila, R. Sanchez-Reillo, Iris-based biometric recognition using dyadic wavelet transform. IEEE Aerosp. Electron. Syst. Mag. **17**, 3–6 (2002)
28. C. Sanchez-Avila, R. Sanchez-Reillo, Two different approaches for iris recognition using Gabor filters and multiscale zero-crossing representation. Pattern Recognit. **38**, 231–240 (2005)
29. Z. Sun, T. Tan, X. Qiu, Graph Matching Iris Image Blocks with Local Binary Pattern, vol. 3832 (2005), pp. 366–372
30. R. Wildes et al., A machine-vision system for iris recognition. Mach. Vis. Applic. **9**, 1–8 (1996)
31. L. Yu et al., Multiscale Wavelet Texture Based Iris Verification (2003), pp. 200–205
32. Z. Zhou, Y. Du, C. Belcher, Transforming traditional iris recognition systems to work in non-ideal situations. IEEE Trans. Industr. Electron. **56**(8), 3203–3213 (2009)
33. Y.W.Y. Zhu, T. Tan, Biometric Personal Identification Based on Iris Patterns (2000), pp. 805–808

Chapter 9
Application of Correlation Filters for Iris Recognition

**B.V.K. Vijaya Kumar, Jason Thornton, Marios Savvides,
Vishnu Naresh Boddeti and Jonathon M. Smereka**

Abstract Excellent recognition accuracies have been reported when using iris images, particularly when high-quality iris images can be acquired. The best-known strategy for matching iris images requires segmenting the iris from the background, converting the segmented iris image from Cartesian coordinates to polar coordinates, using Gabor wavelets to obtain a binary code to represent that iris and using the Hamming distances between such binary representations to determine whether two iris images match or do not match. However, some of the component operations may not work well when the iris images are of poor quality, perhaps as a result of the long distance between the camera and the subject. One approach to matching images with appearance variations is the use of correlation filters (CF). In this chapter, we discuss the use of CFs for iris recognition. CFs exhibit important benefits such as shift-invariance and graceful degradation and have proven worthy of consideration in other pattern recognition applications such as automatic target recognition. In this chapter, we will discuss the basics of CF design and show how CFs can be used for iris segmentation and matching.

9.1 Introduction

Among the many biometric modalities proposed to recognize individuals, iris recognition [1] has become a major research direction because of the excellent accuracy iris recognition methods seem to offer [2] particularly when the iris images are of high quality. As shown in Fig. 9.1, iris refers to the texture-rich region of the eye surrounded by the black pupil (inside) and the white sclera region (outside). It is believed that iris patterns do not change substantially over life time and that an iris

B.V.K. Vijaya Kumar (✉) · M. Savvides · V.N. Boddeti · J.M. Smereka
Carnegie Mellon University, Pittsburgh, PA, USA
e-mail: kumar@ece.cmu.edu

J. Thornton
MIT Lincoln Laboratory, Lexington, MA, USA

© Springer-Verlag London 2016
K.W. Bowyer and M.J. Burge (eds.), *Handbook of Iris Recognition*,
Advances in Computer Vision and Pattern Recognition,
DOI 10.1007/978-1-4471-6784-6_9

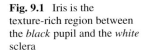

Fig. 9.1 Iris is the
texture-rich region between
the *black* pupil and the *white*
sclera

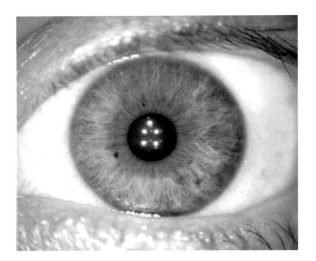

pattern is unique to an eye, i.e., iris patterns from the left eye and the right eye of the
same individual are different.

The original iris recognition method pioneered by Daugman [3] consists of the
following major components:

- Segmenting the iris from the pupil and the sclera by determining its inner and outer
  boundaries,
- Mapping the segmented iris pattern from Cartesian coordinates to polar coordinates
  to normalize for iris size variations caused by the pupil dilation and other factors,
- Producing a binary code from the phases of the inner products of Gabor wavelets
  (of different widths, orientations, locations, and frequencies) with the mapped
  (also called unwrapped) iris pattern, and
- Using the normalized Hamming distance (NHD) between the binary code of an
  enrolled iris image and the binary code of a query (also called probe) iris image
  as an indicator of the quality of the match between the two iris patterns.

Above iris recognition method based on comparing the resulting binary codes is
attractive for its high-speed matching and its excellent accuracy when the training
and testing iris images are of good quality. However, iris images require near infrared
(NIR) illumination to produce images with good contrast and NIR illumination levels
cannot be too high because of safety considerations. As a result of the limitations
on illumination levels, the iris images acquired from distance are not expected to be
of sufficiently good contrast. To add to this challenge, iris images can also exhibit
degradations such as occlusions caused by eye lids, non-frontal gazes, and specular
reflections. In such challenging iris images, traditional binary code matching methods
may not work well because iris regions cannot be easily segmented from the pupil
and the sclera regions.

One attractive method to deal with degraded query images is based on correlating the query images with a template carefully designed from training images [4]. This method, known as correlation filter (CF) [5], has proven useful in other challenging image matching applications such as automatic target recognition [6] and face recognition [7]. In this chapter, we will discuss the basics of CF design and show how CFs can be used for iris segmentation and matching.

The rest of this chapter is organized as follows. Section 9.2 provides a brief review of CF design and Sect. 9.3 shows how CFs can be used for iris segmentation. CFs can be used for matching segmented iris images as well as unsegmented images and this is discussed in Sect. 9.4. Section 9.5 discusses using CF outputs in a Bayesian graphical model to improve the recognition performance and Sect. 9.6 provides a summary.

9.2   Correlation Filter Background

A straightforward measure of the similarity between a probe image $p[m, n]$ and a reference image $r[m, n]$ is the inner product between the two two-dimensional arrays or the inner product between column vectors $\mathbf{p}$ and $\mathbf{r}$ obtained by lexicographically scanning $p[m, n]$ and $r[m, n]$. If this inner product (after appropriate normalization) is large, it indicates a high degree of similarity, whereas if this value is small, it suggests that the probe and the reference images are not a good match. However, in practice, the probe image $p[m, n]$ may be a shifted version of the reference $r[m, n]$ necessitating that the inner product be evaluated for all possible shifts between the two images. This leads to the following correlation output $c[x, y]$ which measures the similarity between $r[m - x, n - y]$ and $p[m, n]$ for all possible shifts x and y.

$$c[x, y] = \sum_{m} \sum_{n} p[m, n]\, r[m - x, n - y] \tag{9.1}$$

It can be shown that if the probe image $p[m, n]$ is exactly equal to $r[m - x_0, n - y_0]$ then $c[x, y]$ will have its highest value (called *correlation peak*) at $x = x_0, y = y_0$. Thus the relative shift between the probe image and the reference image can be determined by locating the peak in the correlation output. If the probe image is from a different class than the class of the reference image, then the resulting $c[x, y]$ will not exhibit a dominant correlation peak indicating that the two images may come from different classes. The cross-correlation operation above is more efficiently implemented in the frequency domain, i.e., $c[x, y]$ is the 2-D inverse discrete Fourier Transform (DFT) of the product of $P[u, v]\, R[u, v]$ where $P[u, v]$ and $R[u, v]$ are the 2-D DFTs of $p[m, n]$ and $r[m, n]$, respectively. Here u and v denote the spatial frequencies corresponding to m and n, respectively and we use upper case italics to denote frequency-domain functions and lower case italics to denote image domain functions. The 2-D DFTs are efficiently implemented using fast Fourier transform

(FFT) algorithm. This implementation of the cross-correlation operation via the frequency domain is the main reason for this operation to be termed *correlation filtering*.

In practice, the probe image $p[m, n]$ will differ from the reference image $r[m, n]$ in multiple ways including additive noise, shifts, rotations, scale differences, illumination changes, partial occlusions and other differences. All these differences cause the correlation peaks to become lower and broader, making it harder to determine the similarity between the two images and to determine the location of the reference image in the probe scene. One method developed to deal with the appearance changes due to such distortions is to design a correlation filter $H[u, v]$ (or equivalently the template $h[m, n]$ in the image domain) that exhibits the following properties of the correlation output $c[x, y]$.

- Correlation output $c[x, y]$ should exhibit large and consistent values at the center in response to centered training images from the authentic class.
- Correlation output $c[x, y]$ should exhibit small values throughout the correlation plane in response to training images from the impostor class.
- Correlation output $c[x, y]$ should take on small values in the rest of the correlation plane so that the controlled values stand out (i.e., yield peaks) in response to centered images from the authentic class.
- Correlation output $c[x, y]$ should exhibit low sensitivity to noise in the probe or query image input.

Over the years, many correlation filter designs have been developed to achieve the above-desired properties. For reasons of space, we will focus on the design of one type of correlation filter known as *optimal trade-off synthetic discriminant function* (OTSDF) filter [8]. More details about CF designs can be found elsewhere [5].

Let $r_1[m, n], r_2[m, n], \ldots, r_L[m, n]$ denote L training images (assumed to be centered) from the authentic class with each image of size $M \times N$. The 2-D DFTs of these images are lexicographically scanned to yield column vectors $\mathbf{r}_1, \mathbf{r}_2, \ldots, \mathbf{r}_L$ each containing $d = MN$ elements. Matrix $\mathbf{R}$ of size $d \times L$ contains $\mathbf{r}_1, \mathbf{r}_2, \ldots, \mathbf{r}_L$ as its column vectors. Similarly, let $\mathbf{h}$ denote a d-dimensional column vector containing as its elements the scanned version of the correlation filter $H[u, v]$. The goal is to find CF vector $\mathbf{h}$ to meet the above objectives.

The OTSDF design requires that the filter vector $\mathbf{h}$ satisfy the following inner product constraints.

$$\mathbf{h}^T \mathbf{r}_i = c_i, \quad i = 1, 2, \ldots, L \qquad (9.2)$$

Typically c_i is set to 1 for all training images from the authentic class and to 0 for training images from the other classes. It is expected that the resulting CF will yield correlation output values (at the origin) close to 1 for centered nontraining (i.e., test) images from the authentic class and values close to 0 for other images. The linear constraints in Eq. (9.2) are under-determined in that there are L constraints and d unknowns, where d (the number of pixels in the training images) is usually much larger than L (the number of training images). Thus, there are infinite solutions to Eq. (9.2). Among these infinite solutions, the OTSDF design tries to find the vector

h that leads to sharp correlation peaks (sharp peaks make it easy to detect and locate the objects) for authentic-class images and that have good tolerance to input noise.

One way to obtain sharp correlation peaks is to force the correlation output values to be small while constraining the value of the peak (i.e., the correlation output at origin given that the input image is a centered training image from the authentic class) to be 1. Mahalanobis et al. [9] tackled this problem by minimizing the average correlation energy (ACE) defined as follows.

$$
\begin{aligned}
\text{ACE} &= \frac{1}{L} \sum_{i=1}^{L} \sum_{x} \sum_{y} |c_i(x,y)|^2 \propto \frac{1}{L} \sum_{i=1}^{L} \sum_{u} \sum_{v} |C_i(u,v)|^2 \\
&= \frac{1}{L} \sum_{i=1}^{L} \sum_{u} \sum_{v} |H(u,v) R_i(u,v)|^2 \\
&= \sum_{u} \sum_{v} |H(u,v)|^2 \left\{ \frac{1}{L} \sum_{i=1}^{L} |R_i(u,v)|^2 \right\} \qquad (9.3) \\
&= \sum_{u} \sum_{v} |H(u,v)|^2 D(u,v)
\end{aligned}
$$

$$
\text{where } D(u,v) = \frac{1}{L} \sum_{i=1}^{L} |R_i(u,v)|^2
$$

The ACE term in Eq. (9.3) can be more compactly expressed as $\mathbf{h}^+ \mathbf{D} \mathbf{h}$ where $\mathbf{h}$ is a d-dimensional column vector containing the filter $H(u,v)$ and $\mathbf{D}$ is a $d \times d$ diagonal matrix whose diagonal entries are $D(u,v)$. Minimizing ACE in Eq. (9.3) subject to the peak constraints in Eq. (9.2) leads to the following CF known as the *minimum average correlation energy* (MACE) filter [9].

$$
\mathbf{h} = \mathbf{D}^{-1} \mathbf{R} \left(\mathbf{R}^+ \mathbf{D}^{-1} \mathbf{R} \right)^{-1} \mathbf{c} \qquad (9.4)
$$

where superscript + denotes conjugate transpose and where the L-dimensional column vector $\mathbf{c}$ is defined as $\mathbf{c} = \begin{bmatrix} c_1 & c_2 & \cdots & c_L \end{bmatrix}^T$. Since $\mathbf{D}$ is diagonal, forming $\mathbf{D}^{-1}$ is easy and the computation of $\left(\mathbf{R}^+ \mathbf{D}^{-1} \mathbf{R} \right)^{-1}$ involves an $L \times L$ matrix.

While the MACE filter in Eq. (9.4) produces sharp correlation peaks in response to training images from the authentic class, it exhibits high sensitivity to input noise and other appearance variations. This is mainly because MACE filters tend to be high frequency-emphasis filters (in order to produce sharp correlation peaks) which end up amplifying noise. One way to reduce the noise sensitivity of a CF is to reduce the output noise variance (ONV) defined as follows. If the input image is corrupted by a wide-sense stationary noise $w[m,n]$ with power spectral density $P_w[u,v]$, then the variance of the correlation output is given as follows:

$$
\begin{aligned}
\text{ONV} &= \text{var}\{c\,(x,\,y)\} = \sum_u \sum_v P_c\,(u,\,v) \\
&= \sum_u \sum_v P_w\,(u,\,v)\,|H\,(u,\,v)|^2
\end{aligned}
\tag{9.5}
$$

where $P_c\,[u,\,v]$ is the power spectral density of the noise in the correlation output. Once again, the ONV can be expressed as $\mathbf{h}^+\mathbf{P}\mathbf{h}$ where $\mathbf{P}$ is a $d \times d$ diagonal matrix whose diagonal entries are $P_w\,[u,\,v]$. Minimizing ONV in Eq. (9.5) subject to the constraints in Eq. (9.2) leads to the following CF known as the minimum variance synthetic discriminant function (MVSDF) filter [10].

$$
\mathbf{h} = \mathbf{P}^{-1}\mathbf{R}\left(\mathbf{R}^+\mathbf{P}^{-1}\mathbf{R}\right)^{-1}\mathbf{c}
\tag{9.6}
$$

While the MACE filter in Eq. (9.4) exhibits sharp correlation peaks and high noise sensitivity, the MVSDF filter in Eq. (9.6) typically exhibits broad correlation peaks and good noise tolerance. Refregier [8] introduced the following optimal trade-off synthetic discriminant function (OTSDF) filter formulation that trades off peak sharpness for noise tolerance.

$$
\mathbf{h} = \mathbf{T}^{-1}\mathbf{R}\left(\mathbf{R}^+\mathbf{T}^{-1}\mathbf{R}\right)^{-1}\mathbf{c}
\tag{9.7}
$$

where $\mathbf{T} = \alpha\mathbf{D} + \sqrt{1-\alpha^2}\,\mathbf{P}$ with $0 \leq \alpha \leq 1$ is a scalar that controls the trade-off between peak sharpness and noise tolerance. For $\alpha = 0$, the OTSDF filter is same as the MVSDF filter and for $\alpha = 1$, the OTSDF filter is same as the MACE filter. For other values of α, we achieve a compromise between the two extremes. In practice, we find that α values close to but not equal to 1 (e.g., 0.999) usually produce the best results.

Over the past two decades, CF designs have advanced in many ways [5]. Some examples of these advances are:

- Relaxing the hard constraints in Eq. (9.2) by maximizing the average correlation output value (at the origin) rather than requiring that the correlation output take on specific values,
- Designing the CF based on the entire correlation output rather than just the value at the origin,
- Applying nonlinear operations to input images in the form of point nonlinearities and in the form of quadratic correlation filters and
- Combining the shift-invariance properties of the CFs with the good generalization properties of support vector machine (SVM) classifiers in the form of maximum margin correlation filters (MMCFs)

In the next section, we discuss how CFs can be used for iris segmentation.

9.3   Iris Segmentation

Before two iris patterns can be compared, they need to be segmented from the rest of the image. Most iris segmentation approaches rely on the fact that, in gray scale images, the pupil (that is interior) to the iris is usually darker than the iris region and the sclera (on the outside) is brighter than the iris. So, iris boundaries can be detected by looking for regions with large gradient magnitudes (e.g., from pupil to iris and from iris to sclera) as was proposed originally in using integro-differential operators for iris boundary detection. Another useful feature of iris boundaries is that they may be nearly circular suggesting the use of circular Hough transforms to identify iris boundaries. More recently, improved iris segmentation results have been obtained using active contours techniques. In this section, we discuss a cross-correlation based method for iris segmentation.

As discussed above, one way to locate the iris boundaries is to determine regions of high radial gradients of the circular Hough transform [11]. For eye image $E[m, n]$, the circular Hough transform is defined as

$$Z[m, n, r] = \sum_{\theta \in I_\theta} E[m + r\cos\theta, n + r\sin\theta] \qquad (9.8)$$

where I_θ is a subinterval of $\theta \in [0°, 360°]$. In practice, we do not integrate across the entire circle because the upper and lower regions are unreliable due to eyelid interference. Instead, we integrate over symmetric left and right lateral regions extending from $45°$ to $150°$ from the top of the circle. This exclusion of the eyelid region leads to a more robust edge detector. Since the iris may not be centered in the image, we need to compute $Z[m, n, r]$ for every possible triplet $[m, n, r]$. This can be computationally prohibitive, as its complexity is order $O(M^4)$ for an $M \times M$ image. As an example, consider the following naive approach to computing the discrete circular Hough transform: for every possible center location $[m, n]$, the polar transform (requiring $O(M^2)$ operations) of the image is obtained using $[m, n]$ as the origin, followed by summing over the angle within the specified angular interval I_θ. This requires M^2 repetitions of the polar transform leading to $O(M^4)$ complexity. This complexity can be reduced by using cross-correlation operation to produce an approximation to the Hough transform, as described below.

For a given triplet $[m_0, n_0, r_0]$, the value of the discrete Hough transform is a sum of pixel intensities that fall along the circular arc of radius r_0 centered at $[m_0, n_0]$. This summation can be approximated as the inner product of the image $E[m, n]$ with a binary template $C_r[m, n]$ that equals 1 along this contour and 0 everywhere else, as shown in Fig. 9.2. The inner product of the eye image with the binary template in Fig. 9.2 yields one value $Z[m_0, n_0, r_0]$.

To determine $Z[m, n, r_0]$ for all $[m, n]$ values, we must compute inner products with all shifted versions of the binary contour, which is equivalent to spatial cross-correlation. So one 2D cross-section of the discrete Hough transform can be obtained as

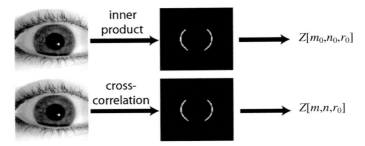

Fig. 9.2 Circular Hough transform approximations using contour filters. An inner product yields a single value, and a cross-correlation yields a 2D cross-section of values

$$Z\,[m,\,n,\,r_0] = E\,[m,\,n] \otimes C_{r_0}\,[m,\,n] \tag{9.9}$$

where cross-correlation is denoted by the $\otimes$ symbol. The cross-correlation in Eq. (9.9) can be efficiently implemented using fast Fourier transform (FFT) algorithm. The computational complexity of the 2-D FFT is $O\left(M^2 \log_2 M\right)$. It should be noted that this technique only produces an approximation to the actual Hough transform values, since the use of discrete Fourier transform results in a *circular* cross-correlation. This means that the contour of integration will wrap around when shifted beyond the edge of the image. Fortunately, this does not present a problem in practice. We can either assume that the iris is completely contained within the eye image or we can zero-pad the eye image if we expect part of the iris to be cut off.

To determine the iris boundaries, the starting point is to build a coarse approximation to the discrete Hough transform. Using a coarse approximation reduces computation time, but allows for a reasonable initial estimate of the boundary locations. First, the input eye image is down-sampled to a low resolution image, e.g., 100 by 100 pixels. Then it is passed through a correlation filter bank where each filter is a binary contour filter of different radius. The output from each filter yields the plane of all Hough transform values at a fixed radius, so concatenating all outputs together gives us the entire discrete Hough space. This is illustrated in Fig. 9.3.

Because the image dimension is low, we need only to use 50–100 radial values. The resulting Hough transform is fairly coarse but is usually sufficient for detecting the approximate boundary locations. Each contour filter's frequency response is computed before hand and stored. Also, the eye image is converted to the frequency domain once, at the beginning of the filtering process. As a result, we only have to compute one inverse FFT for each contour filter. The entire computation has complexity $O\left(KL^2 \log_2 L\right)$ when using K contour filters applied in the low-dimensional space of size $L \times L$. This is significantly better than the $O\left(M^4\right)$ complexity of straightforward computation of the circular Hough transform.

The approximate Hough transform is multiplied by $1/r$ to normalize for the circumference. Because we are detecting circular edges, we need the radial gradients of the normalized Hough space. A smoothed difference operator is applied along

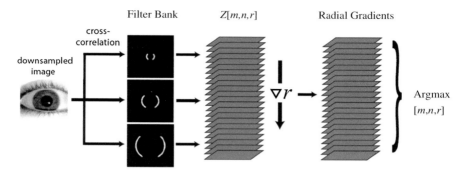

Fig. 9.3 Cross-correlation-based circular boundary detection

the radial direction to get these radial gradients. After this step, we have a 3D set of values which indicate the presence of a circular iris boundary at a range of possible positions. First, a search is conducted for the inner iris boundary, which, depending upon the darkness of the pupil, typically produces the highest radial gradient. We locate the maxima of the gradient, with the minor constraint that the boundary cannot be very near the edge of the image since it is the inner boundary. Once established, the location of the first boundary places a prior on the location of the second boundary. This affects the search in two ways: (1) any potential boundary locations which do not completely surround the inner boundary by some minimal margin are ruled out, and (2) the gradient values are weighted by a Gaussian function, such that the Gaussian is centered on the inner boundary center. The second condition allows for slightly nonconcentric boundaries, but makes the detection of extremely nonconcentric boundaries unlikely. Then the maximum of the weighted gradients are associated with the outer boundary.

At this point in the algorithm, we have coarse estimates for the location of both boundaries. In order to fine-tune these estimates, the detection process is repeated at a higher resolution. The higher resolution contour filters are more computationally expensive to apply, but we do not have to apply the entire filter bank. Instead, we only apply the few filters which have radii in the immediate neighborhood of the coarse estimates. This allows us to refine our estimates without adding significant computation. After deriving the final boundary estimates, the iris pattern is "unwrapped" into normalized pseudo-polar coordinates. We note that the objectives of cross-correlation-based segmentation algorithm are consistent with other iris segmentation algorithm that estimate the iris boundaries by finding the regions of high radial gradients. It is the use of correlation filter bank to efficiently obtain the Hough transform approximation, which differs from other implementations.

We tested the iris segmentation algorithm on an iris image database collected at CMU [12]. Some examples of iris images from CMU database are shown in Fig. 9.4. CMU iris image database contains high-resolution (950×1419) iris images acquired under visible wavelength illumination. This database contains 2390 images from 101

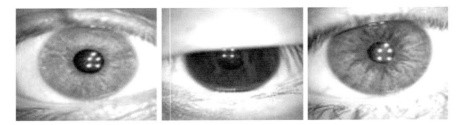

Fig. 9.4 Sample images from CMU database

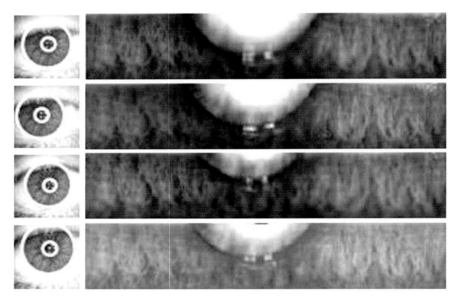

Fig. 9.5 Example cross-correlation-based iris segmentation results (*left*) and resulting unwrapped iris images (*right*)

different eyes with 20–25 images per class. Although the CMU database images have high resolution, they tend to be more difficult for pattern matching because of greater intra-class variation (especially with regard to focus and occlusion). As can be seen from Fig. 9.4, upper eyelid can cause partial occlusion in the iris image.

In Fig. 9.5, we show example segmentation results from the cross-correlation-based method as well as the corresponding unwrapped iris images. The white regions in the top–middle portion of the unwrapped images are due to the occlusion from the eyelids. The results of automatic segmentation were compared against manual segmentation and it was observed that nearly 99 % of the images were properly segmented by the cross-correlation-based algorithm. The few segmentation errors observed were mostly a result of heavy eyelid occlusion obscuring the iris boundaries.

This discussion about iris segmentation would not be complete without mentioning the real-world challenges in segmenting the iris images. Iris segmentation is degraded by impairments such as non-frontal gaze, specular reflections, and occlusion due to eyelids and eyelashes.

9.4   Iris Matching

Cross-correlation is a powerful tool for quantifying the similarity between two images. So, it can be used for matching iris images as illustrated in Fig. 9.6. Segmented and unwrapped training iris patterns from one class (i.e., one eye) are used to determine a correlation filter such as the MACE filter (Eq. (9.4)) or OTSDF filter (Eq. (9.7)). When a query iris image is presented, it is also segmented and unwrapped and then cross-correlated using the designed CF. The resulting correlation output should contain a sharp peak if the query image is from the same class as the training images used for designing the correlation filter, and no such peak if the query image is from an impostor, as depicted in Fig. 9.6.

The sharpness of the correlation peak can be quantified by the peak-to-correlation energy (PCE) defined as a ratio of square of the peak to correlation energy. Since the PCE is a ratio, multiplying the input query image by any constant will not affect the PCE, making it invariant to constant illumination changes. If the PCE is above a pre-specified threshold, the input image is classified as authentic and otherwise as coming from an impostor. By varying the PCE threshold, one can trade off false accept rate (FAR) for false reject rate (FRR).

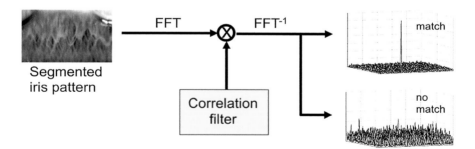

Fig. 9.6 Correlation-based matching of unwrapped iris images

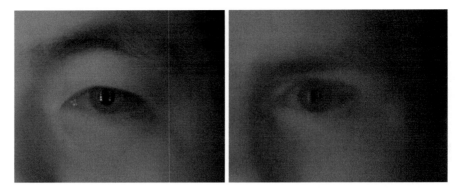

Fig. 9.7 Sample ocular images from the Face and Ocular Challenge Set (FOCS) dataset [14]

We demonstrated [13] that correlation filters can offer excellent iris recognition performance. We investigated the performance of OTSDF correlation filter on the CMU iris database. Three images from each iris class were used as reference images to define the class, and the rest were used for testing. The testing generated similarity scores for a number of authentic and impostor comparisons. We measured the Equal Error Rate (EER), the point at which FRR equals FAR. The EER using correlation filters was 0.61 %, whereas the EER using Gabor wavelet-based binary codes was 1.04 %.

Since correlation filters are applied to unwrapped iris images, the shift-invariance of CFs corresponds to shifts in the polar domain, i.e., the CF method can handle in-plane rotations in the original image (before mapping to polar coordinates). However, the challenge is that iris regions have to be segmented from their surrounding regions before obtaining the unwrapped versions. One of the advantages of CFs is that they can be applied to the original eye images without any need for segmentation.

In Fig. 9.7, we show two example ocular images from the Face and Ocular Challenge Set (FOCS) [14] that contain the iris region as well as surrounding regions such as eyebrow, some part of nose bridge, skin near the eye, and part of the forehead region. Using these additional regions can improve the recognition rate. In Fig. 9.8, we show the correlation outputs for an authentic ocular image pair and an impostor ocular image pair. It is clear that correlation is stronger for the authentic pair. We also show the correlation output when the filter is same, but the probe image is an iris-occluded version of the authentic ocular image and we can see that the correlation peak is still visible even though the iris is occluded.

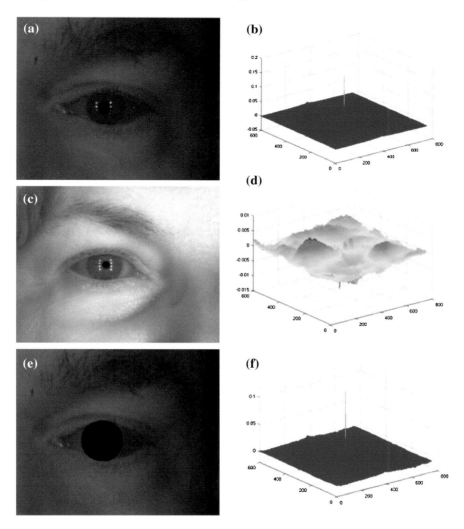

Fig. 9.8 **a** authentic ocular image, **b** resulting correlation output, **c** an impostor ocular image, **d** resulting correlation output, **e** iris-occluded authentic ocular image, and **f** resulting correlation output

9.5 Bayesian Graphical Models for Iris Recognition

One of the reasons for the degradation of match score between two iris images (acquired at different times) from the same eye is that the two images can exhibit non-linear deformations, e.g., different regions of the unwrapped iris images may move differently, as illustrated in Fig. 9.9. Such nonlinear deformation can also be caused

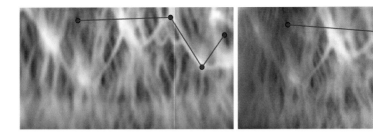

Fig. 9.9 Close-ups of segmented patterns from same eye (*landmark points* illustrate relative deformation)

by slight differences in the segmentation boundaries produced for the two images. When segmentation boundaries differ, corresponding regions of the two unwrapped images may move by different amounts because the mapping from Cartesian coordinates to polar coordinates very much depends on where the inner and outer boundaries are.

Another challenge in matching two iris images from the same eye are that one may exhibit more occlusions caused by eye lid and the other may exhibit less occlusion, affecting the match score. If such occluded regions can be excluded or weighted less in determining a match score, then that should lead to a more robust match score. Toward this goal, Thornton et al. [15] proposed the use of Bayesian graphical models for improved iris matching.

The main idea of Bayesian graphical models can be summarized as follows. The two iris images being compared are divided into nonoverlapping patches as shown in Fig. 9.10 (top) where the unwrapped iris image is divided into 36 patches. Different patches from the probe image may be shifted by different amounts compared to the corresponding patches of the template, as shown in Fig. 9.10 (middle) by white arrows. The length of the arrow indicates the magnitude of the shift and the direction of the arrow indicates the direction of the shift. Also, some of the probe image patches may be occluded, as shown by the gray squares in Fig. 9.10 (bottom). To estimate these patch shifts and to estimate whether a patch is occluded or not, the corresponding patches from the two regions are cross-correlated. If both patches are unoccluded and from the same eye, the resulting correlation peak should be large and the location of the correlation peak should indicate the relative shift between the corresponding patches from the two images. Thus, the cross-correlations between the patches from the two images provide clues about patch shifts between the two images and occlusions.

The graphical model corresponding to the patch structure in Fig. 9.10 is shown in Fig. 9.11. Shaded nodes $O_1, O_2, \ldots, O_{36}$ denote the observations (e.g., PCE values and peak locations from patches) and represent evidence about both the similarity between the template and query iris patterns and the presence of eyelids across the iris plane whereas hidden variables $\mathbf{d}_1, \mathbf{d}_2, \ldots, \mathbf{d}_{36}$ indicate the shift of probe image patches from corresponding template image patches and binary-valued hidden

Fig. 9.10 Hidden states of the model: Sample iris plane partition (*top*), deformation vector field (*center*), and binary occlusion field (*bottom*)

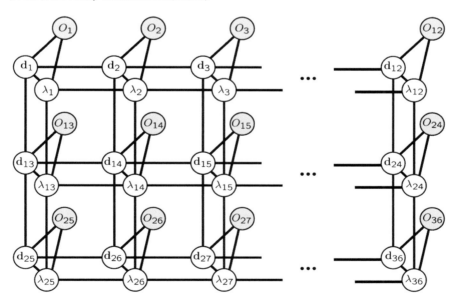

Fig. 9.11 Graphical model structure, for a 3 by 12 iris plane partition. *Shaded nodes* represent observed variables and *non-shaded nodes* represent hidden variables

variables $\lambda_1, \lambda_2, \ldots, \lambda_{36}$ indicate whether a patch is occluded (i.e., $\lambda = 1$) or not occluded (i.e., $\lambda = 0$).

Once the hidden variables (indicated by set H) and the observed variables (indicated by set O) are identified, the objective is to learn a joint probability distribution over these variables so that we may perform inference on the hidden states. In order to do this, we make some assumptions about the dependencies between variables. If we assume a fully connected model (i.e., every variable is directly dependent upon every other variable), learning and inference would be completely intractable. Therefore, we simplify the model by assuming direct dependence only between variables which have an intuitive or empirical statistical connection. This is common practice in the field of probabilistic graphical models [16], which provides a general framework for working with complicated joint distributions. In keeping with conventional graphical model notation, a variable is represented visually as a node, and a direct dependence between two variables is represented as an edge connecting two nodes.

We start by considering the relationship between the hidden deformation variables. Figure 9.12 shows two examples of deformation vector fields which might align a probe image to a template image. The alignment at the top is more "reasonable" than the alignment at the bottom, by which we mean that the top vector field is more likely to approximate the effect of real iris image movement. Part of what makes the second vector field more unlikely, besides the increased magnitude of the vectors, is the fact that many vectors from adjacent regions have conflicting directions. We would expect adjacent iris regions to exhibit similar motion, and we want a model capable of learning this tendency from iris data. Therefore, we allow for direct dependence between each vector and its spatial neighbors in the vector field. We formulate this dependence scheme as a Markov random field (MRF), which is an undirected graph structure on the variable set [17]. We arrange our variables in an MRF framework

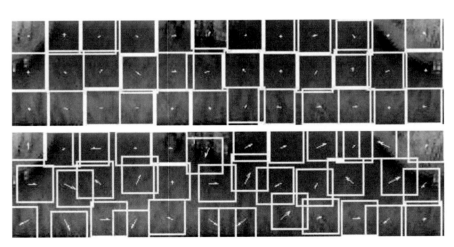

Fig. 9.12 Contrasting deformation field examples. *Top* A "reasonable" field with higher likelihood in our model. *Bottom* An "unreasonable" field with lower likelihood

Table 9.1 False accept rate (FAR) for different false reject rates (FRRS)

Algorithm	FRR = 1 %	FRR = 0.1 %	FRR = 0.01 %
Baseline	0.23 %	1.16 %	1.85 %
BGM	0	0	0.46 %

because it makes learning and inference more tractable. Specifically, we form a 2D lattice MRF on the deformation variables, in which each node is connected to its neighbors on the lattice (illustrated in Fig. 9.11).

The graphical model parameters are learnt using training images via Expectation-Maximization (EM) algorithm [18]. Use of the graphical model for an iris pattern comparison is a two-step process: (1) we infer distributions on the hidden variables of the model, and (2) we use this information to compute a match score between template and query. For space reasons, we do not discuss the details, but they can be found elsewhere [12].

The Bayesian graphical model approach was tested using CMU iris database containing high-resolution (950 × 1419) iris images acquired under visible wavelength illumination. This database contains 2390 images from 101 different eyes with 20 to 25 images per class. Table 9.1 shows the false alarm rates (FAR) for three different false reject rate (FRR) levels for the Bayesian graphical model (BGM) approach and the baseline algorithm. The baseline algorithm is the standard approach of iris segmentation followed by a binary code derived from the phases of Gabor wavelet inner products. As can be seen from Table 9.1, the Bayesian graphical model-based matching algorithm offers improved recognition performance.

9.6 Summary

Correlation filters (CFs) have long been researched for automatic target recognition applications where the targets can appear in different orientations, scales, locations, and with occlusions and obscurations. Advanced CF designs have been developed to deal with such image impairments. Also, CFs have built-in advantages such as shift-invariance and graceful degradation. Since one of the challenges in real-world iris recognition is that the iris images exhibit impairments such as non-frontal gaze, occlusions due to eye lids and eyelashes, specular reflections and nonuniform illuminations, CFs can be beneficial in dealing with such impairments. In this chapter, we discussed how correlation filters (CFs) can play an important role in iris recognition.

We discussed how CFs can provide an alternative method for iris segmentation and how they can be used for matching both unwrapped iris images (in polar coordinates) and iris images in the original Cartesian coordinates. The use of CFs can be extended to iris image patches so that the patch cross-correlations can provide information to a Bayesian graphical model (BGM) that outputs match scores that are adjusted for impairments such as nonlinear deformations and occlusions. We showed that BGM offers improved iris recognition performance compared to a baseline binary code-based matching.

References

1. R. Wildes, Iris recognition, in *Biometric Systems*, ed. by J. Wayman, A. Jain, D. Maltoni, D. Maio (Springer, 2005), ch. 3, pp. 63–95
2. J. Daugman, Probing the uniqueness and randomness of IrisCodes: results from 200 billion iris pair comparisons. Proc. IEEE **94**(11), 1927–1935 (2006)
3. J. Daugman, High confidence visual recognition of persons by a test of statistical independence. IEEE Trans. Pattern Anal. Mach. Intell. **15**(11), 1148–1161 (1993)
4. B.V.K. Vijaya Kumar, C. Xie, J. Thornton, Iris verification using correlation filters, in *Proceedings of 4th International Conference on Audio- and Video-Based Biometric Person Authentication (AVBPA)*, LCNS, vol. 2688 (Springer, Berlin, 2003), pp. 697–705
5. B.V.K. Vijaya Kumar, A. Mahalanobis, R. Juday, in *Correlation Pattern Recognition* (Cambridge University Press, United Kingdom, 2005)
6. A. Mahalanobis, L. Ortiz, B.V.K. Vijaya Kumar, Performance of the MACH/DCCF algorithms on the 10-class public release MSTAR data set. Proc. SPIE **3721**, 285–291 (1999)
7. B.V.K. Vijaya Kumar, M. Savvides, C. Xie, Correlation pattern recognition for face recognition. Proc. IEEE **94**(11), 1963–1976 (2006)
8. P. Refregier, Filter design for optical pattern recognition: multicriteria optimization approach. Opt. Lett. **15**(15), 854–856 (1990)
9. A. Mahalanobis, B.V.K. Vijaya Kumar, D. Casasent, Minimum average correlation energy filters. Appl. Opt. **26**, 3630–3633 (1987)
10. B.V.K. Vijaya Kumar, Minimum variance synthetic discriminant functions. JOSA-A **3**, 1579–1584 (1986)
11. R.D. Duda, P.E. Hart, Use of the Hough transform to detect lines and curves in pictures. Commun. ACM **15**, 11–15 (1972)
12. J. Thornton, Iris pattern matching: a probabilistic model based on discriminative cues, Ph.D. dissertation, Carnegie Mellon University (2007)
13. J. Thornton, M. Savvides, B.V.K. Vijaya Kumar, Robust iris recognition using advanced correlation techniques, in *Proceedings of International Conference on Image Analysis and Recognition ICIAR)* (2005)
14. http://www.nist.gov/itl/iad/ig/focs.cfm, Face and ocular challenge series (FOCS)
15. J. Thornton, M. Savvides, B.V.K. Vijaya Kumar, A unified Bayesian approach to deformed pattern matching of iris images. IEEE Trans. Pattern Anal. Mach. Intell. **29**, 596–606 (2007)
16. B.J. Frey, *Graphical Models for Machine Learning and Digital Communication* (MIT Press, Cambridge, 1998)
17. S. Geman, D. Geman, Stochastic relaxation, Gibbs distributions and the Bayesian restoration of images. IEEE Trans. Pattern Anal. Mach. Intell. **6**(6), 721–741 (1984)
18. M.I. Jordan, *Learning in Graphical Models* (M.I.T. Press, Cambridge, 1999)

Chapter 10
Introduction to the IrisCode Theory

Adams Wai Kin Kong, David Zhang and Mohamed Kamel

Abstract IrisCode is the most successful iris recognition method. Developed for over 18 years, IrisCode still dominates the market even though numerous iris recognition algorithms have been proposed in the academics. Currently, more than 60 million people have been mathematically enrolled by this algorithm. Its computational advantages, including high matching speed, predictable false acceptance rates and robustness against local brightness and contrast variations, play a significant role in its commercial success. To further these computational advantages, researchers have modified this algorithm to enhance iris recognition performance and recognize other biometric traits (e.g. palmprint). Many scientific papers on iris recognition have been published, but its theory is almost completely ignored. In this chapter, we will report our most recent theoretical work on the IrisCode.

10.1 Introduction

[1]IrisCode has drawn considerable attention in the past 18 years [2–4] because of its commercial success, and outstanding performance in terms of speed and

---

[1]In this paper, IrisCode is used interchangeably for both the method and features of iris recognition developed by Daugman. Recently, this method has also been dubbed the Daugman algorithm.

Mohamed Kamel—Deceased

A.W.K. Kong (✉)
Biometrics and Forensics Laboratory, School of Computer Science and Engineering,
Nanyang Technological University, Nanyang Avenue, Singapore 639798, Singapore
e-mail: AdamsKong@ntu.edu.sg

D. Zhang
Biometrics Research Centre Department of Computing,
The Hong Kong Polytechnic University, Kowloon, Hong Kong

M. Kamel
Pattern Analysis and Machine Intelligence Research Group, University of Waterloo,
200 University Avenue West, Ontario, Canada

© Springer-Verlag London 2016   229
K.W. Bowyer and M.J. Burge (eds.), *Handbook of Iris Recognition*,
Advances in Computer Vision and Pattern Recognition,
DOI 10.1007/978-1-4471-6784-6_10

accuracy. The success of IrisCode is due to the characteristics of the human iris (e.g., it contains rich texture information and is stable for a long period of time), and also its algorithmic design. IrisCode, which is an algorithm based on coarse phase information in irises, has a number of desirable properties, including rapid matching, binomial impostor distribution, robustness against contrast and brightness variations, and a predictable false acceptance rate. Therefore, researchers have modified this algorithm to enhance iris recognition performance and recognize other biometric traits. It is extremely important to completely understand IrisCode because over 60 million people are using this algorithm and many other biometric algorithms are extended from IrisCode.

In the past two decades, numerous papers on iris recognition have been published, but our understanding of IrisCode is still very incomplete because very limited work has been devoted to its theory. In the original paper on the IrisCode, Daugman reported that the bits of "0" and "1" in IrisCodes are equally probable and the importer hamming distance of IrisCode follows a binomial distribution with a high degree of freedom [3]. In addition to Daugman, Yao et al. investigated the relationship between the distributions of bits and the bandwidth of the Gabor filter [18]. In contrast to Daugman's conclusion, they stated that the bits of "0" and "1" in IrisCodes are not equally probable. Their study was based on a nonzero DC Gabor filter, while Daugman's analysis was based on zero DC Gabor filters. Hollingsworth et al. attempted to look for the most stable bits in their codes, which were not generated from 2D Gabor filters [6].

Many people believe that the inequality generating bit pairs are the core of the IrisCode, because they quantize the phase information in bitwise format for high-speed matching. Thus, some researchers have replaced the Gabor filters with other linear filters or functions to design their new coding methods. Due to the operators "≤" and ">", some researchers claim that IrisCode is an ordinal feature. This claim is controversial because the bit pairs in IrisCodes are generated from a periodic feature of the Gabor phase (see Sect. 10.2 in this chapter). Furthermore, some researchers believe that the imposter distributions of their coding methods also follow binomial distributions [14]. One clear weakness of the current understanding is that only one bit of information can be extracted from each filtering. It is an inflexible representation. In this chapter, we will summarize our recent theoretical work for a better understanding of the IrisCode [7–9].

Before reporting on our theoretical work, we will offer a brief computational summary of the IrisCode [3] for the sake of presentation convenience and consistency of notations. Two-dimensional Gabor filters with zero DC is applied to an iris image in a dimensionless polar coordinate system, $I(\rho, \phi)$. The complex Gabor response is quantized into two bits using the following inequalities:

$$h_{\text{Re}} = 1 \quad if \quad \text{Re} \left(\int_\rho \int_\phi I(\rho, \phi) e^{-(r_0-\rho)^2/\alpha^2} e^{-(\theta_o-\phi)^2/\beta^2} e^{-i\omega(\theta_0-\phi)} \rho d\rho d\phi \right) \geq 0,$$

$$(10.1)$$

$$h_{\mathrm{Re}} = 0 \quad if \quad \mathrm{Re}\left(\int_{\rho}\int_{\phi} I(\rho,\phi)e^{-(r_0-\rho)^2/\alpha^2}e^{-(\theta_o-\phi)^2/\beta^2}e^{-i\omega(\theta_o-\phi)}\rho d\rho d\phi\right) < 0,$$

$$(10.2)$$

$$h_{\mathrm{Im}} = 1 \quad if \quad \mathrm{Im}\left(\int_{\rho}\int_{\phi} I(\rho,\phi)e^{-(r_0-\rho)^2/\alpha^2}e^{-(\theta_o-\phi)^2/\beta^2}e^{-i\omega(\theta_o-\phi)}\rho d\rho d\phi\right) \geq 0,$$

$$(10.3)$$

$$h_{\mathrm{Im}} = 0 \quad if \quad \mathrm{Im}\left(\int_{\rho}\int_{\phi} I(\rho,\phi)e^{-(r_0-\rho)^2/\alpha^2}e^{-(\theta_o-\phi)^2/\beta^2}e^{-i\omega(\theta_o-\phi)}\rho d\rho d\phi\right) < 0,$$

$$(10.4)$$

where $r_0, \theta_0, \omega, \alpha$, and β are the parameters of the Gabor filters [4]. Initially, Daugman used the bitwise hamming distance defined as $HD = \sum_{i=1}^{2048}(A_i \otimes B_i)/2048$, where A_i and B_i are the bits in two IrisCodes and $\otimes$ represents the bitwise operator, XOR. Currently, masks are employed to exclude the corrupted bits from eyelashes, reflections, eyelids, and low signal-to-noise ratios [4]. The hamming distance between two IrisCodes is redefined as

$$HD = \frac{\sum_{i=1}^{2048}((A_i \otimes B_i) \cap (A_i^M \cap B_i^M))}{\sum_{i=1}^{2048}(A_i^M \cap B_i^M)}, \qquad (10.5)$$

where A^M and B^M are the masks of IrisCodes A and B, respectively and $\cap$ represents bitwise operator AND.

The rest of this chapter is organized as follows. Section 10.2 will report a recent theory on the IrisCode. Section 10.3 will demonstrate an application of the theory. Section 10.4 gives some concluding remarks.

10.2   Theoretical Properties of IrisCode

In this section, we will prove that the IrisCode is a clustering algorithm with four prototypes; the locus of a Gabor function is a two-dimensional ellipse with respect to a phase parameter and can be approximated by a circle in many cases; the Gabor function can be considered as a phase-steerable filter, and the bitwise hamming distance can be regarded as a bitwise phase distance. Moreover, we will present a unified framework to link different coding methods.

10.2.1 IrisCode is a Clustering Process

Let us define a filter-generating function, $Z(\varphi, \rho, \phi) = (\cos(\varphi)M_R(\rho, \phi) + \sin(\varphi)$
$M_I(\rho, \phi))$, where

$$M_R(\rho, \varphi) = e^{-(r_0 - \rho)^2 / \alpha^2} e^{-(\theta_o - \varphi)^2 / \beta^2} \left(\cos(-\omega(\theta_0 - \varphi)) \right), \qquad (10.6)$$

$$M_I(\rho, \varphi) = e^{-(r_0 - \rho)^2 / \alpha^2} e^{-(\theta_o - \varphi)^2 / \beta^2} \left(\sin(-\omega(\theta_0 - \varphi)) \right), \qquad (10.7)$$

represent the real and imaginary parts of a Gabor filter, respectively. For the sake of convenience, we use $Z(\varphi)$, M_R and M_I to denote $Z(\varphi, \rho, \phi)$, $M_R(\rho, \varphi)$ and $M_I(\rho, \varphi)$, respectively. The same notations for other symbols will be used in the rest of this chapter. It should be noted that $Z(\varphi)$ is a periodic function with respect to the phase parameter φ, i.e., $Z(\varphi) = Z(\varphi + 2\pi)$ and M_R is not a zero DC filter. In this chapter, we will suppose that the DC of iris patches for filtering has been removed and therefore, we can retain the DC components in Eq. 10.6.

By substituting $5\pi/4$, $7\pi/4$, $\pi/4$, and $3\pi/4$ to φ, we can obtain four filters:

$$Z_0 = Z(5\pi/4) = -(M_R + M_I)/\sqrt{2}, \qquad (10.8)$$

$$Z_1 = Z(7\pi/4) = (M_R - M_I)/\sqrt{2}, \qquad (10.9)$$

$$Z_2 = Z(\pi/4) = (M_R + M_I)/\sqrt{2}, \qquad (10.10)$$

$$Z_3 = Z(3\pi/4) = -(M_R - M_I)/\sqrt{2}. \qquad (10.11)$$

Note that $Z_0 = -Z_2$ and $Z_1 = -Z_3$. These four filters shown in Fig. 10.1 will be considered as four cluster centers. To cluster an input iris image, we define $j = \arg\max_i \int_\rho \int_\varphi \rho I Z_i d\rho d\varphi / \|\rho I\| \|Z_i\|$ as a clustering condition, where j is called the winning index and I is the iris image in the dimensionless polar coordinate system. The clustering condition is in fact the cosine measure between Z_i and ρI. Because $\|Z_u\| = \|Z_v\|$ for all u and v, the clustering condition can be simplified as:

$$j = \arg\max_i \left(\int_\rho \int_\phi \rho I Z_i d\rho d\phi \right). \qquad (10.12)$$

To prove that $\|Z_u\| = \|Z_v\|$ for all u and v, the orthogonal property between M_R and M_I i.e., $\int_\rho \int_\phi M_I M_R d\rho d\phi = 0$ should be used. Using the coding table under heading "Coded winning indexes" in Table 10.1 to encode the winning indexes and comparing the resultant bits with the bits of IrisCodes, we can easily note that these

(a)   (b)

(c)   (d)

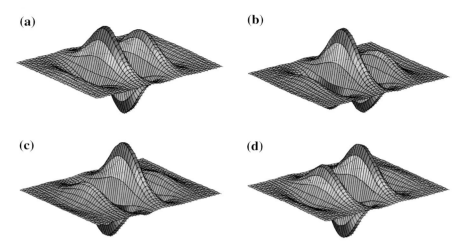

Fig. 10.1   The four filters used in the IrisCode, **a** Z_0, **b** Z_1, **c** Z_2 and **d** Z_3

Table 10.1   Comparison of IrisCode, winning index and coded winning index

Winning index	Coded winning indexes		IrisCode	
	Bit 2	Bit 1	h_{Im}	h_{Re}
1	0	0	0	0
2	0	1	0	1
3	1	1	1	1
4	1	0	1	0

two sets of bits are equivalent. In other words, IrisCode is a clustering process, in which the cosine measure is used as a clustering criterion and Z_0, Z_1, Z_2 and Z_3 are the four prototypes.

10.2.2   Properties of The Filter Generating Function

In this subsection, we will provide the properties of the filter generating function. First of all, we will discuss the physical meaning of Z, and then the locus of φ. Next, we will demonstrate that filters generated from the filter generating function can be regarded as phase-steerable filters. Finally, we will pinpoint the relationship between

φ and $\tan^{-1}\left(\int\limits_{\rho} \int\limits_{\varphi} \rho IM_I d\rho d\phi \middle/ \int\limits_{\rho} \int\limits_{\varphi} \rho IM_R d\rho d\phi \right)$ which is commonly employed

as a feature in image-based applications.

10.2.2.1   The Physical Meaning of Z and the Locus of φ

By substituting Eqs. 10.6 and 10.7 into Z and using a compound angle formula, we can derive that

$$Z(\phi) = e^{-(r_0-\rho)^2/\sigma^2} e^{-(\theta_0-\varphi)^2/\beta^2} \cos(-\omega(\theta_0-\varphi)-\phi). \qquad (10.13)$$

Clearly, Z is a Gabor function and φ is its phase.

Now, we will prove that the locus of φ is an ellipse. First, we discretize M_R, M_I and Z to obtain three vectors, $\vec{M}_R, \vec{M}_I$ and $\vec{Z}(\phi)$, respectively. The unit vectors of $\vec{M}_R$ and $\vec{M}_I$ are defined as $\vec{v}_R = \vec{M}_R / \left\| \vec{M}_R \right\|$ and $\vec{v}_I = \vec{M}_I / \left\| \vec{M}_I \right\|$. Using them to decompose $\vec{Z}(\phi)$, we can obtain

$$\vec{Z}(\phi) = (\cos(\phi) \left\| \vec{M}_R \right\| \vec{v}_R + \sin(\phi) \left\| \vec{M}_I \right\| \vec{v}_I). \qquad (10.14)$$

Clearly, $\vec{Z}(\phi)$ is in a two-dimensional space spanned by $\vec{v}_R$ and $\vec{v}_I$ and its coordinate in this space is $(\|M_R\| \cos(\phi), \|M_I\| \sin(\phi))$, which fulfill the equality

$$\frac{(\|M_R\| \cos(\phi))^2}{\|M_R\|^2} + \frac{(\|M_I\| \sin(\phi))^2}{\|M_I\|^2} = 1, \qquad (10.15)$$

Eq. 10.15 pinpoints that the locus of φ is an ellipse. It can be proven that $\lim_{k \to \infty} (\|M_R\|^2 - \|M_I\|^2) = 0$, where $k = \omega\beta$, which is to say that the locus of φ is a circle because Eq. 10.15 can be simplified as $(\|M_R\| \cos(\phi))^2 + (\|M_I\| \sin(\phi))^2 = \|M_R\|^2$. The proof is given in Appendix 1. Figure 10.2 illustrates the loci and the filters.

10.2.2.2   Gabor Function and Phase-Steerable Filter

By substituting $Z(\varphi, \rho, \phi) = (\cos(\varphi)M_R(\rho, \phi) + \sin(\varphi)M_I(\rho, \phi))$ into $\iint_{\rho} \int_{\varphi} \rho I Z(\varphi) d\rho d\varphi$, we can obtain

$$\cos(\varphi) \int_{\rho} \int_{\varphi} \rho I M_R d\rho d\varphi + \sin(\varphi) \int_{\rho} \int_{\varphi} \rho I M_I d\rho d\varphi. \qquad (10.16)$$

Equation 10.16 pinpoints that no matter how many filters are generated from Z, two filtering operations $\int_{\rho} \int_{\varphi} \rho I M_R d\rho d\varphi$ and $\int_{\rho} \int_{\varphi} \rho I M_I d\rho d\varphi$ are enough to perform

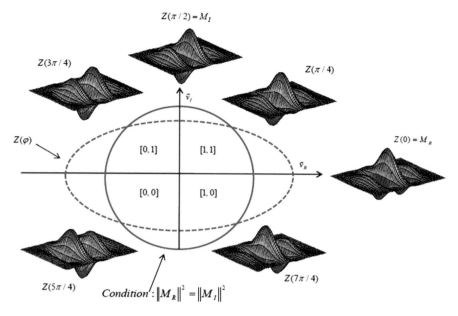

Fig. 10.2 Illustration of the loci of φ and filters generated from Z

the clustering calculation based on $j = \arg\max_i \int_\rho \int_\varphi \rho I Z(\varphi_i) d\rho d\varphi / \|\rho I\| \|Z(\varphi_i)\|$

because $\|Z(\varphi_i)\|$ can be pre-computed. Clearly, Z is a phase-steerable filter.

10.2.2.3   The Difference Between Gabor Phase and ϕ

Let $\phi_c = \tan^{-1} \left(\int_\rho \int_\varphi \rho I M_I d\rho d\varphi \Big/ \int_\rho \int_\varphi \rho I M_R d\rho d\varphi \right)$ be a Gabor phase.
Researchers generally consider ϕ_c as a phase of a local patch, instead of ϕ. Their relationship is not clear. It can be proven that $|\varphi - \phi_c| \leq \tan^{-1}(\frac{1}{\sqrt{K}}) - \tan^{-1}(\sqrt{K})$, where $K = \|M_I\|^2 / \|M_R\|^2$. This proof is given in [8], which is lengthy. Note that when $K=1$, $\phi_c = \varphi$ and the locus of φ is a circle.

10.2.3 Phase Distance and Its Relationship with Bitwise Hamming Distance

In this subsection, we will demonstrate that the phase distance can be represented as the bitwise hamming distance. Assume that we generate a number of filters from Z for clustering based on the cosine measure. If the number of filters are more than four, we need a new distance measure to compare the prototypes, i.e., $\vec{Z}(\omega)$ and $\vec{Z}(\gamma)$. In Sect. 10.2.2.1, we have already shown that Z is on a two-dimensional space and the locus of φ is an ellipse and therefore, $\vec{Z}(\omega)$ and $\vec{Z}(\gamma)$ can be measured by the phase distance between ω and γ defined as $\min(|\omega - \gamma|,\ 2\pi - |\omega - \gamma|)$. If ω and γ are generated from uniform sampling, i.e., $\omega = 2\pi p/2n$ and $\gamma = 2\pi q/2n$, where p and q are two integers between 0 and $2n - 1$, the phase distance can be rewritten as $\min\left(\frac{\pi}{n}|p - q|,\ \frac{\pi}{n}(2n - |p - q|)\right)$. n is called the order of the coding scheme. This formula can be further simplified as $\min(|p - q|,\ (2n - |p - q|))$ if we consider π/n as one unit distance. Note that n is equal to 2 for the IrisCode because it uses four prototypes in the clustering process. Figure 10.3 illustrates the phase distance and winning indexes.

The relationship between the bitwise hamming distance employed in the IrisCode and phase distance based on the integer representations of ω and γ is still not clear. Using the coding scheme given in Fig. 10.4 to encode p and q, the phase distance can be computed through bitwise hamming distance, i.e., $\sum_{i=1}^{n} b_{i,q} \otimes b_{i,p} = \min(|p - q|,\ 2n - |p - q|)$. The proof of this equation is given in Appendix 2. Table 10.2 shows the coding tables for $n = 3$ and $n = 4$. It clearly indicates that the difference between two adjacent winning indexes is only one bit and most importantly, this coding scheme retains the phase distance. It should be emphasized that

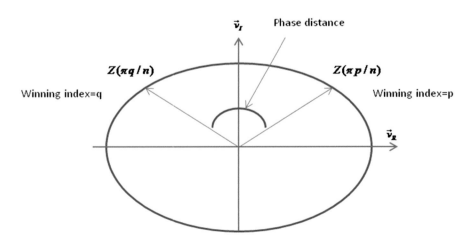

Fig. 10.3 Illustration of phase distance

$$\textit{if} \quad j \le n \quad \textit{and} \quad 1 \le i < j,$$

$$b_{i,j} = 1$$

$$\textit{elseif} \quad j > n \quad \textit{and} \quad j - n \le i \le n,$$

$$b_{i,j} = 1$$

$$\textit{else}$$

$$b_{i,j} = 0$$

Fig. 10.4 Pseudo code of the coding table

Table 10.2 The coding tables for (a) $n = 3$ and (b) $n = 4$

(a)

Winning indexes	Bit 2	Bit 1	Bit 0	
0	0	0	0	
1	0	0	1	
2	0	1	1	
3	1	1	1	
4	1	1	0	
5	1	0	0	

(b)

Winning indexes	Bit 3	Bit 2	Bit 1	Bit 0
0	0	0	0	0
1	0	0	0	1
2	0	0	1	1
3	0	1	1	1
4	1	1	1	1
5	1	1	1	0
6	1	1	0	0
7	1	0	0	0

in rotating between any adjacent phase quadrant, only a single bit in the IrisCode changes, while in rotating between one phase quadrant to the opposite phase quadrant, both two bits in the IrisCode change, which is to say that the distances between phase quadrants in the IrisCode are also retained. By exploiting the relationship between the bitwise hamming distance and the phase distance, we can extend the IrisCode from using the four prototypes in the clustering process to using $2n$ prototypes and high speed matching.

10.2.4 A Generalized Framework from the IrisCode

Many coding methods that are very similar to the IrisCode [1, 5, 12, 13, 15–17, 19] have been proposed for iris and palm print recognition. A common approach is to substitute other linear transforms or filters for the Gabor filters in the IrisCode. We have already proven that the IrisCode is a clustering with four prototypes. It is not surprising that these coding methods can also be considered as clustering algorithms, but with two prototypes. Mathematically, these methods can be represented by the following two equations,

$$h = 1 \quad if \quad \int_{\rho} \int_{\varphi} FId\rho d\varphi \geq 0, \tag{10.17}$$

$$h = 0 \quad if \quad \int_{\rho} \int_{\varphi} FId\rho d\varphi < 0, \tag{10.18}$$

where h is a resultant bit and F is a linear filter employed in these methods. Let $(-1)^{\upsilon+1}F$ be a filtering generating function, where $\upsilon \in \{0, 1\}$. It can only generate two filters, F and $-F$. Note that these two filters have the same power, i.e., $\|F\| = \|-F\|$, the clustering criterion based on the cosine measure can be simplified as

$$j = \arg \max_{i} \left(\int_{\rho} \int_{\varphi} (-1)^{i+1} FId\rho d\varphi \right). \tag{10.19}$$

If $\int_{\rho} \int_{\varphi} FId\rho d\varphi > \int_{\rho} \int_{\varphi} -FId\rho d\varphi, j = 1$ and $\int_{\rho} \int_{\varphi} FId\rho d\varphi > 0$. If $\int_{\rho} \int_{\varphi} -FId\rho d\varphi > \int_{\rho} \int_{\varphi} FId\rho d\varphi, j = 0$ and $\int_{\rho} \int_{\varphi} FId\rho d\varphi < 0$. Using the first-order coding scheme defined in Fig. 10.4 to encode the winning index j, we get back Eqs. 10.17 and 10.18.

   In addition to these coding schemes, other coding methods that use log Gabor filters and Gabor filters employ the order 2 coding scheme, which is to say that in their clustering processes, they have four prototypes, as with IrisCode [17, 19]. Our Competitive Code for palmprint identification [11] uses the negative real part of a Gabor function as a filter generating function to produce six filters for the clustering process. It is the first coding method that uses an order higher than 2. All of these coding methods can be put into a unified framework, which is composed of a filter generating function, clustering, coding scheme, and bitwise phase matching as illustrated in Fig. 10.5.

Fig. 10.5 A common framework employed by most of the existing coding methods

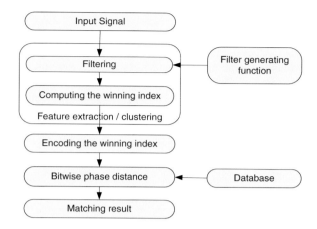

10.3   An Application Based on the Theoretical Results

To demonstrate the theoretical results that have an impact on applications, an algorithm that uses higher precision to present the Gabor phase was designed to improve matching accuracy for iris recognition. Its computational steps are given below

1. Compute $\displaystyle\int_\rho\int_\varphi \rho I M_R d\rho d\varphi$ and $\displaystyle\int_\rho\int_\varphi \rho I M_I d\rho d\varphi$.

2. Use the results in Sect. 10.2.2 i.e., $\cos(i\pi/n)\displaystyle\int_\rho\int_\varphi \rho I M_R d\rho d\varphi + \sin(i\pi/n)$

   $\displaystyle\int_\rho\int_\varphi \rho I M_I d\rho d\varphi$ to compute the winning index, $j = \arg$

   $\displaystyle\max_i \int_\rho\int_\varphi \rho I Z(i\pi/n) d\rho d\varphi / \|\rho I\| \|Z(i\pi/n)\|$.

3. Use the results in Sect. 10.2.3 to encode the winning indexes and bitwise hamming distance to perform high speed matching.

The algorithm is called precise phase representation, which inherits the properties of the IrisCode (e.g., high speed matching). The precision of the phase is controlled by the parameter n. In total, n bits are allocated for a phase value. Note that the IrisCode uses two bits.

10.3.1 Database

The CASIA-1 iris database that contains 756 images from 108 irises is used for this evaluation. One hundred and forty images were used to train the parameters of the Gabor filters. The remaining was used for the following tests. In these experiments, we used d' index and receiver operating characteristic (ROC) curves as a plot of the genuine acceptance rates against the false acceptance rates for all possible operating points as performance indexes. The experimental results based on the West Virginia University (WVU) iris database are reported in [7].

10.3.2 Experimental Results

We compared the original IrisCode and precise phase representations for $n = 3$, 4, and 5 to demonstrate the effectiveness of the latter. Irises from the same and different individuals were matched to respectively obtain 1,848 genuine hamming distances and 187,572 impostor hamming distances for each representation. These distances were used to estimate the genuine and impostor distributions. The genuine and impostor distributions of the IrisCode and precise phase representations for $n = 3$, 4, and 5 are given in Fig. 10.6a–d, respectively. Figure 10.7 depicts the corresponding ROC curves for comparison. It shows that the precise phase representation of the order 4 always provides the best results. Its equal error rate is 0.32 %. In a comparison of the IrisCode and the precise phase representation of the order 4, the latter has a 3.1 % improvement in the genuine acceptance rate when the false acceptance rate is 5.3×10^{-4} %. However, an increase in the precision of the phase does not always improve accuracy, because some encoded bits are in fact, not stable. It is also the case in Eigenface in which increasing numbers of principle components do not always increase accuracy. Note that the matching speed of the precise phase representation of the order 4 is slower than the IrisCode; roughly speaking, it is half of that of the IrisCode since the latter only uses two bits to represent a phase value while the former requires four bits. For some applications, such as identifying a person in a mid-sized company for access control, one million comparisons per second is not necessary. We can use the precise phase representation to obtain high accuracy for these applications. It should be emphasized that the precise phase representation is a flexible representation to balance speed and accuracy.

10.4 Conclusion

The IrisCode has been developed for nearly two decades and more than 60 million people are using this algorithm. Although numerous papers on iris recognition have been published, our theoretical understanding of the IrisCode is not yet complete

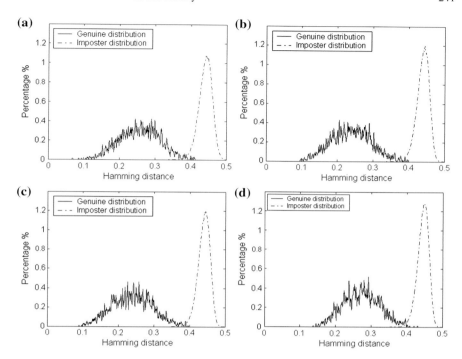

Fig. 10.6 Genuine and impostor distributions for **a** the IrisCode, **b–d** precise phase representations for $n = 3$–5, respectively

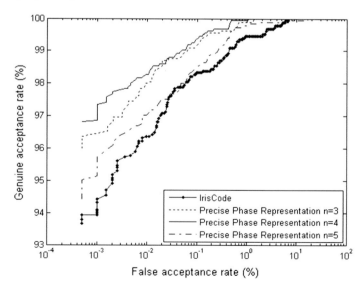

Fig. 10.7 ROC curves of the IrisCode and precise phase representations for $n = 3, 4$ and 5

because only limited research efforts have been put into analyzing the IrisCode. In this chapter, we have summarized our recent work that fills this knowledge gap [7–9]. If readers are interested in this theoretical development, please keep track of the author's publications.

Acknowledgments We would like to thank CASIA for sharing their database. This work is partially supported by the Ministry of Education, Singapore through AcRF Tier 1.

Appendix 1

This appendix proves that $\|M_R\| = \|M_I\|$, when $k \to \infty$, where $k = \omega\beta$.
  Considering $\|M_R\|^2 - \|M_I\|^2$

$$= \int\int \left(e^{-\frac{\rho^2}{\alpha^2}}e^{-\frac{\varphi^2}{\beta^2}}\cos(\omega\varphi)\right)^2 d\rho d\varphi - \int\int \left(e^{-\frac{\rho^2}{\alpha^2}}e^{-\frac{\varphi^2}{\beta^2}}\sin(\omega\varphi)\right)^2 d\rho d\varphi$$

$$= \int\int e^{-\frac{2\rho^2}{\alpha^2}}e^{-\frac{2\varphi^2}{\beta^2}}\left(\cos^2(\omega\varphi) - \sin^2(\omega\varphi)\right) d\rho d\varphi$$

$$= \int e^{-\frac{2\rho^2}{\alpha^2}} d\rho \int e^{-\frac{2\varphi^2}{\beta^2}}\left(\cos^2(\omega\varphi) - \sin^2(\omega\varphi)\right)d\varphi$$

$$= \frac{\alpha\sqrt{2\pi}}{2}\int e^{-\frac{2\varphi^2}{\beta^2}}\left(\cos^2(\omega\varphi) - \sin^2(\omega\varphi)\right)d\varphi$$

Let $\gamma = \frac{k}{\beta}\varphi$. Thus

$$= \frac{\alpha\beta\sqrt{2\pi}}{2k}\int e^{-\frac{2\gamma^2}{k^2}}\left(\cos^2(\gamma) - \sin^2(\gamma)\right)d\gamma$$

$$= \frac{\alpha\beta\sqrt{2\pi}}{2k}\int e^{-\frac{2\gamma^2}{k^2}}\cos(2\gamma)d\gamma$$

Let $2\gamma = \tau$

$$= \frac{\alpha\beta\sqrt{2\pi}}{4k}\int e^{-\frac{\tau^2}{2k^2}}\cos(\tau)d\tau$$

$$= \frac{\alpha\beta\sqrt{2\pi}}{4k}\sqrt{2\pi}ke^{-\frac{k^2}{2}}$$

$$= \frac{1}{2}\alpha\beta\pi e^{-\frac{k^2}{2}}$$

$\|M_R\|^2 - \|M_I\|^2$ is always greater than zero because α, β, and k are greater than zero. Note that $\lim\limits_{k\to\infty} \left(\|M_R\|^2 - \|M_I\|^2 \right) = \lim\limits_{k\to\infty} \frac{1}{2}\alpha\beta\pi e^{-\frac{k^2}{2}} = 0$.

Appendix 2

This appendix shows that the phase distance can be calculated through bitwise hamming distance.

Let two winning indexes be $j - 1$, and $j - 1 + k$, where $1 \leq j \leq j + k < 2n$. Their phase distance is $\min(k, \ 2n - k)$. By using the coding scheme given in Fig. 10.4, they are represented by the jth and $j + k$th column vectors of matrix B. We would like to prove that

$$\sum_{i=1}^{n} b_{i,j} \otimes b_{i,j+k} = \min(k, \ 2n - k).$$

Because all $b_{i,j}$ are either one or zero, $\displaystyle\sum_{i=1}^{n} b_{i,j} \otimes b_{i,j+h} = \sum_{i=1}^{n} \left| b_{i,j} - b_{i,j+k} \right|$

Case 1: If $j \leq n$ and $j + k \leq n$

From the definition of A, we know $\displaystyle\sum_{i=1}^{n} \left| b_{i,j} - b_{i,j+k} \right| = k$

Case 2: If $j > n$ and $j + k > n$

As in Case 1, we know $\displaystyle\sum_{i=1}^{n} \left| b_{i,j} - b_{i,j+k} \right| = k$

Case 3: If $j \leq n$ and $j + k > n$ and $k \leq n$

$$\text{Consider } b_{i,j} = 1 \text{ and } b_{i,j+k} = 1 \tag{10.20}$$

From the definition of A, we have $1 \leq i < j$ and $j + k - n \leq i \leq n$

Then, $j + k - n \leq i < j$
The number of i that satisfies condition (10.20) is

$$\max(0, \ j - (j + k - n)). \tag{10.21}$$

Since $k \leq n$, $\max(0, \ j - (j + k - n)) = n - k$

$$\text{Consider } b_{i,j} = 0 \text{ and } b_{i,j+k} = 0 \tag{10.22}$$

From the definition of A, we have $i \geq j$ and $i < j + k - n$

Then $j \leq i < j + k - n$

The number of i that satisfies condition (10.22) is

$$\max(0, \; j + k - n - j) \tag{10.23}$$

Since $k \leq n$, $\max(0, \; k - n) = 0$

Thus, $\sum_{i=1}^{n} \left| b_{i,j} - b_{i,j+k} \right| = n - (n - k) = k$

Case 4: If $j \leq n$ and $j + k > n$ and $k > n$

$$\text{Consider } b_{i,j} = 1 \text{ and } b_{i,j+k} = 1. \tag{10.24}$$

From (10.21), the number of i that satisfies condition (10.24) is
$\max(0, \; j - (j + k - n))$
Since $k > n$, $\max(0, \; n - k) = 0$

$$\text{Consider } b_{i,j} = 0 \text{ and } b_{i,j+k} = 0, \tag{10.25}$$

From (10.23), the number of i that satisfies condition (10.25) is
$\max(0, \; j + k - n - j)$
Since $k > n$, $\max(0, \; k - n) = k - n$
Thus, $\sum_{i=1}^{n} \left| b_{i,j} - b_{i,j+k} \right| = n - (k - n) = 2n - k$

Thus, $\sum_{i=1}^{n} b_{i,j} \otimes b_{i,j+k} = k$ for Cases, 1–3 and $\sum_{i=1}^{n} b_{i,j} \otimes b_{i,j+k} = 2n - k$ for Case 4.

Since $2n - k \geq k$ for Cases 1–3 and $2n - k < k$ for Case 4, $\sum_{i=1}^{n} b_{i,j} \otimes b_{i,j+k} = $
$\min(k, \; 2n - k)$.

References

1. K. Bea, S. Noh, J. Kim, Iris feature extraction using independent component analysis, in Lecture Notes in Computer Science, vol. 2688 (Springer, 2003), pp. 838–844
2. J. Daugman, Probing the uniqueness and randomness of IrisCode: results from 200 billion iris cross-comparisons. Proc. IEEE **94**(11) (2006)
3. J.G. Daugman, High confidence visual recognition of persons by a test of statistical independence. IEEE Trans. Pattern Anal. Mach. Intell. **15**(11), 1148–1161 (1993)

4. J. Daugman, How iris recognition works. IEEE Trans. Circuits Syst. Video Technol. **14**(1), 21–30 (2004)
5. T. Ea, A. Valentian, F. Rossant, F. Amiel, A. Amara, Algorithm implementation for iris identification, in *Proceedings of 48th Midwest Symposium on Circuits and Systems*, pp. 1207–1210, 2005
6. K.P. Hollingsworth, K.W. Bowyer, P.J. Flynn, The best bits in an iris code. IEEE Trans. Pattern Anal. Mach. Intell. **31**(6), 964–973 (2009)
7. A.W.K Kong, D. Zhang, M. Kamel, An analysis of IrisCode. IEEE Trans. Image Process. **19**(2), 522–532 (2010)
8. A. Kong, An analysis of Gabor detection, in *International Conference on Image Analysis and Recognition, (ICIAR)*, Halifax, Canada, 6–8 July 2009
9. A.W.K. Kong, Palmprint identification based on generalization of IrisCode. Ph.D. thesis, University of Waterloo (2007)
10. A.W.K. Kong, D. Zhang, M. Kamel, Palmprint identification using feature-level fusion. Pattern Recogn., 478–487 (2006)
11. A.W.K. Kong, D. Zhang, M. Kamel, An analysis of brute-force break-ins of a palmprint authentication system. IEEE Trans. Syst. Man Cybern. Part B **36**(5), 1201–1205 (2006)
12. E. Krichen, M.A. Mellakh, S. Garcia-Salicetti, B. Dorizzi, Iris identification using wavelet packets, in *Proceedings of International Conference on Pattern Recognition*, vol. 4, 2004, pp. 226–338
13. L. Ma, T. Tan, Y. Wang, D. Zhang, Efficient iris recognition by characterizing key local variations. IEEE Trans. Image Process. **13**(6), 739–750 (2004)
14. L. Masek, Recognition of human iris patterns for biometric identification. Bachelor thesis, The University of Western Australia
15. S.I. Noh, K. Bae, Y. Park, J. Kim, A novel method to extract features for iris recognition system, in Lecture Notes in Computer Science, vol. 2688 (Springer, 2003), pp. 861–868
16. C.H. Park, J.J. Lee, S.K. Oh, Y.C. Song, D.H. Choi, K.H. Park, Iris feature extraction and matching based on multiscale and directional image representation. Lecture Notes in Computer Science, vol. 2695 (Springer, 2004), pp. 576–583
17. E. Rydgren, T.E.A.F. Amiel, F. Rossant, A. Amara, Iris features extraction using wavelet packets, in *Proceedings of International Conference on Image Processing*, vol. 2, 2004, pp. 861–864
18. P. Yao, J. Li, X. Ye, Z. Zhuang, B. Li, An analysis and improvement of an iris identification algorithm, in *Proceedings of the 18th ICPR*, vol. 4, 2006, pp. 362–365
19. P.F. Zhang, D.S. Li, Q. Wang, A novel iris recognition method based on feature fusion, in *Proceedings of the Third International Conference on Machine Learning and Cybernetics*, 2004, pp. 26–29
20. D. Zhang, W.K. Kong, J. You, M. Wong, On-line palmprint identification. IEEE Trans. Pattern Anal. Mach. Intell. **25**(9), 1041–1050 (2003)

Chapter 11
Robust and Secure Iris Recognition

Jaishanker K. Pillai, Vishal Patel, Rama Chellappa and Nalini Ratha

Abstract Iris biometric entails using the patterns on the iris as a biometric for personal authentication. It has additional benefits over contact-based biometrics such as fingerprints and hand geometry. However, iris biometric often suffers from the following three challenges: ability to handle unconstrained acquisition, privacy enhancement without compromising security, and robust matching. This chapter discusses a unified framework based on sparse representations and random projections that can address these issues simultaneously. Furthermore, recognition from iris videos as well as generation of cancelable iris templates for enhancing the privacy and security is also discussed.

11.1 Introduction

Iris recognition deals with using the patterns on the iris as a biometric for identification or verification. Iris is the colored region of the eye, which controls the amount of light entering the eye. It encloses the darker pupil and is surrounded by a white region called the sclera. Iris and the pupil are protected by a transparent membrane called the cornea. Figure 11.1 shows the different parts of the human eye.

J.K. Pillai · R. Chellappa
University of Maryland, College Park, Maryland, MD, USA
e-mail: jsp@umiacs.umd.edu

R. Chellappa
e-mail: rama@umiacs.umd.edu

V. Patel (✉)
Department of Electrical and Computer Engineering Rutgers, The State University of New Jersey, 508 CoRE 94 Brett Road, Piscataway, NJ 08854, USA
e-mail: pvishalm@umiacs.umd.edu

N. Ratha
IBM Watson Research Center, Hawthorne, NY, USA
e-mail: Ratha@us.ibm.com

© Springer-Verlag London 2016
K.W. Bowyer and M.J. Burge (eds.), *Handbook of Iris Recognition*,
Advances in Computer Vision and Pattern Recognition,
DOI 10.1007/978-1-4471-6784-6_11

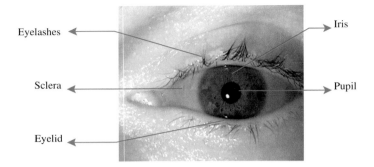

Fig. 11.1 Different parts of the eye

Human iris typically has a rich set of patterns, which are believed to be formed randomly during the fetal development of the eye. The iris patterns are observed to differ for different individuals and remain stable for long periods of time, making it a good biometric. Iris-based human authentication deals with using these iris patterns to recognize individuals. It is a noncontact biometric, which is more hygienic than a contact biometric like finger print. Also it is protected from wear and tear by the cornea, which ensures its stability over years. However, an iris-based personal authentication system requires close proximity of the eye and a cooperative subject. When acquired correctly, iris-based biometric is highly accurate.

11.1.1   Components of an Iris Recognition System

A generic iris recognition system has five main components, as shown in Fig. 11.2. They are the acquisition unit, segmentation unit, quality estimation unit, feature extraction unit, and the matching unit. Since the most well-known iris recognition system is the one by Daugman [9], we use it as an example to explain the different steps below.

The first step in an iris recognition system is the image acquisition, where the iris image of the user is obtained. Near infrared illumination is normally used as it reveals the detailed structure of the iris much better that visible light. Visible light gets absorbed by the melanin pigments on the iris where as the longer near infrared radiations get reflected by them. After the image is obtained, the segmentation algorithm extracts the region of the image corresponding to the iris, for further processing. In

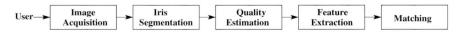

Fig. 11.2 Parts of an iris recognition system

Daugman's method, the inner and outer boundaries of the iris (known as the pupil-lary and limbic boundaries, respectively) are obtained by approximating them by circles and finding their parameters. Each of the boundaries is obtained for an image $I(x, y)$ by integro-differential operators, which find the parameters (r, x_0, y_0) having the highest blurred partial derivatives in a circular arc of width ds along a circle of center (x_0, y_0) and radius r, given by

$$max_{(r, x_0, y_0)} |G_\sigma(r) * \frac{\partial}{\partial r} \oint_{r, x_0, y_0} \frac{I(x, y)}{2\pi r} ds|$$

where $G_\sigma(r)$ denotes a smoothing operator like the Gaussian with scale σ and $*$ denote convolution. After obtaining these boundaries, further processing is per-formed to remove the eye lids and eye lashes present in the iris region. To make the iris template invariant to changes in size, the extracted iris region is mapped to a normalized coordinate system, where the pupillary boundary is mapped to zero and the limbic boundary is mapped to 1. So any pixel in the new coordinate system is defined by an angle between 0 and 360° and a radial coordinate from 0 to 1.

The quality estimation stage estimates the quality of the acquired iris sample and decides whether to further process the image for recognition or reject the sample. Energy of the high-frequency Fourier coefficients can be used as a measure of blur in the acquired image. A blurred image will not have high-frequency components and hence have lower energy in those coefficients.

If the acquired image is accepted by the quality estimation module, feature extrac-tion unit computes features from the iris region, which captures the identity of the person. The texture patterns on the iris contain the information unique to each indi-vidual. To capture this, the extracted and normalized iris region is convolved with two dimensional Gabor filters of the form

$$G(r, \theta) = \exp^{-i\omega(\theta - \theta_0)} \exp^{-\frac{(r - r_0)^2}{\alpha^2}} \exp^{-\frac{(\theta - \theta_0)^2}{\beta^2}}$$

where (r, θ) denote the polar coordinates. (r_0, θ_0) denote the location, ω the scale and (α, β) the width of the Gabor filter, respectively.

To improve the speed of matching, the extracted Gabor features are encoded into a binary vector. Each complex Gabor feature is represented by two bits—the first bit is 1 if the real part of the Gabor feature is positive and zero otherwise. Similarly, the second bit captures the sign of the imaginary part of the Gabor feature. Normalized Hamming distance is then used as a measure of similarity between two iris images. It is defined as the fraction of the bits for which the two iris codes differ. The distance is computed only for those pixels for which both the iris codes are not occluded. To account for the in-plane rotation, the distance is computed for several rotations of the iris vector. The smallest among all those scores is used as the final similarity score.

The source code for a typical generic iris recognition system, similar to the one described above has been released by Masek and Kovesi [21]. We refer the reader to [5] for an excellent survey of the recent efforts in iris recognition.

11.1.2 Cancelable Iris Biometric

An important aspect in iris biometrics is security and privacy of the users. When
the texture features of one's iris are stored in a template dictionary, a hacker could
possibly break into the dictionary and steal these patterns. Unlike credit cards, which
can be revoked and reissued, biometric patterns of an individual cannot be modified.
So, directly using iris features for recognition is extremely vulnerable to attacks. To
deal with this, the idea of cancelable iris biometrics has been introduced [3, 15, 28],
which can protect the original iris patterns as well as revoke and reissue new patterns
when the old ones are lost or stolen.

The concept of cancelable biometrics was first introduced by Ratha et al. [3, 28].
A cancelable biometric scheme intentionally distorts the original biometric pattern
through a revocable and noninvertible transformation. The objectives of a cancelable
biometric system are as follows [15]:

- Different templates should be used in different applications to prevent cross matching.
- Template computation must be noninvertible to prevent unauthorized recovery of biometric data.
- Revocation and reissue should be possible in the event of compromise, and
- Recognition performance should not degrade when a cancelable biometric template is used.

In [10], Hash functions were used to minimize the compromise of the private biometric data of the users. Cryptographic techniques were applied in [13] to increase
the security of iris systems. In [17], error correcting codes were used for cancelable
iris biometrics. A fuzzy commitment method was introduced in [16]. Other schemes
have also been introduced to improve the security of iris biometric. See [10, 13,
15–17, 33] and the references therein for more details.

The pioneering work in the field of cancelable iris biometric was done by Zuo
et al. [36]. They introduced four noninvertible and revocable transformations for cancelability. While the first two methods utilized random circular shifting and addition,
the other two methods added random noise patterns to the iris features to transform
them. As noted by the authors, the first two methods gradually reduce the amount of
information available for recognition. Since they are essentially linear transformations on the feature vectors, they are sensitive to outliers in the feature vector that
arises due to eyelids, eye lashes, and specular reflections. They also combine the
good and bad quality regions in the iris image leading to lower performance. The
proposed random projections-based cancelability algorithm works on each sector
of the iris separately, so outliers can only affect the corresponding sectors and not
the entire iris vector. Hence, it is more robust to common outliers in iris data when
compared to [36].

11.1.3   Iris Recognition from Videos

Though research in iris recognition has been extremely active in the past decade, most of the existing results are based on recognition from still iris images [14]. Multiple iris images have been used in the past to improve performance. Du et al. [12] demonstrated higher rank one recognition rates using three gallery images instead of one. Ma et al. [20] also enrolled three iris images and averaged the three Hamming distances to obtain the final score. Krischen et al. [18] used the minimum of the three Hamming distance as the final score. Schmid and Nicolo [31] demonstrated that fusing the scores using log likelihood ratio gave superior performance when compared to average Hamming distance. Liu and Xie [19], Roy and Bhattacharya [30] used multiple iris images for training classifiers.

The distortions common in iris image acquisition like occlusion due to eyelids, eye lashes, blur, and specular reflections will differ in various frames of the video. So by combining the different frames in the video efficiently, the performance could be improved. The only work towards using the temporal continuity in iris videos for improving the performance is done by Hollingsworth et al. [14]. The authors introduced a feature level fusion by averaging the corresponding iris pixels and a score level fusion algorithm combining all the pairwise matching scores. Though averaging reduces the noise and improves the performance, it required images to be well segmented and aligned, which may often not be possible in a practical iris recognition system.

11.1.4   Publicly Available Datasets

When the iris acquisition conditions are not constrained, many of the acquired iris images suffer from defocus blur, motion blur, occlusion due to the eyelids, specular reflections, and off angle distortions. Numerous datasets are now available for the research community, containing varying degrees of these artifacts.

One of the earliest ones was the CASIA version 1 [32]. It contains 108 subjects and seven images per person. The images in the database are clean, without significant occlusion, blur or specular reflection on the iris. But the pupil has been edited in these images and replaced by a black region, which masks the specular reflections in the pupil region. A larger dataset containing some of the unedited images is now available under the name CASIA version 3 [32]. It has 1500 subjects and more than 2200 iris images.

Two large datasets have been collected by the University of Notre Dame for the Iris Challenge Evaluation (ICE) in 2005 and 2006. The ICE 2005 dataset [22] has two hundred and forty-four subjects and close to three thousand iris images in all. The ICE 2006 dataset [22] has four hundred and eighty subjects and sixty thousand images in all. A super set of the ICE 2005 and ICE 2006 datasets is now available called the ND-IRIS-04-05 dataset [4] (ND dataset). It contains iris images with occlusion due to shadows and eyelids, blur due to motion of the subject and

(a)   **(b)**   **(c)**   **(d)**

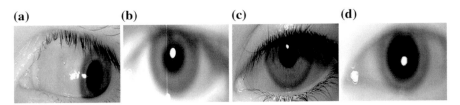

Fig. 11.3 Poorly acquired iris images from the ND dataset. Note that image **a** has specular reflections on the iris and is difficult to be segmented correctly due to the tilt and noncircular shape. Images **b** and **d** suffer from blurring, whereas image **c** is occluded by the *shadow* of the eyelids

defocus, specular reflections and in-plane rotations. Some of these images are shown in Fig. 11.3. Gazed iris images with off angle distortions are available in the West Virginia University iris dataset [34].

11.2 Sparsity-Motivated Selection and Recognition

Some of the challenges in unconstrained iris recognition have been addressed recently using the ideas of sparse representations and random projections [26]. This method provides a unified framework for image quality estimation, recognition, and privacy in iris biometrics.

The idea is to create a dictionary matrix of the training samples as column vectors. The test sample is also represented as a column vector. Different dimensionality reduction methods are used to reduce the dimension of both the test vector and the vectors in the dictionary. It is then simply a matter of solving an ℓ_1 minimization problem in order to obtain the sparse solution. Once the sparse solution is obtained, it can provide information as to which training sample the test vector most closely relates to.

Let each image be represented as a vector in $\mathbb{R}^n$, A be the dictionary (i.e., training set) and y be the test image. The general Sparse Representation-based Classification (SRC) algorithm is as follows [26, 35]:

1. Create a matrix of training samples $A = [A_1, \ldots, A_C]$ for C classes, where A_i are the set of images of each class.
2. Reduce the dimension of the training images and a test image by any dimensionality reduction method. Denote the resulting dictionary and the test vector as $\tilde{A}$ and $\tilde{y}$, respectively.
3. Normalize the columns of $\tilde{A}$ and $\tilde{y}$.
4. Solve the following ℓ_1 minimization problem

$$\hat{\alpha} = \arg\min_{\alpha'} \| \alpha' \|_1 \quad \text{subject to} \quad \tilde{y} = \tilde{A}\alpha', \tag{11.1}$$

5. Calculate the residuals

$$r_i(\tilde{y}) = \|\tilde{y} - \tilde{A}\delta_i(\hat{\alpha})\|_2,$$

for $i = 1, \ldots, C$ where δ_i a characteristic function that selects the coefficients associated with the ith class.

6. Identify$(y) = \arg\min_i r_i(\tilde{y})$.

The assumption made in this method is that given sufficient training samples of the kth class, $\tilde{A}_k$, any new test image y that belongs to the same class will approximately lie in the linear span of the training samples from the class k. This implies that most of the coefficients not associated with class k in $\hat{\alpha}$ will be close to zero. Hence, $\hat{\alpha}$ is a sparse vector. Note that ℓ_1-norm used to solve the above problem is an approximation to the ℓ_0-norm. This approximation is necessary as solving the above problem with ℓ_0-norm is not practical. Furthermore, it has been shown that if the solution is sparse enough and the dictionary A satisfies some properties, then solving the above problem with either ℓ_1-norm or ℓ_0-norm is equivalent. This algorithm can also be extended to deal with occlusions and random noise. Furthermore, a method of rejecting invalid test samples can also be introduced within this framework [35]. In particular, to decide whether a given test sample is a valid sample or not, the notion of Sparsity Concentration Index (SCI) has been proposed [35]. The SCI of a coefficient vector α is defined as

$$SCI(\alpha) = \frac{\frac{C \cdot \max \|\delta_i(\alpha)\|_1}{\|\alpha\|_1} - 1}{C - 1}. \tag{11.2}$$

SCI takes values between 0 and 1. SCI values close to 1 correspond to the case when the test image can be approximately represented using only images from a single class. Thus, the test vector has enough discriminating features of its class and hence has high quality. If SCI $= 0$, then the coefficients are spread evenly over all classes. Hence, the test vector is not similar to any of the classes and hence is of poor quality.

11.2.1   Sector-Based Recognition of Iris Images

Different regions of the iris have different qualities [8]. So instead of recognizing the entire iris image directly, the idea proposed in [26] is to recognize the different regions separately and combine the results depending on the quality of the region. This reduces the computational complexity of the above method as the size of the dictionary is greatly reduced, and the recognition of the different regions can be done in parallel. Also, since occlusions affect only local regions on the iris which can only lower the quality of certain regions, the robustness of the recognition algorithm to occlusion due to eyelids and eye lashes is improved. A direct way of doing this would be to recognize the sectors separately and combine the results by voting [25]. This, however, does not account for the fact that different regions are recognized with different confidences. To deal with this, a score level fusion approach for recognition

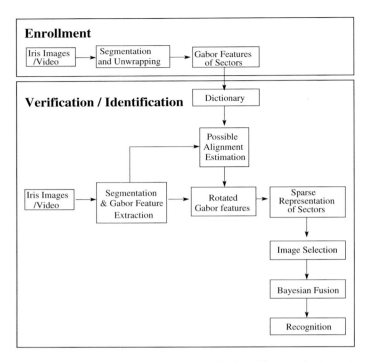

Fig. 11.4 A block diagram illustrating the Bayesian Fusion based image selection and recognition

was proposed in [26] where the recognition results of different sectors are combined based on the recognition confidence using the corresponding SCI values. Figure 11.4 illustrates the different steps involved in the proposed approach.

The iris region is segmented using existing techniques and are divided into different sectors. Each sector is recognized separately using SRC. Here the Gabor features obtained from the sectors form the columns of the dictionary. SCI is used as a quality measure for each sector. Sectors with low SCI values are rejected.

A Bayesian fusion technique is then employed to combine the results from the remaining sectors, based on their quality. Let $\mathbf{C}$ be the set of possible class labels and M be the number of sectors retained after rejection. Let $d_1, d_2, \ldots, d_M$ be the class labels of the retained sectors. The final class label is given by

$$\tilde{c} = \arg\max_{c \in \mathbf{C}} CSCI(c) \tag{11.3}$$

where

$$CSCI(c_l) = \frac{\sum_{j=1}^{M} SCI(d_j) \cdot \delta(d_j = c_l)}{\sum_{j=1}^{M} SCI(d_j)} \tag{11.4}$$

CSCI of a class is the sum of the SCI values of all the sectors identified by the classifier as belonging to that class. Therefore, the optimal estimate is the class having the highest CSCI. Thus higher weighting is given to the labels predicted by the better quality sectors when compared to the rest. To address the issue of in-plane rotation in the test iris image, the same formulation is extended by including sectors obtained after rotating the test iris image [26].

11.2.2 Recognition from Video

When test videos are available, the sectors of the different frames of the video can be combined based on their quality in a similar manner. Let $Y = \{y^1, y^2, \ldots, y^J\}$ be the J vectorized frames in the test video. As before, each frame is divided into $\hat{M}$ sectors and recognized separately by the SRC algorithm. Let M_i be the number of sectors retained by the selection scheme in the ith frame. Let y_j^i be the jth retained sector in the ith frame. Similar to the sector-based recognition approach, one can derive the MAP estimate for video as

$$\tilde{c} = \arg \min_{c \in \mathbf{C}} \sum_{i=1}^{J} \sum_{j=1}^{M_i} SCI(d_j^i) \cdot \delta(c = d_j^i) \tag{11.5}$$

where d_j^i is the class label assigned by the classifier to $\mathbf{y}_j^i$. Equation (11.5) can be alternatively written as

$$\tilde{c} = \arg \min_{c \in \mathbf{C}} CSCI(c)$$

where CSCI of a class c_l is given by

$$CSCI(c_l) = \frac{\sum_{i=1}^{J} \sum_{j=1}^{M_i} SCI(d_j^i) \cdot \delta(d_j^i = c_l)}{\sum_{i=1}^{J} \sum_{j=1}^{M_i} SCI(d_j^i)}.$$

As before, the MAP estimate consists of selecting the class having the highest cumulative SCI value, with the difference that the sectors of all the frames in the test video will be used while computing the CSCI of each class. Note that unlike existing feature level and score level fusion methods available for iris recognition, the CSCI incorporates the quality of the frames into the matching score. Hence, when the frames in the video suffer from acquisition artifacts like blurring, occlusion, and segmentation errors, the CSCI-based matching score gives higher weights to the good frames, at the same time, suppressing the evidence from the poorly acquired regions in the video.

The different modes of operation of the proposed algorithm are illustrated in Fig. 11.5. Both the probe and the gallery can be separate iris images or iris videos. The iris images are segmented and unwrapped to form rectangular images. The Gabor

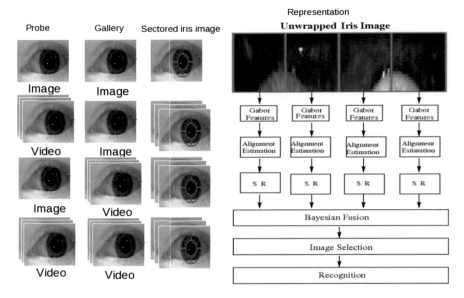

Fig. 11.5 A block diagram illustrating the different modes of operation of the proposed algorithm. Both the probe and the gallery can be individual iris images or iris video. Here, SR stands for Sparse Representation

features of the different sectors are computed, and SRC algorithm is used to select the good iris images. The good sectors are separately recognized and combined to obtain the class of probe image or video as described above.

11.2.3   Generation of Cancelable Iris Templates

Let Φ be an $m \times N$ random matrix with $m \leq N$ such that each entry $\phi_{i,j}$ of Φ is an independent realization of q, where q is a random variable on a probability measure space (Ω, ρ). Consider the following observations:

$$a \doteq \Phi y = \Phi A \alpha + \eta', \qquad (11.6)$$

where $\eta' = \Phi \eta$ with $\| \eta' \|_2 \leq \varepsilon'$. a can be thought of as a transformed version of the biometric y. One must recover the coefficients α to apply the SRC method for recognition. As m is smaller than N, the system of equations (11.6) is underdetermined and the unique solution of α is impossible. Given the sparsity of α, one can approximate α by solving the BPDN problem. It has been shown that for sufficiently sparse α and under certain conditions on ΦA, the solution to the following optimization problem will approximate the sparsest near-solution of (11.6) [29]

$$\hat{\alpha} = \arg\min_{\alpha'} \| \alpha' \|_1 \quad \text{s.t.} \quad \|a - \Phi A \alpha'\|_2 \le \varepsilon'. \tag{11.7}$$

One sufficient condition for (11.7) to stably approximate the sparsest solution of (11.6), is the Restricted Isometry Property (RIP) [1, 6, 7]. A matrix ΦA satisfies the RIP of order K with constants $\delta_K \in (0, 1)$ if

$$(1 - \delta_K) \| v \|_2^2 \le \| \Phi A v \|_2^2 \le (1 + \delta_K) \| v \|_2^2 \tag{11.8}$$

for any v such that $\| v \|_0 \le K$. When RIP holds, ΦA approximately preserves the Euclidean length of K-sparse vectors. When A is a deterministic dictionary and Φ is a random matrix, we have the following theorem on the RIP of ΦA.

Theorem 11.1 ([29]) *Let $A \in \mathbb{R}^{\mathbb{N} \times (n.L)}$ be a deterministic dictionary with restricted isometry constant $\delta_K(A)$, $K \in \mathbb{N}$. Let $\Phi \in \mathbb{R}^{m \times N}$ be a random matrix satisfying*

$$P\left(|\|\Phi v\|^2 - \|v\|^2| \ge \varsigma \|v\|^2\right) \le 2e^{-c\frac{n}{2}\varsigma^2}, \quad \varsigma \in (0, \frac{1}{3}) \tag{11.9}$$

for all $v \in \mathbb{R}^{\mathbb{N}}$ and some constant $c > 0$ and assume

$$m \ge C\delta^{-2} \left(K \log((n.L)/K) + \log(2e(1 + 12/\delta)) + t\right) \tag{11.10}$$

for some $\delta \in (0, 1)$ and $t > 0$. Then, with probability at least $1 - e^{-t}$, the matrix $\Phi\mathbf{D}$ has restricted isometry constant

$$\delta_K(\Phi A) \le \delta_K(A) + \delta(1 + \delta_K(A)). \tag{11.11}$$

The constant satisfies $C \le 9/c$.

The above theorem establishes how the isometry constants of A are affected by multiplication with a random matrix Φ. Note that one still needs to check the isometry constants for the dictionary A to use this result. However, for a given dictionary, A, it is difficult to prove that A satisfies a RIP. One can empirically check the equivalence between the ℓ_0-norm and ℓ_1-norm by plotting the phase transition diagrams [2, 11].

The following are some matrices that satisfy (11.9) and hence can be used as random projections for cancelability.

- $m \times N$ random matrices Φ whose entries $\phi_{i,j}$ are independent realizations of Gaussian random variables $\phi_{i,j} \sim N\left(0, \frac{1}{m}\right)$.
- Independent realizations of ± 1 Bernoulli random variables

$$\phi_{i,j} \doteq \begin{cases} +1/\sqrt{m}, & \text{with probability } \frac{1}{2} \\ -1/\sqrt{m}, & \text{with probability } \frac{1}{2}. \end{cases}$$

- Independent realizations of related distributions such as

$$\phi_{i,j} \doteq \begin{cases} +\sqrt{3/m}, & \text{with probability } \frac{1}{6} \\ 0, & \text{with probability } \frac{2}{3} \\ -\sqrt{3/m}, & \text{with probability } \frac{1}{6}. \end{cases}$$

- Multiplication of any $m \times N$ random matrix Φ with a deterministic orthogonal $N \times N$ matrix D, i.e. ΦD.

Note that RPs meet the various constraints required for cancelability, mentioned in Sect. 11.1.2. Using different RP matrices, one can issue different templates for different applications. If a transformed pattern is compromised, one can reissue a new pattern by applying a new random projection to the iris vector. The RIP properties together with the sparsity of α ensure that the recognition performance is preserved. In the application database, only the transformed dictionary ΦA is stored. If a hacker illegally obtains the transformed dictionary ΦA and the transformed iris patterns of the user, a, he or she will have access to the person's identity. However, it is extremely difficult to obtain the matrix A from ΦA, and without A one cannot obtain the original iris patterns y. Hence, RP-based cancelable scheme is noninvertible as it is not possible to obtain the original iris patterns from the transformed patterns. Furthermore, since this method is based on pseudorandom number generation, one only needs to consider the state space corresponding to the value taken by the seed of the random number generator. Hence, instead of storing the entire matrix, only the seed used to generate the RP matrix needs to be stored.

11.2.3.1   Random Cancelable Iris Biometric

Permutation-Based

As discussed earlier, when the iris image has good quality, only the training images corresponding to the correct class will have high coefficients (Fig. 11.6). If the training images of different classes are randomly arranged as columns of the dictionary, both the dictionary and the order of the training images are required for correct recognition. This can be used to enhance the security of the proposed iris recognition system [26].

When a new user is enrolled, his training images are divided into sectors and placed at random locations in the dictionary. In Fig. 11.7, we show the dictionary for a trivial example of four users. Note that the different sectors of each training image of the user are kept at different random locations in the dictionary. Without prior knowledge of these locations, it is impossible to perform recognition.

An array indicating the column numbers of the training images of the correct class is generated for each user. This array is stored in a hash table, and the corresponding hash code is given to the user during enrollment. During verification, the system acquires the iris image of the person and extracts the features. For each sector of

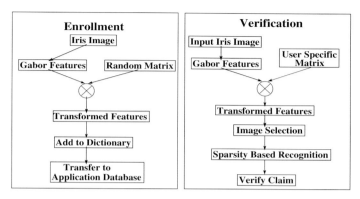

Fig. 11.6 Block diagram of the Random Projections based cancelable system

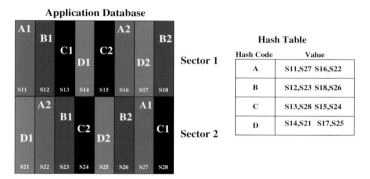

Fig. 11.7 Sample Dictionary and hash table for a four user example. The four users *A*, *B*, *C*, and *D* are indicated by colors *green*, *blue*, *black*, and *red*, respectively. *A1* and *A2* are the two training images corresponding to the first user. *Sij* denote that the *j*th location and the *i*th sector. *D1* at *S*14 means that the first sector of the user D is at location *S*14

the iris vector, the sparse coefficients are obtained using this shuffled dictionary. The user also has to present the hash code to the system. Using the hash code, the indices of training images are obtained from the hash table and the coefficients belonging to different classes are grouped. Then, SCI is computed and used to retain or reject the images. If the image is retained, the CSCI values of the different classes are computed and the class having the lowest CSCI value is assigned as the class label of the user. A block diagram of the security scheme is presented in Fig. 11.8

If the hash code presented is incorrect, then the obtained indices of the training images for each class will be wrong. So the coefficients will be grouped in a wrong way, and all the classes will have similar energy leading to a low SCI value and the subsequent rejection of the image. Even if by chance, one of the classes happened to have high energy and the image is retained, the probability of that class being the correct class is very low ($\frac{1}{N}$). Thus, with high probability, the user will not be

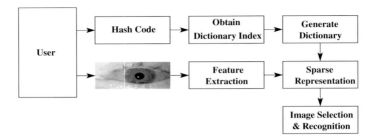

Fig. 11.8 Block diagram of the proposed cancelability scheme using random permutations

verified. Hence, if a hacker illegally acquires the iris patterns of a legitimate user, without having the hash code, he or she will not be able to access the system. Also, even if the hacker obtains the iris dictionary stored in the application database, the iris patterns of the user cannot be accessed without knowing the correct hash codes, because different sectors of an iris patterns reside at different random locations. If the hash code is compromised, the dictionary indices of the user can then be stored at a new location, and a new hash code can be issued to the user. Also, different applications can have different dictionaries. Thus, the user will have a different hash code for each application, preventing cross matching.

It should be noted that the additional security and privacy introduced by these techniques come at the expense of storing additional seed values. In applications requiring higher security, this can be stored with the user, so that a hacker will not get the original templates even if he gets hold of the cancelable patterns in the template database. For applications with greater emphasis on usability, the seed can be stored securely in the template database, so that the user will not have to carry it.

11.3 Experimental Results

To show the effectiveness of the sparsity promoting methods for iris recognition, we highlight some of the results presented in [26] on the ICE2005 dataset [22], ND-IRIS-0405 (ND) dataset [4] and the MBGC videos [24].

To illustrate the robustness of the algorithm to occlusion due to eyelids and eyelashesv, a simple iris segmentation scheme was performed, detecting just the pupil and iris boundaries and not the eyelids and eye lashes. Publicly available code of Masek and Kovesi [21] for detecting these boundaries was used. To study the variation of SCI in the presence of common distortions during image acquisition like occlusion and blur, they were simulated on the clean iris images from the ND dataset. Fifteen clean iris images of the left eye of eighty persons were selected. Twelve such images per person formed the gallery and distortions were simulated on the remaining images to form the probes. Seven different levels of distortion for each case were considered with level one indicating no distortion and level seven indicating maximum distortion. The dictionary was obtained using the gallery images, and evaluated the SCI of the various sectors of the test images.

Figure 11.9 shows some of the simulated images from the ND dataset. The first column includes images with distortion level one (no distortion). The middle column contains images with distortion level three (moderate distortions). The right most column contain images with distortion level five (high distortion). The first row contains images with blur while the second contains images with occlusion. Images with simulated segmentation error and specular reflections are shown in the third and fourth rows, respectively.

Figure 11.10 illustrates the variation of SCI with the common acquisition distortions. It can be observed that good images have high SCI values whereas the ones with distortion have lower SCI values. So by suitably thresholding the SCI value of the test image, one can remove the bad images before the recognition stage. The relatively lower decrease in SCI with occlusion and specular reflection demonstrates the increased robustness attained by the proposed algorithm by separately recognizing the individual sectors and combining the results, as discussed earlier.

11.3.1 Recognition Performance

In the first set of experiments, 80 subjects were selected from the ND dataset. Fifteen clean images of the left iris were handpicked for each person. Of these 15 images per person, twelve were randomly selected to form the gallery and the remaining three images per person were used as probes. Image selection was not performed for this experiment.

The proposed algorithm was compared to a nearest neighbor-based recognition algorithm (NN) that uses the Gabor features and the Masek's implementation. Since we use tough segmentation conditions retaining the eyelids and eye lashes in the iris vector, direct application of NN and Masek's method produced poor results. For fair comparison, the iris images were divided into different sectors, obtained the results using these methods separately on each sectors and combined the results by voting. Recognition rate of 99.15 % is achieved compared to 98.33 % for the NN and 97.5 % for the Masek's method.

To evaluate the recognition performance of the proposed algorithm on poorly acquired images, images with blur, occlusion, and segmentation errors were handpicked. Fifteen clean images per person were used to form the gallery. Probes containing each type of distortion were applied separately to the algorithm. Image selection was performed followed by recognition. The recognition rates are reported in Table 11.1.

In the second set of experiments, we used images from the ICE 2005 dataset. The proposed algorithm is compared with the existing results on the ICE 2005 dataset corresponding to Experiment 1. Experiment 1 has 1425 iris images corresponding to 120 different classes. Ten images per class were used in the gallery and remaining iris images were used as the test images. Segmentation was performed using

(a)　　　　　　　**(b)**　　　　　　　**(c)**

(d)　　　　　　　**(e)**　　　　　　　**(f)**

(g)　　　　　　　**(h)**　　　　　　　**(i)**

(j)　　　　　　　**(k)**　　　　　　　**(l)**

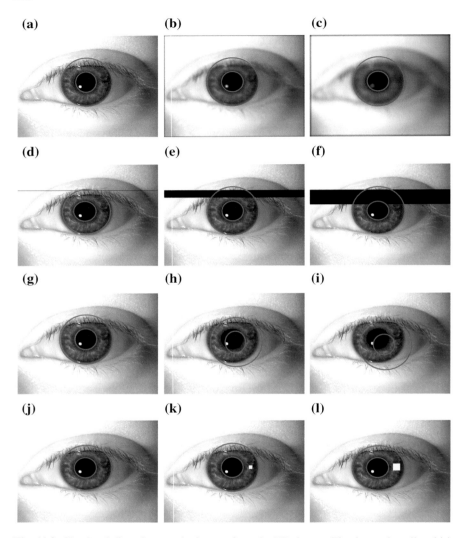

Fig. 11.9 Simulated distortions on the images from the ND dataset. The detected pupil and iris boundaries are indicated as *red circles*

Masek's code and the Gabor features of the segmented iris images were applied to the proposed algorithm. No image selection was performed. The performance of the proposed algorithm was compared with the existing results [23] in Table 11.2, where the verification rates are indicated at a false acceptance rate of 0.001.

Fig. 11.10 Plot of the variation in SCI values with common distortions in iris image acquisition. Note that the SCI falls monotonically with increasing levels of blur and segmentation errors in the iris images. It is also robust to occlusions and specular reflections

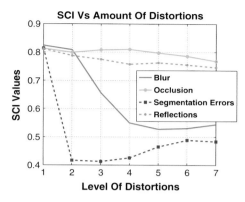

Table 11.1 Recognition rate on the ND dataset

Image quality	NN	Masek's implementation	Proposed method
Good	98.33	97.5	99.15
Blurred	95.42	96.01	98.18
Occluded	85.03	89.54	90.44
Seg. error	78.57	82.09	87.63

Table 11.2 Verification rate at an FAR of 0.001 on the ICE 2005 dataset

Method	Verification rate (%)
Pelco	96.8
WVU	97.9
CAS 3	97
CAS 1	97.8
CMU	99.5
SAGEM	99.8
Proposed method	98.13

11.3.2 Cancelability Results

We present the cancelability results on the clean images from the ND dataset. The iris region obtained after segmentation was unwrapped into a rectangular image of size 10×80. The real part of the Gabor features were obtained and concatenated to form an iris vector of length 800. The random Gaussian matrix was used to generate random projections. In [27], it was shown that the application of the random projections separately on each sector performed better performance when compared to the application of a single random projection on the entire iris vector. The real part of the Gabor features of each sector of the iris image is first vectorized, random projections were then applied, and finally the random projected vectors are concatenated to

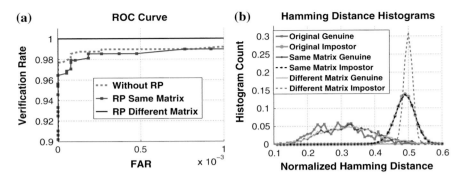

Fig. 11.11 **a** ROC characteristics for the ND dataset. The same matrix performance is close to the performance without cancelability. Using different matrices for each class gives better performance. **b** Comparison of the distribution of the Genuine and impostor normalized Hamming distances for the original and transformed pattern

obtain the cancelable iris biometric. Either the same random Gaussian matrix for all the users or different random matrices for different users were applied to obtain the RP "Same Matrix" and "Different Matrix" vectors, respectively. Having obtained the random vectors from the Gabor features of the iris image, the sparsity-based recognition algorithm was performed.

Figure 11.11a plots the Receiver Operating Characteristic (ROC) characteristics for the iris images in the ND dataset for the original and transformed iris patterns. As demonstrated, using different matrices for each class performs better than using the same matrix for all classes. In the "Different Matrix" case, it is assumed that the user provided the correct matrix assigned to him. So the performance exceeds even the original performance as class specific random projections increases the interclass distance, still retaining the original intraclass distance. In Fig. 11.11b, the distribution of the genuine and impostor normalized Hamming distance for the original and transformed iris patterns is compared. It can be seen that the distribution of the genuine Hamming distance remains almost the same after applying the random projections. The original and Same Matrix cases have similar impostor Hamming distance distributions. However the Different Matrix case has an impostor distribution that is more peaked and farther from the genuine distribution, indicating superior performance.

Table 11.3 provides the statistics of the normalized Hamming distance between the original and the transformed iris vectors. As can be seen, the mean of the normalized Hamming distance is very close to 0.5 with a very low standard deviation.

To evaluate the performance of the proposed cancelable method using dictionary permutations, the following three possible scenarios on the clean images from the ND dataset are considered. In the first case, the user provides the iris image and the correct hash code. In this case, the recognition performance was the same as that of the original method on the ND dataset, which is 99.17 %. In the second case, the user provides the iris image but a wrong hash code. Here the recognition performance dropped to 2 %, which is only slightly better than chance. This is equivalent to the case when a hacker illegally obtains the iris image of a valid user and tries to gain access into the system with a guess about the hash code. The low recognition performance clearly reflects the additional security introduced by the permutations, as a hacker needs to now have not only the iris image but also the hash code of a valid user to gain access. In the third experiment, the closeness between the Gabor features of the original iris images and the new feature vectors obtained by permutations of the Gabor features in the dictionary is found. As before, the normalized Hamming distance between the iris codes obtained from these vectors is used as the measure of similarity. The histogram of the normalized Hamming distance between the original and the randomly permuted iris vectors are shown in Fig. 11.12. The mean and standard deviation of the Hamming distance histogram are indicated in the last row of the Table 11.3. Note that the mean is close to 0.5, indicating that the permutations differ significantly different from the original iris images. Even if a hacker can use the dictionary from the application database, he or she will be unable to extract information about the original iris images without knowing the hash code of each user.

11.3.3   Results on Iris Video

In this section, the results on the MBGC videos [24] are presented [26]. Given the 30 classes, 28 classes that contained at least five good images were used in

Table 11.3 Statistics of the normalized Hamming distance

Methods	Mean	Standard deviation
Without RP	0	0
Same matrix	0.5002	0.0123
Different matrix	0.4999	0.013
Dictionary permutations	0.4913	0.0254

Fig. 11.12 Plot of the histograms of the Normalized Hamming Distance between the original and transformed vectors. Note that the histogram peaks around 0.5 indicating that the original and transformed iris codes are significantly different

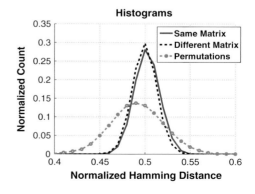

the experiments. Five clean images from the iris videos in the training set were handpicked which formed the dictionary. In the test videos, batches of five frames were given as a probe to the algorithm. Using 28 available videos and 60 frames from each test video, one could form 336 probes. Only a basic segmentation of the iris and pupil using the Masek's code was performed. Also, the poorly segmented iris images were not removed before performing the recognition.

The performance of the proposed algorithm was compared with four other methods. The ROC plots for the different methods are displayed in Fig. 11.13. In Method 1, each frame of the video is considered as a different probe. It gave the worst performance, indicating that using multiple frames available in a video can improve the performance. Method 2 averages the intensity of the different iris images. Though it performs well when the images are clean, a single image which is poorly segmented or blurred could affect the entire average. In Methods 3 and 4, all possible pair wise Hamming distances between the video frames of the probe videos and the gallery videos belonging to the same class are computed. Method 3 uses the average of these Hamming distance as the score. In Method 4, the minimum of the pairwise Hamming distance was used as the score. In the proposed method, the CSCI values were computed for each class for each probe video and the probe video is assigned to the class having the highest CSCI value. For a fair comparison of the proposed quality measure in videos, none of the frames were rejected. The proposed method performed better than other methods. One of the reasons for the superior performance could be the fact that the algorithm is incorporating the quality of the different frames while computing the CSCI. Frames which are poorly segmented or blurred will have a low SCI value and hence will not affect the score significantly. In all the other methods,

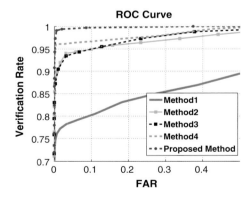

Fig. 11.13 ROC plots for video based iris recognition. *Method 1* treats each frame in the video as a different probe. *Method 2* averages all the frames in the probe video. *Methods 3* and *4* use the average and minimum of all the pairwise Haming distance between the frames of the probe and gallery videos respectively. The *Proposed Method* uses CSCI as the matching score. Note that the introduced quality-based matching score outperforms the existing fusion schemes, which do not incorporate the quality of the individual frames in the video

the image quality was not effectively incorporated into the matching score, so all frames are treated equally irrespective of their quality.

11.4   Discussion and Conclusion

In this chapter, we introduced a general framework for iris image selection and recognition based on sparse representation and random projections. The introduced method has numerous advantages over existing techniques when sufficient number of training data are available. It was shown that the selection algorithm can handle common distortions in iris image acquisition such as occlusions, blur, and segmentation errors. Also, a quality-based matching score was introduced and its effectiveness was demonstrated on the MBGC iris video dataset. Finally, random projection and random permutation were incorporated into the algorithm to prevent the compromise of sensitive biometric information of the subjects.

Acknowledgments   This work was partially supported by a MURI grant N00014-08-1-0638 from the Office of Naval Research.

References

1. R. Baraniuk, Compressive sensing. IEEE Sig. Process. Mag. **24**(4), 118–121 (2007)
2. J.D. Blanchard, C. Cartis, J. Tanner, The restricted isometry property and ℓ_q regularization: phase transition for sparse approximation. preprint
3. R.M. Bolle, J.H. Connel, N.K. Ratha, Biometrics perils and patches. Pattern Recogn. **35**(12), 2727–2738 (2002)
4. K.W. Bowyer, P.J. Flynn, The ND-IRIS-0405 Iris Image Dataset
5. K.W. Bowyer, K. Hollingsworth, P.J. Flynn, Image understanding for iris biometrics: a survey. Comput. Vis. Image Underst. **110**(2), 281–307 (2008)
6. E. Candes, J. Romberg, T. Tao, Robust uncertainty principles: exact signal reconstruction from highly incomplete frequency information. IEEE Trans. Inform. Theor. **52**(2), 489–509 (2006)
7. E. Candes, J. Romberg, T. Tao, Stable signal recovery from incomplete and inaccurate measurements. Commun. Pure Appl. Math. **59**, 1207–1223 (2006)
8. Y. Chen, S.C. Dass, A.K. Jain, Localized iris image quality using 2-D wavelets, in Lecture Notes in Computer Science, vol. 3832 (Springer, 2006), pp. 373–381
9. J. Daugman, High confidence visual recognition of persons by a test of statistical independence. IEEE Trans. Pattern Anal. Mach. Intell. **15**, 1148–1161 (1993)
10. G.I. Davida, Y. Frankel, B.J. Matt, On enabling secure applications through off-line biometric identification, in *IEEE Symposiam on Security and Privacy* (1998), pp. 148–157
11. D.L. Donoho, High-Dimensional centrally symmetric polytopes with neighborliness proportional to dimension. Discrete Comput. Geom. **35**(4), 617–652 (2006)
12. Y. Du, N.L. Thomas, E. Arslanturk, Multi-level iris video image thresholding, in *IEEE Workshop on Computational Intelligence in Biometrics: Theory, Algorithms, and Applications, (CIB)* (Mar. 2009), pp. 38–45
13. F. Hao, R. Anderson, J. Daugman, Combining crypto with biometrics effectively. IEEE Trans. Comput. **55**(9), 1081–1088 (2006)

14. K.P. Hollingsworth, K.W. Bowyer, P.J. Flynn, *Image Averaging for Improved Iris Recognition*. Lecture Notes in Computer Science, vol. 5558 (2009)
15. A.K. Jain, K. Nandakumar, A. Nagar, Biometric template security. EURASIP J. Adv. Sig. Process. Spec. Issue Biometrics **2008**(113), 1–17 (2008)
16. A. Juels, M. Wattenberg, A fuzzy commitment scheme, in *ACM Conference on Computers and Communications Security* (1999), pp. 28–36
17. S. Kanade, D. Petrovska-Delacretaz, B. Dorizzi, Cancelable iris biometrics and using error correcting codes to reduce variability in biometric data, in *Computer Vision and Pattern Recognition* (2009)
18. E. Krichen et al., *Specific texture analysis for iris recognition*. Lecture Notes in Computer Science, vol 3546 (Springer, Heidelberg, 2005), pp. 23–30
19. C. Liu, M. Xie, Iris recognition based on DLDA, in *International Conference on Pattern Recognition* (2006), pp. 489–492
20. L. Ma et al., Efficient iris recognition by characterizing key local variations. IEEE Trans. Image Process. **13**(6), 739–750 (2004)
21. L. Masek, P. Kovesi, *MATLAB Source Code for a Biometric Identification System Based on Iris Patterns* (2003)
22. E.M. Newton, P.J. Phillips, Meta-analysis of third-party evaluations of iris recognition. IEEE Trans. Syst. Man Cybern. **39**(1), 4–11 (2009)
23. P.J. Phillips, *FRGC and ICE Workshop* (2006)
24. P. Phillips et al, Overview of the multiple biometrics grand challenge, in *Advances in Biometrics* (2009), pp. 705–714
25. J.K. Pillai, V.M. Patel, R. Chellappa, Sparsity Inspired Selection and Recognition of Iris Images, in *Third IEEE International Conference on Biometrics–Technology and Systems* (2009)
26. J.K. Pillai, V.M. Patel, R. Chellappa, Sparsity inspired selection and recognition of iris images, in *IEEE 3rd International Conference on Biometrics: Theory, Applications, and Systems (BTAS)* (Sept. 2009), pp. 1–6
27. J.K. Pillai et al, Sectored random projections for cancelable iris biometrics, in *International Conference on Acoustics, Speech, and Signal Processing* (2009)
28. N.K. Ratha, J.H. Connel, R.M. Bolle, Enhancing security and privacy in biometrics-based authentication systems. IBM Syst. J. **40**(3), 614–634 (2001)
29. H. Rauhut, K. Schnass, P. Vandergheynst, Compressed sensing and redundant dictionaries. IEEE Trans. Inform.Theor. **54**(5), 2210–2219 (2008)
30. K. Roy, P. Bhattacharya, Iris recognition with support vector machines, in *International Conference on Biometrics* (2006), pp. 486–492
31. N.A. Schmid, F. Nicolo, A method for selecting and ranking quality metrics for optimization of biometric recognition systems, in *Computer Vision and Pattern Recognition Workshops (CVPR Workshops)* (June 2009), pp. 126–133
32. Specification of CASIA Iris Image Database(ver 1.0), Chinese Academy of Sciences (Mar. 2007), http://www.nlpr.ia.ac.cn/english/irds/irisdatabase.htm
33. A. Teoh, A. Goh, D. Ngo, Random multispace quantization as an analytic mechanism for biohashing of biometric and random identity inputs. IEEE Trans. Pattern Anal. Mach. Intell. **28**(12), 1892–1901 (2006)
34. West Virginia University Iris Dataset
35. J. Wright et al., Robust face recognition via sparse representation. IEEE Trans. Pattern Anal. Mach. Intell. **31**(2), 210–227 (2009)
36. J. Zuo, N. Ratha, J. Connell, Cancelable Iris Biometric, in *Proceeding of International Conference on Pattern Recognition* (2008), pp. 1–4

Chapter 12
Multispectral Iris Fusion
and Cross-Spectrum Matching

Mark J. Burge and Matthew Monaco

Abstract Traditionally, only a narrow band of the Near-Infrared (NIR) spectrum
(700–900 nm) is utilized for iris recognition since this alleviates any physical discomfort from illumination, reduces specular reflections, and increases the amount
of texture captured for some iris colors. However, previous research has shown that
matching performance is not invariant to iris color and can be improved by imaging
outside the NIR spectrum. Building on this research, we demonstrate that iris texture
increases with the frequency of the illumination for lighter colored sections of the
iris and decreases for darker sections. Using registered visible light and NIR iris
images captured using a single-lens multispectral camera, we illustrate how physiological properties of the iris (e.g., the amount and distribution of melanin) impact
the transmission, absorbance, and reflectance of different portions of the electromagnetic spectrum and consequently affect the quality of the imaged iris texture.
We introduce a novel iris code, Multispectral Enhanced irisCode (MEC), which uses
pixel-level fusion algorithms to exploit texture variations elicited by illuminating
the iris at different frequencies, to improve iris matcher performance, and reduce
Failure To Enroll (FTE) rates. Finally, we present a model for approximating an NIR
iris image using features derived from the color and structure of a visible light iris
image. The simulated NIR images generated by this model are designed to improve
the interoperability between legacy NIR iris images and those acquired under visible
light by enabling cross wavelength matching of NIR and visible light iris images.

12.1 Introduction

Traditionally, only a narrow band of the Near-Infrared (NIR) spectrum (700–900 nm)
is utilized for iris recognition [6] since this alleviates any physical discomfort
from illumination, reduces specular reflections and increases the amount of texture

M.J. Burge (✉) · M. Monaco
Noblis, Falls Church, VA, USA
e-mail: Mark.Burge@Noblis.org; burge@ieee.org

M. Monaco
e-mail: Matthew.Monaco@Noblis.org

© Springer-Verlag London 2016
K.W. Bowyer and M.J. Burge (eds.), *Handbook of Iris Recognition*,
Advances in Computer Vision and Pattern Recognition,
DOI 10.1007/978-1-4471-6784-6_12

captured for some iris colors. However, previous research has shown [7] that matching performance is not invariant to iris color and can be improved by imaging outside of the NIR spectrum and that physiological properties of the iris (e.g., the amount and distribution of melanin) impact the transmission, absorbance, and reflectance of different portions of the electromagnetic spectrum and the ability to image well-defined iris texture [1].

Texture-based encoding of the iris is commonly used to create a biometric template that can be quickly and accurately matched against large datasets. Prior to recognition, the iris must be localized and segmented from the overall image. Localization is typically done by finding landmark features of the iris (e.g., the limbic boundary and the pupil) and removing background features (e.g., eyelids, eye lashes, sclera). Once the iris is segmented, it is unwrapped using a polar transformation from its natural circular form into a fixed-size Cartesian rectangle. Once in this form, a quantification of the textural content of the iris is computed using 2D Gabor wavelet filters [4] to create a template, commonly referred to as an IrisCode.

Phasors, which contain information on the orientation, spatial frequency, and position of texture within the image are used to create templates and masks. Since an iris template can be represented by a fixed-size array of bits, efficient large-scale matching can be accomplished by computing a circularly shifted, unmasked, and normalized Hamming distance between two templates over some range. This Hamming distance measure can then be used as a test of the statistical independence between the two iris images to determine if they can be deemed to be from different subjects [3].

Gabor-based iris encoding algorithms are robust because they quantify the phase structure of the iris for encoding and discard the amplitude. Note that the use of the amplitude, and not the phase, in the figures in this paper is solely for illustrative purposes. The actual measurements used in our fusion and transformation algorithms are based on phase information extracted using multiscalar log-Gabor filter banks.

12.2 Outline

Section 12.3 presents the design of single-lens and stereo rig multispectral cameras capable of simultaneously acquiring registered four channel (i.e., 460, 550, 670, and 800 nm) images of an iris. Section 12.4 demonstrates that iris texture increases with the frequency of the illumination for lighter colored sections of the iris and decreases for darker sections. Section 12.5 presents a model for approximating an NIR iris image using features derived from the color and structure of a Visible Light (VL) iris image. Section 12.6 introduces a novel iris code which uses pixel-level fusion algorithms to exploit texture variations elicited by illuminating the iris at different frequencies to improve iris matcher performance and reduce FTE rates. Section 12.7 summarizes our results and describes our ongoing evaluation and assessment.

12.3   Multispectral Iris Cameras

We are using a single-lens multispectral camera and stereo imaging rig capable of simultaneous acquisition across the VL and NIR portions of the spectrum. These cameras are being used to collect a database of pixel-level registered multispectral iris images. The multispectral iris images, Fig. 12.1, are used to develop and evaluate supervised learning algorithms for the pixel-level transformation of VL iris images into a form suitable for matching against existing NIR iris images and fusion algorithms which exploit texture variations elicited by illuminating the iris at different frequencies to improve iris matcher performance and reduce FTE rates.

The multispectral acquisition system shown in Fig. 12.2a utilizes a single-lens camera where four images are simultaneously captured across four different wavelengths by two Sony ICX205AL sensors (with spectral response ranges between 400 and 1000 nm with a peak of 550 nm) to capture the IR and red components and two Sony RGBICX205 sensors (blue response ranging from 400 to 550 nm with a peak at 460 nm and a green response from 400 to 650 nm with a peak at 550 nm) to acquire the green and blue channels. Optimal imaging parameters across all wavelengths of interest are obtained by illuminating the iris using a broadband (350–1100 nm) quartz halogen ring-light located between the imaging device and the subject.

The stereo rig illustrated in Fig. 12.2b is built from two Hitachi KP-F120 cameras, selected for their sensitivity across the 400–1000 nm band. Each camera is equipped with VL-cut filters enabling the selective acquisition of (NIR, NIR), (NIR, VL), and (VL, VL) stereo pairs. Iris specularities are limited to a small portion of the pupil using a cluster of NIR (750–950 nm) LED illuminators centered between the cameras together with adaptive illumination which varies in intensity based on ambient lighting conditions. Since the intrinsic (i.e., image point from camera to pixel coordinates) and extrinsic (i.e., relative position and orientation of the two cameras) parameters of the stereo rig are known *a priori*, it is possible to solve the correspondence problem and reconstruct a 3D depth map of the iris.

12.4   Multispectral Iris Texture

The amount of texture information extractable from a given iris color cluster is dependent on the wavelength under which it is illuminated. In the case of lighter colored clusters, more information is available at shorter wavelengths than at longer wavelengths and conversely for darker colored clusters. Figure 12.3 illustrates this with details from registered images of "green" (left) and "blue" (right) irises acquired at 460, 670, and 800 nm. In the darker "green" iris, the crypt is clearly visible at 800 nm but by 460 nm has deteriorated to noise, while the opposite occurs in the lighter "blue" iris where the crypt is clearly visible at 460 nm but is much less pronounced by 800 nm.

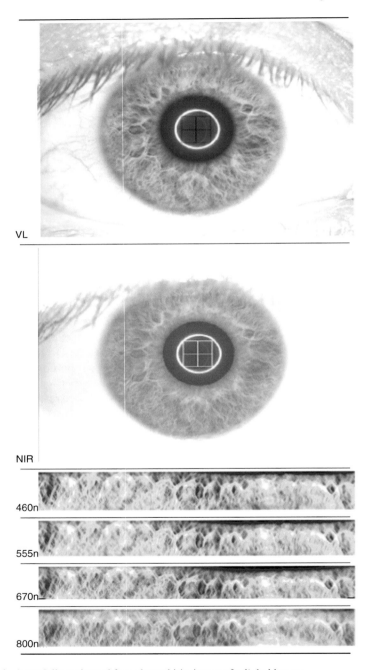

Fig. 12.1 A spatially registered four-channel iris image of a *light blue eye*

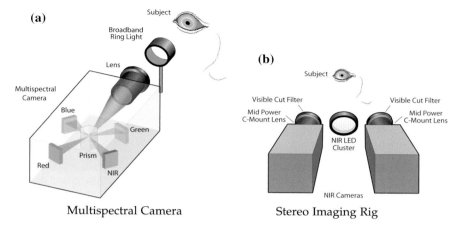

Fig. 12.2   a Simultaneous acquisition of spatially registered iris images is carried out using four optically aligned sensors, two Sony ICX205AL and two Sony RGBICX205 (n.b., internal optics simplified for illustrative purposes). Since these multispectral iris images are spatially registered at the sensor level it is possible to observe, with the aim of modeling, the effect of wavelength on the imaging of iris structure. **b** The stereo rig provides known camera geometry for the simultaneous acquisition of (NIR, NIR), (NIR, VL), and (VL, VL) iris pairs with slightly different spatial orientations. Since the intrinsic (i.e., image point from camera to pixel coordinates) and extrinsic (i.e., relative position and orientation of the two cameras) parameters of the stereo rig are known *a priori*, it is possible to solve the correspondence problem and reconstruct a 3-D depth map of the iris

Our hypothesis is that across the portion of the spectrum under consideration, the texture of lighter colored clusters of the iris increases with the frequency of the illumination and decreases in a similar way for darker clusters. This relation is demonstrated in Fig. 12.3 using the following texture measures derived from the gray-level co-occurence matrix [5] where $P_{\theta,d}(a, b)$ [8] describes how frequently two pixels with gray-levels a, b appear in a window separated by distance d in direction θ

$$T_{asm} = \sum_{a,b} P_{\theta,d}^2(a, b) \tag{12.1}$$

angular second moment,

$$T_c = \sum_{a,b} |a - b|^2 P_{\theta,d}^1(a, b) \tag{12.2}$$

contrast, and

$$T_e = \sum_{a,b} P_{\theta,d}(a, b) \log_2 P_{\theta,d}(a, b) \tag{12.3}$$

"Green" Iris Detail Texture **increases** with wavelength	"Blue" Iris Detail Texture **decreases** with wavelength

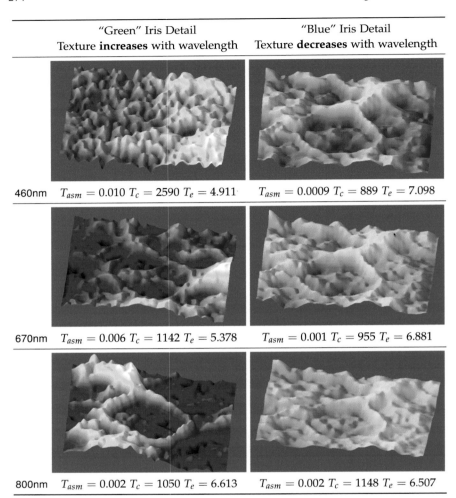

	"Green"	"Blue"
460nm	$T_{asm} = 0.010\ T_c = 2590\ T_e = 4.911$	$T_{asm} = 0.0009\ T_c = 889\ T_e = 7.098$
670nm	$T_{asm} = 0.006\ T_c = 1142\ T_e = 5.378$	$T_{asm} = 0.001\ T_c = 955\ T_e = 6.881$
800nm	$T_{asm} = 0.002\ T_c = 1050\ T_e = 6.613$	$T_{asm} = 0.002\ T_c = 1148\ T_e = 6.507$

Fig. 12.3 In this example, details from "*green*" (*left*) and "*blue*" (*right*) irises from registered images acquired at 460, 670, and 800 nm are shown as heat-coded height maps where hotter colors (e.g., *white*, *yellow*, and *red*) indicate higher values and cooler colors (e.g., *purple*, *blue*, *black*) indicate lower values. In the darker "*green*" iris, the crypt is clearly visible at 800 nm but by 460 nm has deteriorated to noise, while the opposite occurs in the lighter "*blue*" iris where the crypt is clearly visible at 460 nm but is much less pronounced at 800 nm. Our hypothesis is that the information content of the image increases with the frequency of the illumination for lighter colored sections of the iris and decreases for darker sections. This relation is demonstrated using the gray-Level co-occurence matrix [5] derived texture measures: angular second moment T_{asm} (Eq. 12.1), contrast T_c (Eq. 12.2), and entropy T_e (Eq. 12.3). *Note* T_{asm} and T_c decreases with information content while T_e increases

entropy. Note, the texture measures T_{asm} and T_c decrease with information content while T_e increases. We combine these, and other texture measures derived from multiscale log-Gabor filter banks, to create the texture function $T(I_w(x, y))$ defined in Eq. 12.5.

12.5 Modeling NIR Iris Images

Due to the reflectance properties of melanin, which is partially responsible for the color of the iris, commercial-off-the-shelf, iris acquisition devices (e.g., HIIDE, IrisAccess) acquire iris images using NIR illumination. While NIR images enable improved matching performance, especially for darker eyes, it can be difficult to directly match the templates derived from these images to those derived from irises which have been imaged in the visible spectrum.

We present a model for approximating an NIR iris image using features derived from the color and structure of a VL iris image. The simulated NIR images generated by this model are designed to improve the interoperability between legacy NIR iris images and those acquired under VL by enabling cross wavelength matching of NIR and VL iris images.

Eye color does not vary smoothly across the iris, but instead is arranged in clusters of similar colors which can have abrupt boundaries that arise from physiological structures within the anterior and posterior layers of the iris. Given that overall eye color arises from the montage of small color patches found in the iris (e.g., hazel eyes are a combination of many color patches), building a single model, or even a small collection of models, for each "eye color" is not sufficient (See Fig. 12.4).

A multistage supervised learning process is used to develop a set of mathematical models for approximating NIR iris images from VL iris images. In the first stage of our approach, the cluster analysis in the $L^*a^*b^*$ color space [2] on the VL channels of the multispectral iris images is used to identify a set of n representative color clusters. Next, for each of the n clusters, a set of tuples

$$(L^*, a^*, b^*, NIR)$$

is constructed that associates the $L^*a^*b^*$ and NIR values of the registered images. These tuples are then augmented with local structural information derived from k multiscalar log-Gabor filters $G(w)$, where w is the filter's center frequency,

$$(G(w_1), G(w_2), \ldots, G(w_k), L^*, a^*, b^*, NIR)$$

such that, for each of the n clusters, a mathematical model,

$$f(G(w_1), G(w_2), \ldots, G(w_k), L^*, a^*, b^*)_n \approx NIR \qquad (12.4)$$

Iris (Visible Light)	Color Distribution (L*a*b* Color Space)	Color Clusters (k-Means)

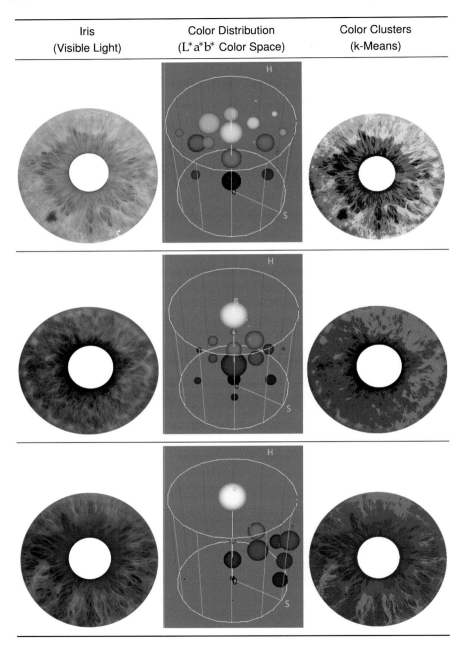

Fig. 12.4 Intra-eye color distribution. Eye color does not vary smoothly across the iris, but instead is grouped in clusters of similar colors that correspond to physiological structures across the anterior and posterior layers of the iris. The color clusters used in the supervised learning phase are derived from a k-means clustering in the L*a*b* color space of a boosted sampling drawn from the registered multispectral images

can be constructed using supervised learning to approximate the final NIR term given the first $k + 3$ terms.

Finally, each of the n learned functions which have been tuned to transform a small range of iris colors into approximations of their NIR values are combined to build a model for approximating an NIR iris image using features derived from the color and structure of a VL iris image.

12.6 Multispectral Iris Fusion

By analyzing the reflectance of the iris at each band of the multispectral image and selecting the areas of the iris image that have the highest probability of resulting in an accurate match, a single high confidence image, or Multispectral Enhanced irisCode (MEC), can be fused. Figure 12.5 illustrates the generation of such a MEC

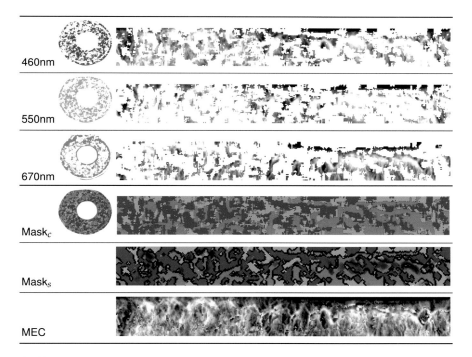

Fig. 12.5 Image-Level Fusion in Multispectral Iris Images. The first three images show the original and unwrapped distribution within each wavelength, of the image patches exhibiting the highest texture (Eq. 12.5) responses across all the imaged wavelengths. The last three images are of the channel and structural Masks (Eq. 12.6) and the MEC (Eq. 12.5) generated by applying these masks and fusing the regions with the highest information (i.e., maximum texture) from each wavelength to create a single enhanced image. The 800 nm NIR image is not shown, as a very light blue iris was used to illustrate the point that stronger texture is available outside of the NIR band and for this particular iris, the texture elicited under VL was more pronounced at every point than under NIR

by image-level fusion of multispectral iris images. For each wavelength w, a mask M_w is generated which is set if and only if the texture measure T_e, across all imaged wavelengths, is highest at that location in wavelength w. More formally, let I_w be an iris imaged at wavelength w and $T(I_w(x, y))$ be a monotonically increasing measure of the texture at a given position (x, y) in the image I_w, then we define a MEC as an image where,

$$I_{\text{mec}}(x, y) = \arg\max\left(T(I_w(x, y))\right) \tag{12.5}$$

and the mask M_w as,

$$M_w(x, y) = \begin{cases} 1 & \iff \arg\max\left(T(I_w(x, y))\right) \\ 0 & otw. \end{cases} \tag{12.6}$$

12.7 Conclusions

We illustrated the design of a single-lens multispectral camera and used spatially registered multispectral iris images acquired from it to demonstrate that iris texture increases with the frequency of the illumination for lighter colored sections of the iris and decreases for darker sections. We presented a model for approximating an NIR iris image using features derived from the color and structure of a VL iris image. The simulated NIR images generated by this model are designed to improve the interoperability between legacy NIR iris images and those acquired under visible light by enabling cross wavelength matching of NIR and visible light iris images. Finally, we introduced the MEC, a novel iris code which uses pixel-level fusion algorithms to exploit texture variations elicited by illuminating the iris at different wavelengths to improve iris matcher performance and reduce FTE rates. We are currently evaluating the performance of both the VL to NIR transform and the MEC iris code and will report a comprehensive assessment in a follow-on paper.

References

1. C. Boyce et al., Multispectral iris analysis: a preliminary study, in *Proceedings of IEEE Computer Society Workshop on Biometrics* (June 2006)
2. W. Burger, M.J. Burge, *Digital Image Processing: An Algorithmic Introduction using Java* (Springer, Nov. 2007)
3. J. Daugman, How Iris Recognition Works, in *IEEE Transaction on CVSVT* (2004), pp. 21–30
4. J.G. Daugman, Complete discrete 2-D gabor transforms by neural networks for image analysis and compression. IEEE Trans. Acoust. Speech Sig. Process. **36**(7), 1169–1179 (1988)
5. R.M. Haralick, K. Shanmugam, I. Dinstein, Textural features for image classification. IEEE Trans. Syst. Man Cybern. **3**(6), 610–621 (1973)
6. A. Jain, R. Bolle, S. Pankanti, Introduction to Biometrics, in *Biometrics: Personal Identification in a Networked Society*, ed. by A. Jain, R. Bolle, S. Pankanti (Kluwer Academic Publishers, 1999)

7. M. Monaco, Color Space Analysis for Iris Recognition, MSEE Dissertation. West Virginia University, 2007
8. M. Sonka, V. Hlavac, R. Boyle, *Image Processing, Analysis, and Machine Vision* (Thomson-Engineering, 2007)

Chapter 13
Iris Segmentation for Challenging Periocular Images

Raghavender Jillela, Arun A. Ross, Vishnu Naresh Boddeti,
B.V.K. Vijaya Kumar, Xiaofei Hu, Robert Plemmons and Paúl Pauca

Abstract This chapter discusses the performance of five different iris segmentation algorithms on challenging periocular images. The goal is to convey some of the difficulties in localizing the iris structure in images of the eye characterized by variations in illumination, eyelid and eyelash occlusion, de-focus blur, motion blur, and low resolution. The five algorithms considered in this regard are based on the (a) integro-differential operator; (b) hough transform; (c) geodesic active contours; (d) active contours without edges; and (e) directional ray detection method. Experiments on the Face and Ocular Challenge Series (FOCS) Database highlight the pros and cons of the individual segmentation algorithms.

13.1 Introduction

The iris is a moving object with a small surface area that is located within the independently movable eyeball. The eyeball itself is located within another moving object—the head. Therefore, reliably localizing the iris in eye images obtained at a distance from unconstrained human subjects can be difficult. Furthermore, since the iris is typically imaged in the near-infrared portion (700–900 nm) of the electromagnetic (EM) spectrum, appropriate invisible lighting is required to illuminate it prior

R. Jillela
Digital Signal Corporation, Chantilly, VA, USA
e-mail: Raghavener.Jillela@mail.wvu.edu

A.A. Ross (✉)
Integrated Pattern Recognition and Biometrics Lab (i-PRoBe), Michigan State University,
East Lansing, MI, USA
e-mail: arun.ross@mail.wvu.edu

V.N. Boddeti · B.V.K. Vijaya Kumar
Carnegie Mellon University, Pittsburgh, PA, USA

X. Hu · R. Plemmons · P. Pauca
Wake Forest University, Winston-Salem, NC, USA

© Springer-Verlag London 2016   281
K.W. Bowyer and M.J. Burge (eds.), *Handbook of Iris Recognition*,
Advances in Computer Vision and Pattern Recognition,
DOI 10.1007/978-1-4471-6784-6_13

to image acquisition. This poses a problem when the illuminator is at a considerable distance from the subject.

In order to mitigate this concern and to extend the depth-of-field of ocular-based biometric systems, the use of a small region around the eye has been proposed as an additional biometric cue. This use of this region—referred to as the *periocular* region—has several benefits:

1. In images where the iris cannot be reliably obtained (or used), the surrounding skin region may be used to either confirm or refute an identity.
2. The use of the periocular region represents a good trade-off between using the entire face region and using only the iris for recognition. When the entire face is imaged from a distance, the iris information is typically of low resolution; this means the matching performance due to the iris modality will be poor. On the other hand, when the iris is imaged at close quarters, the entire face may not be available thereby forcing the recognition system to rely only on the iris.
3. The periocular region can offer information about eyeshape that may be useful as a soft biometric.
4. The depth-of-field of iris systems can be increased if the surrounding ocular region were to be included as well.

The use of the periocular region is especially significant in the context of IOM (Iris On the Move) systems where the eye of a moving subject can be imaged when the individual passes through a choke point (e.g., a portal). Figure 13.1a shows the image acquisition setup used by an Iris On the Move (IOM) system.

A sample periocular image is shown in Fig. 13.1b. Periocular image acquisition depends on the following two factors:

1. Sensor parameters (e.g., field of view, zoom factor, resolution, view angle, etc.),
2. Stand-off distance (distance between the sensor and the subject).

(a)   **(b)**

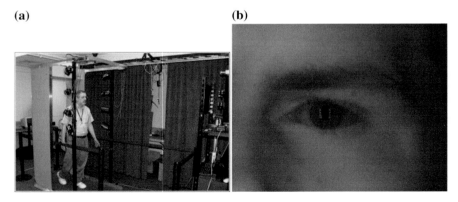

Fig. 13.1 a Image acquisition setup used by the Iris On the Move (IOM) system. Image source: Matey et al. [7]. ©IEEE and **b** sample periocular image. **a** A, **b** B

(a)   (b)

(c)   (d)

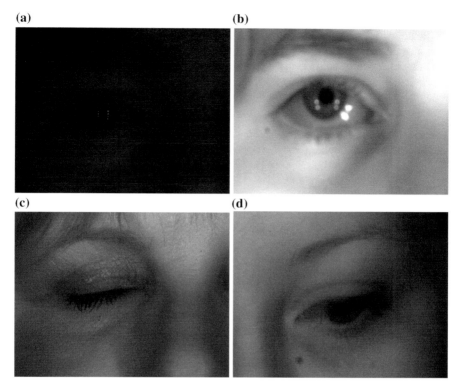

Fig. 13.2 Periocular images exhibiting some of the nonideal attributes referred to in the narrative. **a** Poor illumination. **b** Blur. **c** Occlusion. **d** Off-angle iris

To perform iris recognition using periocular images, the iris region has to be segmented successfully. However, performing iris segmentation in periocular images can be very challenging. This is due to the fact that images acquired from moving subjects in a relatively unconstrained environment can be of poor quality. Such images often exhibit nonideal attributes such as off-axis iris, occlusions, blur, poor illumination, etc. Some challenging periocular images are shown in Fig. 13.2.

However, there are several benefits in segmenting the iris in nonideal periocular images:

1. **Defining the area of the periocular region**: In images that contain poor quality iris, periocular information can be used to improve the recognition performance [16]. However, it is very important to define a rectangular region of fixed size, from which the periocular features can be extracted. The width and height of this region are often expressed as a function of the iris radius [9], which in turn can be determined by iris segmentation.

2. **Selective quality enhancement**: If the iris region is of poor quality in a given periocular image, image enhancement techniques can be applied exclusively within

the iris region. This operation can lead to improved iris recognition performance. The appropriate region for applying selective enhancement can be determined by first segmenting the iris.

3. **Periocular image alignment**: In some cases, it is possible to encounter rotated periocular images, caused by head tilt. The center of the iris, determined by iris segmentation, can be used as an anchor point to perform rotation and to register the images appropriately.

Toward this end, this chapter discusses various techniques that can be used to perform iris segmentation in challenging periocular images.

13.1.1 Periocular Region

The word periocular is a combination of *peri* (meaning, the vicinity) and *ocular* (meaning, related to the eye). In general, the periocular region refers to the skin, and the anatomical features (e.g., eyebrows, birthmarks, etc.) contained within a specified region surrounding the eye. Periocular recognition describes the process of using the discriminative information contained in the periocular region to perform human recognition.

The region defining the periocular biometric has not been precisely defined in the biometric literature. However, Park et al. [10] suggest that a rectangular region centered at the iris center and containing the eyebrows will be the most beneficial size for recognition. Active research is being carried out to study the performance of periocular recognition under various conditions (e.g., distance [1], types of features that can be used [8], etc.). It has to be noted that the periocular region can be considered to be a soft biometric trait. The present chapter focuses exclusively on performing iris segmentation in periocular images, and does not deal with periocular recognition.

13.1.2 Iris Segmentation

Iris segmentation refers to the process of automatically detecting the pupillary (inner) and limbus (outer) boundaries of an iris in a given image. This process helps in extracting features from the discriminative texture of the iris, while excluding the surrounding regions. A periocular image showing the pupillary and limbus boundaries can be seen in Fig. 13.3. Iris segmentation plays a key role in the performance of an iris recognition system. This is because improper segmentation can lead to incorrect feature extraction from less discriminative regions (e.g., sclera, eyelids, eyelashes, pupil, etc.), thereby reducing the recognition performance.

A significant number of iris segmentation techniques have been proposed in the literature. Two most popular techniques are based on using an integro-differential

Fig. 13.3 A sample periocular image with the pupillary (*inner*) and limbus (*outer*) boundaries highlighted

operator [3] and the Hough transform [15], respectively. The performance of an iris segmentation technique is greatly dependent on its ability to precisely isolate the iris from the other parts of the eye. Both the above listed techniques rely on curve fitting approach on the edges of the image. Such an approach works well with good quality, sharply focused iris images. However, under challenging conditions (e.g., nonuniform illumination, motion blur, etc.), the edge information may not be reliable.

In this chapter, the following techniques are considered for performing iris segmentation in challenging periocular images:

1. Integro-differential operator
2. Hough transform
3. Geodesic Active Contours
4. Active contours without edges
5. Directional ray detection

The first two curve fitting techniques are classical approaches that are computationally inexpensive. The other three techniques present relatively newer approaches for iris segmentation and are more suited for nonideal periocular images. The above selection of techniques, ensures a good combination between contour fitting and curve evolution-based approaches for performing iris segmentation in a challenging database.

13.2   Face and Ocular Challenge Series (FOCS) Database

13.2.1   Database

The Face and Ocular Challenge Series (FOCS) database was collected primarily to study the possibility of performing iris and periocular recognition in images obtained under nonideal conditions. Periocular images of resolution 750×600 pixels were captured from subjects walking through a portal in an unconstrained environment.

Fig. 13.4 A set of images showing the significant variations in illumination caused by varying stand-off distance

Fig. 13.5 Sample images in FOCS database showing the padding with zero pixels (by the distributors of the database) to maintain a fixed resolution of 750×600 pixels

The image acquisition system contained a set of Near Infra Red (NIR) sensors and illuminators. The degree of illumination observed in an image varied significantly across images due to variations in the stand-off distance, which in turn was caused by subject movement. Figure 13.4 shows some images exhibiting this effect. Some of the other challenges observed in the images include:

1. out-of-focus blur;
2. specular reflections;
3. partially or completely occluded iris;
4. off-angled iris;
5. small size of the iris region, compared to the size of the image;
6. smudged iris boundaries;
7. sensor noise.

In some cases, the size of the periocular images was smaller than 750×600 pixels. Such images were padded with pixels of zero intensity (by the distributors of the database) in order to maintain a constant image resolution (Fig. 13.5). All these factors render FOCS to be a challenging database.

13.2.2 Preprocessing

As the image quality of the FOCS database was very poor, two image preprocessing schemes were used to improve the iris segmentation performance: (i) illumination normalization, (ii) eye center detection.

13.2.2.1 Illumination Normalization

For a majority of the images in the FOCS database, it is very difficult, even for a human expert, to determine the precise location of the iris boundaries. This is caused by low illumination in the images. In such cases, the image contrast is very low and the iris boundaries are obscured. To alleviate this problem, illumination normalization was performed prior to iris segmentation. This was done by adjusting the histogram of the image using the *imadjust* command in MATLAB. This step helps in increasing the contrast of the image and highlights the intensity variation across the iris boundaries. Figure 13.6 shows sample images before and after illumination normalization.

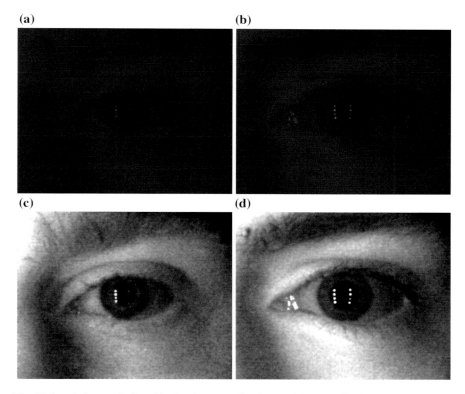

Fig. 13.6 a, b Images before illumination normalization. **c, d** Images after illumination normalization. Notice that the iris boundaries are better distinguishable only after performing illumination normalization

(a)   **(b)**   **(c)**

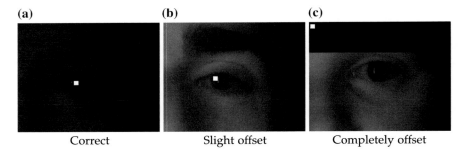

Correct   Slight offset   Completely offset

Fig. 13.7 Results of the eye center detector on sample images in FOCS data set (shown by a *white dot*). **a** Correctly detected eye center. **b, c** Incorrect output

13.2.2.2   Eye Center Detection

Many iris segmentation techniques determine the rough location of the pixels lying within the pupil region by a simple image thresholding process. This is based on the fact that the pixels corresponding to the pupil area, in a uniformly illuminated image, are usually of the lowest intensity. In nonideal images, however, such an approach may not work due to the presence of nonuniform illumination. In this work, an eye center detector [5, 14] was used to output the 2D location of the center of the iris in a given image. The eye center detector is based on the shift-invariance property of the correlation filters.

The correlation filter for the eye center detector was trained on 1000 images, in which the eye centers were manually labeled. When the correlation filter is applied to a given periocular image, a peak is observed, whose location corresponds to the center of the eye. The output of the detector was observed to be reliable in a majority of images, and can be used as an anchor point (a) to perform geometric normalization of the images, and (b) to initialize contours in the curve evolution-based techniques.

The eye center detector can be of significant use in nonideal images containing off-centered or occluded eyes. Figure 13.7a shows a sample periocular image, with the eye center detector output marked by a white dot. Figure 13.7b, c show examples of some rare cases where the eye center was not accurately determined.

13.3   Integro-Differential Operator

Given a preprocessed image, $I(x, y)$, Daugman's integro-differential operator [3] can be used to first determine the limbic boundary of the iris. This operation can be mathematically expressed as:

$$\mathbf{max}(r, x_0, y_0) \left| G_\sigma(r) * \frac{\partial}{\partial r} \oint_{r,x_0,y_0} \frac{I(x, y)}{2\pi r} ds \right|, \tag{13.1}$$

where

$$G_\sigma(r) = \frac{1}{\sqrt{2\pi}\sigma} \exp^{-\left(\frac{(r-r_0)^2}{2\sigma^2}\right)} \tag{13.2}$$

represents a radial Gaussian with a center r_0, standard deviation σ, and the symbol $*$ denotes the convolution operation. Convolving the image with a Gaussian operator helps in smoothing the image, thereby highlighting the edge information. The term r denotes the radius of the circular arc ds, centered at (x_0, y_0). To normalize the circular integral with respect to its perimeter, it is divided by a factor of $2\pi r$. In short, Daugman's integro-differential operator performs circular edge detection, which can be controlled by the parameter set $\{x_0, y_0, r\}$. The computational expense associated with an iris boundary search process can be minimized by providing a range of estimates for the parameter r, that are close to the actual boundary radius.

Once the limbus boundary is detected, the search process for the pupillary boundary is carried out only within the predetermined limbus region. Daugman suggests that the radius of the pupillary boundary can range from 0.1 to 0.8 of the limbus

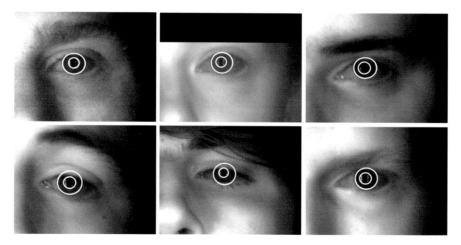

Fig. 13.8 Images showing successful iris segmentation output obtained using the integro-differential operator technique

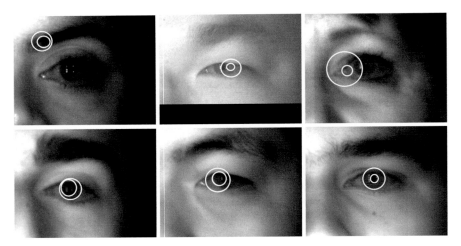

Fig. 13.9 Images showing unsuccessful iris segmentation output obtained using the integro-differential operator technique

boundary radius. Figure 13.8 shows some images in which the iris boundaries are successfully segmented using an integro-differential operator. Some examples of poorly segmented boundaries using this technique are shown in Fig. 13.9.

13.4 Hough Transform

Given a preprocessed image, $I(x, y)$, a Canny edge detector is first used to determine the edges contained in the image. Consider the set of edge points obtained by the Canny edge detector to be (x_i, y_i), where $i = 1, 2, \ldots, n$. Since this set of edge points could represent a noncontinuous or noncircular contour, a voting procedure is used to fit a circle to the boundary. For this purpose, Hough transform [4], a standard contour fitting algorithm, is used. The voting procedure in the Hough transform technique is carried out in a parameter space, from which object candidates (in this case, circular contours) are obtained as local maxima in an accumulator space constructed by the algorithm. In the field of iris recognition, Wildes et al. [15] demonstrated the use of Hough transform to determine the iris boundaries.

For a given set of edge points, (x_i, y_i), $i = 1, 2, \ldots, n$, Hough transform can be used to fit a circle with center (x_c, y_c), and radius r, as follows:

$$H(x_c, y_c, r) = \sum_{i=1}^{n} h(x_i, y_i, x_c, y_c, r) \tag{13.3}$$

where

$$h(x_i, y_i, x_c, y_c, r) = \begin{cases} 1, & \text{if } g(x_i, y_i, x_c, y_c, r) = 0 \\ 0, & \text{otherwise.} \end{cases} \tag{13.4}$$

and

$$g(x_i, y_i, x_c, y_c, r) = (x_i - x_c)^2 + (y_i - y_c^2) - r^2. \tag{13.5}$$

For each edge point contained in the set (x_i, y_i), $g(x_i, y_i, x_c, y_c, r)$ is considered to be 0, if the parameter triplet (x_c, y_c, r) represents a circle through that point. $H(x_c, y_c, r)$ is an accumulator array and its values (indexed by discretized values for x_c, y_c, and r) are incremented as per the equations above. The parameter triplet that corresponds to the largest value in the array is considered to be the most suitable parameter set for the circle that fits the given contour. Equation 13.5 can be modified to accommodate various contours such as circle, parabola, or ellipse. However, the computational complexity associated with a parabola or an ellipse is much higher than for a circle.

Similar to the integro-differential operator, Hough transform-based segmentation first detects the limbus boundary of the iris. To detect the pupillary boundary, the region within the limbus boundary is used for localization purposes. Figure 13.10

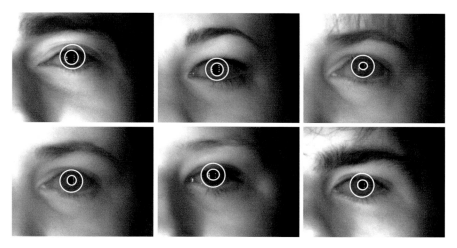

Fig. 13.10 Images showing successful iris segmentation output obtained using the Hough transform technique

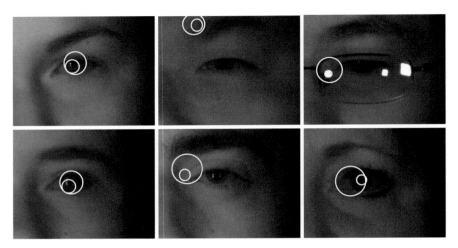

Fig. 13.11 Images showing unsuccessful iris segmentation output obtained using the Hough transform technique

shows some sample images in which the segmentation was successful using Hough transform. On the other hand, unsuccessful segmentation outputs are shown in Fig. 13.11.

13.5   Geodesic Active Contours (GAC)

This approach is based on the relation between active contours and the computation of geodesics (minimal length curves). The strategy is to evolve an arbitrarily initialized curve from within the iris under the influence of geometric properties of the iris boundary. GACs combine the energy minimization approach of the classical "snakes" and the geometric active contours based on curve evolution [12].

Let $\gamma(t)$ be the curve, that has to gravitate toward the outer boundary of the iris, at a particular time t. The time t corresponds to the iteration number. Let ψ be a function measuring the signed distance from the curve $\gamma(t)$. That is, $\psi(x, y)$ = distance of point (x, y) to the curve $\gamma(t)$.

$$\psi(x, y) = \begin{cases} 0 & \text{if (x,y) is on the curve;} \\ <0 & \text{if (x,y) is inside the curve;} \\ >0 & \text{if (x,y) is outside the curve.} \end{cases} \tag{13.6}$$

Here, ψ is of the same dimension as that of the eye image $I(x, y)$. The curve $\gamma(t)$ is called the level set of the function ψ. Level sets are the set of all points in ψ where ψ is some constant. Thus $\psi = 0$ is the zeroth level set, $\psi = 1$ is the first level set, and so on. ψ is the implicit representation of the curve $\gamma(t)$ and is called the embedding function since it embeds the evolution of $\gamma(t)$. The embedding function evolves under the influence of image gradients and the region's characteristics so that the curve $\gamma(t)$ approaches the desired boundary of the iris. The initial curve $\gamma(t)$ is assumed to be a circle of radius r just beyond the pupillary boundary. Let the curve $\gamma(t)$ be the zeroth level set of the embedding function. This implies that

$$\frac{d\psi}{dt} = 0.$$

By the chain rule,

$$\frac{d\psi}{dt} = \frac{\partial\psi}{\partial x}\frac{dx}{dt} + \frac{\partial\psi}{\partial y}\frac{dy}{dt} + \frac{\partial\psi}{\partial t},$$

i.e.

$$\frac{\partial\psi}{\partial t} = -\nabla\psi \cdot \gamma'(t).$$

Splitting the $\gamma'(t)$ in the normal $(N(t))$ and tangential $(T(t))$ directions,

$$\frac{\partial\psi}{\partial t} = -\nabla\psi \cdot (v_N N(t) + v_T T(t)).$$

Now, since $\nabla\psi$ is perpendicular to the tangent to $\gamma(t)$,

$$\frac{\partial\psi}{\partial t} = -\nabla\psi \cdot (v_N N(t)). \qquad (13.7)$$

The normal component is given by

$$N = \frac{\nabla\psi}{\|\nabla\psi\|}.$$

Substituting this in Eq. (7.9),

$$\frac{\partial\psi}{\partial t} = -v_N\|\nabla\psi\|.$$

Let v_N be a function of the curvature of the curve κ, stopping function K (to stop the evolution of the curve) and the inflation force c (to evolve the curve in the outward direction) such that,

$$\frac{\partial\psi}{\partial t} = -(\mathrm{div}(K\frac{\nabla\psi}{\|\nabla\psi\|}) + cK)\|\nabla\psi\|.$$

Thus, the evolution equation for ψ_t[1] such that $\gamma(t)$ remains the zeroth level set is given by

$$\psi_t = -K(c + \epsilon\kappa)\|\nabla\psi\| + \nabla\psi \cdot \nabla K, \qquad (13.8)$$

where, K, the stopping term for the evolution, is an image dependant force and is used to decelerate the evolution near the boundary; c is the velocity of the evolution; ϵ indicates the degree of smoothness of the level sets; and κ is the curvature of the level sets computed as

$$\kappa = -\frac{\psi_{xx}\psi_y^2 - 2\psi_x\psi_y\psi_{xy} + \psi_{yy}\psi_x^2}{(\psi_x^2 + \psi_y^2)^{\frac{3}{2}}}.$$

Here, ψ_x is the gradient of the image in the x direction; ψ_y is the gradient in the y direction; ψ_{xx} is the 2nd order gradient in the x direction; ψ_{yy} is the 2nd order gradient in the y direction; and ψ_{xy} is the 2nd order gradient, first in the x direction and then in the y direction. Equation (7.10) is the level set representation of the geodesic active contour model. This means that the level set C of ψ is evolving according to

$$C_t = K(c + \epsilon\kappa)\mathbf{N} - (\nabla K \cdot \mathbf{N})\mathbf{N} \qquad (13.9)$$

where N is the normal to the curve. The term $\kappa\mathbf{N}$ provides the smoothing constraints on the level sets by reducing their total curvature. The term $c\mathbf{N}$ acts like a balloon force and it pushes the curve outward toward the object boundary. The goal of the stopping function is to slow down the evolution when it reaches the boundary. However, the evolution of the curve will terminate only when $K = 0$, i.e., near an ideal edge. In most images, the gradient values will be different along the edge, thus requiring the use of different K values. In order to circumvent this issue, the third geodesic term $((\nabla K.\mathbf{N}))$ is necessary so that the curve is attracted toward the boundary (∇K points toward the middle of the boundary). This term makes it possible to terminate the evolution process even if (a) the stopping function has different values along the edges, and (b) gaps are present in the stopping function.

The stopping term used for the evolution of level sets is given by

$$K(x, y) = \frac{1}{1 + \left(\frac{\|\nabla(G(x,y)\star I(x,y))\|}{k}\right)^\alpha} \qquad (13.10)$$

where $I(x, y)$ is the image to be segmented, G(x,y) is a Gaussian filter, and k and α are constants. As can be seen, $K(x, y)$ is not a function of t (Figs. 13.12 and 13.13).

Consider an iris image to be segmented as shown in Fig. 7.19a. The stopping function K obtained from this image is shown in Fig. 7.19b (for $k = 2.8$ and $\alpha = 8$). Assuming that the inner iris boundary (i.e., the pupillary boundary) has already been detected, the stopping function K is modified by deleting the circular edges

---

[1]The subscript t denotes the iteration number.

(a)   (b)

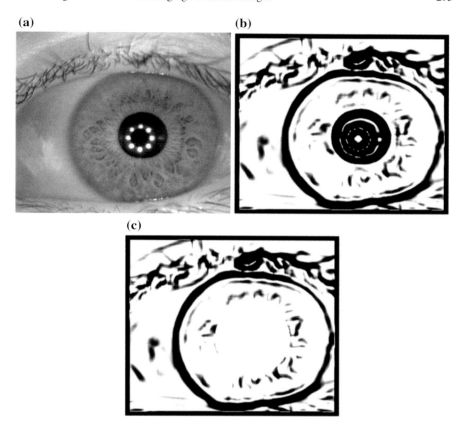

(c)

Fig. 13.12 Stopping function for the geodesic active contours. **a** Original iris image, **b** stopping function K, and **c** modified stopping function K'

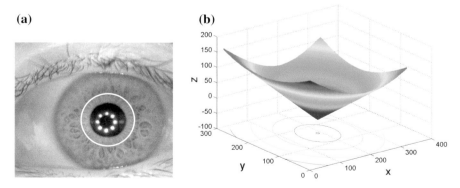

Fig. 13.13 Contour initialization for iris segmentation using GAC. **a** Zeroth level set (initial contour), **b** mesh plot denoting the signed distance function ψ

corresponding to the pupillary boundary, resulting in a new stopping function K'. This ensures that the evolving level set is not terminated by the edges of the pupillary boundary (Fig. 7.19c).

A contour is first initialized near the pupil (Fig. 7.20a). The embedding function ψ is initialized as a signed distance function to $\gamma(t = 0)$ which looks like a cone (Fig. 7.20b). Discretizing Eq. 7.10 leads to the following equation:

$$\frac{\psi_{i,j}^{t+1} - \psi_{i,j}^t}{\Delta t} = -cK_{i,j}'\|\nabla\psi^t\| - K_{i,j}'(\epsilon\kappa_{i,j}^t\|\nabla\psi^t\|) + \nabla\psi_{i,j}^t \cdot \nabla K_{i,j}'^t, \quad (13.11)$$

where Δt is the time step (e.g., Δt can be set to 0.05). The first term $(cK_{i,j}'\|\nabla\psi^t\|)$ on the right hand side of the above equation is the velocity term (advection term) and, in the case of iris segmentation, acts as an inflation force. This term can lead to singularities and hence is discretized using upwind finite differences. The upwind scheme for approximating $\|\nabla\psi\|$ is given by

$$\|\nabla\psi\| = \sqrt{A},$$
$$A = \min(D_x^- \psi_{i,j}, 0)^2 + \max(D_x^+ \psi_{i,j}, 0)^2 +$$
$$\min(D_y^- \psi_{i,j}, 0)^2 + \min(D_y^+ \psi_{i,j}, 0)^2.$$

$D_x^- \psi$ is the first order backward difference of ψ in the x-direction; $D_x^+ \psi$ is the first order forward difference of ψ in the x-direction; $D_y^- \psi$ is the first order backward difference of ψ in the y-direction; and $D_y^+ \psi$ is the first order forward difference of ψ in the y-direction. The second term $(K_{i,j}'(\epsilon\kappa_{i,j}^t\|\nabla\psi^t\|))$ is a curvature-based smoothing term and can be discretized using central differences. In our implementation, $c = 0.65$ and $\epsilon = 1$ for all iris images. The third geodesic term $(\nabla\psi_{i,j}^t \cdot \nabla K_{i,j}'^t)$ is also discretized using the central differences.

After evolving the embedding function ψ according to Eq. (7.13), the curve begins to grow until it satisfies the stopping criterion defined by the stopping function K'. But at times, the contour continues to evolve in a local region of the image where the stopping criterion is not strong. This leads to over-evolution of the contour. This can be avoided by minimizing the thin plate spline energy of the contour. By computing the difference in energy between two successive contours, the evolution scheme can be regulated. If the difference between the contours is less than a threshold (indicating that the contour evolution has stopped at most places), then the contour evolution process is terminated. The evolution of the curve and the corresponding embedding functions are illustrated in Fig. 13.14.

Since the radial fibers may be thick in certain portions of the iris, or the crypts present in the ciliary region may be unusually dark, this can lead to prominent edges in the stopping function. If the segmentation technique is based on parametric curves,

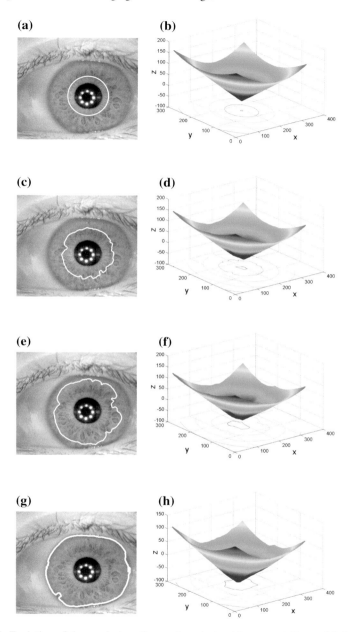

Fig. 13.14 Evolution of the geodesic active contour during iris segmentation. **a** Iris image with initial contour, **b** embedding function ψ (X and Y axes correspond to the spatial extent of the eye image and the Z axis represents different level sets), **c–f** contours after 600 and 1400 iterations, and their corresponding embedding functions, and **g, h** final contour after 1800 iterations (contours shown in *white*)

(a)   **(b)**

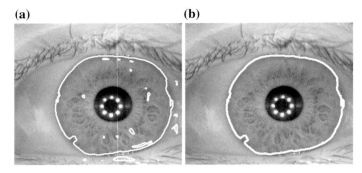

Fig. 13.15 The final contour obtained when segmenting the iris using the GAC scheme. **a** Example of a geodesic contour splitting at various local minima, **b** final contour (contours shown in *white*)

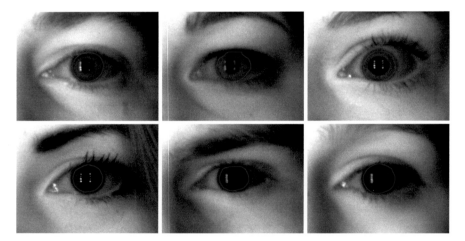

Fig. 13.16 Sample images showing successful segmentation output obtained using the Geodesic Active Contours technique

then the evolution of the curve might terminate at these local minima. However, geodesic active contours are able to split at such local minima and merge again. Thus, they are able to effectively deal with the problems of local minima, thereby ensuring that the final contour corresponds to the true limbus boundary (Fig. 13.15).

Figures 13.16 and 13.17 show sample images corresponding to successful and failed segmentation outputs, respectively, obtained using the Geodesic Active Contours technique.

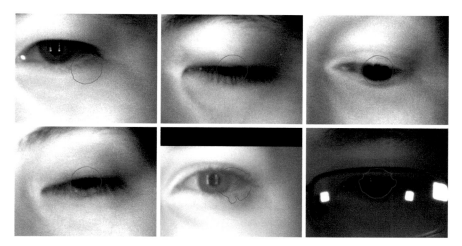

Fig. 13.17 Sample images showing failed segmentation output obtained using the Geodesic Active Contours technique

13.6 Active Contours Without Edges

As explained in Sect. 13.1.2, the classical iris segmentation algorithms depend on edge information to perform boundary detection. However, in poor quality images of FOCS database, the sharp edges required for iris segmentation are smudged to the point that there is no discernible edge information. This problem can be alleviated to an extent by basing the segmentation algorithm on the statistics of different regions of the eye (e.g., pupil, iris, etc.), instead of the sparse edge information. To this end, a region-based active contour segmentation algorithm is developed, which is inspired by the seminal work of Chan and Vese [2]. In this technique, the contour evolution is governed by the image statistics of the *foreground* and *background* regions of a considered contour. Such an approach has been shown to work very well in cases where both the *foreground* (the region that has to be segmented) and the *background* are homogeneous, but is known to fail when the regions are not homogeneous.

For iris images, the foreground inside the contour (pupil or iris) is homogeneous, while the background is not, due to the presence of skin, eyelashes, and eyelids. Recently, Sundaramoorthi et al. [13] addressed this issue by defining a *lookout region*. This lookout region is typically a region just outside the region of interest, from which the background statistics are computed as a function of the foreground. The basic idea behind this, is that for a Gaussian distributed data (assumption for the foreground), the region outside the foreground (that is required to detect a transition from the foreground to background) is dependent on the image statistics of the foreground region. More precisely, the lookout region for the quickest change detection for Gaussian distributed data is given by $\Delta_{\sigma(I|\Omega)}\Omega\backslash\Omega$, where Δ_σ denotes dilation by $\sigma(I|\Omega)$.

13.6.1 Description of the Technique/Contour Formulation

The proposed technique segments the image based on the distribution of pixel intensities or features extracted from the eye image from a region both inside and outside the contour rather than looking for sharp edges, making it more robust to blurring and illumination variations than an edge-based active contour. The segmentation involves two steps: pupil segmentation, followed by iris segmentation. The pupil segmentation algorithm is posed as a energy minimization problem, with the objective to be minimized defined as follows:

$$E(\Omega, \mu, \bar{\mu}, \lambda_1, \lambda_2) = \int_{\Delta_{\sigma(I|\Omega)}\Omega\backslash\Omega} |I(x) - \bar{\mu}|^2 dx + \lambda_1 \int_\Omega |I(x) - \mu|^2 dx + \lambda_2 \Gamma(\Omega)$$

$$(13.12)$$

where $I(x)$ is the eye image. For simplicity reason, $I(x)$ is used instead of $I(x, y)$. Ω is the current contour, $\sigma(I|\Omega) = \frac{\int_\Omega |I(x) - \mu|^2 dx}{\int_\Omega dx}$ computes the statistics of the region within a contour which is then used to define the lookout region $\Delta_{\sigma(I|\Omega)}\Omega\backslash\Omega$ outside the current contour, $\Gamma(\Omega)$ is the regularization term, μ is the mean pixel intensity within the contour, $\bar{\mu}$ is the mean pixel intensity in the lookout region and λ_1 and λ_2 are scalars weighting the different criteria defining the contour energy. The output of the eye center detection is used to initialize a contour for pupil segmentation. Once the pupil is segmented, a contour is initialized just outside the pupil. However, Eq. 13.12 may not be used directly because the pupil region needs to be excluded from within the current contour. This leads to the following energy formulation for detecting the outer boundary:

$$E(\Omega, \mu, \bar{\mu}, \lambda_1, \lambda_2) = \int_{\Delta_{\sigma(I|\Omega)}\Omega\backslash\Omega} |I(x) - \bar{\mu}|^2 dx + \lambda_1 \int_{\bar{\Omega}} |I(x) - \mu|^2 dx + \lambda_2 \Gamma(\Omega)$$

$$(13.13)$$

where $\bar{\Omega} = \Omega\backslash\Omega_{\text{pupil}}$ defines the region within the current contour excluding the pupil. Due to occlusions like specular reflections, eye lashes, etc. as part of the contour evolution many small contours are also formed along with the pupil or iris contours. These extraneous contours are pruned based on their regional statistics like size of region, eccentricity of region etc. Further, the final contour is smoothed by applying a simple moving average filter to the contour. Figures 13.18 and 13.19 show some examples of successful and unsuccessful iris segmentation outputs, respectively.

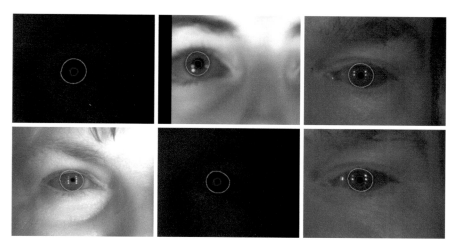

Fig. 13.18 Some examples showing successful segmentation of iris regions under challenging conditions (poor illumination and blur) using the active contours without edges technique on the FOCS database

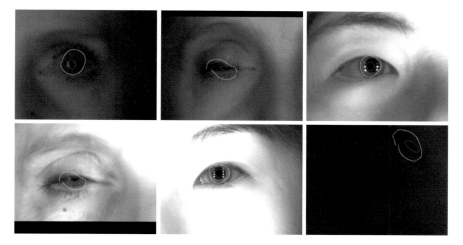

Fig. 13.19 Some examples showing unsuccessful segmentation of iris regions under challenging conditions (poor illumination and blur) using the active contours without edges technique on the FOCS database. Some of the mistakes are due to eye-detection failure and closed eye

13.7 Directional Ray Detection Method

This section presents an iris segmentation technique for low quality, and off-angle iris images that is based on a novel directional ray detection segmentation scheme. This method can employ calculus of variations or directional gradients to better approximate the boundaries of the pupillary and limbic boundaries of the iris. variational segmentation methods are known to be robust in the presence of noise and can be combined with shape-fitting schemes when some information about the object shape is known a priori. Quite commonly, circle-fitting is used to approximate the boundaries of the iris, but this assumption may not necessarily hold for noncircular boundaries or off-axis iris data. For computational purposes, this technique uses directional gradients and circle-fitting schemes, but other shapes can also be easily considered.

This technique extends the work by Ryan et al. [11], who approach the iris segmentation problem by adapting the Starburst algorithm to locate pupillary and limbic feature pixels used to fit a pair of ellipses. The Starburst algorithm was introduced by Li et al. [6], for the purpose of eye tracking. The proposed method involves multiple stages of an iterative ray detection scheme, initialized at points radiating out from multiple positions around eye region, to detect the pupil, iris, and eyelid boundaries. The scheme also involves the use of a correlation filter method for eye center detection.

13.7.1   Description of the Technique

The proposed segmentation approach includes the following four sequential steps:

1. The location of the eye center is first estimated using a specially designed correlation filter.
2. The circular boundary of the pupil is obtained by uniform key point extraction and Hough transformation.
3. The iris boundary is determined by the directional ray detection scheme.
4. Finally, the eyelid boundary is also determined by directional ray detection scheme, applied at multiple points.

13.7.1.1   Eye Center Detection

Given a periocular image, the location of the eye center is obtained using the correlation-based eye center detector described in Sect. 13.2.2.2. It is noticed that the accuracy of the current iris segmentation technique is crucially related to the correctness of the eye center detector output.

13.7.1.2   Pupil Segmentation

In this step, it is assumed that the eye center (x_c, y_c) of image $I(x, y)$ is located within the pupil. Iterative directional ray detection is then applied within a square region $I_p(x, y)$ of size of $2(r_p + R_p)$ centered at (x_c, y_c), where $0 < r_p < R_p$ are

(a) **(b)** **(c)** **(d)**

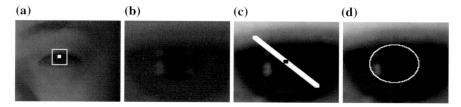

Fig. 13.20 One iteration of iterative directional ray segmentation for pupil detection. **a** $I(x, y)$. **b** $I_p(x, y)$. **c** Directional ray. **d** Segmented pupil

pupil radius bounds determined experimentally from the data set. A sample square region $I_p(x, y)$ containing a pupil is shown in Fig. 13.20b.

Each iteration includes ray detection to extract structural key points and the Hough transformation to estimate the circular pupil boundary. As shown in Fig. 13.20c, a number of rays are chosen starting at the estimated eye center (x_c, y_c) along m directions $\theta \in \Theta$, where Θ is a subset of $[0, 2\pi]$. For the FOCS data set, the value of Θ is set as $\Theta = [\frac{\pi}{4}, \frac{3\pi}{4}] \cup [\frac{5\pi}{4}, \frac{7\pi}{4}]$, to select pixel information contained along the vertical direction. The directional gradient difference along these rays is then calculated. Locations for which the gradient difference reaches an absolute maximum are then selected as key points. The Hough transform is performed to find the circular pupil boundary, the estimated pupil center (x_p, y_p), and the radius of the pupil $\hat{r}_p$ as shown in Fig. 13.20d.

Gradient calculation is notoriously sensitive to image noise. To compensate for the presence of noise, an adaptive approach is implemented that:

1. enhances the edges at the location of selected key points,
2. uses the estimated pupil center (x_p, y_p) instead of the eye center location (x_c, y_c), and
3. properly sets up the length of test rays to vary towards $\hat{r}_p$.

In the present implementation, at most 3 iterations are needed to obtain a very reliable and accurate pupil segmentation, as shown in Fig. 13.20d.

13.7.1.3 Iris Segmentation

In this step, the estimate pupil center (x_p, y_p) and pupil radius $\hat{r}_p$ are used to select a square region of size $2(\hat{r}_p + R_I)$ centered at (x_p, y_p), where $R_I > \hat{r}_p$ is a bound parameter determined experimentally from the data set. Iterative directional ray detection is then applied within this region. Specifically, a set of rays are chosen to emanate from a set of points Γ along n directions $\theta \in \Theta$, where $\Gamma = \{(x, y)|x = x_p + (1 + \alpha)\hat{r}_p; y = y_p + (1 + \alpha)\hat{r}_p\}$, $\Theta = [-\frac{\pi}{6}, \frac{\pi}{6}] \cup [\frac{5\pi}{6}, \frac{7\pi}{6}]$, and $\alpha = 0.5$. As shown in Fig. 13.21a, the directions of test rays in this stage are close to the horizontal axis to avoid the upper and lower eyelid regions. Similarly, to perform pupil segmentation, the key points are determined using the adaptive gradient different

(a)   **(b)**   **(c)**   **(d)**

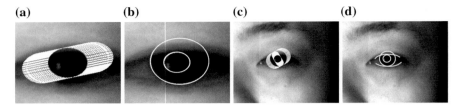

Fig. 13.21 Iterative directional ray detection results for iris and eyelids. **a** Rays ($\theta = \frac{pi}{6}$). **b** Segmented iris. **c** Rays (multiple pos.). **d** Eyelids detection

scheme, and Hough transform is applied to find the iris, as shown in Fig. 13.21b. The main advantage of this approach is a reduced sensitivity to light reflection and other impurities in the iris region as well as increased computational efficiency of the Hough transform.

13.7.1.4 Eyelid Boundary Detection

Detecting the eyelid boundaries is an important step in the accurate segmentation of the visible iris region as well as for the determination of iris quality metrics. For this, a two-step directional ray detection approach from multiple starting points is used. As shown in Fig. 13.21c, the testing rays are set to emanate from the boundaries of the pupil and iris regions. Two groups of rays are chosen roughly along the vertical and horizontal directions. Gradient differences are computed along these rays and key points are appropriately selected. A least squares best fitting model is then applied to the binary key points map and a first-step fitting estimation to the eyelid boundary is produced. To improve accuracy of the estimation in the previous step, the noisy key points are removed outside the estimated eyelid boundary, and the edges are enhanced around the remaining key points. Applying ray detection from multiple positions, a new set of key points is obtained. The least squares fitting model is then applied again, resulting in an improved estimation of eyelids, shown in Fig. 13.21d.

The proposed iterative directional ray detection method is a promising segmentation approach as it has been shown be robust in the segmentation of poor quality data. An adaptive gradient difference scheme is used as a core procedure to select key points in specific image regions, simplifying the overall problem into simpler more manageable pieces. The computational cost for this technique is comparable to other existing techniques in the literature. Figure 13.22 provides examples of successful segmentation obtained by the directional ray detection technique. Figure 13.23 provides images of unsuccessful examples.

Fig. 13.22 Directional ray detection method—some successful examples from the FOCS data set

Fig. 13.23 Directional ray detection method—some unsuccessful examples from the FOCS data set

13.8 Experimental Evaluation

The total number of images contained in the FOCS database is 9581. However, performing an evaluation of iris segmentation algorithms using the entire database. This is due to the high number of images and the computational cost aspects involved. Therefore, a subset of 404 images was chosen from the FOCS database, and used to determine the best performing iris segmentation algorithm. It was ensured that the sample dataset was representative of the full FOCS database, in terms of the challenges posed (e.g., nonuniform illumination, blur, occlusion, etc.). The resolution of the images was unaltered (750 × 600 pixels). The number of unique subjects contained in this 404 image dataset was 108, with the number of samples per subject ranging from 1 to 11.

13.8.1 Segmentation Accuracies

The correlation filter approach for detecting the eye centers, when applied on the full FOCS data set, yielded a success rate of over 95 %. The output of the eye center detector was used only for three techniques: Geodesic Active Contours, active contours without edges, and directional ray detection techniques. The performance of an iris segmentation technique was measured by computing the *segmentation accuracy*, defined as follows:

$$\text{Segmentation accuracy} = \frac{\text{Number of correctly segmented images}}{\text{Number of input images provided}} \times 100 \quad (13.14)$$

The types of iris segmentation technique used, and their corresponding segmentation accuracies are summarized in the table below.

Technique	Images	Correct	Accuracy (%)
Integro-diff.	404	207	51.2
Hough transform	404	210	52.0
Geodesic active contours	404	358	88.6
Active contours	404	365	90.3
Ray detection	404	343	84.9

From the results obtained on the 404 image dataset, it was observed that the techniques based on active contours resulted in the best performance among the considered set of techniques.

13.8.2 *Analysis*

The preprocessing schemes appear to have a significant role in the segmentation performance for all the techniques. Illumination normalization helps in increasing the contrast of the image, thereby highlighting the iris boundaries. Similarly, eye center detector helps in localizing a region for iris boundary search process.

The considered set of iris segmentation techniques ensures a balance between the classical approaches, and the relatively newer approaches to handle challenging iris images. Both the integro-differential operator and Hough transform require relatively less computations, when compared to the other three techniques. However, their performance was observed to be low, due to the poor quality input data. On the other hand, Geodesic Active Contours, active contours without edges, and directional ray detection algorithm provide better performance, at the expense of higher computational complexity.

Geodesic Active Contours can be effectively used to evolve a contour that can fit to a noncircular iris boundary (typically caused by eyelids or eyelash occlusions). However, edge information is required to control the evolution and stopping of the contour. The performance of Geodesic Active Contours for this database was limited to 88.6 % due to the lack of edge information, which is caused by poor illumination levels.

13.9 Summary

Performing iris recognition at a distance is a challenging task. Significant amount of research is being conducted toward improving the recognition performance in iris images acquired under unconstrained conditions. Employing better image acquisition systems can significantly improve the quality of input images and, thereby, the recognition performance. However, for practical purposes, it is necessary to develop algorithms that can handle poor quality data. In this regard, the present chapter discusses the problem of iris segmentation in challenging periocular images. A set of 5 iris segmentation techniques were evaluated on a periocular database containing various nonideal factors such as occlusions, blur, and significant illumination variations. This work helps serve two main purposes: (a) it describes a real world problem of uncontrolled iris image acquisition and the associated challenges, and (b) it highlights the need for robust segmentation techniques to handle poor quality iris images.

Acknowledgments This work was sponsored under IARPA BAA 09-02 through the Army Research Laboratory and was accomplished under Cooperative Agreement Number W911NF-10-2-0013. The views and conclusions contained in this document are those of the authors and should not be interpreted as representing of official policies, either expressed or implied, of IARPA, the Army Research Laboratory, or the U.S. Government. The U.S. Government is authorized to reproduce and distribute reprints for Government purposes notwithstanding any copyright notation herein.

References

1. S. Bharadwaj et al., Periocular biometrics: when iris recognition fails, in *Fourth IEEE International Conference on Biometrics: Theory Applications and Systems (BTAS). BTAS'10* (IEEE Press, Piscataway, NJ, USA, 2010)
2. T. Chan, L. Vese, Active contours without edges. IEEE Trans. Image Process. **10**(2), 266–277 (2001)
3. J. Daugman, How iris recognition works **1** (2002)
4. J. Illingworth, J. Kittler, A survey of the Hough transform. Comput. Vis. Graph. Image Process. **44**(1), 87–116 (1988)
5. B.V.K.V. Kumar, L. Hassebrook, Performance measures for correlation filters. Appl. Opt. **29**(20), 2997–3006 (1990)
6. D. Li, J.S. Babcock, D. Parkhurst, openEyes: a low-cost headmounted eye-tracking solution, in *ETRA* (2006), pp. 95–100
7. J. Matey et al., Iris on the move: acquisition of images for iris recognition in less constrained environments. Proc. IEEE **94**(11), 1936–1947 (2006)
8. P. Miller et al., Performance evaluation of local appearance based periocular recognition, in *Fourth IEEE International Conference on Biometrics: Theory Applications and Systems (BTAS). BTAS'10* (IEEE Press, Piscataway, NJ, USA, 2010)
9. U. Park, A. Ross, A.K. Jain, Periocular biometrics in the visible spectrum: a feasibility study, in *Proceedings of the 3rd IEEE International Conference on Biometrics: Theory, Applications and Systems. BTAS'09* (IEEE Press, Piscataway, NJ, USA, 2009), pp. 153–158
10. U. Park et al., Periocular biometrics in the visible spectrum. IEEE Trans. Inf. Forensics Secur. **6**(1), 96–106 (2011)

11. W. Ryan et al., Adapting starburst for elliptical iris segmentation, in *Proceedings of the 2rd IEEE International Conference on Biometrics: Theory, Applications and Systems. BTAS'08.* (IEEE Press, Piscataway, NJ, USA, 2008)
12. S. Shah, A. Ross, Iris segmentation using geodesic active contours. IEEE Trans. Inf. Forensics Secur. **4**(4), 824–836 (2009)
13. G. Sundaramoorthi, S. Soatto, A.J. Yezzi, Curious snakes: a minimum latency solution to the cluttered background problem in active contours, in *CVPR* (2010), pp. 2855–2862
14. J. Thornton, M. Savvides, B.V.K. Vijayakumar, Robust iris recognition using advanced correlation techniques, in *Conference on Image Analysis and Recognition (ICIAR)*, vol. 3656 (2005), pp. 1098–1105
15. R. Wildes et al., A system for automated iris recognition, in *Proceedings of the Second IEEE Workshop on Applications of Computer Vision* (1994), pp. 121–128
16. D.L. Woodard et al., Appearance-based periocular features in the context of face and non-ideal iris recognition. Signal Image Video Process. **5**(4), 443–455 (2011)

Chapter 14
Periocular Recognition from Low-Quality Iris Images

Josh Klontz and Mark J. Burge

Abstract Definitions of the periocular region vary, but typically encompass the skin covering the orbit of the eye. Especially in cases where the iris has not been acquired with sufficient quality to reliably compute an IrisCode, the periocular region can provide additional discriminative information for biometric identification. The NIR periocular images which form NIST's Face and Ocular Challenge Series (FOCS) are characterized by large variations in illumination, eyelid and eyelash occlusion, de-focus blur, motion blur, and low resolution. We investigate periocular recognition on the FOCS dataset using three distinct classes of features: photometric, keypoint, and frequency-based. We examine the performance of these features alone, in combination, and when fused with classic IrisCodes.

14.1 Introduction

Section 14.2 introduces NIST's Face Ocular Challenge Series (FOCS) dataset, which is characterized by large variations in illumination, eyelid and eyelash occlusion, de-focus blur, motion blur and low resolution. Section 14.3 identifies some of the properties which make the FOCS dataset difficult for IrisCode systems. Section 14.4 investigates three alternatives to IrisCodes which take advantage of the periocular information available in the FOCS images: Gabor Wavelets, Local Binary Patterns (LBP), Scale Invariant Feature Transformation (SIFT). Section 14.5 demonstrates how applying a sequence of Principle Component Analysis (PCA) and Local Discriminant Analysis (LDA) to the alternative feature encodings can improve match performance. Finally, Sect. 14.6 explores the result of fusing our alternative encodings with traditional IrisCodes.

J. Klontz · M.J. Burge (✉)
The MITRE Corporation, McLean, VA, USA
e-mail: mburge@mitre.org; Mark.Burge@Noblis.org

J. Klontz
e-mail: jklontz@mitre.org

© Springer-Verlag London 2016   309
K.W. Bowyer and M.J. Burge (eds.), *Handbook of Iris Recognition*,
Advances in Computer Vision and Pattern Recognition,
DOI 10.1007/978-1-4471-6784-6_14

14.2 Face Ocular Challenge Series (FOCS)

The FOCS dataset is an example of low-quality iris images which exhibit a high rate of failure to acquire (i.e., failure to enroll) on commercial iris systems. A NIST document http://www.nist.gov/itl/iad/ig/focs.cfm describes the rational for the FOCS dataset as "A significant amount research has gone into iris recognition from 'high' quality iris images captured from cooperative subjects. The results of this research are commercially available products for matching 'high' quality iris images. The cutting edge of research is recognition from images that contain the eye region of the face and the iris. The iris in these images can be of variable quality." [14] We investigate using the periocular area of the FOCS images to improve match performance.

NIST's FOCS dataset was commissioned by IARPA to serve as a challenge set for performers in the ocular track of the IARPA BEST program. It consists of NIR frames extracted from the Iris on the Move [12] (IoM) videos (See Fig. 14.1) of the MBGC Portal Track V2. It contains 4792 left and 4789 right eyes of 136 subjects. Images are of a single iris (See Fig. 14.2) and the surrounding periocular region. They are encoded as 750×600, 8-bit grayscale, JPEG quality 100 images.

The COIR [16] ocular collection was a precursor to the FOCS dataset which was developed "to compensate for the lack of a dedicated ocular dataset and to leverage the large amount of existing face and iris image and video data already available." [16]. In contrast to the FOCS dataset, COIR used visible light images extracted from NIST's MBGC [18] series.

14.3 FOCS: A Difficult Dataset for IrisCodes

FOCS images pose a number of challenges (e.g., large variations in illumination, eyelid and eyelash occlusion, de-focus blur, motion blur, and low resolution) which make them difficult for traditional IrisCode systems. Two traditional IrisCode algorithms were used in the study, NIST's VASIR [9] system, and a commercial algorithm. The iris-pupil and -sclera boundary were manually located and the coordinates were pro-

Fig. 14.1 The FOCS dataset consists of frames extracted from NIST's Multi-Biometrics Grand Challenge (MBGC) IoM (Iris on the Move) NIR video sequences

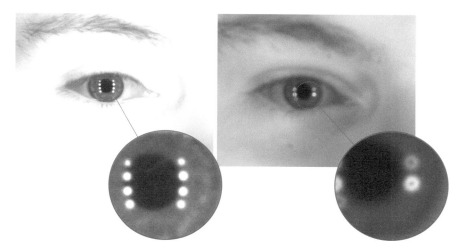

Fig. 14.2 Example FOCS images. The image on the *left* 05301d128_06_r was enrollable by commercial algorithms, while the image on the *right* 05301d116_09_r was not

vided to both algorithms. Without this information both systems failed to enroll over 90 % of the FOCS images.

After localizing the iris-sclera boundary (Fig. 14.3a, b), the first step in a traditional IrisCode algorithms is to segment and unwrap the iris texture. Figure 14.3d gives an example of the quality and resolution of a typical unwrapped FOCS images and can be compared to that of a typical "high" quality iris images such as that of CASIA V1, Fig. 14.3c.

14.3.1   IrisCode Performance

While both VASIR [9] and the commercial algorithm were easily able to separate match and non-match scores,[1] on the higher quality CASIA images, they failed to enroll nearly all FOCS images.

14.3.2   Dynamic Range

The dynamic range of an image can be defined as the difference between the image's highest and lowest pixel values. In cases where a small number of outlier values skew the distribution, a number of more robust variations, such as discarding 0.5 %

---

[1]As can be expected for one of the earlier standard test sets like CASIA [17], the commercial algorithm was able to perfectly separate match and non-match pairs.

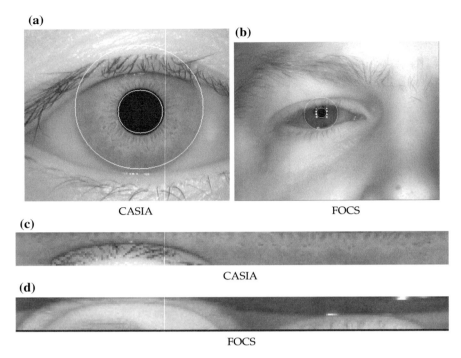

Fig. 14.3 Example of the segmentation of **a** "high" quality NIR iris image CASIA and **b** a "lower" quality FOCS images **c** unwrapped CASIA **d** unwrapped FOCS

of both tails, can be used. A low dynamic range can indicate acquisition problems such as insufficient illumination on target or nonoptimal sensor bias settings.

Figure 14.4 graphs the mean $\bar{x}$ and standard deviation σ of all the pixel values (i.e., each graph point corresponds to the mean and sigma of a single image) in each of 2,000 NIR iris images sampled from the ND-IRIS [19] and FOCS datasets. Figure 14.4 illustrates how the distribution of the dynamic range of the FOCS dataset differs from that of a typical NIR iris dataset like ND-IRIS. The low dynamic range of the FOCS images makes both segmentation and feature extraction challenging. Figure 14.5 shows the increasing dynamic range of the FOCS image, note that 1/4 of the images have a σ less than 23 and a $\bar{x}$ of less than 76.

14.4 Alternatives to IrisCodes

Using a Bayesian graphical model to find the correlations between patches on the FOCS images, Boddeti [3] reported an Equal Error Rate (EER) of 26.81 % for the left ocular region, 23.83 % for the right ocular region, and 30.8 % for a customized IrisCode implementation. This established that the ocular region could be used to

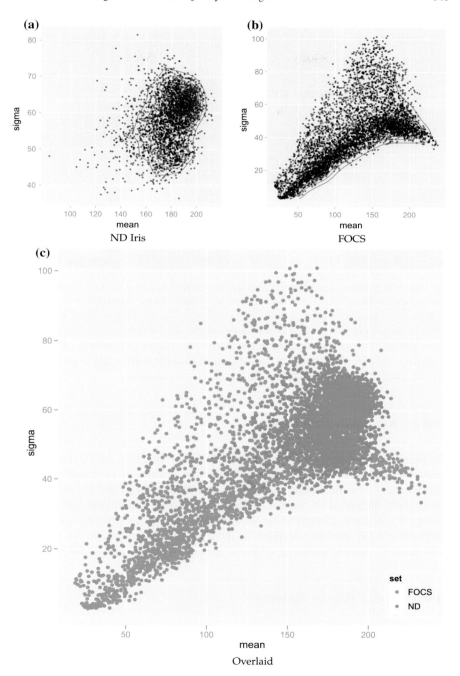

Fig. 14.4 Mean $\bar{x}$ and standard deviation σ of all the pixel values in each of 2,000 NIR iris images from **a** ND-IRIS and **b** FOCS, **c** overlay of ND-IRIS (*teal*) and FOCS (*red*). Each point represents the $\bar{x}$ and σ of a single image

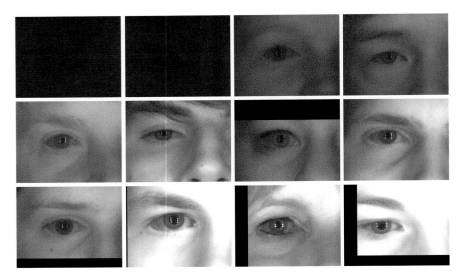

Fig. 14.5 FOCS images sorted (increasing) by the standard deviation of their dynamic range, equally sampled (i.e., 4/12 of the images have a σ less than the *upper-right* image)

improve match performance over IrisCodes alone. To further assess the usefulness of periocular information for recognition, three alternatives to IrisCodes, we investigated the used of Gabor Wavelets, Local Binary Patterns (LBP), and Scale Invariant Feature Transformation (SIFT) features for ocular recognition.

14.4.1 Key Point Descriptors

The skin texture in periocular images contains discriminating marks arising from variations in the skin surface. In general, keypoint descriptors are those which are able to identify edge-like features which persist over scale variations. In the following experiments, the Speed-Up Robust Features (SURF) [24] variation of the SIFT [11] descriptor was used. Compared to SIFT, SURF uses integral images to decrease computation time and Haar wavelets to increase robustness. Feature vectors were constructed by densely sampling a 11×11 grid of 24 pixel radius SURF features.

14.4.2 Local Binary Patterns

A seminal method in face recognition is the use of local binary patterns [15] (LBP) to represent the face [1]. Local Binary Patterns are Level 2 features that represent small patches across the face with histograms of binary patterns that encode the structure and texture of the face. In this experiment, we encode the periocular region using LBPs.

Local binary patterns describe each pixel using a p-bit binary number. Each bit is determined by sampling p pixel values at uniformly spaced locations along a circle of radius r, centered at the pixel being described. For each sampling location, the corresponding bit receives the value 1 if it is greater than or equal to the center pixel, and 0 otherwise.

A special case of LBP, called the uniform LBP [15], is generally used in face recognition. Uniform LBP (LBP U2) assigns any nonuniform binary number to the same value, where uniformity is defined by whether more than u transitions between the values 0 and 1 occur in the binary number. In the case of $p = 8$ and $u = 2$, the uniform LBP has 58 uniform binary numbers, and the 59th value is reserved for the remaining $256 - 58 = 198$ nonuniform binary numbers. Thus, each pixel will take on a value ranging from 1 to 59. Overlapping histograms of LBP U2 patterns were extracted from window sizes ranging from 32 to 256 pixels (See Table 14.1) and the resulting histograms were compared using a ChiSquared distance metric. Table 14.1 gives the match results from five variations

In the context of periocular recognition, LBP values are first computed at each pixel in the (normalized) periocular image. The image is tessellated into patches with a height and width of 12 pixels. For each patch i, a histogram of the LBP values $S'_i \in \mathbb{Z}^{d_s}$ is computed (where $d_s = 59$). This feature vector is then normalized to the feature vector $S_i \in \mathbb{R}^{d_s}$ by

$$S_i = \frac{S'_i}{\sum_i^{d_s} S'_i}.$$

Finally, we concatenate the N vectors into a single vector x of dimensionality $d_s \cdot N$. Note, in our implementation, the illumination filter proposed by Tan and Triggs [23] is used prior to computing the LBP codes in order to suppress nonuniform illumination variations.

14.4.3 Gabor Wavelets

Gabor features are one of the first Level 2 facial features [8] to have been used with wide success in representing facial images [10, 22, 25]. One reason Gabor features are popular for representing both facial and natural images is their similarity with human neurological receptor fields [13, 20].

Table 14.1 Performance of LBP on FOCS

	$LBP^{u2}_{256,8}$	$LBP^{u2}_{128,8}$	$LBP^{u2}_{64,8}$	$LBP^{u2}_{48,8}$	$LBP^{u2}_{32,8}$
FAR $= 10^{-3}$	0.04	0.26	0.52	**0.53**	0.43
FAR $= 10^{-2}$	0.16	0.49	0.65	**0.66**	0.58

(a) Impact of LBP window size on match performance. (b) Highest scoring LBP variation (i.e., $LBP^{u2}_{48,8}$ vs. VASIR. Note LBP's TAR of 0.61 vs. VASIR's TAR of 0.06 at the same FAR of 10^{-2}

A Gabor image representation is computed by convolving a set of Gabor filters with an image (in this case, a periocular image). The Gabor filters are defined as

$$G(x, y, \theta, \eta, \gamma, f) = \frac{f^2}{\pi \gamma \eta} e^{-\left(\frac{f^2}{\gamma^2}x'^2 + \frac{f^2}{\gamma^2}y'^2\right)} e^{(j2\pi fx')} \tag{14.1}$$

$$x' = x\cos\theta + y\sin\theta \tag{14.2}$$

$$y' = -x\sin\theta + y\cos\theta \tag{14.3}$$

where f sets the filter scale (or frequency), θ is the filter orientation along the major axis, γ controls the filter sharpness along the major axis, and η controls the sharpness along the minor axis. Typically, combinations across the following values for the scale f and orientation θ are used: $f = \{0, 1, \ldots, 4\}$ and $\theta = \{\pi/8, \pi/4, 3\pi/8, \ldots, \pi\}$. This creates a set (or bank) of filters with different scales and orientations. Given the bank of Gabor filters, the input image is convolved with each filter, which results in a Gabor image for each filter. The combination of these scale and orientation values results in 40 different Gabor filters, which in turn results in 40 Gabor images (for example).

In this paper, the recognition experiments using a Gabor image representation operate by: (i) performing illumination correction using the method proposed by Tan and Triggs [23], (ii) computing the phase response of the Gabor images with $f = \{8, 16, 32\}$, and $\theta = 0, \pi/4, \pi/2, 3\pi/4$, (iii) tessellating the Gabor image(s) into patches of size 12×12, (iv) quantizing the phase response (which ranges from 0 to 2π) into 24 values and computing the histogram within each patch, and (v) concatenating the histogram vectors into a single feature vector. Given two (aligned) periocular images, the distance between their corresponding Gabor feature vectors is used to measure the dissimilarity between the two periocular images.

14.5 Improving Performance Using Learning

The trainable algorithm used in this study is the Spectrally Sampled Structural Subspace Features algorithm [7], which is abbreviated as 4SF@. This algorithm uses multiple discriminative subspaces to perform recognition. After geometric normalization of a periocular image illumination correction is performed using the illumination correction filter presented by Tan and Triggs [23]. Periocular images are then represented using histograms of local binary patterns at densely sampled patches [1] (to this point, 4SF is the same as the non-trainable LBP algorithm described in Sect. 14.4.2). For each patch, principal component analysis (PCA) is performed so that 95.0 % of the variance is retained.

Given a training set of subjects, multiple stages of weighted random sampling are performed, where the spectral densities (i.e., the eigenvalues) from each face patch are used for weighting. The randomly sampled subspaces are based on Ho's original method [5], however, the proposed approach is unique in that the sampling is

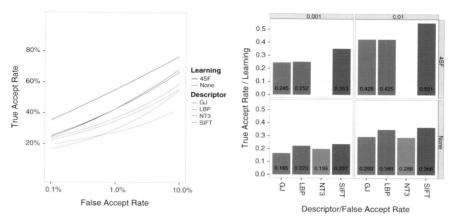

Fig. 14.6 Performance of a commercial iris code system (NT), Gabor Wavelets (GJ), Local Binary Patterns (LBP), and keypoint descriptors (SIFT), with (*solid line*) and without (*dashed line*) learning

weighted based on the spectral densities. For each stage of random sampling, LDA [2] is performed on the randomly sampled components. The LDA subspaces are learned using subjects randomly sampled from the training set (i.e., bagging [4]). Finally, distance-based recognition is performed by projecting the LBP representation of periocular images into the per-patch PCA subspaces, and then into each of the learned LDA subspaces. The sum of the Euclidean distance in each subspace is the dissimilarity between two periocular images (Fig. 14.6).

14.6 Fusing Periocular Features with Iris Codes

Ross et al. [21] reported recognition rates on the FOCS dataset based on fusing results from Gradient Orientation Histogram (GOH), SIFT, and Probabilistic Deformation Model (PDM). In Table 14.2 we present the results of ZScore fusing [6] combinations of LBP, SURF, Gabor wavelets, and traditional IrisCodes on the FOCS dataset.

Table 14.2 Fusion method for the following was ZScore score normalization then weighing the higher performing descriptor 2:1

	w/o learning				w/learning			
	GJ	LBP	SIFT	NT	GJ	LBP	SIFT	NT
GJ	0.293	0.357	0.357	0.398	0.398	0.546	0.485	0.506
LBP	0.357	0.348	0.381	0.430	0.546	0.430	0.556	0.488
SIFT	0.357	0.381	0.366	0.445	0.485	0.556	0.445	0.591
NT	0.398	0.430	0.445	0.288	0.506	0.488	0.591	na

14.7   Conclusions

The NIR periocular images which form NIST's Face and Ocular Challenge Series (FOCS) are characterized by large variations in illumination, eyelid and eyelash occlusion, de-focus blur, motion blur, and low resolution. We investigated periocular recognition on the FOCS dataset using three distinct classes of features: photometric, keypoint, and frequency-based. We examined the performance of these features alone, in combination, and when fused with classic IrisCodes. We demonstrated that in cases where the iris has not been acquired with sufficient quality to reliably compute an IrisCode (as in NIST's FOCS dataset), the periocular region can provide additional discriminative information for biometric identification.

References

1. T. Ahonen, A. Hadid, M. Pietikainen, Face description with local binary patterns: application to face recognition. IEEE Trans. Pattern Anal. Mach. Intell. **28**(12), 2037–2041 (2006)
2. P. Belhumeur, J. Hespanda, D. Kriegman, Eigenfaces vs. fisherfaces: recognition using class specific linear projection. IEEE Trans. Pattern Anal. Mach. Intell. **19**(7), 711–720 (1997)
3. V. Boddeti, J. Smereka, B. Kumar, A comparative evaluation of iris and ocular recognition methods on challenging ocular images. IEEE (2011)
4. L. Breiman, Bagging predictors. Mach. Learn. **24**(2), 123–140 (1996)
5. T.K. Ho, The random subspace method for constructing decision forests. IEEE Trans. Pattern Anal. Mach. Intell. **20**(8), 832–844 (1998)
6. A. Jain, K. Nandakumar, A. Ross, Score normalization in multimodal biometric systems. Pattern Recognit. **38**(12), 2270–2285 (2005)
7. B. Klare, Spectrally Sampled Structural Subspace Features (4SF), in *Michigan State University Technical Report*, MSU-CSE-11-16 (2011)
8. B. Klare, A. Jain, On a taxonomy of facial features, in *Proceedings of IEEE Conference on Biometrics: Theory, Applications and Systems* (2010)
9. Y. Lee et al., Robust iris recognition baseline for the grand challenge, in *National Institute of Standards and Technology, NISTIR 7777* (2011)
10. C. Liu, H. Wechsler, Gabor feature based classification using the enhanced fisher linear discriminant model for face recognition. IEEE Trans. Image Process. **11**(4), 467–476 (2002)
11. D.G. Lowe, Distinctive image features from scale-invariant keypoints. Int. J. Comput. Vis. **60**(2), 91–110 (2004)
12. J.R. Matey et al., Iris on the move: acquisition of images for iris recognition in less constrained environments. Proc. IEEE **94**(11), 1936–1947 (2006)
13. E. Meyers, L. Wolf, Using biologically inspired features for face processing. Int. J. Comput. Vis. **76**(1), 93–104 (2008)
14. NIST, Face and Ocular Challenge Series. www.nist.gov/itl/iad/ig/focs.cfm
15. T. Ojala, M. Pietikäinen, T. Mäenpää, Multiresolution gray-scale and rotation invariant texture classification with local binary patterns. IEEE Trans. Pattern Anal. Mach. Intell. **24**(7), 971–987 (2002)
16. V.P. Pauca et al., in *Challenging Ocular Image Recognition*, vol. 8029(1), ed. by S.O. Southern et al. (SPIE, 2011), p. 80291V
17. P. J. Phillips et al., Comments on the CASIA version 1.0 iris dataset. IEEE Trans. Pattern Anal. Mach. Intell. **29** (2007)

18. P.J. Phillips et al., Overview of the multiple biometrics grand challenge, in *Proceedings of the Third International Conference on Advances in Biometrics. ICB '09* (Springer, Berlin, 2009), pp. 705–714
19. P. Phillips et al., FRVT 2006 and ICE 2006 large-scale experimental results. IEEE Trans. Pattern Anal. Mach. Intell. **32**(5), 831–846 (2010)
20. M. Riesenhuber, T. Poggio, Hierarchical models of object recognition in cortex. Nat. Neurosci. **2**(11), 1019–1025 (1999)
21. A. Ross et al., Matching highly non-ideal ocular images: an information fusion approach, in *Proceedings of the 5th IAPR International Conference on Biometrics (ICB)* (2012)
22. L. Shen, L. Bai, A review on Gabor wavelets for face recognition. Pattern Anal. Appl. **9**, 273–292 (2006)
23. X. Tan, B. Triggs, Enhanced local texture feature sets for face recognition under difficult lighting conditions. IEEE Trans. Image Process. **19**(6), 1635–1650 (2010)
24. B. Thomee, E.M. Bakker, M.S. Lew, TOP-SURF: a visual words toolkit, in *ACM Multimedia'10* (2010), pp. 1473–1476
25. L. Wiskott et al., Face recognition by elastic bunch graph matching. IEEE Trans. Pattern Anal. Mach. Intell. **19**(7), 775–779 (1997)

Chapter 15
Unconstrained Iris Recognition in Visible Wavelengths

Hugo Proença

Abstract One of the most challenging goals in biometrics research is the development of recognition systems to work in unconstrained environments and without assuming the subjects' willingness to be recognized. This has led to the concept of *noncooperative recognition*, which broaden the application of biometrics to forensics/criminal seek domains. In this scope, one active research topic seeks to use as main trait the ocular region acquired at visible wavelengths, from moving targets and large distances. Under these conditions, performing reliable recognition is extremely difficult, because such *real-world* data have features that are notoriously different from those obtained in the classical constrained setups of currently deployed recognition systems. This chapter discusses the feasibility of iris/ocular biometric recognition: it starts by comparing the main properties of near-infrared and visible wavelength ocular data, and stresses the main difficulties behind the accurate segmentation of all components in the eye vicinity. Next, it summarizes the most relevant research conducted in the scope of visible wavelength iris recognition and relates it to the concept of *periocular* recognition, which is an attempt to augment classes separability by using—apart from the iris—information from the surroundings of the eye. Finally, the current challenges in this topic and some directions for further research are discussed.

15.1 Introduction

The iris is one of the most valuable traits for human identification and growing efforts have been concentrated in the development of this technology [6]. Fundamentally, three reasons justify this interest: (1) it is a naturally protected internal organ that is visible from the exterior; (2) it has a near circular and planar shape that turns easier its segmentation and parameterization and (3) its texture has a predominantly phenotypic or chaotic appearance that is stable over lifetime. The accuracy of the deployed

H. Proença (✉)
IT: Instituto de Telecomunicações, University of Beira Interior, Covilhã, Portugal
e-mail: hugomcp@di.ubi.pt

© Springer-Verlag London 2016
K.W. Bowyer and M.J. Burge (eds.), *Handbook of Iris Recognition*,
Advances in Computer Vision and Pattern Recognition,
DOI 10.1007/978-1-4471-6784-6_15

321

iris recognition systems is remarkable: a study of 200 billion cross-comparisons conducted by Daugman [13] reported false acceptance rates of order 10^{-6} with false rejections of 1 %. Other independent evaluations [21, 37] confirmed these results.

Current systems require high illumination levels, sufficient to maximize the signal-to-noise ratio in the sensor and to capture images of the discriminating iris features with sufficient contrast. However, if similar processes were used to acquire iris images from large distances, acceptable depth-of-field values would demand significantly higher f-numbers for the optical system, corresponding directly (squared) with the amount of light required for the process. Similarly, the motion factor will demand very short exposure times, which again will require too high levels of light. The American and European standards councils [16, 31] proposed safe irradiance limits for near-infrared (NIR) illumination of near 10 mW/cm^2. In addition to other factors that determine imaging system safety (blue light, nonreciprocity, and wavelength dependence), these limits should be taken into account, as excessively strong illumination can cause permanent eye damage. The NIR wavelength is particularly hazardous, because the eye does not instinctively respond with its natural mechanisms (aversion, blinking, and pupil contraction).

The pigmentation of the human iris consists mainly of two molecules: brown-black eumelanin (over 90 %) and yellow-reddish pheomelanin [49]. Eumelanin has most of its radiative fluorescence under the visible wavelength (VW), which—if properly imaged—enables the capture of a much higher level of detail, but also of many more artefacts, including specular and diffuse reflections and shadows. Also, the spectral reflectance of the sclera is significantly higher in the VW than in the NIR and the spectral radiance of the iris in respect of the levels of its pigmentation varies much more significantly in the VW than in the NIR. These optical properties are the biological roots behind the higher heterogeneity of the VW iris images, when compared with the traditional NIR data. Also, the types and number of artefacts likely to appear in VW and NIR data are notoriously different, which justify the need for specialized recognition strategies.

Figure 15.1 illustrates the variations in appearance of NIR and VW images, with respect to the levels of iris pigmentation. These images were acquired using a multispectral device in a synchronous way. It is particularly interesting to observe the inverse relation between the levels of minutia captured in NIR and VW data, with respect to the levels of iris pigmentation: while for light pigmented irises, much more detail is perceived in VW than in NIR images, it occurs the opposite for heavily pigmented irises (leftmost image). Note that this is a particularly concerning problem, as the large majority of the world population has heavily pigmented irises.

15.2   VW Iris Recognition: Summary of Research Works

Tan et al. [80] performed biometric recognition according to both iris and periocular data. Global color-based features and local ordinal measures were used to extract discriminating data from the iris region, later fused to periocular data extracted from

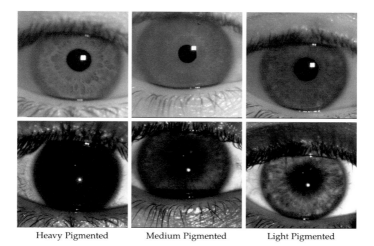

Heavy Pigmented   Medium Pigmented   Light Pigmented

Fig. 15.1 Comparison between the appearance of the iris texture acquired in a synchronous way using multispectral sensors. The *upper row* gives the iris data in near-infrared (NIR) wavelengths, while the *bottom row* gives the corresponding data in visible wavelengths (VW). Note the inverse relationship in the NIR and VW data regarding the levels of iris pigmentation and the captured iris minutia

texton representations. Finally, fusion is performed by the sum rule using the normalized scores generated for the different types of features. Wang et al. [85] used an adaptive boosting algorithm to build a strong iris classifier learned from a set of bi-dimensional Gabor-based set of features, each corresponding to a specific orientation and scale and operating locally. Later, given the fact that the pupillary boundary is especially difficult to segment in VW data, the authors trained two distinct classifiers: one for irises deemed to be accurately segmented and another for cases in which the pupillary boundary was not accurately segmented. Santos and Hoyle [71] fused a set of recognition techniques that can be divided in two main categories: wavelet-based textural analysis methods applied to the iris region, complemented by distribution-based (histogram of oriented gradients and local binary patterns) and scale invariant feature transforms that analyze the periocular region, which was recently suggested as an important addition for handling degraded samples, essentially because it is less vulnerable to problems resulting from deficient illumination or low-resolution acquisition. Shin et al. [74] started by classifying the left and right eyes by their eyelash distributions, which they used to reduce the search space. Further, they coupled two encoding and matching strategies based on color and textural analysis to obtain multiple distance scores fused by means of a weighted sum rule, which is claimed to improve the separation between *match* and *non-match* distributions. Li et al. [43] used a novel weighted co-occurrence phase histogram to represent local textural features. This method is claimed to model the distribution of both the phase angle of the image gradient and the spatial layout, which overcomes the major weakness of the traditional histogram. A matching strategy based on the Bhattacharyya distance measures the goodness of match between irises. Finally, the authors concluded that the performance is improved when a simple image registration scheme accounts for the image deformation. Marsico et al. [47] proposed the use of implicit equations to approximate both the pupillary and limbic iris boundaries and perform image normalization. Next, they exploited local feature extraction techniques such as linear binary patterns and discriminable textons to extract information from vertical and horizontal bands of the normalized image. Li and Ma [42] introduced an image registration method based on the Lucas–Kanade algorithm to account for iris pattern deformation. Operating on the filtered iris images, this method divides the images into small subimages and solves the registration problem for each small subimage. Later, a sequential forward selection method searches for the most distinctive filters from a family of Gabor filters, concluding that a very small number of selected features are able to obtain satisfactory performance. Finally, Szewczyk et al. [77] presented a semiempirical approach based on a reverse bi-orthogonal dyadic wavelet transform, empirically selecting a compactly supported bi-orthogonal spline wavelet for which symmetry is possible with FIR filters and three vanishing moments. The authors concluded that such a method produces a short biometric signature (324 bits) that can be successfully used for recognition under such challenging conditions, improving its reliability.

Du et al. [18] aimed at robustness and used the SIFT transform and Gabor wavelets to extract iris features, which were used for local feature point description. Then two feature region maps were designed to locally and globally register the feature points, building a set of deformable iris subregions that takes into account the pupil dilation/contraction and deformations due to off-angle data acquisition.

15.3 Data Acquisition: Frameworks and Major Problems

The term *constraint* refers to one of the factors that currently deployed systems impose, in order to perform recognition with enough confidence: subjects distance, motion and gaze direction, and lighting conditions of the environment. These constraints motivate growing research efforts and became the focus of many recent proposals, among which the "Iris-on-the-move" project [48] should be highlighted: it is a major example of engineering an image acquisition system to make the recognition process less intrusive for subjects. The goal is to acquire NIR close-up iris images as a subject walks at normal speed through an access control point. *Honeywell Technologies* applied for a patent [30] on a very similar system, which was also able to recognize irises at a distance. Previously, Fancourt et al. [19] concluded that it is possible to acquire sufficiently high-quality images at a distance of up to 10 m. Narayanswamy et al. [52] used a wavefront coded optic to deliberately blur images in such a way that they do not change over a large depth of field. Removing the blur with digital image processing techniques makes the trade-off between signal-to-noise ratio and depth of field linear. Also, using wavefront coding technology, Smith et al. [75] examined the iris information that could be captured in the NIR and

VW spectra, addressing the possibility of using these multispectral data to improve recognition performance. Park and Kim [55] acquired in-focus iris images quickly at a distance, and Boddeti and Kumar [7] suggested extending the depth of field of iris imaging frameworks by using correlation filters. He et al. [23] analyzed the role of different NIR wavelengths in determining error rates. More recently, Yoon et al. [90] presented an imaging framework that can acquire NIR iris images at a distance of up to 3 m, based on a face detection module and on a light-stripe laser device used to point the camera at the proper scene region. Boyce and Kumar [5] studied the image acquisition wavelength of revealed components of the iris, and identified the important role of iris pigmentation. Although concluding that illumination inside the 700–900 nm optimally reveals the richness of the iris structure, they observed that irises with moderate levels of pigmentation could be imaged in the visible light with good quality.

15.3.1 Proof-of-Concept

This section reports one possible solution for acquiring data of the ocular region from moving subjects in outdoor environments and large distances (between 10 and 40 m), without requiring subjects' willingness to be recognized. A prototype was developed, with two cameras mounted on the exterior wall of the *SOCIA Lab.: Soft Computing and Image Analysis Lab.*,[1] located in Covilhã, University of Beira Interior, Portugal. Cameras are at a first-floor level (approximately 5 m above the ground), and pointing toward a parking lot. A master–slave configuration was adopted, i.e., a wide-view (static) camera (*Canon VB-H710F* in our prototype) covers the whole scene and provides data for human detection and tracking modules, which enables to point the PTZ camera (*Hikvision DS-2DE5286-AEL*) to subjects' faces. Figure 15.2 illustrates the environmental conditions in this prototype and the data acquired by both the wide-view and PTZ devices.

In order to automatically obtain information from the subjects faces/ocular regions, the whole processing chain is composed by five modules: (1) at first, the SOBS [46] is used to discriminate between the background/foreground objects in the scene. Next, (2) a human detection algorithm based on the widely known Haar-based Viola and Jones algorithm [83] enables to obtain a set of regions of interest (ROI), which feed a (3) object tracking module, based on the KLT algorithm [73] and in the omega shape of the head and shoulders region as primary source of keypoints. This tracker gives as output a set of point lists, each one describing the 2D position of one subject in the scene. Such positions are used by a (4) time series predictor that estimates the subsequent positions of subjects in the scene, which is where the PTZ should be pointed to. A (5) camera calibration/synchronization module is capable of

---

[1]http://socia-lab.di.ubi.pt.

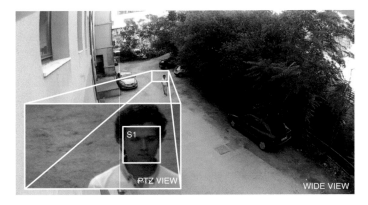

Fig. 15.2 Image automatically captured using a master–slave configuration that obtains high-resolution face images with inter-pupillary distance greater than 60 pixels, being subjects at 40 m away from the cameras

accurately estimating the PTZ pan-tilt parameters without depending on additional constraints. Our approach exploits geometric cues to estimate subjects height and avoids depth ambiguity, obtaining the subject's 3D position in the scene. As main result of this processing chain, we get images similar to the ones illustrated in the bottom-left corner of Fig. 15.2.

In order to establish a baseline comparison between the performance attained by face and ocular recognizers, considering two classical algorithms: (1) the face recognition strategy proposed by Turk and Pentland [81], which introduced the concept of *eigenface* that became extremely popular in the computer vision literature; and (2) the periocular recognition algorithm due to Park et al. [56], defining a grid around the iris, from where histograms of oriented gradients, local binary patterns, and scale-invariant features are extracted. Data from 25 persons were collected, with subjects from 15 to 30 m away from the camera. In this case, only samples with relatively frontal pose (yaw $\pm\pi/10$) and *neutral* expression were kept, resulting in a total of 78,960 images pairwise comparisons. Figure 15.3 compares the Receiver Operating Characteristic (ROC) curves obtained for the face and ocular recognition experts, being evident the better results of the ocular expert in the low *false acceptances* (FA) region, in contrast to the high FA region, where the facial recognition expert outperformed. In terms of the Area Under Curve (AUC) values, the ocular expert got 0.857, and the face expert 0.854, which are too close to provide statistically relevant conclusions about the *best* trait for this kind of environments. Note that in – this experiment—all subjects had neutral facial expression, which otherwise would decay more the recognition performance of face than of the ocular region. Anyway, the main purpose of this experiment was exclusively to obtain a baseline performance that could be substantially improved by using more sophisticated recognition algorithms.

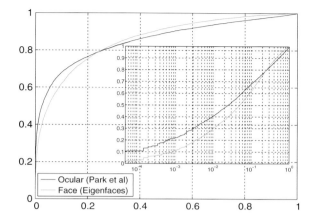

Fig. 15.3 Comparison between the recognition performance observed for two classical face and ocular recognition algorithms, using data acquired in outdoor environments, under conditions that are currently associated to visual surveillance

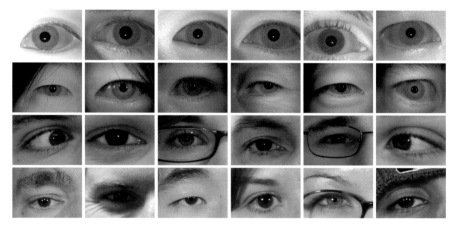

Fig. 15.4 Examples of the data sets used in the experiments are reported in this chapter. From *top* to *bottom rows* BATH, CASIA-Iris-Distance, UBIRIS.v2, and FRGC data sets

15.3.2 *NIR Versus VW Data: Amount of Information Acquired*

As illustrated in Fig. 15.4, four freely available data sets were selected for all experiments reported in this chapter, each one representing a different data acquisition setup/scenario:

- The University of Bath data set[2] contains 32,000 NIR images from 800 subjects. From these, 6,000 images from 1.000 different classes (eyes) with very good quality were considered, to represent the optimal conditions for a recognition system. All irises are sharp without relevant occlusions and in frontal view.
- The CASIA-Iris-Distance set[3] was collected by the CASIA long-range device in a relatively unconstrained setup. Images feature blink, motion blur, off-axis gaze, and other small anomalies, representing NIR data of moderate quality. A set of 9,521 images (127 subjects, 814 classes) were used, for which segmentation and noise detection was confirmed by visual inspection.
- The UBIRIS.v2 [66] data set has 11,102 images from 261 subjects, acquired at visible wavelengths between 3 and 8 m away, under dynamic lighting conditions and unconstrained setups. Images are high heterogeneous in terms of quality, with glossy reflections across the iris, significant occlusions due to eyelids and eye-lashes, off-angle, and blurred data. 5,340 images from 518 classes were selected from this data set, all of them accurately segmented. All these images were con-verted to grayscale.
- The FRGC [57] data set served initially for face recognition experiments and is a specially hard set for iris recognition due to its limited resolution. The still images subset from both the controlled/uncontrolled setups were used. Images are typically frontal, with varying amounts of light, shadows, and glossy reflections that occlude portions of the irises. 4,360 images from 868 classes were selected from this data set. All these images were reasonably segmented, according to visual inspection, and were converted to grayscale.

The first experiment comprised the comparison between the amount of informa-tion available in small iris patches, which was measured by the Shannon entropy criterion, quantifying (in terms of bits) the expected value for the amount of infor-mation in square regions $p \times p$ of the normalized image I:

$$h(I_{p\times p}) = - \sum_i P(I_{p\times p} = i) \ \log_2 \big(P(I_{p\times p} = i)\big), \tag{15.1}$$

where $P(I_{p\times p} = i)$ is the probability for the ith intensity in the patch.

Figure 15.5 quantifies the amount of information in $p = 9$ patches. Even noting that the comparison between data sets might be unfair (the original images have different resolution), the immediate conclusion is the higher homogeneity of values observed in NIR data than in the VW case. Note that the average values are also much higher in NIR than in VW data, which actually implies that the NIR images provide more heterogeneity in terms of intensities in iris patches than VW data.

[2]http://www.smartsensors.co.uk/products/iris-database/32-000-full-set/.
[3]http://biometrics.idealtest.org/.

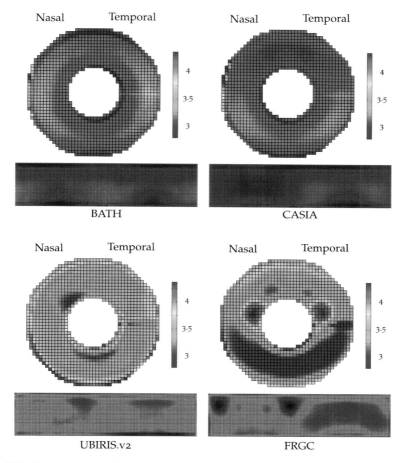

Fig. 15.5 Average amount of information (Shannon entropy in 9×9 patches of the normalized images) across the different regions of the irises in the BATH, CASIA-Iris-Distance, UBIRIS.v2, and FRGC data sets. Values are expressed in bits, and enable to perceive the gap of information between NIR (BATH and CASIA) and VW (UBIRIS.v2 and FRGC) iris data

Also, we observed that the pupillary regions are the most valuable in NIR images, which is not evident in VW. Regarding the FRGC data set, there are two regions near the pupillary boundary with values notoriously higher than the remaining regions. We confirmed that they are due to frequent reflections not detected by the noise-free segmentation phase. Also, we noticed that in the FRGC set the bottom parts of the irises have evidently smaller amounts of information than the upper parts, probably due to the lighting sources from above that cause shadows in these regions.

15.4   Iris Segmentation

15.4.1   Comparison of NIR Versus VW Issues

In order to acquire iris data from large distances and under unconstrained protocols, acceptable depth-of-field values demand high f-numbers for the optical system, corresponding directly (squared) with the amount of light required. Similarly, the motion factor demands very short exposure times, which again increases the amounts of light required. It is known that excessively strong illumination cause permanent eye damage and the NIR wavelength is particularly hazardous, because the eye does not instinctively respond with its natural mechanisms: aversion, blinking, and pupil contraction.

The above points were the major motivations for using visible light to *in-the-wild* iris biometrics, even though such light spectrum increases the challenges in performing reliable recognition. As stated above, the pigmentation of the human iris enables to capture much higher level of detail in VW than in NIR, but also more noisy artefacts, including specular and diffuse reflections and shadows. In practice, this supports the uniqueness of the iris texture acquired in the visible light spectrum (in a way similar to the empirically suggested for the near-infrared setup in previous studies [13]), but also stresses the difficulties in obtaining good quality data.

15.4.2   Why Is It so Difficult?

There are four families of factors that affect the quality of VW iris biometric data not acquired under the classical *stop-and-stare* protocol: (A) blur; (B) occlusions; (C) perspective and (D) lighting. By working in a broad range of distances and on moving targets, blurred (A.1) and low-resolution (A.2) images are highly probable. Also, portions of the iris texture are occluded by eyelids (B.1), eyelashes (B.2), and glossy reflections (B.3) from the surrounding environment. Camera-to-subject misalignments may occur due to subjects gaze (C.1) and pose (C.2). Finally, variations in light intensity (D.1), type (D.2), and incident angles (D.3) reinforce the broadly varying features of this kind of data.

Considering that periocular biometrics uses data not only from the iris but also from the surroundings of the eye (e.g., eyelids, eyebrows, eyelashes, and skin), particular attention should be paid to additional data degradation factors, such as (E.1) makeup, (E.2) piercings, and (E.3) occlusions (e.g., due to glasses or hair).

Figure 15.6 illustrates the four families of factors that primarily affect the quality of data that is not acquired under the classical *stop-and-stare* protocol. By working in a broad range of distances and on moving targets, blurred (I.a) and low-resolution images (I.b) are highly probable. Also, portions of the iris texture are occluded by eyelids, eyelashes (II.c), and by glossy reflections from the surrounding environment (II.d). Camera-to-subject misalignments might occur due to varying subjects gaze

I. Amount of Information   **(a)** blur   **(b)** resolution

II. Occlusions   **(c)** eyelids   **(d)** glossy reflections

III. Perspective   **(e)** gaze   **(f)** pose

IV. Lighting   **(g)** absence   **(h)** saturation

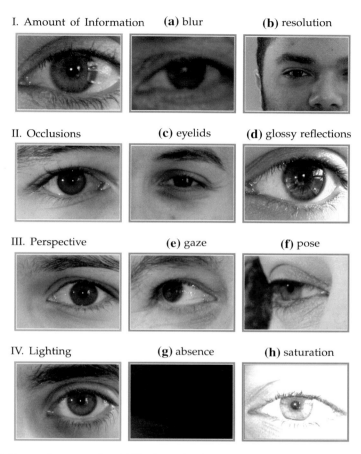

Fig. 15.6 Four major types of variability in ocular data acquired in non-constrained setups. The amount of information highly varies, due to optical defocus, motion blur, and data resolution (group I). Portions of the iris texture are often occluded by eyelids, eyelashes, and reflections (group II) and subjects are misaligned with respect to cameras (group III). Finally, light sources of different types, intensity and 3D angles may exist in the environment (group IV)

(III.e) and pose (III.f). Finally, variations in light intensity, type, and angle (IV. g and h) reinforce the broadly varying features of the resulting data.

15.4.3   Iris Segmentation: Summary of Research Works

Segmentation is undoubtedly perhaps the most concerning phase of the processing chain, in terms of the ability of the whole system to deal with data that is degraded, due to the unconstrained acquisition setup. Also, as it is one of the earliest phases of the recognition process, it is the one that more directly has to deal with data variability and supports the whole process, with any error in segmentation (even small inaccuracies in one of the detected boundaries), easily propagating though the processing chain and substantially increasing the recognition error rates [64]. Here we briefly summarize some of the most relevant researches in the iris segmentation topic, not only covering methods for VW data, but also describing the approaches designed for NIR images, in order to stress the typical differences between both kinds of methods.

In Table 15.1 we give an overview of the main techniques behind several recently published iris segmentation methods. We compare the methods according to the data sets used in the experiments, categorized by the order in which they segment iris borders. The "Experiments" column contains the iris image databases used in the experiments. "Preprocessing" lists the image preprocessing techniques used before segmentation. "Ord. Borders" lists the order in which the iris borders are segmented, where P denotes the pupillary borders and S denotes the scleric iris borders ($x \rightarrow y$ denotes the segmentation of y after x and x, y denotes independent segmentation, i.e., when no information from one parameterized border is used in the segmentation of the other). "Pupillary Border" and "Scleric Border" columns refer to the main methods used to segment that iris border.

Noting that the significant majority of the methods were designed to work with NIR images. These methods expect to find typically a high contrast between the pupil (almost black) and the iris, which justifies the order in which almost all of these NIR method segment both boundaries ($P \rightarrow S$). In contrast, methods that were particularly designed to handle VW data almost invariantly segment the outer iris boundary first, and then use this information to constrain the region where the pupillary boundary is searched, as there is almost no contrast between the pupil and the iris, in case of heavily pigmented irises, imaged with reduced amounts of light. Among the relevant innovations in this topic, techniques such as the use of active contour models, either geodesic [69], based on Fourier series [14] or based on the snakes model [2] can be highlighted. Noting that these techniques require previous detection of the iris to properly initialize contours, they are associated with heavy computational requirements. Modifications to known form fitting methods have also been proposed, essentially to handle off-angle images (e.g., [82, 95]) and to improve performance (e.g., [17, 44]). Finally, the detection of non-iris data that occludes portions of the iris ring has motivated the use of parabolic, elliptical, and circular models (e.g., [3, 17]) and the modal analysis of histograms [14]. Even so, in unconstrained conditions, several authors have suggested that the success of their methods is limited to cases of image orthogonality, to the nonexistence of significant iris occlusions, or to the appearance of corneal reflections in specific image regions.

Table 15.1 Summary of the most relevant iris segmentation techniques

Method	Data	Processing	Order	Pupillary border	Scleric border
Zuo et al. [95]	CASIA.1, ICE, WVU (NIR)	Specular reflections detected (threshold), PDE and inpainting	P→S	Randomized Elliptical Hough Transform	Weighted Integro-differential operator
Puhan and Jiang [67]	UBIRIS (VW)	Image binarization (Fourier spectral density)	S	–	Construction of a set of unidimensional signals, gradient analysis
Ross and Shah [69]	CASIA.1, WVU (NIR)	2-D Median filter	P→S	Binarization (threshold), Circular Hough Transform	Geodesic Active Contours
Poursaberi and Araabi [58]	CASIA.1 (NIR)	Negative image, inpainting	P	Iterative expansion/shrink of the detected border based on morphological operators	–
Morimoto et al. [50]	– (NIR)	Not described	P→S	Images difference	Images cascade at different scales, Sobel edges detection, elliptical form fitting
Liu et al. [44]	ICE	Not described	P→S	Angular constrained Canny, Hough-based	Hough-based, hypothesis and test
Kennell et al. [38]	BATH (NIR)	Histogram equalization, image binarization (threshold)	P→S	Morphological operators, integro-differential operator	Image binarization based on pixels + neighborhood variance, form fitting
Vatsa et al. [82]	UBIRIS, CASIA.3 (NIR, VW)	Not described	P→S	Rough estimation according to an elliptical model, followed by a modified Mumford–Shah functional	Process similar to the pupillary border

(continued)

Table 15.1 (continued)

Method	Data	Processing	Order	Pupillary border	Scleric border
Proenca and Alexandre [63]	UBIRIS (VW)	Histogram equalization	S→P	Feature extraction (pixel position + intensity) and fuzzy clustering to reduce image heterogeneity, Canny edges detection and circular Hough transform	Process similar to the pupillary border
Zaim [91]	CASIA.1 (NIR)	Morphologic operators to eliminate eyelashes	S→P	Split and merge localize regions of uniform intensity	Image normalization based on pupil coordinates, Sobel filtering, detection of horizontal edges in the normalized image
Broussard et al. [8]	BATH (NIR)	Not described	P, S	Extraction of local texture features, neural network	Process similar to the pupillary border
He et al. [22]	– (NIR)	Image binarization, morphologic operations	P→S	Geometrical projection, Sobel filtering, form fitting	Canny edge extraction, Hough transform
Basit and Javed [3]	BATH (NIR)	Image binarization, morphologic operations	P→S	Iterative bijections-based method	Maximization of the difference of intensities of radial direction
Arvacheh and Tizhoosh [2]	CASIA.1 (NIR)	Not described	P→S	Near circular active contour model (snakes), interpolation process to improve performance	Integro-differential operator
Daugman [14]	ICE (NIR)	Not described	P→S	Active contours based on 17 Fourier coefficients	Active contours based on 4 Fourier coefficients
He et al. [24]	CASIA.1 (NIR)	Not described	P→S	Adaboost, iterative circumference shifting	Image normalization, Sobel and Canny filtering, line fitting

(continued)

Table 15.1 (continued)

Method	Data	Processing	Order	Pupillary border	Scleric border
Zheng et al. [93]	SJTU (VW)	Conversion into HSV color space	P→S	Assume existence of specular reflections, maximization of integral projections, integro-differential operator	Iterative shift, shrink and expand circumference process to minimize average intensity
Xu and Shi [87]	CAS-PEAL (VW)	Not described	P→S	Integral projection functions, median filtering, circumference shifting intensity minimization	Sobel filtering, Edges weighting according to position and curvature
Honeywell [29]	CASIA.1 (NIR)	Not described	P	Search for radial texture discontinuities	–
Dobes et al. [17]	AR, CVL (VW)	Histogram equalization, Gaussian blur	S	–	Canny edges detection, Angular constrained Hough transform
Shuckers et al. [72]	WVU (NIR)	Remove specular reflections (threshold), impainting	P→S	Elliptical integro-differential operator	Elliptical integro-differential operator
Tan et al. [79]	UBIRIS v1&2	Image clustering to perform rough eye localization	P, S	Integro-differential constellation	Integro-differential constellation
Proenca [59]	UBIRIS.v2, FERET, FRGC (VW), ICE	Sclera Detection	S→P	Local hue, blue luminance, red chroma, neural network classification, constrained polynomial fitting	Local hue, blue luminance, red chroma, neural network classification, constrained polynomial fitting

15.5 Image Quality Assessment

The concept of *good* metric is not trivial to determine, although the best one should maximally correlate with recognition effectiveness. Previous studies reported significant decays in effectiveness when data is degraded by each of the factors listed in Table 15.2. Here, we overview the main techniques used to assess iris image quality with respect to each factor and compare them according to the spectrum of light used, the type of analyzed data (*raw* image, *segmented* or *normalized* iris region) and their output (*local* or *global*), as they operate at the pixel or image level. We note that most of the methods operate on NIR images and assess quality in the segmented data (either in the Cartesian or polar coordinate systems). Exceptions are usually related with focus measurement, obtained by one of two approaches: (1) measuring the high-frequency power in the 2D Fourier spectrum through a high-pass convolution kernel or wavelet-based decomposition [9, 14, 32]; (2) analyzing the sharpness of the iris borders through the magnitude of the first- and second-order derivatives [1, 92]. Another key characteristic is the level of analysis: some methods operate globally (at the image level), usually to determine focus, gaze, or motion blur [32, 35, 84]. As image quality varies across the iris, others operate at the pixel level to determine local obstructions [1, 33, 62]. Motion is estimated by detecting interlaced raster shear that might be due to significant movements during the acquisition of a frame [15, 45, 86, 97]. Other approaches rely on the response of the convolution between the image and directional filters, being observed that linear motion blurred images have higher central peak responses than sharp ones [33, 36]. Gaze is estimated by 3D projection techniques that maximize the response of the Daugman's integro-differential operator [33] and by the length of the axes of a bounding ellipse [97]. Eyelids are detected by means of line and parabolic Hough transforms [25], active contours [39], and machine learning frameworks [62, 89]. The modal analysis of the intensities histogram enables the detection of eyelashes [14, 25], as do spectral analysis [45] and edge-based methods [33]. As they usually are the brightest regions of images, specular reflections are detected by thresholds [33], while diffuse reflections are exclusive of VW data and more difficult to discriminate, being reported a method based on texture descriptors and machine learning techniques [62]. Proença proposed a method [60] to assess the quality of VW iris samples captured in unconstrained conditions, according to the factors that are known to determine the quality of iris biometric data: focus, motion, angle, occlusions, area, pupillary dilation, and levels of iris pigmentation. The key insight is to use the output of the segmentation phase in each assessment, which permits to handle severely degraded samples that are likely to result of such imaging setup.

Table 15.2 Overview of the most relevant methods published to assess the quality of iris biometric data

Method	Data	Images	Analysis	Quality assessment
Abhyankar and Schuckers [1]	CASIA.v3, BATH, WVU and Clarkson (NIR)	S	L, G	Occlusion (frequency analysis); focus (second order derivatives); contrast (hard threshold) and angular deformation (assigned manually)
Chen et al. [9]	CASIA.v3, WVU (NIR)	S	L, G	Focus and amount of information (2D isotropic Mexican hat wavelet-based frequency analysis)
Daugman and Downing [15]	ICE (NIR)	R	G	Effect of image compression; motion (interlaced raster shear)
Daugman [14]	ICE-1 (NIR)	S	L, G	Focus (magnitude of the response to a 5 × 5 high-pass kernel); off-angle (projective deformation that maximizes the circular shape of the pupil); eyelashes (intensities histogram modality)
Grabowski et al. [20]	–	S, N	G	Focus (entropy in the iris ring)
He et al. [25]	CASIA.v3 (NIR)	S	L	Eyelid (line Hough transform); eyelashes (intensities histogram modality)
Hollingsworth et al. [27]	Univ. Notre Dame (NIR)	S	G	Effect of pupil dilation
Jang et al. [32]	Yonsei (NIR, UBIRIS.v1 (VW)	R	G	Focus (ratio between the higher and lower frequency components, resultant of the dyadic discrete wavelet transform)
Kalka et al. [33]	CASIA.v3, WVU, ICE (NIR)	S	L, G	Focus (response to the Daugman's 8 × 8 high pass kernel); occlusion (morphologically dilated horizontal edges); motion blur (response to directional filters in Fourier space); off-angle (maximization of the circular integro-differential operator); specular reflection (threshold); lighting variation (intensities variance within small iris blocks); iris size (proportion of occluded pixels)
Kang and Park [34]	CASIA.v2(NIR)	R	G	Focus (magnitude of the response to a 5 × 5 high-pass kernel)
Kang and Park [35]	CASIA (NIR)	S	L	Eyelids (parabolic form fitting); focus (magnitude of the high frequency components; eyelashes (adaptive criteria according to the image blurring, convolution kernel for multiple eyelashes, first order differential for separable eyelashes)
Kang and Park [36]	CASIA.v3 (NIR)	S	L, G	Iris size; reflections (threshold); eyelids (parabolic form fitting scheme); eyelash (template matching based on continuity); motion blur (directional filters) and focus (frequency analysis)

(continued)

Table 15.2 (continued)

Method	Data	Images	Analysis	Quality assessment
Krishen et al. [39]	ICE (NIR)	S, N	L	Eyelids and eyelashes (gradient vector flow-based active contours method); focus (Gaussian mixture model learned from a set of image intensity histograms)
Nandakumar et al. [51]	WVU (NIR)	S, N	L, G	Focus and amount of information (2D isotropic Mexican hat wavelet-based frequency analysis)
Lu et al. [45]	CASIA.v3 (NIR)	S, N	L, G	Focus (energy of the frequency components resultant of a wavelet packet decomposition); motion blur (average difference of intensities between adjacent rows); eyelids (hard threshold) and eyelashes (frequency analysis in the upper and lower iris extremes)
Proença and Alexandre [62]	UBIRIS.v1 (VW)	S, N	L	Glossy and specular reflections, eyelids and eyelashes (extraction of an 8D feature set, neural network classification scheme)
Proença. [60]	UBIRIS.v2 (VW)	S	L, G	Focus (response kernel), motion (directional derivative analysis), angle (analysis of bounding box), iris pigmemtation (HSV analysis)
Wan et al [84]	SJTU-IDB (NIR)	R	G	Focus (magnitude of the response to a 2D isotropic Laplacian of Gaussian kernel)
Wei et al. [86]	CASIA.v2 (NIR), UBIRIS.v1 (VW)	R, S	G	Focus (magnitude of high frequency components); motion blur (average difference of intensities between adjacent rows) and occlusions (thresholds)
Ye et al. [89]	CASIA, CASIA.v2 (NIR)	R	G	Iris occlusions and focus (pixels intensity feed neural network that detects the iris contour. A second network gives the data quality).
Zhang and Salganicoff [92]	–	S	G	Focus (sharpness of a portion of the pupillary border, based in the gradients' magnitude)
Zuo and Schmid [96]	CASIA.v2, WVU (NIR)	S	G	Pupil size (threshold); pupillary and scleric borders sharpness (cumulative gradient along the boundaries) and ROI homogeneity (difference between average intensities of the iris, pupil and sclera)
Zuo and Schmid [97]	ICE, MBGC (NIR)	S	L, G	Interlacing (average difference between odd and even rows); illumination (average intensity of the segmented iris); lighting (intensity variance over small iris blocks); occlusions (proportion of occluded iris pixels); area (pixel count); pupil dilation (proportion between the iris and pupil); off-angle (ratio between the major and minor axis of a bounding ellipse) and blur (magnitude of the high frequency components)

15.6   Feature Encoding

Feature encoding is a particularly interesting subtopic in the *unconstrained recognition* domain, due to the reduced quality of the data that is expected to be acquired. Here, a fundamental property of the iris texture should be considered, being one of the major reasons that justify the interest on this trait for this kind of scenarios: most of the discriminating information between the iris texture of different subjects lies in the lowest and middle-low frequency components, which are (luckily) those that are most easy to capture under outdoor environments and unconstrained acquisition protocols.

A particularly interesting advance is the use of multilobe differential filters, which are claimed to adapt better than the traditionally used Gabor filters to data of reduced quality and can be used at reduced computational cost. On the other way, they lie in a parameterization space of much higher dimension than the one of Gabor filters, making it more difficult to obtain good parameterizations for a specific recognition system/environment.

15.6.1   Gabor Versus Multilobe Differential Filters

The discriminating power provided by each region of VW and NIR iris images was assessed with respect to two families of filters: (1) Gabor kernels, which faithfully model simple cells in the visual cortex of mammalian brains [11] and are used in the most acknowledged iris recognition algorithm; and (2) Multilobe differential filters (MLDF), which were recently reported as a relevant advance in the iris recognition field [76].

The impulse response of a Gabor kernel is defined by the multiplication of a harmonic and a Gaussian function:

$$G[x, y, \omega, \varphi, \sigma] = \exp\left[\frac{-x^2 - y^2}{\sigma^2}\right] \exp[2\pi \omega i \Phi], \qquad (15.2)$$

where $\Phi = x\cos(\varphi) + y\sin(\varphi)$, ω is the spatial frequency, φ is the orientation and σ the standard deviation of a Gaussian kernel (isotropic in our experiments, $\sigma = 0.65\omega$). A more general form of Gabor filters can be found in the literature (e.g., [13]), allowing for different scales along the axes (σ_x and σ_y). In this chapter, to keep the dimension of the parameterization space moderate, only filters with the same scale along the axes are considered.

Regarding the MLDF filters, they can be parameterized in terms of the number of positive/negative lobes, location, scale, orientation, and interlobe distance. To keep the number of possibilities moderately low, only Gaussian kernels with balanced number of positive/negative lobes (1/1, 2/2, …) and equal scale for both types of lobes are considered. Hence, the MLDF filters are expressed by:

$$\mathbf{m}[\mathbf{x_j}, \mu_\mathbf{j}, \sigma_\mathbf{j}] = \sum_{j=1}^{t_l} (-1)^{j+1} \frac{1}{\sqrt{2\pi}\,\sigma_j} \exp\left[\frac{-(\mathbf{x_j} - \mu_\mathbf{j})^2}{2\sigma_j}\right], \qquad (15.3)$$

where $\mathbf{x_j} = (\mathbf{x_j}, \mathbf{y_j})$ is the center of each of the t_l lobes. Next, $k = \{m, g\}$ filters were convolved with each normalized iris image I, providing a set of coefficients. The sign of the coefficients was obtained, i.e., C is the vector representation of sgn($I * k$). In terms of parameterizations tested per filter, for Gabor kernels the wavelength (px.) $\omega : \{1 : 1 : 14\}$, the orientation $\varphi : \{0, \pi/4, \pi/2, 3\pi/4\}$ and the Gaussian sigma $\sigma : 0.65\omega$. Regarding MLDFs, the number of lobes $t_l : \{1/1, 2/2, 3/3, 4/4\}$ and the Gaussian sigma $\sigma : \{1, 2, 3, 4, 5, 6\}$.

Figure 15.7 illustrates the filters used and Table 15.3 summarizes the range of parameters considered, with ($\{a : b : c\}$ denoting values in the $[a, c]$ interval, with steps of size b).

Figure 15.8 expresses the variations in discriminability with respect to each parameter of the filters. The continuous lines represent the BATH data set, the dashed lines with the diamond marks regard the CASIA-Iris-Distance. The UBIRIS.v2 is

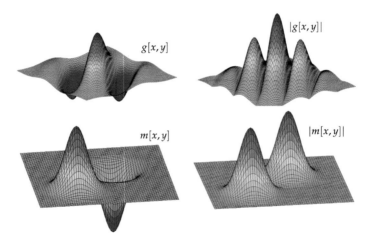

Fig. 15.7 Illustration of the filters used in experiments ($\{g, m\}$) and of the filters that give the contribution of each position in the iris to the coefficient in the iris code $\{|g|, |m|\}$

Table 15.3 Types and range of the filters parameters varied in our experiments

Gabor filters $g[.,.]$	
Wavelength (px.)	$\omega : \{1 : 1 : 14\}$
Orientation	$\varphi : \{0, \pi/4, \pi/2, 3\pi/4\}$
Gaussian sigma	$\sigma : 0.65\omega$
MLDF filters $m[.,.]$	
Num. Lobes	$t_l : \{1/1, 2/2, 3/3, 4/4\}$
Gaussian sigma	$\sigma : \{1, 2, 3, 4, 5, 6\}$

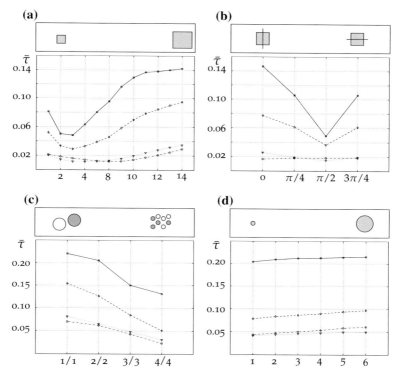

Fig. 15.8 Average discriminability $\bar{\tau}$ of the bits in iris codes regarding filters parameterization. The *upper row* regards the Gabor kernels (wavelength and orientation parameters) and the *bottom row* corresponds to the MLDF filters (number of lobes and sigma of the Gaussian kernel). **a** Wavelength. **b** Orientation. **c** Num. lobes. **d** Sigma Gaussian

given by the dotted lines with triangular marks and the FRGC data set by the dashed lines with circular marks. Above each plot we illustrate a normalized iris image and represent the filters that correspond to the nearby positions in the plot. Generally, the discriminability was substantially higher for MLDF than for Gabor filters. In case of the latter filters, larger wavelengths consistently increased the discriminability, essentially because they have a reduced sensitivity to outlier values due to acquisition artefacts. Orientation is another relevant parameter for Gabor kernels, where filters that analyze features that spread radially in the normalized data provided much better results. Regarding MLDF filters, filters with more lobes got worse results, which might be due to the *cross-elimination* effect of differences between lobes. Surprisingly, the variation in results with respect to the sigma of the Gaussian kernel are not so evident as in the case of Gabor kernels.

15.6.2 Analysis of Iris Codes: Comparison Between NIR and VW Data

The discriminability τ of each bit extracted from NIR and VW images was obtained. Note that the iris patches evolved in the convolution for each bit contribute to the result in different degrees, according to the magnitude of the kernel at each point, i.e., if a kernel has very small value at a specific position, the corresponding intensity on the patch almost does not affect the result. This way, the contribution of each location $[x, y]$ in the iris to the bit value is given by:

$$\Psi[x, y] = \frac{\sum_i \left(|k_i[x - r_i, y - c_i]| \, \tau(i) \right)}{\sum_i |k_i[x - r_i, y - c_i]|}, \tag{15.4}$$

where $[r_i, c_i]$ is the central position of the ith filter k_i and $\tau(i)$ is the discriminability of the ith bit, given by:

$$\tau(i) = P(C_i^{(p)} \oplus C_i^{(q)} = 0 \,|H_a) - P(C_i^{(p)} \oplus C_i^{(q)} = 0 \,|H_0), \tag{15.5}$$

with $P(C_i^{(p)} \oplus C_i^{(q)} = 0 \,|H_a)$ expressing the probability that the ith bit of an iris code is equal in two intersubject samples, and $P(C_i^{(p)} \oplus C_i^{(q)} = 0 \,|H_0)$ expressing the same probability for intrasubject samples.

Figure 15.9 gives the discriminability provided by each region of the iris in the Cartesian and polar coordinate systems when using Gabor filters. Complementary, Fig. 15.10 expresses the similar statistics when using MLDF filters. The immediate conclusion is that the maximal values are observed for the NIR data sets, both for Gabor and MLDF filters. Interestingly, in all cases the lower parts of the iris are better than the upper parts, which are more frequently occluded by eyelids. Globally, MLDF filters provided more homogeneous values than Gabor filters. For VW data, regions nearby the pupillary boundary are worse than the middle and outer bands, probably due to the difficulty in obtaining reliable estimates of the pupillary boundary in VW images.

Regarding the radial bands in the iris, even though the maximal discriminability was observed for the middle bands, this might not be due to biological properties of the iris texture. Instead, the middle bands are the regions where the largest filters can be applied without surpassing the iris boundaries. As illustrated in Fig. 15.8, large filters tend to produce more discriminant bits, which accords with the results given in [28].

It is interesting to note the reduced correlation between the amounts of information in iris patches and the discriminability of each patch. For the BATH data set, the observed levels of linear correlation between variables $h[x, y]$ and $\Psi[x, y]$ are –0.12/–0.38 (Gabor/MLDF filters), and –0.40/–0.22 for the CASIA-Iris-Distance

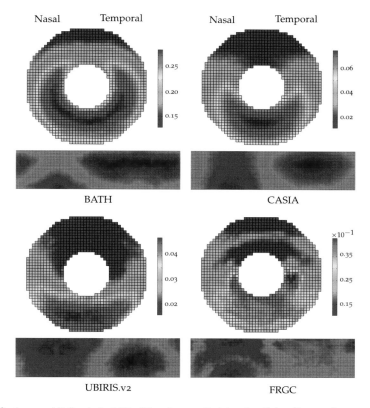

Fig. 15.9 Average bit discriminability $\Psi[x, y]$ across the iris using Gabor filters as feature encoders. Values are given for the Cartesian and polar coordinate systems for the four data sets considered: BATH and CASIA-Iris-Distance (NIR) and UBIRIS.v2 and FRGC (VW)

set. Regarding the VW data, values are 0.16/–0.02 for the UBIRIS.v2 and –0.34/–0.41 for the FRGC data sets. These low correlation values in terms of magnitude and sign (negative in 7/8 of the cases) give space for additional research about iris feature extraction/matching strategies that profit in a better way from the amount of information that is locally available.

In summary, MLDFs appear to provide better performance than Gabor kernels due to their ability of exploiting nonadjacent patterns. This property is particularly interesting for tissues with interlacing fibers, such as the human iris; (2) there is a strong agreement between the best iris regions obtained for MLDF and Gabor filters, suggesting that the choice for the best regions to perform iris recognition is relatively independent of the kind of filters used.

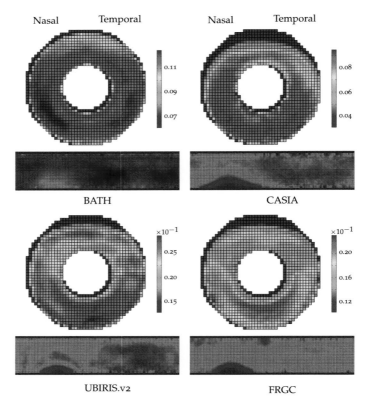

Fig. 15.10 Average bit discriminability Ψ[*x*, *y*] across the iris, using Multilobe Differential Filters as feature encoders. Values are given for the Cartesian and polar coordinate systems for the four data sets considered: BATH and CASIA-Iris-Distance (NIR) and UBIRIS.v2 and FRGC (VW)

15.6.3 Codes Quantization: Is Too Much Information Lost?

In the most acknowledged iris recognition algorithm, only phase information is used in recognition. Amplitude information is not considered reliable, as it depends of imaging contrast, illumination and camera gain. Accordingly, Hollingsworth et al. [28] observed that most inconsistencies in iris codes are due to the coarse quantization of the phase response, and disregarded bits from filter responses near the axes.

Even considering the above arguments reasonable, we assessed the amounts of discriminating information contained in the filter responses near the axes. With respect to the traditional strategy of keeping only the sign of coefficients (function A) in Fig. 15.11), two other strategies are considered: a linear mapping of the magnitude of the responses, yielding real-valued coefficients matched by the ℓ_2 norm (function C) in Fig. 15.11); and a trade-off of both strategies, according to a sigmoid-based transform that maps large magnitude values to the 0/1 values, but weights values near

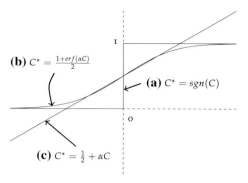

Fig. 15.11 Three different strategies for code quantization: **a** binary; **b** sigmoid function; and **c** linear mapping

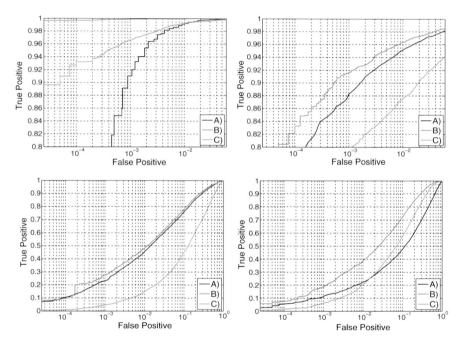

Fig. 15.12 Rcognition performance with respect to A, B, C code quantization strategies for BATH (*upper-left plot*), CASIA-Iris-Distance (*upper-right*), UBIRIS.v2 (*bottom-left*), and FRGC data sets (*bottom-right*)

the axes to real values in the [0, 1] interval. In this case, the ℓ_2 norm was also used as matching function.

The ROC curves given at the right side of Fig. 15.12 compare the recognition performance with respect to each quantization strategy and Table 15.4 summarizes the results, giving the Area Under Curve (AUC) and the decidability index d' that,

Table 15.4 Variations in recognition performance with respect to different strategies for code quantization

Data set	Features	(A) sign()		(B) sigmoid()		(C) linear (no quantization)	
		d'	AUC	d'	AUC	d'	AUC
BATH	Gabor	**8.79 ± 0.01**	**0.994 ± 0.001**	7.08 ± 0.01	0.992 ± 0.001	6.52 ± 0.01	0.990 ± 0.001
BATH	MLDF	**9.15 ± 0.01**	**0.994 ± 0.001**	8.82 ± 0.01	0.993 ± 0.001	5.89 ± 0.01	0.988 ± 0.001
CASIA-Iris-Distance	Gabor	**3.20 ± 0.01**	**0.982 ± 0.001**	3.16 ± 0.01	0.982 ± 0.001	3.05 ± 0.02	0.971 ± 0.001
CASIA-Iris-Distance	MLDF	3.89 ± 0.01	0.990 ± 0.001	**4.12 ± 0.01**	**0.984 ± 0.001**	3.13 ± 0.01	0.982 ± 0.001
UBIRIS.v2	Gabor	**1.23 ± 0.01**	**0.813 ± 0.006**	1.16 ± 0.02	0.793 ± 0.007	0.82 ± 0.02	0.720 ± 0.006
UBIRIS.v2	MLDF	1.88 ± 0.01	0.904 ± 0.003	**1.96 ± 0.01**	**0.917 ± 0.003**	1.02 ± 0.01	0.766 ± 0.009
FRGC	Gabor	**1.12 ± 0.02**	**0.792 ± 0.006**	1.01 ± 0.02	0.770 ± 0.008	0.83 ± 0.01	0.731 ± 0.007
FRGC	MLDF	1.74 ± 0.01	0.892 ± 0.006	**1.88 ± 0.02**	**0.908 ± 0.002**	1.47 ± 0.02	0.849 ± 0.007

as suggested by Daugman [12], measures how well separated the genuine/impostor distributions are:

$$d' = \frac{|\mu_G - \mu_I|}{\sqrt{\frac{1}{2}(\sigma_I^2 + \sigma_G^2)}}, \tag{15.6}$$

where $\mu_I = \frac{1}{k}\sum_i d_i^I$ and $\mu_G = \frac{1}{m}\sum_i d_i^G$ are the means of the genuine (G) and impostor (I) scores and $\sigma_I = \frac{1}{k-1}\sum_i(d_i^I - \mu_I)^2$ and $\sigma_G = \frac{1}{m-1}\sum_i(d_i^G - \mu_G)^2$ their standard deviations.

Two opposite conclusions can be drawn: for Gabor filters, the best results are observed when using the traditional sign() quantization function. In this case, using scalars instead of sign bits even decreased the recognition performance. Oppositely, for MLDF filters, the best results are observed when using the proposed sigmoid function, i.e., when the coefficients of small magnitude are also considered for the matching process. This points toward the conclusion that there is actually reliable discriminating information in the coefficients near the origin. However, these coefficients are less reliable than those with large magnitude, as in no case the linear mapping strategy got results close to any of the remaining strategies.

Note that the above conclusions result from the reported AUC and d' values, which in the large majority of the cases are in agreement. The exceptions occur mostly in cases where the shape of the genuine/impostor distributions are the farthest from Gaussian distributions. For these particular cases, we relied mostly on the AUC value, as it does not require a specific data distribution to report meaningful results.

15.7 Ocular Recognition

As an attempt to increase the robustness of iris recognition in visible light data, the concept of *periocular* biometrics has emerged, which compensates for the degradation in iris data by considering the discriminating information in the surroundings of the eye (eyelids, eyelashes, eyebrows, and skin texture). Currently, the most relevant algorithms work in a holistic way: they define a region of interest (ROI) around the eye and use a feature encoding/matching algorithm regardless of the biological component in each point of the ROI. However, this augments the probability of sensitivity to some data covariate and the correlation between the scores extracted from the different points in the ROI.

15.7.1 Weak/Strong Ocular Experts

Under an atomistic criterion, two experts that use disjoint data can be devised, with radically different recognition strategies and attaining very different effectiveness.

Here, the term *weak* is employed to refer to a recognition system that yields a poor separable decision environment, i.e., where the distributions of the genuine/impostor pairwise scores largely overlap. The term *strong* refers to a system where the distributions of genuine and impostor scores almost do not overlap, resulting in a clearly separable decision environment and low error rates.

In this dual ensemble, the strong expert analyzes the multispectral information in the iris texture, according to an automatically optimized set of multilobe differential filters (MLDF). Complementary, the weak expert parameterises the boundary of the visible cornea and defines a dimensionless ROI that comprises the eyelids, eyelashes, and the surrounding skin. This expert helps to discriminate between individuals and has three interesting properties: (1) it analyzes data that has an appearance independent of the iris texture; (2) it shows reduced sensitivity to the most problematic iris image covariates; and (3) it exclusively analyzes traits that cannot be easily forged by anyone not willing to be recognized, which is in contrast to the traits classically used in periocular recognition (e.g., the shape of eyebrows). We encode the shape of eyelids, the distribution and shape of the eyelashes and the morphology of the skin wrinkles/furrows in the eyelids, which are determined by the movements of the *orbicularis oculi* muscles family. Figure 15.13 overviews the information sources used in such recognition ensemble.

It is evident that using multiple sources for biometric recognition is not a new idea and some controversy remains: is it actually an effective way to improve performance? It is argued that when a stronger and a weaker expert are combined, the resulting decision environment is averaged and the performance will be somewhere between that of the two experts considered individually [12]. Due to the way such a strong/weak ensemble was designed, our experiments support a radically different conclusion: even when the fused responses come from experts with very distant performance, the ensemble attains much better performance than the stronger expert (iris). This is due to the fact that both experts produce quasi-independent responses and are not particularly sensitive to the same image covariate, augmenting the robustness against degraded data.

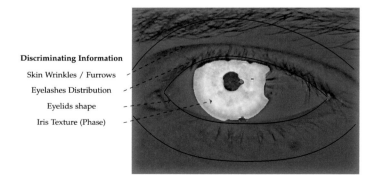

Fig. 15.13 Overview of the components in the vicinity of the human eye that can be used to extract discriminating information, useful for biometric recognition purposes

15.7.2   Relevant Ocular Recognition Algorithms

Concluded in 2011, the *NICE: Noisy Iris Challenge Evaluation* [65] promoted the research about iris/ocular recognition in visible light data. It received over one hundred participations and the best performing teams described their approaches in two special issues of the *Image and Vision Computing*[4] and *Pattern Recognition Letters*[5] journals. This event has documented the state-of-the-art recognition performance, having the best algorithm achieved d-prime values above 2.57, area under curve around 0.95 and equal error rates of 0.12. This method (due to Tan et al. [80]) is actually a *periocular* recognition algorithm: texton histograms and semantic rules encode information from the surroundings of the eye, while ordinal measures and color histograms analyze the iris. The second best approach was due to Wang et al. [85] and is quite more classical: it employs an AdaBoost feature selection scheme from a large set of quantized Gabor-based features, matched by the Hamming distance.

The most relevant recognition algorithms for VW images can be divided with respect to their data source: (1) the iris; or (2) the periocular region. Regarding the first family, Raffei et al. [68] preprocessed the iris to remove reflections and represented the normalized data at multiple scales, according to the Radon transform. The score from each scale was matched by the Hamming distance and fused by weighted nonlinear combination. Rahulkar and Holambe [26] derived a wavelet basis for compact representation of the iris texture (triplet half-band filters), with coefficients matched by the minimum Cambera distance. A post-classifier outputs a match when more than k regions give a positive response. Roy et al. [70] used a feature selection technique from game theory, based on coefficients from the Daubechies wavelet decomposition. The Hausdorff distance yields the matching score between two feature sets. Kumar and Chan [40] approached the problem from the data representation perspective, having used a quaternionic sparse coding scheme solved by convex optimization. Quaternion image patches were extracted from the RGB channels and the basis pursuit algorithm used to find the quaternion coefficients. In another work [41], the same authors were based on the sparse representation for classification algorithm, using the output of a local Radon transform as feature space.

The second family of algorithms considers other data beside the iris (sclera, eyebrows, and skin texture), and its popularity has been increasing since the work of Park et al. [56]. Bharadwaj et al. [4] fused a global descriptor (GIST) based on five perceptual dimensions (image naturalness, openness, roughness, expansion, and ruggedness) to circular local binary patterns. The Chi-squared distance matched both types of features and a fusion scheme (score level) yielded the final matching value.

Crihalmeanu and Ross [10] used the sclera patterns as biometric trait. The sclera was segmented according to the pixel-wise proportion between the NIR and green channel values. After enhancing the blood vessels by a line filter, SURF, minutiae,

---

[4]http://www.sciencedirect.com/science/journal/02628856/28/2.

[5]http://www.sciencedirect.com/science/journal/01678655/33/8.

and correlation-based schemes produced the matching scores that were fused subsequently. Similarly, Zhou et al. [94] enhanced the blood vessels in the sclera by Gabor kernels and encoded features by line descriptors. The accumulated registration distance between pairs of line segments yielded the matching score. Also, Oh and Toh [53] encoded the information in the sclera by local binary patterns (LBP) in angular grids, concatenated in a single feature vector. Then, a normalized Hamming distance produced the matching score.

In terms of hybrid approaches, Oh et al. [54] combined the sclera to periocular features. Directional features from the former region were extracted by structured random projections, complemented by binary features from the sclera. Tan and Kumar [78] fused iris information (encoded by Log-Gabor filters) to an overcomplete representation of the periocular region (LBP, GIST, Histogram of Oriented Gradients and Leung-Malik Filters). Both representations were matched independently and fused at the score level (Table 15.5).

Proença recently proposed a recognition ensemble [61] composed by two experts. The strong expert analyzes the multispectral information in the iris texture, according to an automatically optimized set of multilobe differential filters (MLDF). Complementary, the weak expert parameterises the boundary of the visible cornea and defines a dimensionless ROI that comprises the eyelids, eyelashes, and the surrounding skin. This expert helps to discriminate between individuals and has three interesting properties: (1) it analyzes data that has an appearance independent of the iris texture; (2) it shows reduced sensitivity to the most problematic iris image covariates; and (3) it exclusively analyzes traits that cannot be easily forged by anyone not willing to be recognized, which is in contrast to the traits classically used in periocular recognition (e.g., the shape of eyebrows).

The weak expert encodes the shape of eyelids, the distribution and shape of the eyelashes, and the morphology of the skin wrinkles/ furrows in the eyelids, which are determined by the movements of the *orbicularis oculi* muscles family. With respect to related works, the main advantage of this method is that the responses of the iris (strong) and ocular (weak) experts are practically independent, in result of the disjoint regions analyzed and in the fully disparate algorithms used in feature encoding/matching. This way, even by using relatively simple fusion techniques that work at the score level, it is possible to use the weak biometric expert as a valuable complement of the iris expert, particularly in cases where this expert produces matching scores that are near the borderline accept/reject regions. This kind of complementarity between experts is illustrated in Fig. 15.14, showing pairwise comparisons that are intrasubject (upper row) and intersubject (bottom row), with P_s, P_w denoting the posterior probability of acceptance (by the strong s and weak w experts) of the *null hypothesis* H_0 that both images are from the same subject.

Table 15.5 State-of-the-art algorithms for recognizing degraded ocular data acquired in visible light environments

Method	Traits	Feat. encoding	Feat. matching	Performance
Bharadwaj et al. [4]	Periocular (Holistic)	GIST, CLBP	Chi-square distance	73 % rank-1 (UBIRIS.v2)
Crihalmeanu and Ross [10]	Sclera	SURF, Minutiae (vessel bifurcations)	Euclidean distance, data correlation	EER < 1.8 % (Own data set)
Kumar and Chan [40]	Iris	Quaternion sparse orientation code	Shift alignment	48 % rank-1 (UBIRIS.v2)
Kumar et al. [41]	Iris	Radon local transform	Sparse representation for classification	40 % rank-1 (UBIRIS.v2), 33 % rank-1 (FRGC)
Oh and Toh [53]	Sclera	LBP	Hamming distance	EER 0.47 % (UBIRIS.v1)
Oh et al. [54]	Periocular (Holistic), Sclera	Multi resolution LBP (Sclera), Directional Projections (Periocular)	Hamming and Euclidean distance	EER 5 % (UBIRIS.v2)
Proença [61]	Periocular (Piecewise)	MLDF (iris), shape and texture descriptors (eyelashes, eyelids)	Modified Hamming (iris), Histogram distance (eyelids, eyelashes)	EER 2.97 % (UBIRIS.v2)
Raffei et al. [68]	Iris	Multiscale local Radon transform	Hamming distance, weighted non-linear score combination	AUC 88 % (UBIRIS.v2)
Holambe et al. [26]	Iris	Triplet half-band filter bank	Canbera distance, k-out-of-n post classifier	ACC > 99 % (UBIRIS.v1)
Roy et al. [70]	Iris	Daubechies wavelet, Modified Contribution feature selection	Hausdorff distance	TPR 97.43 % @ 0.001 % FPR (UBIRIS.v1)
Tan and Kumar [78]	Iris, Periocular (Holistic)	Log-Gabor filters (Iris), SIFT, GIST, LBP, HOG and LMF (Periocular)	Chi-square and Euclidean distances	39.4 % rank-1 (UBIRIS.v2)
Tan et al. [80]	Iris, Eye	Texton Histograms, Semantic information (Eye), Ordinal Filters, Color Histogram (Iris)	Chi-square, Euclidean, Diffusion and Hamming distances	AUC 95 % (UBIRIS.v2)
Wang et al. [85]	Iris	Gabor filters, AdaBoost feature selection	Hamming distance	AUC 88 % (UBIRIS.v2)
Zhou et al. [94]	Sclera	Line (sclera vessels) description	Accumulated line registration cost	EER 3.83 % (UBIRIS.v2)

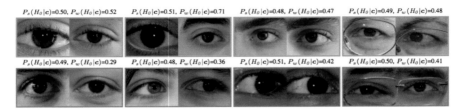

Fig. 15.14 Examples of image pairwise comparisons that fall in the uncertainty region of the strong (iris) biometric expert ($P_s(H_0|x) \approx 0.5$). In most cases, the weak (periocular) biometric expert provides valuable information P_w to distinguish between intrasubject (*green* frames) and intersubject comparisons (*red* frames)

15.8 Fusion of Multiple Recognition Systems

Considering that the type of biometric recognition systems discussed in this chapter should work covertly, meaning that no conscious human effort will be required of subjects during the recognition processes, there is a theoretically interesting possibility of using multiple recognition systems regularly spaced across an airport terminal hallway or a city street. This section reports the (optimistic) performance that such a recognition ensemble would attain, considering as baseline recognizers the current state-of-the-art solutions for *noncooperative ocular recognition*.

It is known that not all subjects perform consistently in terms of false matches and non-matches of a biometric system. Based on their intrinsic features, some are difficult to match (*goats*), while others are particularly vulnerable to impersonation (*lambs*) and consistently increase the probability of false matches [88]. We oversimplify the problem and regard all subjects of a population $\mathbb{P} = \{s_1, \ldots, s_n\}$ as *sheep*, i.e., subjects that tend to follow the system averages: they match relatively well against themselves and poorly against others. Let us consider k ocular recognition systems with roughly similar performance, with a sensitivity of α at a false match rate of β. Here we introduce the concept of *exogenous independence*, hypothesizing that purposely changing the lighting conditions in the environment (by using different levels of light or types of illuminants) and the acquisition protocols (poses, distances) should potentiate the independence between the system outputs. Assuming that the independence of each system provides an upper bound on the performance that would be attainable by the fusion of multiple systems, the binomial distribution can be used to obtain the probability that a subject s_i is screened by k recognition systems and correctly recognized by k' of these, $1 \leq k' \leq k$:

$$P(R_{k'}) = \frac{k!}{k'! \, (k - k')!} \, \alpha^{k'} \, (1 - \alpha)^{k - k'}. \tag{15.7}$$

Fig. 15.15 Expected
sensitivity of an ensemble of
ocular recognition systems
working covertly and
consecutively (e.g., in an
airport terminal hallway or a
city street), with different
required values for the false
acceptance rates. Note that
this is an *optimistic* estimate
of the ensemble
performance, as it assumes
that the responses given by
baseline recognizers are
statistically independent

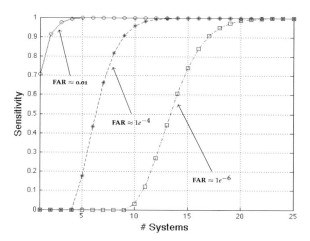

For different values of k', the probability that a reported match is false is given by $\beta^{k'}$, assuming that false matches in each of the k recognition systems are independent events. Accordingly, a *match* will be reported *iff* a minimum of k' recognition systems output a match:

$$P(R_{\geq k'}) = \sum_{j=k'}^{k} P(R_j)$$

$$= \sum_{j=k'}^{k} \frac{k!}{j!\,(k-j)!}\, \alpha^j\, (1-\alpha)^{k-j}, \tag{15.8}$$

provided that all events are mutually exclusive. Considering the average performance for a baseline recognizer that fuses at the score level the responses given by four state-of-the-art algorithms [71, 74, 80, 85], Fig. 15.15 gives the expected sensitivity of a *multipoint* biometric system, with respect to the number of baseline recognizers used, considering different false match rates. However, note that this analysis provides an upper bound estimate of the ensemble performance, as it assumes that the responses given by individual experts are independent, Even though, this *optimistic* assumption would enable to conclude that around five independent recognition systems would be enough to attain almost full sensitivity at a false acceptance rate β of 0.01. This value substantially increases when a lower number of false alarms is convenient (large-scale applications), requiring between 13 and 23 independent recognition systems to operate, respectively, at FAR $1e^{-4}$ and $1e^{-6}$.

15.9 Conclusions and Current Challenges

There is no doubt that concerns about the "security" and "safety" of crowded urban areas have been increasing significantly, particularly due to terrorist attacks such as the 2001 New York 9/11, the 2004 Madrid train bombing and the 2013 Boston marathon attacks. These concerns raised the interests on biometrics and made it one the most popular topics in the Pattern Recognition/Computer Vision domains. However, there are still not biometric recognition systems that work effectively using data acquired in totally uncontrolled environments and without assuming subjects' willingness to be recognized.

This chapter discussed such extremely ambitious kind of biometric recognition and advocated the use of the ocular region as basis trait due to several reasons: being a naturally protected internal organ visible from the exterior, it has a near circular and planar shape that turns easier its segmentation and parameterization. Also, its texture has a predominantly phenotypic or chaotic appearance that is stable over lifetime, which—particularly important—discriminating information between subjects lies in the lowest and middle-low frequency components, i.e., those that are easier to capture in unconstrained data acquisition protocols. Finally, the ocular region is less sensitive to facial expressions (than the whole face), and has a relatively small probability of being occluded due to hair, facial hair, and clothing.

We started by summarizing the most relevant research works devoted to increasing the recognition robustness with respect to data of reduced quality, and hereinafter, focused particularly in the major issues behind each of the phases that compose the recognition chain: data acquisition, segmentation, feature encoding, and matching. Also, we summarized some of the most relevant works in the *periocular recognition* domain. In this topic, we stressed two key properties of an ocular recognition ensemble: (1) the *weak* (periocular) recognizer should provide as much independent scores (responses) as possible with respect to the *strong* (iris) recognizer; and (2) experts should not share particular sensitivity to the same data covariates, in order to actually improve recognition robustness.

Finally, the obstacles remaining in every phase of a fully *noncooperative ocular recognition* system were discussed, particularly the difficulty in real-time detecting and segmenting all the components in the ocular region, which is important not only for developing non-holistic feature encoding/matching strategies, but also to estimate pose and data quality.

Acknowledgments The financial support given by "IT: Instituto de Telecomunicações" in the scope of the UID/EEA/50008/2013 project is acknowledged.

References

1. A. Abhyankar, S. Schuckers, Iris quality assessment and bi-orthogonal wavelet base decoding for recognition. Pattern Recogn. **42**, 1878–1894 (2009)
2. E. Arvacheh, H. Tizhoosh, A study on Segmentation and Normalization for Iris Recognition (2006)
3. A. Basit, M. Javed, Iris localization via intensity gradient and recognition through bit planes, in *Proceedings of the International Conference on Machine Vision* (2007), pp. 23–28
4. S. Bharadwa et al., Periocular biometrics: when iris recognition fails, in *Proceedings of the International Conference on Biometrics: Theory, Applications and Systems. U.S.A* (2010), pp. 1–6
5. N. Boddeti, B.V.K.V. Kumar, Extended depth of field iris recognition with correlation filters, in *Proceedings of the Computer Vision and Pattern Recognition Workshop on Biometrics. U.S.A* (2006), pp. 51–59
6. K. Bowyer, K. Hollingsworth, P.J. Flynn, Image understanding for iris biometrics: a survey. Comput. Vis. Image Underst. **110.2**, 281–307 (2008)
7. C. Boyce et al., Multispectral iris analysis: a preliminary study, in *Proceedings of the First IEEE International Conference on Biometrics: Theory, Applications, and Systems. U.S.A* (2008), pp. 1–8
8. R. Broussard et al., Using artificial neural networks and feature saliency techniques for improved iris segmentation, in *Proceedings of the International Joint Conference on Neural Networks* (2007), pp. 1283–1288
9. Y. Chen, S.C. Dass, A.K. Jain, Localized iris image quality using 2-D wavelets, in *Proceedings of the International Conference on Biometrics* (2006), pp. 373–381
10. S. Crihalmeanu, A. Ross, Multispectral scleral patterns for ocular biometric recognition. Pattern Recogn. Lett. **33.14**, 1860–1869 (2012)
11. J. Daugman, Uncertainty relation for resolution in space, spatial frequency, and orientation optimized by two-dimensional visual cortical filters. J. Opt. Soc. America A **2.7**, 1160–1169 (1985)
12. J. Daugman, Biometric decision landscapes. University of Cambridge Technical Report, UCAM-CL-TR-1476-2986 482 (2000)
13. J. Daugman, Probing the uniqueness and randomness of IrisCodes: results from 200 billion iris pair comparisons. Proc. IEEE **94.11**, 1927–1935 (2006)
14. J. Daugman, New methods in iris recognition. IEEE Trans. Syst. Man Cybern.—Part B: Cybern. **37.5**, 1167–1175 (2007)
15. J. Daugman, C. Downing, Effect of severe image compression on iris recognition performance. IEEE Trans. Inform. Forensic Secur. **3.1**, 52–61 (2008)
16. C.I. de l'Eclarirage, Photobiological safety standards for safety standards for lamps (CIE-99), Report of TC 6 (1999), pp. 134–38
17. M. Dobes et al., Human eye localization using the modified hough transform. Optik **117**, 468–473 (2006)
18. Y. Du, C. Belcher, Z. Zhou, Scale Invariant gabor descriptor-based noncooperative iris recognition. EURASIP J. Adv. Signal Process. 2010.ID 936512 (2010)
19. C. Fancourt et al., Iris recognition at a distance, in *Proceedings of the 2005 IAPR Conference on Audio and Video Based Biometric Person Authentication. U.S.A* (2005), pp. 1–13
20. K. Grabowski et al., Focus assessment issues in iris image acquisition system, in *Proceedings of the 14th International Conference MIXDES 2007* (2007), pp. 628–631
21. I. B. Group
22. X. He, P. Shi, A new segmentation approach for iris recognition based on hand-held capture device. Pattern Recogn. **40**, 1326–1333 (2007)
23. Y. He, T. Tan, J. Cui, Y. Wang, Key techniques and and methods for imaging iris in focus, in *Proceedings of the IEEE International Conference on Pattern Recognition. Hong Kong* (2006), pp. 557–561

24. Z. He, T. Tan, Z. Sun, Iris localization via pulling and pushing, in *Proceedings of the 18th International Conference on Pattern Recognition*, vol. 4 (2006), pp. 366–369
25. Z. He et al., Robust eyelid, eyelash and shadow localization for iris recognition, in *Proceedings of the International Conference on Image Processing* (2009), pp. 265–268
26. R.S. Holambe, A.D. Rahulkar, Half-Iris feature extraction and recognition using a new class of biorthogonal triplet half-band filter bank and flexible k-out-of-n:A postclassifier. IEEE Trans. Inform. Forensics Secur. **7.1**, 230–240 (2012)
27. K.P. Hollingsworth, K.W. Bowyer, P.J. Flynn, The Importance of small pupils: a study of how pupil dilation affects iris biometrics, in *Proceedings of the International Conference on Biometrics* (2008), pp. 1–6
28. K. Hollingsworth, K. Bowyer, P.J.J.J. Flynn, Pupil dilation degrades iris biometric performance. Comput. Vis. Image Underst. **113**(1), 150–157 (2009)
29. H. I. Inc. Invariant radial iris segmentation (2007)
30. H. I. Inc
31. A. N. S. Institute. American national standard for the safe use of lasers and LEDs used in optical fiber transmission systems (1988)
32. J. Jang et al., New focus assessment method for iris recognition systems. Pattern Recogn. Lett. **29**(13), 1759–1767 (2008)
33. N. Kalka et al., Estimating and fusing quality factors for Iris biometric. IEEE Trans. Syst. Man Cybern. Part A **40**(3), 509–524 (2010)
34. B.J. Kang, K.R. Park, A study on iris image restoration. in *Proceedings of the International Conference on Audio- and Video-Based Biometric Person Authentication* (2005), pp. 31–40
35. B.J. Kang, K.R. Park, A Robust eyelash detection based on iris focus assessment. Pattern Recogn. Lett. **28.13**, 1630–1639 (2007)
36. B.J. Kang, K.R. Park, A new multi-unit iris authentication based on quality assessment and score level fusion for mobile phones. Mach. Vis. Appl. (2009)
37. G. Kelly, T. Mansfield, D. Chandler, J. Kane, Biometric product testing final report. issue 1.0 (2001)
38. L. Kennell, R. Ives, R.M. Gaunt, Binary morphology and and local statistics applied to iris segmentation for recognition, in *Proceedings of the IEEE International Conference on Image Processing* (2006), pp. 293–296
39. S. Krichen E. Garcia-Salicetti, B. Dorizzi, A new probabilistic iris quality measure for comprehensive noise detection, in *Proceedings of the International Conference on Biometrics: Theory, Applications, and Systems* (2007), pp. 1–6
40. A. Kumar, T.-S. Chan, Iris recognition using quaternionic sparse orientation code (QSOC), in *Proceedings of the Computer Vision and Pattern Recognition Workshops* (2012), pp. 59–64
41. A. Kumar, T.-S. Chan, C.-W. Tan, Human identification from at-adistance face images using sparse representation of local iris features, in *Proceedings of the International Conference on Biometrics* (2012), pp. 303–309
42. P. Li, H. Ma, Iris recognition in non-ideal imaging conditions. Pattern Recogn. Lett. **33.8**, 1012–1018 (2012)
43. P. Li, X. Liu, N. Zhao, Weighted co-occurrence phase histogram for Iris recognition. Pattern Recogn. Lett. **33.8**, 1000–1005 (2012)
44. X. Liu, K.W. Bowyer, P.J. Flynn, Experiments with an improved iris segmentation algorithm, in *Proceedings of the Fourth IEEE Workshop on Automatic Identification Advanced Technologies* (2005), pp. 118–123
45. G. Lu, J. Qi, Q. Liao, A new scheme of Iris image quality assessment, in *Proceedings of the Third International Conference on International Information Hiding and Multimedia Signal Processing*, vol. 1 (2007), pp. 147–150
46. L. Maddalena, A. Petrosino, The Sobs algorithm: what are the limits?, in *Proceedings of the Computer Vision and Pattern Recognition Workshops* (2012), pp. 21–26
47. M. Marsico, M. Nappi, D. Riccio, Noisy Iris recognition integrated scheme. Pattern Recogn. Lett. **33.8**, 1006–1011 (2012)

48. J.R. Matey et al., *Iris Recognition In Less Constrained Environments*. Advances in Biometrics: Sensors, Algorithms and Systems (Springer, 2007) pp. 107–131
49. P. Meredith, T. Sarna, The physical and and chemical properties of eumelanin. Pigm. Cell Res. **19**, 572–594 (2006)
50. C.H. Morimoto, T.T. Santos, A.S. Muniz, Automatic iris segmentation using active near infra red lighting, in *Proceedings of the Brazilian Symposium on Computer Graphics and Image Processing (SIBGRAPI 2005)* (2005), pp. 37–43
51. K. Nandakumar et al., Quality based score level fusion in multibiometric systems, in *Proceedings of the International Conference on Pattern Recognition* (2006), pp. 473–476
52. R. Narayanswamy et al., Extending the imaging volume for biometric iris recognition. Appl. Opt. **44**(5), 701–712 (2005)
53. K. Oh, K.-A. Toh, Extracting sclera features for cancellable identity verification, in *Prooceedings of the International Conference on Biometrics* (2012), pp. 245–250
54. K. Oh et al., Combining sclera and and periocular features for multi-modal identity verification. Neurocomputing (2013)
55. K. Park, J. Kim, A real-time focusing algorithm for iris recognition camera. IEEE Trans. Syst. Man Cybern. **35.3**, 441–444 (2005)
56. U. Park et al., Periocular biometrics in the visible spectrum. IEEE Trans. Inf. Forensics Secur. **6**(1), 96–106 (2011)
57. P. Phillips et al., Overview of the face recognition grand challenge, in *Proceedings of the IEEE Conference on Computer Vision and Pattern Recognition*, vol. 1 (2005), pp. 947–954
58. A. Poursaberi, B.N. Araabi, Iris recognition for partially occluded images methodology and sensitivity analysis. EURASIP J. Adv. Signal Process. 20–32 (2007)
59. H. Proenca, Iris recognition: on the segmentation of degraded images acquired in the visible wavelength. IEEE Trans. Pattern Anal. Mach. Intell. **32.8**, 1502–1516 (2010)
60. H. Proenca, Quality assessment of degraded iris images acquired in the visible wavelength. IEEE Trans. Inform. Forensics Secur. **6.1**, 82–95 (2011)
61. H. Proenca, Ocular biometrics by score-level fusion of disparate experts. IEEE Trans. Image Process. **31.12**, 5082–5093 (2014)
62. H. Proença, L.A. Alexandre, A method for the identification of noisy regions in normalized iris images, in *Proceedings of the International Conference on Pattern Recognition*, vol. 4 (2006), pp. 405–408
63. H. Proença, L.A. Alexandre, Iris segmentation methodology for noncooperative iris recognition. IEE Proc. Vis. Image Signal Process. **153.2**, 199–205 (2006)
64. H. Proença, L.A. Alexandre, Iris recognition: analysis of the error rates regarding the accuracy of the segmentation stage. Image Vis. Comput. **28**, 202–206 (2010)
65. H. Proença, L.A. Alexandre, Toward covert iris biometric recognition: experimental results from the NICE contests. IEEE Trans. Inform. Forensics Secur. **7.2**, 798–808 (2012)
66. H. Proença et al., The UBIRIS.v2 a database of visible wavelength iris images captured on-the-move and at-a-distance. IEEE Trans. Pattern Anal. Mach. Intell. **32**(8), 1529–1535 (2010)
67. N. Puhan, X. Jiang, Robust eyeball segmentation in noisy iris images using fourier spectral density, in *Proceeding of the 6th IEEE International Conference on Information, Communications and Signal Processing* (2007), pp. 1–5
68. A. Raffei et al., Feature extraction for different distances of visible reflection iris using multi-scale sparse representation of local Radon transform. Pattern Recogn. **46**, 2622–2633 (2013)
69. A. Ross, S. Shah, in *Proceedings of the IEEE 2006 Biometric Symposium*
70. K. Roy, P. Battacharya, C.Y. Suen, Iris recognition using shape-guided approach and game theory. Pattern Anal. Appl. **14**, 329–348 (2011)
71. G. Santos, E. Hoyle, A fusion approach to unconstrained Iris recognitio. Pattern Recogn. Lett. **33.8**, 984–990 (2012)
72. S. Schuckers et al., On techniques for angle compensation in nonideal iris recognition. IEEE Trans. Syst. Man Cybern.-Part B: Cybern. **37**(5), 1176–1190 (2007)
73. J. Shi, C. Tomasi, Good features to track, in *Proceedings of the IEEE Computer Society Conference on Computer Vision and Pattern Recognition* (1994)

74. K. Shin et al., New iris recognition method for noisy iris images. Pattern Recog. Lett. **33**(8), 991–999 (2012)
75. K. Smith et al., Extended evaluation of simulated wavefront coding technology in iris recognition, in *Proceedings of the First IEEE International Conference on Biometrics: Theory, Applications, and Systems. U.S.A* (2007), pp. 1–7
76. Z. Sun, T. Tan, Ordinal measures for iris recognition. IEEE Trans. Pattern Anal. Mach. Intell. **23.12**, 2211–2226 (2009)
77. R. Szewczyk et al., Reliable iris recognition algorithm based on reverse biorthogonal wavelet transform. Pattern Recog. Lett. **33**(8), 1019–1026 (2012)
78. C.-W. Tan, A. Kumar, Towards online Iris and periocular recognition under relaxed imaging constraints. IEEE Trans. Image Process. **22.10**, 3751–3765 (2013)
79. T. Tan, Z. He, Z. Sun, Efficient and and robust segmentation of noisy iris images for non-cooperative segmentation. Image Vis. Comput. **28.2**, 223–230 (2010)
80. T. Tan et al., Noisy iris image matching by using multiple cues. Pattern Recog. Lett. **33**(8), 970–977 (2012)
81. M. Turk, A. Pentland, Eigenfaces for recognition. J. Cognitive Neurosci. **3.1**, 71–86 (1991)
82. M. Vatsa, R. Singh, A. Noore, Improving iris recognition performance using segmentation, quality enhancement, match score fusion, and indexing. IEEE Trans. Syst. Mans Cybern.-B **38.4**, 1021–1035 (2008)
83. P. Viola, M. Jones, Rapid object detection using a boosted cascade of simple features, in *Proceedings of the 2001 IEEE Computer Society Conference on Computer Vision and Pattern Recognition*, vol. 1 (2001)
84. J. Wan, X. He, P. Shi, An iris image quality assessment method based on laplacian of gaussian operation, in *Proceedings of the IAPR Conference on Machine Vision Applications* (2007), pp. 248–251
85. Q. Wang et al., Adaboost and and multi-orientation 2D Gaborbased noisy iris recognition. Pattern Recog. Lett. **33**, 978–983 (2012)
86. Z. Wei et al., Robust and fast assessment of iris image quality, in *Proceedings of the International Conference on Biometrics* (2006), pp. 464–471
87. Z. Xu, P. Shi, A robust and and accurate method for pupil features extraction, in *Proceedings of the 18th International Conference on Pattern Recognition*, vol. 1 (2006), pp. 437–440
88. N. Yager, T. Dunstone, The biometric menagerie. IEEE Trans. Pattern Anal. Mach. Intell. **32**(2), 220–230 (2010)
89. X. Ye et al., Iris image realtime pre-estimation using compound neural network, in *Proceedings of the International Conference on Biometrics* (2006), pp. 450–456
90. S. Yoon, K. Bae, K.R. Park, J. Kim, *Pan-tilt-zoom Based Iris Image Capturing System for Unconstrained User Environments at a Distance*. Lecture Notes in Computer Science, vol. 4642 (2007), pp. 653-662
91. A. Zaim, Automatic segmentation of iris images for the purpose of identification, in *Proceedings of the IEEE International Conference on Image Processing*, vol. 3 (2005), pp. 11–14
92. G. Zhang, M. Salganicoff, Method of measuring the focus of close-up image of eyes (1999)
93. Z. Zheng, J. Yang, L. Yang, A robust method for eye features extraction on color image. Pattern Recog. Lett. **26**, 2252–2261 (2005)
94. Z. Zhou et al., A new human identification method: sclera recognition. IEEE Trans. Syst. Man Cybern.—Part A: Syst. Humans **42**(3), 571–583 (2012)
95. J. Zuo, N. Kalka, N.A. Schmid, A robust iris segmentation procedure for unconstrained subject presentation, in *Proceedings of the Biometric Consortium Conference* (2006), pp. 1–6
96. J. Zuo, N.A. Schmid, An automatic algorithm for evaluating the precision of iris segmentation, in *Proceedings of the IEEE Conference on Biometrics: Theory, Applications and Systems* (2008), pp. 1–6
97. J. Zuo, N.A. Schmid, Global and and local quality measures for NIR iris video, in *Proceedings of the International Conference On Computer Vision and Pattern Recognition* (2009), pp. 120–125

Chapter 16
Design Decisions for an Iris Recognition SDK

Christian Rathgeb, Andreas Uhl, Peter Wild and Heinz Hofbauer

Abstract Open-source software development kits are vital to (iris) biometric research in order to achieve comparability and reproducibility of research results. In addition, for further advances in the field of iris biometrics the community needs to be provided with state-of-the-art reference systems, which serve as adequate starting point for new research. This chapter provides a summary of relevant design decisions for software modules constituting an iris recognition system. The proposal of general criteria and adequate concepts is complemented by a detailed description of how according design decisions are implemented in the University of Salzburg Iris Toolkit, an open-source iris recognition software which contains diverse algorithms for iris segmentation, feature extraction, and comparison. Building upon a file-based processing chain, the provided open-source software is designed to support rapid prototyping as well as integration in existing frameworks achieving enhanced usability and extensibility. In order to underline the competitiveness of the presented iris recognition software, experimental evaluations of segmentation and feature extraction algorithms are carried out on a publicly available iris database and compared to a commercial product.

C. Rathgeb (✉)
Biometrics and Internet Security Research Group, Hochschule Darmstadt,
Darmstadt, Germany
e-mail: christian.rathgeb@h-da.de

A. Uhl · H. Hofbauer
Multimedia Signal Processing and Security Lab, Department of Computer Sciences,
University of Salzburg, Salzburg, Austria
e-mail: uhl@cosy.sbg.ac.at

H. Hofbauer
e-mail: hhofbaue@cosy.sbg.ac.at

P. Wild
Safety and Security Department, AIT Austrian Institute of Technology GmbH,
Seibersdorf, Austria
e-mail: peter.wild@ait.ac.at

© Springer-Verlag London 2016   359
K.W. Bowyer and M.J. Burge (eds.), *Handbook of Iris Recognition*,
Advances in Computer Vision and Pattern Recognition,
DOI 10.1007/978-1-4471-6784-6_16

16.1 Introduction

In past decades, iris recognition [7, 11, 42] has emerged as a rapidly growing field of research. Due to its intricate structure, the iris constitutes one of the most powerful biometric characteristics utilized by iris recognition algorithms to extract discriminative biometric reference data (templates). Existing approaches to iris recognition achieve auspicious biometric performance, reporting recognition rates above 99 % and equal error rates (EERs) of less than 1 % on diverse (publicly available) iris data sets acquired under active participation of captured subjects. Deployments of iris recognition in diverse large-scale application scenarios, such as border control, underline its tremendous inroads [46]. The Unique IDentification Authority of India (UIDAI) [12] represents the world's largest national identification number project, which aims at collecting iris as well as fingerprint data of 1.2 billion Indian residents, where iris recognition accuracy is reported to exceed that of fingerprint. Similar national projects are also under way in Indonesia and in several smaller countries [42], which confirms that iris recognition is here to stay.

In order to drive forward the advances made in iris recognition over the past decades, researches will have to solve remaining challenges such as processing eye images in less than ideal conditions and accurately localizing the iris's spatial extent in poor quality images [46]. One driving factor behind rapid progress of research in computer science and its reproducibility is the provision of open-source software [44, 48, 53]. Focusing on iris biometrics, open-source iris recognition software development kits (SDKs) should provide an adequate starting point for researchers working on improvements of different key components of an iris recognition system such as iris image segmentation or feature extraction. Hence, the design of open-source SDKs in terms of software architecture, functionality, platform-dependence, etc., represents a crucial factor with respect to usability, broad applicability, and straight forward extensibility. In this chapter, we provide insights into general design decisions to be dealt with during the development of an iris recognition SDK. Moreover, we provide a detailed description of how to realize design decisions for distinct modules of an iris recognition SDK; in particular, the University of Salzburg Iris Toolkit (USIT)[1] [42]. In addition, experimental evaluations of corresponding key components are carried out on the publicly available CASIAv4 iris database.

The remainder of this chapter is organized as follows: Sect. 16.1 briefly introduces the constitutive modules forming an iris recognition system as well as the current landscape regarding open-source iris recognition SDKs. Section 16.2 provides a detailed summary of design decisions for an iris recognition SDK which are implemented in USIT, where focus is put on general aspects, image preprocessing, feature extraction, and comparison. Experimental evaluations of different modules of USIT are presented in Sect. 16.3. Finally, conclusions are drawn in Sect. 16.4.

---

[1]University of Salzburg Iris Toolkit (USIT), available at http://www.wavelab.at/sources/ Rathgeb12e/.

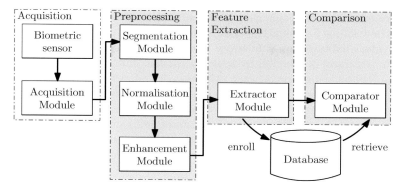

Fig. 16.1 The processing chain of a generic iris recognition system comprising image acquisition, image preprocessing, iris texture feature extraction, and comparison

16.1.1 Modules of an Iris Recognition System

The ever-increasing demand on biometric systems has entailed continuous proposals of different iris recognition techniques [7]. Still, the processing chain of traditional iris recognition systems has remained almost unaltered. In particular, generic iris recognition systems consist of four major modules

1. Iris image acquisition
2. Image preprocessing
3. Iris texture feature extraction
4. Comparison (feature matching)

Figure 16.1 depicts a flowchart of a generic iris recognition system. With respect to image acquisition, good quality images are necessary to provide a robust iris recognition system. Still, most current deployments of iris recognition systems require users to fully cooperate with the system. At preprocessing, the pupil and the outer boundary of the iris are detected. Subsequently, the vast majority of iris recognition algorithms "un-roll" the iris ring to a normalized rectangular iris texture. To complete the preprocessing, the contrast of the resulting iris texture is enhanced; e.g., by applying histogram stretching methods. In addition, parts of the iris texture which are occluded by eyelids, eyelashes or reflections are detected and stored in a corresponding bit-mask.

Based on the preprocessed iris texture, feature extraction is applied. The vast majority of feature extraction algorithms follow the approach of Daugman [11] in which a binary feature vector is extracted by applying adequate filters to the iris texture in a row-wise manner. The resulting biometric template is commonly referred to as "iris code". While Daugman suggests to apply 2D Gabor filters in the feature extraction stage, many different methods have been proposed [7, 42].

In most iris biometric comparators, pairs of iris-codes are compared by applying the bit-wise XOR-operator to count miss-matching bits, masked (AND'ed) by both of their corresponding mask templates to prevent occlusions from influencing comparisons. The resulting fractional Hamming distance indicates the grade of dissimilarity (small values indicate high similarity). In order to compensate against head tilts, template alignment is achieved by applying circular shifts in both directions. The minimal Hamming distance between two iris-codes refers to an optimal alignment. Hence, the comparison of iris-codes can be performed in an efficient process, which can be parallelized easily. In contrast to other biometric systems based on different modalities requiring a more complex comparator, millions of comparisons can be done within one second. With respect to biometric recognition systems operating in identification mode, iris recognition algorithms are capable of handling large-scale databases.

While image acquisition plays a fundamental role in iris recognition, for the development of an iris recognition SDK focus is merely put on image preprocessing, iris texture feature extraction, and comparison (marked gray in Fig. 16.1).

16.1.2   Open-Source Iris Recognition Landscape

While iris recognition represents an active field of biometric research [21] the availability of open-source iris recognition SDKs turns out to be rather disappointing. Hence, the research program in most laboratories either relies on in-house software solutions, existing open-source software, which might be noncompetitive and hardly maintained, or even commercial products. Further, a single point of reference which summarizes available open-source iris recognition SDKs is currently nonexistent, unlike for other biometric characteristics such as face, see [13]. It is important to note that, while the processing chain of iris recognition systems is rather specific, other systems which process different biometric characteristics, where recognizing individuals can be reduced to texture modeling/recognition tasks, e.g., face or palm, certainly benefit from advances in different fields of image processing.

One of the widely used open-source iris SDK is the implementation of the Bachelor Thesis by Libor Masek [29]. This iris recognition system consists of a segmentation module that is based on the Hough transform which should be able to localize circular iris and pupil boundaries, occluding eyelids and eyelashes, as well as reflections. The extracted iris region is normalized into a rectangular block of fixed dimensions and the phase data of 1D Log-Gabor filters is extracted and quantised to four levels to generate iris-codes. The software was developed in MATLAB® using its image processing tool-box. Due to the fact that this SDK has remained unmaintained for more than ten years, its usefulness for state-of-the-art research is doubtful. Similarly, the Project Iris SDK [8], which was developed by a group of students at the Imperial College London in 2010, represents a reimplementation of Daugman's algorithms. Implemented in C++ using the Qt framework for the visual representation, this SDK turns out to be hard to extend and, like the system of Masek, must

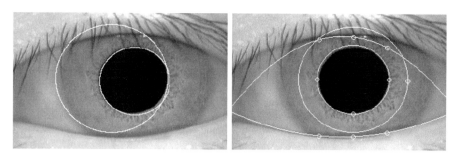

Fig. 16.2 Example of segmentation errors on a single image of the CASIAv1 database for the open-source SDKs of Masek (*left*) and the Project Iris (*right*)

not be considered as state-of-the-art iris recognition system. To emphasis this fact, Fig. 16.2 shows segmentation errors of both SDKs for the same sample image of the CASIAv1 database [19] for which the segmentation task is considered rather simple for today's iris segmentation algorithms, since original images have been modified to have a digital circle of constant pixel value for the pupil region [36].

In contrast to the aforementioned type of iris recognition SDKs, OSIRIS (Open Source for IRIS) [23] represents a more sophisticated open-source iris recognition SDK. Initially developed in the framework of the BioSecure project [6] the SDK is maintained on a regular basis. Implemented in C++ using OpenCV for image processing, the SDK comprised four processing modules such as segmentation, normalization, feature extraction, and comparison. At segmentation, a Viterbi algorithm [49] is employed to detect the boundaries of the iris and the pupil. In the feature extraction step, a bank of customizable Gabor filters is applied to 256 application points within the iris texture at various resolutions. Finally, comparison is performed by XORing two iris-codes incorporating their corresponding bit-masks. The current version of OSIRIS offers enhanced extensibility and obtains practical biometric performance on various publicly available databases, e.g., CASIAv4 [19] or ICE [30].

Further open-source iris recognition SDKs might exist, e.g., VISAR [26], however, at this point we only intended to provide a coarse impression of the present open-source iris recognition landscape. Focusing on current challenges in iris biometrics one major shortcoming applies to all of the above-mentioned SDKs: only one algorithm is provided for each module of the iris biometric processing chain. Iris recognition under nonideal conditions may call for a fusion of algorithms at various processing steps in order to improve accuracy. In summary, while some open-source iris recognition SDKs can be considered useless for open issues and challenges in iris recognition, others require further extension. Researchers should be provided with an easily extendible pool of different algorithms for each element in the iris biometric processing chain which can be employed for different scenarios or biometric fusion.

16.2   Design Decisions for an Iris Recognition SDK

When designing SDKs for iris recognition systems, target platform, programming interface, and scope are of crucial importance. Considering the rapid change in the field with regards to external input to be considered in the decision process (e.g., biometric quality, counter-spoofing information, biometric fusion) and yet lacking standardization for such support, USIT aims at providing a baseline reference system based a desktop CPU allowing for easy wrapping into biometric frameworks, but also allowing for white-box adaption building custom processing chains. Building on C++ with compilation scripts for Windows, Linux (and MacOS via macports) operating systems, relying on well-supported libraries (OpenCV,[2] Boost[3]) USIT—University of Salzburg Iris Toolkit is a software package for iris recognition, made publicly available as additional material to [42]. The software follows the module-based design of the traditional iris processing chain introduced in Fig. 16.1 and comes with implementations for each of the stages preprocessing, feature extraction, and comparison, providing a set of reference implementations of standard baseline approaches.

16.2.1   General

While USIT is not aimed at providing a biometric framework, it is designed to support rapid prototyping and evaluation, as well as integration in standardized systems via a lightweight library concept following a file-based processing chain. While not natively provided, wrappers for biometric frameworks as BioAPI (Version 2.0 specified in ISO/IEC 19784-1:2006), an important standard for biometric processing APIs in industrial applications, can be implemented using the provided library. In BioAPI, biometric functionality (sensor, archive, processing algorithms, and verification algorithms) can be provided in modules called Biometric Service Providers. These can be used by the framework via service provider interfaces in a rather flexible way, allowing for several implementations supporting a modular concept and permitting to replace individual modalities easily.

CPU-based implementations still dominate the board, but recently field-programmable gate arrays (FPGA) and graphical processing unit (GPU) implementations for iris APIs have become an important research topic [17, 40, 47], especially since image-based processing heavily relies on arithmetic logic units (ALU) processing, a scarce resource in current multi-core architectures. The idea is to parallelize most time-consuming operations, with reported speedups in Daugman-based iris recognition of 10–300 times in FPGAs [40] and 10–15 (single parts, 1.3 overall) in GPUs [47], compared to CPU-only implementations following key characteristics as [40]: size and shape (small form-factor), speed, power, and accuracy.

---

[2]OpenCV library website: http://opencv.willowgarage.com/.
[3]Boost library website: http://www.boost.org/.

Design criteria for USIT were (1) usability supporting ease of use and reproducibility, (2) accuracy, and (3) performance focusing on CPU. The USIT library
can be used by anyone agreeing to the Berkeley Software Distribution (BSD) license
agreement[4] and citing [42] in all the technical reports and papers that report experimental results using this software. The software package includes C++ algorithms
for iris preprocessing, feature extraction, and comparison. Input and output rely on
files following the provided command line tools. Listed algorithms coincide with
the list of provided source files, i.e., each algorithm represents a stand-alone application. Supporting batch processing or iris biometric databases, command line tools
enable auto-search in directories and folders (note, that for this feature, globbing in
Linux has to be deactivated via `set -o noglob`). In filenames, `*` can be used
as a wildcard character to match any character sequence. If `*` is used as a wildcard (one or multiple times), `?1`, `?2`, `...` in other related attributes refer to the
contents of the n-th `*`. Example: `hdverify -i files/class*/*.tiff ?1`
`-t -s -7 7 -r roc.dat` processes each of the directories `files/class1`,
`files/class2, ... files/class999` and each file ending in `.tiff` in
each of these directories. As class label, the `?1` refers to the contents of the matched
character sequence, i.e., 1 for `files/class1`, 2 for `files/class2`, etc.

16.2.2 Image Preprocessing

As biometric systems without active participation of users become more and more
important, iris image preprocessing is at the heart of the problem of efficient and
robust iris recognition from noisy iris images [51]. While the iris as a biometric
modality is known for its high uniqueness, certainly quality has a drastic impact
on recognition [18] and therefore usually receives central attention in iris recognition toolkits and has particularly affected revisions in related software packages,
as OSIRIS [23]: in OSIRIS-v2 iris segmentation involves the steps of pupil pre-
localization (using morphological operations) and Hough circle detection (on the
Canny edge image), masks to discard occlusions (eyelids,eyelashes) were not considered [16]. In OSIRIS-v3 GMM-based local quality estimators around each pixel
were introduced and OSIRIS-v4 even more emphasized on processing time and edges
introducing the Viterbi [49] algorithm applied on the gradient map at high and low
resolutions to refine detections. USIT provides a set of different implementations in
the same software release, allowing to interchange certain algorithms and modules,
where necessary. Table 16.1 lists available preprocessing tools in USIT, which are
discussed and analyzed with regards to design decisions.

---

[4]BSD license: http://opensource.org/licenses/bsd-license.php.

Table 16.1 Overview of tools in the image preprocessing module

Name	Title and description	Input	Output
gfcf	**Gaussian Face and Face-part Classifier Fusion** locates eyes via fusion of face(-part) detectors [50]	Image with face	Eye, face regions
caht	**Contrast-adjusted Hough Transform** employs classic Hough transform iris segmentation [42]	Eye image	Normalized texture, masks
wahet	**Weighted Adaptive Hough and Ellipsopolar Transform** fast two-stage iris segmentation [51]	Eye image	Normalized texture, masks
miss	**Manual Iris Segmentation Software** GUI for marking iris boundaries [18]	Iris database	Ground truth files
manuseg	**Manual Unrolling for Segmentation** for two-stage fast iris segmentation [18]	Eye image, gr.-truth files	Normalized texture, masks

16.2.2.1 Face/Face-Part Detection

While OpenCV already comes with implementations of Haar-based face and face-part detectors detecting regions of interest within images, in order to (1) eliminate the unsatisfactory high number of false positives, (2) increase speed when processing high-resolution images, and (3) avoid contradicting information when applying object detectors (face, face-part) trained on heterogeneous (e.g., VW vs. NIR) datasets in nested or parallel configuration, the tool **GFCF** (Gaussian Face and Face-part Classifier Fusion) provides a learning-based implementation of geometric co-occurrence of detection results. Quality criteria outlined in [50] are offset (window's center should be close to the iris center, e.g., within 10 % of the inter-eye distance), containment (found window should fully include the iris), and robustness (each trained classifier is prone to different types of errors and trained on different datasets). Fusion is employed to combine individual detectors using prior knowledge on geometrical positions of detection results. The training stage learns object relationships of detection results by fitting Gaussian distributions $\mathcal{N}_x, \mathcal{N}_y, \mathcal{N}_s$ and z-normalizing to the parameters of each detector f_i (accounting for symmetry), for each of n training images $I_j \in \mathcal{I}$, and m object detectors $f_i \in \mathcal{F}$ recording regions $b \in f_i(I_j)$, coordinate-size triples $b = (x, y, s)$ wrt. face coordinates (origin R, inter-eye unit S). The tool in Table 16.2 executes the following steps:

1. **Combinations**: For each $i \leq m$ all $\binom{i}{k}$ classifier combinations are tested;
2. **Prediction**: the face size/location $(R = (X, Y), S)$ is predicted from the t-th detector result (x, y, s) using trained models $\mathcal{N}_x, \mathcal{N}_y, \mathcal{N}_s$:

$$X := x - \mu_x \cdot s, \ Y := y - \mu_y \cdot s, \ S := \frac{s}{\mu_s}. \tag{16.1}$$

Table 16.2 Gaussian face and face-part classifier fusion

Source	`gfcf.cpp`
Task	Face detection and eye localization within (NIR and VW) portrait images, generating cropped eye images for further iris segmentation
Synopsis	`./gfcf -i picture -o face left eye right eye`
Example	`./gfcf -i *.tiff -o ?1 face.png ?1 eyeleft.png ?1 eyeright.png -q -t`

3. **Average model location**: Using $\alpha := \sigma_x \cdot S$, $\beta := \sigma_y \cdot S$, $\gamma := \sigma_s \cdot S$ for a set of m model locations $L_i = (X_i, Y_i, S_i, \alpha_i, \beta_i, \gamma_i)$ we define the average model location $\mathrm{Avg}(\mathcal{L})$:

$$\mathrm{Avg}(\mathcal{L}) = (X_{\mathrm{Avg}}, Y_{\mathrm{Avg}}, S_{\mathrm{Avg}}), \quad X_{\mathrm{Avg}} := \left(\sum_{i=1}^{m} \frac{1}{\alpha_i} \right) \cdot \left(\sum_{i=1}^{m} X_i \cdot \frac{1}{\alpha_i} \right),$$

$$Y_{\mathrm{Avg}} := \left(\sum_{i=1}^{m} \frac{1}{\beta_i} \right) \cdot \left(\sum_{i=1}^{m} Y_i \cdot \frac{1}{\beta_i} \right), \quad S_{\mathrm{Avg}} := \left(\sum_{i=1}^{m} \frac{1}{\gamma_i} \right) \cdot \left(\sum_{i=1}^{m} S_i \cdot \frac{1}{\gamma_i} \right).$$

$$(16.2)$$

4. **Location energy**: Finally, for each tested subset of detection results we estimate, how likely the subset represents the detection of a face

$$E(\mathcal{L}) := \frac{1}{m} \sqrt{1 + \sum_{i=1}^{m} \max \left(\frac{|X_i - X_{\mathrm{Avg}}|}{\alpha_i}, \frac{|Y_i - Y_{\mathrm{Avg}}|}{\beta_i}, \frac{|S_i - S_{\mathrm{Avg}}|}{\gamma_i} \right)} \quad (16.3)$$

GFCF uses the predicted face localisation of the best subset to report a cropped ROI for the face region as well as left and right eye regions.

16.2.2.2   Iris Segmentation

Iris segmentation aims to locate (1) pupillary and limbic boundary curves $P, L :$ $[0, 2\pi) \rightarrow [0, m] \times [0, n]$ for normalization using the rubbersheet map and (2) eyelash boundaries, location of eyelids, reflections, etc., for noise suppression masking occluded iris texture in a noise mask image, see Fig. 16.3 for a visualization of segmentation data stages. Segmentation problems comprise quality degrading factors like uneven illumination (classical approaches require 700–900nm sensing), resolution (minimum iris diameter of 140–200 pixels as of ISO/IEC 29794-6), motion blur or defocus (restoration for images with low quality), off-axis (non-frontal-view)

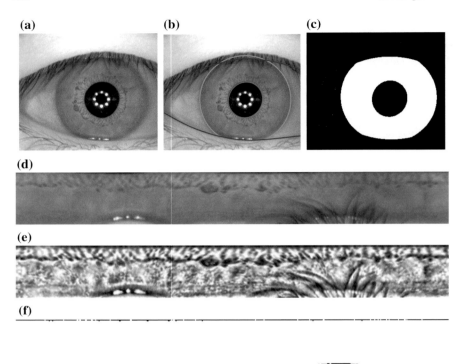

Fig. 16.3 Segmentation locates (**b**) boundaries and (**c**) occlusions, which are used to create (**d**) unrolled and (**e**) enhanced texture and (**f**) noise masks via Rubbersheet transform. **a** Original, **b** segmented, **c** mask, **d** texture bef. enhancement, **e** normalized texture, **f** noise mask

images, eyeglasses, restrictions on wavelength (NIR versus VW), and performance issues, like real-time processing requirements, data compression impact, or "fast" screening. Especially the impact of wavelength on iris processing has to be considered, e.g., clear pupillary (between pupil and iris) but weaker limbic (between iris and sclera) boundaries in NIR, but clear limbic and weak pupillary boundaries and reflections in VW (see Fig. 16.4).

Algorithms for iris segmentation differ in their robustness to challenges in recording conditions and segmentation accuracy, yet the environment (attended vs. unattended, controlled vs. uncontrolled) can have a huge impact on whether it is advisable to employ simpler or advanced models, as higher degrees of flexibility (e.g., elliptical models) do not necessarily have a positive effect if the flexibility provided is not required by the recording setup, exposing a higher risk of segmentation failures [50]. On the other hand, unattended enrollment and especially off-axis acquisition need very flexible models. USIT therefore offers a set of algorithms for this task (see Tables 16.3, 16.4) differing in the complexity of the employed model, taking an eye image as input and offering an integrated segmentation (creating boundaries),

(a)

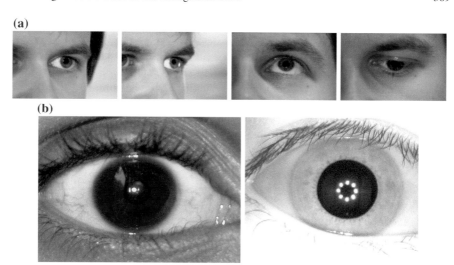

(b)

Fig. 16.4 Examples of challenges in segmentation processing for iris images. **a** perspective distortion due to off-axis iris image acquisition, **b** boundary contrast in VW (*left*, UBIRIS-v2) versus NIR (*right*, Casia-v4-Interval)

Table 16.3 Weighted adaptive Hough and Ellipsopolar transform

Source	`wahet.cpp`
Task	Two-stage fast iris segmentation using iterative Hough transform for coarse circle detection and fine ellipsopolar transform-based boundary detection in unrolled image
Synopsis	`./wahet -i file.tiff -o texture.png -s 512 64 -e`
Example	`./wahet.exe -i *.tiff -o ?1 texture.png -m ?1 mask.png -s 512 64 -e`

Table 16.4 Contrast-adjusted Hough transform

Source	`caht.cpp`
Task	Iris segmentation using pupillary boundary and sequential iris boundary Hough circle detection after contrast adjustment
Synopsis	`./caht -i eye image -o texture -m mask -s width height`
Example	`./caht.exe -i *.tiff -o ?1 texture.png -m ?1 mask.png -s 512 64 -e`

normalization (unrolling), and enhancement module, see Fig. 16.3. While early reim-plementations of the algorithms of Wildes' (based on Hough transform) and Daug-man (based on integrodifferential operator) traditionally needed database-specific assumptions on iris/ pupil size to reduce search space and were likely affected by reflections and low limbic contrast, implementations have been refined by a lot of researchers [42], and multi-stage implementations have seen high popularity.

The **WAHET** (Weighted Adaptive Hough and Ellipsopolar Transform) [50] algo-rithm adopts this strategy of decoupled coarse center and fine boundary detection and is composed of the following steps:

1. **Reflection removal and inpainting**: Reflection spots cause bright edges, which may affect subsequent center search. In this common stage for segmentation algorithms, a reflection mask $M : [0, m] \times [0, n] \to \{0, 1\}$ is computed (here via adaptive thresholding using relative excess $e = 60$ in a 23×23 neighborhood), followed by region size filtering ($10 \leq$ area ≤ 1000) and morphological post-processing (dilation with 11×11 structuring element). Inpainting (OpenCV's provided *Navier-Stokes* method) reconstructs the selected image area from the pixel near the area boundary (e.g., using bilinear interpolation), see Fig. 16.5.

2. **Gradient extraction**: Not only edge magnitude, but also orientation (see Fig. 16.6) may provide useful information to determine the eye center. However, for bound-ary detection it is useful to suppress gradients from eyelashes and eyelids first (see Fig. 16.7). Eyelash tests like the following one employ the block-wise mean gradient $\{\overline{G_x}\}_{i,j}$, $\{\overline{G_y}\}_{i,j}$ to determine, whether a block contains eyelashes

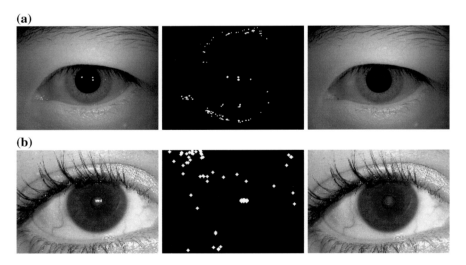

(a)

(b)

Fig. 16.5 Effect of reflection removal (*left* original, *center* mask, *right* inpainted) and inpainting on different datasets. **a** Casia-v4 lamp, **b** UBIRIS-v1

Fig. 16.6 Gradient magnitude versus orientation. Images from *left* to *right* indicate $(1+2)$ strongest gradients, and $(3+4)$ orientation via hue channel

(a)

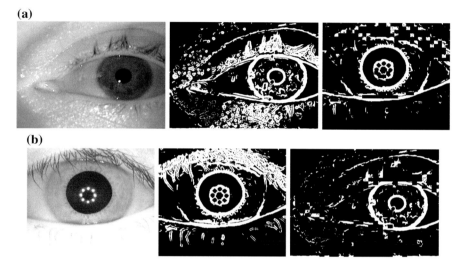

(b)

Fig. 16.7 Eyelash removal. **a** ND eyelash removal, **b** CASIA eyelash removal

$$e(i, j) := \begin{cases} 1, \text{ if } \sqrt{\{\overline{G}_x\}_{i,j}{}^2 + \{\overline{G}_y\}_{i,j}{}^2} \geq \eta \\ 0, \text{ else.} \end{cases}$$

Phase $\phi \in [0, 2\pi)$ and magnitude $m \in \mathbb{R}_0^+$ for each pixel are computed for the top 20 % (magnitude) candidates with no dominant mean orientation only (to save computational time), using 7×7 Sobel kernels on the normalized image.

3. **Weighted Adaptive Hough Transform**: Uses gradients to find the center of the most pronounced circle in the image. Following [9], for an $m_i \times n_i$ ROI R_i (initially $R_0 = I'$), a $w \times h$ grid accumulator A_i (covering R_i) is initialized with 0. All candidate edge points $P_j \in E_{i-1}$ (initially $E_{-1} = \{(x, y) : E(x, y) = 1\}$), whose gradient lines g_j do not intersect with R_i, are rejected in E_i. In a subsequent voting step, cells in A_i crossed by a gradient line g_j of a candidate point in E_i are incremented using the absolute gradient value. WAHET uses Bresenham's line algorithm and searching for the maximum supercell of 4 cells for this task. In order to favor center positions, A_i is downscaled, multiplied by Gaussian G, the

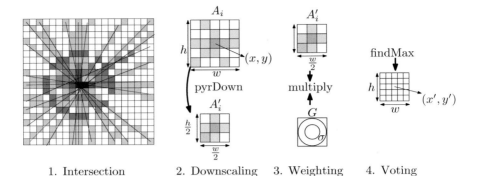

1. Intersection   2. Downscaling   3. Weighting   4. Voting

Fig. 16.8 Steps in weighted adaptive Hough transform. **1** Intersection, **2** downscaling, **3** weighting, **4** voting

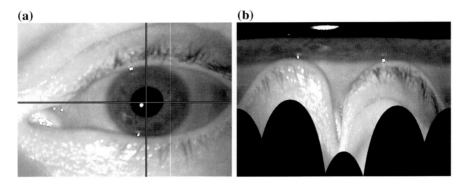

Fig. 16.9 Center detection and polar transform. **a** Center, **b** unrolling

cell of maximum value is found and R_{i+1} is centered in the cell's center (x', y'). The process is repeated as long as R_{i+1} (with $m_{i+1} = \frac{m_i}{2}, n_{i+1} = \frac{n_i}{2}$) is larger than a predefined threshold, updating the center point $C = (x', y')$. Figure 16.8 illustrates the processing stages.

4. **Polar transform**: Center C is used to polar unwrap the iris image I' using the following formula (see Fig. 16.9).

$$T : [0, 2\pi) \times \mathbb{R}_0^+ \to \mathbb{R}^2, \quad T \begin{pmatrix} \theta \\ r \end{pmatrix} := \begin{pmatrix} x + r\cos\theta \\ y + r\sin\theta \end{pmatrix} \tag{16.4}$$

5. **Initial boundary localization**: The polar transformed I_p is convolved with 21×21 Gabor kernels (using parameters $\lambda = 8\pi, \psi = \frac{\pi}{2}, \sigma = 6, \gamma = 0.5, \theta = -\frac{\pi}{2}$). An approximate first contour in polar domain is localized using radial fitting (polar contour series $(b_\theta)_{\theta=0}^{k-1}$ is initialized by the radius r_{max} with maximum gradient sum over $\theta \in [0, k-1] \cap \mathbb{N}$) and angular fitting (within local radial window

$W = [-15, 15] \cap \mathbb{N}$, the contour gradient is maximized yielding a refined contour $(b'_\theta)_{\theta=0}^{k-1}$ such that $\forall \theta : b'_\theta = b_\theta + \max_{i \in W} \arg \left(G_p(\theta, b_\theta + i) \right)$. Finally, exploiting the periodic nature of the contour series, Fourier fitting is executed (smoothing using 1D Fourier series expansion keeping initially the first 2, and then 4 coefficients after rerunning angular fitting again).

6. **Ellipsopolar transform**: This transformation maps concentric ellipses (center (x, y), ref. half axes a, b and angle of inclination α) to axis-parallel lines.

$$T_E : [0, 2\pi) \times \mathbb{R}_0^+ \rightarrow \mathbb{R}^2$$

$$T_E \begin{pmatrix} \theta \\ r \end{pmatrix} := \begin{pmatrix} x \\ y \end{pmatrix} + \begin{pmatrix} \cos \alpha & -\sin \alpha \\ \sin \alpha & \cos \alpha \end{pmatrix} * \begin{pmatrix} ra \cos(\theta - \alpha) \\ rb \sin(\theta - \alpha) \end{pmatrix} \quad (16.5)$$

7. **Inner ($r < 1$) & Outer ($r > 1$) boundary**: Using boundary localization steps introduced before, candidate boundaries are searched on either side of the already found boundary (initialization favors elliptic boundary concentric to B). Gaussian weighting (applied to the sum) depending on radial distance r wrt. reference contour B helps to favor boundaries close to an expected pupil-to-iris ratio ($\mu_i = 0.66$, $\sigma_i = 0.44$ for inner search, $\mu_o = 2.5$, $\sigma_o = 1$ for outer boundary search). Boundary selection is via Hypothesis testing, whether $H_0 : B = P$ or $H_1 : B = L$ holds is estimated by evaluating the gradient energy function e for an ellipsopolar sampled boundary curve X with respect to ellipse B

$$e(X) := \sum_{\theta=0}^{k-1} M_E \left(X(\theta) \right) * W(\mu, \sigma, r(X, \theta, B)) \quad (16.6)$$

If $e(P') > e(L')$ we set $P = P'$, otherwise $L = L'$.

8. **Rubbersheet transform**: The resulting boundary curves P and L are subjected to Daugman's rubbersheet model assigning—regardless of pupillary dilation and iris size—each pair (θ, r) of angle θ and pupil-to-limbic radial distance r the corresponding originating location $R(\theta, r)$ within I

$$R : [0, 2\pi) \times [0, 1] \rightarrow [0, m] \times [0, n] \quad (16.7)$$

$$R(\theta, r) := (1 - r) \cdot P(\theta) + r \cdot L(\theta) \quad (16.8)$$

Finally, the texture is enhanced using contrast-limited adaptive histogram equalization (CLAHE), see Fig. 16.10. Typical iris features track radial and concentric furrows, i.e., the textural pattern, not color, is used for identification. In order to achieve higher recognition rates, a normalization of the iris texture is highly desirable.

The **CAHT** (Contrast-adjusted Hough Transform) [15] algorithm is a much simpler, Masek-like [29] custom implementation of an approach following Hough

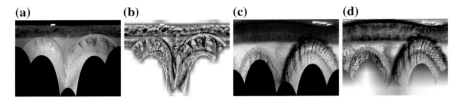

Fig. 16.10 Effect of contrast-limited adaptive histogram equalization enhancement. **a** NIR original, **b** NIR enhanced, **c** VW original, **d** VW enhanced

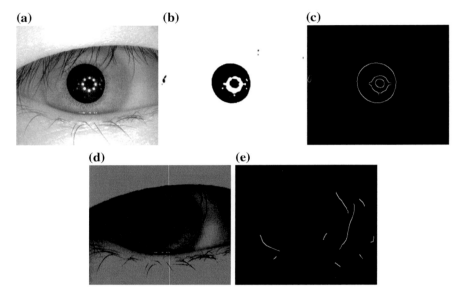

Fig. 16.11 CAHT processing chain. **a** Original, **b** after step 1, **c** after step 2, **d** after step 4, **e** after step 5

Transform. However, note, that its strict model assumptions (pupil intensity distribution, circular models, etc.) make it an excellent candidate for datasets captured under good conditions, for example CASIA.v4-Interval. It is based on the following steps, illustrated in Fig. 16.11 for a concrete example

1. **Pupillary contrast adjustment**: Exploiting the fact that the pupil is usually among the darkest regions in a NIR iris image under constrained acquisition, luminance of the image is adjusted in place so that the result has at least 2
2. **Pupillary Canny edge detection** using a Gaussian 15×15 kernel with $\sigma = 3$, followed by removal of streaks and limiting the maximal length of streaks.
3. **Hough transform for pupillary boundary detection**: As aimed for NIR segmentation, this boundary should be easier to detect (using Hough threshold 200), limiting outcomes to the best circle following geometrical constraints.

4. **Limbic image enhancement**: In order to assist detection and concentrate on the traditionally weaker (in NIR) iris-to-sclera boundary, the pupil is blacked out suppressing pupillary gradients. Further, contrast adjustment similar to the first step ensures that the blacked-out pupil is ignored for contrast purposes, enhancing the limbic biundary, followed by iterative summation to make areas brighter.
5. **Limbic Canny edge detection** Using a similar processing as in stage 2, followed by removal of streaks and limiting the maximal length of streaks. Further, dimming of pixels far above the horizontal line through the pupil center is executed, since the actual circle outline can mostly contribute from the center.
6. **Hough transform for limbic boundary detection** in a small window of interest for radius values (e.g., minimum iris radius is 1.5 times the pupillary radius) only.
7. **Rubbersheet transform** is applied, following the same algorithmic approach as WAHET.

When comparing iris segmentation algorithms, besides efficiency (robust segmentation of less intrusively captured irides) and independence of sensors (avoiding the problem of database-specific optimizations), especially speed with its growing demand for real-time capable solutions is an important characteristic. With WAHET's iterative center search exploiting the fact that the required eye center is the unique center of multiple concentric rings, a rather transparent processing for NIR and visible range images (either pupil or iris boundary may contribute to a larger extent) is generally possible. However, with the Gaussian weighting step, model-specific prior knowledge can be considered—for higher accuracy on particular datasets the user might want to adjust certain parameters: the Gaussian weighting process during adaptive HT can be used to successfully tune the algorithm for particular datasets with a known iris-to-pupillary radius. Further, in the design of iris segmentation software, it is useful to notice the drastic effect of reflections on accuracy without corresponding integrated counter mechanisms, as can be seen in Fig. 16.12. While boundary detection in polar domain has the advantage of an alignment of relevant gradients in almost horizontal orientation, reflections can significantly impact on boundary detection causing errors.

Finally, during the segmentation process, sometimes feedback loops (e.g., using a refined center to rerun stages based on refined parameters) can be a successful way if processing time requirements are not too high. As a general observation, iris segmentation algorithms are often optimized with respect to databases, neglecting the need for high usability and reproducibility of segmentation algorithms when applied to different databases [50]. Less constrained images usually cause drastic increase in EERs (1.2–12.9 % WAHET, 0.7–28.8 % CAHT in [50]).

In surveillance environments or for on-the-move capture, off angle iris images and insufficient illumination challenge even state-of-the-art iris segmentation algorithm. For such cases and in order to compare accuracy of segmentation algorithms, the authors of USIT introduced a manual segmentation tool in [18]: **MISS** (Manual Iris Segmentation Software, see Fig. 16.13) is a graphical user interface-based segmentation software that generates parameter files for a successful segmentation. The parameters recorded present points along pupillary and limbic boundaries as well as

(a)

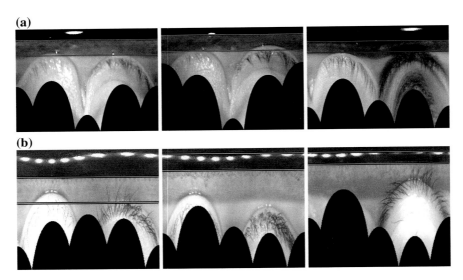

Fig. 16.12 Boundary detection problems if large reflections are not removed/ignored. **a** Notre Dame, **b** Casia-v4-interval

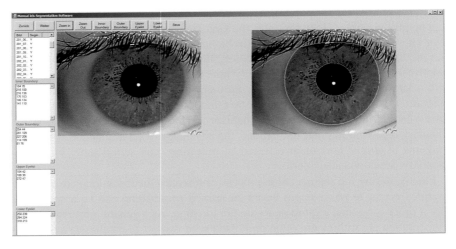

Fig. 16.13 Manual iris segmentation softwares

upper and lower eyelids. For the pupillary and limbic boundaries, an elliptical model is employed, requiring a minimum of five user-labeled boundary points, which are used to fit an ellipse based on OpenCV's Fitzgibbon's best ellipse fitting. Allowing zooming functionality and displaying results interactively in two windows (original image and visual segmentation feedback) users can correct segmentations or add further boundary points where necessary. Parameters for eyelids define polynomials

Table 16.5 Manual iris segmentation rubbersheet mappings

Source	`manuseg.cpp`
Task	Rubbersheet mapping and texture enhancement for manually segmented iris images

Synopsis	`./manuseg -i picture -c`
	`inner outer upper lower -o`
	`texture -m mask`

Example	`./manuseg -i *.tiff -c`
	`?1.inner.txt ?1.outer.txt`
	`?1.upper.txt ?1.lower.txt -o`
	`?1.norm.png -m ?1.mask.png`
	`-q -t`

and are encouraged to take the best possible separation of iris and eyelid in the iris region into consideration (rather than approximating the entire eyelid, i.e., outside the iris region deviations from the true boundary are not relevant). The output of coordinate files for upper and lower eyelids as well as inner and outer boundaries (click positions with regards to the employed models) serves as an input to the provided **MANUSEG** (Manual Iris Segmentation Rubbersheet Mapping) software, executing the same rubbersheet normalization (and potentially enhancement) stage as for the automated segmentation techniques WAHET and CAHT, see Table 16.5.

16.2.3 Feature Extraction

USIT includes several feature extraction techniques, which are summarized in Table 16.6. While some of these represent custom reimplementations of traditional approaches, e.g., 1D-Log-Gabor or quadratic spline wavelet, others are in-house developments, e.g., local intensity variations or context-based comparator. Further, USIT provides other types of feature extractors, which do not follow the typical processing flow of iris biometric feature extractors, e.g., scale-invariant feature transform or local binary patterns. In order to provide an appropriate insight to available feature extraction techniques, we restrict to describe only a subset of these in detail, while a guidance for all feature extractors is provided in the manual and source code of the SDK.

The **QSW** (Quadratic Spline Wavelet) [28] and the **LG** (Log-Gabor) [29] algorithm follow a similar processing chain while different types of wavelets are applied. Both algorithms, which are shown in Tables 16.7 and 16.8, respectively, are based on the following steps:

1. **Texture-decomposition to 1D signal**: in the first step the normalized iris texture is divided into ten vertical texture stripes of same height. Within the default

Table 16.6 Overview of tools in the feature extraction module

Name	Title and description	Input	Output
lg	**Log-Gabor** extracts iris-code applying a 1D-Log-Gabor filter [29]	Normalized iris texture	Iris-code
qsw	**Quadratic Spline Wavelet** extracts iris-code applying quadratic spline wavelet [28]	Normalized iris texture	Iris-code
dct	**Discrete Cosine Transform** generates iris-code employing DCT [31]	Normalized iris texture	Iris-code
cg	**Complex-Gabor** extracts iris-code applying a complex 2D-Gabor filter [11]	Normalized iris texture	Iris-code
ko	**Cumulative Sums of Gray-scale Blocks** generates iris-codes by encoding cumulative sums of neighboring texture blocks [22]	Normalized iris texture	Iris-code
cr	**Local Intensity Variations** generates iris-code by encoding pixel neighboring intensities within texture stripes [41]	Normalized iris texture	Iris-code
cb	**Context-based Extractor** extracts iris-codes for context-based comparator [43]	Normalized iris texture	Iris-code
sift	**Scale-Invariant Feature Transform** extracts SIFT-based key points [27]	Normalized iris texture	Set of SIFT points
surf	**Speeded Up Robust Features** extracts SURF-based key points [5]	Normalized iris texture	Set of SURF points
lbp	**Local Binary Patterns** extracts spectral histograms using uniform LBPs [33]	Normalized iris texture	Sequence of spectral histograms

Table 16.7 Quadratic spline wavelet

Source	`qsw.cpp`
Task	Extract iris-code based on a row-wise processing of normalized iris textures applying a quadratic spline wavelet
Synopsis	`./qsw -i texture -o template`
Example	`./qsw -i *.tiff -o ?1qsw.png -q -t`

Table 16.8 1D Log-Gabor

Source	`lg.cpp`
Task	Extract iris-code based on a row-wise processing of normalized iris textures applying a Log-Gabor wavelet
Synopsis	`./lg -i texture -o template`
Example	`./lg -i *.tiff -o ?1qsw.png -q -t`

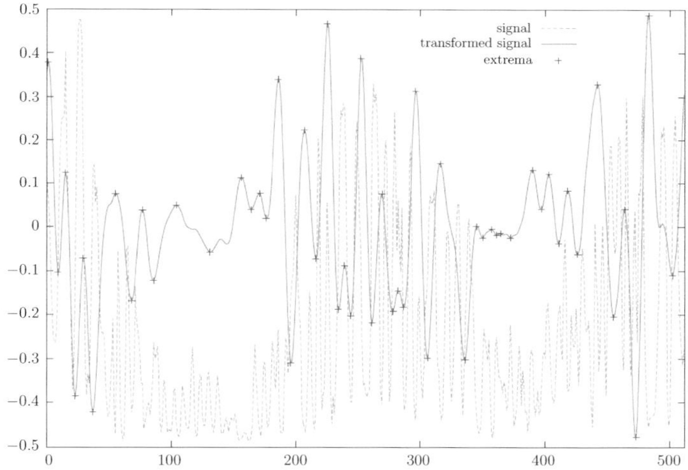

Fig. 16.14 Example of a one-dimensional signal extracted from a 512×5 pixel texture stripe and the corresponding filter responses and local extrema for applying a quadratic spline wavelet

configuration of segmentation tools, e.g., WAHET, normalized textures comprise 512×64 pixels which are divided into ten stripes of 512×5 pixels, hence, the upper 512×50 pixel of preprocessed iris textures is analyzed. Subsequently, the average gray-scale value of each 1×5 is estimated and normalized in an adequate range in order to obtain a one-dimensional signal.

2. **Wavelet filtering**: within **QSW** a quadratic spline wavelet transform is performed on the ten signals, and two fixed subbands are selected resulting in a total number of 20 subbands. An example of applying a quadratic spline wavelet transform on a sample texture stripe is depicted in Fig. 16.14. In **LG** a convolution with a complex Log-Gabor filter is performed.

3. **Binary encoding**: focusing on **QSW**, local extrema, i.e., minima and maxima of the filter responses, are detected (as shown in Fig. 16.14) and descending and ascending sequences are encoded with 0 and 1, respectively. In the **LG** algorithm the phase angle of the resulting complex values for each signal is discretized into 2 bits. Therefore, both feature extractors extract iris-codes consisting of

(a)

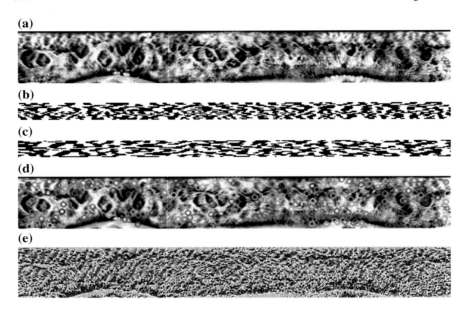

(b)

(c)

(d)

(e)

Fig. 16.15 Examples of features extracted by different types of feature extraction techniques. **a** Enhanced normalized iris texture, **b** iris-code using quadratic spline wavelet, **c** iris-code using 1D Log-Gabor wavelet, **d** SIFT keypoints, **e** uniform LBP

$512 \times 20 = 10240$ bits. Examples of resulting iris-codes for the iris texture of Fig. 16.15a are shown in Fig. 16.15b, c.

Representing global feature extractors, further approaches in particular, **DCT**, **CG**, **KO**, **CR** and **CB**, work similarly as these processing normalized iris textures in a row- or block-wise manner extracting different types of features. In contrast, **SIFT** (Scale Invariant Feature Transform) [27] and **SURF** (Speeded Up Robust Features) [5] extract sets of local features, i.e., keypoints, which are of variable length. For details on these algorithms we refer to [5, 27]. Generic algorithms like **SIFT** can be applied to various types of input images while in USIT these algorithms are optimized for processing normalized iris textures as suggested in [54], see Table 16.9. Still, these techniques can easily be applied to other types of input images, e.g.,

Table 16.9 Scale-invariant feature transform

Source	`sift.cpp`
Task	Extract a set of SIFT keypoints of variable length from a normalized iris texture
Synopsis	`./sift -i texture -o template`
Example	`./sift -i *.tiff -o ?1.sift -q -t`

Table 16.10 Local binary patterns

Source	`lbp.cpp`
Task	Extract spectral histograms form a normalized iris texture using uniform LBPs
Synopsis	`./lbp -i texture -o template`
Example	`./lbp -i *.tiff -o ?1` `lbp.png -q -t`

segmented cropped eye images as suggested in [4], or even VW iris images. It is generally conceded that these types of general purpose texture descriptors tend to obtain worse biometric performance compared to the aforementioned traditional schemes. However, it has been shown that, within multi-algorithm fusion scenarios, fusions of scores obtained from local and global features significantly improve the overall biometric performance of the system [55], which motivates the provision of nontraditional schemes. Keypoint extractors of the **SIFT** as well the **SURF** algorithm are provided by OpenCV and can be employed using default setting. Figure 16.15d shows detected SIFT keypoints for the sample texture of Fig. 16.15a. It is important to note that the **SIFT** feature extractor requires significant computational cost. Alternatively, **SURF** can be employed which is computationally more efficient [5].

In addition, USIT also provides classical texture description algorithms, in particular **LBP** (Local Binary Patterns) [33] which is shown in Table 16.10. Based on a block-wise processing of (8, 1) pixel neighborhoods **LBP** extracts 256 different values which are mapped to 59 different uniform LBPs which have been found to be more robust in biometric recognition [1]. The resulting biometric template consists a sequence of spectral histograms. Again, this algorithm is optimized for processing normalized iris textures, for the sample texture of Fig. 16.15a the according output is depicted in Fig. 16.15e. It is important to note that, similar to **SIFT**, **LBP** is not expected to obtain practical biometric performance as opposed to traditional schemes. However, again spectral histogram features may provide supplement information which can be employed within fusion scenarios.

16.2.4 Comparators

A list of comparators provided in USIT is shown in Table 16.11. The traditional **HD** (Hamming Distance) comparator, as proposed in [10], is shown in Table 16.12. The simple Boolean exclusive-OR operator (XOR) applied to a pair of binary biometric feature vectors, and masked (AND'ed) by both of their corresponding mask templates to prevent occlusions caused by eyelids or eyelashes from influencing comparisons. The XOR operator $\oplus$ detects disagreement between any corresponding pair of bits, while the AND operator $\cap$ ensures that the compared bits are both deemed to have

Table 16.11 Overview of tools in the comparison module

Name	Title and description	Input	Output
hd	**Hamming Distance** calculates a Hamming distance-based score between two iris-codes incorporating corresponding bit-masks applying circular bit shifts for alignment [10]	Iris-codes	Score
dctc	**Discrete Cosine Transform Comparator** estimates a dissimilarity score between two DCT-based iris-codes applying circular bit shifts for alignment [31]	Iris-codes	Score
koc	**Cumulative Sums of Gray-scale Blocks Comparator** estimates a dissimilarity score between two iris-codes extracted by the reimplementation of the algorithm proposed in [22]	Iris-codes	Score
cbc	**Context-based Comparator** performs a context-based comparison for iris-codes considering clusters of (non)matching bits [43]	Iris-codes	Score
siftc	**Scale-Invariant Feature Transform Comparator** estimates a dissimilarity score by matching two sets of SIFT keypoints trimming false matches [27]	Sets of SIFT keypoints	Score
surfc	**Speeded Up Robust Features Comparator** estimates a dissimilarity score by matching two sets of SURF keypoints trimming false matches [5]	Sets of SURF keypoints	Score
lbpc	**Local Binary Patterns Comparator** estimates a dissimilarity score by comparing sequences of spectral histogram using χ^2-distance [33]	Sequences of spectral histograms	Score

Table 16.12 Hamming distance

Source	hd.cpp
Task	Estimate the fractional Hamming distance between two iris-codes incorporating their corresponding masks for several bit shifts
Synopsis	`./hd -i first template second template -m first mask second mask -s left shift right shift -a algorithm -o result log`
Example	`./hd -i *.png *.png -a minHD -s -8 8 -o result.txt -q -t`

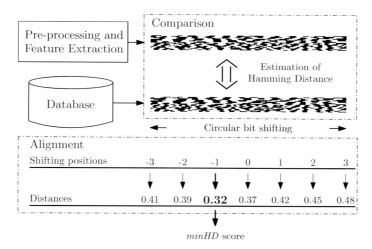

Fig. 16.16 Iris-biometric comparator: Iris-codes are circularly shifted in order to obtain an optimal alignment (minimal dissimilarity score)

been uncorrupted by noise. The norm $(|| \cdot ||)$ of the resulting bit vector and of the AND'ed mask template are then measured in order to compute a fractional Hamming distance (HD) as a measure of the dissimilarity between pairs of binary iris-codes {codeA, codeB} and the according mask bit vectors {maskA, maskB} [10]:

$$HD = \frac{||(\text{codeA} \oplus \text{codeB}) \cap \text{maskA} \cap \text{maskB}||}{||\text{maskA} \cap \text{maskB}||}. \qquad (16.9)$$

To compensate for small head tilts HD scores are estimated at different shifting positions and the best score, which corresponds to an optimal alignment, is returned. The entire process is schematically illustrated in Fig. 16.16. Several of the afore-mentioned feature extractors in particular, **QSW**, **LG**, **CG**, and **CR**, use **HD** for estimating comparison scores between pairs of iris-codes. Further feature extractors, e.g., **DCT**, **CB**, or **KO**, require distinct comparators which are termed according to the associated feature extractor, e.g., **DCTC**, **CBC**, or **KOC**.

The **SIFTC** (Scale Invariant Feature Transform Comparator) [27] as well as the **SURFC** (Speeded Up Robust Features Comparator) [5] are designed to compare two sets of keypoints detected on pairs of normalized enhanced iris textures. As shown in [54], SIFT is expected to obtain best biometric performance when applied to enhanced iris textures, see Table 16.13. It is based on the following steps:

1. **Brute-force keypoint matching**: given two sets of keypoints $\mathcal{S}$ and $\mathcal{T}$ the brute force matching algorithm available in OpenCV returns a set $\mathcal{M}$ of k matching keypoint tuples $\mathcal{M} = \{(m_{\mathcal{S}}, m_{\mathcal{T}})_1, (m_{\mathcal{S}}, m_{\mathcal{T}})_2, \dots, (m_{\mathcal{S}}, m_{\mathcal{T}})_k\}$.
2. **Trimming of false matches**: as suggested in [4], false matches should be eliminated by forcing pairs of matching key points to be within a certain area of

Table 16.13 SIFT-based comparison

Source	`siftc.cpp`
Task	Matching two sets of SIFT keypoints considering geometric constraints
Synopsis	`./siftc -i first template second template -o result log`
Example	`./siftc -i *.sift *.sift -o result.txt -q -t`

the texture. Thresholds, ϵ_x and ϵ_y, define maximum deviations allowed with respect x- and y-coordinates of matching keypoint tuples. The resulting set of keypoint tuples $\mathcal{M}'$ is defined as, $\mathcal{M}' = \{(m_\mathcal{S}, m_\mathcal{T})_i : |m_\mathcal{S}(x) - m_\mathcal{T}(x)| < \epsilon_x \wedge |m_\mathcal{S}(y) - m_\mathcal{T}(y)| < \epsilon_y, \forall i = 1, \ldots, k\}$.

3. **Score estimation**: finally, for the purpose of score-level fusion, it is important to estimate a normalized score. The dissimilarity score between two sets of keypoints is estimated as the number of matching keypoint pairs in $\mathcal{M}'$ normalized by the average amount of detected keypoints in both iris textures:

$$s(\mathcal{S}, \mathcal{T}) = 1 - \frac{|\mathcal{M}'|}{\text{avg}(|\mathcal{S}|, |\mathcal{T}|)}. \qquad (16.10)$$

Figure 16.17 shows pairs of matching SIFT keypoints where false matches were eliminated in order to improve biometric performance.

LBPC (Local Binary Pattern Comparator) [33], shown in Table 16.14, employs the χ^2-distance to compare pairs of sequences of spectral histograms consisting of K histograms extracted from $n \times n$ pixel cells. Again, the obtained comparison score is normalized according to the number of histograms and the number of processed pixels within each cell

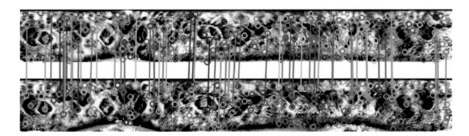

Fig. 16.17 Matching SIFT keypoints considering geometrical constraints ($\epsilon_x = 6, \epsilon_y = 2$) for two sample iris textures of the same subject

Table 16.14 LBP-based comparison

Source	`lbpc.cpp`
Task	Comparing sequences of spectral histograms of uniform LBPs
Synopsis	`./lbpc -i first template second template -o result log`
Example	`./lbpc -i *.png *.png -o result.txt -q -t`

$$\chi^2(\mathcal{S}, \mathcal{T}) = \frac{1}{K} \sum_{k=1}^{K} \sum_{b=1}^{B} \frac{\left((\mathcal{S}_{kb} - \mathcal{T}_{kb})/(n-2)^2\right)^2}{2 * (\mathcal{S}_{kb} + \mathcal{T}_{kb})/(n-2)^2}. \tag{16.11}$$

Finally, it is important to note that periocular biometrics is gaining more and more attention [34, 35]. Unconstrained environmental conditions call for a biometric fusion, thus, we believe that the provision of generic texture description algorithm improves the dissemination and applicability of an open-source iris recognition SDK. Independent of the type of input image algorithms like **LBP** or **SIFT** can be easily used for biometric fusion, e.g., extracting features from eyebrows. Finally, the inclusion of such algorithms provides a reference point for extension, in order to include improved texture description schemes, e.g., Local Phase Quantisation (LPQ) [2] or Binarized Statistical Image Features (BSIF) [20].

16.3 Experimental Evaluation

In this section, we present an evaluation of a selection of algorithms included in the USIT. In order to properly evaluate them we choose a well-known database with good quality images. This lets us evaluate the overall tool chain rather than having to differentiate between errors introduced in segmentation and feature extraction. The database used throughout this section is the CASIA Iris Image Database version 4.0,[5] or more specifically the interval subset.

The CASIA Iris-Interval subset of the CASIA version 4.0 database contains 2639 iris images of 320×280 pixels from 249 subjects which were taken over two sessions. The total number of classes in the database is 395, differentiating between left and right eye. The images were acquired with a close-up infrared iris camera in an indoor environment, having images with very clear iris texture details thanks to a circular NIR LED array. Figure 16.18 shows some examples of recorded iris images.

---

[5]http://biometrics.idealtest.org.

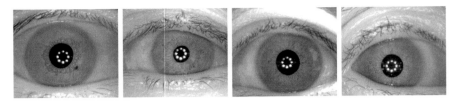

Fig. 16.18 Examples from the CASIA Iris-Interval database

16.3.1 Iris Segmentation

Iris recognition challenges for on-the-move and less constrained acquisitions, like the Noisy Iris Challenge Evaluation (NICE) [39], and Multiple Biometrics Grand Challenge (MBGC), illustrated the importance of robust iris segmentation in latest-generation iris biometric systems. Iris verification rates as low as 44.6% [45] are reported for unconstrained applications, and image quality has been shown to play a critical role in the segmentation and normalization process [3]. The performance of automated segmentation algorithms raises further questions, especially questions related to stability if algorithms fail: Accurate results of a cohort of segmenters might be severely affected by a single segmentation error. The ability to evaluate the segmenters in an individual test setup can help to identify such segmentation errors and help to improve on the segmentation process.

To evaluate the segmentation without utilizing the further steps in the iris-biometric tool chain requires the availability of ground truth data regarding iris segmentation. Iris segmentation ground truth is available for a number of databases and different segmentation modes. The IRISSEG-CC dataset[6] provides parameters for circular segmentation, i.e., circular pupil and iris boundaries as well as circular eyelid maskings. The IRISSEG-EP[7] provides parameters for elliptical pupil and iris boundaries and polynomial eyelid maskings. Both datasets are described in more detail in Hofbauer et al. [18]. The iris databases covered by the ground truth datasets are

IRISSEG-CC:

- **Biosec Baseline database** [14] available at:
  http://atvs.ii.uam.es/databases.jsp.
- **CASIA Iris Image Database version 3.0** available at:
  http://biometrics.idealtest.org.
- **MobBIO Database** [32] available at:
  http://paginas.fe.up.pt/~mobbio2013.

---

[6]http://islab.hh.se/mediawiki/index.php/Iris_Segmentation_Groundtruth.
[7]http://www.wavelab.at/sources/Hofbauer14b/.

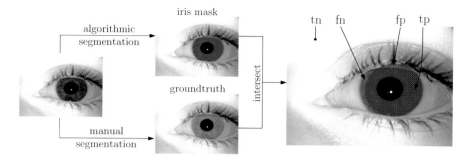

Fig. 16.19 Example of the split between *tp*, *fp*, *tn*, and *fn* for an iris image segmentation

IRISSEG-EP:

- **CASIA Iris Image Database version 4.0** available at:
  http://biometrics.idealtest.org.
- **IIT Delhi Iris Database version 1.0** [24, 25] available at:
  http://www4.comp.polyu.edu.hk/~csajaykr/IITD/Database_Iris.htm.
- Parts of the **ND-IRIS-0405 Database** [37] available at:
  http://www3.nd.edu/~cvrl/CVRL/Data_Sets.html.
- Parts of the **UBIRIS.v2 Database** [38] available at:
  http://iris.di.ubi.pt/ubiris2.html.

The usual way to evaluate the iris segmentation is to differentiate between the number of iris pixels returned by the algorithm in relation to the number of pixels which are part of the iris according to the ground truth. To do so we split the mask produced by an algorithm into four result groups (illustrated in Fig. 16.19): true positives (*tp*), the number of iris pixels which were correctly detected; false positives (*fp*), the number of non-iris pixels which were detected as iris pixels; false negative (*fn*), the number of iris pixels which were not detected; and true negative (*tn*), the number of correctly detected non-iris pixel.

Based on this differentiation there are a number of ways to calculate a score per algorithmically generated mask (A_i) to the masks provided by the ground truth (G_i) for image index i with a uniform dimension of $M \times N$ pixels.

Methods as suggested by the Noisy Iris Challenge Evaluation — Part I (NICE.I) are the error rates E_1 and E_2. The error

$$E_1 := \frac{fp + fn}{MN}, \tag{16.12}$$

refers of the rate of pixel disagreement between ground truth and segmentation noise masks. In contrast,

$$E_2 := \frac{1}{2}\left(\frac{fp}{fp+tn}\right) + \frac{1}{2}\left(\frac{fn}{fn+tp}\right), \tag{16.13}$$

accounts for the disproportion between a priori probabilities.

The measures utilized in [18] are the precision, recall, and F-measure, which are well-known measures from the field of information retrieval [52].

The precision, defined as

$$\text{Precision} = \frac{tp}{tp+fp}, \tag{16.14}$$

gives the percentage of retrieved iris pixels which are correct. The recall

$$\text{Recall} = \frac{tp}{tp+fn}, \tag{16.15}$$

gives the percentage of iris pixels in the ground truth which were correctly retrieved. Since the target is to optimize both recall and precision these two scores are combined by the F-measure, which is the harmonic mean of precision and recall,

$$f = \frac{2 \cdot \text{recall} \cdot \text{precision}}{\text{recall} + \text{precision}}. \tag{16.16}$$

From the equations, we can see that recall is a measure for the original iris content retrieved by an algorithm, it can also be maximized by overestimating the iris. Precision on the other hand can be optimized by underestimating the iris and is a measure of the non-iris content of the retrieved iris mask. The F-measure combines precision and recall in a way that will prevent optimization of results by over-fitting or under-fitting the iris.

While the overall performance over a database is a good performance measure, it is often more useful to know border cases when developing an algorithm. Iris masks which are especially good or especially bad show faults and strengths of an algorithm better than the overall performance. Especially during development this information can be utilized to further improve an algorithm. In order to find outliers, rather than natural fluctuations of the algorithm, [18] suggests the following methods.

To detect single image outliers, the E_1, E_2, precision, recall or F-measure are calculated for every image I in a given database $\mathcal{D}$. The z-score for a given measure $m \in \{\text{recall}, \text{precision}, f, E_1, E_2\}$ and image I can be calculated as

$$z(I, \mathcal{D}) = \frac{m(I) - \mu(m_{i \in \mathcal{D}}(i))}{\sigma(m_{i \in \mathcal{D}}(i))}. \tag{16.17}$$

A given mask is defined as an outlier if $|z| > 3$, i.e., the score is outside of $\mu \pm 3\sigma$. This can be done on a user basis as well as for individual iris images, i.e., find users which overall exhibit interesting properties regarding an algorithm. In this way, the distinction can be made between single image performance, which may be a result of image quality or unfortunate occlusions occurring only in a single image and a systemic problem related to a user. To do this, the database $\mathcal{D}$ is partitioned into groups $\mathcal{G}$, where each group contains all iris images of one user. Another possibility is to partition the groups by user and eye id, either left or right. Then the group outliers, for $G \in \mathcal{G}$, can be calculated as

$$z(G, \mathcal{G}) = \frac{\mu(m_{i \in G}(i)) - \mu(\mu_{g \in \mathcal{G}}(m_{i \in g}(i)))}{\sigma(\mu_{g \in \mathcal{G}}(m_{i \in g}(i)))}. \tag{16.18}$$

It should however be noted that the outlier detection on a per group basis can be easily influenced when a low number of images are in a given group.

An example of this can be seen in Fig. 16.20a based on the F-measure for the CAHT algorithm. Figure 16.21 gives the three iris mask images generated by the CAHT algorithm, as can be seen two images are clearly well segmented, but the third is faulty and drags the group average down enough to be counted as outlier. In terms of recognition rate this results in the performance shown in Table 16.15 for two algorithms. For both algorithms the mis-segmentation is enough to push the feature response above the threshold (at the EER) which would reject ID 3. For a comparison of other genuine and imposter scores see the distribution plots in Sect. 16.3.2.

Typical errors in segmentation are shown in Fig. 16.22, and can be classified as follows. Total segmentation errors where no borders are detected or both border are wrongly detected (Fig. 16.22a) are rare. More typical are errors which only miss the iris to sclera boundary. The most typical of this type of error is to mistakenly identify the collarette, the boundary between the pupillary and ciliary zone, as the outer iris boundary (Fig. 16.22c). This happens most frequently if the iris to sclera boundary is occluded by cilia or eyelid (Fig. 16.22b). Another error with the outer iris boundary is that the transition from iris to sclera is of low contrast and a random structure in the iris image is detected (Fig. 16.22d).

We have presented a somewhat in-depth overview of the performance of the CAHT segmentation algorithm on the CASIA Iris-Interval database based on the F-measure. The remaining results are given in a more concise form, by giving the average score over the database, in Table 16.16.

16.3.2 Feature Extraction

In this section, we will give an overview of the performance of selected feature extraction methods, which are described in more detail in Sect. 16.2. Instead of utilizing a large number of databases and presenting a cursory overview, only a single database, the CASIA Iris-Interval, will be used and all the relevant details are presented. In Fig. 16.23 the receiver–operator characteristics (ROC) are given, in logarithmic scale to pull out details, which give the true positive rate over the false positive rate. The ROC gives all possible operating points at which the iris-tool chain can be operated,

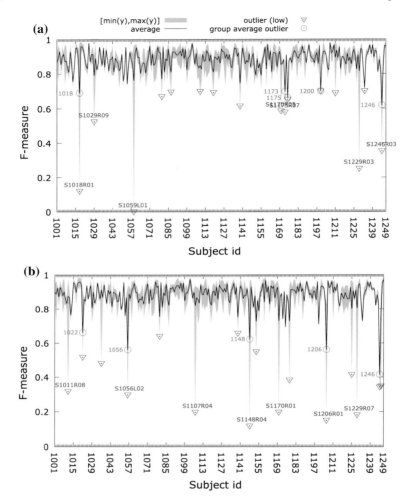

Fig. 16.20 Outlier detection for single images and group averages based on the CAHT algorithm on the CASIA Iris-Interval database. **a** CAHT compared to ground truth, **b** WAHET compared to ground truth

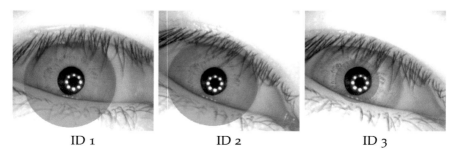

ID 1   ID 2   ID 3

Fig. 16.21 Mask of user 1246 from the CASIA Iris-Interval database as segmented by CAHT

Table 16.15 Response of the LG and QSW algorithms for the CAHT segmentation of user ID 1246 on the CASIA Iris-Interval database

Maseki, Kovesi (LG)				Ma et al. (QSW)			
	ID 1	ID 2	ID 3		ID 1	ID 2	ID 3
ID 1	—	0.4493	0.4910	ID 1	—	0.4563	0.4910
ID 2		—	0.4710	ID 2		—	0.4846
ID 3			—	ID 3			—

Threshold at EER is 0.446.   Threshold at EER is 0.46.

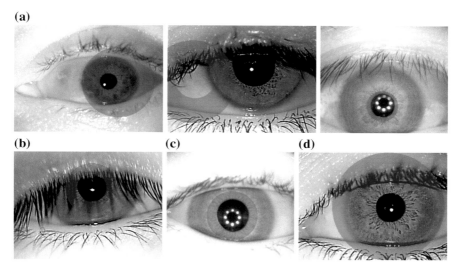

Fig. 16.22 Examples of different types of iris boundary segmentation errors. **a** Total segmentation failure, **b** heavy occlusion by cilia, **c** detection of collarette as iris boundary, **d** misdetection due to low contrast

Table 16.16 Segmentation performance of the CASIA Iris-Interval database, with ground truth of operator A of the IRISSEG-EP database

Algorithm	Precision (%)	Recall (%)	f (%)	E_1 (%)	E_2 (%)
CAHT	97.677	82.894	89.268	6.294	9.010
WAHET	94.718	85.444	89.134	6.065	8.305

but usually this is not a realistic scenario. The operation point is usually determined by the application scenario, high security areas would operate in a mode with a low false match rate, e.g., FMR= 0.1 % or even FMR= 0.01 %. Access points where only screening or high throughput is required operate at a low non-match rate point, e.g., FNMR= 0.1 %. The third option is to balance both by choosing the operation point at the equal error rate, i.e., FNMR=FMR. In Table 16.17 we summarize these

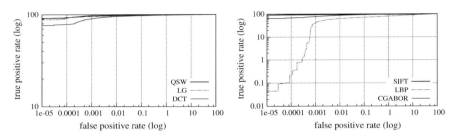

Fig. 16.23 Receiver–operator characteristics for CG, DCT, LBP, LG, SIFT, and QSW features extraction methods

Table 16.17 Key points of the ROC at equal error rate, false non-match rate at false match rates 0.1 % and 0.01 % as well as false match rate for false non-match rate of 0.1 % for selected algorithms on the CASIA Iris-Interval database

	EER (%)	FNMR (%) at FMR=0.1 %	FNMR (%) at FMR=0.01 %	FMR (%) at FMR=0.1 %
QSW	0.989	**1.361**	1.702	91.479
LG	1.220	**2.022**	3.159	92.759
DCT	1.342	**2.535**	4.235	95.605
CG	**3.24**	7.186	12.533	97.707
SIFT	4.161	**5.851**	6.455	97.089
LBP	**10.011**	28.624	36.989	99.960

operation points for the presented feature extraction algorithms. It can clearly be seen that the FNMR= 0.1 % operation point is tainted by a high FMR. Apart from that, the different methods are differently able to handle the balanced or high security operation points. The operation point where the overall error (FNMR+FMR) is lowest is marked in the table by a bold entry, i.e., the EER operation point is preferred if 2 EER < FNMR + FMR. Finally, Fig. 16.24 shows the distribution of feature comparison responses which resulted in the ROCs in Fig. 16.23. The distribution plots give an overview over the genuine and imposter comparison distributions and the overall performance of separating these two.

16.3.3 Comparison to Commercial Product

While the USIT performance cannot compare to the performance of commercial systems like the VeriEye Software by Neurotechnology,[8] it provides an implementation of algorithms from scientific literature with the goal of flexibility. This enables reproducible research and replacement of single elements in the iris-tool chain in order to focus research on a single part of the chain. The clear disadvantage is

---

[8]http://www.neurotechnology.com/verieye.html.

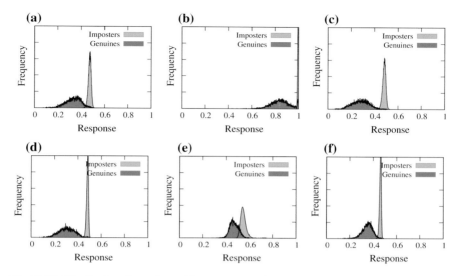

Fig. 16.24 Distribution of genuine and imposter scores based on algorithm. **a** CG, **b** SIFT, **c** LG, **d** QSW, **e** LBP, **f** DCT

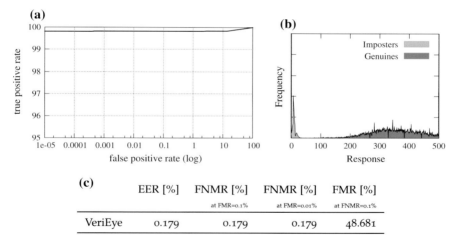

	EER [%]	FNMR [%]	FNMR [%]	FMR [%]
		at FMR=0.1%	at FMR=0.01%	at FNMR=0.1%
VeriEye	0.179	0.179	0.179	48.681

Fig. 16.25 Receiver–operator characteristic and genuine/imposter distribution for the Neurotechnology Biometric 5.1 SDK VeriEye. **a** Receiver–operator characteristic, **b** genuine/imposter distribution

that the respective parts of the tool chain are not specifically tailored to each other. As an example if a researcher wants to implement a new feature extraction algorithm it is simple to use a segmentation- and comparison-tool from the USIT while replacing the feature extraction. Since the segmentation tool is general purpose the resulting textures enhancement is of a general nature instead of being tailored to the newly implemented feature extraction, which might impact overall performance of the tool chain. This impact is immediately evident when comparing the EER and receiver–operator characteristics of the various USIT configurations to the finely tuned VeriEye, compare Fig. 16.25.

16.4 Conclusions

In this chapter, we discussed different aspects regarding design decisions of an iris recognition SDK. While several criteria, such as platform independence or usability, apply to the vast majority of (open source) software, distinct requirements have to be fulfilled by open-source iris recognition SDKs in order to support wide dissemination of them and, thus, support comparable and reproducible research. For instance, focusing on iris segmentation in unconstrained environments, which represents an unsolved research challenge, stand-alone feature extraction and comparison software are required to evaluate the overall performance of the biometric system, which highlights the importance of a tool chain-based software architecture. In order to provide a deep insight in how to realize design decisions accordingly, we describe in detail how these are implemented in the open-source USIT SDK. Hence, this chapter provides an overview of essential software-related decisions to be taken into account when designing (iris) biometric SDKs as well as a guidance and detailed description of algorithms implemented in USIT. In order to underline the relevance of USIT it is shown that contained algorithms obtain practical biometric performance on a publicly available iris database. The provision of an open-source iris recognition SDK in combination with a comprehensive technical manual will further leverage usability and extension of the reference system by researchers in the field of iris biometrics.

Acknowledgments This work was partially supported by the European FP7 FIDELITY project (SEC-2011-284862), the Center for Advanced Security Research Darmstadt (CASED) and the Austrian Science Fund, project no. P26630.

References

1. T. Ahonen, A. Hadid, M. Pietikainen, Face description with local binary patterns: application to face recognition. IEEE Trans. Pattern Anal. Mach. Intell. **28**(120, 2037–2041 (2006)
2. T. Ahonen et al., Recognition of blurred faces using local phase quantization, in *International Conference on Pattern Recognition* (2008), pp. 1–4
3. F. Alonso-Fernandez, J. Bigun, Quality factors affecting iris segmentation and matching, in *Proceedings of International Conference on Biometrics (ICB'13)* (2013)
4. F. Alonso-Fernandez et al., Iris recognition based on SIFT features, in *International Conference on Biometrics, Identity and Security (BIdS)* (2009), pp. 1–8
5. H. Bay et al., Speeded-up robust features (SURF). Comput. Vis. Image Underst. **110**(3), 346–359 (2008)
6. BioSecure project. Accessed June 2015

7. K.W. Bowyer, K. Hollingsworth, P.J. Flynn, Image understanding for iris biometrics: a survey. Comput. Vis. Image Underst. **110**(2), 281–307 (2007)
8. M. Boyd et al., Project Iris: free software for iris recognition (2010). Accessed June 2015
9. J. Cauchie, V. Fiolet, D. Villers, Optimization of an Hough transform algorithm for the search of a center. Pattern Recogn. **41**(2), 567–574 (2008)
10. J. Daugman, High confidence visual recognition of persons by a test of statistical independence. IEEE Trans. Pattern Anal. Mach. Intell. **15**(11), 1148–1161 (1993)
11. J. Daugman, How iris recognition works. IEEE Trans. Circ. Syst. Video Technol. **14**(1), 21–30 (2004)
12. Unique Identification Authority of India, Aadhaar, http://uidai.gov.in/. Accessed June 2015
13. Face Recognition Homepage. Source Codes. Accessed June 2015
14. J. Fierrez et al., BioSec baseline corpus: a multimodal biometric database. Pattern Recogn. **40**(4), 1389–1392 (2007)
15. J. Hämmerle-Uhl, E. Pschernig, A. Uhl, Cancelable iris biometrics using block re-mapping and image warping, in *Proceedings of 12th International Information Security Conference*, ed. by P. Samarati et al. vol. 5735. LNCS. (Springer, 2009), pp. 135–142
16. R. Hentati et al., Measuring the quality of IRIS segmentation for Improved IRIS recognition performance, in *2012 Eighth International Conference on Signal Image Technology and Internet Based Systems (SITIS)* (2012), pp. 110–117
17. R. Hentati, M. Abid, B. Dorizzi, Software implementation of the OSIRIS iris recognition algorithm in FPGA, in *2011 International Conference on Microelectronics (ICM)* (2011), pp. 1–5
18. H. Hofbauer et al., A ground truth for iris segmentation, in *2014 22nd International Conference on Pattern Recognition (ICPR)* (2014), pp. 527–532
19. Institute of Automation, Chinese Academy of Sciences (CASIA). Biometrics Ideal Test. Accessed June 2015
20. J. Kannala, E. Rahtu, BSIF: binarized statistical image features, in *IEEE International Conference on Pattern Recognition* (2012), pp. 1363–1366
21. K.P.H. Kevin, W. Bowyer, P.J. Flynn, A survey of iris biometrics research: 2008–2010, in *Handbook of Iris Recognition* (Springer, 2013), pp. 15–54
22. J.-G. Ko et al., A novel and efficient feature extraction method for iris recognition. ETRI J. **29**(3), 399–401 (2007)
23. E. Krichen et al., A biometric reference system for iris. OSIRIS version 4.1 (2013). Accessed June 2015
24. A. Kumar, A. Passi, Comparison and combination of iris matchers for reliable personal identification. Proc. CVPR **2008**, 21–27 (2008)
25. A. Kumar, A. Passi, Comparison and combination of iris matchers for reliable personal authentication. Pattern Recogn. **43**(3), 1016–1026 (2010)
26. Y. Lee et al., VASIR: an open-source research platform for advanced iris recognition technologies. J. Res. NIST **118**, 218–259 (2013). Accessed June 2015
27. D.G. Lowe, Distinctive image features from scale-invariant keypoints. Int. J. Comput. Vis. **60**(2), 91–110 (2004)
28. L. Ma et al., Efficient iris recognition by characterizing key local variations. IEEE Trans. Image Process. **13**(6), 739–750 (2004)
29. L. Masek, Recognition of human iris patterns for biometric identification, MA Thesis. University of Western Australia (2003)
30. D. Monro, S. Rakshit, D. Zhang, Iris challenge evaluation (2006)
31. D.M. Monro, S. Rakshit, D. Zhang, DCT-based iris recognition. IEEE Trans. Pattern Anal. Mach. Intell. **29**(4), 586–595 (2007)
32. J.C. Monteiro et al., MobBIO 2013: 1st biometric recognition with portable devices competition (2013)
33. T. Ojala, M. Pietikäinen, T. Mäenpää, Multiresolution gray-scale and rotation invariant texture classification with local binary patterns. IEEE Trans. Pattern Anal. Mach. Intell. **24**(7), 971–987 (2002)

34. U. Park, A. Ross, A. Jain, Periocular biometrics in the visible spectrum: a feasibility study, in *IEEE 3rd International Conference on Biometrics: Theory, Applications, and Systems, 2009. BTAS '09* (2009), pp. 1–6
35. U. Park et al., Periocular biometrics in the visible spectrum. IEEE Trans. Inf. Forensics Secur. **6**(1), 96–106 (2011)
36. P. Phillips, K. Bowyer, P.J. Flynn, Comments on the CASIA version 1.0 iris data set. IEEE Trans. Pattern Anal. Mach. Intell. **29**(10), 1869–1870 (2007)
37. P.J. Phillips et al., FRVT 2006 and ICE 2006 large-scale experimental results. IEEE Trans. Pattern Anal. Mach. Intell. **32**(5), 1–1 (2010)
38. H. Proenca et al., The UBIRIS.v2: a database of visible wavelength images captured on-the-move and at-a-distance. IEEE Trans. Pattern Anal. Mach. Intell. **32**(8), 1529–1535 (2010)
39. H. Proença, L. Alexandre, Toward covert iris biometric recognition: experimental results from the NICE contests. IEEE Trans. Inf. Forensics Secur. **7**(2), 798–808 (2012)
40. R. Rakvic et al., Parallelizing iris recognition. IEEE Trans. Inf. Forensics Secur. **4**(4), 812–823 (2009)
41. C. Rathgeb, A. Uhl, Secure iris recognition based on local intensity variations, in *Proceedings of the 7th International Conference on Image Analysis and Recognition—Volume Part II. ICIAR'10* (2010), pp. 266–275
42. C. Rathgeb, A. Uhl, P. Wild, *Iris Recognition: From Segmentation to Template Security*. Advances in Information Security, vol. 59 (Springer, 2013)
43. C. Rathgeb, A. Uhl, Context-based biometric key generation for Iris. IET Comput. Vis. **5**(6), 389–397 (2011)
44. E.S. Raymond, *The Cathedral and the Bazaar*, ed. by T. O'Reilly. 1st edn. (O'Reilly & Associates Inc., 1999)
45. A. Ross et al., Matching highly non-ideal ocular images: an information fusion approach, in *Proceedings of 5th International Conference on Biometrics* (2012)
46. A. Ross, Iris recognition: the path forward. IEEE Comput. **43**(2), 30–35 (2010)
47. F. Sakr, M. Taher, A.Wahba, High performance iris recognition system on GPU, in *Computer Engineering Systems (ICCES)* (2011), 237–242
48. R.M. Stallman, *Free Software, Free Society: Selected Essays of Richard M. Stallman*, ed. by J. Gay (2002)
49. G. Sutra, S. Garcia-Salicetti, B. Dorizzi, The Viterbi algorithm at different resolutions for enhanced iris segmentation, in *2012 5th IAPR International Conference on Biometrics (ICB)* (2012), pp. 310–316
50. A. Uhl, P. Wild, Combining face with face-part detectors under Gaussian assumption, in *Proceedings of 9th International Conference on Image Analysis and Recognition*, vol. 7325. LNCS, ed. by A. Campilho, M. Kamel (Springer, 2012), pp. 80–89
51. A. Uhl, P. Wild, Weighted adaptive hough and ellipsopolar transforms for real-time iris segmentation, in *Proceedings of 5th International Conference on Biometrics* (2012), pp. 1–8
52. C.J. van Rijsbergen, Information retrieval (Butterworth-Heinemann, 1979)
53. P. Vandewalle, J. Kovacevic, M. Vetterli, Reproducible research in signal processing. IEEE Signal Process. Mag. **26**(3), 37–47 (2009)
54. G. Yang et al., SIFT based iris recognition with normalization and enhancement. Int. J. Mach. Learn. Cybern. **4**(4), 401–407 (2013)
55. P.-F. Zhang, D.-S. Li, Q. Wang, A novel iris recognition method based on feature fusion, in *Proceedings of 2004 International Conference on Machine Learning and Cybernetics*, vol. 6 (2004), pp. 3661–3665

Chapter 17
Fusion of Face and Iris Biometrics

Ryan Connaughton, Kevin W. Bowyer and Patrick J. Flynn

Abstract This chapter presents a system which simultaneously acquires face and iris samples using a single sensor, with the goal of improving recognition accuracy while minimizing sensor cost and acquisition time. The resulting system improves recognition rates beyond the observed recognition rates for either isolated biometric.

17.1 Introduction

The practice of using more than one biometric modality, sample, sensor, or algorithm to achieve recognition, commonly referred to as *multi-biometrics*, is a technique that is rapidly gaining popularity. By incorporating multi-biometrics into the recognition process, many of the shortcomings of traditional single-biometric systems can be alleviated and overall recognition accuracy can be improved. Multi-biometrics can inherently increase system robustness by removing the dependency on one particular biometric approach. Further, a system that utilizes more than one biometric feature or matcher may be more difficult to deliberately spoof [16]. Systems that make use of multiple biometric features can also provide redundancy that may lower failure-to-acquire rates. Though multi-biometrics offers many potential advantages over traditional biometric systems, inefficient system design can greatly increase sensor cost, computation time, and data acquisition time.

While research into multi-biometrics has received a large increase in attention over recent years, the task of fusing multiple biometric modalities from a single sensor remains an understudied challenge. Due to a lack of available multi-modal data, many current experiments in multi-biometrics create "chimeric" datasets, in which

R. Connaughton (✉) · K.W. Bowyer · P.J. Flynn
University of Notre Dame, Notre Dame, IN, USA
e-mail: rconnaug@nd.edu

K.W. Bowyer
e-mail: kwb@cse.nd.edu

P.J. Flynn
e-mail: flynn@cse.nd.edu

© Springer-Verlag London 2016
K.W. Bowyer and M.J. Burge (eds.), *Handbook of Iris Recognition*,
Advances in Computer Vision and Pattern Recognition,
DOI 10.1007/978-1-4471-6784-6_17

397

samples of one biometric modality from one set of subjects are arbitrarily paired with a second biometric modality from a separate set of subjects in order to simulate a multi-biometric scenario [2]. This approach, though useful for preliminary experimentation, may mask unknown dependencies between modalities. Further, chimeric datasets simulate a multi-biometric scenario in which samples of each modality are acquired independently. In practice, it is much more desirable to simultaneously acquire multiple modalities from a single sensor if possible for cost and usability reasons.

This chapter presents a system which simultaneously acquires face and iris samples using a single sensor, with the goal of improving recognition accuracy while minimizing sensor cost and acquisition time. The resulting system improves recognition rates beyond the observed recognition rates for either isolated biometric.

17.2 Characteristics of Multi-biometric Systems

The term *multi-biometrics* encompasses a wide range of fusion techniques and its precise meaning is somewhat inconsistent in the literature [2, 17, 21]. In the simplest, traditional single-biometric system, one sensor images a particular body part (i.e., iris, face, or fingerprint) to produce a single image. The image is then processed and matched against a gallery using a specific algorithm to obtain a verification or identification result. A multi-biometric system aims to improve recognition rates (or address some other drawbacks of traditional systems) by providing redundancy at one or more of the steps in this recognition process.

In general, there are five types of multi-biometric systems [15]:

1. **Multi-Sample**: Multi-sample systems collect and process multiple images of the same biometric. Such systems benefit from some of the advantages of multi-biometrics, while minimizing sensor cost.
2. **Multi-Instance**: Similar to multi-sample, multi-instance systems collect and process images of several distinct instances of the same biometric trait. Examples of multi-sample systems include systems that consider multiple fingerprints or both irises for recognition. Alternatively, multi-instance systems may collect multiple images of the same trait with some controlled variation; for example, a system may collect face images with smiling and neutral expressions.
3. **Multi-sensor**: A multi-sensor system images the same biometric trait using more than one sensor. Multi-sensor systems may be considered implicitly multi-sample as well. The incorporation of multiple sensors naturally leads to an increase in system cost, but this approach may help to address a particular bias or shortcoming in a specific sensor by obtaining a cross-sensor consensus.
4. **Multi-algorithm**: Multi-algorithm systems use more than one matching algorithm on the same biometric sample and then fuse the results to improve system performance. Because this approach can make use of the same biometric sample for each matcher, multi-algorithm systems can be cost-effective and help to reduce algorithmic biases.

5. **Multi-modal**: Multi-modal systems consider more than one biometric trait, or modality, in the recognition process. Ko [7] suggests that multi-modal fusion benefits the most when the biometric modalities are orthogonal. Modalities can be considered orthogonal when the match performance of one modality does not predict the performance of the other. In the ideal scenario, all of the biometrics would be orthogonal, simultaneously imaged with the same sensor, and captured at high quality.

While these five classifications can be used to describe many multi-biometric approaches, there are naturally some systems which represent hybrids of more than one multi-biometric approach. Nonetheless, it is useful to have some method of categorizing multi-biometric systems, and understanding the advantages and disadvantages associated with each approach is crucial to good system design.

17.3 Levels of Fusion

In multi-biometric systems, the term *fusion* is often used to describe the process of combining information from more than one source in the recognition process. The previous section described the stages at which multi-biometric systems may use redundancy to improve performance; fusion is used to combine the results of the redundancy so that a single output can be produced. There are five levels at which fusion can occur in a multi-biometric system.

1. **Signal Level**: Using signal-level fusion, multiple samples may be combined together to create one superior sample. An example of signal fusion is a super-resolution technique which combines multiple images of the same iris to achieve a higher quality image.
2. **Feature Level**: In a system that uses feature-level fusion, matching features are first extracted from each biometric sample and fusion is used to condense all of the features into a single-biometric signature.
3. **Score Level**: With score-level fusion indexScore-level fusion, the match scores are combined to produce a final result. Examples include a multi-sample approach in which each sample is matched separately and the resulting scores are fused, or a multi-algorithm approach in which the same sample is matched using multiple matchers and the results of all of matchers are combined.
4. **Rank Level**: Similar to score-level fusion, rank-level fusion combines match rankings, rather than the actual scores, into a final ranking to determine the best match.
5. **Decision Level**: Decision-level fusion applies a matcher to each biometric sample (or the same matcher to multiple samples) to obtain a Boolean response indicating whether or not each comparison is a match. The outputs are then fused using Boolean operators, a voting scheme, or some similar method.

It has been suggested in literature that systems which incorporate fusion at an early stage of the recognition process (e.g., signal or feature-level fusion) have the potential to be more effective than systems which use fusion later in the pipeline [16]. Despite this, many researchers believe that score-level fusion offers the best trade-off between potential performance gain and ease of implementation [11].

17.4 Related Work

The fusion of face and iris modalities is a biometric approach that has gained increasing attention over the past decade, likely due to the popularity of the individual modalities, as well as the natural connection between them. Despite this recent trend, very few studies have been done on fusion of face and iris biometrics from a single sensor.

The most common method of multi-biometric fusion is score-level fusion. Zhang et al. approach the problem of fusing face and iris biometrics under near-infrared lighting using a single sensor [24]. Frontal face images are acquired using a 10 megapixel CCD camera. Eye detection and face alignment are performed using Local Bit Pattern histogram matching as described in Li et al. [9]. The eigenface algorithm and Daugman's algorithm are used to perform face and iris recognition, respectively, and score-level fusion is accomplished via the sum and product rules after min–max normalization. Numerous other score-level fusion approaches have been tested on chimeric datasets. Chen and Te Chu use an unweighted average of the outputs of matchers based on neural networks [4]. Wang et al. test weighted average, linear discriminant analysis, and neural networks for score fusion [22].

Another common approach to biometric fusion is feature-level fusion through concatenation. Rattani and Tistarelli compute SIFT features for chimeric face and iris images and concatenate the resulting feature vectors [14]. The number of matching SIFT features between two vectors (measured by Euclidean distance) is used as a match score for that comparison. Son and Lee extract features for face and iris images based on a Daubechies wavelet transform [18]. Concatenation is used to form a joint feature vector, and Euclidean distance between feature vectors is used to generate match scores.

The Multiple Biometrics Grand Challenge (MBGC) provided a collection of face and iris data to researchers in order to provide a standard test bed for comparing matching and fusion techniques [12, 13]. The MBGC data included a subset of the near-infrared videos used in the experiments being presented in this chapter, as well as face stills, high-quality color face video, iris stills, and iris video. In general, results showed that fusion of face and iris biometrics offered improved accuracy over either biometric alone. The near-infrared videos released as part of the MBGC are also used by Yang et al. [23]. Yang et al. investigate the use of SIFT features to perform alignment between the partial faces present in the dataset in order to facilitate face matching, but do not incorporate these results into a multi-biometric experiment.

The work presented in this chapter differs from previous work in the fusion of face and iris biometrics in several facets. First, this chapter uses only genuine multi-modal data, rather than chimeric data for experimentation. Additionally, the fusion is accomplished using a single sensor. Though Zhang et al. also use a single sensor, the authors also manually acquire each image to guarantee high-quality face and iris samples. In the experiments presented in this chapter, an on-the-move and at-distance sensor is used to acquire data for a high-throughput scenario. The resulting dataset consists of a much wider range of sample quality with incomplete data for some subjects, making the dataset a practical but challenging test bed for fusion experiments. These experiments also differ from work presented on the MBGC data; the near-infrared videos used in the MBGC dataset were manually selected to guarantee the presence of a subject in the field of view, whereas in the experiments shown in this chapter, this process is done automatically. Finally, this work uses multi-modal, multi-sample, and multi-instance approaches to improve system accuracy and robustness.

17.5   Approach

To facilitate the fusion of face and iris biometrics from a single sensor, the Iris on the Move (IOM) sensor was selected for data acquisition. The IOM shown in Fig. 17.1 is a sensor designed for high-throughput stand-off iris recognition [10].

Fig. 17.1 Picture of the Iris on the Move Sensor designed by Sarnoff Corporation. The IOM was used for all probe data collection. Picture reprinted from [1] with permission from Elsevier

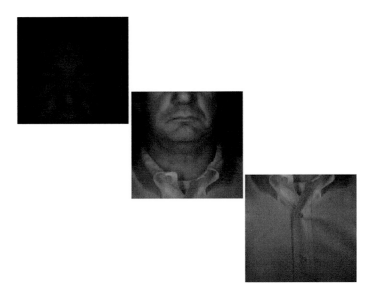

Fig. 17.2 Example of corresponding frames from the IOM as the subject passes through the in-focus region of the portal. The *left* image shows a frame from the *top* camera, the *middle* image shows a frame from the *middle* camera, and the *right* shows a frame from the *bottom* camera

The IOM features a portal which subjects walk through at normal walking pace. As a subject passes through the portal, the subject is illuminated with near-infrared (NIR) LEDs, and frontal video is captured by an array of three vertically arranged, fixed-focus cameras equiped with NIR filters. The presence of multiple cameras allows the system to handle a larger range of subject heights, and the sensor can be extended to include more than three cameras to support an even larger range of subject heights. Though the sensor is intended for iris image acquisition, the face is typically captured as well. While the sides of the portal help to direct subjects into the field of view of the cameras, it is possible for subjects to stray partially out of the video frames, leading to frames with partial faces or only one iris visible. Figure 17.2 shows corresponding frames from each of the three IOM cameras while a subject passes through the in-focus region of the IOM. Each frame captured by one of the IOM cameras is a 2048 by 2048 pixel grayscale image. A typical iris acquired by the system is approximately 120 pixels in diameter.

The general steps used in this work to combine face and iris biometrics from the IOM sensor are outlined in Fig. 17.3. As previously described, when a subject passes through the IOM portal, three videos are collected, with one video coming from each of the IOM cameras. In a preprocessing step, the corresponding frames of the three videos are stitched together to create one virtual video. Next, a series of detection phases are used to locate whole faces and eyes in each frame. Matching is then performed on each face sample and iris sample independently, and the results are fused using several different techniques.

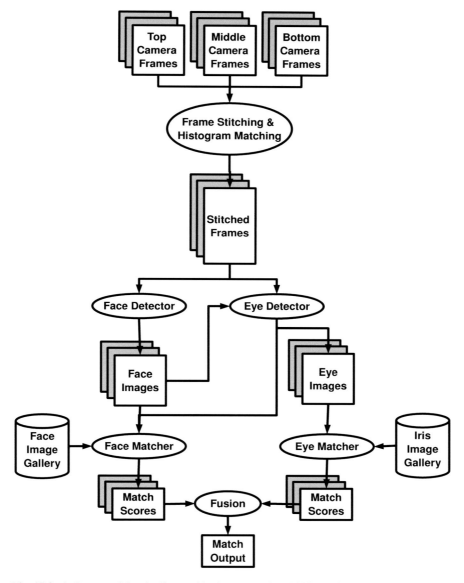

Fig. 17.3 A diagram of the pipeline used in the proposed multi-biometric system

17.5.1 Preprocessing

In order to increase the likelihood of a whole face being captured for each subject, the three videos from each IOM acquisition are "stitched" together to combine corresponding frames. As can be seen in Fig. 17.2, there is significant vertical overlap

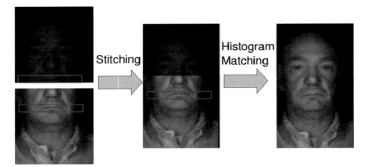

Fig. 17.4 An example of the progression during alignment between corresponding frames from the *top* and *middle* camera. The *top left* image is the frame from the *top* camera with the template marked as a *rectangle*. The *bottom left* image is the frame from the *middle* camera, with the matched region indicated. The *middle* image is the composite image, with the frame from the *top* camera cropped and padded. The overlapping region is indicated. The *right* image shows the final stitching results after histogram matching. A similar approach is used to stitch the frame from the *bottom* camera to the *middle* frame

between the top and middle cameras, as well as between the middle and bottom cameras. Due to imperfect calibration of the individual cameras, some horizontal misalignment between the cameras is also present.

A template matching approach is taken to determine the desired translation to align frames from adjacent cameras. Specifically, the bottom portion of the top frame is cropped and used as a template. This template is then matched against the upper half of the middle frame, and the best match is selected as the desired alignment. This process is repeated for the bottom camera, where the template is created from the top portion of the bottom frame and matched against the lower half of the middle frame.

Finally, noticeable illumination differences were observed between corresponding frames from different cameras. To account for this discrepancy, histogram matching is used to match the top and bottom frame to the illumination observed in the middle frame. Figure 17.4 shows the intermediate and final results of the stitching procedure for an example frame.

17.5.2   Face Detection

Once the frame stitching is completed, the next step in the preprocessing phase is to detect a face in each frame. To accomplish this task, the OpenCV implementation of the Viola-Jones cascade face detector is used [3, 20]. The detector was trained on whole faces, and thus may or may not detect faces which lie only partially within the field of view of the camera.

17.5.3 Eye Detection

The purpose of the eye detection phase is twofold. The primary goal is to detect any eyes present in each frame for iris matching. However, the locations of the eyes that are detected in the faces produced by the face detector are also used for an alignment phase during face matching. A template matching approach is adopted for eye detection. The template used to search for eyes in each frame is based on the specular highlights generated by the reflection of the IOM LEDs.

The eye detection is completed in two phases. First, the template matching is performed on the upper left and upper right quadrants of each face detected by the face detector. This approach guarantees that each detected face will have two eye locations estimated as well.

Because it is possible for eyes to be detected in frames where whole faces were not present (or in frames where the face detector failed to detect the face), a second round of template matching is performed on any stitched frame where a face was not detected. In these frames, the location of the partial face can be crudely estimated by computing the sums of the rows and columns of the image and comparing these sums to appropriate thresholds. This partial face detection step is not required, but reduces the likelihood of false eye detections by limiting the search space to the region of the image that is likely to contain the eyes. An example of a face region being estimated in this manner is shown in Fig. 17.5. Once the partial face region has been estimated, the template matching is performed twice to identify the two best eye locations. Finally, the detected eyes are cropped from the corresponding location in the *original* frames to remove any possible artifacts caused by the histogram matching in the stitching phase. In cases where the detected eye is located in the overlapping region between two cameras, the eye is cropped from *both* camera frames.

17.5.4 Face Matching

In this work, Colorado State University's implementation of the eigenface algorithm is used for face matching [5, 19]. To achieve alignment with the training set, the probe face images are normalized using the eye centers detected by the eye detector. The Mahalanobis cosine metric is used to compute the distance between two feature vectors. Using this metric, match scores can range from -1.0 to 1.0, with -1.0 being a perfect score. The output of the face matcher stage of the pipeline is a distance for every comparison between each probe face image and gallery face image.

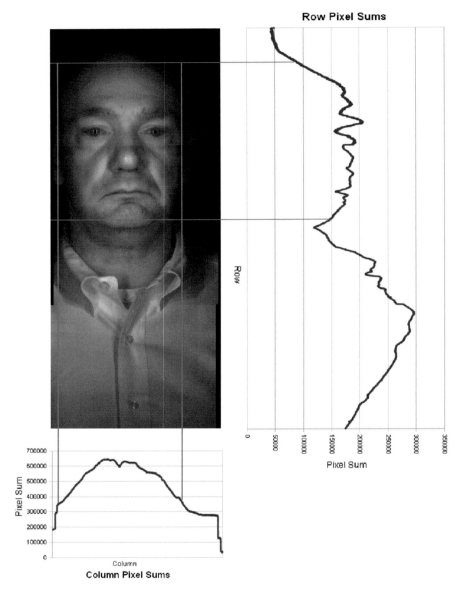

Fig. 17.5 Example of the image projection technique used to estimate the location of the face during eye detection. The graphs on the *right* and *bottom* of the image represent the summations of the pixel values in each row or column, respectively. The projected lines represent the face boundaries determined using appropriate thresholds

17.5.5 Iris Matching

For the iris matcher, a modified version of Daugman's algorithm is used to compare each probe iris image to the gallery [6]. The normalized fractional Hamming distance, referred to simply as the Hamming distance in the rest of this work, ranges from 0.0 to 1.0, with 0.0 being a perfect match. The Hamming distance is normalized to adjust low Hamming distances that occur for comparisons that used relatively few bits. The output of the iris matcher stage of the pipeline is a Hamming distance for every comparison between each probe eye image and gallery iris image.

17.5.6 Fusion

In this framework, the problem is multi-sample (i.e., several faces from each video), multi-modal (i.e., both iris and face samples from each video), and multi-instance (i.e., both left and right irises from each video). Consequently, there are many methods which could be used to combine the face and iris biometrics from each video. Several fusion techniques are considered at both the score and rank level.

The first method considers only one biometric modality in the fusion process, and makes use only of the multi-sample and multi-instance dimensions of the problem by taking the minimum score for a given modality. For example, in the MinIris approach, the minimum score for all of the iris comparisons from a given video is reported as the best match. Similarly, the MinFace approach takes the minimum score for all of the face comparisons from a given video to determine the best match. Equations 17.1 and 17.2 express the MinIris and MinFace fusion rules, respectively, for a given probe video,

$$\text{MinIris} = \text{Min}\{I_{i,j} | i = 1, \dots n, j = 1 \dots G\} \qquad (17.1)$$

$$\text{MinFace} = \text{Min}\{F_{i,j} | i = 1 \dots m, j = 1 \dots G\} \qquad (17.2)$$

where n and m are the number of irises and faces detected in the video, respectively, G is the number of gallery subjects, $I_{i,j}$ is the Hamming distance between the i-th iris and the j-th gallery subject, and $F_{i,j}$ is the score for the comparison between the i-th face and the j-th gallery subject.

The next type of fusion method considered is rank-level fusion, and can incorporate face, iris, or both modalities into the decision process. A Borda count is used to determine a best match across the desired biometric modalities. In a Borda count, the scores for all comparisons from a given sample are sorted such that the first rank corresponds to the best score for that sample. Each sample then casts votes for the top v ranked subjects, where the weight of each vote is inversely proportionate to rank number. Each sample votes in this manner, and the gallery subject with the most votes is taken to be the best match. In these experiments, the BordaIris method considers only the iris scores to perform fusion, and the BordaFace method considers only face scores. The BordaBoth method allows both face and iris samples to vote, with v votes being cast by each iris and face sample.

Two vote weighting schemes are tested for the BordaIris, BordaFace, and BordaBoth fusion methods. In the Linear approach, the vote weight is linearly proportional to the rank; specifically, the weight associated with the rank-n match is described by the equation

$$\text{VoteWeight}_n = v + 2 - n \tag{17.3}$$

and v represents the total number of votes cast by each biometric sample. In the Exponential approach, the weight of the vote is exponentially related to the rank. Specifically, the weight associated with the rank-n match is described by the equation

$$\text{VoteWeight}_n = 2^{v-n} \tag{17.4}$$

The third fusion method again uses score-level fusion, implementing a weighted summation of the iris and face scores. The summation rule can be expressed as Eq. 17.5 for a given probe video,

$$\text{SumScore}_k = \frac{\alpha * \sum_{i=1}^{n} (1 - \text{FNorm}_{i,k}) + \beta * \sum_{j=1}^{m} (1 - \text{INorm}_{j,k})}{\alpha * n + \beta * m} \tag{17.5}$$

where n and m are the number of irises and faces detected in the video, respectively, $\text{INorm}_{j,k}$ is the normalized Hamming distance between the j-th iris and the k-th gallery subject, and $\text{FNorm}_{i,k}$ is the normalized score for the comparison between the i-th face and the k-th gallery subject. Each face and iris score is normalized using min–max normalization, according to the expression

$$\text{Score}' = \frac{\text{Score} - \text{Min}}{\text{Max} - \text{Min}} \tag{17.6}$$

where Min and Max are the minimum and maximum possible values for each score metric, so that all normalized scores fall between 0.0 and 1.0, with 1.0 representing a perfect match. In Eq. 17.5, α and β are coefficients used to weight the face and iris biometrics, respectively. In the presented work, $\alpha = 1 - \beta$ for simplicity. In Eq. 17.5, SumScore_k represents the final match score for the given probe video with gallery subject k; the best match score can be determined by finding the maximum SumScore_k for all k. SumIris is the special case where $\alpha = 0$ and $\beta = 1$, which corresponds to summing only the iris scores to determine the best match. Similarly, SumFace is the case where $\alpha = 1$ and $\beta = 0$, and equates to summing only the normalized face scores.

17.6   Experiments

The previously described multi-biometric system was tested on a probe dataset of 1,886 IOM video sets. Note that here a video "set" refers to the corresponding videos from each of the three IOM cameras, so the dataset is comprised of 5,658 videos in total. The 1,886 videos spanned 363 unique subjects, with an average of about five videos per subject. The most frequently occurring probe subject had 15 videos in the probe set, and the least frequently occurring had one probe video.

The iris gallery contained one left eye and one right eye for each of the 363 gallery subjects. The gallery images were acquired using the LG IrisAccess 4000 (LG4000) [8], a high-quality iris acquisition camera, and the gallery was manually screened for good quality and segmentation. For comparison, Fig. 17.6 shows an example of an image of the same iris acquired from both the LG4000 and the IOM.

The face gallery contained one full face image for each of the 363 subjects. The gallery images were acquired using the IOM. Each of the 363 subjects in the study had an additional IOM video set acquired in which the presence of a whole face was verified manually. The frames were stitched using the process previously described, and then the best frame was manually selected and the coordinates of the eye centers were manually annotated for alignment. The PCA training was performed on the face image gallery.

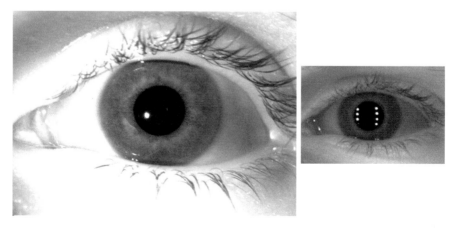

Fig. 17.6   Images of the same iris image using the LG4000 (*left*) and the IOM (*right*). The IOM image shown on the *right* represents a well-focused IOM iris image

17.6.1 Detection Results

Across the entire dataset, 14,829 left irises and 14,711 right irises were detected and successfully segmented, and 9,833 faces were detected with valid eye locations for alignment. In this context, "successful segmentation" simply means that the iris segmentation routine returned pupil and limbic boundaries; it does *not* guarantee correctness. On average, 15.7 ($\sigma = 8.1$) irises, 5.2 ($\sigma = 3.7$) faces, and 20.9 ($\sigma = 20.9$) of either biometric samples were found in each video.

Table 17.1 provides a breakdown of the detection results by frame and video. The 1,886 videos were composed of a total of 28,381 frames. From Table 17.1 it can be seen that while a large number of frames (44.1 %) contained no detected features, a much larger percentage of the probe *videos* (99.3 %) had at least one biometric feature detected. Further, the majority (80.6 %) of the probe videos contained samples of face and both iris features.

17.6.2 Matching Results

Figure 17.7 shows the match and non-match score distributions for all 9,833 detected faces. The mean match score was -0.281 with a standard deviation of 0.213, while the mean non-match score was 0.000 with a standard deviation of 0.676. If each face were treated independently, the rank-one recognition achieved for the 9,833 probes faces would be 51.6 % (5,073/9,833) recognition.

The results from the left and right irises were aggregated, and Fig. 17.8 shows the match and non-match score distributions. The mean match score was 0.398 with a standard deviation of 0.053, while the mean non-match score was 0.449 with a standard deviation of 0.013. Figure 17.8 shows a significant number of match comparisons with fairly high scores. Upon examination of the data, it was found that most of these scores arise from incorrect segmentation. In some cases, these high match scores were caused by severe image defocus. Additionally, there are some false

Table 17.1 Detailed detection results

Modalities detected	Frame count	Video count
Left iris (only)	1,447 (5.1 %)	35 (1.9 %)
Right iris (only)	2,104 (7.4 %)	46 (2.4 %)
Face (only)	900 (3.2 %)	2 (0.1 %)
Left and right irises (only)	2,495 (8.8 %)	209 (11.1 %)
Face and left iris (only)	1,411 (5.0 %)	34 (1.8 %)
Face and right iris (only)	724 (2.6 %)	27 (1.4 %)
Face, left, and right irises	6,798 (24.0 %)	1,522 (80.6 %)
None	12,502 (44.1 %)	11 (0.6 %)

Fig. 17.7 The match and
non-match score
distributions for the face
features from the entire
probe dataset

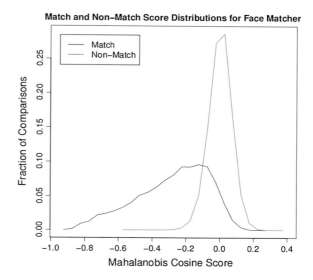

Fig. 17.8 The match and
non-match score
distributions for the *left* and
right iris features from the
entire probe dataset

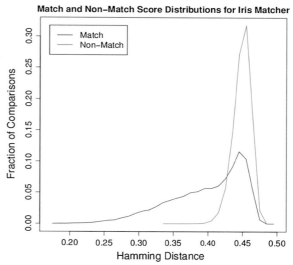

positives from the eye detector (non-eye regions) that contain features that resemble pupil and limbic boundaries according to the segmentation routine. If each iris image were treated independently, the rank-one recognition achieved for all of the probe irises would be 46.6% (13,556/29,112) recognition.

17.6.3   *Fusion Results*

The results of the iris and face matchers were combined using each of the methods previously described. The rank-one recognition rates achieved by each fusion approach are shown in Table 17.2. In the fusion methods based on Borda-counts, the number of votes given to each sample was varied between 1 and 363 (though all samples were given the same number of votes for any given fusion experiment), and the best results for each approach are presented. Similarly, results from the optimal tested values of α and β are presented.

Summarizing, the best single-modality fusion approach was the SumIris approach, which achieved an 87.8 % rank-one recognition rate. The SumBoth approach achieved the overall highest recognition rate (93.2 %), and all multi-modal fusion approaches achieved higher recognition rates than the fusion methods based on a single modality.

Figure 17.9 shows the ROC curves for the best SumBoth and BordaBoth approaches, as well as the MinIris, MinFace, SumFace, and SumIris results for comparison. From this graph, it is clear that the BordaBoth and SumBoth approaches outperform the single-modality fusion methods. Interestingly, while SumBoth achieved the highest rank-one recognition rate, Fig. 17.9 shows that the BordaBoth fusion technique performs better at false positive rates less than 0.06.

In general, the videos that failed to match correctly typically had relatively few face and iris features detected. While the iris proved to be the more accurate of the two modalities in the multi-sample fusion scenarios, Fig. 17.8 indicates that many of the iris features detected are of poor quality, represent false detections from the eye detector, or failed to segment correctly. While the fusion techniques in these experiments were able to overcome these challenges when enough samples were present, videos in which a small number of faces and iris are detected are much less likely to be correctly matched.

Table 17.2 Rank-one recognition rates for fusion approaches

Approach	Fusion parameters	Rank-one (Raw)
MinIris		86.7 % (1,635/1,886)
MinFace		62.6 % (1,180/1,886)
BordaIris-Linear	$v = 3$	86.4 % (1,629/1,886)
BordaIris-Exponential	$v = 20$	86.8 % (1,637/1,886)
BordaFace-Linear	$v = 3$	58.9 % (1,110/1,886)
BordaFace-Exponential	$v = 5$	59.3 % (1,118/1,886)
BordaBoth-Linear	$v = 10$	91.7 % (1,729/1,886)
BordaBoth-Exponential	$v = 10$	92.0 % (1,735/1,886)
SumIris	$\alpha = 0.0, \beta = 1.0$	87.8 % (1,656/1,886)
SumFace	$\alpha = 1.0, \beta = 0.0$	61.3 % (1,156/1,886)
SumBoth	$\alpha = 0.3, \beta = 0.7$	93.2 % (1,757/1,886)

Fig. 17.9 ROC curves for the various fusion methods using the optimal tested parameters for each. The BordaBoth method shown is the BordaBoth-Exponential method

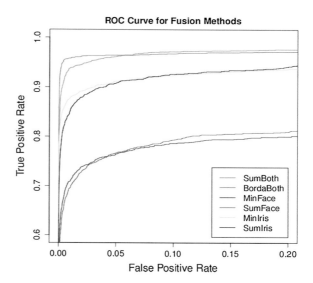

17.7   Conclusions

This chapter presents an investigation into the fusion of face and iris biometrics from a single sensor, a surprisingly understudied problem in current literature. The previously described multi-biometrics framework utilizes multi-sample, multi-instance, and multi-modal fusion techniques to improve recognition rates from a single sensor. The multi-biometric system is tested on a non-chimeric dataset of over 1,886 videos spanning 363 subjects. This represents one of the largest genuine multi-modal experiments that has been conducted to date. Face and iris biometric samples extracted from videos produced from the Iris on the Move sensor were combined using several different fusion methods. In these experiments, the combination of face and iris biometrics via match score summation yielded a 5.4 % increase in recognition rate over the best single-modality approach that was tested, while a modified Borda count approach performed best at lower false positive rates (<0.06).

The multi-biometrics system proposed exploits the face information collected by the IOM, a sensor that is intended for iris recognition purposes, with no modifications to the sensor and no increase in probe data acquisition time. The resulting system is less likely to experience failures to acquire, and the use of multiple modalities could allow the system to identify subjects with incomplete gallery data. This approach could be extended to operate on other stand-off iris sensors, which often detect the face as a preliminary step to iris image acquisition.

Acknowledgments Datasets used in this work were acquired under funding from the National Science Foundation under grant CNS01-30839, by the Central Intelligence Agency, and by the Technical Support Working Group under US Army Contract W91CRB-08-C-0093. The authors were supported by a grant from the Intelligence Advanced Research Projects Activity.

References

1. K.W. Bowyer, K. Hollingsworth, P.J. Flynn, Image understanding for iris biometrics: a survey. Comput. Vis. Image Underst. **110**(3), 281–307 (2008)
2. K.W. Bowyer et al., Multi-modal biometrics: an overview. Presented at the Second Workshop on Multi-Modal User Authentication (MMUA 2006) (2006)
3. G. Bradski, A. Kaehler, *Learning OpenCV*, ed. by M. Loukides (O'Reilly Media, Inc., 2008)
4. C.-H. Chen, C. Te Chu, Fusion of face and iris features for multimodal biometrics, in *Advances in Biometrics* ed. by D. Zhang, A. Jain. Lecture Notes in Computer Science, vol. 3832 (Springer Berlin/Heidelberg, 2005), pp. 571–580
5. Colorado State University, Evaluation of Face Recognition Algorithms (2010)
6. J. Daugman, *High Confidence Visual Recognition of Persons* (1993), pp. 1148–1161
7. T. Ko, Multimodal biometric identification for large user population using fingerprint, face and iris recognition, in *34th Applied Imagery and Pattern Recognition Workshop* (Dec 2005), pp. 218–223
8. LG Iris, LG Iris products and solutions (2010)
9. S.Z. Li et al., Highly accurate and fast face recognition using near infrared images, in *International Conference on Biometrics (ICB 2006)* (2006), pp. 151–158
10. J. Matey et al., Iris on the move: acquisition of images for iris recognition in less constrained environments. Proc. IEEE **94**(11), 1936–1947 (2006)
11. N. Morizet, J. Gilles, A new adaptive combination approach to score level fusion for face and iris biometrics combining wavelets and statistical moments, in *Advances in Visual Computing*, ed. by G. Bebis et al. Lecture Notes in Computer Science, vol. 5359 (Springer, Berlin/Heidelberg, 2008), pp. 661–671
12. National Institute of Standards and Technology (NIST), Portal Challenge Problem—Multiple Biometric Grand Challenge, Preliminary Results of Version 2 (2009)
13. P.J. Phillips et al., Overview of the multiple biometrics grand challenge, in *Proceedings of the Third International Conference on Advances in Biometrics, ICB '09* (Springer-Verlag, Berlin, Heidelberg, 2009), pp. 705–714
14. A. Rattani, M. Tistarelli, Robust multi-modal and multi-unit feature level fusion of face and iris biometrics, in *Advances in Biometrics*, ed. by M. Tistarelli, M. Nixon. Lecture Notes in Computer Science, vol. 5558 (Springer, Berlin/Heidelberg, 2009), pp. 960–969
15. A. Ross, An introduction to multibiometrics, in *15th European Signal Processing Conference (EUSIPCO)*, Poznan, Poland (Sept 2007), pp. 20–24
16. A.A. Ross, K. Nandakumar, A.K. Jain, *Handbook of Multibiometrics* (Springer Science and Business Media, 2006)
17. A. Ross, A.K. Jain, Multimodal biometrics: an overview, in *12th European Signal Processing Conference (EUSIPCO)*, Vienna, Austria (2004), pp. 1221–1224
18. B. Son, Y. Lee, Biometric authentication system using reduced joint feature vector of iris and face, in *6th International Conference on Audio- and Video-Based Biometric Person Authentication (AVBPA'03)*, ed. by T. Kanade, A. Jain, N. Ratha. Lecture Notes in Computer Science, vol. 3546. (Springer, Berlin/Heidelberg, 2005), pp. 513–522
19. M. Turk, A. Pentland, Face recognition using eigenfaces, in *IEEE Computer Society Conference on Computer Vision and Pattern Recognition (CVPR '91)*, June 1991, pp. 586–591
20. P. Viola, M. Jones, Rapid object detection using a boosted cascade of simple features, in *2001 IEEE Computer Society Conference on Computer Vision and Pattern Recognition (CVPR 2001)*, vol. 1 (2001), pp. 511–518
21. R. Volner, P. Bores, Multi-biometric techniques, standards activities and experimenting, in *International Baltic Electronics Conference* (Oct. 2006), pp. 1–4
22. Y. Wang, T. Tan, A.K. Jain, Combining face and iris biometrics for identity verification, in *4th International Conference on Audioand Video-Based Biometric Person Authentication (AVBPA'03)* (Springer, Berlin, Heidelberg, 2003), pp. 805–813

23. J. Yang, S. Liao, S. Li, Automatic partial face alignment in NIR video sequences, in *Advances in Biometrics*, ed. by M. Tistarelli, M. Nixon. Lecture Notes in Computer Science, vol. 5558. (Springer, Berlin/Heidelberg, 2009), pp. 249–258
24. Z. Zhang et al., Fusion of near infrared face and iris biometrics, in *Advances in Biometrics*, ed. by S.-W. Lee, S. Li. Lecture Notes in Computer Science, vol. 4642. (Springer, Berlin/Heidelberg, 2007), pp. 172–180

Chapter 18
A Theoretical Model for Describing Iris Dynamics

Antwan Clark, Scott Kulp, Isom Herron and Arun A. Ross

Abstract We present a theoretical approach using what we know about tissue dynamics to explore the nonlinear dynamics of iris deformation. Current iris recognition algorithms assume a simple transformation to approximate the deformation of the iris tissue. Furthermore, current research work on iris deformation does not take into account the mechanical properties of the iris tissue nor the cause of deformation from the iris muscle activity. By looking at the tissue dynamics, we are able to gain a more comprehensive understanding of this deformation process. The results of this research work can potentially be leveraged into existing iris recognition systems.

18.1 Introduction

Biometrics is the science of recognizing individuals based on the physical or behavioral attributes of an individual such as fingerprints, face, iris, voice, gait, and signature [9]. The deployment of biometric systems in several identity management and access control systems ranging from laptops to border security has demonstrated the potential of using biometrics for human recognition. Iris recognition systems, in particular, are gaining interest because the iris's rich texture offers a strong biometric cue for recognizing individuals [19]. Located just behind the cornea and in front of

A. Clark
West Virginia University, Morgantown, WV, USA
e-mail: aclark.biometrics@gmail.com

S. Kulp (✉)
Climate Central, Princeton, NJ, USA
e-mail: sckulp@cs.rutgers.edu

I. Herron (✉)
Rensselaer Polytechnic Institute, Troy, NY, USA
e-mail: herroi@rpi.edu

A.A. Ross (✉)
Integrated Pattern Recognition and Biometrics Lab (i-PRoBe),
Michigan State University, East Lansing, MI, USA
e-mail: arun.ross@mail.wvu.edu

© Springer-Verlag London 2016
K.W. Bowyer and M.J. Burge (eds.), *Handbook of Iris Recognition*,
Advances in Computer Vision and Pattern Recognition,
DOI 10.1007/978-1-4471-6784-6_18

417

the lens, the iris uses the dilator and sphincter muscles that govern pupil size to control the amount of light that enters the eye. Near-infrared (NIR) images of the iris's anterior surface exhibit complex patterns that computer systems can use to recognize individuals. Because NIR lighting can penetrate the iris's surface, it can reveal the intricate texture details that are present even in dark-colored irides. The iris's textural complexity and its variation across eyes have led scientists to postulate that the iris is unique across individuals. Further, the iris is the only internal organ readily visible from the outside. Thus, unlike fingerprints or palm prints, environmental effects cannot easily alter its pattern.

The history of iris recognition dates back to 1936, but was revolutionized in the mid-1990s when Daugman [3] developed an algorithm to automate the process of iris recognition. Most iris recognition systems consist of five basic modules leading to a decision [19]:

1. The *acquisition* module obtains a 2D image of the eye using a monochromatic CCD camera sensitive to the NIR light spectrum.
2. The *segmentation* module localizes the iris's spatial extent in the eye image by isolating it from other structures in its vicinity, such as the sclera, pupil, eyelids, and eyelashes. Typically, a variant of the integro-differential operator is used for this purpose (Fig. 18.1).
3. The *normalization* module invokes a geometric normalization scheme to transform the segmented iris image from Cartesian coordinates to polar coordinates.
4. The *encoding* module uses a feature extraction routine to produce a binary code.
5. The *matching* module determines how closely the produced code matches the encoded features stored in the database.

The role of the normalization module is to convert the localized iris from a near-circular entity to a rectangular entity. The process, often called iris unwrapping, has three advantages:

1. It accounts for variations in pupil size due to changes in external illumination that might influence iris size.
2. It ensures that the irides of different individuals are mapped onto a common image domain in spite of the variations in pupil size across subjects.

Fig. 18.1 Iris segmentation using an integro-differential operator. *White lines* are used to denote the output of the *circle* fitting algorithm

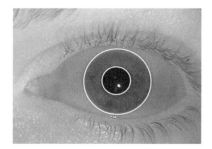

3. It enables iris registration during the matching stage through a simple translation operation that can account for in-plane eye and head rotations.

The normalization module, denoted by $I(x(r, \theta), y(r, \theta)) \longmapsto I(r, \theta)$, is given by the following transformation:

$$x(r, \theta) = (1 - r)x_p(\theta) + rx_l(\theta) \qquad (18.1)$$
$$y(r, \theta) = (1 - r)y_p(\theta) + ry_l(\theta)$$

where (x_p, y_p) and (x_l, y_l) correspond to the Cartesian coordinates of the pupil and limbus boundary respectively. Figure 18.2 denotes the normalization process. After applying (18.1) to normalize the dilation effects, encoding is performed (typically using Gabor wavelets) in order to convert the information in the iris texture to a bit sequence used for comparison. Current commercial systems use Daugman's algorithms, which has demonstrated good matching accuracy on large datasets. However, there still exist challenges in iris recognition, including the effect of varying levels of pupil dilation. Recently, researchers showed that changes in pupil dilation have the potential to degrade iris recognition performance. Hence, there is a need to explore ways to counteract iris deformation caused by pupil dilation.

18.1.1   Related Work

The problem of pupil dilation and iris deformation has recently been explored and noted by researchers in biometrics as well as other areas. In their work, Ma et al.

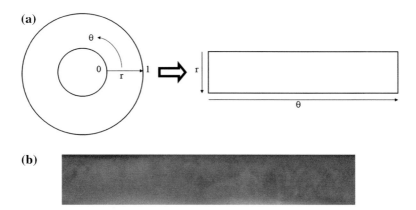

Fig. 18.2 Iris normalization. **a** The normalization routine converts the pixel coordinates in the annular region between the pupillary and limbus boundaries to pseudo-polar coordinates. This addresses the problem of variations in pupil size across multiple images. **b** Example of a normalized iris

noticed that there were a number of false non-matches due to pupil dilation. Later, Thornton et al. [21] took pupil dilation into account in their work by using Bayesian estimation to recover the level of iris deformation. Their results illustrated that estimating the level of iris deformation leads to an improvement in iris recognition performance. In addition, Wei et al. [23] attempted to consider the effects of pupil dilation by modeling the nonlinear iris stretch as the sum of a linear stretch and Gaussian deviation term. Hollingsworth et al. [8] investigated this problem further by conducting experiments that demonstrated the impact of varying degrees of pupil dilation on iris recognition performance.

Pupil dilation has been explored in other fields to including mathematical biology and, more recently, computer graphics. Previous research has shown that in addition to changes in light intensity pupil motion is also dictated by levels of consciousness; focal length; heart rate; respiration; emotional factors; disease; and drug use. However, physiological models were created by taking variations of illumination into account since there is a large amount of data supporting this factor. Modeling pupil dynamics began with empirical studies based on varying ambient light intensity. One of the famous models is due to Moon and Spence [13] who proposed the following model based on experimental data:

$$D = 4.9 - 3\tanh(0.4(\log_{10}(L_b - 0.5))) \qquad (18.2)$$

where D is the pupil diameter (expressed in mm) and L_b is the background luminance (expressed in *Blondels*). Later, it was realized that it is necessary to explore the pupil dynamics in order to understand the changes in pupil size given the varying levels of illumination. Therefore, more experimental studies have been conducted to explore this effect rather than simply relying on changes in pupil size. Ellis [4] performed experiments to determine the average latency as well as the maximum constriction and dilation velocities of the pupil for a given light intensity. As a result, he found that the latency τ (expressed in *ms*) can be described as

$$\tau(L_{cd}) = 445.7 - 22.9L_{cd} + 76.2L_{cd}^2 \qquad (18.3)$$

and the constriction V_c and dilation V_d velocities (expressed in *mm/s*), respectively, can be described as:

$$V_c(L_{cd}) = 0.15 + 2.0L_{cd} - 0.17L_{cd}^2 \qquad (18.4)$$

and

$$V_d(L_{cd}) = 0.16 + 0.72L_{cd} - 0.07L_{cd}^2. \qquad (18.5)$$

In Eqs. (18.3), (18.4), and (18.5) the variable L_{cd} represents the intensity of the light measured in *candelas/m²*. Furthermore Link and Stark [11] empirically determined the pupillary latency, the time delay between the light pulse reaching the retina and the beginning of the pupillary reaction, which yields the following equation:

$$\tau(R, L_{fL}) = 253 - 14\ln(L_{fL}) + 70R - 29R\ln(L_{fL}) \tag{18.6}$$

where τ is the latency in ms, L_{fL} is the luminance in $foot - Lambert$, and R is the frequency in Hz.

From the empirical models came the physiologically based models derived from the physiological and anatomical observations without the reliance on experimental data. Usui and Stark [22] developed a parametric model of the iris to describe the pupil characteristics in response to light while using probability distribution functions to describe the random fluctuations. Later, Stark [20] concluded that the pupillary response can be viewed as a negative feedback dynamical system. Though this expression of the pupil dynamics is attractive, it was Longtin et al. [12] who were the first to express the dynamics of the pupil light reflex as a nonlinear delay differential equation given by

$$\frac{dg}{dA}\frac{dA}{dt} + \alpha g(A) = \gamma \ln\left[\frac{\phi(t-\tau)}{\overline{\phi}}\right] \tag{18.7}$$

where A is the pupil area; ϕ is the retinal light flux; and $\overline{\phi}$ is the light level when there is no pupillary response. Furthermore, τ is the time delay due to retinal processing, which includes responses from the midbrain nuclei; and $\gamma > 0$ is an arbitrary constant. In the derivation of Eq. (18.7), $g(A)$ takes into account the inverse relationship between the pupil area and iris muscle activity. The direct relationship is given by

$$A = f(x) \tag{18.8}$$

where $f(x)$ represents the activity of the iris muscle. Longtin defines this activity in terms of the Hill function expressed as

$$f(x) = \frac{\beta_1 \theta^n}{\theta^n + x^n} + \beta_2 \tag{18.9}$$

where β_1 is the minimum pupil area; $\beta_1 + \beta_2$ is the maximum pupil area; and θ and n are positive constants. In his work, Longtin chose the Hill function because it best represents the fact that the pupil area is positive and has finite limits while accounting for the elastic properties of the iris muscle. In computer graphics, Pamplona [15] recently looked at Longtin's equation of the pupil light reflex in order to simulate the varying degrees of pupil dilation as well as iridal pattern deformation in animated human characters in order to enhance facial animation. In his work, Pamplona notes that though Longtin's model is well cited, there are ambiguities in estimating the various parameters ($\alpha, \beta_1, \beta_2, \gamma, \theta, n, \overline{\phi}$). The selection of these parameters are important to guarantee convergence as well as ensure that the simulations are as realistic as possible. By using the steady-state formulation of Eq. (18.7), making the comparison with the Moon and Spencer model, as well as making the appropriate conversions to the dynamic case yields

$$\frac{\mathrm{d}M}{\mathrm{d}D}\frac{\mathrm{d}D}{\mathrm{d}t} + 2.3026M(D) = 0.45 \ln\left[\frac{\phi(t-\tau)}{\bar{\phi}}\right] \qquad (18.10)$$

where D is the pupil diameter and the function $M(D) = \tanh^{-1}\left(\frac{D-4.9}{3}\right)$.

Although pupil dynamics has been studied in different communities outside of biometrics, modeling iridal dynamics has received limited attention. It appears that Rohen [18] was the first researcher to study the collagen form of the iris. In his work, he proposed a model for the collagen fibers assuming that they are arranged in a series of parallel arcs, connecting the iris root to the pupil border in both clockwise and counter clockwise fashions. Later, Wyatt [24] used Rohen's formulation and created a mathematical expression for iris deformation as the sum of a linear stretch and nonlinear deviation in order to demonstrate the wear and tear of the collagen fibers in the iris region. Wei et al. [23] used pattern recognition approaches and concluded that the nonlinear deviation is Gaussian. Finally, Pamplona used an imaged-based model for iridal deformation by tracking points on the pupil border as well as various feature points throughout the iris region. Based on this, he calculated the distance from the pupil center; the distance of the points from the pupil border; and the percentage of the points in the iris region with respect to the pupil diameter. With these results, he concluded that approximating the iridal deformation as a linear function is good enough to generate a realistic simulation.

18.1.2 Our Approach and Motivation

One of our main motivations for this work comes from Hollingsworth et al. [8]. Their results show that there is a need to explore the possibility of correcting various degrees of pupil dilation in order to improve iris recognition. Our other motivation comes from the observation that the impact of pupil dilation on the dynamics of the iris is not well studied in the literature. Though Thornton [21] and Wei [23] took dilation into account in their corrections, it appears that they did not consider the varying degrees of pupil dilation. Furthermore, both Thornton and Wei used pattern recognition approaches, which are limiting because they depend on a particular dataset and are not necessarily based on the physiology of the iris. We also found Pamplona's image-based model for iridal deformation to be incomplete since it cannot account for the nonlinearity in iris deformation. Having a realistic simulation might prove beneficial in computer graphics; however, the desire in biometrics and other biologically related fields is to be physically accurate as possible. Finally, Wyatt is also aware that his mathematical model is limiting because he stresses that his work is only a "meshwork skeleton" and does not form the basis for both linear and nonlinear iridal stretch, which comes from the variations in the elastic properties of the iris as well as the iris musculature. Thus, the work of Wei et al. is also limiting in this regard since they apply the "meshwork skeleton" to determine that the nonlinear stretch is Gaussian.

Here we present a novel approach to mathematically model iris deformation by using what we know about biomechanics – the application of continuum mechanics to biological medium [5, 6]. With biomechanics, we can predict the nonlinear dynamics of the iris while considering the varying degrees of pupil dilation. Such an approach removes the reliance on pattern recognition principles alone and incorporates the changes in the elastic properties of the iris while considering the muscle activity. After formulating our model, we will perform a mathematical analysis on it within the confines of the annular region of the iris. Our mathematical analysis is done in two parts: we first look at the entire orthotropic case. Next, we consider the assumption that the iris region is isotropic. Though we adopt the assumption by Lei et al. [10] that the iris region is orthotropic, exploring the isotropic case could prove beneficial because we do not have to be concerned about the variation of the material properties of the iris while gaining some insight into the orthotropic case.

18.2   Mathematical Formulation

We begin our mathematical formulation by viewing the iris region as a thin cylindrical shell, where the thickness in the z dimension is much smaller compared to that of the r and θ directions. Hence, we can look at the region in terms of a thin plate where the loads are applied uniformly over the z dimension. With this thin plate formulation, we can also make the assumption that the normal stress in the z direction, σ_z, as well as the shear stresses, τ_{rz} and $\tau_{\theta z}$, are negligible. This simplification reduces the dynamics of the iris region to the two-dimensional r-θ plane. Therefore, the Cauchy-Euler equations become [14]

$$\epsilon_r = \frac{\partial u_r}{\partial r} - \frac{1}{2}\left\{ \left(\frac{\partial u_r}{\partial r}\right)^2 + \left(\frac{\partial u_\theta}{\partial r}\right)^2 \right\} \tag{18.11}$$

$$\epsilon_\theta = \frac{1}{r}\frac{\partial u_\theta}{\partial \theta} + \frac{u_r}{r} - \frac{1}{2r^2}\left\{ \left(\frac{\partial u_\theta}{\partial \theta}\right)^2 + \left(\frac{\partial u_r}{\partial \theta}\right)^2 - 2\frac{\partial u_r}{\partial \theta}u_\theta + 2\frac{\partial u_\theta}{\partial \theta}u_r + u_r^2 + u_\theta^2 \right\}$$
$$\tag{18.12}$$

$$\gamma_{r\theta} = \frac{1}{r}\frac{\partial u_r}{\partial \theta} + \frac{\partial u_\theta}{\partial r} - \frac{u_\theta}{r} - \frac{1}{r}\left\{ \left(\frac{\partial u_r}{\partial \theta}\right)\left(\frac{\partial u_r}{\partial r}\right) + \left(\frac{\partial u_\theta}{\partial r}\right)\left(\frac{\partial u_\theta}{\partial \theta}\right) + \frac{\partial u_\theta}{\partial r}u_r - \frac{\partial u_r}{\partial r}u_\theta \right\}$$
$$\tag{18.13}$$

where ϵ_r and ϵ_θ ,in (18.11) and (18.12), are the normal strains and $\gamma_{r\theta}$, in (18.13), is the shear strain. Also, u_r and u_θ are the radial and azimuthal components of the displacement vector in the annular region. Consequently, the equilibrium conditions are expressed as [14]

$$\frac{\partial \sigma_r}{\partial r} + \frac{1}{r}\frac{\partial \tau_{r\theta}}{\partial \theta} + \frac{(\sigma_r - \sigma_\theta)}{r} = 0 \qquad (18.14)$$

$$\frac{\partial \tau_{r\theta}}{\partial r} + \frac{2}{r}\tau_{r\theta} + \frac{1}{r}\frac{\partial \sigma_\theta}{\partial \theta} = 0$$

where σ_r and σ_θ are the normal stresses and $\tau_{r\theta}$ is the shear stress. Another observation is that the iris muscles (both the sphincter and dilator muscles) are equally distributed throughout the annular region. Furthermore, the pupillary response causes these muscles to produce an axisymmetric load throughout the iris region. Therefore, mathematically, we can also make the assumptions that $\frac{\partial}{\partial \theta}$ and u_θ are negligible, and consequently it follows that the shear stress $\tau_{r\theta}$ is also negligible [2]. We next consider the fact that soft biological tissues, like the iris, experience finite (or large) strain. This affects the Cauchy relationships because the relationship between the strain components ϵ_r and ϵ_θ and the displacement are completely nonlinear. With these assumptions, the Cauchy-Euler equations become

$$\epsilon_r = u' - \tfrac{1}{2}(u')^2 \qquad (18.15)$$

$$\epsilon_\theta = \tfrac{u}{r} - \tfrac{1}{2}\left(\tfrac{u}{r}\right)^2$$

and the equilibrium condition reduces to

$$\frac{d\sigma_r}{dr} + \frac{\sigma_r - \sigma_\theta}{r} = 0. \qquad (18.16)$$

In Eq. (18.15), we have dropped the subscripts because our problem now simplifies to only examining variations in the radial displacement u_r. We also use the primes $()'$ to denote ordinary differentiation with respect to r because the displacement now only depends on the radial component (i.e., $u = u(r)$). Adopting Lei et al.'s assumption that the iris material is orthotropic, the relationship between the stress vector $\overrightarrow{\sigma} = \langle \sigma_r, \sigma_\theta \rangle$ and the strain vector $\overrightarrow{\epsilon} = \langle \epsilon_r, \epsilon_\theta \rangle$ can be expressed in the following manner:

$$\epsilon_r = \tfrac{\sigma_r}{E_r} - \tfrac{v_{r\theta}}{E_\theta}\sigma_\theta \qquad (18.17)$$

$$\epsilon_\theta = -\tfrac{v_{\theta r}}{E_r}\sigma_r + \tfrac{\sigma_\theta}{E_\theta}$$

where E_r and E_θ are the Young's moduli (i.e., the material properties of the iris region); $v_{r\theta}$ is the Poisson's ratio in the azmuthal direction; and $v_{\theta r}$ is the Poisson's ratio in the radial direction. It needs to be noted that for orthotropic formulation $v_{r\theta} \neq v_{\theta r}$; however, due to the symmetry with the stress and strain tensors, the following relationship must hold:

$$\frac{v_{\theta r}}{E_r} = \frac{v_{r\theta}}{E_\theta}. \qquad (18.18)$$

Since the Poisson's ratio $\nu_{\theta r}$ is known [10], we use the relationship given from (18.18) to simplify Eq. (18.17) to be

$$\epsilon_r = \frac{\sigma_r}{E_r} - \frac{\nu_{\theta r}}{E_r}\sigma_\theta \tag{18.19}$$
$$\epsilon_\theta = -\frac{\nu_{\theta r}}{E_r}\sigma_r + \frac{\sigma_\theta}{E_\theta}.$$

Solving for the stress terms σ_r and σ_θ results in

$$\sigma_r = \frac{E_r}{(1-\zeta\nu^2)}(\epsilon_r + \zeta\nu\epsilon_\theta) \tag{18.20}$$
$$\sigma_\theta = \frac{E_\theta}{(1-\zeta\nu^2)}(\nu\epsilon_r + \epsilon_\theta)$$

where $\nu = \nu_{\theta r}$ and $\zeta = \frac{E_\theta}{E_r}$. Substituting Eq. (18.15) into Eqs. (18.17) and (18.16) yields the following differential equation:

$$u'' + \frac{u'}{r} - \frac{\zeta u}{r^2} - \frac{(1-\nu\zeta)}{2r}(u')^2 - \frac{(\nu-1)\zeta}{2r}\left(\frac{u}{r}\right)^2 - \frac{1}{2}\frac{d}{dr}(u')^2 - \frac{\nu\zeta}{2}\frac{d}{dr}\left(\frac{u}{r}\right)^2 = 0 \tag{18.21}$$

where ζ is given by

$$\zeta = \frac{E_\theta}{E_r} \tag{18.22}$$

and E_r and E_θ are the radial and azimuthal Young's moduli, respectively. The boundary conditions in Eq. (18.21) on the annular domain $r \in (r_1, r_2)$ are

$$u(r_1) = \mu_1, \mu_1 > 0 \tag{18.23}$$

and

$$u(r_2) = 0. \tag{18.24}$$

Examining Eq. (18.21) shows that iris deformation is nonlinear. However, we will like to perform a theoretical analysis of the displacement $u(r)$ inside of the annular region $r \in (r_1, r_2)$ by examining (18.21) given the boundary conditions (18.23) and (18.24). Providing such a mathematical analysis results in the overall theoretical picture of the iridal dynamics.

18.2.1 Mathematical Analysis—Orthotropic Deformation

In order to begin our mathematical analysis of Eq. (18.21) with the boundary conditions (18.23) and (18.24), we first perform the following normalization:

$$\hat{u} = u/\mu_1, \quad \hat{r} = r/r_2. \tag{18.25}$$

Thus, Eq. (18.21) becomes

$$\hat{u}'' + \frac{1}{\hat{r}}\hat{u}' - \frac{\zeta}{\hat{r}^2}\hat{u} + \lambda \left[\frac{\nu\zeta - 1}{2\hat{r}} (\hat{u}')^2 + \frac{(1-\nu)\zeta}{2\hat{r}^3}\hat{u}^2 - \frac{1}{2}\frac{\mathrm{d}}{\mathrm{d}\hat{r}} \left\{ (\hat{u}')^2 + \nu\zeta \left(\frac{\hat{u}}{\hat{r}} \right)^2 \right\} \right] = 0.$$

(18.26)

and the normalized boundary conditions become

$$\hat{u}(\eta) = 1, \quad \hat{u}(1) = 0.$$

(18.27)

where

$$\lambda = \frac{\mu_1}{r_2}, \quad \eta = \frac{r_1}{r_2},$$

(18.28)

and the primes $()'$ denote the differentiation with respect to $\hat{r}$. It is important to note that the existence of the solution to Eq. (18.21) with boundary conditions defined in (18.23) and (18.24) is to be expected from the rational derivation of the equations in solid mechanics [1]. However, the question of uniqueness needs to be explored in more detail [16], so that we can apply a maximum principle for nonlinear differential operators. The idea is based on the maximum principle for linear operators of which the linearized problem ($\lambda = 0$) is an example. For nonlinear operators we take advantage of the following theorem [16] to show uniqueness:

Theorem 18.1 *Let $u(r)$ be a solution of the boundary value problem*

$$u'' + H(r, u, u') = 0, \quad a < r < b,$$

(18.29)

$$\left. \begin{array}{l} u(a) = \gamma_1, \\ u(b) = \gamma_2. \end{array} \right\}$$

(18.30)

Suppose that $H, \partial H/\partial u, \partial H/\partial u'$ are continuous and that $\partial H/\partial u \leq 0$. Then a solution to (18.29) which also satisfies (18.30) is unique.

In order to take advantage of Theorem 18.1 we expand Eq. (18.26) to obtain the following:

$$\left(1 - \lambda\hat{u}' \right)\hat{u}'' + \frac{1}{\hat{r}}\hat{u}' - \frac{\zeta}{\hat{r}^2}\hat{u} + \lambda \left[\frac{\nu\zeta - 1}{2\hat{r}} (\hat{u}')^2 + \frac{(1+\nu)\zeta}{2\hat{r}^3}\hat{u}^2 - \nu\zeta\frac{\hat{u}'\hat{u}}{\hat{r}^2} \right] = 0.$$

(18.31)

which is in the same form as in (18.29) with H being defined as

$$H = \frac{1}{\left(1 - \lambda\hat{u}' \right)} \left\{ \frac{1}{\hat{r}}\hat{u}' - \frac{\zeta}{\hat{r}^2}\hat{u} + \lambda \left[\frac{\nu\zeta - 1}{2\hat{r}} (\hat{u}')^2 + \frac{(1+\nu)\zeta}{2\hat{r}^3}\hat{u}^2 - \nu\zeta\frac{\hat{u}'\hat{u}}{\hat{r}^2} \right] \right\} = 0$$

(18.32)

with the boundary conditions defined in (18.27). Looking at the annular domain of the iris region $r \in (r_1, r_2)$, it is noted that as the pupil dilates the iris tissue is compressed due to the iris musculature. Therefore, we can physically expect that $\hat{u}' \leq 0$ making the expression $1 - \lambda \hat{u}' > 0$. Furthermore, since the rest of the expression inside of the braces in Eq. (18.32) is in polynomial form, we can deduce that H and its derivatives are continuous.

Next, we compute $\partial H / \partial \hat{u}$ and get the following expression:

$$\frac{\partial H}{\partial \hat{u}} = \frac{\zeta}{(1 - \lambda \hat{u}')} \left\{ -\frac{1}{\hat{r}^2} + \lambda \left[(1 + \nu) \frac{\hat{u}}{\hat{r}^3} - \nu \frac{\hat{u}'}{\hat{r}^2} \right] \right\}. \tag{18.33}$$

Looking at Eq. (18.33) we see that since $\zeta / (1 - \lambda \hat{u}') > 0$ the condition $\partial H / \partial u \leq 0$ is satisfied when

$$\lambda \left[(1 + \nu) \frac{\hat{u}}{\hat{r}^3} - \nu \frac{\hat{u}'}{\hat{r}^2} \right] \leq \frac{1}{\hat{r}^2}. \tag{18.34}$$

Now we have $\eta \leq \hat{r} < 1$ and, since $\hat{u}' \leq 0$ and $\hat{u} \leq 1$, so condition (18.34) is satisfied as long as

$$\lambda \left[(1 + \nu) \frac{1}{\eta} + \nu |\hat{u}'| \right] \leq 1. \tag{18.35}$$

Though the conditions of the theorem are sufficient for uniqueness and are seemingly satisfied for the smaller values of λ, it does indicate the prominent role played by the nonlinearity. In Eq. (18.26) we perform a regular perturbation expansion to describe the behavior of the nonlinearity. For small values of λ, we can perform the perturbation expansion of $\hat{u}$ as follows:

$$\hat{u}(\hat{r}; \lambda) = \hat{u}_0(\hat{r}) + \lambda \hat{u}_1(\hat{r}) + \lambda^2 \hat{u}_2(\hat{r}) + \cdots \tag{18.36}$$

with simple boundary conditions $\hat{u}_0(\eta) = 1$, $\hat{u}_0(1) = 0$, $\hat{u}_1(\eta) = \hat{u}_1(1) = \hat{u}_2(\eta) = \hat{u}_2(1) = \cdots = 0$. Thus $\hat{u}_1$ is given by

$$\hat{u}_1'' + \frac{1}{\hat{r}} \hat{u}_1' - \frac{\zeta}{\hat{r}^2} \hat{u}_1 = \frac{(1 - \nu \zeta)}{2\hat{r}} \left(\hat{u}_0' \right)^2 - \frac{(1 + \nu) \zeta}{2\hat{r}^3} \hat{u}_0^2 + \nu \zeta \frac{\hat{u}_0' \hat{u}_0}{\hat{r}^2} := f_0(\hat{r}). \tag{18.37}$$

Each term can actually be represented as an integral such as

$$\hat{u}_n(\hat{r}) = \int_\eta^1 G(\hat{r}, \rho) f_{n-1}(\rho) d\rho, \quad n = 1, 2, \ldots, \tag{18.38}$$

where $G(\hat{r}, \rho)$ is the Green's function satisfying

$$\left(\hat{r} G_{\hat{r}} \right)_{\hat{r}} - \frac{\zeta}{\hat{r}} G = \delta(\hat{r} - \rho), \quad G(\eta, \rho) = G(1, \rho) = 0. \tag{18.39}$$

Therefore, the term of order 1 we have the following expression:

$$\hat{u}_1(\hat{r}) = \int_\eta^1 G(\hat{r}, \rho) \left[\frac{(1 - \nu\zeta)}{2\rho} \left(\hat{u}_0'(\rho)\right)^2 - \frac{(\nu + 1)\,\zeta}{2\rho^3} \hat{u}_0^2(\rho) + \nu\zeta \frac{\hat{u}_0(\rho)\hat{u}_0'(\rho)}{\rho^2} \right] d\rho.$$

(18.40)

Likewise, successive terms of (18.36) may be determined in this regular perturbation expansion.

18.2.2 Mathematical Analysis—Isotropic Deformation

The isotropic case, though different physically is really only a special case analytically, by taking $\zeta = 1$ in Eq. (18.26). The uniqueness theorem therefore holds in the same way as before. The perturbation solution is a little simpler to write down. The appropriate Green's function in this case is explicitly:

$$G(\hat{r}, \rho) = \begin{cases} [3(1 - \eta^2)]^{-1} \left(\hat{r} - \frac{\eta^2}{\hat{r}}\right)\left(\rho - \frac{1}{\rho}\right), & \hat{r} < \rho \\ [3(1 - \eta^2)]^{-1} \left(\rho - \frac{\eta^2}{\rho}\right)\left(\hat{r} - \frac{1}{\hat{r}}\right), & \hat{r} > \rho \end{cases}$$

(18.41)

The solution of the perturbation expansion proceeds with

$$\hat{u}_0(\hat{r}) = \frac{\eta}{(\eta^2 - 1)}\left(\hat{r} - \frac{1}{\hat{r}}\right), \quad \hat{u}_0'(\hat{r}) = \frac{\eta}{\eta^2 - 1}\left(\frac{1}{\hat{r}^2} + 1\right),$$

(18.42)

and the equation for $\hat{u}_1$ is the expression (18.40) with $\zeta = 1$.

18.3 Numerical Results and Simulation

The numerical simulation of the iris deformation for both the orthotropic and isotropic cases was done using the Finite Element Method (FEM) [7, 17]. The simulation could be implemented via other numerical methods; however, we found that the FEM offers greater flexibility with regard to mesh generation. The FEM implementation consisted of converting Eq. (18.21) into a variational form; and discretizing our annular domain into 100 vertices that are uniformly spaced from the inner radius r_1 to the outer radius r_2 (r_2 is set to 6 mm to represent the limbus boundary). Because the average pupil size at constriction is 3 mm in diameter we initialize the inner radius to 1.5 mm and solve numerically for $u(r)$. As we vary the inner radius we continue to numerically solve for $u(r)$ noting the level of deformation of the iris tissue. Furthermore, due to the fact that the average pupil size at dilation is approximately 9.6 mm diameter (or 4.8 mm in radius), we use that as our stopping point. Each time we solve for $u(r)$ we compare that to the linear assumption. To visualize the deformation between our model and the linear approximation, we begin by adding concentric circles that are evenly spaced in the annular region. Next, once numerically solving for $u(r)$, we move the ring located at the starting radius r to the final position located at radius $u(r) + r$.

We adopt Pamplona's metrics [15] as follows: the distance from the interior point to the center of the annular region; the distance from the interior point to the pupil boundary; and the ratio of the distance between the tracked interior point to the pupil border and the local width of the iridal disk (otherwise known as the invariance). Doing so enables us to further analyze the nonlinear effects of the interior points of the annular region for both the orthotropic and isotropic cases.

18.3.1   Numerical Results—Orthotropic Deformation

For the numerical simulation of the orthotropic deformation, we adopt Lei et al.'s [10] formulation and assumptions for determining the material parameters E_r and E_θ in order to compute ζ for the various degrees of dilation. Because it is found that the Poisson ratio for the iris $\nu \in [0.45, 0.5)$, we chose $\nu = 0.49$ for our simulation. Figures 18.3, 18.4 and 18.5 show the results for each simulation where the inner radius was changed to 2, 3, and 4.5 mm to depict the various levels of iris deformation.

In Fig. 18.3 top left, we compare the solution $u(r)$ to Eq. (18.21) with the inner radius expanded to 2 mm against the previously assumed linear solution. The difference between the nonlinear solution given by (18.21) and the linear approximation is rather apparent in this figure. However, in the top right and bottom of Fig. 18.3, we see a minimum difference between the two methods in the effects of deformation when looking at the final positions $r + u(r)$. Furthermore, our model also shows that the compression of the iris tissue occurs in the innermost regions of the annular region, which is where most of the deformation occurs.

In Fig. 18.4, we see that when the inner radius is moved to 3 mm, there is the apparent difference between the solution $u(r)$ to (18.21) and the linear approximation. However, in this case, we now find that the differences between the linear and nonlinear solutions are more significant. Furthermore, the difference in the visualizations also become more discernible.

In Fig. 18.5 we see the results after the inner radius expands to 4.5 mm. For this case, while the iris boundary is now at 4.5 mm, elements originally at 2.5 mm move to approximately 4.4 mm behind the boundary. We conclude that this behavior is analogous to simulating folds in the iris tissue. It is important to note that these effects occur only in the radial direction due to the fact that we make the assumption that the dynamics in the z direction are negligible.

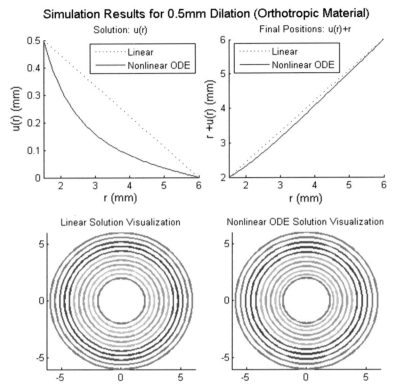

Fig. 18.3 Results in simulating a pupil with orthotropic material properties dilating from 1.5 to 2.0 mm. The solution $u(r)$, of Eq. (18.21) is nonlinear (*top left*); however, the difference in deformation between $u(r)$ and the linear approximation does not appear significant (*top right*). This is further shown in the visualizations (*bottom*)

We then ran the simulation for many more degrees of dilation; tracked several locations on the iris through time; applied Pamplona's metrics; and plotted the results shown in Fig. 18.6. Each line in these graphs represents a single point on the iris that moves as the pupil dilates. The top-left graph represents the invariance, or the percentage that a given point lies within the annular region. So, for example, we see that a point which was originally 10 % in the iris steadily moves inward as the pupil dilates, again suggesting that the inner regions are becoming compressed. In contrast, the point originally 90 % into the iris barely moves at all as the pupil dilates, generating a straight line. We can see that as the pupil diameter exceeds 6.5 mm, the lines originating at 10–30 % begin to intersect the 0 line, demonstrating the effects of folding. The top-right graph shows the final distance from a point to the pupil border after dilation. As expected, points closer to the outer edge of the iris are decreasing nearly linearly as pupil diameter increases, whereas the points closer to the pupil deform nonlinearly, and again cross the horizontal axis. Finally, the bottom-center

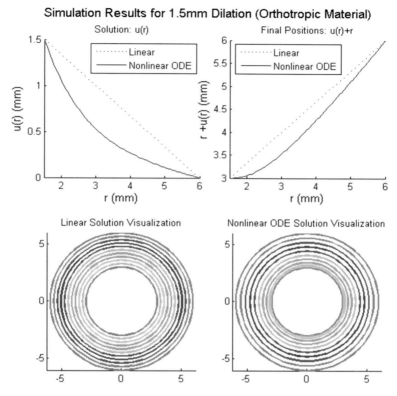

Fig. 18.4 Results in simulating a pupil with orthotropic material properties dilating from 1.5 to 3.0 mm. The solution $u(r)$, to (18.21), continues to remain nonlinear (*top left*); however, the differences between $u(r)$ and the linear approximation become significant (*top right*). This is further shown in the visualizations (*bottom*)

graph shows the distance from the center of the pupil to points within the iris. We once again see that near the outer iris edge, points are moving very little compared to those near the pupil border.

18.3.2   *Numerical Results—Isotropic Deformation*

Our approach to simulate the isotropic deformation was the same as that for the orthotropic case except that we set $\zeta = 1$ to account for the material parameters being the same in all directions. The Poisson ratio ν was chosen to be 0.49 for our simulations for the same reason as that of the orthotropic case. Similar to the orthotropic case, Figs. 18.7, 18.8 and 18.9 show the results for each simulation where

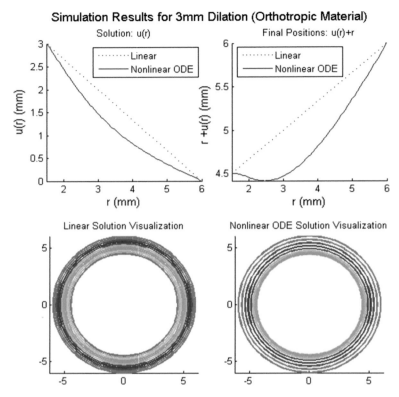

Fig. 18.5 Results in simulating a pupil with orthotropic material properties dilating from 1.5 to 4.5 mm. Note in the *top right*, the iris tissue moves backward, behind the pupil border, suggesting the need for three-dimensional simulations

the inner radius was changed to 2, 3, and 4.5 mm depicting the various levels of deformation in the annular region.

Analogous to the orthotropic case, Fig. 18.7 shows that for the case when the inner radius is expanded to 2 mm, the solution $u(r)$ is nonlinear compared to the linear approximation. However, just as in the orthotropic case, the distinctions between $u(r)$ and the linear approximation are not significant. Furthermore, compared to the orthotropic simulation, $u(r)$ does not appear to fall as rapidly at the beginning, and so we can conclude that the iris tissue is slightly less compressed in the inner regions.

We reach similar conclusions for the medium deformation case in Fig. 18.8. Again we see that the nonlinear deformation is starting to be significantly different than the linear deformation.

Finally, in Fig. 18.9, we again see that the high degree of dilation is causes the simulation to produce folding results. Just as in the orthotropic case, the reason for these effects is due to our assumption that the dynamics in the z direction are negligible.

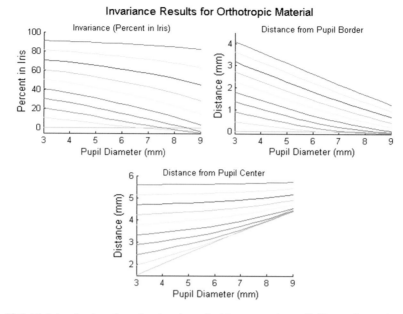

Fig. 18.6 Plot showing how the points interior to the iris move as the pupil dilates, given orthotropic material properties

As in the orthotropic case, we applied Pamplona's metrics to track the interior points of the iris as the inner radius changes (due to pupil dilation) as shown in Fig. 18.10. The behavior is similar to the orthotropic case. However, it appears that the slopes in the invariance graph tend to be lower in this simulation. Furthermore, we see that the graphs exhibit a linear behavior when depicting the distance from the pupil border and the distance from the pupil center respectively. Finally, looking at the invariance graph our results show that folding occurs when the inner diameter is between 7.5 and 8 mm versus 6–6.5 mm in the orthotropic case.

18.4 Conclusions and Future Work

We used the knowledge of biomechanics in order to produce a theoretical two-dimensional mathematical model describing iris deformation. We believe that our model is an improvement from previous work because it takes into account the material properties of the iris as well as the cause of deformation due to the iris muscle activity. Also, by building our model we were able to directly show that the deformation is nonlinear and that, therefore, there is more to the deformation than just a linear approximation. We were able to perform a mathematical analysis of our model by looking at the uniqueness conditions to show the behavior of $u(r)$ with

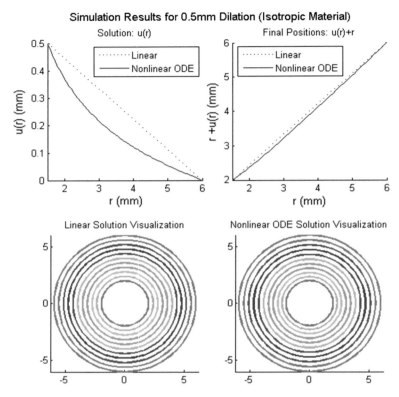

Fig. 18.7 Results in simulating a pupil with isotropic material properties dilating from 1.5 to 2 mm. Analogous to the orthotropic case, the nonlinear solution $u(r)$ to (18.21) with $\zeta = 1$ is nonlinear (*top left*); however, the difference in deformation between $u(r)$ and the linear approximation does not appear to be significant (*top right*). This is further shown in the visualizations of the iris deformation (*bottom*)

various degrees of dilation. This analysis strengthens our model because we were able to relate the biology of the iris to the mathematical theory. In our numerical experiments, we were able to visually compare the level of deformation against the linear assumption: this not only showed the level of nonlinearity, but also the potential folds in the iris tissue. Furthermore, we were able to apply the metrics in Pamplona's [15] work to show that our model, as well as our approximation, behaves similarly to Pamplona's image model and is also consistent with Wyatt's results. However, using Pamplona's metrics we were able to further show the nonlinearity as well as potential folds in the iris region. These folds are more accurate in describing the iridal dynamics as the pupil dilates. Finally, through our mathematical analysis and numerical experiments, we were able to show the similarity in behavior between the isotropic and orthotropic case and conclude that the isotropic formulation could serve as a practical approximation because the nonlinear dynamics are still preserved.

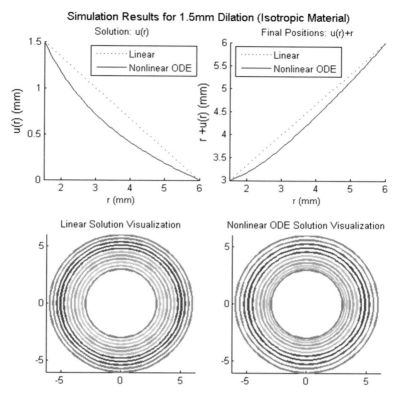

Fig. 18.8 Results in simulating a pupil with isotropic material properties dilating from 1.5 to 3 mm. Analagous to the orthotropic case, the nonlinear solution $u(r)$ to Eq. (18.21) with $\zeta = 1$ is nonlinear; however, the distinctions between $u(r)$ and the linear approximation become significant (*top right*). This is displayed further in the visualizations (*bottom*)

Our model can be useful to the biometrics and biology communities. In the biometrics community this model can serve as an analytical description for describing the level of iris deformation. Thornton et al.'s [21] work showed through pattern recognition models that if there is knowledge of the level of deformation one should be able to correct its effects. Our model would be an improvement to their technique because it can be used to show the level of deformation in the iris region at both micro and macro levels. Our model can also serve to explore the possible enhancement of Daugman's rubber sheet model, which uses a simple transformation to unwrap the iris while accounting for dilation. Though Daugman's model is used in commercial systems, the current challenge in iris recognition is accounting for variations in pupil dilation. Therefore, our model can be applied to design an enhanced rubber sheet model that counteracts iridal deformation. In biology, our model can be used for exploring other effects of iris deformation. Finally, our model can also be applied

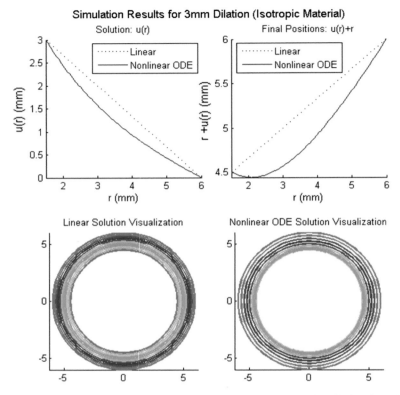

Fig. 18.9 Results in simulating a pupil with isotropic material properties dilating from 1.5 to 4.5 mm. Analogous to the orthotropic case, the iris tissue moves backward, behind the pupil border, suggesting the need for three-dimensional simulations

to the computer graphics arena to simulate realistic response in animated characters due to variations in illumination.

Though the numerical simulation of our model gives promising results, there are also a couple of areas for future work that need to be explored. First, there is a need to explore testing our model extensively on actual data to draw a more accurate comparison. Doing so will afford us the opportunity to explore the deformation pragmatically, thereby connecting our theoretical model to actual data. Pamplona [15] tested his model with actual data and concluded that the deformation is mostly linear when tracking certain feature points; however, our model shows that this conclusion is not necessarily complete. Second, for the extreme cases of dilation, we noticed the significant impact of the effects of folding. This is not completely shown in our two-dimensional model because we had assumed that the dynamics within the thickness of the iris is negligible. Therefore, there is a need to build a mathematical model that also takes into consideration the thickness of the iris as the pupil dilates. Doing so will enable us to have a more complete perspective of iris dynamics.

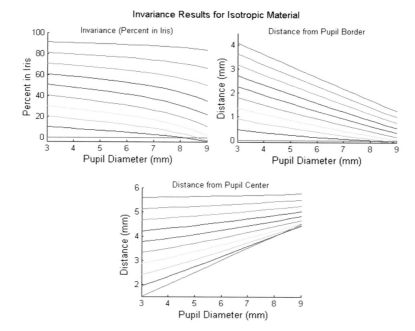

Fig. 18.10 Plot showing how the points interior to the iris move as the pupil dilates, given isotropic material properties

Acknowledgments This material is based upon work supported by the U.S. Department of Homeland Security under Grant Award Number 2007-ST-104-000006. The views and conclusions contained in this document are those of the authors and should not be interpreted as necessarily representing the official policies, either expressed or implied, of the U.S. Department of Homeland Security. Arun Ross was supported by US National Science Foundation CAREER Grant No. IIS 0642554

References

1. S. Antman, *Nonlinear Problems of Elasticity* (1994)
2. W.F. Carroll, *A Primer for Finite Elements in Elastic Structures* (Wiley, 1999)
3. J. Daugman, *High Confidence Visual Recognition of Persons* (1993), pp. 1148–1161
4. C.J. Ellis, The pupillary light reflex in normal subjects. Br. J. Opthamol. **65**(11), 754–759 (1981)
5. Y.C. Fung, *Biomechanics* (Springer, 1997)
6. Y.C. Fung, *A First Course in Continuum Mechanics* (Prentice Hall, 1994)
7. D. Henwood, J. Bonet, *Finite Elements: A Gentle Introduction* (1996)
8. K. Hollingsworth, K.W. Bowyer, P.J. Flynn, Pupil dilation degrades iris biometric performance. Comput. Vis. Image Underst. **113**(1), 150–157 (2009)
9. A.K. Jain, P.J. Flynn, A. Ross, *Handbook of Biometrics* (2007)

10. Y. Lei et al., Experimental research on the mechanical properties of porcine iris. Clin. Biomech. **23**, 83–87 (2008)
11. N. Link, L. Stark, Latency of the pupillary response. IEEE Trans. Bio. Eng. **35**(3), 214–218 (1988)
12. A. Longtin, J.G. Milton, Modelling autonomous oscillations in the human pupil light reflex using nonlinear delay-differential equations. Bull. Math. Biol. **51**(5), 605–624 (1989)
13. P. Moon, D. Spencer, *On the Stiles-Crawford Effect*, vol. 34 (1944), pp. 319–329
14. A. Palazotto, *Nonlinear Analysis of Shell Structures* (AIAA Education Services, 1992)
15. V. Pamploma, Photorealistic models for pupil light reflex and iridal pattern deformation (2008)
16. H. Protter, H.F. Weinberger, *Maximum Principles in Differential Equations* (Springer-Verlag, 1984)
17. J.N. Reddy (Oxford University Press, 2004)
18. H. Rohen, Der Bau der Regenbogenhaut beim Menschen und einigen Säugern. Gegenbaur Morphol. **91**, 140–181 (1951)
19. A. Ross, *Iris Recognition: The Path Forward* (2010), pp. 30–35
20. L. Stark, *The Pupil As a Paradigm for Neurological Control*, vol. 31 (1984), pp. 1925–1939
21. J. Thornton, M. Savvides, B.V.V. Kumar, Bayesian approach to deformed pattern matching of iris images. IEEE Trans. Pattern Anal. Mach. Intell. **29**(4), 596–606 (2007)
22. S. Usui, L. Stark, *A Model for Nonlinear Stochastic Behavior of the Pupil* (1982), pp. 13–21
23. Z. Wei, T. Tan, Z. Sun, Nonlinear iris deformation correction based on gaussian model, in *Advances in Biometrics*. Lecture Notes in Computer Science, vol. 4642, 2007, pp. 780–789
24. H.J. Wyatt, A 'minimum-wear-and-tear' meshwork for the iris. Vis. Res. **40**, 2167–2176 (2000)

Chapter 19
Iris Liveness Detection by Modeling Dynamic Pupil Features

Adam Czajka

Abstract The objective of this chapter is to present how to employ pupil dynamics in eye liveness detection. A thorough review of current liveness detection methods is provided at the beginning of the chapter to make the scientific background and position this method within current state-of-the-art methodology. Pupil dynamics may serve as a component of a wider presentation attack detection in iris recognition systems, making them more secure. Due to a lack of public databases that would support this research, we have built our own iris capture device to register pupil size changes under visible light stimuli, and registered 204 observations for 26 subjects (52 different irides), each containing 750 iris images taken every 40 ms. Each measurement registers the spontaneous pupil oscillations and its reaction after a sudden increase and a sudden decrease of the intensity of visible light. The Kohn and Clynes pupil dynamics model is used to describe these changes; hence, we convert each observation into a point in a feature space defined by model parameters. To answer the question whether the eye is alive (that is, if it reacts to light changes as a human eye) or the presentation is suspicious (that is, if it reacts oddly or no reaction is observed), we use linear and nonlinear support vector machines to classify natural reaction and spontaneous oscillations, simultaneously investigating the goodness of fit to reject bad modeling. Our experiments show that this approach can achieve a perfect performance for the data we have collected; all normal reactions are correctly differentiated from spontaneous oscillations. We investigated three variants of modeling to find the simplest, yet still powerful configuration of the method, namely (1) observing the pupil reaction to both the positive and negative changes in the light intensity, (2) using only the pupil reaction to positive surge of the light intensity, and (3) employing only the pupil reaction when the light is suddenly turned off. Further investigation related to the shortest observation time required to model the pupil reaction led to the final conclusion that time periods not exceeding 3 s are adequate to offer a perfect performance (on this dataset).

A. Czajka (✉)
Warsaw University of Technology, Warsaw, Poland
e-mail: aczajka@elka.pw.edu.pl

A. Czajka
Research and Academic Computer Network (NASK), Warsaw, Poland

© Springer-Verlag London 2016
K.W. Bowyer and M.J. Burge (eds.), *Handbook of Iris Recognition*,
Advances in Computer Vision and Pattern Recognition,
DOI 10.1007/978-1-4471-6784-6_19

439

19.1 Introduction

For more than a decade, liveness detection has been an important element of international discussion on biometric security. According to ISO/IEC, it concerns 'measurement and analysis of anatomical characteristics or involuntary or voluntary reactions, in order to determine if a biometric sample is being captured from a living subject present at the point of capture' [18]. The ability to check the liveness is crucial to any biometric sensor. Even its name, *biometric*, is the synonym for dealing with living and authentic biological traits, and not with nonliving artifacts. Once the biometric sensor accepts artifacts or nonliving body parts, the entire system deploying such sensor becomes moot.

Liveness detection refers to the detection of living symptoms, and hence is a special case of a wider class of techniques aiming at detection of any presentation attack. ISO/IEC defines the presentation attack as the 'presentation to the biometric data capture subsystem with the goal of interfering with the operation of the biometric system' [18]. This means that any subversive action (i.e., with the *intention* to subvert an intended operation of a biometric system) should be detected as a presentation attack. However, the intention of the attacker cannot be inferred. Hence the presentation attack becomes a very broad-ranging field that includes presentation of fake objects, as well as cadaver parts, incongruous, or coerced presentations, and even zero-effort impostor attempts performed in a justified hope that nonzero error rates must allow occasional false acceptances. This unknown intention also causes false alarms by classifying some suspicious actions as potential presentation attacks, e.g., non-conformant presentation due to illness, fatigue, presentation of artificial objects for cosmetic or health reasons, or due to a lack of experience with this particular system. This complicates the classification of attacks and stimulates on-going scientific discussion in the field of how to efficiently deal with these problematic cases and implement an efficient presentation attack detection (abbreviated further as PAD).

This chapter focuses on iris liveness detection, i.e., identification of liveness symptoms that could prove the authenticity of the eye and the willingness of the subject to be registered by the sensor. Instead of more commonly used static properties of the eye or its tissue, we use dynamics of the pupil registered under visible light stimuli. Since the pupil reacts involuntarily when the light intensity changes, it is difficult to conceal or change this behavior. As will be shown in the chapter, the pupil dynamics are not trivial, making it difficult for artificial object to mimic them. In our tests we decided not to use static objects such as iris paper printouts or static prosthetic eyeballs, since in such cases we would be assured of success (static objects do not present significant dynamics, apart from some measurement noise, and thus are easily recognizable when dynamics is the key). Instead, to assess the proposed method performance, we classify spontaneous pupil oscillations (often called *hippus*) and normal pupil reactions to a positive and negative surges of visible light, thus making the tests more realistic.

This chapter is an extension of our earlier work [5, 7, 8] devoted to the use of pupil dynamics for liveness detection, which is evaluated on dynamic, real objects rather than static artifacts. It gives a complete view on how to employ dynamics of the pupil, observed under step changes of the light intensity, to build a presentation attack detection technique. In particular, we aim at suggesting a minimum observation time required to correctly identify the dynamic model and providing the simplest possible (but not simplistic) combination of model complexity and stimulus to achieve a perfect discrimination between authentic eye reactions and noise signals.

The remainder of this chapter is organized as follows. Section 19.2 gives a brief summary of error metrics used in this work. Section 19.3 quotes and categorizes the most important past work on PAD related to iris recognition. Section 19.4 describes a database of eye movies collected for this research and the way the data was divided to provide samples of normal and odd reactions of the eye. In Sect. 19.5, we provide theoretical backgrounds of the data preprocessing and modeling of pupil dynamics. Section 19.6 presents experimental results. In Sect. 19.7, we discuss merits and limitations of the proposed method, suggesting a space for applications and further developments.

19.2   Error Metrics Used

False rejections and false acceptances are common errors in biometrics. These refer to mistakenly rejecting or accepting a claimed identity. In theory, we could use the same nomenclature in the context of liveness detection by a simple change of the claim from 'identity' to 'liveness'. However, an international discussion in this field suggests distinguishing error estimators related to presentation attack detection from those describing the biometric recognition due to different nature and sources of the errors and hence different techniques that must be used in estimation. In this chapter, we follow the most recent ISO/IEC proposal [19] and describe system performance at the PAD level by the following estimators:

Attack Presentation Classification Error Rate (APCER): proportion of presentation attacks incorrectly classified as normal presentations,
Normal Presentation Classification Error Rate (NPCER): proportion of normal presentations incorrectly classified as presentation attacks.

Occasionally in this chapter, there will be a need to present a system's performance at a specific operating point describing jointly the APCER and NPCER. One of such points is an **Equal Error Rate (EER)**, namely a value of APCER and NPCER when they are equal. It is analogous to the EER estimator used in recognition performance analysis, which employs equality of false rejections and false acceptances.

19.3 Presentation Attack Detection in Iris Recognition: Past Work

19.3.1 First Demonstrations of Vulnerabilities

Sixteen years have passed since Daugman's first proposal on how the iris recognition system can be spoofed by the eye printout [9]. Three years later, this idea was proved due to the first security evaluation of commercial iris recognition systems by Thalheim et al. [35]. During these tests, simple iris printouts with a hole cut in place of the pupil were used. This gimmick made it possible to stultify an iris detection method implemented in the tested device. Disjoint frequency ranges employed in the tested iris coding (low frequencies) and in the printing process (high frequencies) made the printing artifacts 'invisible' to the iris feature extraction processes. This allowed them to print, present, and positively verify a given iris. Pioneer research by Thalheim et al. stimulated others presenting their own security evaluation of additional, previously untested hardware, and again showing an alarming lack of effective countermeasures in the commercial equipment [25, 27].

19.3.2 Scientific Papers

From these first findings, we observe a constant full bloom of PAD methods, characterized by a different sophistication level and kind of signals that may be analyzed when observing the eye. To summarize the current state of the art, we introduce four categories of the PAD methods characterized by a way of measurement and dynamics of the observed object: passive or active measurement of a static or dynamic object. In the following subsections, we provide the most prominent research results for each category.

19.3.2.1 Passive Measurement of a Static Object

Methods of this kind employ a still image, typically the one used further in iris recognition, and are able to reveal only static eye features. No additional active measurement steps are performed. These approaches are still very attractive because no additional investment is made in iris capture hardware, even at the cost of limited reliability. What is important from the user point of view, the iris image acquisition process is unchanged when compared to systems lacking the PAD technique. These advantages are probably the main reason of the highest population in the literature.

The pioneer idea for this kind of PAD methodology comes from Daugman [9], who noticed that the amplitude spectrum of the printed irides contains fake patterns, as opposed to smooth spectra obtained for authentic eyes. The first proposal on how to automatically find these 'fake frequencies' within the amplitude spectrum was probably made by Pacut and Czajka [27], and involved follow-up investigations [4, 15] that finally reported correct recognition of more than 95 % of iris printouts (when no false rejections of alive samples were encountered). Wei et al. [38] are probably the first authors to analyze three iris image properties to detect a patterned contact lens: image sharpness, Gabor-based filtering, and second-order iris region statistics. The authors report good performance for the latter two approaches (98.3 % and 100 % of correct recognition rate, correspondingly), although admitting their high dependency on the printed contact lens pattern type. The small number (20) of artificial irides used should be taken into account when generalizing these results. He et al. [14] use wavelet packets analysis to calculate the liveness features classified by SVM (Support Vector Machine) with radial basis kernel. The authors report correct recognition of iris paper printouts even if intentionally blurred due to motion. He et al. [16] employ AdaBoost learning to select the best LBP-based (Local Binary Patterns) liveness features and Gaussian kernel density estimation is used to generalize the AdaBoost classifier. The authors report 99.33 % correct recognition of fakes at the alive rejection rate of 2.64 %, calculated for the evaluation database gathering 300 images of 20 different kinds of contact lenses, a few printouts and glassy eyes. Zhang et al. [41] use SVM to classify authentic iris images and patterned contact lenses within the LBP feature space. Authors report CCR = 99.14 % (correct classification rate) calculated for 55 different types of contacts worn by 72 subjects and averaged through four different capture devices. This promising CCR drops to 88.05 % in cross-validation scenario (when training and testing procedures are performed on samples captured by different cameras). Gragnaniello et al. [13] analyze a multitude of different local image descriptors (including LBP, WLD, LPQ, BSIF, LCPD, SIFT, DAISY, SID, and variants of those) to recognize paper printouts (two disjoint datasets were used) and patterned contact lenses (four different datasets were applied). The authors report more than 90 % correct classification, on average across the datasets, for all descriptors, with the best descriptor (SID) enabling recognition of 98.4 % of iris artifacts. However, there is no interoperability analysis in the paper to determine how methods trained on one set perform on the other datasets. Since statistical descriptors are known to be sensitive to local image properties, the interoperability may be limited.

Those all promising, yet single image properties discussed above, were later used jointly to form multidimensional, image quality-based liveness indicators. Galbally et al. [12] apply feature selection methodology to find the best combination of liveness features among 22 proposed simple iris geometrical or frequency descriptors. Although they report perfect recognition of printouts and alive eyes, this may be specific to the low quality of printouts applied, as this result was based solely on segmentation outcomes (information on occlusions fused with pupil-to-iris radii ratio). We should rather expect the fake samples to result in correct segmentation, if they are used in real attacks. Nevertheless, the idea of merging different quality covariates has high potential and it was applied later by Galbally et al. [11] along with quadratic discriminant analysis to detect 99.75 % of iris printouts, simultaneously falsely rejecting 4.2 % of the authentic eyes. They selected 25 quality measures that are complementary in detecting different attack types and that could be calculated efficiently in real time. This approach was also able to detect 99.2 % of synthetic irides at NPCER = 3.4 %. Sequeira et al. [33] use a collection of different feature extractors, including those based on high image frequency power, image contrast, and statistical descriptors, to detect paper printouts and patterned contact lenses. The best combination of features is then selected by sequential forward floating selection (SFFS) technique, which finds suboptimal feature sets by series of forward and backward inclusions and removals of features, followed by an assessment of each such feature set in terms of the classification performance. The authors used five different datasets of fake and authentic images, and report a correct detection rate ranging from 88.6 to 99.5 % depending of the dataset. The positive outcome of this work is that the segmentation (unpredictable for iris artifacts) is not crucial in iris liveness detection.

Researchers at the University of Notre Dame proposed in recent years a series of methods for detecting textured contact lenses. One of their significant contributions, presented in selected papers, is the proposal to use an ensemble of weaker classifiers to construct a stronger one, similar to the well-known boosting methods in machine learning. Doyle et al. [10] use Local Binary Patterns, modified to enhance the generalization capabilities of these descriptors. The authors stress the problem of limited PAD interoperability in detection of patterned contact lenses, which is the consequence of a dependence on different texture characteristics present in lenses produced by different manufacturers. They report 83 and 96 % of correct detection of artifacts for two disjoint dataset used in their work, and a significant drop in accuracy to 42 and 53 % when inter-class analysis is performed (i.e., the methods trained on the first dataset are applied to samples of the second set, and vice versa). Yadav et al. [39] apply similar modifications to LBP and a ensemble of classifiers to correctly detect more than 90 % of textured contact lenses in three different datasets. Again, limited accuracy (dropping to approximately 60 % of correct classification) is reported for inter-dataset analysis. These may suggest that features based on LBP, even modified, do not generalize well in this task.

Last but not least, an interesting approach proposed by Menotti et al. [26] is to recognize static artificial irides, fingerprints, and faces by the use of deep learning related to architecture and weights of the convolution networks. The authors report correct detection of more than 98 % fake iris images for three disjoint datasets (gathering paper printouts only).

19.3.2.2 Active Measurement of Static Object

Methods of this kind realize the active measurement (besides the normal process of iris recognition) revealing some additional structural properties of the eye, yet not using eye dynamics. A typical example is detection of Purkinje reflections, i.e., specular spots generated by illumination at inner and outer boundaries of the cornea and the eye lens. The idea originally proposed by Daugman [9] had been elaborated later by Lee et al. [23], who use two collimated NIR light sources (additional to the illuminants used for iris recognition) to generate and measure the Purkinje reflections.

Experiments done for eye images of 30 persons (including 10 wearing glasses and 10 wearing contact lenses), 10 samples of paper printouts, 2 samples of printed contact lens, and 2 samples of 3D eye models lead to promising EER = 0.33 %. However, one should note that detection of Purkinje spots requires high image sharpness, far better than normally required by iris recognition methods.

Connell et al. [3] use the fact that the authentic iris (when analyzed in low resolution) is roughly flat, in contrary to a printed contact lens that reveals a convex shape. Hence, the authors use a structured light (popular in 3D facial imaging) generated by a miniature projector to capture three-dimensional properties of the anterior part of the eyeball. This approach presented perfect recognition of fakes; however, it was tested for images captured for only one subject and six different contact lenses.

When zooming in on the iris to see its muscle fibers, we end up with a structure that is no longer flat. When observed in higher resolution the trabeculae generate shadows when illuminated by light coming from different directions. Such shadows should not be present when smooth imitations (like paper printouts) are observed, hence some researchers use this concept to distinguish flat artifacts from ragged, alive iris muscle. The first approach known to us on how to utilize the three dimensionality of the iris to determine its authenticity comes from Lee et al. [22]. The authors used wavelet decomposition to find 3D liveness features classified by SVM. Reported EER = 0.33 % was achieved for 600 live samples collected for 60 volunteers (some of them wearing glasses or contact lens) and for 600 fake samples prepared for different artifact types (printouts, photographs, printouts with contact lens, artificial images made from silicon or acrylic, and patterned contact lens). Hughes et al. [17] noticed that wearing patterned contact lens makes the observed iris pattern more convex (i.e., lying on the lens surface), in contrast with the unobstructed, authentic iris, whose pattern lies roughly on a plane. Hence, they transformed a liveness detection problem into a problem of classifying the surface shape observed within the iris region. The authors captured stereo images of the iris in visible light for 4 persons, and additionally asked two of those four volunteers to wear contact lens (transparent and patterned) when capturing the images. They report perfect recognition of irides not equipped with contact lenses (or when transparent lenses are worn) from those wearing textured contacts.

Park et al. [29] proposed an interesting solution using a few multispectral iris images instead of a typically applied single image taken in near infrared. The authors used a specialized tunable crystal filter offering very selective (10 nm band) illumination starting from 650 nm up to 1100 nm. The image used in recognition results in a gradient-based image fusion and presents no iris structure if it is the image of a printout, unlike authentic images providing useful iris features. The authors claim perfect performance, yet tests are shown for 4 different eyes only. Lee et al. [24] also use differences in multispectral light absorption by the eye tissues. The authors first calculate the ratio of iris-to-sclera image intensity (in preselected iris and sclera small regions). Since both the iris and the sclera have different light absorption properties depending on the wavelength of the illuminating light, this ratio differs when the light wavelength changes. Indeed, one may judge the authenticity of the sample by calculating the quotient of these ratios for two different illuminant wavelengths

(750 nm and 850 nm are used in the paper). The authors demonstrate zero APCER and a small NPCER $=0.28\%$ for 2800 authentic iris images, 400 images of paper printouts and 30 images of plastic eyes. Not surprisingly however, this method falsely accepts 40% of colored (and not textured) contact lenses due to their transparency to the multispectral light applied in this work.

19.3.2.3 Passive Measurement of Dynamic Object

In this group we detect dynamic properties of the measured object, yet without its stimulation. A natural example is detection of *hippus*, i.e., spontaneous pupil size oscillations [9]. Although the idea of using hippus for liveness detection has existed for years and is often cited in papers, it is difficult to find reliable implementations to date. Additionally Pacut et al. suggest (after observing their own measurements) that the visibility of hippus is subject to the individual, and hence its reliability may be limited when applied to larger populations. A successful deployment of the hippus is shown by Fabiola et al. [37], however in the context of user authentication and not in liveness detection. EER $=0.23\%$ achieved by the authors when analyzing hippus in 50 persons suggests that the spontaneous movements of the pupil may deliver individual features. When added to the iris biometric template, they could serve as liveness indicators. The paper, however, does not include any tests with fake eyes to prove this hypothesis. If the iris image contains also the eyelids, one may adapt a spontaneous eye blinking detection, popular in face recognition and face liveness detection. Reported accuracy of blinks recognition is high (98% claimed by Cohn et al. [2] for 10 volunteers, or 88.8% for 20 subjects reported by Pan et al. [28]). One should note, however, that spontaneous blinks happen every few seconds; they are irregular and their frequency is subject dependent. Hence, when iris capture time plays an important role, detection of stimulated blinks (instead of spontaneous) seems to be a more adequate approach. Rigas et al. [31] present a concept based on analysis of eye gaze in a challenge-response scenario to detect static paper printouts. The authors follow the eye gaze for 15 s using a specialized eye tracker device. The reported correct classification rate of artifact detection reaches 95.7%. This interesting proposal has a potential to be adapted in real scenarios if the acquisition time is shorter and the eye gaze tracking could be realized by the same camera which captures the iris image for recognition purposes.

19.3.2.4 Active Measurement of Dynamic Object

The last group of methods comprises those stimulating the object and analyzing its dynamics. The human eye delivers at least two types of dynamic features: those related to the entire eyeball and those describing changes in pupil size. Komogortsev et al. observe the eye's horizontal saccade trajectories to differentiate authentic eyeballs and simulated behavior of mechanical replicas. The stimulus is a jumping point that had to be followed by system users. The smallest EER $=5\%$ is achieved for

32 volunteers participating in the experiment, and when the eye movement model is unknown to the attacker. The EER grows to 20 % when the occulomotor plant characteristics are available to imitate the eye's saccade. Some researchers employ the iris muscle deformations under changing illumination, like Kanematsu et al. [20] who calculate the iris image brightness variations after the light stimuli in the predefined iris regions. They report perfect recognition of alive irides and a few paper printouts. Puhan et al. [30] calculate the differences in iris texture for dilated and constricted irides, claiming that these differences should be large for an authentic eye and small for a printed contact lens. This claim, although correct in principle, has no proof of concept in the paper since the authors show results for two authentic eyes only and not for artifacts.

Conference debates and scientific literature often suggest an attack with the use of an active LCD panel (displaying an eye movie) as a candidate for successful mimicking of eye dynamics. However, no successful realization of this forgery is known so far and it is doubtful to observe such successful attack in future. The rationale behind this statement is the following. The iris acquisition equipment illuminates the eye by near-infrared light (typical operating wavelength starts at 700 nm and ends at 900, as recommended by ISO/IEC 29794-6) and implements optical filters to cut the light outside this range. On the other hand, the LCD displays aim at presenting the contents to the user, and hence must operate in visible light (with wavelength not exceeding 700 nm). This causes the iris recognition cameras to be 'blind' to what is displayed by the LCD. We do not know any off-the-shelf LCD displays operating in near-infrared light that could be used to play an eye movie. A far better idea, not yet verified, is to use passive LCD displays, such as those used in electronic book readers.[1] They do not block a light of any particular wavelength, hence they should reflect an active NIR illumination produced by iris recognition cameras. A resolution of 300 PPI ('pixel per inch') offered by typical readers seems to be enough to present iris features with adequate quality. Namely, according to ISO/IEC 29794-6, the minimum scanning resolution should be at least 120 pixel across the iris diameter. Assuming a typical iris radius equal to 12 mm gives the minimum resolution of 10 pixels per mm, i.e., approximately 254 PPI. Hence, in theory, this kind of attack could be possible. In practice, however, due to high regularity of elements of the passive LCD displays, they should be easily detected by methods based on passive measurement and using static features of the eye (as presented in Sect. 19.3.2.1).

One should note that no pupil dynamic features are estimated in the studies presented above. Although the obvious idea to use pupil dynamic features for liveness detection has existed for years, there is only a small amount of research presenting proof of this concept along with adequate experimental results. Pacut et al. [27] used a dynamic pupil reaction model and neural classifier to perfectly recognize the authentic eyes and the iris printouts based on an image sequence database collected for 29 volunteers and more than 500 paper artifacts. At the same time, the authors

---

[1] This interesting variant of the LCD-based attack was suggested from the audience by an anonymous participant during Norwegian Biometrics Laboratory Annual Workshop on Presentation Attack Detection in Biometrics, Gjøvik, Norway, March 2, 2015.

applied for a patent in Poland [8], which was later extended to the USA [7]. Since they used the iris printouts in the research, which can be recognized by easier approaches, the potential of the method was neither appreciated nor presented. Czajka extended this study to show how this method recognizes the odd (or no) reactions of the eye [5] when a positive surge of the light is used as the stimulus for pupil reaction. This chapter gives a thorough description of these findings to date and presents extended research employing positive and negative changes in light intensity as stimuli.

19.3.3 Supporting Activities

Besides the scientific endeavors, it is worth noting some other initiatives related to iris liveness detection. Clarkson University (USA), University of Notre Dame (USA), and Warsaw University of Technology (Poland) organized the first international iris liveness competition in 2013 [40]. This competition is a follow-up to three earlier liveness competitions, all devoted to fingerprint biometrics. The competition organizers used paper iris printouts (815 images in total) and printed contact lenses (2240 images in total) in testing. Approximately 62 % of contact lens images and 25 % of paper printout images have been offered to participants as a training set, and the remaining data were used in evaluation of the delivered methods. Three universities decided to send their algorithms. Competition results demonstrate some interesting phenomena. First, it is clear that patterned contact lenses are much harder to detect when compared to recognition of paper printouts (0.65 % of paper printout acceptance vs. 9.32 % on average of printed contact lens acceptance achieved for the winning method). Second, the competition results show a clear dissonance between laboratory results presented by most of the scientific papers (typically showing perfect, or almost perfect recognition of fakes and alive samples) and third-party evaluation reporting average classification errors at a 10 % level for a winning solution. These findings reinforce the importance of independent evaluations. This is why the second edition of this competition was organized in 2015 [32] and other initiatives came out after LivDet 2013, such as MobiLive 2014 [34] focusing on mobile environment. One of the positive outcomes of these competitions is the availability of specific datasets that can be used as valuable benchmarks once the competitions are concluded.

One may be also interested in TABULA RASA [36], a European project that is solely devoted to liveness detection. Some of the impressive project outcomes are devoted to iris recognition, e.g., already cited deployment of iris image quality features in artifacts detection [12]. Biometrics Institute is an initiator of the Biometric Vulnerability Assessment Expert Group [1], an international group of experts that aims at raising the awareness about the importance of biometric vulnerability assessments and exchanging subject-related experiences. ISO/IEC JTC sub-committee No. 37 (Biometrics) is also about to issue a separate international multipart standard devoted in full to presentanotion attack detection. These examples show that liveness detection in biometrics is t a fully solved issue or the results obtained to date do not satisfy both science and industry.

19.4   Database of Iris Movies

19.4.1   Collection Stand

To our best knowledge, there are no public collections of iris movies that would allow for this study of pupil dynamics. We decided to build suitable measuring equipment and gather our own set of *eye movies* captured in near-infrared light. The core of the collection stand is the IrisCUBE camera [6] embedding The Imaging Source DMK 4002-IR b/w camera equipped with a SONY ICX249AL 1/2" CCD interline sensor of increased infrared sensitivity. The scene was illuminated by two near-infrared illuminants ($\lambda = 850$ nm) placed horizontally and equidistantly to the lens. Our equipment applies a near-infrared filter to cut any light with a wavelength lower than 800 nm. The IrisCUBE captures 25 full frames per second, and the iris image quality significantly exceeds minimal ISO/IEC 19794-6 and ISO/IEC 29794-6 recommendations related to those aspects that are independent of the imaged subject. Since we wanted to guarantee repeatable capture conditions in the entire experiment, we enclosed the camera in a large, shaded box with a place where the subject positions his or her eyes for acquisition of the image. The distance between the camera lens and the subject's eyes was thus fixed and equal to approximately 30 cm. We used visible LEDs, embedded into the frontal part of the camera case, which normally help the user in positioning the head, as a visible light stimulus. This configuration guarantees the repeatable measurements in a fixed and controlled environment. It allows us to measure the pupil's reaction in complete darkness (regardless of external lighting conditions) as well as during the visible light step stimulation. However, one should be aware that pupil reaction may be less distinct when the eye is observed under bright ambient light (due to higher pupil constriction before the stimuli is applied), and it may also fluctuate as the ambient light changes.

19.4.2   Database Properties

This research is based on a unique database of eye movies collected for 52 distinct irides of 26 subjects. For 50 irides we acquired 4 movies, and only 2 movies for a single person, making for 204 eye movies in total. Each movie lasts 30 s and presents spontaneous oscillations of the pupil size (first 15 s) and reaction to a step increase of light intensity (next 5 s), as well as the reaction to a negative step change in the illumination (last 10 s). Since we capture 25 frames per second, the database volume sums up to $204 \times 30 \times 25 = 153{,}000$ iris images illustrating pupil dilation and constriction processes.

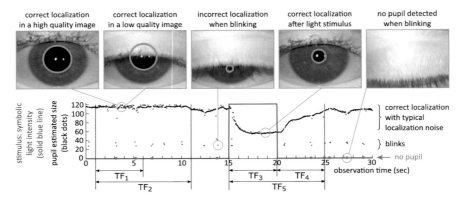

Fig. 19.1 Pupil size (*black dots*) measured automatically during a single experiment under the light stimuli (*blue solid line*). Note that capture of a real object results in a nonideal sequence of pupil size due to blinks (*black dots* departing from the expected sequence), eye closure (*red dots* of zero ordinate denoting that no pupil is detected), or fluctuations of the segmentation process (revealing as a 'noise' in the sequence). Illustrating exemplars are shown at the *top* and linked to the corresponding moments of the sequence. Five different time frames (denoted as $TF_1, ..., TF_5$) are also shown, indicating different parts of each time series used in this research

Figure 19.1 presents example frames and illustrates the moments when visible LED are turned on and off. It is worth noting that 30 s movies deliver good quality iris images as well as those acquired when blinking. Additionally, despite the fact that head position was roughly fixed owing to the hardware setup, typical head (and thus eye) micro movements were still present during image capture, also visible in Fig. 19.1. All these deviations from ideal presentation of the eye provide additional challenges for further data processing.

19.4.3   Representation of Actual and Odd Pupil Reactions

In all research devoted to presentation attack detection there is a common difficulty in finding the classification function that divides liveness feature space into two subspaces corresponding to authentic and fake samples. Since typically these classifiers are built by some learning procedures, we need samples representing those classes. This, unfortunately, leads to methods that are specific to some kinds of fake objects. Generalization is almost impossible since we cannot predict the fantasy and determination of the counterfeiters. In particular, past work summarized in Sect. 19.3 is devoted mainly to detection of static artifacts, typically iris printouts, contact lenses or eye prosthetic models. Application of pupil dynamics for detection of paper printouts should lead to perfect performance, since static objects demonstrate no dynamics.

This work goes beyond this limitation and presents the method that may recognize correct pupil dynamics and reject any behavior that mimics real pupil movements, or presents some odd, unexpected oscillations. In this research we decided to analyze the alive eyes only and to treat the spontaneous oscillations of the pupil as odd reactions to hypothetical (nonexistent in this case) light stimuli. This approach perfectly corresponds to what is understood under the 'liveness' term, namely the detection of vital symptoms of the analyzed object. Only an alive and authentic eye should demonstrate correct dynamics specific to a human organ. If after a sudden visible light impulse (positive, negative, or both in a row) nothing but *hippus* is observed, this may denote that a nonliving eye is observed. To organize the data according to our assumptions, we consequently crop sub-movies from each 30 s eye movie gathered in the database to make samples useful for modeling the pupil reaction to positive, negative and both light stimuli. Simultaneously we need to have data representing odd reactions of the same length. Hence, the following options are considered (denoted as five different time frames in Fig. 19.1: TF_1, ..., TF_5):

(1) sub-movies representing **odd eye reactions** starting 1 s after the measurement takes off and ending after the sixth (TF_1) or eleventh (TF_2) second of the measurement,
(2) sub-movies representing actual eye reaction to **positive** change in the light intensity, starting in the sixteenth second of the measurement, i.e., exactly when the eye is stimulated by a visible light, and lasting 5 s (TF_3),
(3) sub-movies representing actual eye reaction to **negative** change in the light intensity, starting in the twenty-first second of the measurement, i.e., exactly when the light stimulus is turned off, and lasting 5 s (TF_4),
(4) sub-movies representing actual eye reaction to **positive and negative** changes in the light intensity, starting in the sixteenth second of the measurement and lasting 10 s (TF_5).

Certainly, we have 204 sub-movies in each option as all the acquired data (for all subjects) were used. The analysis of pupil reaction will be further realized in the selected time frame pairs. We define three scenarios of data usage:

S1 pupil reaction to both positive and negative stimuli versus odd reaction: TF_5 versus TF_2.
S2 pupil reaction to negative stimulus versus odd reaction: TF_4 versus TF_1,
S3 pupil reaction to positive stimulus versus odd reaction: TF_3 versus TF_1,

One should be aware that the spontaneous oscillations of the pupil observed in complete darkness, or in a very bright ambient light, may have lower amplitude when compared to oscillations captured under a regular ambient light. The latter case allows the pupil to constrict and dilate with no distinct limitations, while complete darkness or a very bright ambient light causes the pupil to be already excessively constricted or dilated, hence allowing for only a limited change in its size.

19.5 Recognition of Pupil Dynamics

19.5.1 Data Preprocessing

19.5.1.1 Pupil Detection, Segmentation and Calculation of Its Size

Pupil dynamics is expressed by changes of its size. The *pupil size* is however an imprecise and general dimension that may be calculated in various ways. In this work, we decided to use the most common, circular approximation of its—possibly irregular—shape. This is done intentionally due to three factors: (a) high speed of circular segmentation, (b) commonness of circular modeling in already deployed iris recognition methods, and (c) unimportance of noncircular deviations when describing the dynamics.

Having no ground truth related to iris location, the pupil is detected localized in each frame independently. While *detection* refers to a statement of whether the pupil exists within the frame, the *localization* delivers its position. To localize a boundary between the pupil and the iris, we applied a Hough transform operating on *directional image*, that is estimation of an image gradient delivering both a gradient value and its direction [6]. The transform is parametrized to make it sensitive to dark circular shapes and almost unresponsive to other dark shapes and light circles, such as specular reflections. Use of gradient and sensitivity to circular shapes makes this method surprisingly robust even if the pupil is 50 % covered by eyelids. Consequently each eye movie is transformed into a time series of pupil radii, Fig. 19.1. We do not use gradient values that do not exceed a minimum threshold (set experimentally to the hardware setup that was employed). If there is no single gradient value exceeding the threshold, the method reports that no pupil could be detected. The latter realizes pupil detection, and helps to identify time moments when the eye is completely covered by eyelids.

19.5.1.2 Artifacts Removal

Raw sequences of pupil radii are not perfect due to segmentation inaccuracy. In general, we encounter two kinds of disruptions: (a) pupil detection errors (typically due to blinks fully covering the eye), and (b) pupil segmentation noise (typically due to blinks in which the pupil is partially covered, eye motion, off-axis gaze, highly noncircular pupil shape that results in small oscillations of the estimated pupil size, or simply algorithm mistakes). Errors of the first kind are identified by the pupil detection process. Those erroneous points can be easily omitted when modeling the pupil dynamics (marked as red dots lying on the horizontal axis in Fig. 19.1). However, the segmentation errors can be identified only to some extent when the pupil radius diverges significantly when compared to its neighboring values. These sudden collapses in pupil radius are mostly caused by partial blinks and—due to the speed of blink relative to 25 frames per second—they typically occupy several

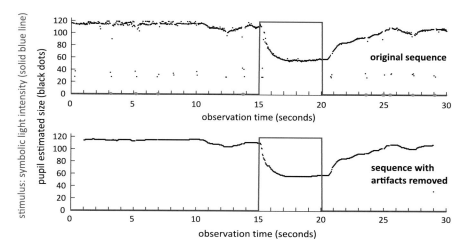

Fig. 19.2 *Upper graph* Original measurement of the pupil size (*upper graph*) as shown in Fig. 19.1 with artifacts caused by blinks (visualized by *black dots* significantly diverging from the trend, and *red dots* representing frames with no pupil detected). *Lower graph* The same sequence after median filtering. Most of the isolated deviations in the estimated pupil size were removed, simultaneously the character of pupil dynamics is retained (both the reaction to light stimuli and the spontaneous oscillations are visible). *Blue line* symbolizing the intensity of visible light (the stimulus) is also shown in both graphs

(or even isolated) values. Thus a median filtering with 1 s (i.e., 25 frames) sliding window was applied to smooth the pupil reaction functions, Fig. 19.2.

19.5.2   Modeling of Pupil Dynamics

Light intensity surges generate obvious pupil constriction and dilation. Kohn and Clynes [21] noticed an asymmetry in pupil response depending on whether the flash is positive (from darkness to brightness) or negative, and proposed a reaction model that can be graphically envisioned as a two-channel transfer function of a complex argument s, Fig. 19.3.

Fig. 19.3 Pupil dynamics model deployed in this work and derived from an original proposal of Kohn and Clynes [21]. Graph adapted from [7]

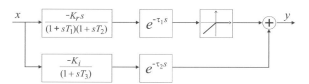

The upper channel consists of a second-order inertia with time constants T_1 and T_2, and a lag element characterized by τ_1. It models a transient behavior of the pupil only for positive light stimuli, what is guaranteed by a nonlinear function placed after the lag element and cutting down the channel response for negative stimuli. The channel gain is controlled by K_r. In turn, the lower channel is responsible for modeling long-term and persistent changes in pupil size, and answers by setting a new pupil radius after both the negative or positive light stimuli. It contains a first-order inertia (with its speed controlled by T_3) and a lag element characterized by τ_2. The lower channel gain is controlled independently of the upper channel by K_i.

Calculating the inverse Laplace transform, we may easily obtain the model response $y(t; \phi)$ in time domain. Note the nonlinear element in the upper channel causing the model response to be different for positive and negative light stimuli. Namely, assuming a positive light stimuli at $t = 0$, the model output is a sum of the upper and lower channel responses, $y_{\text{upper}}(t; \phi_1)$ and $y_{\text{lower}}(t; \phi_2)$, respectively:

$$y(t; \phi) = y_{\text{upper}}(t; \phi_1) + y_{\text{lower}}(t; \phi_2) \tag{19.1}$$

where

$$y_{\text{upper}}(t; \phi_1) = \begin{cases} -\frac{K_r}{T_1^2}(t - \tau_1)e^{-\frac{t-\tau_1}{T_1}} & \text{if } T_1 = T_2 \\ \frac{K_r}{T_2-T_1}\left(e^{-\frac{t-\tau_1}{T_1}} - e^{-\frac{t-\tau_1}{T_2}}\right) & \text{otherwise} \end{cases}$$

$$y_{\text{lower}}(t; \phi_2) = -K_i\left(1 - e^{-\frac{t-\tau_2}{T_3}}\right) \tag{19.2}$$

and

$$\phi = [\phi_1, \phi_2]^T = [K_r, T_1, T_2, \tau_1, K_i, T_3, \tau_2]^T \tag{19.3}$$

However, in case of a negative light stimuli at $t = 0$, the model output is built solely by the lower channel $y_{\text{lower}}(t; \phi_2)$:

$$y(t; \phi) = y_{\text{lower}}(t; \phi_2) \tag{19.4}$$

where

$$y_{\text{lower}}(t; \phi_2) = K_i\left(1 - e^{-\frac{t-\tau_2}{T_3}}\right) \tag{19.5}$$

and

$$\phi = \phi_2^T = [K_i, T_3, \tau_2]^T \tag{19.6}$$

Note the 'minus' sign disappeared from Eq. (19.5) when compared to Eq. (19.2) due to inverse polarity of the stimulus. The vector ϕ consists of *liveness features*, i.e., the vector of parameters setting the model response. Thus, the observed pupil dynamics (time series) is transformed to a single point in seven- or three-dimensional (depending on the stimulus used), liveness feature space by solving the **model fitting problem**.

19.5.3   Searching for Liveness Features: Fitting the Model

Optimal model parameters $\widehat{\phi}$ for each eye movie are identified by solving a nonlinear least-squares curve fitting problem of the form:

$$\widehat{\phi} = \text{argmin}_{\phi \in \Phi} \sum_{i=1}^{N} (\widehat{y}(t; \phi) - y(t))^2 \tag{19.7}$$

where Φ is the set of possible values of ϕ, $y(t)$ is real (observed) change in the pupil size, $\widehat{y}(t; \phi)$ is the model response given the parameters ϕ and estimated for a given $y(t)$, and $t = 0, \ldots, t_{max}$. The definition of Φ is made by setting the following box constraints on model parameters:

$$0 \leq K_r \leq 1000$$
$$0 \leq T_1 \leq 100$$
$$0 \leq T_2 \leq 100$$
$$0 \leq \tau_1 \leq 20$$
$$0 \leq K_i \leq 1000$$
$$0 \leq T_3 \leq 100$$
$$0 \leq \tau_2 \leq 20$$

Kohn and Clynes [21] suggest the following model parameters of a typical pupil dynamics: $T_1 = 0.25$ s, $T_2 = T_3 = 0.4$ s, $\tau_1 = 0.28$ s and $\tau_2 = 0.35$ s. These values (along with the channel gains) are used as the starting point $\widehat{\phi}_0$ in optimization procedure (19.7) for each type of stimuli, namely:

$$\widehat{\phi}_0 = [100, 0.25, 0.4, 0.28, 100, 0.4, 0.35]^T$$

We found that $t_{max} \leq 1.5$ s makes this model useless. Hence, in this work we analyze a multitude of optimization horizons starting from $t_{max} = 1.6$ s and finishing with the maximum $t_{max} = 5$ s for positive or negative stimuli, or $t_{max} = 10$ s if both stimuli are jointly taken into account in modeling. Figure 19.4 illustrates how the observation horizon influences the quality of modeling.

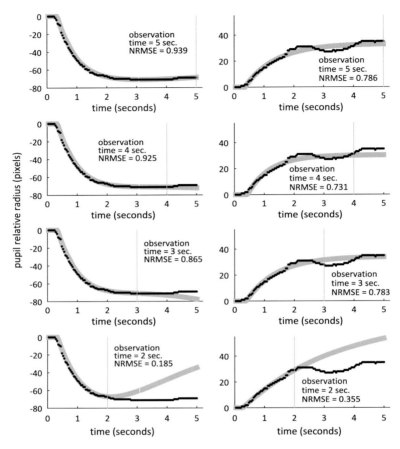

Fig. 19.4 Kohn and Clynes model responses (*solid* and *thick gray line*) calculated for preprocessed measurement (*black dots*). In each case, the modeling starts in $t = 0$. *Top left graph* presents the model output after 5 s observation, achieved for $\widehat{\phi} = [387.38, 0.54, 5.99, 0.30, 45.90, 2.78, 0.65]^T$ and positive light stimulus. *Top right graph* shows the model output for negative stimulus, achieved for $\widehat{\phi} = [33.09, 1.02, 0.32]^T$. Remaining graphs illustrate the degradation in modeling accuracy when the optimization horizon decreases, for both the positive and negative light stimuli. Normalized root mean square error (NRMSE) for each model is also shown, calculated for the entire 5 s horizon in each case. NRMSE close to 1 denotes a good fit, while values around 0 suggest that the model is not better than a straight line

19.5.4 Goodness of Fit

Modeling of pupil dynamics may certainly be erroneous and result in poor fits. These inadequate sets of model parameters should be identified and not used in further classification. To assess the goodness of fit, we use normalized root mean square error, namely

$$\text{GoF} = \max\left(0, \, 1 - \frac{\|y(\cdot) - \widehat{y}(\cdot; \phi)\|}{\|y(\cdot) - \bar{y}(\cdot)\|}\right) \tag{19.8}$$

where $\bar{y}$ is the mean of y, and $\|\cdot\|$ indicates the 2-norm of a vector. GoF limits from 0, when $\widehat{y}$ is no better than a straight line fitting y, to 1 for a perfect fit.

19.5.5   Classification of the Liveness Features

Sample values of the liveness features calculated for three scenarios (S1, S2 and S3, defined in Sect. 19.4.3) are shown in Figs. 19.5, 19.6 and 19.7, respectively. It is clear that the discrimination power of the liveness features is heterogeneous, and some of them perform better that others. In high-dimensional feature spaces, it would be reasonable to apply a feature selection methodology to narrow the problem dimensionality. However, in our case there is no practical rationale behind narrowing the feature set. First, when identifying the model, we need to set all parameters, hence no calculations can be simplified even if a feature subset is smaller. Second, all liveness features have a solid interpretation in terms of the modeling, and dropping any of them would make the model incomplete.

   To build a classification function, we use the support vector machine as one of the best off-the-shelf classifiers performing well in low-dimensional feature spaces (as in our case). To approximate linear and nonlinear classification boundaries, we deployed linear SVM as well as those with nonlinear kernels: quadratic, radial basis function and polynomial. That is, we have four different classifiers in each of three scenarios that are analyzed and compared in this work.

19.6   Experiments and Results

19.6.1   Generating Gallery and Probe Samples

In order to minimize the risk of underestimating the performance errors, we divide our dataset into two disjoint subsets used to train and evaluate a given method. The training subset is often called the *gallery*, while the subset used to evaluate the trained algorithm is called the *probe*. In the ideal situation, we have ample sizes of both gallery and probe subsets to provide statistical guarantees of the calculated errors that satisfy our needs. In a typical situation, however, the sizes of those sets are far below the ideal, and—depending on the original database size—different cross-validation techniques are used to answer how the specific results would generalize on the independent and unknown data. In biometrics we commonly use the k-fold and leave-n-out cross-validations, setting $k = 2$ in the former (two folds, possibly of equal size, corresponding to the gallery and probe subsets) and setting $n = 1$ in the

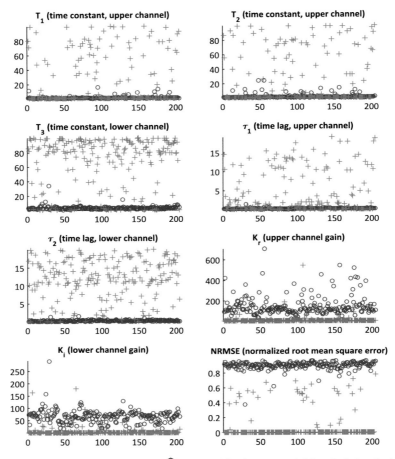

Fig. 19.5 Values of the liveness features $\widehat{\phi}$ calculated for the expected (*blue circles*) and odd (*red crosses*) pupil reactions for positive and negative light stimuli and 10 s observation time (scenario S1). Results for all 204 eye movies are shown. Normalized root mean square error (NRMSE) is also shown in the *bottom right* graph, suggesting a far better fit for normal pupil reactions when compared to odd ones

latter (the gallery consists of $n-1$ samples, while the remaining one sample forms a probe set).

In this work leave-one-out cross-validation is used in all evaluations, but leaving out *all* samples of a given person instead of using a single sample (i.e., single time series). This scenario generates $n = 26$ runs in each scenario (S1, S2 and S3) of training-testing experiments (which is equal to the number of distinct subjects) instead of 204 (i.e., number of all samples), but due to statistical dependency among samples of the same person, we believe in obtaining evaluation results unbiased by person-dependent factors shared between the train and test data.

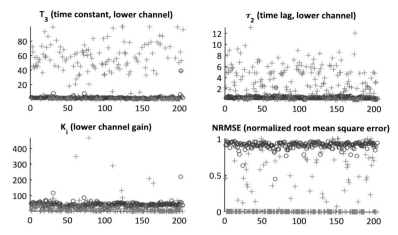

Fig. 19.6 Same as in Fig. 19.5, except the stimulus is a negative step of light intensity and the observation time is 5 s (scenario S2)

19.6.2   Decision Making

Relying solely on the classifier output is insufficient since some odd reactions of the eye may result in model parameters falling into the subspace representing authentic eye reactions. It is a good idea to analyze the goodness of fit simultaneously with the classifier output, as erroneously accepted samples may result from poor model identification. This builds a two-dimensional decision plane with classifier response on one axis and the goodness of fit on the other providing four decision regions, Fig. 19.8. In consequence, we accept the observed object as alive only when the classifier decision is positive *and* the model fit is accurate (the NRMSE is above the threshold).

19.6.3   Assessment of the Method Performance

We had two objectives of the experiments: (a) to assess the performance of the method, select the most reliable SVM kernel and combination of the stimuli, and (b) to find a minimum pupil observation time that is necessary to offer reasonable accuracy. The former answers the question of whether there is a theoretical potential in this approach. The latter estimates the chances of practical deployments in a biometric system, since the expected iris capture times should be short (not exceeding a few seconds).

Application of a leave-one-out procedure (leaving out all the samples for a given person) leads us to $n = 26$ estimation-evaluation experiments realized in each scenario. That is, in each experiment we train four different SVMs (linear, quadratic,

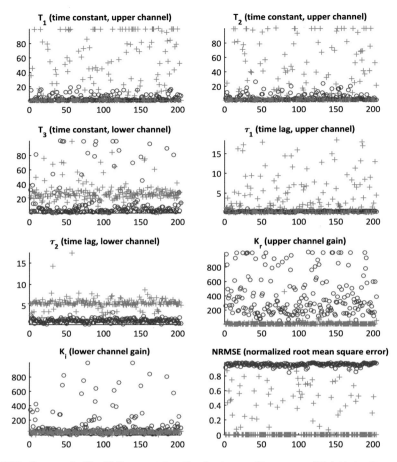

Fig. 19.7 Same as in Fig. 19.5, except the stimulus is a positive surge of light intensity and the observation time is 5 s (scenario S3)

polynomial, and radial basis), along with eventual parameter optimization (in particular: order of polynomial kernel and attenuation parameter for radial basis kernel) using all samples for $n - 1$ subjects. We then evaluate these SVMs on the unknown samples of the remaining nth subject. In each estimation experiment, we also set the goodness of fit threshold for later use in evaluating the classifier with the remaining samples. We decided to set the GoF threshold so as not to increase false rejections of authentic eyes due to liveness detection, i.e., we minimized NPCER. There is an important rationale behind this approach rather than minimizing the false acceptances of nonliving eyes that comes both from theory and practice. Theoretical deliberations suggest that predicting the nature of—and hence resulting statistics related to—all the possible attacks is impossible. On the other hand, it is easier to develop statistical models for authentic biometric samples. Thus, it is reasonable to focus on authentic

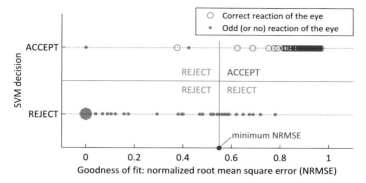

Fig. 19.8 Decision plane defined by the SVM output and the estimate of goodness of fit (GoF). This example shows that requiring some minimum value of GoF when calculating the liveness features may improve the final decision: the method correctly rejected a few odd reactions mistakenly accepted by the SVM (represented by the *red dots*) but resulting from an inaccurate model (GoF below the threshold), thus lowering the APCER. Simultaneously, only one falsely rejected authentic sample constitutes to a slight growth in NPCER. This example is generated for all 204 samples classified by the linear SVM during 10 s observation period when both positive and negative stimuli are use (scenario S1)

data when approximating a classification function and to accept that this classifier may generate some errors for fakes. This approach is more robust than an opposite approach in which we would fix the classification function tightly around specific fake samples, since the generality for other kinds of fakes would be weak and would decrease accuracy for authentic samples. This corresponds to practice, since the system developers are more resistant to the increased probability of false rejection and they are more likely to a higher probability of accepting the fakes, which is very high with no liveness detection anyway, and which always decreases when even a weak PAD method is applied.

Consequently, we performed $n = 26$ independent evaluations in three scenarios and calculated the NPCER and APCER, with and without GoF, Table 19.1. These results show a few interesting outcomes. First, in all scenarios there is at least one classifier variant that does not introduce false rejections of authentic pupil reaction (NPCER $= 0$ for all 26 evaluations). Second, it seems that using only the lower channel of the Kohn and Clynes model (and hence, only three-dimensional liveness feature space—scenario S2) gives worse general results when compared to the use of both channels (and hence seven-dimensional feature space—scenarios S1 and S3). In particular, there is no classifier variant presenting zero APCER in scenario S2. Third (minor), the SVM with polynomial kernel presents the best performance, with a linear SVM variant reaching closely its accuracy. This may be important from the practical point of view, since implementation of a linear classifier should engage less computational resources when compared to the use of nonlinear kernels.

Table 19.1 Sample error rates achieved in three different scenarios of stimulus usage

	SVM kernel	NPCER	APCER	APCER with GoF
Scenario S1 (positive and negative stimuli)	Linear	0	0.0098	0.0049
	Quadratic	0.0098	0	0
	Polynomial (p=4)	0	0	0
	RBF ($\sigma = 4.4$)	0	0.0147	0.0049
Scenario S2 (only negative stimulus)	Linear	0.0049	0.0245	0.0245
	Quadratic	0.0049	0.0049	0.0049
	Polynomial (p=4)	0	0.0049	0.0049
	RBF ($\sigma = 1.4$)	0.0049	0.0049	0.0049
Scenario S3 (only positive stimulus)	Linear	0	0	0
	Quadratic	0	0.0147	0
	Poly (p=3)	0	0	0
	RBF ($\sigma = 1.2$)	0.0049	0	0

All numbers are calculated for maximum time horizon available in each scenario, i.e., 10 s in S1, and 5 s in S2 and S3. It is evident that when the quality of the model fitting (GoF) is considered, the erroneous acceptance of odd eye reactions as authentic reactions is lower

Table 19.1 shows that we may resign from using both stimuli, and hence waiting 10 s to measure pupil dynamics during iris image acquisition, and select scenario S2 or S3 as a satisfactory one, shortening the acquisition time to 5 s. One may be happy with this 5-s acquisition time, or—remembering that this choice comes from the data collection procedure—may look for even shorter observation times that still offer reasonable performance. The average error rates are presented for each variant of the SVM and a series of observation times (starting from 1.6 s and stopping at 5 s) in Figs. 19.9 and 19.10. When modeling the reaction to negative stimulus (i.e., using only three-parameter model) we do not achieve a perfect performance for any of time horizons used for modeling, Fig. 19.9. However, this simplified model starts to perform reasonably well when the modeling horizon is not greater than 3 s, presenting the APCER and NPCER below of equal to 1 %. However, if practical considerations call for even better performance, the best decision is to use a model for positive stimulus. Three-second observation is enough to get the perfect recognition of authentic and odd reactions of the pupil for all four SVM kernels, Fig. 19.10.

19.7 Discussion: Merits and Limitations

The outcomes shown in the last section suggest that pupil dynamics may deliver interesting liveness features when observing the eye for a short time (relative to the typical acquisition time of a few seconds in iris recognition). Mimicking pupil

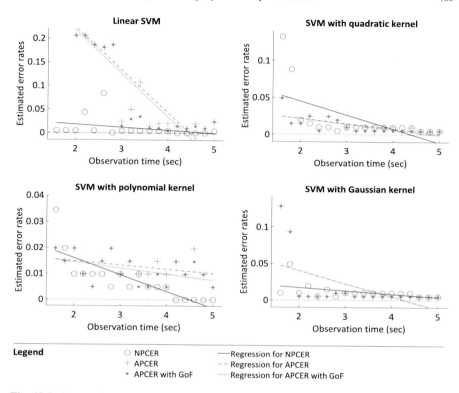

Fig. 19.9 Averaged error rates as a function of the observation time (calculations made every 200 ms starting from 1600 ms and ending after 5000 ms), achieved for **negative light stimulus** and three-parameter model. Each graph represents the results obtained for one of four variants of the SVM kernel. *Blue circles* show the average (for 26 independent evaluations) proportion of authentic presentations incorrectly classified as attacks. *Red crosses* show averaged proportion of attack presentations that were incorrectly classified as authentic ones when we rely solely on the SVM output. *Red dots* suggest far better accuracy when the goodness of fit is analyzed along with the classification decisions. Regression lines were added to illustrate linear trends as a function of the observation time

dynamics is difficult, and concealing one's own pupil reaction is impossible due to its involuntary nature. The medical literature reports also that the pupil reaction may change under stress. Therefore, we may even formulate the hypothesis that this is one of few methods that could recognize the capture under coercion.

Implementation of the proposed approach may have an additional, positive side effect. It is known that the accuracy of iris recognition may be affected by inconsistencies in pupil size, especially when the pupil dilation differs significantly in the enrollment and authentication processes. The approach presented in this chapter can paradoxically compensate for this phenomenon at no cost, in particular not introducing additional acquisition time. Namely, once the iris movie is captured, the biometric system can select one (or a few) iris images with different sizes of the pupil to per-

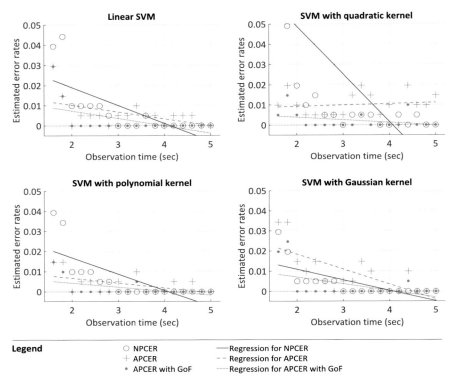

Fig. 19.10 Same as in Fig. 19.9 except that **positive light stimulus** and the seven-parameter model are used

form the biometric recognition (no additional capture is needed). If the same system records the pupil size observed at the enrollment along with the reference template, it can select the frame with similar pupil size at the authentication stage. If there are no pupil size data connected to the reference template, the system can deploy multiple authentication images presenting different pupil sizes and select the lowest distance between the template and the authentication sample. This should significantly lower within-class variance of the iris comparison score distribution.

To complete our conclusions, we should also analyze the darker side of the coin. First, the measurement of dynamic features takes time. Not all applications allow for additional 3 s when capturing the iris. Second, limitation may come from the variability of dynamic features across different populations and more subtle changes in pupil size for elderly people. Since the database used in this study does not contain any measurement from elderly people, reported errors may be underestimated in their case. The third limitation may refer to the possible nonstationarity of pupil dynamics as a consequence of ingestion of different substances (e.g., drugs or alcohol), an altered psychological state (e.g., stress, relaxation, drowsiness or mental load). We do not know of scientific results that would thoroughly discuss the influence of these factors on pupil dynamics, yet it is easy to imagine that they are not unimportant. Since this work presents research results for people who are not stressed and who have not ingested any substance that could modify pupil reaction, we cannot guarantee that pupil dynamics is unaltered in these abnormal circumstances. Lest we also forget the surrounding environment, since the starting pupil size (and thus the amplitude of the reaction) depends on the intensity of ambient light. This research used data collected in darkness before applying light stimuli.

To conclude, this method seems to be a good candidate for robust liveness detection and has a high potential for practical applications. Keeping in mind its limitations, one may obtain an interesting element of the PAD implementation that is sensitive to features not offered by methods detecting static artifacts.

Acknowledgments The author would like to thank Mr. Rafal Brize, who collected the database of iris images used in this work under his Master's degree project lead by this author. The author is cordially grateful to Prof. Andrzej Pacut of Warsaw University of Technology for valuable remarks that significantly contributed to this research. The application of Kohn and Clynes model was inspired by research of Mr. Marcin Chochowski, who used parameters of this model as individual features in biometric recognition. This author, together with Prof. Pacut and Mr. Chochowski, has been granted a US patent No. 8,061,842 which partially covers the idea deployed in this work.

References

1. Biometric Institute, Biometric Vulnerability Assessment Expert Group (BVAEG). (2015) http://www.biometricsinstitute.org
2. J. Cohn et al., Automatic recognition of eye blinking in spontaneously occurring behavior. Behav. Res. Methods Instrum. Comput. **35**(3), 420–428 (2003)
3. J. Connell et al., Fake iris detection using structured light, in *2013 IEEE International Conference on Acoustics, Speech and Signal Processing (ICASSP)* (2013), pp. 8692–8696
4. A. Czajka, Database of iris printouts and its application: Development of liveness detection method for iris recognition, in *2013 18th International Conference on Methods and Models in Automation and Robotics (MMAR)* (2013), pp. 28–33
5. A. Czajka, Pupil dynamics for iris liveness detection. IEEE Trans. Inf. Forensics Secur. **10**(4), 726–735 (2015)
6. A. Czajka, A. Pacut, Iris recognition system based on Zak-Gabor wavelet packets. J. Telecommun. Inf. Technol. **4**, 10–18 (2010)
7. A. Czajka, A. Pacut, M. Chochowski, Method of eye aliveness testing and device for eye aliveness testing. US Patent No. 8.061.842. November 22, 2011
8. A. Czajka, A. Pacut, M. Chochowski, Sposob testowania zywotnosci oka i urzadzenie do testowania zywotnosci oka (Method of Eye Aliveness Testing and Device for Eye Aliveness Testing). Polish Patent Application No. P380581. September 7, 2006
9. J. Daugman, Countermeasures against subterfuge, in *Biometrics: Personal Identication in Networked Society*, ed. by Jain, Bolle, and Pankanti (Kluwer, Amsterdam, 1999), pp. 103–121
10. J. Doyle, K. Bowyer, P.J. Flynn, Variation in accuracy of textured contact lens detection based on sensor and lens pattern. in *2013 IEEE Sixth International Conference on Biometrics: Theory, Applications and Systems (BTAS)* (2013), pp. 1–7
11. J. Galbally, S. Marcel, J. Fierrez, Image quality assessment for fake biometric detection: application to iris, fingerprint, and face recognition. IEEE Trans. Image Process. **23**(2), 710–724 (2014)

12. J. Galbally et al., Iris liveness detection based on quality related features, in *2012 5th IAPR International Conference on Biometrics (ICB)* (2012), pp. 271–276
13. D. Gragnaniello et al., An investigation of local descriptors for biometric spoofing detection. IEEE Trans. Inf. Forensics Secur. **10**(4), 849–863 (2015)
14. X. He, Y. Lu, P. Shi, A new fake iris detection method, in *Advances in Biometrics*, ed. by M. Tistarelli and M. Nixon. Lecture Notes in Computer Science, vol. 5558. (Springer, Berlin, 2009), pp. 1132–1139
15. Y. He, Y.H.H. Yang, H. He, An elimination method of light spot based on iris image fusion. Commun. Comput. Inf. Sci. **15**(12), 415–422 (2008)
16. Z. He et al., Efficient iris spoof detection via boosted local binary patterns, in *Advances in Biometrics*. ed. by M. Tistarelli and M. Nixon. Lecture Notes in Computer Science, vol. 5558. (Springer, Berlin, 2009), pp. 1080–1090
17. K. Hughes, K.W. Bowyer, Detection of contact-lens-based iris biometric spoofs using stereo imaging, in *2013 46th Hawaii International Conference on System Sciences (HICSS)* (2013), pp. 1763–1772
18. ISO/IEC JTC 1/SC 37 Text of 3rd Working Draft 30107-1. Information Technology - Presentation Attack Detection—Part 1: Framework. April 13, 2015
19. ISO/IEC JTC 1/SC 37 Text of 3rd Working Draft 30107-3. Information Technology - Presentation Attack Detection—Part 3: Testing and reporting. February 18, 2015
20. M. Kanematsu, H. Takano, K. Nakamura, Highly reliable liveness detection method for iris recognition, in *SICE, 2007 Annual Conference* (2007), pp. 361–364
21. M. Kohn, M. Clynes, Color dynamics of the pupil. Ann. NY Acad. Sci. **156**(2), 931–950 (1969). Available online at Wiley Online Library (2006)
22. E.C. Lee, K.R. Park, Fake iris detection based on 3D structure of iris pattern. Int. J. Imaging Syst. Technol. **20**(2), 162–166 (2010)
23. E. Lee, K. Park, J. Kim, Fake iris detection by using Purkinje image, in *Advances in Biometrics*. ed. by D. Zhang and A. Jain. Lecture Notes in Computer Science, vol. 3832 (Springer, Berlin, 2005), pp. 397–403
24. S.J. Lee, K.R. Park, J. Kim, Robust fake iris detection based on variation of the reflectance ratio between the iris and the sclera, in *2006 Biometrics Symposium: Special Session on Research at the Biometric Consortium Conference* (2006), pp. 1–6
25. T. Matsumoto, Artificial fingers and irises: importance of vulnerability analysis, in *Proceedings of the Seventh International Biometrics Conference and Exhibition. London, United Kingdom* (2004)
26. D. Menotti et al., Deep representations for iris, face, and fingerprint spoofing detection. IEEE Trans. Inf. Forensics Secur. **10**(4), 864–879 (2015)
27. A. Pacut, A. Czajka. Aliveness detection for iris biometrics, in *40th Annual IEEE International Carnahan Conference on Security Technology* (2006), pp. 122–129
28. G. Pan, Z. Wu, L. Sun, Liveness Detection for Face Recognition, in *Recent Advances in Face Recognition*, ed. by K. Delac, M. Grgic, M.S. Bartlett (Springer, Berlin, 2008), pp. 109–124
29. J. Park, M. Kang, Iris recognition against counterfeit attack using gradient based fusion of multi-spectral images, in *Advances in Biometric Person Authentication*, ed. by S. Li et al. Lecture Notes in Computer Science, vol. 3781 (Springer Berlin, 2005), pp. 150–156
30. N. Puhan, N. Sudha, A. Suhas Hegde, A new iris liveness detection method against contact lens spoofing, in *2011 IEEE 15th International Symposium on Consumer Electronics (ISCE)* (2011), pp. 71–74
31. I. Rigas, O. Komogortsev, Gaze estimation as a framework for iris liveness detection, in *2014 IEEE International Joint Conference on Biometrics (IJCB)* (2014), pp. 1–8
32. S. Schuckers, A. Czajka, K.W. Bowyer, LivDet-Iris 2015—Iris Liveness Detection Competition (2015). http://iris2015.livdet.org
33. A. Sequeira, J. Murari, J. Cardoso, Iris liveness detection methods in the mobile biometrics scenario, in *2014 International Joint Conference on Neural Networks (IJCNN)* (2014), pp. 3002–3008

34. A.F. Sequeira et al., MobiLine 2014 1st Mobile Iris Liveness Detection Competition (2014). http://mobilive2014.inescporto.pt
35. L. Thalheim, J. Krissler, P.-M. Ziegler, Biometric access protection devices and their programs put to the test. Available online in c't Magazine, No. 11/2002 (2002), p. 114
36. Trusted Biometrics under Spoofing Attacks (TABULA RASA), Project funded by the European Commission, under the Seventh Framework Programme (2013). http://www.tabularasa-euproject.org
37. F.M. Villalobos-Castaldi, E. Suaste-Gómez, A new spontaneous pupillary oscillation-based verification system. Expert Syst. Appl. **40**(13), 5352–5362 (2013)
38. Z. Wei et al., Counterfeit iris detection based on texture analysis, in *19th International Conference on Pattern Recognition* (2008)
39. D. Yadav et al., Unraveling the effect of textured contact lenses on iris recognition. IEEE Trans. Inf. Forensics Secur. **9**(5), 851–862 (2014)
40. D. Yambay et al., LivDet-iris 2013—Iris Liveness Detection Competition 2013, in *2014 IEEE International Joint Conference on Biometrics (IJCB)* (2014), pp. 1–8
41. H. Zhang, Z. Sun, T. Tan, Contact lens detection based on weighted LBP, in *2010 20th International Conference on Pattern Recognition (ICPR)* (2010), pp. 4279–4282

Chapter 20
Iris Image Reconstruction from Binary Templates

Javier Galbally, Marios Savvides, Shreyas Venugopalan and Arun A. Ross

Abstract This chapter explores the possibility of recovering iris *images* from binary iris *templates*. It has been generally assumed that the binary iris code is irreversible, i.e., the original iris *texture* cannot be derived from it. Here, we discuss two distinct approaches to reconstruct the iris texture from the binary iris code. Next, we discuss a method to detect such synthesized iris textures. Finally, we discuss some of the advantages and risks of generating iris texture from iris codes in the context of data privacy and security.

20.1 Introduction

A classical biometric system acquires the biometric trait of an individual, extracts salient features from the trait, and compares the extracted features against those in a database in order to *verify* a claimed identity or to *identify* an individual. For security and privacy reasons, biometric systems typically do not store the raw biometric data that may disclose sensitive information about the subjects (e.g., race, diseases, etc.). Rather, they store the extracted template (feature set) containing the information about the individual that is most relevant for recognition purposes. However, recent research has looked into the possibility of recovering the original biometric data

J. Galbally
European Commission-Joint Research Centre, 21027 Ispra, VA, Italy
e-mail: javier.galbally@jrc.ec.europa.eu

M. Savvides · S. Venugopalan
Cylab Biometrics Center, Carnegie Mellon University, Pittsburgh, PA, USA
e-mail: marioss@andrew.cmu.edu

S. Venugopalan
e-mail: svenugop@alumni.cmu.edu

A.A. Ross (✉)
Integrated Pattern Recognition and Biometrics Lab (i-PRoBe),
Michigan State University, East Lansing, MI, USA
e-mail: rossarun@cse.msu.edu

© Springer-Verlag London 2016
K.W. Bowyer and M.J. Burge (eds.), *Handbook of Iris Recognition*,
Advances in Computer Vision and Pattern Recognition,
DOI 10.1007/978-1-4471-6784-6_20

from the reduced template [26, 32, 64]. Such studies, which are also relevant from an information theory perspective (i.e., what is the amount of information necessary to reverse engineer a biometric template?) have set a new research trend in biometrics known as *inverse biometrics*.

One of the biggest challenges faced by researchers in the field of inverse biometrics is the iris. Among the various biometric traits that have been considered in the literature for personal authentication purposes, iris is traditionally regarded as one of the most reliable and accurate [44]. After some preprocessing steps in which the iris is localized, segmented and normalized, the vast majority of iris recognition systems perform some type of filtering operation in order to generate the iris template (e.g., using 2-D Gabor wavelets). The phase information of the filtered normalized image is quantized to produce the final binary template (i.e., iris code) which is stored in the database during enrollment. Then, in the authentication or recognition phase, iris codes are compared using bit-based metrics like the Hamming distance [14]. This way, in most cases, iris recognition is accomplished based only on phase-related information, while the amplitude data is discarded due to its sensitivity to external factors such as imaging contrast, illumination or camera gain.

The iris code has been adopted as a *de facto* standard by most iris-based systems, as it is a very efficient and compact representation of the discriminative characteristics contained within a person's iris pattern. It has been a common belief in the biometric community that binary templates do not have sufficient information to reconstruct the original iris image from them [43]. Furthermore, iris codes from *real* iris images have been demonstrated to be significantly unique across individuals [16].

Are iris codes really resilient to being reverse-engineered in order to recover the original iris pattern from them? Is it possible to generate different *synthetic* iris-like patterns which yield iris codes very similar to the one given? In summary, can we generate *synthetic* images that match a specific binary template thereby potentially deceiving an iris recognition system? The present chapter addresses these questions by reviewing the two inverse biometric methods that have been proposed in the literature for the generation of iris-like synthetic patterns whose corresponding iris codes match that of a given genuine user. Two main goals are pursued by these reconstruction methods:

- On the one hand, explore whether the phase information embedded in the iris code is sufficient to reconstruct an iris image that can be successfully matched to the real one from which the template was generated.
- On the other hand, determine if it is possible to generate not just one, but a class of synthetic patterns with very similar iris codes to that of a real one (i.e., exhibiting similarities in phase but differences in magnitude with respect to the original genuine pattern).

Given that the aforementioned goals are realized, it would imply that it is possible to generate synthetic iris images that are visually different from the original iris sample but which produce iris codes that fall within the intra-class tolerance of a genuine user. These synthetic irides can be potentially used for a number of different purposes such as:

- Vulnerability studies: The synthetic iris images could be used by an attacker to impersonate the genuine user as the reconstructed sample would be positively matched to the original one since their respective iris codes would be sufficiently alike [67].
- Increase of biometric data: The reconstructed images could also be applied to synthetically increase the amount of available biometric samples of a given user. Such a strategy has proven to potentially increase the performance of recognition systems in other biometric traits such as the signature [20].
- Pseudo-identities generation: The reconstructed samples could also be used as enrolled templates. This way, the users could still access the system (since their iris would match the synthetic image stored), while preserving their privacy as it would not be needed to keep their real biometric data [56].
- Entropy studies: From an information theory standpoint, the synthetic images may be useful to conduct experiments on the individuality of the iris trait [7, 40], helping to assess the entropy of the information present in iris templates and to develop methods that compress and reliably store the intrinsic individual-related data conveyed within an iris pattern.

To date, from the different potential applications mentioned above, the synthetic irides have only been considered within vulnerability studies in order to assess the resilience of iris recognition systems to such type of threat. For this reason, in the present chapter, we also present a brief survey of possible countermeasures to detect an attack carried out with reconstructed iris images, as well as an experimental case study assessing the performance of one of those protection techniques.

It should be emphasized that, throughout the chapter, inverse biometric approaches are conceived from a computer-based perspective, that is, the final objective is not to reconstruct a biometric sample which visually resembles the original one (in order to deceive a human observer), but rather, that it is incorrectly recognized as the original sample by an automatic authentication algorithm.

20.2 Inverse Biometrics Within Synthetic Biometric Generation

As already introduced, this chapter is focused on the review of inverse biometric methods in iris recognition. The present section gives a general overview of the very broad field of synthetic biometric generation. The overall taxonomy considered in the chapter regarding the different techniques proposed so far to produce synthetic biometrics is shown in Fig. 20.1. This way, the reader can better understand where inverse biometric algorithms stand within the larger domain of biometric synthetic generation.

Historically, *manually* produced *physical* biometric traits such as fingerprints, signatures or forged handwriting have been a point of concern for experts from a forensic point of view [55, 70]. More recently, such physically produced synthetic

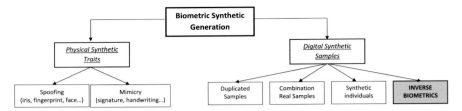

Fig. 20.1 General classification of biometric synthetic generation methods considered in the present contribution. The area of inverse biometrics, main focus of the chapter, is highlighted in *gray*

traits have been largely utilized for vulnerability and spoofing assessment studies in traits such as the iris [49], the fingerprint [47] or the face [28].

However, it has not been until the recent development of the biometric technology when the *automatic* generation of *digital* synthetic samples has been considered. Over the last years, a growing interest has arisen in the scientific community in this new field of research and different algorithms have been proposed for the synthetic generation of biometric samples in traits such as iris [10, 46, 65, 71, 76], fingerprints [8], face [59], voice [18], handwriting [45], or online [24] and offline signature [19].

It should be emphasized that, as shown above, although there are multiple works which address the problem of generating synthetic digital biometric samples [53, 73], not all of them consider the term *synthetic* in the same way. In particular, four different trends for producing synthetic biometric samples can be found in the current literature:

- **Duplicated samples**. In this case the generation algorithm takes as input one *real* sample of a given user and, through different transformations, produces different synthetic (or duplicated) samples corresponding to the same person. This type of algorithms are useful to artificially *increase* the amount of already acquired biometric data [59, 61]. Such approaches have been used, for instance, to synthetically augment the size of the enrollment set of data in identification and verification systems, a critical parameter in traits such as the signature [20]. A particular case of this type of approaches is described in [29], where the authors generate synthetic offline signature images starting from the dynamic information contained in the corresponding real online templates.
- **Combination of different real samples**. This is the approach followed by most speech [6] and handwriting synthesizers [45]. This type of algorithms start from a pool of *real* units, n-phones (isolated or combination of sounds) or n-grams (isolated or combination of letters), and using some type of concatenation procedure combine them to form the synthetic samples. These techniques have been used in applications such as text-to-speech, typewriting-to-handwriting, or CAPTCHAs (Completely Automatic Public Turing Test to tell Computers and Humans Apart).
- **Synthetic individuals**. In this case, some kind of *a priori* knowledge about a certain biometric trait is learned from a development set of real samples (e.g., iris structure, minutiae distribution, signature length, etc.) and then used to create

a model that characterizes that biometric trait for a population of subjects. New synthetic individuals can then be generated by sampling the constructed model. In a subsequent stage of the algorithm, multiple instances of the synthetic users can be generated using any of the methods for creating duplicated samples. These algorithms are therefore able to generate completely synthetic databases and constitute a very effective tool to overcome the usual shortage of biometric data without undertaking highly resource-consuming acquisition campaigns. Different performance evaluation studies have been conducted on this type of synthetic datasets for traits such as the iris [10, 65, 76], the fingerprint [8], or the signature [23].

- **Inverse biometrics**. As already mentioned in the introduction, the term inverse biometrics refers to those methods that aim at producing a synthetic biometric sample whose template matches a specific real template of a given user. In other words, they may be considered as reverse engineering techniques that reconstruct a synthetic sample from the information conveyed in a real biometric template. This way, according to one or more recognition systems, the synthetic sample will be considered to belong to the genuine user. Such methods have already been developed for traits such as the iris [26, 67], the fingerprint [9, 39, 64], the face, [1, 2, 21, 50] or the hand geometry [32]. Most of these techniques have been used in the framework of vulnerability-related studies.

Regarding the specific area of inverse biometrics, which is the main focus of the present chapter, different studies may be found in the current literature. In one of the pioneering works, Hill reported an experiment that challenged the notion of nonreversibility of fingerprint minutiae templates [39]. His study suggested that the information contained in minutiae templates might allow for the reconstruction of images that are somewhat similar to the original fingerprints. Since that study, various researchers have successfully undertaken the challenge of generating a fingerprint image from minutiae points alone [9, 64]. More recently, researchers have succeeded in manufacturing a physical gummy finger from minutiae templates [22].

In the field of face recognition, different approaches have been used by researchers to reconstruct face images from raw templates [1, 2, 21, 50]. It was Adler who first suggested that even quantized scores could be used as feedback to recursive hill climbing algorithms in order to recover the original face image [1, 2]. This recursive hill climbing approach has later been used in several works, including a recent study that has shown the feasibility to recover the hand geometry image from its encoded templates [32].

In the context of iris recognition, two recent studies have been the first to address the problem of reconstructing iris images from binary iris codes [26, 67]. These two works are reviewed in detail in the next sections. We also discuss methods that can be used to detect the artificial irises, and so avoid potential attacks carried out with them.

20.3 Inverse Biometrics Methods in Iris

The two iris reconstruction methods reviewed in the present section have been developed from a computer-based perspective. This means that the goal is not to generate iris images that could deceive a human expert; rather, the goal is to successfully match the synthesized iris images with their true counterparts using automated iris matchers. Even so, different strategies to make the synthetic patterns look as realistic as possible have also been explored in both works, presenting some statistical results regarding the visual perception that experts and nonexperts have of the reconstructed images.

Each of the two methods is reviewed in the next subsections following the chronological order of their publication. The main differences between the two works may be summarized as follows:

- **Type of approach**. The method proposed in [67], is a deterministic one, which means that, given an iris code and a fixed set of parameter values, the resulting reconstructed synthetic pattern is always the same. On the other hand, the algorithm described in [26] is probabilistic. As such, given an iris code and a fixed set of parameters it is capable of producing different iris-like patterns with very similar iris codes.
- **Knowledge required**. In the development stage, the method proposed in [67] requires knowledge of the feature-extraction scheme being used by the recognition system (i.e., type of filters). On the other hand, the technique presented in [26] needs to have access in the development stage to the output score of an iris matcher (which can be a publicly available one) to reconstruct the image. This last algorithm will be most effective if the development matcher and the final test matcher use a similar feature extraction strategy. This is usually the case, as most iris recognition methods are based on the principles first introduced by Daugman [14]. However, as shown in Sect. 20.3.2.1, the algorithm has also been successfully used to bypass black-box commercial systems with unknown feature-extraction algorithms.
- **Images required**. In order to generate realistic iris-like patterns, both algorithms rely on information extracted from a pool of real iris samples which can be obtained, for instance, from one of the many publicly available iris databases.

To extend formality to the problem being addressed, some mathematical notations that will be used throughout the next sections are introduced here. Let $\mathbf{B}$ represent the iris code of the user whose iris image is being reconstructed, $\mathbf{I_R}$ represent the reconstructed *normalized* iris image which is a solution to the problem, $\mathbf{B_R}$ be its associated iris code and δ the matching threshold that determines if two iris images come from the same eye.

20.3.1 Deterministic Approach Based on Gabor Filtering

In the work described in [67], the authors take advantage of the prior knowledge of the feature extraction scheme used by the recognition system (i.e., functions defining the filters used during feature extraction) in order to reverse engineer the iris code. Then, real images are used to impart a more realistic appearance to the synthetic iris patterns. The feature extraction scheme used is based on the method outlined by Daugman [16], which computes the convolution between normalized iris images and Gabor functions. The knowledge of this extraction scheme is used to generate user-specific discriminating patterns from their respective iris code templates. These patterns may be estimated based on the original Gabor filter used for feature extraction or based on actual iris patches from an exemplar image, that resembles this Gabor filter.

20.3.1.1 Person-Specific Discriminating Pattern

In the following discussion, the tuple (r, θ) is used to refer to the normalized polar coordinate system. From an input eye image in the Cartesian coordinate system, the iris is segmented and normalized into a polar representation as pointed out in [67]. In this representation, r represents the radial direction and θ represents the direction along the circumference of the iris. The filtering process, during feature extraction, quantifies the presence of the spatially reversed version of the Gabor function $G(r, \theta)$, at every pixel location. The reason, as pointed out by the authors, is that convolution is equivalent to correlation of one function with the reversed version of the other (in other words, the filtering process acts as a matched filter implementation, with the matched filter's role being adopted by the reversed version of the Gabor function). If $R(r, \theta)$ is the output of filtering the normalized iris image, the authors define a *person-specific discriminating iris pattern*, as a weighted sum of spatially shifted and reversed versions of the Gabor function, i.e. $G(-r, -\theta)$. The weights at each shift of $G(-r, -\theta)$ are determined by the corresponding pixel value in $R(r, \theta)$. The 'person specificity' of this output pattern comes from the fact that it is unique to the person that generated $R(r, \theta)$ as a result of the filtering operation. This pattern $I_{R1}(r, \theta)$ can be represented as

$$I_{R1}(r, \theta) = \int_{i=1}^{m} \int_{j=1}^{n} R(i, j) G(r - i, \theta - j) di \, dj \qquad (20.1)$$

where $m \times n$ is the support of $R(r, \theta)$. If the pattern $I_{R1}(r, \theta)$ is used as the input to an iris feature extraction module, then the result of filtering it with $G(r, \theta)$ can be expressed as,

$$R_E(r, \theta) = I_{R1}(r, \theta) * G(r, \theta)$$

$$= \int_{i=1}^{m} \int_{j=1}^{n} \left\{ \int_{k=1}^{m} \int_{l=1}^{n} R(k, l)G(-k + i, -l + j)dk \, dl \right\}$$

$$G(-r + i, -\theta + j)di \, dj$$

$$= \int_{k=1}^{m} \int_{l=1}^{n} R(k, l)g(r, \theta, k, l)dk \, dl$$

The last line in the expression above is obtained by rearranging the order of integrals; where $g(r, \theta, k, l) = \int_{i=1}^{m} \int_{j=1}^{n} G(-k + i, -l + j)G(-r + i, -\theta + j)di \, dj$. This term can be interpreted as a correlation of the Gabor function with itself. Gabor functions used in iris feature extraction have a small support, as a result $R_E(r, \theta) \approx R(r, \theta)$. The original work [67] provides empirical evidence for this statement, by comparing the iris verification performance when I_{R1} is used *vs* when the original normalized iris texture is used.

In a similar manner, instead of using the original filter response $R(r, \theta)$, the stored iris code of an individual can be used as the weighting function when generating a person-specific discriminating pattern. This iris code template is simply a quantized form of $R(r, \theta)$ and, for the purpose of this discussion, it is represented as $R_Q(r, \theta)$. This new pattern can be obtained by replacing $R(r, \theta)$ with $R_Q(r, \theta)$ in Eq. (20.1). For the experiments presented later, these patterns are referred to as $I_{R2}(r, \theta)$. In addition, instead of using the reversed version of the Gabor function, in order to generate these person-specific patterns, another possibility is to use real iris patches of the same size as the Gabor function, cropped out from a pool of development irides. Such patches $P(r, \theta)$ can be estimated by a cross-correlation operation between the iris texture and $G(-r, -\theta)$. Examples of both $I_{R1}(r, \theta)$ as well as patterns generated using $P(r, \theta)$ (for the purpose of this text, the latter pattern is labeled as $I_{R3}(r, \theta)$) are shown in Fig. 20.2.

20.3.1.2 Embedding the Pattern in an Iris Texture

Once the person-specific pattern has been estimated, it is embedded in a background iris texture, so that the final spoof pattern has a higher level of visual realism. By controlling the ratio between the background texture and the discriminating texture, the spoof pattern can be hidden in the background. Let $S(r, \theta)$ be the background and let $I_{R3}(r, \theta)$ from the previous section be the person-specific discriminating texture. Then, the final spoof texture is given by

$$I_{R_F}(r, \theta) = p_1 S(r, \theta) + p_2 I_{R3}(r, \theta) \tag{20.2}$$

$$p_1, p_2 \in [0, 1]$$

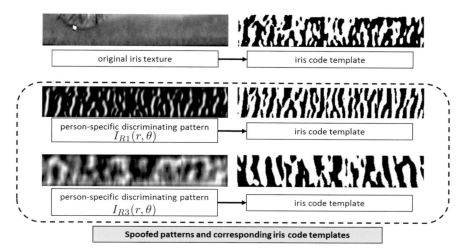

Fig. 20.2 Two examples of person-specific spoof patterns generated by the method described in Sect. 20.3.1. The *top row* shows the original iris texture along with the corresponding iris code. The *second* and *third rows* show two different spoof patterns generated using this iris code. The corresponding 'spoofed' iris codes do not differ significantly from the original as is shown by empirical iris verification evidence presented by Venugopalan et al. [67]. In a latter stage, the reconstructed iris patterns are embedded in a background iris texture to obtain a higher visual realism as described in Sect. 20.3.1.2 and shown in Fig. 20.3

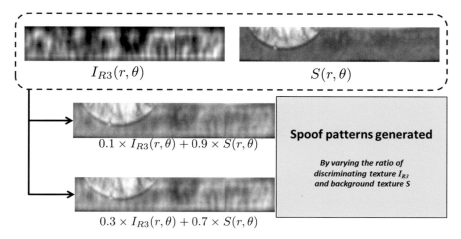

Fig. 20.3 Two examples of a *spoof pattern* I_{R3} embedded within a background texture S. The *first spoof pattern* uses $p_1 = 0.9$; $p_2 = 0.1$ and the second uses $p_1 = 0.7$; $p_2 = 0.3$. As a result, the pattern is better hidden in the first case compared to the second case. However, as seen from Eq. 20.3, the second case elicits a response from the feature extractor that is similar to the response of I_{R3}. Hence, there is a trade-off to be made between the similarity of the response to that of I_{R3} and to what extent the reconstructed pattern is hidden within S

When the pattern $I_{R_F}(r, \theta)$ is fed as input to the Gabor filter-based feature extraction module, the resulting output is as follows

$$
\begin{aligned}
R_F(r, \theta) &= I_{R_F}(r, \theta) * G(r, \theta) \\
&= (p_1 S(r, \theta) + p_2 I_{R3}(r, \theta)) * G(r, \theta) \\
&= p_1 R_S(r, \theta) + p_2 R_{E3}(r, \theta)
\end{aligned} \tag{20.3}
$$

where $R_S(r, \theta) = S(r, \theta) * G(r, \theta)$ and $R_{E3}(r, \theta) = I_{R3}(r, \theta) * G(r, \theta)$. There is a trade-off to be made between the value of p_2 and the value of p_1. If $p_1 > p_2$, the pattern can be effectively hidden within $S(r, \theta)$, however at the same time, if $p_1 \gg p_2$, then the effect of $R_{E3}(r, \theta)$ diminishes the filter response $R_F(r, \theta)$. This, in effect, means that the person-specific pattern will not be processed by the feature extraction algorithm and hence this pattern cannot be used to spoof the system. The authors in the original work, empirically selected a value of $p_1 = 0.7$ and $p_2 = 0.3$. Figure 20.3 shows examples of $I_{R_F}(r, \theta)$ for $p_1 = 0.9$; $p_2 = 0.1$ and $p_1 = 0.7$; $p_2 = 0.3$. Figure 20.4 shows examples of genuine eye images and eye images with embedded spoof patterns.

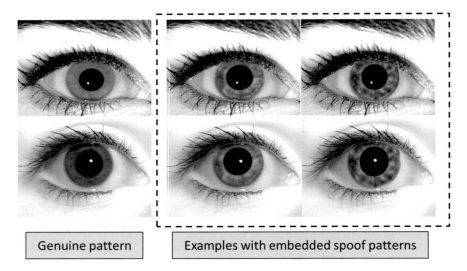

Genuine pattern   Examples with embedded spoof patterns

Fig. 20.4 Two examples of embedded *spoof patterns* within an eye image. The *first column* shows the genuine eye images, while the *second* and *third columns* show reconstructed patterns embedded into the respective iris patterns, using the method described in Sect. 20.3.1.2

20.3.1.3   Evaluation of the Reconstruction Method

In order to assess the performance of the reconstruction method presented in this section, experiments were run on the database released by NIST as part of the Iris Challenge Evaluation (ICE) database [58]. Spoof textures were generated for every image contained in the set of left eyes in this database; $S(r, \theta)$ for this experiment was chosen at random to be any image of a different class from which the spoof pattern was generated.

Figure 20.5 compares the verification performance using the spoof patterns I_{R1}, I_{R2}, and I_{R3} with the performance using the original left eye images from the dataset. A proprietary implementation of the Daugman matcher [16] was used for these experiments. It may be observed that, for very low values of false accept rates, the true accept rate remains high for all three methods.

Figure 20.6 compares the performance for the case in which embedded spoof patterns within true patterns are used, as described in Eq. (20.2). Examples of images generated using this method, with $p_1 = 0.7$; $p_2 = 0.3$ are shown in Fig. 20.4. The verification rates remain high in this case too, for very low values of the false acceptance rate, showing the ability of this method to circumvent conventional iris recognition systems.

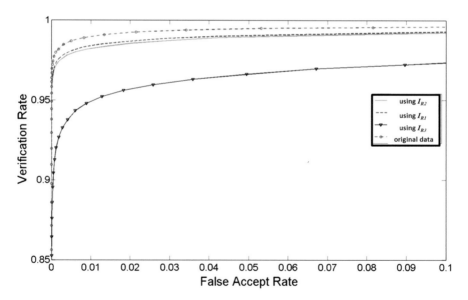

Fig. 20.5 Receiver operating characteristic (ROC) curves showing comparable subject verification performance when reconstructed patterns are used versus when the original iris textures are used. The left eye images from the ICE dataset [58] were used for these experiments

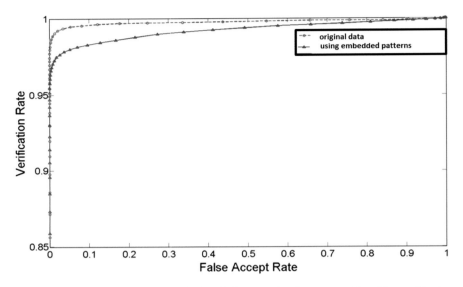

Fig. 20.6 Receiver operating characteristic (ROC) curves showing comparable subject verification performance when *spoof patterns* embedded in a person's iris texture are used *vs* when the original iris texture images are used. The left eye images from the ICE dataset [58] were used for these experiments. Examples of embedded *spoof patterns* are shown in Fig. 20.4

20.3.2 Probabilistic Approach Based on Genetic Algorithms

The challenging reverse engineering problem of reconstructing an iris pattern from its iris code, was solved in [26] using a probabilistic approach based on genetic algorithms. In the following the method is described in detail.

Problem statement. Consider a $R \times C$ dimensional matrix $\mathbf{I_R}$ of real values, which is divided into $H \times L$ square blocks of dimension R/H $\times$ C/L, with $H \leq R$ and $L \leq C$. This matrix is mapped by some unknown function $\mathcal{F}$ to a binary matrix $\mathbf{B_R}$ (i.e., $\mathbf{B_R} = \mathcal{F}(\mathbf{I_R})$) of dimensions $K \times W$ (K is a multiple of R and W is a multiple of C).

Consider the problem of finding an $\mathbf{I_R}$ matrix such that, its associated $\mathbf{B_R}$ matrix (unknown), produces a similarity score (s) greater than a certain threshold δ, when it is compared to a *known* binary matrix $\mathbf{B}$ according to some unknown matching function $\mathcal{J}$, i.e., $\mathcal{J}(\mathbf{B}, \mathbf{B_R}) > \delta$.

For clarity, we will define a new function $\mathcal{V}$ as: $\mathcal{V}(\mathbf{B}, \mathbf{I_R}) = \mathcal{J}(\mathbf{B}, \mathcal{F}(\mathbf{I_R})) = \mathcal{J}(\mathbf{B}, \mathbf{B_R}) = s$

Assumptions. Let us assume that we have access to the evaluation of the function $\mathcal{V}(\mathbf{B}, \mathbf{I_R})$ for several trials of $\mathbf{I_R}$.

Algorithm. The problem stated above may be solved using a genetic algorithm to optimize the similarity score given by the system, according to the general diagram shown in Fig. 20.7. Genetic algorithms, which have shown remarkable performance

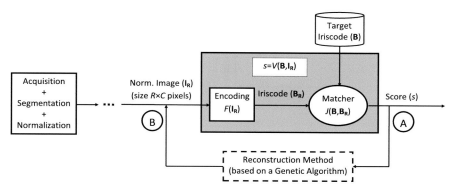

Fig. 20.7 General diagram of the scheme followed in [26]. A detailed diagram of the reconstruction approach (*dashed rectangle*) is given in Fig. 20.8 where points A and B show, respectively, the input and output of the algorithm

in optimization problems [31], are search methods that iteratively apply certain rules inspired by biological evolution to a population of individuals (possible solutions) according to a given fitness function. During each iteration the algorithm moves towards better solutions in terms of the fitness function which has to be optimized. In our particular problem, the following observations ought to be made.

- The fitness value associated with each individual (normalized iris image) is the matching score, $s = \mathcal{V}(\mathbf{B}, \mathbf{I_R})$.
- Usually genetic algorithms operate with individuals that are binary vectors. In this problem, the genetic algorithm has been modified to work with matrices of real values (i.e., $\mathbf{I_R}$) where each of the $H \times L$ blocks represents a gene of the individual.

As can be seen in Fig. 20.8, the steps followed by the reconstruction algorithm are:

1. Generate an initial population P_0 with N individuals of size $R \times C$ (i.e., dimensions of the normalized iris images), and tessellate each individual into $H \times L$ rectangular blocks.
2. Compute the similarity scores s^i of the individuals ($\mathbf{I_R}^i$) of the population P_0, $s^i = \mathcal{V}(\mathbf{B}, \mathbf{I_R}^i)$, with $i = 1, \ldots, N$.
3. Four rules are used at each iteration to create the next generation P_n of individuals from the current population:

   a. **Elite**: The two individuals with the maximum similarity scores are retained unaltered for the next generation.
   b. **Selection**: Certain individuals, the *parents*, are chosen by stochastic universal sampling [4]. Therefore, the individuals with the highest fitness values (similarity scores) are more likely to be selected as parents for the next generation: one subject can be selected 0 or many times. From the original N

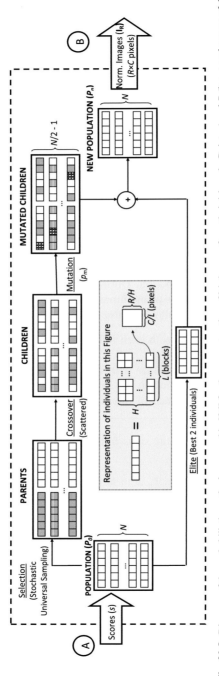

Fig. 20.8 Diagram of the probabilistic method proposed in [26] for the reconstruction of iris images from their iris code. Points *A* and *B* (input and output of the reconstruction algorithm respectively) may be seen for reference in Fig. 20.7. As is shown in the *shaded chart* in the center of the figure, although individuals are represented as vectors for simplicity, strictly they are matrices of size $R \times C$ pixels divided into $H \times L$ blocks

individuals, only $N - 2$ are eligible (as the best two are retained as elite) from which N/2−1 *fathers* and N/2−1 *mothers* are chosen.

c. **Crossover**: Parents are combined to form $N - 2$ *children* for the next generation by employing a scattered crossover method: a random binary matrix of size $H \times L$ is created and the genes (blocks) for the first child are selected from the first parent if the value of an entry is 1, and from the second when it is 0 (vice versa for the second child).

d. **Mutation**: Random changes are applied to the blocks of the new children with a mutation probability p_m. When a certain block is selected for mutation, the equivalent block in the individual of the population with the highest fitness value is changed by the same block of the highest scoring individual.

4. Redefine $P_0 = P_n$ and return to step 2.

Stopping criteria. The algorithm stops when: (i) the best fitness score of the individuals in the population is higher than the threshold δ (i.e., the image has been successfully reconstructed); (ii) the variation of the similarity scores obtained in successive generations is lower than a previously fixed value; or (iii) when the maximum number of generations (iterations) is exceeded.

Additional note. There are some important characteristics of the reconstruction method presented above that should be highlighted:

- Due to the probabilistic nature of the four rules being applied, the algorithm produces different solutions at each execution, even when the initialization and parameter values are the same. This facilitates the reconstruction of multiple normalized iris images ($\mathbf{I_R}$) whose iris codes ($\mathbf{B_R}$) are very similar to the target ($\mathbf{B}$).
- The algorithm does not require prior knowledge of the mapping function $\mathcal{F}$ between the normalized iris images ($\mathbf{I_R}$) and their corresponding iris codes ($\mathbf{B_R}$).
- The algorithm does not require knowledge of the matching function $\mathcal{J}$.
- The algorithm does not require knowledge of the function $\mathcal{V}$, but just its output to the given inputs.

A genetic search algorithm was used in [26], since the nature of the search space is unknown. Specifically, it is not clear if the objective function results in a smooth or even a continuous search space. Consequently, the efficiency of classical stochastic gradient descent methods would be at least unclear. Although previous work in [62] partially supports the assumption of smoothness/continuity, this could not be easily substantiated for the current problem. Therefore, by simultaneously searching for multiple solutions in the solution space, genetic algorithms are more likely to avoid potential minima or even plateaus in the search space (much like simulated annealing schemes).

In Fig. 20.9 we show some real iris images (two upper rows) and synthetic iris samples (two lower rows) generated following the probabilistic method described in [26].

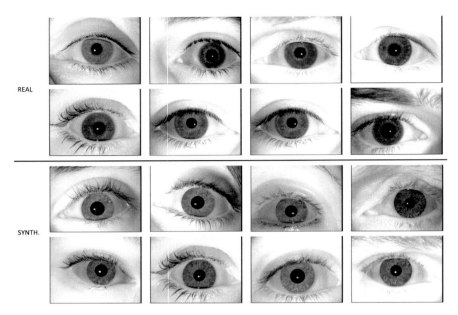

Fig. 20.9 Examples of real images (*two upper rows*) and synthetic iris images generated following the method described in [26] (*two lower rows*)

20.3.2.1 Evaluation of the Reconstruction Method

The experimental framework used to assess the performance of the iris reconstruction method presented above is designed to estimate its compliance with the main objective of inverse biometric algorithms: can iris images reconstructed using the proposed method be successfully matched with the original iris?

With this goal in mind, the evaluation is carried out on the iris subset of the desktop dataset contained in the multimodal Biosecure DB [54]. This iris subset includes four grayscale images (two per session) per eye, all captured using the Iris Access EOU3000 sensor from LG. In the experiments the two eyes of each subject have been considered as separate users (i.e., $210 \times 2 = 420$ users), resulting in a total of $420 \times 4 = 1680$ iris samples.

In the development stage, one sample of each of the 420 users present in the database was randomly selected and their iris codes computed according to the publicly available iris recognition system developed by Masek and Kovesi [48]. Then, in a subsequent step, Masek's matcher was used to compute the matching scores needed by the optimization algorithm, in order to generate five different reconstructed images of each binary template (i.e., the algorithm was applied 5 times to reconstruct 5 images from each iris code), thus leading to a database of $5 \times 420 = 2,100$ synthetic iris samples.

The iris images reconstructed in the development stage are then used to test the vulnerabilities of the VeriEye iris matcher [51]. This commercial system operates as a black-box, i.e., given an input, it returns an output with no information about the internal algorithms used to obtain that final result.

The attack to VeriEye is performed matching all five reconstructed images against each of the three samples of the same user present in the Biosecure DB, not used in the development phase. Therefore, the total number of attacks performed is $A_T = 420 \times 3 = 1,260$. The attack is successful if at least one of the synthetic images matches against the real image. This represents the most likely attack scenario analyzed in other related vulnerability studies [9]; here, the iris code of a legitimate user in the database is compromised and the intruder reconstructs multiple images of the iris to try and break the system. The attacker will gain access if any one of the reconstructed images results in a positive score.

The efficiency of the attack (and therefore the performance of the reconstruction algorithm) is measured in terms of its Success Rate (SR), which is defined as the percentage of successful attacks (A_s) out of the total carried out (A_T), i.e., SR $= A_s/A_T \times 100$.

In general, the success of an attack is highly dependent on the false acceptance rate (FAR) of the system. Thus, the vulnerability of VeriEye to the attacks with the reconstructed images is evaluated at three operating points corresponding to FAR = 0.1, FAR = 0.05, and FAR = 0.01 %, which, according to [3], correspond to a low, medium and high security application, respectively. For completeness, the system is also tested at a very high security operating point corresponding to FAR $\ll$ 0.01 %. The results of the validation experiments carried out on VeriEye are shown in Table 20.1 from which different observations can be made:

- The high performance of the proposed reconstruction algorithm is confirmed, reaching an average SR of around 91 % for the three usual operating points considered.
- Even for an unrealistically high security point (i.e., FAR = 0.0001 %), the reconstructed images would have, on average, almost 83 % chance of breaking the system.
- The reconstructed images present a high probability of breaking the system even when the stored templates are not the one from which they were recovered (i.e., the images used for development and test are different).

Table 20.1 SR of the evaluation experiments carried out on the VeriEye matcher at the four operating points tested

SR (%)—VeriEye				
FAR = 0.1 %	FAR = 0.05 %	FAR = 0.01 %	FAR = 0.0001 %	Average
92.8	91.4	90.9	82.9	89.5

Table 20.2 Percentage of successful attacks where *n* out of the total five reconstructed images were positively matched against each of the three iris samples of the same user that were not used for their reconstruction

FAR	SR_n (%)—VeriEye				
	$n = 1$	$n = 2$	$n = 3$	$n = 4$	$n = 5$
0.1 %	1.5	5.1	12.8	23.3	50.1
0.05 %	2.1	6.3	13.1	26.1	44.0
0.01 %	3.1	5.8	13.1	26.6	42.3
0.0001 %	7.2	6.3	21.4	23.4	31.2
Average	3.5	5.9	15.1	24.8	41.9

Results are given for the four operating points tested on VeriEye

The results presented in Table 20.1 confirm the main objective set for the proposed algorithm: iris patterns may be recovered from their iris codes, and the reconstructed images represent a threat to the integrity of automatic recognition systems.

Recall that an important characteristic of the probabilistic reconstruction approach described in Sect. 20.3.2 is its ability to generate several iris patterns with iris codes very similar to a real one. In order to assess this point, the experimental results are presented in Table 20.2 from a different perspective. In this case we report in each column the percentage of attacks in which only *n* out of the 5 reconstructed images (with $n = 1, \ldots, 5$) were positively matched to the real image. In each case, the total number of attacks performed is $A_{Tn} = 420$ and the success rate is denoted as SR_n.

Averaging over the four operating points, all five reconstructed images were positively matched to the original image in 41.9 % of the cases. This increases to 66.7 % if we consider $n = \{4, 5\}$, and to 81.8 % when taking into account $n = \{3, 4, 5\}$. These results confirm the ability of the probabilistic reconstruction method proposed in [26] to generate multiple iris patterns that match successfully against one specific iris code.

20.4 Detection of Iris Reconstructed Images

Since inverse biometrics is a relatively novel field of research, very few works have been published so far regarding the specific detection of reconstructed biometric samples [30]. However, many of the techniques developed for the protection against the largely studied spoofing attacks can potentially be used to detect also attacks with reversed engineered samples.

Biometric spoofing is widely understood in the specialized literature as the ability to fool a biometric system into recognizing an illegitimate user as a genuine one, by means of presenting to the sensor a physical synthetic forged version (i.e., artifact) of the original biometric trait, as shown in Fig. 20.10. Typical spoofing attacks in

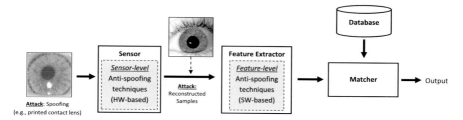

Fig. 20.10 General diagram of a biometric system specifying the modules where the two most common types of anti-spoofing techniques are usually integrated (sensor-level and feature-level). Also displayed are the two different types of attacks for which anti-spoofing techniques may offer protection: spoofing (both sensor-level and feature-level techniques can detect these attacks) and attacks carried out with reconstructed samples (only feature-level techniques give protection for this threat)

iris are carried out with printed iris pictures, printed contact lenses or even replayed videos of the iris [49, 69].

Given the above spoofing definition, an anti-spoofing method is usually accepted to be any technique that is able to automatically distinguish between real biometric traits presented to the sensor and synthetically produced artifacts. Such protection methods may be classified as (see Fig. 20.10):

- *Sensor-level techniques*, also referred to as hardware-based. These methods are integrated in the sensor (see Fig. 20.10). In these approaches some specific device is usually integrated to the scanner in order to detect particular properties of a living trait (e.g., specific reflection properties of the eye or dilation and contraction movements of the pupil).
- *Feature-level techniques*, also referred to as software-based. In this case, the fake trait is detected once the sample has been acquired with a standard sensor. As such, features used to distinguish between real and fake traits are extracted from the biometric sample (i.e., an image in the iris case), and not directly from the human body as in the case of sensor-level techniques. These methods are integrated after the sensor, usually as part of the feature extractor module (see Fig. 20.10).

While sensor-level anti-spoofing methods are of little use for the detection of reconstructed samples (since they interact with real physical traits/artifacts in the analogue domain), feature-level techniques can be an effective tool to prevent inverse biometric attacks (which are committed already in the digital domain).

Over the last few years valuable efforts to enhance iris-based systems security have been carried out, leading to different feature-level iris anti-spoofing methods that can be also useful in the detection of reversed engineered samples.

Daugman, regarded as the father of automatic iris recognition due to his pioneering and very successful early works in the field [12], presented some of the first ideas regarding anti-spoofing countermeasures for iris biometrics [13, 15], where the suggested feature-level methods were presented as a theoretical framework. Daugman pointed out that the printing process can leave detectable traces on spoofing artifacts (e.g., photographs or lenses), and that a simple 2-D Fourier analysis of the acquired image can expose that unnatural behavior. Pacut and Czajka [57], Czajka [11], and He et al. [36], have developed automated feature-level methods to analyze artificial frequencies in printed iris images. Following the same line, the Wavelet Transform has also been used, combined with a support vector machine (SVM) classifier, as a way to extract discriminative features from the iris frequency spectrum in the task of detecting photo-attacks [37].

From those initial works based on the iris image spectral analysis, different image processing methods have been applied to iris images acquired with standard sensors, as an alternative to extract features that allow differentiating between real and fake traits.

For instance, in [35] four features based on the grey level values of the outer region of fake contact lenses are proposed for software-based spoofing detection. Similarly, in a subsequent work, grey level values of the iris texture are studied in order to characterize the visual primitives of the iris complementing them with measures related to the iris edge sharpness [72]. The analysis of the iris texture primitives of real and fake iris images was also considered in [75] using a hierarchical visual codebook to represent the extracted SIFT descriptors and tested against attacks carried out with printed photos, contact lenses, and even plastic eyes.

One of the most recent trends in image processing is the use of local binary patterns (LBPs) for representation of the image texture. This approach, which is one of the most successful in face anti-spoofing has also been successfully applied to the iris trait in several works [38, 74], where the efficiency of different configurations of LBPs has been evaluated against a number of known attacks (e.g., contact lenses, photo-attacks, artificial physical irises).

The use of image quality assessment metrics has also been studied for iris liveness-detection. Several iris-specific and general image quality metrics were studied in [25] and in [27] to distinguish between real iris images and those acquired in photo-attacks.

The next subsection describes a practical study on the ability to detect iris reconstructed samples of a feature-level countermeasure initially designed as protection against spoofing attacks. Although several of the techniques mentioned above could be applied, just as a proof of concept, we have conducted the experiments based on the method introduced in [27], which is based on the use of general image quality measures.

The use of image quality assessment (IQA) for anti-spoofing and/or inverse bio-metrics detection is motivated by the assumption that: "It is expected that a fake image involved in an attack attempt will have different quality than a real sample acquired in the normal operation scenario for which the sensor was designed." Following this "*quality-difference*" hypothesis, in the present case study we explore the potential of *general* image quality assessment as a way to detect reconstructed iris samples.

Expected quality differences between real and synthetic samples may include: degree of sharpness, color and luminance levels, local artifacts, structural distortions or natural appearance. For example, reconstructed iris images are more likely to present unnatural local acquisition artifacts such as spots and patches that may be difficult to differentiate for the untrained human eye.

20.4.1 Case Study: Detection Method Based on Image Quality Features

The problem of detecting reconstructed biometric samples can be seen as a two-class classification problem where an input biometric sample has to be assigned to one of two classes: real or fake (i.e., synthetically reconstructed). The key point of the process is to find a set of discriminant features in order to build an appropriate classifier capable of reliably estimating the probability of the image "realism". In the present case study we apply the parameterization based on 25 general image quality measures (IQM) proposed in [27].

A general diagram of the detection approach is shown in Fig. 20.11. In order to keep its generality and simplicity, the system needs only one input: the biometric sample to be classified as real or fake (i.e., the same image acquired for biometric recognition purposes). Furthermore, as the method operates on the whole image, without searching for any trait-specific properties, it does not require any preprocessing steps (e.g., iris detection, pupil segmentation, iris normalization) prior to the computation of the IQ features. This characteristic minimizes its computational load. Once the feature vector has been generated, the sample is classified as real (generated by a genuine trait) or fake (synthetically reconstructed), using some simple classifiers. In particular, for the present experimental evaluation, a standard implementation in Matlab of the Quadratic Discriminant Analysis (QDA) classifier has been considered.

The parameterization used in this case study comprises 25 image quality measures, both full-reference and blind [27]:

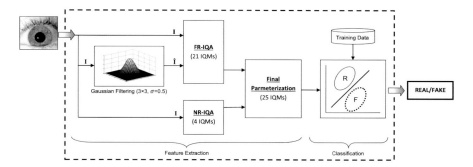

Fig. 20.11 General diagram of the biometric protection method based on Image Quality Assessment (IQA) applied in the present work to the detection of reconstructed iris images. IQM stands for image quality measure, FR for full-reference, and NR for no-reference. The original approach is thoroughly described in [27]

- Full-reference image quality assessment (FR-IQA) methods rely on the availability of a clean undistorted reference image to estimate the quality of the test sample. In the problem of fake detection addressed in this work such a reference image is unknown, as the detection system only has access to the input sample. In order to circumvent this limitation, as shown in Fig. 20.11, the input image $\mathbf{I}$ (of size $N \times M$) is filtered with a low-pass Gaussian kernel ($\sigma = 0.5$ and size 3×3), generating this way a smoothed version $\hat{\mathbf{I}}$ of the image. Then, the quality between both images ($\mathbf{I}$ and $\hat{\mathbf{I}}$) is computed according to the corresponding full-reference IQA metric.
- Unlike full-reference IQA methods, in general, the human visual system does not require of a reference sample to determine the quality level of an image. Following this same principle, automatic no-reference image quality assessment (NR-IQA) algorithms aim at addressing the very complex and challenging problem of assessing the visual quality of images, in the absence of a reference. Presently, NR-IQA methods generally estimate the quality of the test image according to some pre-trained statistical models.

As mentioned above, the task in the performance assessment experiments is to automatically distinguish between real and fake samples. Results are reported in terms of: the False Genuine Rate (FGR), which accounts for the number of reconstructed samples that were classified as real; and the False Fake Rate (FFR), which gives the probability of an image coming from a genuine sample being considered as synthetic. The half total error rate (HTER) is computed as HTER $= (\text{FGR} + \text{FFR})/2$.

The experiments are conducted on the same databases described in Sects. 20.3.1.3 and 20.3.2.1 for the evaluation of the two iris reconstruction methods reviewed in the present chapter. For each of the inverse biometric algorithms the corresponding database is divided into two totally independent (in terms of users) sets: train set, used to train the classifier of the detection method; and test set, used to evaluate the performance of the protection approach. The final results are reported after applying twofold cross validation.

The results achieved by the protection approach appear in Table 20.3. It can be observed that the method is able to correctly classify over 87 % of the synthetic samples generated following the deterministic method described in [67], and almost 90 % of the synthetic samples produced with the probabilistic algorithm proposed in [26]. It is also worth noticing that the FGR and FFR are quite balanced, which suggests that the detection algorithm does not favor one class (i.e., real or synthetic) over the other.

These results show the feasibility of applying feature-level anti-spoofing methods to the detection of reconstructed iris samples and open a promising future line of research in the protection of iris-based recognition systems against this type of threat.

Table 20.3 Results (in percentage) obtained by the evaluated biometric protection method based on IQA for the two type of reconstructed iris images considered: those generated following the deterministic method described in [67] (top row) and those generated following the probabilistic method described in [26] (bottom row)

	Results: Iris		
	FFR	FGR	HTER
Iris-Synthetic [67]	13.8	11.6	12.7
Iris-Synthetic [26]	10.9	9.5	10.2

20.5   Conclusions, Facts and Challenges

The present chapter has shown that the phase information summarized in iris codes is sufficient to generate synthetic iris-like images with very similar binary templates as that of the original iris pattern. The experimental findings of the two iris reconstruction algorithms reviewed in the chapter indicate that an eventual attack against iris matchers using such reconstructed images would have a very high chance of success. Since iris codes, in general, only encode phase-related data of the original iris image and discard the amplitude information [17], there are visual differences between the reconstructed iris and the original iris. However, results indicate that it may be possible to deceive a human expert with the reconstructed samples even though the synthetic grayscale iris patterns are not a fully accurate reproduction of the original patterns.

The experimental findings have also shown that, following a probabilistic reconstruction approach, it is possible to generate not just one, but multiple synthetic samples from a given iris code. This not only significantly increases the chances of generating a synthetic image that is recognized as the original one by iris recognition systems, but it also opens up the possibility of other potential applications for inverse biometric algorithms:

- These approaches may be used to synthetically increase the amount of available data of a subject (i.e., the number of training samples) in order to improve the performance of iris recognition systems [20].
- Biometric samples are personal data and different privacy concerns have arisen regarding their distribution and protection [60]. The proposed reconstruction method is able to generate synthetic iris patterns visually different to the original which are, nevertheless, positively matched to the user's identity. This means that the synthetic samples may be considered as an alternative representation of the user's identity and, as such, may be stored in the database thereby avoiding some of the possible privacy issues.

- From an information theory standpoint, the reconstruction methods may be useful to conduct experiments on the individuality of the iris trait [7, 40], helping to assess the entropy of the information present in iris templates and to develop methods that compress and reliably store the intrinsic individual-related data conveyed within an iris pattern.

Furthermore, the work has reinforced the need for including template protection schemes in commercial iris systems as well as adopting a verification strategy that confirms if the biometric samples presented to the system are those of a genuine eye and not that of a digital or physical artifact of the iris.

It may be argued that the reconstruction approaches considered in this chapter can be successful only when the template stored in the database is compromised. This may be difficult (although possible) in classical biometric systems where the enrolled templates are kept in a centralized database. In this case, the attacker would have to access the database and extract the information, or intercept the communication channel when the stored template is released for matching. However, the threat is heightened in Match-on-Card (MoC) applications where an individual's biometric template is stored in a smartcard possessed by the person. Such applications are rapidly growing due to several appealing characteristics such as scalability and privacy [5]. Similarly, biometric data is being stored in many official documents such as the new biometric passport [41], some national ID cards [34], the US FIPS-201 Personal Identity Verification inititatives (PIV) [52] and the ILO Seafarers Identity Card Program [42]. In spite of the clear advantages that these type of applications offer, templates are more likely to be compromised as it is easier for the attacker to have physical access to the storage device and, as has already been demonstrated [68], fraudulently obtain the information contained inside. This makes MoC systems potentially more vulnerable to the type reconstruction algorithms described in this chapter especially when the biometric data is stored without any type of encryption [52], or printed in the clear on plastic cards as 2D barcodes [42].

Thus, there is an acute need to deflect the type of attack outlined in this chapter. This can be accomplished using two complementary approaches:

- **Prevention**. Here the goal is to avoid the users' templates from being compromised, for example by securely storing biometric data using encrypted templates [33, 63] or protecting the communication channels through encryption [66].
- **Protection**. Here the goal is to minimize the probability of a successful attack even when a template is compromised. This could be accomplished by using biometric-based countermeasures to distinguish synthetic images from real iris images or to employ liveness-detection techniques [27, 28].

Research work, such as the one presented in this chapter, or previous studies dealing with other modalities like fingerprint [9, 64], face [21, 50] or hand [32], bring to the fore the difficulty in estimating the amount of information present within a biometric trait and the issue of biometric template generation and protection.

Furthermore, from a security perspective, we believe that these examples may serve as a wake-up call for vendors and developers to be aware of the potential risks of not securing biometric templates, as is the case in some operational systems already installed in sensitive areas. There is an urgent need to design effective template protection algorithms that minimize the effects of these threats and increase the confidence of the end users in this rapidly emerging technology.

References

1. A. Adler, Sample images can be independently restored from face recognition templates, in *Proceedings of Canadian Conference on Electrical and Computer Engineering (CCECE)*, vol 2 (2003), pp. 1163–1166
2. A. Adler, Images can be regenerated from quantized biometric match score data, in *Proceedings of Canadian Conference on Electrical and Computer Engineering (CCECE)* (2004), pp. 469–472
3. ANSI-NIST. ANSI X9.84-2001, Biometric Information Management and Security (2001)
4. J.E. Baker, Reducing bias and inefficiency in the selection algorithm, in *Proceedings of International Conference on Genetic Algorithms and their Application (ICGAA)* (L. Erlbaum Associates Inc., 1987), pp. 14–21
5. C. Bergman, in *Advances in Biometrics: Sensors, Algorithms and Systems*, ed. by N. Ratha, V. Govindaraju. Chap. Match-on-card for Secure and Scalable Biometric Authentication (Springer, 2008), pp. 407–422
6. A. Black, N. Campbell, Optimizing selection of units from speech database for concatenative synthesis, in *Proceedings of European Conference on Speech Communication and Technology (EUROSPEECH)* (1995), pp. 581–584
7. R. Bolle et al., Iris individuality: a partial iris model, in *Proceedings of International Conference on Pattern Recognition* (2004), pp. 927–930
8. R. Cappelli, in *Handbook of Fingerprint Recognition*, ed. by D. Maltoni et al. Chap. Synthetic Fingerprint Generation (Springer, 2003), pp. 203–231
9. R. Cappelli et al., Fingerprint image reconstruction from standard templates. IEEE Trans. Pattern Anal. Mach. Intell. **29**, 1489–1503 (Sept. 2007)
10. J. Cui et al., An iris image synthesis method based on PCA and super-resolution. in *Proceedings of IAPR International Conference on Pattern Recognition (ICPR)* (2004) pp. 471–474
11. A. Czajka, Database of iris printouts and its application: development of liveness detection method for iris recognition, in *Proceedings of International Conference on Methods and Models in Automation and Robotics (MMAR)* (2013), pp. 28–33
12. J. Daugman, High confidence visual recognition of persons by a test of statistical independence. IEEE Trans. Pattern Anal. Mach. Intell. **15**, 1148–1161 (1993)
13. J. Daugman, in *Biometrics. Personal Identification in a Networked Society*, ed. by A. K. Jain, R. Bolle, S. Pankanti (Kluwer Academic Publishers, 1999). Chap. Recognizing Persons by their Iris Patterns, pp. 103–121
14. J. Daugman, How iris recognition works. IEEE Trans. Circuits Syst. Video Technol. **14**, 21–30 (2004)
15. J. Daugman, Iris recognition and anti-spoofing countermeasures, in *Proceedings of International Biometrics Conference on (IBC)* (2004)
16. J. Daugman, Probing the uniqueness and randomness of iris codes: results from 200 billion iris pair comparisons. Proc. IEEE **94**, 1927–1935 (2006)
17. J. Daugman, in *Encyclopedia of Biometrics*, ed. by S. Z. Li (Springer, 2009). Chap. Iris encoding and recognition using gabor wavelets, pp. 787–797
18. T. Dutoit, *An Introduction to Text-to-speech Synthesis* (Kluwer Academic Publishers, 2001)

19. M.A. Ferrer, M. Diaz-Cabrera, A. Morales. Static signature synthesis: a neuromotor inspired approach for biometrics. IEEE Trans. Pattern Anal. Mach. Intell. **37**, 667–680 (2015)
20. J. Galbally et al., Improving the enrollment in dynamic signature verification with synthetic samples, in *Proceedings of IAPR International Conference on Document Analysis and Recognition (ICDAR)* (2009)
21. J. Galbally et al., On the vulnerability of face verification systems to hill-climbing attacks. Pattern Recogn. **43**, 1027–1038 (2010)
22. J. Galbally et al., An evaluation of direct and indirect attacks using fake fingers generated from ISO templates. Pattern Recogn. Lett. **31**, 725–732 (2010)
23. J. Galbally et al., Synthetic on-line signature generation. Part II: experimental validation. Pattern Recogn. **45**, 2622–2632 (2012)
24. J. Galbally et al., Synthetic on-line signature generation. Part I: methodology and algorithms. Pattern Recogn. **45**, 2610–2621 (2012)
25. J. Galbally et al., Iris liveness detection based on quality related features, in *Proceedings of IAPR International Conference on Biometrics (ICB)* (2012), pp. 271–276
26. J. Galbally et al., Iris image reconstruction from binary templates: an efficient probabilistic approach based on genetic algorithms. Comput. Vis. Image Underst. **117**, 1512–1525 (2013)
27. J. Galbally, S. Marcel, J. Fierrez, Image quality assessment for fake biometric detection: application to iris, fingerprint and face recognition. IEEE Trans. Image Process. **23**, 710–724 (2014)
28. J. Galbally, S. Marcel, J. Fierrez, Biometric Anti-spoofing Methods: A Survey in Face Recognition. IEEE Access **2**, 1530–1552 (2014)
29. J. Galbally et al., On-line signature recognition through the combination of real dynamic data and synthetically generated static data. Pattern Recogn. **48**, 2921–2934 (2015)
30. J. Galbally et al., Securing iris recognition systems against masquerade attacks, in *Proceedings of SPIE Biometric and Surveillance Technology for Human and Activity Identification X (BSTHAI)* (2013), 87120E
31. D.E. Goldberg, *Genetic Algorithms in Search Optimization and Machine Learning* (Addison Wesley, 1989)
32. M. Gomez-Barrero et al., A novel hand reconstruction approach and its application to vulnerability assessment. Inform. Sci. **268**, 103–121 (2014)
33. M. Gomez-Barrero et al., Protected facial biometric templates based on local gabor patterns and adaptive bloom filters, in *Proceedings of IAPR/IEEE International Conference on Pattern Recognition (ICPR)* (2014), pp. 4483–4488
34. Government of Spain. Ministry of Interior. http://www.dnielectronico.es/
35. X. He, S. An, P. Shi, Statistical texture analysis-based approach for fake iris detection using support vector machines, in *Proceedings of IAPR International Conference on Biometrics (ICB)* (Springer LNCS-4642, 2007), pp. 540–546
36. X. He, Y. Lu, P. Shi, A fake iris detection method based on FFT and quality assessment, in *Proceedings of IEEE Chinese Conference on Pattern Recognition (CCPR)* (2008)
37. X. He, Y. Lu, P. Shi, A new fake iris detection method, in *Proceedings of IAPR/IEEE International Conference on Biometrics (ICB)* (Springer LNCS-5558, 2009), pp. 1132–1139
38. Z. He et al., Efficient iris spoof detection via boosted local binary patterns, in *Proceedings of IEEE International Conference on Biometrics (ICB)* (2009)
39. C.J. Hill, *Risk of Masquerade Arising from the Storage of Biometrics*, MA Thesis (Australian National University, 2001)
40. K. Hollingsworth, K. Bowyer, P. Flynn, The best bits in an iris code. IEEE Trans. Pattern Anal. Mach. Intell. **31**, 964–973 (2009)
41. ICAO. ICAO Document 9303, Part 1, Volume 2: Machine Readable Passports—Specifications for electronically enabled passports with biometric identification capability (2006)
42. ILO. ILO SID-0002, Finger Minutiae-Based Biometric Profile for Seafarers Identity Documents, International Labour Organization (2006)
43. International Biometric Group. Generating images from templates. White paper (2002)
44. A. Jain, P. Flynn, A. Ross (eds.), *Handbook of Biometrics* (Springer, 2008)

45. A. Lin, L. Wang, Style-preserving English handwriting synthesis. Pattern Recogn. **40**, 2097–2109 (2007)
46. S. Makthal, A. Ross, Synthesis of iris images using markov random fields, in *Proceedings of 13th European Signal Processing Conference (EUSIPCO)* (2005)
47. E. Marasco, A. Ross, A survey on anti-spoofing schemes for fingerprints. ACM Comput. Surv. **47**, 1–36 (2014)
48. L. Masek, P. Kovesi, *MATLAB Source Code for a Biometric Identification System Based on Iris Patterns*. MA thesis (School of Computer Science and Software Engineering, University of Western Australia, 2003)
49. T. Matsumoto, Artificial irises: importance of vulnerability analysis, in *Proceedings of Asian Biometrics Workshop (AWB)* (2004)
50. P. Mohanty, S. Sarkar, R. Kasturi. From scores to face templates: a model-based approach. IEEE Trans. Pattern Anal. Mach. Intell. **29**, 2065–2078 (2007)
51. NeuroTechnology. "VeriEye SDK." Accessed form http://www.neurotechnology.com/verieye.html
52. P. Grother, W. Salamon, R. Chandramouli, *NIST Special Publication 800-76-2. Biometric Specifications for Personal Identity Verification* (National Institute of Standards and Technology (NIST) 2013). Accessed from http://dx.doi.org/10.6028/NIST.SP.800-76-2
53. N.M. Orlans, D.J. Buettner, J. Marques, A survey of synthetic biometrics: capabilities and benefits, in *Proceedings of International Conference on Artificial Intelligence (ICAI)* (2004), pp. 499–505
54. J. Ortega-Garcia et al., The multi-scenario multi-environment biosecure multimodal database (BMDB). IEEE Trans. Pattern Anal. Mach. Intell. **32**, 1097–1111 (2010)
55. A. Osborn, *Questioned Documents* (Boyd Printing Co, Albany, NY, 1929)
56. A. Othman, A. Ross, On mixing fingerprints. IEEE Trans. Inf. Forensics Secur. **8**, 260–267 (2013)
57. A. Pacut, A. Czajka, Aliveness detection for iris biometrics, in *Proceedings of IEEE International Carnahan Conference on Security Technology (ICCST)* (2006), pp. 122–129
58. P. Phillips et al., The Iris Challenge Evaluation 2005, in *IEEE International Conference on Biometrics: Theory, Applications and Systems* (Oct. 2008), pp. 1–8
59. N. Poh, S. Marcel, S. Bengio, Improving face authentication using virtual samples, in *Proceedings of IEEE International Conference on Acoustics, Speech and Signal Processing (ICASSP)* (2003)
60. S. Prabhakar, S. Pankanti, A.K. Jain, Biometric recognition: security and privacy concerns. IEEE Secur. Priv. **1**, 33–42 (2003)
61. C. Rabasse, R. M. Guest, M.C. Fairhurst, A method for the synthesis of dynamic biometric signature data, in *Proceedings of IAPR International Conference on Document Analysis and Recognition (ICDAR)* (2007)
62. C. Rathgeb, A. Uhl, Attacking Iris Recognition: An Efficient Hill-Climbing Technique, in *Proceedings of International Conference on Pattern Recognition (ICPR)* (2010), pp. 1217–1220
63. A. Ross, A. Othman, Visual cryptography for biometric privacy. IEEE Trans. Inform. Forensics Secur. **6**, 70–81 (2011)
64. A. Ross, J. Shah, A.K. Jain, From template to image: reconstructing fingerprints from minutiae points. IEEE Trans. Pattern Anal. Mach. Intell. **29**, 544–560 (2007)
65. S. Shah, A. Ross, Generating synthetic irises by feature agglomeration, in *Proceedings of IEEE International Conference on Image Processing (ICIP)* (2006), pp. 317–320
66. U. Uludag et al., Biometric cryptosystems: issues and challenges. Proc. IEEE **92**, 948–960 (2004)
67. S. Venugopalan, M. Savvides, How to generate spoofed irises from an iris code template. IEEE Trans. Info. Forensics Secur. **6**, 385–394 (2011)
68. J. van Beek, ePassports reloaded, in *Black Hat USA Briefings* (2008)
69. U.C. von Seelen, Countermeasures against iris spoofing with contact lenses, in *Proceedings of Biometrics Consortium Conference* (2005)

70. A. Wehde, J.N. Beffel, *Finger-prints Can be Forged* (Tremonia Publish Co., 1924)
71. Z. Wei, T. Tan, Z. Sun, Synthesis of large realistic iris databases using patch-based sampling, in *Proceedings of IAPR International Conference of Pattern Recognition (ICPR)* (2008), pp. 1–4
72. Z. Wei et al., Counterfeit iris detection based on texture analysis, in *Proceedings of IAPR International Conference on Pattern Recognition (ICPR)* (2008)
73. S.N. Yanushkevich et al., (eds.), Image pattern recognition. *Synthesis and Analysis in Biometrics* (World Scientific, 2007)
74. H. Zhang, Z. Sun, T. Tan, Contact lense detection based on weighted LBP. in *Proceedings of IEEE International Conference on Pattern Recognition (ICPR)* (2010), pp. 4279–4282
75. H. Zhang et al., Learning Hierarchical Visual Codebook for Iris Liveness Detection, in *Proceedings of IEEE International Joint Conference on Biometrics (IJCB)* (2011)
76. J. Zuo, N.A. Schmid, X. Chen, On generation and analysis of synthetic iris images. IEEE Trans. Inf. Forensics Secur. **2**, 77–90 (2007)

Chapter 21
Off-Angle Iris Correction Methods

David S. Bolme, Hector Santos-Villalobos, Joseph Thompson,
Mahmut Karakaya and Chris Bensing Boehnen

Abstract In many real-world iris recognition systems, obtaining consistent frontal images is problematic do to inexperienced or uncooperative users, untrained operators, or distracting environments. As a result many collected images are unusable by modern iris matchers. In this chapter, we present four methods for correcting off-angle iris images to appear frontal which makes them compatible with existing iris matchers. The methods include an affine correction, a retraced model of the human eye, measured displacements, and a genetic algorithm optimized correction. The affine correction represents a simple way to create an iris image that appears frontal but it does not account for refractive distortions of the cornea. The other method account for refraction. The retraced model simulates the optical properties of the cornea. The other two methods are data-driven. The first uses optical flow to measure the displacements of the iris texture when compared to frontal images of the same subject. The second uses a genetic algorithm to learn a mapping that optimizes the Hamming Distance scores between off-angle and frontal images. In this paper, we hypothesize that the biological model presented in our earlier work does not adequately account for all variations in eye anatomy and therefore the two data-driven approaches should yield better performance. Results are presented using the commercial VeriEye matcher that show that the genetic algorithm method clearly improves over prior work and makes iris recognition possible up to 50° off-angle.

21.1 Introduction

Iris recognition is one of the most accurate biometric identification techniques and has addressed many military and civilian security needs. For example, iris recognition has recently been adopted in the travel industry as a way to verify a traveler's identity and reduce the wait time at customs or security checkpoints. It has also been adopted by the US military as a tool in the war on terror because it can be used to track

D.S. Bolme (✉) · H. Santos-Villalobos · J. Thompson · M. Karakaya · C.B. Boehnen
Oak Ridge National Laboratory, Oak Ridge, TN, USA
e-mail: bolmeds@ornl.gov

© Springer-Verlag London 2016
K.W. Bowyer and M.J. Burge (eds.), *Handbook of Iris Recognition*,
Advances in Computer Vision and Pattern Recognition,
DOI 10.1007/978-1-4471-6784-6_21

497

Fig. 21.1 Illustration of eye components important for iris recognition. (*Top*) Frontal image of iris. (*Bottom*) Cross-section of iris captured with an Optical Coherent Tomography system

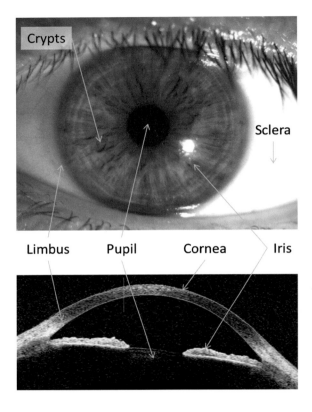

the movement of individuals, identify potential terrorists, and verify the identity of people accessing military installations.

Under ideal collection conditions iris recognition is extremely accurate [8]. In addition, as shown in Fig. 21.1, the iris is the only human internal organ visible to the outside world. Therefore, the iris pattern is difficult to change and research shows that for high quality images the iris pattern is virtually stable [11]. Another advantage of iris recognition is that systems can operate with very low false accept rates even exceeding one in a billion [8]. Maintaining high levels of accuracy requires that high quality iris images are collected using a high-resolution sensor of a subject that is looking directly at the sensor. There are a variety of commercial systems that can accurately and quickly match irises, but they depend on accurately aligning the iris textures. Since iris-matching algorithms are exploiting high frequency patterns in the iris texture even small errors in the segmentation and alignment of the iris texture can cause failures in the matching process.

One of the biggest problems in iris recognition is recognizing non-frontal iris images. Non-frontal images can come from a variety of sources. To produce high-quality images most sensors have the subjects position their faces close to the camera and look directly at the lens. In practice, however, many of the users or operators of these systems are inexperienced and often capture images where the subjects are looking in the wrong direction due to inadvertent eye movement. There is also an increasing interest in standoff iris collection that automatically images a subject's eyes from a distance without any explicit participation. In such cases, the subjects could be looking in almost any direction and therefore the ability to recognize non-frontal irises is necessary for the operation of the system.

The problem with non-frontal images is that the corneal refraction produces complex distortions preventing images from being easily transformed to align to frontal images. Most recognition algorithms operate under the false assumption that the iris texture lies on a plane and under such assumptions it can be aligned to frontal images using techniques like elliptical or rubber sheet unwrapping [7, 40]. We have found that these techniques are adequate for correcting off-angle images up to around 20–30°, but for larger angles there are 3D and optical effects that cause alignment problems. In this research, we are focusing on correcting the iris texture for images taken from 30° to 50° off-angle, however the techniques could be applied to a broader range of angles with further development. Thirty degrees was selected as a lower bound, because it is where simple correction methods fail. Fifty degrees was selected as an upper bound, because about 50° the cornea is self-occluding which makes accurately segmenting the far limbus boundary impossible. Without the far limbus boundary, alignment and correction requires an additional level of complexity.

As the angle increases, there are a number of physical and anatomical factors that cause distortions in the iris image and makes alignment difficult

- Cornea Refraction—As light passes through the cornea it is refracted. Because the iris is an approximate plane behind an approximately spherical cornea the rays of light are bent in ways that cause the iris texture to shift in different directions and by different amounts depending on the viewpoint [25, 30, 35].
- The Limbus Effect—The limbus, which is the semi-opaque outer boundary of the cornea, is slightly elevated relative to the iris plane. As a result, it occludes different parts of the iris boundary as the viewing angle changes [17].
- 3D Iris Shape—The iris is not strictly a plane but has an approximately toroid shaped surface. Additionally the iris texture is three-dimensional including crypts, ridges, and contraction folds that cause the appearance of the texture to change when viewed from different angles [34].
- Dilation—As the iris sphincter and dilator muscles constrict or relax for pupil dilation, collarette and ciliary zones move and the iris crypts are distorted [28, 33]. In addition, as shown in medical glaucoma studies the volume (3D thickness) of the iris changes by 50 % [27], which also distorts the iris texture.
- Accommodation—During the normal focusing process of the eye, the lens is sometimes pushed against the iris. This is called accommodation and it moves the center of the iris closer to the cornea, which causes additional distortion when viewed from off-angle images [13].

In this work we have looked at four methods for correcting off-angle iris images. Our techniques are based on transforming the iris images to appear frontal by correcting for the complex distortions caused by the cornea and 3D structure of the

500 D.S. Bolme et al.

iris. By correcting the images, these techniques can be used to preprocess off-angle images and do not require costly modification of existing commercial systems. Our four methods are based on

1. A simple affine correction.
2. Measuring the texture displacement from off-angle images using optical flow techniques.
3. Learning corrections using a Genetic Algorithm (GA) that optimizes the Hamming Distance scores for off-angle image comparisons.
4. Modeling the refractive process of the cornea to compensate for optical distortions [35].

Although our techniques do not currently compensate for all of the challenges associated with non-frontal images, the techniques significantly improve the scores for the commercial VeriEye iris matcher. Our hypothesis is that the cornea modeling process used by Thompson [35] does not account for all the previously-mentioned challenges and therefore the two data-driven approaches offer significant performance improvements. We will show that by applying these techniques we can demonstrate significant improvements in performance for off-angle images up to 50°.

The remainder of this paper will discuss related work and background information in Sect. 21.2. Four methods for remapping the iris texture from off-angle to frontal will be discussed in Sect. 21.3. Experimental data and results will be presented in Sect. 21.4. Finally, concluding remarks and suggestions for future work can be found in Sect. 21.5.

21.2 Related Works

The first problem with off-angle iris recognition is segmenting the noncircular iris and pupil boundaries. As the eye becomes increasingly off-angle those boundaries become increasingly elliptical. Many nonideal iris recognition systems handle off-angle images by improving segmentation and unwrapping but ignore other effects such as cornea refraction.

In the early history of iris biometrics, Daugman and Wildes were the two key pioneers of the field. Daugman suggested finding the iris boundaries with an integro-differential operator, normalizing the segmented texture by polar unwrapping, generating the iris code by convolving the normalized iris with 2D Gabor filters, and matching iris codes with a Hamming Distance metric [9]. On the other hand, Wildes proposed segmenting the iris with an edge detector and the Hough transform, then generating iris codes or templates from multiscale Laplacian Filters, and matching the templates with normalized correlation [39]. Although several iris segmentation techniques have been derived from Wildes's approach, today most iris recognition algorithms and commercial systems rely on a Daugman-style iris recognition pipeline due to its simple implementation [4, 28]. Both approaches assumed a high-quality iris image and circular and centered iris and pupil boundaries.

It was noted early on that the shape of the iris and pupil were not exactly circular and the centers of the iris boundary and pupil boundary were not the same. On average, the pupil center tends to be located below and slightly nasal of the iris center [7]. In addition, previous research has shown that the accuracy of an iris recognition system depends greatly on the quality and segmentation of the iris image [26]. Therefore, a number of different methods have been developed to approximate the noncircular boundaries and polar unwrappings. For example, for near frontal, Daugman represents the noncircular inner and outer iris boundaries with active contours based on the discrete Fourier series expansion of the contour data [7]. Another iris segmentation example is the work of Shah and Ross, who combine "snakes" segmentation with geometric active contours [32]. Active contour methods are ideal for irregular shapes like the iris boundary. However, the edge threshold parameters that define the contour are image dependent and hard to generalize. Zuo et al. developed a system for automatically segmenting nonideal iris images using intensity, shape, and localization features from the iris and pupil [40]. Their ellipse-based representation for the iris and pupil boundaries demonstrated significant performance improvements on challenging datasets; one of the datasets included irises with gaze up to $30°$ [40]. The noncircular iris can also be segmented with morphological operations as described by Kennell et al. [18]. Although in their work Kennell et al. fitted a circle to the morphological segmentation, the segmentation could also be fitted with an ellipse model as done by Zuo et al. There are several other methods for segmentation, normalization, and feature extraction of the iris. For a more complete review of existing methods, please refer to [4–6, 14, 15, 28].

Probably the best understood problem with off-angle iris recognition is that when the angle deviates significantly from frontal the elliptical appearance of the iris boundary is more evident. Schuckers et al. estimate the gaze angle by computing an affine transformation that maps the elliptical iris boundary to a circle [31]. The affine transformation is applied to the off-angle image in order to approximate a frontal view of the iris. Daugman extends this approach by employing a method he named "Fourier-based trigonometry [7]." Daugman's method does not constrain the corrected frontal view iris to a circular boundary and accounts for occlusions. There are several other approaches for off-angle iris recognition that deviate from Daugman's recognition pipeline. For example, Thorton proposed the use of correlation filters to address iris nonidealities like occlusions, dilation, and perspective distortion [36]. Vatsa et al. employ different support vector machines (SVM) to enhance the quality of segmented irises, to select the features with rich information, and to match a fusion of texture and topological iris features [37]. Roy et al. extract and select important iris features with Daubechies wavelets and a Genetic Algorithm, respectively, and employ adaptive asymmetrical support vector machines for iris matching [29]. Miyazawa et al. claim that the phase components of the 2D Discrete Fourier Transform can also be used to match nonideal irises [21]. A last example is the work of Belcher and Du [1], which uses the Scale-Invariant Feature Transform (SIFT) to match two irises. These approaches outperform Schuckers's and Daugman's off-angle methods, because they inherently take into account distortion generated by cornea refraction, limbus occlusion, and the nonplanar surface of the iris. On the other hand, one drawback of these approaches is that they are not compatible with most commercial matchers and databases, because they "re-define" Daugman's matching approach. These 're-defining' solutions may not be practical to implement in existing enterprise solutions that have already heavily invested in costly commercial algorithms that require frontal irises.

As mentioned above, a flaw in Schuckers's and Daugman's methods is the assumption that a perspective projection is enough to transform/correct an off-angle iris to its frontal view. The iris is a 3D nonplanar organ visible through a semi-transparent and refractive interface i.e., the cornea, and previous work has reported the impact of the cornea on iris recognition performance. For example, Price et al. developed a generalized eye model to correct for perspective and refractive distortion of the iris pattern using ray tracing techniques [25]. They reported a median reduction of Hamming Distance of 27.4 % for synthetic eyes with gaze up to 60°. Kennell et al. tested Price et al. method on real off-angle irises up to 40° and found a tenfold reduction of false match rates. The work from Price et al. was later extended by Santos-Villalobos et al. [30], who discovered a number of issues with the original eye model, which include the incorporation of an aspheric corneal shape and the limbus component. Price et al. employ a spherical model for the cornea. This model does not resemble the typical shape found in the human cornea, which is an aspheric or a melon-shaped surface [22]. The eye model used in Santos-Villalobos et al. was primarily based on research motivated by ophthalmology and correcting vision, and therefore is concerned with correcting the rays of light that pass through the cornea, pupil, and lens and produce an image on the fovea. Adjustments were needed to better account for light rays passing only through the cornea and intercepting the iris plane. In addition, as the gaze increases, the limbus region occludes iris features or generate shadows that alter the biometric signature of the iris pattern. This phenomena was named the *limbus effect*. The limbus effect was further studied by Karakaya et al., who show that by taking in account the limbus effect and improving segmentation Hamming Distances could be increased up to 40 % [17]. About the same time, Thompson et al. compared the Oak Ridge National Laboratory (ORNL) eye model and Schuckers's affine transformation method using the commercial VeriEye matcher, and showed that by correcting for corneal distortion the match score distribution mean increased by 15.48 and 32.47 % for real off-angle irises with 40° and 50° of gaze, respectively [35].

One of the most challenging aspects of frontal view reconstruction through ray tracing models is ensuring accurate alignment of the eye model to the iris image in order to obtain a good ray traced reprojection. In addition, the eye models discussed above assume a planar iris surface, which differs from the real 3D and dynamic structure of the iris. For example, Thompson et al. studied the impact of iris accommodation on iris recognition and showed that even for a frontal view, different iris curvature has a significant adverse impact on recognition [34]. We argue that to increase recognition performance for irises with gaze greater than 30°, the recognition system should take into account the following factors: cornea diffraction, iris 3D shape and curvature, and the limbus effect. In the hopes of better understanding these effects present in off-angle images, in the research presented here we investigate two data-driven approaches for correcting off-angle iris images and compare those results to Thompson's ray tracing approach.

21.3 Algorithm Development

In this paper, we have investigated four methods for the correction of off-angle iris images. Those methods are

1. **Affine**: a simple affine correction that makes the iris appear circular.
2. **Measured**: measuring the displacements of the iris texture using optical flow.
3. **Genetic Algorithm**: finding optimal displacement mappings that minimize the Hamming Distances between frontal and off-angle images.
4. **Refractive**: modeling the cornea refraction using ray tracing.

The four techniques are used as a preprocessing step that corrects the iris image such that it appears as if it was frontal. In this way, the irises can be further processed using unmodified back end matchers. This work is tested using the Neurotechnology VeriEye matcher. Although the VeriEye algorithm is robust to off-angle images, we show that our techniques further improve VeriEye scores and extend the useful range of the algorithm out to 50° off-angle.

Baseline performance is represented by comparing to an unmodified image or the affine correction. VeriEye has some tolerance to non-frontal images, so using an unmodified image represents the performance of the algorithm with no correction. VeriEye had difficulty segmenting the iris images as the angle neared 50°. The simple affine correction serves as the other baseline. This correction makes the iris appear frontal by adjusting the pupil boundary to appear approximately circular. This adjustment effectively compensates for perspective distortions assuming a planar iris, but it will not correct for cornea refraction or other nonlinear distortions. We believe this is a good stand-in for most elliptical or rubber sheet unwrapping techniques. It also corrects the appearance of the iris so that VeriEye has no issues with segmentation.

21.3.1 Affine Correction

The affine correction used in this paper was designed to operate with some of the more difficult iris images and are used for preprocessing for the Measured and Genetic Algorithm corrective techniques. Most iris recognition algorithms assume that the eye is facing approximately frontal and the pupil and limbus boundaries are approximately circular. For off-angle images those boundaries are elliptical and much of the boundary is not visible due to occlusion from the eye lids.

The portions of the iris that are visible vary depending not only upon the eye gaze direction, but also the face gaze direction. When the face gaze direction is different

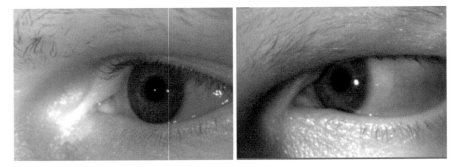

Fig. 21.2 The *left* image illustrates our laboratory setup where the subject is looking directly forward and the camera is positioned off-angle. The *right* image shows the same subject where their face is oriented towards the camera but their eye gaze is off-angle. The *right* image introduces many challenges related to segmentation that are beyond the scope of this paper but are often encountered in operational data

from the eye gaze direction, portions of the iris can become occluded by the left and right portions of the eye socket as shown in Fig. 21.2. On the left, when the face and eye gaze concur, this issue does not arise. However, on the right, when the eye gaze and face gaze are different, the left portion of the iris becomes occluded.

In our laboratory setup, the subject's head and eyes have the same gaze simplifying the problem. However, for some of the commercial sensors the camera is positioned directly in front of the subject's head and then the subject is asked to look to the left and right to obtain off-angle data. The differences between these collections are illustrated in the images below where the left image is collected by the laboratory setup and the right image is collected using a commercial sensor. A similar issue exists when the eye gaze is shifted away from the nose so that the other corner of the eyelids occludes the limbus boundary. For this paper, we exclusively use the laboratory setup for training and testing, because it shows more of the iris. In the future, we would like to further investigate the segmentation issues and other challenges with the data collected using the commercial sensor. For examples, see Fig. 21.2.

Because large portions of the limbus boundary are often occluded in off-angle imagery, a technique is used that geometrically normalizes the image based only on the pupil boundary and the iris width. This technique applies an affine transformation to the iris that causes the pupil to appear circular and centered in a 640×640 image, while the limbus is scaled to have a width of 512 pixels. Because the limbus width is constrained, it eliminates the need to segment the entire limbus boundary. As seen in Fig. 21.2, both sides of the limbus boundary may not be available, so in the future this technique may need to be extended to better handle those cases. For now, the method described below is adequate for the test set used in this particular research.

To determine the affine transformation the following steps are applied:

1. The iris is first automatically segmented using the method proposed by Karakaya et al. [16]. This provides a good estimate of the pupil and limbus boundaries. For our tests the automatic segmentations were corrected manually to ensure that the ellipses fit to the boundaries were accurate.
2. Ellipses are fit to the boundaries of the pupil and iris using the technique described by Fitzgibbon et al. [12]. This provides parameters for the ellipse which include the x and y center point, a major and minor axis, and a rotation angle.
3. Four control points for the transformation are defined as the end points of the major and minor axes. To correct the pupil to appear circular an affine transformation is computed that translates the center of the ellipse to the center of the 640×640 image and rescales the major and minor axis to have equal length. The orientation of those axes is preserved so that there is no rotation of the iris texture due to the transformation.
4. Once the image has been stretched so that the pupil is circular, an additional uniform scaling is applied such that the limbus boundary is 512 pixels across.

21.3.2 Measuring Displacements

To better understand distortions produced by off-angle cornea refraction, a technique was developed to measure the distortions directly from images of irises. The idea is to associate points from the off-angle images with points on the frontal images using optical flow. This provides a mapping from the off-angle to frontal images which can be analyzed to better understand how the texture of the iris is distorted as the pose of the eye changes.

Before measuring displacements the affine transformation described in Sect. 21.3.1 is applied. All of the irises are aligned to the center of the image by applying the affine transformation, which results in an iris pattern that is much closer to circular. The result of the affine transformation is that the limbus boundary of the irises will always be in the same position.

After the affine transformation the irises are centered, stretched, and scaled but differences in the dilation levels of the iris can cause large texture misalignments near the pupil. To correct this, the image is radially stretched such that a ring 256 pixels from the center of the image does not move but the pixels near the center of the image are artificially dilated or contracted such that the pupil is a circle with a radius of 80 pixels. After the dilation correction, it is estimated that the texture translates by at most 15 pixels for the majority of the off-angle dataset.

Three techniques were tried to compute optical flow associations between the off-angle and frontal textures, which included Lucas Kenade Tracking [20], Farneback optical flow [10], and Minimum Output Sum of Squared Error (MOSSE) correlation filter tracking [3]. It was found that the latter produced the best results because Minimum Output Sum of Squared Error (MOSSE) filters were more sensitive to

Table 21.1 The number of point tracked by the Minimum Output Sum of Squared Error (MOSSE) filter

Degrees off-angle	Tracked points
30	32626
40	18261
50	7708

Measured Displacements - 30 Degrees

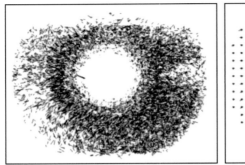 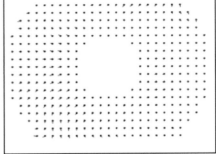

Original Displacements   Smoothed Displacements

Fig. 21.3 The *left* image shows the associated pixel values used to compute the distortion mapping. The *right* plot shows the approximate distortion map using the RBF projection to average the data

the low contrast iris texture. In addition, Minimum Output Sum of Squared Error (MOSSE) tracking also produces a quality score based on the peak-to-sidelobe ratio that was used to drop many erroneous point associations from the dataset.

Table 21.1 shows the number of points tracked for each partition of the dataset. The plot shows that as the angle increases, it is harder to produce good associations between images and therefore the number of tracked points drops. In order to best represent the local effects of the cornea, point associations are translated back to the dilation level of the frontal image. Each of the tracked points provides a measurement of how much the local region in the normalized off-angle image should be corrected in order to align the iris texture.

Figure 21.3 shows the results of the Minimum Output Sum of Squared Error (MOSSE) filter tracking for the 30° off-angle portion of the training set. The left image shows the original data produced by the Minimum Output Sum of Squared Error (MOSSE) tracking. Computing the flow between two images can result in many inconsistent measurements across the whole training set. This data was smoothed by computing local averages using a weighted sum of Radial Basis Functions (RBF). The RBFs two-dimensional Gaussian functions laid out in a grid in the normalized iris image with a spacing of 40 pixels and a sigma of 40 pixels. For each pixel location in the distortion map, the weights of the RBFs are rescaled to sum to 1.0. Finally, a least-squares regression is run to determine a fit to the point association data. Once the approximation to the distortion map is generated it is used to create dense look-up tables that remap the off-angle images to frontal. The resulting smooth mapping is shown on the right side of the Fig. 21.3 and shows a trend that is consistent with the other two methods of cornea correction.

21.3.3 Genetic Algorithm Optimization

As an alternative to measuring displacements between the off-angle and frontal images, it is possible to evaluate look-up tables based on how they affect the Hamming Distances produced between the two images. Here we describe a genetic algorithm that we used to optimize look-up tables (LUTs) to produce improved Hamming Distance scores for the off-angle images.

For training we used the same images of 25 subjects that were used for testing, however, to control for over fitting threefold cross validation was used. In other words, the 25 subjects were partitioned into three groups. For each of three tests one partition was used as a testing set while the other two partitions were used for the Genetic Algorithm (GA) optimization process. This resulted in three Look-Up Tables (LUTs) that were computed for each angle: 30°, 40°, and 50°.

Like the Measured technique, the Genetic Algorithm (GA) starts out using the same 640×640 affine corrected images. The LUT transform is based on a 9×9 grid of 81 control points. Each control point has an x and y displacement for a total of 162 parameters that are optimized by the Genetic Algorithm (GA). The Genetic Algorithm (GA) tunes these parameters in order to make corrections for the cornea refraction and other distortions which misalign the iris texture.

The fitness function that is optimized is based on a Daugman-like iris recognition algorithm [7]. For each subject in the training set there are five frontal images and five off-angle images. The recognition algorithm converts the unmodified frontal images and corrected off-angle images into an iris bit-code by convolving the unwrapped irises with Gabor wavelets at three scales and then thresholds the results. The final fitness function value is the average Hamming Distance between the frontal and off-angle images after correction.

The genetic algorithm is based on the GENITOR [38] and the specific implementation used comes from the PyVision library [2]. The GENITOR algorithm used a population where only the best 100 individuals were retained in the population. This applies more evolutionary pressure than traditional algorithms and can result in faster convergence. The population was initialized with control points that had only small displacements relative to the affine correction. Therefore the Genetic Algorithm (GA)'s initial population performed approximately as well as the Affine transformation alone.

Each Genetic Algorithm (GA) ran for 10000 fitness function evaluations. Figure 21.4 shows the convergence of the Genetic Algorithm (GA) for 50° off-angle images where the average Hamming Distance was reduced from about 0.33–0.23. In

Fig. 21.4 This figure shows the convergence of one of the genetic algorithm runs. The score is the Average Hamming Distance for the tuning dataset and each Iteration is one fitness function evaluation

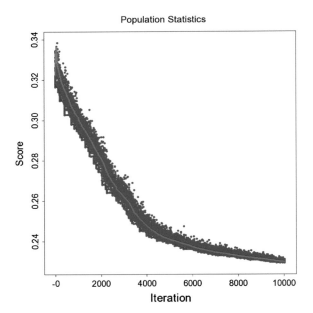

these results, the blue dots represent each fitness function evaluation. The green line represents the best individual in the population and the red line is the worst individual in the population at each time step. The fitnesses of individuals were evaluated in parallel on a 64 core machine where each of the nine Genetic Algorithm (GA) runs completed after approximately 17 h.

Three of the LUTs are shown in Fig. 21.5 for 30°, 40°, and 50° where the left side of the LUTs corresponds to the part of the eye that is furthest from the camera and needs the most correction. It can be seen that as the angle increases so does the magnitude of the correction, while the direction of the corrections remain mostly unchanged.

21.3.4 Refractive Eye Model

The final method we are using to correct for off-angle distortion models the refractive properties of the cornea and uses ray tracing to correct for refraction and to render a corrected frontal view of the off-angle irises. We are using the Oak Ridge National Laboratory (ORNL) eye model that was originally proposed by Price et al. [25] and was later extended by Santos Villalobos et al. [30] and then Thompson et al. [35]. The details of the eye model used for this work are discussed in Thomson's paper [35], which includes a carefully constructed model of the cornea and iris geometry.

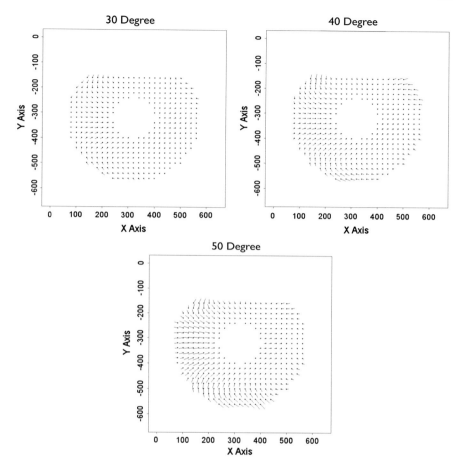

Fig. 21.5 The three look-up tables produced by the genetic algorithm. The distortions become stronger as the angle increases

The model used includes a quadratic surface for the anterior cornea as defined by Navarro [22]. The posterior cornea was a sphere based on the work of Le Grand et al. [19]. The cornea thickness is 0.5 mm at the apex. An index of refraction of 1.36 was used for the cornea and 1.33 for the aqueous humor. The iris is modeled as a plane with an anterior corneal depth of 3.6 mm. The iris is tilted slightly outward at an angle of 2.5°. The limbus extends along the cornea up to 0.5 mm above the cornea.

To transform an image from non-frontal to frontal using the eye model, the limbus boundary needs to be aligned to the limbus of the three-dimensional model. To do this would typically require adjusting the camera parameters and the eye model location to match our laboratory setup. To improve performance our approximate laboratory setup was replicated in the 3D geometry of the ray tracer. In other words, the camera had a focal length of 150 mm and it was located 340 mm from the eye. The off-angle eye was always rendered in the center of the image and then an affine transformation was used to transform the limbus of the original off-angle image to align to the limbus in the ray traced image.

The eye model was originally designed using POV-Ray [24]. The projection process involves first tracing the rays from the camera, through the cornea to the iris plane for the off-angle image. This creates a texture for the iris plane. The eye model and camera geometry are then modified to a frontal configuration and a frontal view of the eye is then rendered using the newly created iris plane texture. The result is a view of the iris as it would appear in a frontal image. For this most recent work, the iris plane was extended beyond the cornea so that the texture includes the ocular region. When corrected to frontal, the ocular region is corrected with a perspective transformation while the iris, which is within the cornea bubble, includes additional correction for optical refraction. The resulting image looks like a frontal image of an eye, which is easily segmented by the iris matcher.

21.4 Results

21.4.1 Dataset

We used a set of iris images that are taken of the left eye of 25 subjects at six angles ranging from 50° to the left of the subject to frontal (0°). For collection, the subjects were asked to sit in a chair and place their face in a chin rest with forehead support to reduce head motion. The subject is asked to remain steady and not change their gaze during data capture. The camera, which was mounted on a robotic arm with a radius of 50 cm, moved from left to right collecting images. Five images were collected at six angles that were separated by 10° increments. This resulted in a dataset of 30 images for each subject for a total of 750 images.

The images were collected using a Toshiba Teli CleverDragon series camera with a focal length of 150 mm. The camera features a 12 megapixel (4096×3072) monochrome CMOS sensor with NIR sensitivity. The size of the captured irises ranged from 750 to 1000 pixels in diameter. A 720 nm long-pass filter fitted to the lens blocks ambient light while allowing most of the NIR illumination to pass. For illumination, two infrared light sources were attached to both sides of the camera and were directed at the subject's eyes.

The 750 images selected for these experiments came from a larger collection. The subjects and images were selected because they were all high-quality images without any blinks or focus problems. Dilation levels were not controlled but are typical of indoor illumination. The pupil and iris boundaries were hand-segmented to avoid any complications with automatic segmentation. As a result of this selection process, all images in the dataset should be easily matched except for the challenges due to off-angle images.

21.4.2   Iris Matching

Iris matching is performed using the commercial VeriEye 2.5 Algorithm from the Neurotech SDK. VeriEye is a complete iris recognition system that includes detection, segmentation, and matching capabilities. Although the algorithm details are proprietary, VeriEye's product literature claims the system is robust to common issues with iris quality including off-angle images [23]. In our experiments, we have verified that VeriEye performs well on our unmodified test dataset and produces high match scores for most images in our testing set including images in the 30° and 40° partitions. The unmodified 50° images cause significant issues for VeriEye and it is clear that many of the failures are caused by difficulty in segmentation.

To test our correction methods images that have been preprocessed using our methods are given to the VeriEye SDK. VeriEye computes similarity scores for each pair of irises where irises that have higher scores indicate a better match. Examples of the images used for testing are shown in Fig. 21.6. As can be seen the Affine, Refracted, and Genetic Algorithm methods appear approximately frontal. There are also less noticeable corrections in the Refracted and Genetic Algorithm images that account for effects like cornea refraction. There are also noticeable distortions near the top and bottom eyelids in the Genetic Algorithm image that are somewhat random. Those regions are often masked out in the fitness function computation and have little effect on iris matching.

21.4.3   Distribution Box Plots

Figure 21.7 shows score distributions for the five preprocessing methods across three pose bins. In this plot, higher scores are better. Scores labeled 'Unmodified' are from VeriEye that run on the original images. 'Affine' results are from images

Original   Affine

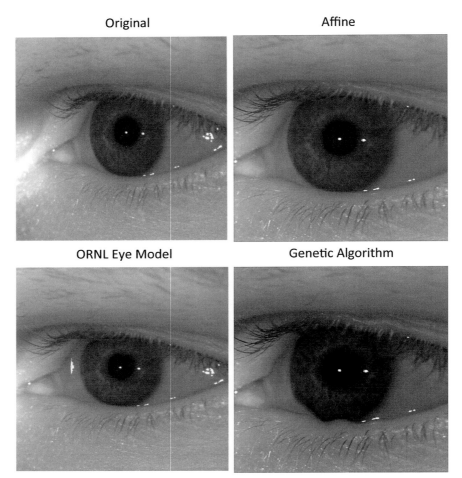

ORNL Eye Model   Genetic Algorithm

Fig. 21.6 This shows the original eye image of the iris and compares that image to the methods for correcting corneal refraction. Although the Genetic Algorithm method provides the best results, it also has noticeable visible artifacts near the *top* and *bottom* of the image

using a simple affine transformation described in Sect. 21.3.1 and we believe the improvement is mostly due to improved segmentation. 'Measured' shows the results of using corrective look-up tables computed from optical flow results as described in Sect. 21.3.2. 'Genetic Algorithm' uses corrections from the genetic algorithm from Sect. 21.3.3. Finally, 'Refracted' used ray tracing to correct for cornea refraction as published by Thompson et al. [35].

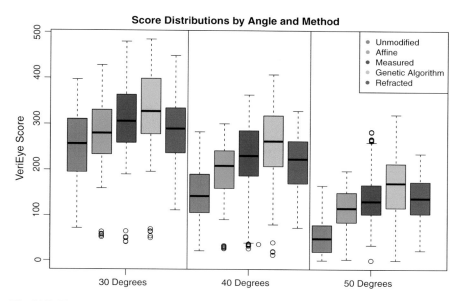

Fig. 21.7 These plots show how the VeriEye scores change are based on the method used correct for corneal refraction. Higher scores are better. The *circles* indicate outliers

A different way to look at these results is shown in the scattered plots in Fig. 21.8. These plots show the VeriEye scores for the unmodified images on the x-axis verse the scores for our techniques shown on the y-axis. In short, all the points plotted above the diagonal line represents scores that were improved by applying our methods. It can also be easily seen in this plot that there are many matches that are correctly verified using our technique that would have failed using the unmodified images. These are the mostly blue points to the left and above the dashed 0.001 False Accept Rate (FAR) threshold lines. Our techniques also improve significantly over the Affine projection. This can be seen where the scores in the 50–150 range are mostly above the diagonal line for both the Genetic Algorithm (GA) method and the refracted method. Finally, the results show that there is no significant effect on the nonmatch population as illustrated by the small gray block of nonmatch scores in the lower left of the plot and also the fact that there is no significant shift to the 0.001 False Accept Rate (FAR) position.

The results shown here clearly indicate that the corrective methods that we have developed improve the match scores for off-angle irises. Of the four techniques, the Genetic Algorithm (GA) method appears to be the best and improves on the unmodified score by 120 points and the affine score by 50 points. By applying this technique, many off-angle images that would not have been recognized can now be easily matched.

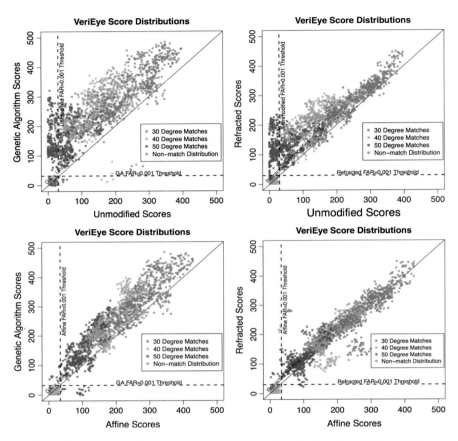

Fig. 21.8 These show the changes to the scores for the Genetic Algorithm (GA) and Refracted when compared to the unmodified and affine transformed images

Figure 21.9 shows that all the corrective methods perform well up to the 1/10000 FAR threshold which we estimate to be a VeriEye Score of 40. The 50° plot shows one interesting result that is not obvious from the other visualizations. The Genetic Algorithm (GA) method outperforms all other methods except for on 50° images with score thresholds between 0 and 60. However, as the score threshold gets higher, the GA is clearly the best performer. It is unclear why this would be the case, especially in light of the fact that that at lower angles the Genetic Algorithm (GA) was clearly the better performer. It is possible that this could be related to only the 50° Look-Up Table (LUT) and that retraining on a different dataset would eliminate that problem. The plots also illustrate that as the score threshold is raised to accommodate larger datasets, the need for corrective methods becomes apparent.

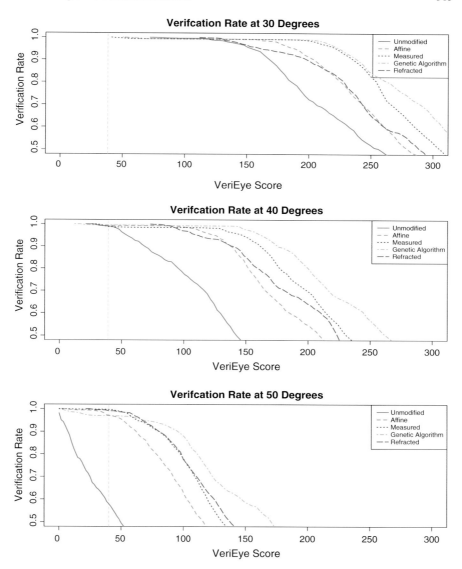

Fig. 21.9 These plots compare the performance of the methods at various thresholds of the VeriEye score. The *vertical dashed line* indicates the 1/10000 FAR threshold which is the strictest threshold that is supported by our nonmatch score distribution

21.5 Conclusion

There are still a number of areas where future work is needed. The most obvious is that the techniques applied here could be extended to larger distances off-angle and more finely defined pose bins. The methods presented here also assume that the pose angle of the eye only varies in one dimension and that should be extended to handle vertical angles as well. In addition, work is needed to handle cases where the subject's face is looking directly at the sensor but the eye gaze is elsewhere. In many of these cases, we believe that the challenge will be just as much with segmentation as with correcting for off-angle effects.

In this paper, we have investigated four methods for correcting corneal refraction in off-angle iris images. All of these methods showed significant improvements to the match scores while having no real effect on the nonmatch distribution. Results on the Verieye matcher showed that the Genetic Algorithm (GA)-based corrections performed the best. We suspect this is because the Genetic Algorithm (GA) can better compensate for the complexity of the eye's anatomy and therefore produce a more general transformation. Because our techniques produce a corrected iris image, those images can easily be passed as input to any preexisting iris matcher with little or no modification to that software.

References

1. C. Belcher, Y. Du, Region-based SIFT approach to iris recognition. Opt. Lasers Eng. **47**(1), 139–147 (2009)
2. D.S. Bolme, S. O'Hara, PyVision—Computer Vision Toolkit (2008), http://pyvision.sourceforge.net
3. D.S. Bolme et al., Visual object tracking using adaptive correlation filters, in *2010 IEEE Conference on Computer Vision and Pattern Recognition (CVPR)*. IEEE (2010), pp. 2544–2550
4. K. Bowyer, K. Hollingsworth, P.J. Flynn, A survey of iris biometrics research: 2008-2010. English, in *Handbook of Iris Recognition*, ed. by M.J. Burge, K.W. Bowyer. Advances in Computer Vision and Pattern Recognition (Springer, London, 2013), pp. 15–54
5. K. Bowyer, K. Hollingsworth, P.J.J. Flynn, Image understanding for iris biometrics: a survey. Comput. Vis. Image Underst. **110**(2), 281–307 (2008)
6. J. Daugman, New methods in iris recognition. IEEE Trans. Syst. Man Cybern. **37**(5), 1167–1175 (2007)
7. J. Daugman, How iris recognition works. Circuits Syst. Video Technol. **14**(1), 21–30 (2004)
8. J. Daugman, Probing the uniqueness and randomness of IrisCodes: results from 200 billion iris pair comparisons. Proc. IEEE **94**(11), 1927–1935 (2006)
9. J.G. Daugman, High confidence visual recognition of persons by a test of statistical independence. Pattern Anal. Mach. Intell. **15**(11), 1148–1161 (1993)
10. G. Farnebäck, Two-frame motion estimation based on polynomial expansion, in *Image Analysis* (Springer, 2003), pp. 363–370
11. S. Fenker, K. Bowyer, Experimental evidence of a template aging effect in iris biometrics, in *Applications of Computer Vision (WACV)* (2011), pp. 232–239
12. A. Fitzgibbon, M. Pilu, R.B. Fisher, Direct least square fitting of ellipses. Pattern Anal. Mach. Intell. **21**(5), 476–480 (1999)

13. A. Glasser, in *Optics of the Eye*, ed. by D. Dartt, R. Dana, J. Besharse. Encyclopedia of the Eye (Academic Press, Oxford, 2010), pp. 8–17
14. R. Jillela, A.A. Ross, Methods for iris segmentation. English, in *Handbook of Iris Recognition*, ed. by M.J. Burge, K.W. Bowyer. Advances in Computer Vision and Pattern Recognition (Springer, London, 2013), pp. 239–280
15. R. Jillela et al., Iris segmentation for challenging periocular images, in *Handbook of Iris Recognition*, ed. by M.J. Burge, K.W. Bowyer. Advances in Computer Vision and Pattern Recognition (Springer, London, 2013), pp. 281–308
16. M. Karakaya et al., An iris segmentation algorithm based on edge orientation for off-angle iris recognition, in *IS&T/SPIE Electronic Imaging* (2013)
17. M. Karakaya et al., Limbus impact on off-angle iris degradation, in *International Conference on Biometrics* (2013)
18. L. Kennell, R. Ives, R. Gaunt, Binary morphology and local statistics applied to iris segmentation for recognition, in *International Conference on Image Processing*, Oct 2006, pp. 293–296
19. Y. Le Grand, M. Millodot, G.G. Heath, in *Form and Space Vision*, vol. 3 (Indiana University Press, Bloomington, 1967)
20. B. D. Lucas, T. Kanade, et al., An iterative image registration technique with an application to stereo vision, in *IJCAI*, vol. 81 (1981), pp. 674–679
21. K. Miyazawa et al., An effective approach for iris recognition using phase-based image matching. IEEE Trans. Pattern Anal. Mach. Intell. **30**(10), 1741–1756 (2008)
22. R. Navarro, L. González, J.L. Hernández, Optics of the average normal cornea from general and canonical representations of its surface topography. JOSA A **23**(2), 219–232 (2006)
23. NeuroTechnology, VeriEye SDK 2.5: Iris Identification for PC and Web Solutions. Software Brochure (2012)
24. Persistence of Vision Pty. Ltd., Persistence of Vision Raytracer (Version 3.6) [Computer software] (2004), http://www.povray.org/download/
25. J.R. Price et al., On the efficacy of correcting for refractive effects in iris recognition, in *Computer Vision and Pattern Recognition* (2007)
26. H. Proenca, Quality assessment of degraded iris images acquired in the visible wavelength. IEEE Trans. Inf. Forensics Secur. **6**(1), 82–95 (2011)
27. H.A. Quigley et al., Iris cross-sectional area decreases with pupil dilation and its dynamic behaviour is a risk factor in angle closure. J. Glaucoma **18**(3), 173–179 (2009)
28. A. Ross, Iris recognition: the path forward. Computer **43**(2), 30–35 (2010)
29. K. Roy, P. Bhattacharya, C.Y. Suen, Towards nonideal iris recognition based on level set method, genetic algorithms and adaptive asymmetrical SVMs. Eng. Appl. Artif. Intell. **24**(3), 458–475 (2011)
30. H.J. Santos-Villalobos et al., ORNL biometric eye model for iris recognition, in *Biometrics: Theory, Applications and Systems*. IEEE (2012), pp. 176–182
31. S.A.C. Schuckers et al., On techniques for angle compensation in nonideal iris recognition. Syst. Man Cybern. Part B: Cybern. **37**(5), 1176–1190 (2007)
32. S. Shah, A. Ross, Iris segmentation using geodesic active contours. Inf. Forensics Secur. **4**(4), 824–836 (2009)
33. S. Thainimit, L. Alexandre, V. de Almeida, Iris surface deformation and normalization, in *Communications and Information Technologies* (2013), pp. 501–506
34. J. Thompson et al., Effects of iris surface curvature on iris recognition, in *Biometrics: Theory, Applications and Systems* (2013)
35. J. Thompson et al., Off-angle iris correction using a biological model, in *Biometrics: Theory, Applications and Systems* (2013)
36. J. Thornton, M. Savvides, B. Vijayakumar, Robust iris recognition using advanced correlation techniques. English, in *Image Analysis and Recognition*, vol. 3656, ed. by M. Kamel, A. Campilho. Lecture Notes in Computer Science (Springer, Berlin, 2005), pp. 1098–1105
37. M. Vatsa, R. Singh, A. Noore, Improving iris recognition performance using segmentation, quality enhancement, match score fusion, and indexing. IEEE Trans. Syst. Man Cybern. Part B **38**(4), 1021–1035 (2008)

38. D. Whitley, T. Starkweather, Genitor II: a distributed genetic algorithm. Exp. Theor. Artif. Intell. **2**(3), 189–214 (1990)
39. R.P. Wildes, Iris recognition: an emerging biometric technology. Proc. IEEE **85**(9), 1348–1363 (1997)
40. J. Zuo, N.A. Schmid, On a methodology for robust segmentation of nonideal iris images. Syst. Man Cybern. Part B: Cybern. **40**(3), 703–718 (2010)

Chapter 22
Ophthalmic Disorder Menagerie and Iris Recognition

Ishan Nigam, Mayank Vatsa and Richa Singh

Abstract Popularity of iris biometrics has led to large scale deployment of large-scale authentication systems such as India's Aadhar project and UAE border control system. For such projects, maintaining high image quality standards during enrollment as well as recognition becomes important. It is also important to handle diversity in iris patterns so that error rates are reduced and all citizens are enrolled in the system. While traditional covariates such as illumination and pose variations are well explored, challenges due to ophthalmic disorders or medical conditions are overlooked. This chapter focuses on the "Ophthalmic Disorder Menagerie" and its effect on iris recognition. The experimental observations suggest that such conditions should also be considered for large scale iris recognition systems.

22.1 Introduction

Iris is an integral component of the human visual system and its robust functioning is essential towards humans engaging in a myriad of activities. Iris also serves as a physiological biometric trait and has high discriminative capability. Iris recognition has come a long way since Daugman's seminal paper [11] introducing a test of statistical independence as the basis for identifying individuals. Present day biometric systems are being deployed to identify citizens in countries such as India, Canada, and the United Arab Emirates. The largest public biometric endeavor,

---

I. Nigam · M. Vatsa · R. Singh (✉)
IIIT, Delhi, India
e-mail: rsingh@iiitd.ac.in

I. Nigam
e-mail: ishann@iiitd.ac.in

M. Vatsa
e-mail: mayank@iiitd.ac.in

© Springer-Verlag London 2016
K.W. Bowyer and M.J. Burge (eds.), *Handbook of Iris Recognition*,
Advances in Computer Vision and Pattern Recognition,
DOI 10.1007/978-1-4471-6784-6_22

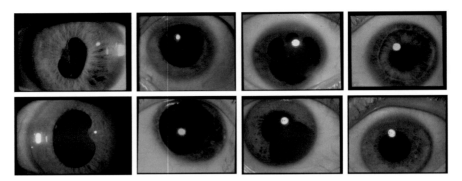

Fig. 22.1 Images of irises suffering from ophthalmic diseases. Iris patterns are distorted and occluded due to surrounding tissue pushing on either the limbic or the pupillary boundary

the *Aadhaar* program, aims to enroll the citizens of India into its system and has registered over 1 billion citizens to date. This program captures all ten fingers, both irises, and face pertaining to each enrollee; however, only iris and fingerprints are used for de-duplication and authentication purposes. The daily enrollment of close to a million citizens under the aegis of the Aadhaar program requires de-duplication matches of the order of 10^{14}. Enlistment of subjects at such a scale makes it inevitable that factors that were previously statistically insignificant in small scale systems are likely to be of consequence in biometric systems of the future.

Among the factors that affect iris recognition, distortions of the iris pattern due to medical conditions occur occasionally. However, it is imperative that the effects of such ocular conditions are ascertained due to the scale at which biometric systems are presently being deployed. As shown in Fig. 22.1, a number of ophthalmic diseases distort and occlude the iris pattern. Using the data collected during the 2010 Somaliland presidential election, a recent study [7] reports that cataract and corneal conditions cause false-non-match results. According to the 2010 US Census data [25], approximately 142.6 million American citizens are above the age of 40. A report by the National Institute of Health [19] suggests that over 36 million of these citizens suffer from one of the major ophthalmic conditions: 24.4 million have cataract patients, 7.7 million diabetic retinopathy patients, 2.7 million glaucoma patients, and more than 2 million patients suffering from age-related macular diseases. The annual number of cataract surgeries performed in the United States is approximately 3 million [1], i.e., nearly 1 % of the American population is annually undergoing ocular surgery which may affect the iris pattern. The number of cataract surgeries performed annually in India is projected to be more than 7.6 million by 2020 [17]. Previous studies have shown that cataract surgeries affect the performance of iris recognition [12, 26]. To mitigate this effect, Seyeddain et al. [22] report that failure in iris recognition due to cataract surgery can be corrected through re-enrollment. This suggests that more than 7 million citizens will require to be re-enrolled in the Aadhaar program every year from 2020 onwards. These statistics also indicate that distortion and occlusion of the iris pattern due to medical conditions is a significant covariate that will likely affect the robustness of large-scale biometric systems in the future.

This chapter explores the effect of ocular medical conditions on the recognition performance of iris biometric systems. The contributions of this research are two-fold: (i) iris datasets which demonstrate the effects of ophthalmic conditions such as diseases, surgeries, and medicinal drugs are introduced and a relative comparison is presented, (ii) using iris image quality assessment, segmentation, and matching algorithms, a detailed analysis is performed to understand the effect of medical conditions on iris recognition. Section 22.2 we describes the ocular medical conditions that affect iris patterns and Sect. 22.3 presents the iris databases that contain images affected due to various medical conditions, including ophthalmic surgeries and diseases. Section 22.4 presents the algorithms used for performance evaluation and Sect. 22.5 discusses the experimental observations and presents analysis on the medical conditions that affect the performance of iris recognition.

22.2 Taxonomy of Medical Conditions

Distortion of iris images, though rare, can occur due to several reasons. The most critical cases of iris distortion are medical conditions which result in partial or complete loss of discriminatory information in the iris pattern. Therefore, ophthalmic disorder menagerie encompasses three broad categories: disorder, surgeries, and pupil dilation/constriction due to medical effects. In this section, we present the taxonomy of medical conditions, including cataract, glaucoma, aniridia, coloboma, uveitis, hyphema, hypopyon, and surgical procedures. Figures 22.2 and 22.3 show some images affected due to different medical conditions and procedures.

22.2.1 Ophthalmic Disorders

Ophthalmic diseases affecting the iris and its surrounding region result from genetic mutations, infections, malfunctioning of the iris, or malfunctioning of other organs that interact with the iris (Fig. 22.2). The following is a list of a few common medical conditions which affect irides:

- *Iritis*: Iritis is caused due to inflammation of the iris. Busacca nodules and mutton-fat keratic precipitates are formed on the iris.
- *Acute anterior uveitis*: Inflammation of the iris and the ciliary body breaks down the blood-ocular barrier, which allows proteins and blood cells to pool in the aqueous chamber.

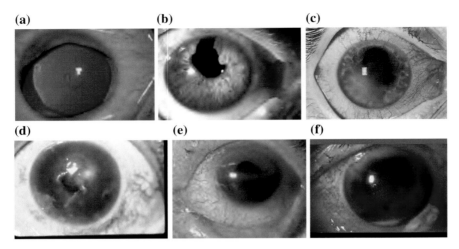

Fig. 22.2 Irises suffering from **a** Aniridia, **b** Coloboma, **c** Anterior uveitis, **d** Corneal ulcer, **e** Hyphema, and **f** Hypopyon

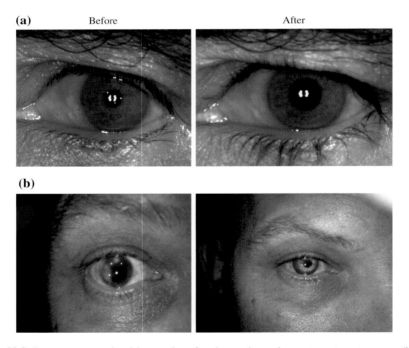

Fig. 22.3 Images representing iris samples of patients who underwent **a** cataract surgery (NIR spectrum), and **b** iris tattoo (visible spectrum). Images in the figure have been brightened for easier visualization

- *Rubeosis iridis*: New vessels form on the iris in patients suffering from rubeosis iridis, which obstruct the outflow of aqueous humor causing glaucoma.
- *Aniridia*: Absence of iris resulting in a large distorted pupil. Usually a hereditary ocular condition, but may also be caused by a mutation in the PAX6 gene.
- *Ciliary body leiomyoma*: A benign muscle tumor originates from the sphincter or the dilator muscles. The muscle tissue distorts the iris pattern.
- *Lisch nodules*: Consist of melanocytic hamartomas and occur as round elevations on the iris surface; common ocular symptoms of Type 1 neurofibromatosis.
- *Iris melanoma*: Results in hemorrhage and elevated intra-ocular pressure. The condition occurs most commonly in pale or blue irides.
- *Heterochromia*: Iris atrophy results in heterochromia. It occurs either with a dark iris (hyperchromic) or with a light iris (hypochromic).
- *Hyphema*: The ocular condition is produced by an injury that disrupts the vasculature supporting the iris or ciliary body. The condition is caused by blunt trauma to the eye, or may be related to surgery.
- *Iris cysts*: Cysts in the iris may be congenital, implanted by surgery, or caused by trauma; cysts are usually stationary and rarely require treatment.
- *Iris prolapse*: Occurs due to defect in the cornea—an iris plug closes off the anterior chamber. The condition may occur due to surgery, infection, or corneal melting.
- *Iridodialysis*: Occurs due to separation of the iris from the attachment at the ciliary body due to blunt trauma. It often results in increased intraocular pressure.

The field of ophthalmic diseases affecting the performance of iris recognition systems has not been studied extensively. A few studies have been conducted, but most of them pertain to studying cataract in human eyes. Trokielewicz et al. [26] present an experimental study which indicates weaker performance of automatic iris recognition methods for cataract-affected eyes compared to healthy eyes. Aslam et al. [3] suggest that iris templates are unlikely to suffer significant changes due to most ophthalmic diseases; however subjects developing anterior uveitis are reported to have iris patterns that cause automated recognition systems to fail. Rennie [20] explores diseases such as neurofibromatosis, epithelial cysts, iris metastasis, peripheral iris melanocytoma and their genesis in the imperfect pigmentation of the iris.

22.2.2 Ophthalmic Surgeries

Surgery may be performed in the ocular organ around the iris or by interacting with the iris itself. Since reconstructive procedures can alter the iris permanently, ophthalmic surgeries have the potential to completely rewrite the iris code. The following is a list of the major forms of ophthalmic surgeries:

1. *Disorder corrective surgery*: Surgery may have to be performed to correct an ophthalmic condition such as cataract, or to avert the adverse effects of injuries caused due to accidents or trauma to the eye. Deviations in the iris pattern may also occur as after-effects of surgeries; these deviations are usually temporary,

but may also be permanent resulting in an irreversible change in the iris pattern. The iris can also be affected by other organs of the eye; for example, a punctured pupil may result in a change in the structure of the iris.

2. *Cosmetic surgery*: Surgery may be performed on the iris either for the purpose of correcting a structural defect or for cosmetic purposes. Figure 22.3b depicts the distorted iris pattern and pupil of a war veteran whose iris is reconstructed to ensure that an optimal amount of light reaches the retina. Even though very few professionals perform such procedures, the surgery has potential for rewriting the iris code patterns of individuals. Ophthalmic (eyeball) tattooing can also be considered as cosmetic surgery which may affect iris segmentation algorithms.

Similar to ophthalmic diseases, very few studies have been conducted to study the effect of different surgeries on human irises. Seyeddain et al. [22] report that standard cataract surgery is not a limiting factor for iris recognition in most cases when recognition is performed within a day of the surgery; though, some patients might require to be re-enrolled after surgery. Dhir et al. [12] also investigate the effect of cataract surgery and pupil dilation in iris recognition, however, recognition experiments are conducted two weeks after the surgery is performed. The authors posit that matching reliability decreases considerably with increase in pupillary dilation.

22.2.3 Pupil Myosis and Mydriasis Due to Medicines

The dilation of the pupil for conducting optometric examinations is a well documented phenomenon [21]. Temporary mydriasis (dilation) or myosis (constriction) of the pupil may be caused due to eyedrops administered to patients to cure ophthalmic infections or for treatment of ocular dryness. Moreover, several medicines are known to cause myosis or mydriasis of the pupil even if the drug is designed to effect another part of the human body. Figure 22.4 presents sample images of subjects under the influence of eyedrops and alcohol. These examples show that administering the medicines affects the iris pattern. Since over-the-counter ocular medicines can affect such changes in the iris pattern, the integrity of large-scale iris recognition systems stands to be compromised due to such medicines.

Lachkar and Bouassida [14] suggest that individuals might suffer from acute angle closure glaucoma—an ocular emergency which receives distinction due to its acute symptoms and need for immediate treatment—if treated with drugs that use adrenergic agents either locally or systemically. Bickel et al. [6] also present a study

(a)   **(b)**

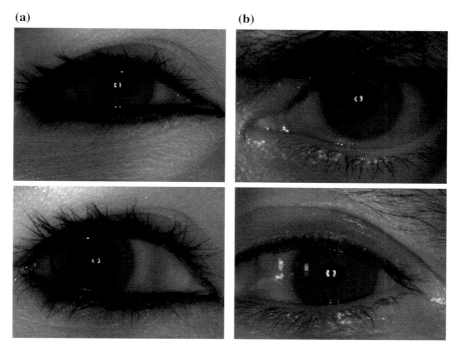

Fig. 22.4 Effect of medicines on the pupil (NIR spectrum): **a** Eyedrops, and **b** Alcohol. Images in the figure have been brightened for easier visualization

on the effect of opioids on the pupillary diameter. Arora et al. [2] report a significant increase in false non-matches for subjects under the influence of alcohol. The above literature clearly indicate that the effect of ocular medicines on the iris pattern is a significant covariate while performing iris recognition.

22.3 Iris Databases Representing Ophthalmic Conditions

Public iris databases in the literature predominantly consist of images of healthy irises and do not capture the effects of distinct medical conditions such as ophthalmic diseases, surgery, or medicines and drugs. We have collected image datasets of irises describing several different ophthalmic conditions. Figure 22.5 shows image samples from these databases and Table 22.1 presents a summary of the characteristics of the databases. These databases will be made available upon request.

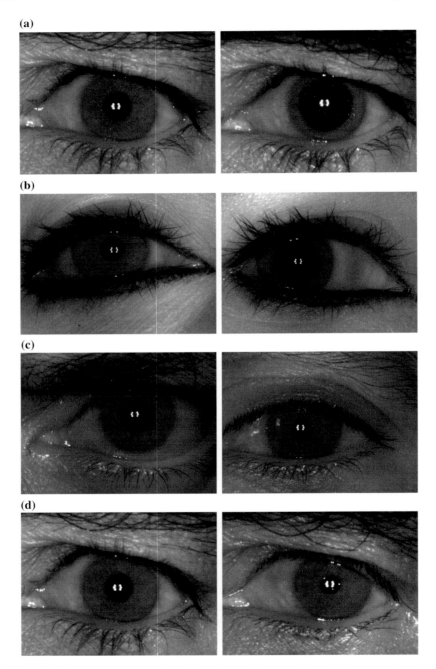

Fig. 22.5 Databases representing irises affected by medical conditions (NIR spectrum): **a** IIITD Iris Cataract, **b** IIITD Iris Eyedrops, **c** IIITD IUAI, and **d** IIITD Iris Surgery. Images in the figure have been brightened for easier visualization

Table 22.1 Characteristics of the IIITD iris databases used in this research

IIITD dataset	Sessions	Subjects/Classes	Samples
Iris cataract	2	40	8
Iris eyedrops	2	88	6
Iris under alcohol influence	2	110	4
Iris surgery	2	49	8

22.3.1 Database Representing Ocular Diseases

The following databases have been collected to represent iris images suffering from ophthalmic diseases:

1. *Composite Ophthalmic Disease Dataset*: Diseases such as glaucoma, aniridia, and uveitis cause the iris pattern to become distorted or occluded. 88 unique iris images are collected from the Cogan Ophthalmic Pathology Collection [9], and 80 unique irises are collated from the Atlas of Ophthalmology [4]. Only one session per iris image is recorded and used in the experiments; image samples from the dataset are presented in Figs. 22.1 and 22.2.
2. *IIITD Iris Cataract Dataset*: The database consists of images of patients suffering from cataract whose irises have been dilated using eyedrops. Images are collected before and after administering eyedrops to study pupil dilation on the cataract patients. Figure 22.5a presents sample images from the dataset.

22.3.2 Database Representing Medicines and Drugs

Section 22.2.3 describes the effect of several medicinal drugs on the size of the pupil. The following datasets are used to study the effects of medicines on the iris pattern:

1. *IIITD Iris under Alcohol Influence (IUAI) Database*: Arora et al. [2] collect images of subjects before and after the consumption of alcohol. A number of medicines consist of alcohol such as cough syrups; thus, this dataset mimics the effect of medicines on human subjects. Figure 22.5c presents sample images from the dataset.
2. *IIITD Iris Eyedrops Dataset*: Tropicacyl Plus, a prescription drug which is used to treat paralysis of the ciliary muscle and to dilate pupils before or after ophthalmic surgery is used to create the dataset. The database consists of images of human subjects captured before and after the medicine is administered by an ophthalmologist. Figure 22.5b presents sample images from the dataset.

22.3.3 Database Representing Surgery

The *IIITD Iris Surgery Dataset* consists of pre-surgery and post-surgery images of patients suffering from cataract. The post-surgery images are captured two to three days after the surgery is performed. Figure 22.5d presents sample images from the dataset.

22.4 Analyzing the Effect of Ophthalmic Disorders and Surgeries

The quality of an iris image can be evaluated in several ways. An iris image can be assessed on the basis of the accuracy of segmentation of the iris pattern, the quality of the input image, and the distribution of the scores obtained while matching gallery and probe iris images. This section discusses approaches used in evaluating the performance of iris recognition capabilities with variations in ophthalmic disorders. Section 22.4.1 presents segmentation analysis framework for iris images, Sect. 22.4.2 discusses iris quality assessment approach used in experiments, and Sect. 22.4.3 briefly presents the matching approach.

22.4.1 Segmentation Analysis

Biometric quality assessment metrics in the literature primarily focus on the pre-processing stage and the fusion of match-scores—accurate iris segmentation is presumed. However, segmentation methods are adversely affected due to distortion and occlusion of the iris pattern, especially in unconstrained acquisition scenarios. Sections 22.4.1.1 and 22.4.1.2 describe two popular algorithms used to assess iris segmentation performance.

22.4.1.1 Non-ideal Iris Segmentation Algorithm

Vatsa et al. [28] propose a two-stage iris segmentation algorithm—the first stage estimates the inner and outer boundaries of the iris using an elliptical model. The approximate boundary of the pupil is empirically determined by iteratively varying the center and the boundary of the elliptical model; the approximate outer boundary of the iris is also detected in a similar manner.

The second stage applies the modified Mumford-Shah functional [8, 27] in a narrow band over the estimated boundaries to compute the exact inner and outer boundaries of the iris. In the proposed curve evolution method for iris segmentation, the model optimizes the following energy functional:

$$Energy(c) = \alpha \int_{\Omega} ||\frac{\partial \hat{C}}{\partial c}|| \phi dc + \beta \int \int_{in(C)} |I(x, y) - c_2|^2 dxdy$$

$$+ \lambda \int \int_{out(C)} |I(x, y) - c_2|^2 dxdy \qquad (22.1)$$

where, $\hat{C}$ is the evolution curve such that, $\hat{C} = \{(x, y) : \hat{\psi}(x, y) = 0\}$, c is the curve parameter, ϕ is the weighting function or the stopping term, Ω represents the image domain, $I(x, y)$ represents the iris image, c_1 and c_2 are the average values of pixels inside and outside $\hat{C}$, respectively, and α, β, and λ are positive constants such that $\alpha < \beta \leq \lambda$. Using this approach, iris and pupil boundaries are obtained and iris is segmented for feature extraction and matching.

22.4.1.2 Random Walker Algorithm for Segmentation of Iris Patterns

Online iris recognition using distantly acquired images in a constrained environment requires the development of efficient iris segmentation approaches that exploit multiple features available for potential identification. Tan and Kumar [24] present an effective solution towards addressing real-world iris segmentation. The developed approach exploits a random walker algorithm to efficiently estimate coarsely segmented iris images. These coarsely segmented iris images are post-processed using a sequence of operations that effectively improve the segmentation accuracy.

22.4.2 Estimation of Quality Factors

The performance of the iris pattern as a biometric modality strongly depends upon the quality of the iris image. Bharadwaj et al. [5] define the biometric quality of an image as:

Quality of a biometric sample is a measure of its efficiency in aiding recognition of an individual, ideally, irrespective of the recognition system in use.

Kalka et al. [13] present an exhaustive framework to assess iris images based on the evaluation of seven parameters—defocus blur, motion blur, off-angle, occlusion, specular reflectance, illumination, and pixel count. These parameters are used to establish a quality factor for the image based on Dempster-Shafer theory [23]. We briefly describe these factors as well as the method for combining these factors below.

Defocus Blur Defocus blur attenuates high spatial frequencies. The defocus blur quality of an image is assessed by measuring high-frequency content in the segmented iris region. Daugman [10] proposed a convolutional kernel to measure the total 2D spectral power in the response. This measure is normalized as follows:

$$f(x) = 100 \frac{x^2}{x^2 + c^2} \tag{22.2}$$

where, x is the spectral power measured by the convolution kernel, and c is the half power of a focus score corresponding to 50 %.

Motion Blur Motion blur results from motion between the object and the camera; it is estimated as the strength and the direction of blur in the image. The Fourier transform, F, of the image, I, and the filter response, H, at orientation Φ, and scale α, is used to assess the blur at multiple steps (δ):

$$\hat{\Phi} = arg \max_{\Phi[0:\delta:\pi]} ||F(I)H(\Phi : \alpha)||^2 \tag{22.3}$$

The strength of the blur is estimated by analyzing the log-magnitude image perpendicular to the estimated angle $(\hat{\Phi})$ of motion blur.

Off-angle blur The circularity of the pupil is used to estimate the direction of the gaze of the iris image, which is estimated using Daugman's integro-differential operator. The pitch (ψ) and yaw (φ) angles for the off-angle iris are estimated by performing a projective transform of the iris about the pupil center and optimizing an objective function for multiple values of ψ and φ:

$$(\hat{\psi}, \hat{\varphi}) = arg \max_{\psi, \varphi} J(\psi, \varphi) \tag{22.4}$$

Occlusion Occlusion is estimated by applying several morphological operations in succession. Horizontal-edge detection is performed in the greyscale image. The horizontal edges are extended and the localized iris is overlaid on the image. Spurious pixels are removed and the occlusion mask is obtained. Discontinuities in the mask are filled, and the percentage of masked pixels is used as a measure for occlusion.

Specular Reflection Occlusions resulting from specular reflection are evaluated on the iris image pattern unaffected by eyelid occlusion. This factor is estimated using hard thresholding based on the respective datasets.

Illumination Variation The unoccluded iris pattern is split into several regions. The mean intensity for each region is computed (X_i) and the variance of their means is used to assess the illumination variation in the iris image:

$$Illumination\ Variation = \frac{\sum_{i=1}^{N}(X_i - \mu_X)^2}{N} \tag{22.5}$$

where, μ_X is the mean of the average intensities (X_i) of the independent regions and N is the number of such independent regions.

Pixel Counts The pixel count of the iris image is measured as the ratio of the number of iris pixels to the combined number of iris pixels and occluded pixels within the iris region:

$$Pixel\ Counts = \frac{X_{\text{estimated}}}{X_{\text{estimated}} + X_{\text{occluded}}} \qquad (22.6)$$

where, X_{occluded} represents the number of pixels occluded due to the eyelids and due to specular reflection, and $X_{\text{estimated}}$ represents the number of estimated iris pixels.

22.4.2.1   Composite Quality Factor

Kalka et al. [13] suggest that the quality metrics are combined to generate a score representing overall quality of the iris pattern based on Dempster-Shafer theory [23]. Shafer's rule assumes that the individual quality factors are independent. Murphy [15, 16] proposed a modification to Shafer's rule so as to use information from the same image which may or may not be correlated:

$$m(C) = \frac{\sum_{A_i \cap B_j = C} p(m_1(A_i)m_2(B_j))}{1 - \sum_{A_i \cap B_j = \phi} p(m_1(A_i)m_2(B_j))} \qquad (22.7)$$

where $p(\cdot)$ is given by

$$p(m_1(A_i)m_2(B_j)) = [m_1(A_i)m_2(B_j)]^n, \ n \in [0, 1] \qquad (22.8)$$

where, n is used to create a balance between independence and correlation of the quality factors: $n = 0.5$ is used in the framework to represent a neutral combination of the individual quality factors.

22.4.3   Iris Recognition

To understand the performance of iris recognition on these databases, we utilize two algorithms: Neurotechnology's VeriEye [18] and Vatsa et al.'s feature extraction and matching algorithm [28]. VeriEye [18] is a commercial iris recognition algorithm and Vatsa et al.'s algorithm uses log polar Gabor with Hamming distance.

22.5   Experimental Observations

The quality of iris patterns must be regulated at time of enrollment as well as recognition in large-scale biometric systems. Traditionally, the quality assessment of an image is based upon the perception of the human visual system. However, the quality of a *biometric image* is interpreted as an indicator of its usefulness as a biometric sample for the purpose of recognition. Distortion and occlusion of the iris image is likely to result in improper segmentation of the iris (Fig. 22.6). It is important to quantify the extent of such irregularities so as to ascertain whether it is appropriate to either perform recognition, or perform pre-processing on the iris pattern, or to

Fig. 22.6 Segmentation applied to an eye: **a** Iris suffering from an ophthalmic disease, **b** Preprocessed iris image, **c** Binary mask to segment iris pattern, and **d** Results for segmented iris and pupil. The *inner* and *outer* boundary of the iris have converged to the inner boundary of the iris, resulting in failed segmentation

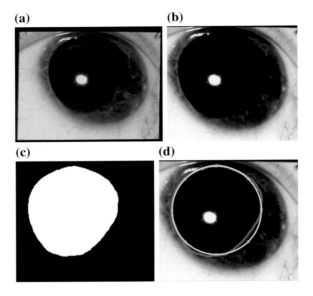

reject the iris pattern entirely. This section presents experimental results pertaining to iris segmentation, quality assessment, and matching with respect to ophthalmic disorders and surgeries.

22.5.1 Segmentation Analysis

Segmentation of the iris pattern is one of the most critical steps in recognizing iris patterns suffering from ophthalmic disorder menagerie. We, therefore, analyze the performance of the two segmentation approaches on iris patterns representing medical conditions. A human expert has examined the segmentation results of the algorithms to determine which irises were correctly segmented and Table 22.2 shows the performance of the segmentation algorithms. It is observed that the algorithms yield good results for normal and healthy images. However, many iris images cap-

Table 22.2 Performance of segmentation algorithms on irises suffering from medical conditions

Dataset	Tan [24] (%)	Vatsa [28] (%)
Composite ophthalmic disease	10.1	38.7
IIITD iris cataract	98.8	99.4
IIITD iris eyedrops	100	100
IIITD iris under alcohol influence	100	100
IIITD iris surgery	96.9	98.2

tured under the influence of ophthalmic diseases fail to be segmented while a few images of irises suffering from cataract and post-surgery are also not segmented. Figure 22.7 illustrates the detection results on sample iris patterns suffering from ophthalmic diseases. The failure instance in Fig. 22.7a occurs due to irregular pigmentation of the iris pattern while Fig. 22.7b shows failure due to extraneous membranes being formed on the eye which confuse the segmentation algorithm apart from irregular pigmentation.

Iris images in the Iris Eyedrops Dataset and the IIITD IUAI Dataset are segmented perfectly and it is possible that the covariates represented by these datasets are not of much significance in affecting iris segmentation; however, the IIITD Iris Cataract Dataset and the IIITD Iris Surgery Dataset suffer from failure of segmentation and it is likely that the iris pattern is being affected due to the respective ocular conditions.

Figure 22.8 presents a visual summary of the quality metrics described in Sect. 22.4.2 for the Composite Ophthalmic Disease Dataset and Fig. 22.9 presents a histogram of the iris segmentation scores. Since Bharadwaj et al. [5] derive meaningful inferences using these quality metrics, the random distribution of the metrics suggests that the dataset suffers from loss in quality due to distortions and occlusions in the iris. The histogram also suggests that majority of the images have very poor segmentation performance and therefore, iris segmentation under ophthalmic disorders is an open research problem.

22.5.2 Matching Analysis

Occlusion and distortion of the iris pattern, as discussed earlier, may be caused due to ophthalmic surgery, medicines such as eyedrops, or the consumption of alcohol. In this section, we present the matching analysis using two approaches, Vatsa et al. [28] and VeriEye. The Receiver Operating Characteristic (ROC) curves in Fig. 22.10 illustrate the performance of iris verification using the algorithm proposed in [28] on the four individual databases. The verification performance is observed to be significantly lower on all the databases, particularly, cataract and surgery ones, indicating that iris image samples have likely endured alterations to a higher degree. Table 22.3 describes the results of VeriEye for intra-session matching (*Pre-Pre* and *Post-Post*) as well as inter-session matching (*Pre-Post*). A drop in accuracy is observed for all the datasets in inter-session comparisons as compared to intra-session matching. This drop in performance indicates a change in the structure of the iris pattern. Intuitively, the post-post accuracy should be higher, however, in cataract and surgery databases the accuracies are in the range of 73.1 % and 65.3 % respectively. The lower accuracy of post-post images is because the images are captured with a difference of few days after surgery and it is observed that, post surgery, the patterns takes time to stabilize. In such cases, the re-enrollment of the iris after surgery may help to address the problem.

The match scores obtained from [28] are also analyzed with respect to the quality and segmentation scores. Figure 22.11 presents the match scores for iris images before and after the effects of medical conditions as a function of the Dempster-Shafer

(a)

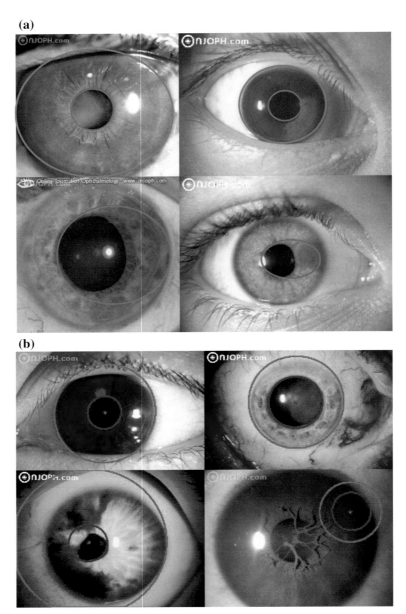

(b)

Fig. 22.7 The result of iris segmentation algorithms: **a** algorithm proposed by Vatsa et al. [28], and **b** algorithm proposed by Tan and Kumar [24]. The *first row* in each sub-diagram shows successful segmentation, while the *second row* shows incorrect segmentation

Fig. 22.8 Quality metrics
versus iris segmentation
score for diseased images
from Atlas of
Ophthalmology and Cogan
Ophthalmic Pathology Clinic

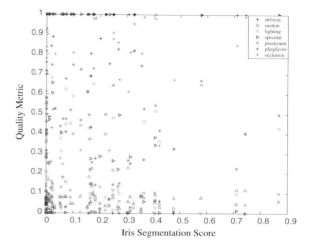

Fig. 22.9 Histogram of iris
segmentation scores
obtained by the algorithm
proposed by Vatsa et al. [28]

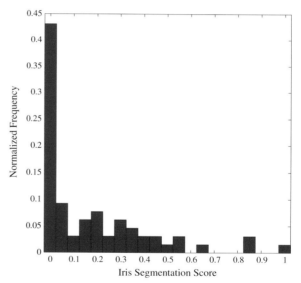

theory based quality factor [13] and the iris segmentation score [28]. Hamming distance based matcher provides a score in the range of 0–1 with 0 representing ideal genuine match and 1 representing ideal impostor match. However, since the number of genuine scores are lower, they are not clearly visible in the plot. We have therefore plotted z-axis as (1-Hamming Distance). The variability in the distributionof

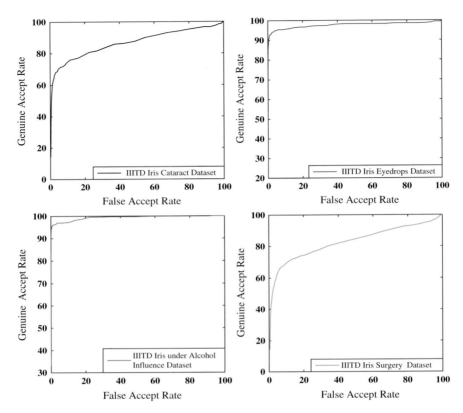

Fig. 22.10 Receiver Operating Characteristic curve for the IIITD Iris Cataract, IIITD Iris Eyedrops, IIITD IUAI, and IIITD Iris Surgery datasets

Table 22.3 VeriEye intra- and inter-session verification accuracy

Dataset	Accuracy		
	Pre-Pre (%)	Post-Post (%)	Pre-Post (%)
Iris cataract	92.2	73.1	40.8
Iris eyedrops	100.0	84.8	70.5
Iris under alcohol influence	99.3	98.7	96.1
Iris surgery	94.6	65.3	55.1

both quality assessment metrics—Dempster-Shafer theory based combined quality factor as well as segmentation score—for all four datasets indicates the large differences in the quality of biometric patterns. This observation assert the requirement of developing algorithms that can account for ophthalmic disorders and surgeries during enrollment and recognition.

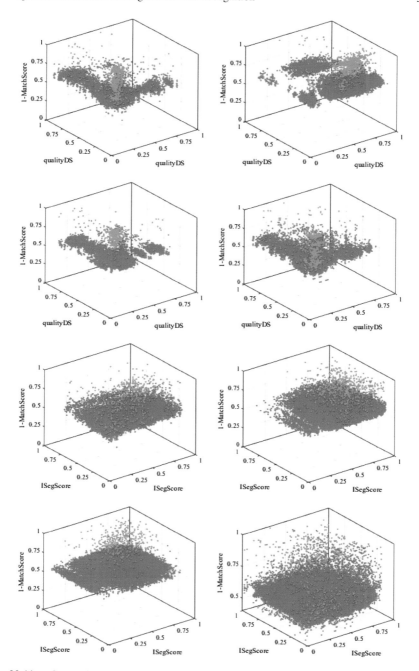

Fig. 22.11 a Comparing the iris quality assessment and segmentation scores against match-scores obtained from [28]. For better visualization, at z-axis, 1-matchscore is used

22.6 Conclusion

Iris patterns can be affected by ophthalmic medical conditions. Ophthalmic diseases can lead to changes in the iris patterns whereas, eye drops can lead to pupil dilation and constriction. In this study, we analyze the effect of five individual medical challenges on the performance of iris segmentation, quality assessment, and matching algorithms. The results suggest that sometimes "Ophthalmic Disorder Menagerie" lead to changes in iris patterns or significant dilation and contraction thereby affecting the performance of iris recognition algorithms.

Acknowledgments This research was partially supported by a grant from the Department of Electronics and Information Technology, Government of India. The authors acknowledge Sunpreet Singh Arora in collecting a part of IIITD iris database used in this research.

References

1. American Academy of Ophthalmology. EyeSmart, in (2014)
2. S.S. Arora et al., Iris recognition under alcohol influence: a preliminary study, in *5th IAPR International Conference on Biometrics (ICB)*. IEEE (2012), pp. 336–341
3. T.M. Aslam, S.Z. Tan, B. Dhillon, Iris recognition in the presence of ocular disease. J. R. Soc. Interface **6**(34), 489–493 (2009)
4. Atlas of Ophthalmology, Online Multimedia Databsae, in (2015)
5. S. Bharadwaj, M. Vatsa, R. Singh, Biometric quality: a review of fingerprint, iris, and face. EURASIP J. Image Video Process. **2014**(1), 1–28 (2014)
6. W.K. Bickel et al., Buprenorphine: dose-related blockade of opioid challenge effects in opioid dependent humans. J. Pharmacol. Exp. Ther. **247**(1), 47–53 (1988)
7. K.W. Bowyer, E. Ortiz, A. Sgroi, Trial somaliland voting register de-duplication using iris recognition, in *11th IEEE International Conference and Workshops on Automatic Face and Gesture Recognition (FG)*, vol. 2. IEEE (2015), pp. 1–8
8. T.F. Chan, L. Vese, Active contours without edges. IEEE Trans. Image Process. **10**(2), 266–277 (2001)
9. Cogan Ophthalmic Pathology Collection, in (2008)
10. J. Daugman, How iris recognition works. IEEE Trans. Circuits Syst. Video Technol. **14**(1), 21–30 (2004)
11. J. Daugman, High confidence visual recognition of persons by a test of statistical independence. IEEE Trans. Pattern Anal. Mach. Intell. **15**(11), 1148–1161 (1993)
12. L. Dhir et al., Effect of cataract surgery and pupil dilation on iris pattern recognition for personal authentication. Eye **24**(6), 1006–1010 (2010)
13. N.D. Kalka et al., Estimating and fusing quality factors for iris biometric images. IEEE Trans. Syst. Man Cybern. Part A: Syst. Hum. **40**(3), 509–524 (2010)
14. Y. Lachkar, W. Bouassida, Drug-induced acute angle closure glaucoma. Curr. Opin. Ophthalmol. **18**(2), 129–133 (2007)
15. R.R. Murphy, Adaptive rule of combination for observations over time, in *International Conference on Multisensor Fusion and Integration for Intelligent Systems*. IEEE (1996), pp. 125–131
16. R.R. Murphy, Dempster-Shafer theory for sensor fusion in autonomous mobile robots. IEEE Trans. Robot. Autom. **14**(2), 197–206 (1998)
17. G. Murthy et al., Current status of cataract blindness and vision 2020: the right to sight initiative in India. Indian J. Ophthalmol. **56**(6), 489 (2008)
18. Neurotechnology VeriEye Software Development Kit

19. Prevalence of Adult Vision Impairment and Age-Related Eye Diseases in America, in (2010)
20. I. Rennie, Dont it make my blue eyes brown: heterochromia and other abnormalities of the iris. Eye **26**(1), 29–50 (2012)
21. M. Rosenfield, N. Logan, K.H. Edwards, *Optometry: Science, Techniques and Clinical Management* (Elsevier Health Sciences, 2009)
22. O. Seyeddain et al., Reliability of automatic biometric iris recognition after phacoemulsification or drug-induced pupil dilation. Eur. J. Ophthalmol. **24**(1), 58–62 (2014)
23. G. Shafer, *A Mathematical Theory of Evidence*, (Princeton University Press, 1976)
24. C.-W. Tan, A. Kumar, Towards online iris and periocular recognition under relaxed imaging constraints. IEEE Trans. Image Process. **22**(10), 3751–3765 (2013)
25. The United States of America Census, in (2010)
26. M. Trokielewicz, A. Czajka, P. Maciejewicz, Cataract influence on iris recognition performance, in *Symposium on Photonics Applications in Astronomy, Communications, Industry and High-Energy Physics Experiments*. International Society for Optics and Photonics (2014), pp. 929020–929020
27. A. Tsai, A. Yezzi Jr., A.S. Willsky, Curve evolution implementation of the Mumford-Shah functional for image segmentation, denoising, interpolation, and magnification. IEEE Trans. Image Process. **10**(8), 1169–1186 (2001)
28. M. Vatsa, R. Singh, A. Noore, Improving iris recognition performance using segmentation, quality enhancement, match score fusion, and indexing. IEEE Trans. Syst. Man Cybern. Part B: Cybern. **38**(4), 1021–1035 (2008)

Chapter 23
Template Aging in Iris Biometrics

**Sarah E. Baker, Kevin W. Bowyer, Patrick J. Flynn
and P. Jonathon Phillips**

Abstract Using a data set with approximately 4 years of elapsed time between the earliest and most recent images of an iris (23 subjects, 46 irises, 6,797 images), we investigate template aging for iris biometrics. We compare the match and non-match distributions for short-time-lapse image pairs, acquired with no more than 120 days of time lapse between them, to the distributions for long-time-lapse image pairs, with at least 1,200 days of time lapse. We find no substantial difference in the non-match, or impostor, distribution between the short-time-lapse and the long-time-lapse data. We do find a difference in the match, or authentic, distributions. For the image dataset and iris biometric systems used in this work, the false reject rate increases by about 50 % or greater for the long-time-lapse data relative to the short-time-lapse data. The magnitude of the increase in the false reject rate varies with changes in the decision threshold, and with different matching algorithms. Our results demonstrate that iris biometrics is subject to a template aging effect.

23.1 Introduction

The term "template aging" refers to degradation of biometric performance that occurs with increased time between the acquisition of an enrollment image and acquisition of the image compared to the enrollment. Template aging effects are known to exist for biometrics such as face and fingerprint [6, 14, 22, 24, 28].

S.E. Baker · K.W. Bowyer (✉) · P.J. Flynn
University of Notre Dame, Notre Dame, IN, USA
e-mail: kwb@cse.nd.edu

S.E. Baker
e-mail: sbaker3@cse.nd.edu

P.J. Flynn
e-mail: flynn@cse.nd.edu

P.J. Phillips
National Institute of Standards and Technology, Gaithersburg, MD, USA
e-mail: jonathon@nist.gov

© Springer-Verlag London 2016   541
K.W. Bowyer and M.J. Burge (eds.), *Handbook of Iris Recognition*,
Advances in Computer Vision and Pattern Recognition,
DOI 10.1007/978-1-4471-6784-6_23

The iris biometrics community has long accepted the premise that the iris is "essentially stable" throughout a person's life, and that this means that template aging does not occur for iris biometrics. Daugman stated the core assumption this way — "As an internal (yet externally visible) organ of the eye, the iris is well protected and stable over time" [7]. This assumption is commonly repeated in research publications dealing with iris biometrics: "[the iris is] stable over an individual's lifetime" [26], "[the iris is] essentially stable over a lifetime" [17], "the iris is highly stable over a person's lifetime" [19]. The commercial iris biometrics literature explicitly connects this to the idea of lifetime enrollment — "only a single enrollment in a lifetime" [25].

Note that claims about stability of the iris texture and "lifetime enrollment" are never presented as dependent on the particular sensor, algorithm, length of time lapse or any other condition. They are presented as universal claims about iris biometrics in general. Thus, a single counter-example is sufficient to disprove the universal claim.

It is well known in the medical literature that the eye and iris undergo a variety of changes with age [2, 5, 11, 18, 29, 30]. Any of these effects could in principle alter details of the imaged iris texture. It is also possible that a template aging effect could be due to aging of the sensor, changes in how a person uses the biometric system, or other factors. The essential question for iris biometrics is—does the quality of a match between two images of the same iris change with increased time between the enrollment image and the image to be recognized? That is, does a template aging effect exist? We present results of the first systematic investigation of this question.

We use an image dataset involving 23 persons (46 irises) with approximately 4 years of time lapse between the earliest and latest images of a given iris. We consider image pairs in a short-time-lapse group, representing no more than 120 days of time lapse between the two images, and in a long-time-lapse group, representing at least 1,200 days of time lapse. We experiment with three iris biometric systems: our modification of the IrisBEE baseline matcher [23], Neurotechnology's VeriEye system [21], and the Cam-2 submission to the Iris Challenge Evaluation 2006 [20]. We find that, for each of the three systems, there is no significant difference in the non-match, or "impostor," distributions between the short-time-lapse and the long-time-lapse data. We also find that, for each of the three systems, the match distribution for the long-time-lapse data is different from that for the short-time-lapse data in a way that results in an increased false reject rate. Thus, we observe clear evidence of a template aging effect for iris biometrics.

23.2 Previous and Related Work

We do not know of *any* experimental study that supports the conclusion that template aging does not occur for iris biometrics. Claims about the stability of iris texture appear to be based on subjective human visual perception of iris texture in visible-light images of the iris. However, it has been shown that humans are able to perceive similarities in iris texture that do not result in closer iris biometric matches [13].

Thus human perception of the general iris texture pattern does not automatically or necessarily imply anything about iris biometric operation.

Gonzalez et al. [27] report an effect of time lapse on iris recognition that may initially seem similar to our results. However, Gonzalez et al. compare matches between images acquired at the same acquisition session with those acquired with at most three months time lapse. They report a better match statistic for images from the same session than for those across sessions. However, they show little change in match statistics when comparing matches with short-time lapses, between two weeks and three months. In our results presented here, we do not consider matches between images acquired in the same acquisition session, as we expect that this is not representative of a real-world biometric scenario. We expect that "same session" images will generally result in atypically good matches. Like Gonzalez et al., we do not find any significant difference in match scores for images with a few months time lapse. However, when considering a longer-time lapse than that examined in Gonzalez et al., we do observe a statistically significant degradation in match scores.

This paper expands upon our initial results [3] in several ways. First, we have increased the number of subjects from 13 to 23 and the number of irises from 26 to 46. Second, in [3] we only considered images from spring 2004 and spring 2008 and the matches within one semester and matches across the 4 years. In this work, we now consider all images acquired from 2004 through 2008 and have set two time thresholds in defining our short-time-lapse and long-time-lapse matches. Third, we have tested the time-lapse effect on two additional iris biometric algorithms: Neurotechnology's VeriEye [21] and the Cam-2 submission to the Iris Challenge Evaluation 2006 from the University of Cambridge [20]. We also test for various possible causes of match score degradation with increased time lapse. Finally, we present ROC curves for short-time-lapse and long-time-lapse matches for each of the three algorithms, and explicitly show the difference in the false reject rates.

23.3 Image Data Set and Algorithms

All of the iris images used in this study were acquired with the same LG 2200 iris imaging system [15], located in the same studio throughout the 4 years of image acquisition. The system had no hardware or software modifications during the 4 years. The LG 2200 model is now discontinued. However, current state-of-the-art iris imaging systems of course did not exist at the time that data acquisition for this experiment started. We are currently pursuing additional work with images acquired using a newer model sensor and initial results [9] are generally consistent with results of this study.

Image acquisition sessions were held at multiple times in each academic semester across the 4 years. At a given acquisition session, for a given subject, six images were acquired of each eye. The image acquisition protocol was the same as that used in the Iris Challenge Evaluation (ICE) 2005 and 2006 [20, 23]. However, it is important to note that while the protocol for the ICE acquisitions allowed for some images that did not pass the normal built-in quality control checks of the LG 2200 [20], *all images used in this study were manually screened for image quality.* Images of noticeably poor quality were excluded from this study; e.g., out-of-focus irises, major portions of the iris occluded, obvious interlace artifacts, etc., were all excluded. Also, images that resulted in a noticeably poor iris segmentation by the IrisBEE algorithm were excluded from the study. (The detailed segmentation was not available from the other systems.)

A total of 23 persons participated in data acquisitions from 2004 through 2008. See Fig. 23.1 for examples of iris images. There are images from both irises of the 23 subjects over the 4 years. Subject age ranges from 22 to 56 years old at the end of the 4-year period. Sixteen subjects are male and seven are female. Sixteen subjects are Caucasian and seven are Asian. The repeated sixteen by seven breakdown is a coincidence; the ethnicity division does not follow the gender division. None of the subjects wore glasses for any of the data acquisition. Five subjects wore contact lenses at all acquisition sessions, and eighteen subjects did not wear contact lenses at any acquisition session. The total number of iris images selected for use in this study was 6,797.

We created two sets of image pairs, a short-time-lapse set and a long-time-lapse set. The short-time-lapse set consists of image pairs where the two images were

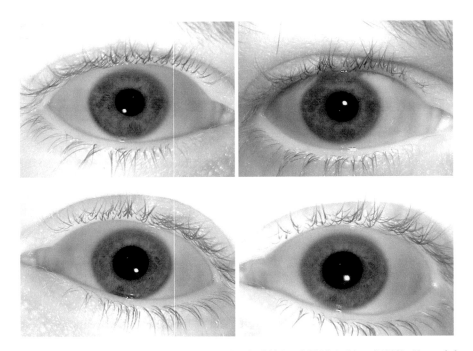

Fig. 23.1 Example iris images of a subject taken in 2004 and 2008 (subject 04233). *Upper left* right iris from 2004; *upper right* right iris from 2008; *lower left* left iris from 2004; and *lower right* left iris from 2008

acquired with no more than 120 days of time lapse between them. The average time lapse in this group is 44 days. The long-time-lapse set consists of image pairs acquired with no less than 1,200 days of time lapse. The average time lapse in this group is 1,405 days. A given iris image can participate in multiple short-time-lapse pairs and multiple long-time-lapse pairs.

23.4 Iris Matching Algorithms

To investigate the generality of any observed effects, three different iris biometric algorithms were included in the study. First, we used our own modified version of the IrisBEE system distributed through the ICE program [20]. This system represents an iris as a $240 \times 10 \times 2$-bit iris code generated from the complex-valued responses of one-dimensional log-Gabor wavelet filters applied to the normalized iris image [16]. For the IrisBEE matcher, the output of matching two iris images is a fractional Hamming distance. The range of the fractional Hamming distance is [0, 1], with zero being a perfect match and 0.5 a random level of match. Second, we used the commercial VeriEye 2.2 Iris SDK from NeuroTechnology [21]. This system produces match scores on a different scale and with a different polarity than systems employing fractional Hamming distance. For the analysis in this paper, we negated the match scores so that lower scores represented better matches. The third system was the Cam-2 submission to the ICE 2006 from the University of Cambridge [20]. The output of the Cam-2 matcher is nominally a fractional Hamming distance. Thus we have used three different algorithms. One is based on a "baseline" source code that was made available to the research community, one is a readily available commercial product, and one was a best performer in the ICE 2006 results.

23.5 False Reject Rates for Short and Long-Time Lapse

We computed the authentic and impostor distributions for each of the three algorithms. The impostor distributions showed no apparent difference between the short-time-lapse data and the long-time-lapse data. However, the authentic distributions for long-time-lapse data were shifted in the direction of the impostor distribution. For each of the three algorithms, the shift in the authentic distribution is such that it causes an increase in the False Reject Rate (FRR) for any practical choice of decision threshold.

Graphs that zoom in on the "tails" of the long-time-lapse and short-time-lapse authentic distributions for each algorithm are shown in Fig. 23.2. These graphs show the tails of the distributions across a range of possible values for the decision threshold. Recall that for the IrisBEE and Cam-2 algorithms, a smaller value (of fractional Hamming distance) represents a better match, while for the VeriEye algorithm a larger value of different units represents a better match.

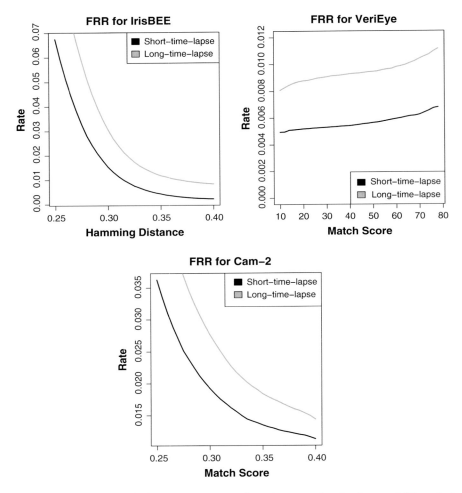

Fig. 23.2 Authentic distributions across a range of match scores, showing increased false reject rates

This figure shows that for all three algorithms, across a broad range of possible threshold values, *the long-time-lapse authentic distribution has a higher false reject rate than the short-time-lapse authentic distribution*. The IrisBEE algorithm shows approximately 150 % increase in the false reject rate across the range of decision thresholds, the VeriEye algorithm shows an approximately 70 % increase, and the Cam-2 algorithm shows an approximately 40 % increase. Thus we observe clear and consistent evidence of a template aging effect for each of three algorithms considered in this study.

23.6 Frequency of Authentic Distribution With Worse Mean Score

We also performed a one-sided sign test to check for statistical significance of the frequency, across the 46 irises, of the long-time-lapse authentic distribution having a worse mean match score than the short-time-lapse authentic distribution. A worse mean score is one closer to the impostor distribution. If time lapse has no effect, then we would expect that the long-time-lapse mean is worse for half of the irises and the short-time-lapse mean is worse for half. This is the null hypothesis for the test. The sign test does not make any distributional assumptions about the means of similarity scores. The one-sided test was selected because we are interested in the alternative hypothesis that the longer-time-lapse data has a larger mean score.

The sign test results are presented in Table 23.1, including the test statistic, p-value, and number of irises for which the mean of the long-time match scores is worse than the mean of the short-time-lapse match scores ($\mu_L(i) > \mu_S(i)$). The results show that we can easily reject the null hypothesis for all three algorithms. The frequency of a worse match score occurring for the long-time-lapse is statistically significant. This indicates that the increased FRR seen in Fig. 23.2 is not the result of a small number of unusual irises in the data set, but is characteristic of the data set in general.

Table 23.1 shows that for IrisBEE there are 42 of 46 irises for which the long-time-lapse mean HD is worse, for VeriEye there are 41 irises for which the long-time-lapse mean match score is worse, and for Cam-2 there are 38 irises for which the long-time-lapse mean HD is worse. One natural question is: how many of these irises are in common? The answers are presented in Table 23.2, which shows the number of irises in common. The last row reports that 34 irises have the time-lapse effect for all three algorithms. A one-sided sign test for 34 of 46 irises showing an effect across

Table 23.1 Sign test for frequency of worse mean match score with longer time lapse

Algorithm	No. irises	Test statistic	p-value
IrisBEE	42	5.75	2.55×10^{-9}
VeriEye	41	5.46	2.20×10^{-8}
Cam-2	38	4.57	4.62×10^{-6}

Table 23.2 Overlap in number of irises for which the mean of the long-time match scores is greater than the mean for the short-time match scores

Algorithms	N of 46 irises in common
IrisBEE-veriEye	38
IrisBEE-Cam2	35
VeriEye-Cam2	35
All three	34

The overlap is reported for all combinations of the three algorithms and for all three algorithms all three algorithms produces a test statistic of 3.391 with a p-value of 8.207×10^{-4}. Thus, even if we use the criteria that all three algorithms must agree on the movement of the means, the null hypothesis is rejected.

23.7   Possible Causes of an Increased False Reject Rate

We considered a variety of factors that could conceivably contribute to causing the observed result. For example, it is known that the presence of contact lenses can adversely affect match quality [4]. If the short-time-lapse data contained image pairs where a subject did not wear contact lenses and the long-time-lapse data contained image pairs where the same subject wore contacts, this could conceivably cause an increased FRR for long-time-lapse relative to short-time-lapse. Similarly, if a person was wearing the same type of contacts in short-time-lapse image pairs, but a different type in long-time-lapse image pairs, this could conceivably cause an increased FRR.

We manually checked for the presence of contact lenses in all images included in this study. We found that each subject in this study either wore contacts for all acquisition sessions, or did not wear contacts to any acquisition session. Also, for the subjects who wore contacts, none appear to have changed the type of contacts worn. Thus we conclude that the wearing contact lenses is not an appreciable factor in our observed results.

Hollingsworth et al. [12] showed that the degree of the pupil dilation, and the difference in pupil dilation between two images, can affect the match distribution. We performed an analysis of the changes in pupil dilation and its possible effect on the difference between long-time-lapse and short-time-lapse data.

The first step in the analysis was to compute the ratio of the pupil diameter to the iris diameter for each image. The second step was to compute the difference in the pupil-to-iris ratio for the iris images in each match pair. Then, for each subject, we computed the average change in the pupil-to-iris ratio over all short-time-lapse match pairs. We denote this by $\rho_S(i)$. Similarly, we computed the average change in the pupil-to-iris ratio for all long-time match pairs, denoted by $\rho_L(i)$. Then for each iris, we computed the difference between the average short-time-lapse change in the pupil-to-iris ratio and the average long-time-lapse change in the pupil-to-iris ratio, denoted by $\rho_L(i) - \rho_S(i)$. For the IrisBEE algorithm, we created a scatter plot of the change in the pupil-to-iris ratio between long-time-lapse and short-time-lapse match pairs and change in match score between long-time-lapse and short-time-lapse. Figure 23.3 is a scatter plot of $\mu_L(i) - \mu_S(i)$ versus $\rho_L(i) - \rho_S(i)$. The corresponding Kendall correlation coefficient is 0.217. If the observed increase in false reject rate could be attributed to a change in pupil dilation, then $\mu_L(i) - \mu_S(i)$ versus $\rho_L(i) - \rho_S(i)$ would be substantially correlated. If $|\rho_L(i)| > |\rho_S(i)|$, then there is a greater difference in diameters of the pupils for long-time match pairs than for short-time match pairs. In turn this implies that match scores should degrade. However, our analysis shows minimal correlation between $\mu_L(i) - \mu_S(i)$ versus

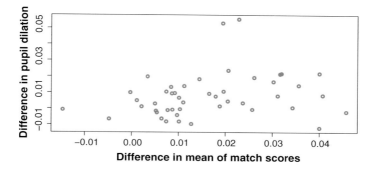

Fig. 23.3 Scatterplot of the change in match score between long-time and short-time lapse for each iris versus the change in the pupil-to-iris ratio between long-time and short-time lapse match pairs $(\mu_L(i) - \mu_S(i)$ versus $\rho_L(i) - \rho_S(i))$. The *horizontal* axis is the change in mean match scores for the long-time and short-time lapse iris pairs. The *vertical* axis is the change in the average short-time change in the pupil-to-iris ratio and the average long-time change in the pupil-to-iris ratio. Each *red circle* is an iris

$\rho_L(i) - \rho_S(i)$. Thus we conclude changes in pupil dilation are not an appreciable factor in our observed result.

The percentage of an iris that is occluded can affect iris matching performance [8]. The more of the iris that is observable, the better the expected performance. Thus one possible factor contributing to the observed increase in the false reject rate is that the percentage of the iris that is observable decreased in the long-time-lapse data relative to the short-time-lapse data.

In the IrisBEE algorithm [20], the fraction of the iris that is visible is indicated by the fraction of the iris code bits that are marked in the iris code mask as representing non-occluded portions of the iris. To determine if there is a change over time in the fraction of the iris that is occluded, we divided the time period over which the data was collected for this study into 30-day intervals. We computed the average number of bits marked as non-occluded in the mask for all images collected in each 30-day interval. We then computed Kendall's correlation coefficient between the average number of bits marked as non-occluded and time. The resulting Kendall's correlation coefficient is -0.131. This indicates that there is no substantial correlation between number of bits marked as non-occluded and elapsed time. Thus, we conclude that change in the amount of iris occluded does not account for the increase in the false reject rate observed in our results.

The iris images in the time-lapse study were collected with the same LG 2200 sensor [15]. It is conceivable that the sensor properties of the LG 2200 could have changed over time in such a way as to cause an increased false reject rate in the long-time-lapse data. To test for this, in the Fall 2008 we collected iris images with a second rarely used LG 2200 camera. We collected approximately 3000 images from 77 subjects (154 irises) who attended three separate acquisition sessions (labeled "session one," "session two," and "section three"). There was approximately two weeks elapsed time between each session. During sessions one and three, iris images

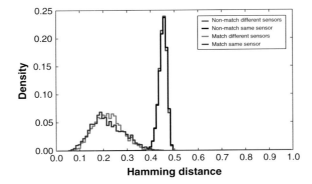

Fig. 23.4 The match and non-match distributions for the within and between sensors experiments. The match and non-match distributions are for the Hamming distance from the IrisBEE algorithm. The mean Hamming distance for match scores collected with the same sensor is 0.2153 and for match scores collected with difference sensors is 0.2167. The mean Hamming distance for non-match scores collected with the same sensor is 0.4483 and for non-match scores collected with difference sensors is 0.4478

were collected with the original camera; during session two the iris images were collected with the second rarely used camera. The first step in our sensor aging analysis was to compute the match and non-match score distributions between iris images collected in session one and session three, both sessions using the original sensor. The second step was to compute the match and non-match score distributions between iris images collected in session one and session two. In session two, the images were collected with the second rarely-used sensor. If the sensor age affects match quality, we would expect a significant degradation in match scores between images collected from the two different sensors compared to image pairs collected with the original sensor. The average match score for image pairs collected with the original sensor is 0.215; the average match score for image pairs collected with the two different sensors was 0.217. Figure 23.4 shows a histogram for the match and non-match distributions for both within and between sensor comparisons. Based on this analysis, we conclude that a sensor aging effect cannot account for the increase in false reject rate that is seen in our results.

The LG 2200 camera actively illuminates the iris using three infrared light emitting diodes (LED) positioned on the left, right, and top of the sensor. When acquiring images, the camera is designed to take three images, one with each LED. In commercial applications, the camera will save the best quality image and discard the other two. For our acquisitions, the system had the capability to save all three images (for a detailed explanation see Phillips et al. [20, 23]). It is conceivable that if there were more matches between images acquired with the same LED in the short-time-lapse group, and more matches between images acquired with different LEDs in the long-time-lapse group, that this could result in an increased false reject rate for the long-time-lapse group.

We grouped the matches into those in which the two images were taken with the same LED and those in which the two images were taken with different LEDs. For both groups, we observed an increased false reject rate of about 50 % across all feasible decision threshold values for the long-time-lapse data over the short-time-lapse data. Thus we conclude that variations in the particular LED illuminating the images is not the cause of the increased false reject rate seen in our results.

23.8   Conclusions and Discussion

For three different matching algorithms, and across the range of practical decision threshold values for each matching algorithm, we found that the false reject rate increases with longer-time lapse between enrollment and verification. This is seen clearly in the difference in the tails of the authentic distributions. Also, the frequency of irises with a worse mean match score for long-time-lapse compared to short-time-lapse is statistically significant. Thus our experimental results show clear and consistent evidence of a template aging effect for iris biometrics. The magnitude of the template aging effect varies between algorithms, with the value of the decision threshold, and other factors.

We were able to test for a variety of factors that could potentially contribute to observing an increased false reject rate with increased time lapse. We concluded that factors such as varying pupil dilation, wearing of contact lenses, differences in amount of iris occluded, and sensor aging are not an appreciable factor in our experimental results.

It is possible that the template aging effect observed in our experimental results is caused by normal aging of the eye. One well-known example of age-related change in the normal eye involves pupil size. Winn et al. studied factors affecting light-adapted pupil size and found that "of the factors investigated, only chronological age had a significant effect on the size of the pupil" [29]. They concluded "the results of this study are consistent with previous reports suggesting that pupil size becomes smaller in an almost linear manner with increasing age" [29]. The iris, of course, controls the pupil size, and so this change in average pupil size reflects a change in the functioning of the iris tissue. As the Merck Manual of Geriatrics describes it, "The iris comprises two sets of muscles that work together to regulate pupillary size and reaction to light. With aging, these muscles weaken and the pupil becomes smaller (more miotic), reacts more sluggishly to light, and dilates more slowly in the dark" [18].

There are also age-related changes in the melanocytes, the cells that produce melanin, in the iris. Eye color is largely determined by the melanocytes in the anterior layer of the iris. For some segments of the population, aging can lead to a noticeable change in the melanocytes, and so the eye color. Bito et al. report that "Most individuals had stable eye color after early childhood. However, there was a subpopulation of white subjects with eye color changes past childhood. Approximately 17 % of twins and 11 % of mothers experienced a change in eye color of 2 U or more. [...] Thus, eye color, and hence, iridial pigmentation, seems to change in some individuals during later years" [5]. They found that the changes in eye color were more similar for identical twins than fraternal twins, indicating a genetic link to this particular element of aging. One element of melanocyte aging can, in rare cases, lead to a cancer. "The melanocytes in the iris are constantly exposed to UV radiation, and this leads to the malignant transformation of these cells to form a specific type of malignant tumor, the uveal melanoma" [11].

Also connected with the melanocytes, iris freckles and nevi can arise in the iris, and can grow over time. "Iris freckles are the most common iris tumors found in children as well as adults. They are collections of benign, but abnormal melanocytes that vary in size and shape. Although congenital, they tend to become more prominently pigmented with age. Iris freckles are clusters of normal melanocytes and have no malignant potential. Nevi efface the iris architecture and may cause clinical structural alterations . . ." [30].

In addition, it is known that the cornea undergoes age-related changes. "The shape and aberrations of the cornea change with age. It is well known that the radius of curvature slightly decreases with age, and the asphericity also changes. On average, the cornea becomes more spherical with age and, as a consequence, spherical aberrations tend to increase" [1]. The iris is imaged through the cornea, thus, corneal changes may affect iris images.

Small, incremental changes in imaged iris texture over time should be considered normal, as ". . . age-related changes take place in all ocular tissues of the human eye . . ." [2]. The relevant question for iris biometrics is the time scale at which normal aging has an appreciable effect on the biometric template computed from the imaged iris texture. To underscore this point, we quote from the Flom and Safir iris recognition patent [10]—"The basic, significant features of the iris remain extremely stable and do not change over a period of many years. Even features which do develop over time, such as the atrophic areas discussed above, usually develop rather slowly, so than an updated iris image will permit identification for a substantial length of time". In this quote, it is clear that Flom and Safir anticipated the possibility that small, incremental changes in iris texture could potentially result in the need for an "updated image" and re-enrollment of the iris template. One interpretation of our results is that they confirm that the possibility that Flom and Safir envisioned is in fact true.

In an attempt to identify the regions of the iris that changed, degrading the match quality, we visually examined the iris images. Visual examination of the iris image pairs with the poorest match scores for the IrisBEE algorithm revealed no drastic or obvious changes in the irises or their textures. This suggests that, if the template aging effect is due to normal aging of the eye, humans may not be able to easily perceive the subtle changes that are involved.

Much additional research remains to be done in the area of template aging for iris biometrics. While we have experimentally observed a template aging effect, and have ruled out several factors as primary causes of the observed effect, we have not conclusively identified a primary cause of the observed template aging. It is important to understand the cause of the observed template aging effect, so that techniques can be developed to mitigate the effect. It would also be valuable to know whether or not iris biometric template aging is constant across different demographic groups, and whether it occurs at a faster or slower rate as a person ages. Studies that collect new and larger data sets, involve a larger pool of subjects, different sensors, a longer time period, and/or a sample of subjects that represent a greater range of demographics would all be important.

Acknowledgments SEB, KWB, and PJF were supported by the National Science Foundation under grant CNS01-30839, by the Central Intelligence Agency, by the Intelligence Advanced Research Projects Activity and by the Technical Support Working Group under US Army contract W91CRB-08-C-0093. PJP acknowledges the support of the the Biometric Task Force, the Department of Homeland Security's Directorate for Science and Technology, the Intelligence Advanced Research Projects Activity (IARPA), the Federal Bureau of Investigation (FBI), and the Technical Support Working Group (TSWG).

The opinions, findings, and conclusions or recommendations expressed in this publication are those of the authors and do not necessarily reflect the views of our sponsors. The identification of any commercial product or trade name does not imply endorsement or recommendation by the authors, the University of Notre Dame, or the National Institute of Standards and Technology.

References

1. P. Artal, Aging effects on the optics of the eye, in *Age-Related Changes of the Human Eye* (Springer, 2008), pp. 35–44
2. D. Atchison et al., Age-related changes in optical and biometric characteristics of emmetropic eyes. J. Vis. **8**(4), 1–20 (2008)
3. S. Baker, K. Bowyer, P. Flynn, Empirical evidence for correct iris match score degradation with increased time-lapse between gallery and probe matches, in *Proceedings of the Third International Conference on Biometrics*, 2009, pp. 1170–1179
4. S. Baker et al., Degradation of iris recognition performance due to non-cosmetic prescription contact lenses. Comput. Vis. Image Underst. **114**(9), 1030–1044 (2010)
5. L. Bito, A. Matheny, O.C.K. Cruickshanksa, D. Nondahl, Eye color changes past early childhood. Arch. Ophthalmol. **115**, 659–663 (1997)
6. J. Carls et al., Biometric enhancements: Template aging error score analysis, in *8th IEEE International Conference on Automatic Face and Gesture Recognition*, 2008, pp. 1–8
7. J. Daugman, IEEE Trans. Circuits Syst. Video Technol., 21–30 (2004)
8. J. Daugman, New methods in iris recognition. IEEE Trans. Syst. Man Cybern. **37**(5), 1167–1175 (2007)
9. S.P. Fenker, Experimental evidence of a template aging effect in iris biometrics (2011)
10. L. Flom, A. Safir, Iris recognition systems. U.S. Patent No. 4641394 (1987)
11. L. Flom, A. Safir, D. Hu, Photobiology of the uveal tract, in *Photobiological Sciences Online* (1987)
12. K. Hollingsworth, K.W. Bowyer, P.J. Flynn, Pupil dilation degrades iris biometric performance. Comput. Vis. Image Underst. (2009)
13. K. Hollingsworth, K.W. Bowyer, P.J. Flynn, Similarity of iris texture between identical twins, in *Computer Vision and Pattern Recognition Biometrics Workshop*, June 2010
14. A. Lanitis, A survey of the effects of aging on biometric identity verification. Int. J. Biometr. **2**(1), 34–62 (2010)
15. LG, (2010)

16. X. Liu, K.W. Bowyer, P. Flynn, Experiments with an improved iris segmentation algorithm, in *Proceedings of the Fourth IEEE Workshop on Automatic Identification Technologies*, Oct 2005, pp. 118–123
17. K. Miyazawa, et al., IEEE Trans. Pattern Anal. Mach. Intell. **30**, 1741–1756 (2008)
18. K. Miyazawa et al., *Aging and the Eye* (2008)
19. D. Monro, S. Rakshit, D. Zhang, DCT-based iris recognition. IEEE Trans. Pattern Anal. Mach. Intell. **4**(29), 586–595 (2007)
20. D. Monro, S. Rakshit, D. Zhang, *Iris Challenge Evaluation* (2006)
21. NeuroTechnology, VeriEye SDK
22. P. Phillips et al., *Face Recognition Vendor Test 2002: Overview and Summary* (2000)
23. P. Phillips et al., The iris challenge evaluation 2005, in *Proceedings of the Second IEEE Conference on Biometrics: Theory, Applications, and Systems* (2008)
24. J. Ryu, J. Jang, H. Kim, Analysis of effect of fingerprint sample quality in template aging, in *NIST Biometric Quality Workshop*, vol. II, 2007, pp. 7–8
25. L. I. T. W. I. I. R. B. Scalability (2009)
26. J. Thornton, M. Savvides, V. Kumar, A Bayesian approach to deformed pattern matching of iris images. IEEE Trans. Pattern Anal. Mach. Intell. **29**(4), 596–606 (2007)
27. P. Tome-Gonzalez, F. Alonso-Fernandez, J. Ortega-Garcia, On the effects of time variability in iris recognition, in *Proceedings of the Second IEEE Conference on Biometrics: Theory, Applications and Systems* (2008)
28. U. Uludag, A. Ross, A. Jain, Biometric template selection and update: a case study in fingerprints. Pattern Recogn. **37**, 1533–1542 (2008)
29. B. Winn et al., Factors affecting light-adapted pupil size in normal human subjects. Investig. Ophthalmol. Visual Sci. **35**(3), 1132–1137 (1994)
30. K. Wright, P. Spiegel, *Pediatric Ophthalmology and Strabismus* (2003)

Afterword to the Second Edition

My first encounter with iris recognition was in the very early 1990s when the Vice President of Technology for my employer—a large technology firm—tasked me to review a paper by one John Daugman, asking "Can this technology be successful?" Neither Dr. Daugman nor iris recognition was familiar to me. The Daugman paper made great claims of accuracy for the method based on a presumed binomial model for the score distributions, with model parameters estimated from only limited data. Further, the method used phase information extracted from localized filters, an old idea which had been much discussed in other areas of automated human recognition but never applied effectively. So my answer to the Vice President's question about the potential for iris recognition success was simply, "I don't know".

Although my response showed no imagination or foresight, it was quite rational within the conservative corporate culture of my employer. Retinal "scanning," which had just undergone a large test funded directly by U.S. Federal legislation, was gaining traction within the government as an eye-based biometric recognition technology and was already being used for access control to classified government spaces. Did we really need another eye-based recognition method and could this iris upstart unseat retinal scanning?

Now, 25 years later, we have seen the answer clearly. The original accuracy claims were verified through large-scale testing and the phase-based implementation turned out to be both novel and ingenious. Retinal scanning systems are no longer used or marketed (although the words "retinal scanning" continue to linger in the press); iris recognition has become the dominant eye-based biometric technology, with applications in National ID systems, border crossing and facility access control; iris systems rival or surpass even fingerprinting in accuracy and ease of use; and, with the expiration of the early patent claims inhibiting adoption, iris systems are now available on a commercially competitive basis.

Although iris recognition has matured from a disruptive technology to what philosophers of science would refer to as "normal science," there is no shortage of continuing research questions. This second edition of the Handbook of Iris Recognition, which is a significant expansion in scope and in length just 4 years after

© Springer-Verlag London 2016
K.W. Bowyer and M.J. Burge (eds.), *Handbook of Iris Recognition*,
Advances in Computer Vision and Pattern Recognition,
DOI 10.1007/978-1-4471-6784-6

the highly successful 2012 first edition, serves to emphasize that point. The four additional chapters and nearly 300 additional pages consider new research in iris template security, eye disorders, SDK development, and off-angle image correction. In the 4 years intervening between editions of this handbook, iris recognition has been applied to a billion persons in India—not in a trial, but within a full-fledged National Identification System.

In a review of the first edition, as published in IET Biometrics, I said, "It is impressive how this human recognition technology has matured scientifically and found a commercial market in such a relatively short time, due in large measure to the effective research, development and advocacy of Prof. Daugman." I continue to stand behind that statement. Although some advancement of eye-based recognition technologies might have been inevitable, the rapid and widespread success of iris recognition must be seen as owing directly to the tenacity and genius of John Daugman. No other biometric technology owes its existence so completely to a single individual. This story should serve as a great inspiration to all of us—a lesson that unwavering passion for a subject can bring tremendous success.

San Jose, California, March 2016   James L. Wayman

Afterword to the First Edition

Since its introduction in 1992, the iris modality has earned acceptance as a highly accurate biometric. As evidenced in the collection of articles in this handbook, the iris itself continues to captivate the inquisitive minds of top researchers in the field of biometrics who seek to unearth all of the secrets this phenomenology has to offer. Probably more importantly, for those who have been leading the charge to promote its utility in a number of scenarios involving security, the iris remains able to boast extremely high rates of accuracy in large-scale national deployments.

Iris recognition systems generally accept for "match processing" images that have passed a predetermined quality threshold. The requirement for meeting this quality threshold has been instrumental in allowing the iris modality to build and preserve credibility as a highly accurate biometric. Image samples not meeting the required quality threshold are generally rejected by the iris recognition system— a result commonly referred to as a "failure to acquire." In many deployments, the "failure to acquire" events are immediately detected and resolved by simply acquiring another image. This process can usually be implemented in such a way that it goes unnoticed by the individual being imaged—they just find themselves waiting a little longer for the success indicator, without necessarily understanding why.

In order to meet the demand to produce high-quality data (i.e., images) sufficient to pass the quality threshold, many of today's iris acquisition systems require highly cooperative or conditioned individuals. In addition to the constraints placed on the individual whose iris is being acquired, the environment where the acquisition takes place must also be controlled; or steps taken to mitigate the adverse effects introduced. That said, there have been some successes in the development of iris recognition systems (e.g., iris-on-the-move (IOM)) that have allowed for greater stand-off distances of operation; and freedom of movement by the individual being imaged. These advancements have mainly been limited to maximizing the performance of mainstream optical designs and sensor technologies through creative engineering of the acquisition platform to meet the desired signal quality of existing algorithms. This approach shifts a significant portion of the burden of conformance

© Springer-Verlag London 2016
K.W. Bowyer and M.J. Burge (eds.), *Handbook of Iris Recognition*,
Advances in Computer Vision and Pattern Recognition,
DOI 10.1007/978-1-4471-6784-6

from the individual onto the acquisition system. And while the performance and operation of these systems is quite impressive, the level of sophistication involved in the design has the adverse consequence of substantially increasing the cost to produce the acquisition system.

In 2008, I was invited to give a presentation entitled "The Science of Biometrics with Relaxed Constraints" at the 2nd Annual IEEE International Conference on Biometrics, Theory, and Systems. During this presentation, I discussed the possibility of exploiting features derived from the periorbital region of the eye to enhance the performance of iris recognition algorithms when confronted with data that is less than ideal (i.e., data of a quality level that falls just short of a predetermined threshold for processing by conventional algorithms.) In an attempt to uphold the reputation of iris recognition for being a highly accurate biometric, and because the exploitation of all features in the vicinity of the eye was being encouraged, the term ocular recognition was used.

The proper implementation of an ocular recognition system would have at its core an iris recognition algorithm. In addition, the data quality requirements for enrollment in an iris system would not only be maintained, but expanded to preserve information contained in the periorbital region of the eye. Methodologies employed to extract and subsequently match features derived from the periorbital region of the eye are only necessary when the data quality is insufficient for processing by conventional iris algorithms. Thus, ocular recognition—not to be confused with face recognition by parts—has the potential to be just as accurate as conventional iris recognition algorithms when processing high-quality data, and yet more robust to minor degradations in signal quality that render them ineffective.

In the years following BTAS 2008, there have been a number of publications at mainstream IEEE conferences on biometrics addressing topics germane to ocular recognition. As is often the case, research progress by scientists on the leading edge of this area has been hampered by the dearth of data that exists. Much of the data that does exist to support investigations into the efficacy of the iris, lacks sufficient detail in the periorbital region of the eye due to cropping techniques designed to isolate the iris or pixels in the periorbital region of the eye being overexposed due to the wavelength used to illuminate the iris and the reflectance properties of human skin. Alternatively, the ocular region was extracted from high resolution photos of the face at visible wavelengths. These photos are not ideally suited for exploiting iris information.

Developments occurred to help to spur new innovations in the area of ocular recognition. First, the National Institute of Standards and Technology released an Ocular Challenge data set as part of its "Face and Ocular Challenge Series (FOCS)" in November of 2010. The stated goal of FOCS "is to engage the research community to develop robust face and ocular recognition algorithms along a broad front." Second, NIST also recently published a report detailing an "Ocular and Iris Baseline Algorithm" (November, 2011). And finally, the Intelligence Advanced Research Projects Activity (IARPA) sponsored research efforts to investigate the utility of advanced ocular recognition algorithms to improve the robustness of biometric exploitation systems on suboptimal (iris) data; as well as next generation sensor technology and innovative optical systems to relax the constraints on iris/ocular acquisition as part of its Biometrics Exploitation Science and Technology (BEST) Program.

As I close, I would like to thank the authors for all of their efforts to assemble this outstanding handbook. One thing is for certain, there are a number of exciting questions that remain unanswered pertaining to understanding the discriminative power of the eye—and all of its complements. These questions, coupled with the quest to build ocular/iris acquisition systems that "adapt to the user, instead of requiring the user to adapt to the technology," will continue to drive bold innovation in this area of biometrics for years to come.

Washington, D.C. April 2012

Michael C. King

Index